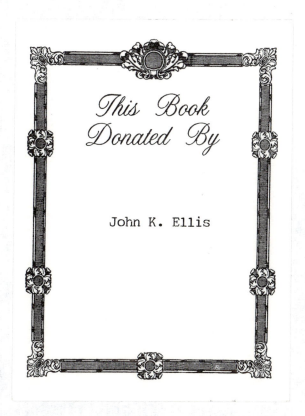

This Book Donated By

John K. Ellis

September 4. 1746.

The Pennsylvania GAZETTE.

Numb. 925:

Containing the freſheſt Ad-vices Foreign and Domeſtick

MERCY. JUSTICE.

ANTWERP, May 29.

THERE has been, in the Courſe of the Motions of the two Armies, ſeveral Skirmiſhes, wherein the Auſtrian Light Troops have generally had the better. On the 22d Inſtant it proved otherwiſe; a Detachment from the Left of the French Army, under M. de Moutiere, being informed of 600 Auſtrian Huſſars lying at Wineg-hem, marched to attack them. The Auſtrians drew up in the open Field, and ſtood their Ground: Montiere thereupon marched towards them with Part of his Detachment, and order'd the other Part to take Poſſeſſion of the Village, which being effected, he attacked the Huſſars, who finding themſelves overpower'd, retreated towards the ſame Vil-lage, where they were attacked again by the French, and to prevent being ſurrounded, rode off again on the Spur, with the loſs of about 80 Men. Couſin d'Euree hid the ſame Day detached from his Body, at Harcarthuis, 300 Men; and M. Graffin being ſent from the main Body of the Army, the two French Parties met, and engaged each other, and ſome Miſchief was done before the Miſtake was diſcovered, by which Means 2 Party of Huſſars who had been in Purſuit of, got ſafe off, with the loſs of two Men.

Paris, May 24. There has lately appeared a kind

Troops ſhall not paſs the Rhine in the ſame Limits to attack any Part of Alſace or the French Territo-ries. Baron Ramſchwag has tranſmitted this to Vi-enna, to know the Senſe of his Court upon it.

Turin, May 11. The French decamped the 10th at Break of Day from the Neighbourhood of Aſti, after ſetting Fire to their Camp, and have retaken Poſſeſſion of their former Poſt. The 400 Men which were in the Caſtle retired the 15th. — The blowing up the Baſtions, &c. — Detachment of Auſtrian Huſſars, which came from Alexan-dria to obſerve their Motions, have brought in too Mules laden with Corn, and ſome Militia; have taken many Priſo-ners. Capt. Ibres, who commanded a Corp of Volun-teers in the King's Service, has made Priſoners 7 Captain of Grenadiers; and 97 French Soldiers, and ſent them to Alexandria. All the King's Troops will daily march as all in Court with the Imperial Army. Many Reports are again current of a new neutral Treaty of the ſame Nature with thoſe ſigned ſome time ſince which 'tis generally thought will be at an end ſoon. Jame Salamon confined.

Compiegny, June 11. About 2 Fortnight ago Commo-dore Mitchell ſhared an Shore near Blanckinburg a large Ship of 54 Guns bound for Dunkirk, ſince ſet at Liberty. Commodore has chaced a French Cutter. She had been in England with Officers and Men of War. She held and had been in England with Officers and Money, and had ſunk her Anchors, miſtook of the Old Ferry; but being order'd away North, was met with at

pens, and by this it evidently appears which Side we lean'd towards during the Courſe of the War. Mr. Giffes, on the Marſhal Zuchian's leaving Antwerp to the Mercy of the French, made the Abbe de la Viſte a complimental Viſit, in which he told him, that he thought his Maſter the happieſt Man in the World; for that he no ſooner appeared before a Town, but the Gates flew open to him. The Abbe replied, And ſo, I doubt not will your Sluices too, with this material Difference, That theſe Gates open to let him in, your Sluices to keep Him out. — There is no Occaſion for that, return'd the Imbaſſador, ſince the States are ready to ſign a Neutrality whenever the King pleaſes. The King, rejoins the Abbe, has no Reaſon to enter his Subjects into Treaties with thoſe he is diſpoſed to treat as Enemies. We ſhould have cheer'd your Neutrality, if we could now, it muſt be upon ſuch Terms as the King ſhall preſcribe, which you ſhall hereafter underſtand.

An Extract of a Letter from Paris, to a foreign Miniſter at the Hague.

Affairs are in a poor Situation in the Capital, as well on Account of the bad News that it daily,

ABSTRACTS FROM
BEN FRANKLIN'S
PENNSYLVANIA GAZETTE,
1728-1748

By

KENNETH SCOTT

CLEARFIELD

Reprinted for
Clearfield Company, Inc. by
Genealogical Publishing Co., Inc.
Baltimore, Maryland
1999

Library of Congress Catalogue Card Number 74-29164
International Standard Book Number: 0-8063-0661-0

Made in the United States of America

INTRODUCTION

When Ben Franklin arrived in Philadelphia at the age of seventeen that city had but one newspaper, *The American Weekly Mercury,* founded in December, 1719, the third paper in British North America, the first being the *Boston News-Letter* (1704) and the second *The New-England Courant,* established by James Franklin.

Ben had been apprenticed to his printer brother James and had worked on the *Courant* until James's "harsh and tyrannical treatment" led the young apprentice to leave Boston and seek a job, first in New York and then in Philadelphia. Employment there with Samuel Keimer and later in London at the printing establishments of Palmer and then of Watts gave young Franklin valuable experience.

Upon his return to Philadelphia from England, Ben set up a printing office in partnership with Hugh Meredith and before long gave serious consideration to the publication of a newspaper, since Bradford's *Mercury* was, in Franklin's opinion, "a paltry thing, wretchedly manag'd, no way entertaining, and yet profitable to him." George White, a journeyman printer, to whom Ben indiscretely confided his project, tipped off Samuel Keimer, who hastened to bring out a newspaper, the first number of which appeared in December, 1728. After three-quarters of a year, however, there were at most ninety subscribers, so that Keimer gladly sold his newspaper to Franklin and Meredith.

Ben soon became sole owner, for Meredith, whom another partner later characterized as "no compositor, a poor pressman, and seldom sober," was glad to dispose of his share in the undertaking. Franklin was justified in asserting that his *Pennsylvania Gazette* had better type and was better printed than Bradford's *Mercury.* The skill and industry of Franklin soon made the paper flourish and take its place as the leading newspaper in America. It helped, moreover, to bring Franklin by 1748 to such financial independence that he took a partner, David Hall, "very able, industrious and honest," who took over "all care of the printing office," enabling Ben to devote himself to public service and philosophical studies.

The present volume presents abstracts of all items pertaining to America in which individuals are mentioned, with omission only of shipping records in and out of the Port of Philadelphia, and this solely to avoid increasing the size of the book. On the other hand, all persons mentioned in shipping news or advertising are recorded.

The *Pennsylvania Gazette* was a weekly, like the other papers of the day, and like them printed foreign news obtained from newspapers, letters or accounts from overseas. Franklin read the newspapers from Boston, New York, Charleston and other cities and reprinted items from them, so that his publication covered happenings from Canada to the West Indies and in all the Colonies. Proceedings of Colonial Assemblies and messages of governors or addresses to them frequently appeared, as they were of concern to all the Colonies.

Once a year, after the elections held at the beginning of October, there appeared in the *Pennsylvania Gazette* the names of representatives, commissioners, sheriffs, coroners and assessors who were chosen. A special feature of the newspaper was the occasional publication, after Ben was appointed postmaster of Philadelphia, of unclaimed letters in the post office, an innovation which provided the names of hundreds of persons, their addresses and, frequently, the indication of their status or that of persons in whose care correspondence was sent.

A recurring matter in the news was Negro unrest in the form of rebellion in the West Indies and conspiracies, genuine or imagined, to kill all Whites in the West Indies, New York, Virginia or South Carolina, where in 1730 a plot was reported, with the comment that at the time South Carolina had 28,000 Negroes but only 3,000 Whites.

War with Spain and then also with France for a time dominated domestic news with the movement of armies and fleets, the exploits of privateers, Indian raids, the taking of Louisburg, recruiting of soldiers, expeditions against the West Indies and Florida.

The pages of the *Gazette* record mutinies, piracies, risings of Negroes on slave ships, fires, hunting accidents, hurricanes, drownings, death from lightning and disease, especially from smallpox and the throat distemper. Crimes were ever newsworthy, murder, assault, rape, burglary, arson and suicide. Jail breaks, desertions from the armed forces on land and sea, runaway slaves and redemptioners, these as a rule appearing among the advertisements, yield a wealth of genealogical information, as is true of confessions of criminals at the gallows.

Births are mentioned rarely, usually in the case of persons of distinction, but notices of marriages are much more frequent, while deaths appear very often. It should be noted that the "Index to the Obituary Notices published in 'the Pennsylvania Gazette,' from 1728-1791" in the *Pennsylvania Magazine of History,* x (1886) is very far from complete.

iv

Advertisements, in addition to those concerned with runaways and deserters, give a listing of merchants, artisans, teachers, shippers, etc.— extremely valuable items at a time when there were no city directories. Rewards for the recovery of lost or stolen horses, cattle, boats or other valuables are of genealogical importance, and the same is true of offers of real estate to be sold or leased, for they yield data concerning present or past owners and their neighbors. Requests for the location of missing heirs or relatives are invaluable. Elopements of wives and requests for the settlement of accounts by the executors or administrators of estates are of obvious significance.

The more than 12,000 persons indexed in this volume are by no means limited to Philadelphia or Pennsylvania but appear in all the Colonies, especially in New Jersey, the Three Lower Counties of Delaware and Maryland. Perusal of the items in the *Pennsylvania Gazette* presents a colorful and accurate picture of life in the first half of the Eighteenth Century. An admirable feature of the newspaper was Franklin's careful exclusion of "all libelling and abuse."

The compiler of this volume wishes to express his gratitude to the New-York Historical Society for making available the reprint edition of the newspaper, to Dr. Kenn Stryker-Rodda for generous assistance in checking the entire index of persons and to Mrs. Joan Sanger for typing the manuscript.

Kenneth Scott

KEIMER, Samuel, printer of Phila. - will publish newspaper (1 Oct.)

NEWTON, Henry, of Newcastle - persons desiring to promote
Keimer's newspaper may send their names to him (1 Oct.)

HEURTIN, Henry, of New York City, goldsmith - same as
above

PHILIPS, Eleazer, of Charlestown in New England, bookseller - same as above

MONTGOMERIE, John, Gov. of New Jersey - address to him on
18 Dec. of Representatives of New Jersey by order of
John Johnston, Speaker (24 Dec.)

HANSEN, Elizabeth (wife of John Hansen, of Knoxmarsh at
Keacheachy in Dover Twp.) - account of her capture,
with her children and maid, by Indians in New England
in 1724 is offered for sale by Samuel Keimer in Phila.
and W. Heurtin, goldsmith, in New York City (24 Dec.)

CAMPBELL, Thomas, lately arrived from Ireland - offers
rugs, blankets, cloth stockings and tools for sale at
Samuel Keimer's in Phila. (24 Dec.)

1729

BAXTER, Capt., lately a half-pay officer, who has taken
up the practice of law - has married at Barbadoes the
Widow Salmon, worth at least 30,000 pounds sterling
(2 Jan.)

READ, Charles - offers for sale land in Bucks Co. (7 Jan.)

SKIT, Elizabeth, servant - runaway from Daniel Prichard,
of Bucks Co. (7 Jan.)

WARE, Capt. - spoke with a ship on the coast to eastward
that had been 15 weeks from England, bound to Rhode
Island - New York item of 28 Dec. 1728 (7 Jan.)

PEARCE, Capt. - his vessel said to be run aground in the bay (7 Jan.)

MONTGOMERIE, John. Gov. of New Jersey - on 14 Jan. dissolved the New Jersey Assembly (21 Jan.)

KNOWLES/KNOLS, Francis, shopkeeper - woman is said to have taken a 12s. bill from his counter (21 Jan.); Knowles denies the story and Keimer reports that it was a gentleman's maid who said she lost the bill (29 Jan.)

CUNDUN, James, Irish servant, age c. 22 - runaway from Richard Whitten, of Dublin, Phila. Co. (29 Jan.)

FERGUSON, Samuel - offers for sale at Widow Fox's in Walnut St., Phila., men and women servants (29 Jan.)

SNELLING, Capt. - brings news from Paris that the King of France has recovered from his late sickness - New York item of 27 Jan. (4 Feb.)

KEIMER, Samuel - denies libel by Andrew Bradford to effect that Keimer claimed he was acquainted with Hudibras, the Secretary of State to Oliver Cromwell (4 Feb.)

SHIPPEN, Edward - sells soap and coffee (4 Feb.)

HATTON, Thomas - sells linens in his store at Thomas Oldman's in Market St., Phila. (11 Feb.)

WAYMAN, Dr. - on 1 Mar., St. David's Day, will preach sermon for persons in Phila. of stock of ancient Bretons, after which the group will partake of a collation at the house of Robert Davis at the Queen's Head in King St. (25 Feb.)

WALBY, John, schoolmaster - sells goods lately imported from Ireland at his house, almost opposite to Samuel Powel's in Second St., Phila. (25 Feb.)

HYNDSHAW, John, whose shop is in Market St., opposite to the Presbyterian Meeting-house in Phila. - sells books and stationery and binds books (25 Feb.)

BENNY, Elizabeth - offers to let her house adjoining the Ship Carpenter's, next to Society Hill in Phila. (25 Feb.)

JONES, Evan, at the Paracelsus's Head in Phila. - asks all persons indebted to him to make payment (25 Feb.); Evan Jones, chemist, is located in Market St. (24 June 1731)

SMITH, William, master of a sloop - arrived in New York
on 17 Feb. in 30 days from Jamaica - New York item of
24 Feb. (4 Mar.)

BLOODWORTH, Capt., and Capt. Fred, joint masters and
owners of the sloop <u>Pearl</u> - arrived in New York 17 Feb.
in 10 days from South Carolina - New York dispatch of
24 Feb. (4 Mar.)

VARDEL, Capt., who sailed last summer for St. Thomas -
his sloop was taken by the Spaniards; his cargo of 700
barrels of flour, besides butter, was owned by M. de
Lancey - New York item of 24 Feb. (4 Mar.)

MORGAN, Benjamin, wine-cooper, a steward of the Welsh
group in Phila. - sells wines, cordials, spirits and
vinegar at his store in King's St. (4 Mar.)

JONES, Evan, chemist - a steward of the Welsh group (4
Mar.)

PEARCE, Edward, attorney-at-law - a steward of the Welsh
group (4 Mar.)

EVANS, Peter - has been chosen a steward of the Welsh
group for next year (4 Mar.)

ELLIS, Robert, merchant - same as above

HOPKINS, John, merchant - same as above

PHILIPS, Capt. Matthew - same as above

ASHMEAD, Nicholas, at the Crown and Shoe, almost over
against the prison in Phila. - offers land for sale
(4 Mar.)

STOWBAR, Jacob - will sell plantation of 600 acres at
Penn's Neck; enquire of John Brick, Esq., or Malachy
Davis (13 Mar.)

BRODERICK, Darby, Irish servant - runaway from Samuel
Wright and Richard Kirby, both of New Hanover, Burlington Co. (13 Mar.)

GREEN, Edward, Irish servant - same as above

BURNET, Gov. - appointed 20 Mar. as day of fasting in
Mass. - Boston item of 24 Feb. (20 Mar.)

LUNDIN, John, master of sloop bound from Carolina to
Provincetown on Cape Cod - lost his life when his ship

was driven ashore on back side of that town - Boston
item of 24 Feb. (20 Mar.)

GODFREY, Capt. was cast away with a cargo of salt near the
same place on Cape Cod - Boston item of 24 Feb. (20
Mar.)

COWMAN, Nathan, master of ship Sizargh, who lately sailed
from Phila. - his ship, with cargo, several passengers
and sailors, was lost near the Irish coast (20 Mar.)

PLUMSTEAD, Hon. Clement - one night this week some mis-
creants did much damage to his gardens (20 Mar.)

BAYNTON, Peter, living at the lower end of Front St.,
Phila. - offers goods for sale (20 Mar.)

THOMPSON, Christopher - will sell 6-acre pasture back of
Spring Garden (20 Mar.)

GORDON, Patrick, Gov. of Pa. - sends message to the House
with the bill for emitting 50,000 pounds in bills of
credit (27 Mar.)

STRETTEL, Abel, of Dublin - his land in West New Jersey
is offered for sale by Thomas Hatton at Thomas Oldman's
in Market St., Phila. (27 Mar.)

WILSON, Mary, servant, a Londoner, mantua-maker - runaway
from Christopher Smith, merchant; reward will be paid
if she is brought to Samuel Ferguson in Walnut St.,
Phila. (27 Mar.)

LAMENON, Patrick, Irish apprentice, cooper, age c. 30 -
runaway from ship Mary, Robert Deglish commander; reward will be paid if he is brought to Deglish or to
John Morrison at Henry Dexter's in Phila. (27 Mar.)

FOLKS, Thomas, Jr. - will sell his plantation on the Post
Road by Crosswicks Bridge and the meeting-house in West
New Jersey (3 Apr.)

CLOUD, Joseph - plantation of 225 acres on Brandywine
Creek, lately belonging to him, is for sale; enquire
of Edward Horne of Phila. (3 Apr.)

BROWNE, Dr., living by York Road near Burlington - will
sell plantation about 5 miles from Burlington (3 Apr.)

MULLINGTON, Richard, in Water St., Phila. - will sell man
servant (4 years to serve) and woman (5¼ years to
serve) (17 Apr.)

DOWDLE, Major John, late of Sasafrax River, Cecil Co., Md.,
dec'd - has left his estate to Richard Dowdle, who is
asked to apply to the printer (17 Apr.)

HARRISON, Joseph - enquire of him to buy new brick house,
adjoining the Sign of the Bear in Market St., Phila.,
or to rent the house next adjoining, in which Owen Owen,
Esq., late sheriff, now lives (17 Apr.)

LLOYD, John - has opened a school in Mulberry St. at the
house of Alderman Carter (17 Apr.)

HARVEY, Capt. Seth - when he was at Porto Rico, the
Spaniards brought in 2 prizes (24 Apr.)

BURNET, Gov. - after his speech at Salem dissolved the
Massachusetts Assembly and set out for New Hampshire -
Boston item of 21 Apr. (1 May)

GRAY, John, English servant - runaway from John Bentley,
of Burmingham,and Richard Clayton, of Concord (1 May)

MIDDLETON, Richard, English servant - same as above

DECOW, Jacob, of Mans, Burlington Co. - sells books (8 May)

CHEYNEYS, John, of Thornbury, near Concord, Chester Co. -
has 2 stills for sale (8 May)

MACNEAL, Neal, Irish servant, age c. 20 - runaway from John
Matlock, of Waterford Twp., Gloucester Co., farmer (22 May)

PALMORE, George, English servant, age 33 - runaway from
Benjamin Armitage, of Bristol Twp., Phila. Co. (22 May)

POWEL, Evan - sells goose feathers at his shop in Chestnut
St., Phila., next door but one to Andrew Hamilton, Esq.
(22 May)

MACKMAMAN, John, Irish servant, age c. 30 - runaway from
Samuel Richardson of Bristol Twp.; reward will be paid
if servant is captured or news of him is given to Hugh
Roberts of Phila. (29 May)

WIT, Christopher, of Germantown - persons indebted to him
are to pay or expect trouble (29 May)

RAWLE, William - sells tea at his house in Water St.,
commonly called Arch St. in Phila. (29 May)

FINLEY, John, servant, farmer, age c. 20 - runaway from Mary
Stockdale of Evesham, Burlington Co.; notice of the run-

6

away is to be given to John Breintnal in Chestnut St.,
Phila. (5 June)

BENNET, Mr., leader of a gang of Irish robbers - steals goods
and horses and sells same in Maryland, Virginia and North
Carolina; one Lynch is a lieutenant and a Dobbs and a
certain Wiggins are members of the gang (12 June)

BUDD, John, at Phila., or, in his absence, Humphrey Murrey
or Edward Shippen - will sell land in Burlington, Gloucester and Cape May Counties and also 9,000 acres in
the Long Valley on the south branch of Rarington River
in New Jersey and likewise 1,500 acres on the west side
of the King's Road from Newcastle to Andrew Peterson's,
joining to said road, and to Col. Harman's manor and to
the lower side of the Welsh Tract, on the head of Duck
Creek (19 June)

VINING, Benjamin, who lives at plantation of 1,000 acres,
2 miles from Salem - offers for sale land in Salem Co.
and in Pennsylvania, including the house at Marcus Hook
where Ralph Hoy lives and a square field on Miamensack
Road, opposite to Philip Johns (19 June)

LEYCRAFT, Capt. - when he was bound out from Jamaica to
the Spanish Coast with a cargo of Negroes and dry goods,
his powder room took fire and blew up, with the loss of
some 50 persons - New York item of 10 July (24 July)

COOPER, Charles, captain of a sloop - when leaving Kingston, Jamaica, on 5 June, the powder took fire and the
ship sank, with about 60 white men and 300 Negroes; the
captain, 19 white men and 40 or 50 Negroes were saved -
Boston item (7 Aug.)

BRYANT, William, master of ship Albany - arrived in New
York City on 3 Aug. from Gibralter in 6 weeks, bringing
news from Europe; he states that Capt. Norris was detained by the Portuguese at Lisbon (7 Aug.)

COPE, John, servant - runaway from Edward Kemble of
Springfield Twp., Burlington Co. (7 Aug.)

SANDIFORD, Ralph, shopkeeper, over against the courthouse in Phila. - intends for England in 2 months
(14 Aug.)

SHAD, Tom, of Phila., who was harsh in collecting debts
- a verse against him is printed (4 Sept.)

NICHOLS, William, High Sheriff of Monmouth Co., N. J. -
offers reward for capture of Joseph Robins, of Mon-

mouth Co., yeoman, who on 19 August escaped from the goal of that county (4 Sept.)

HYDE, Cesar, servant, age 28 - runaway from Daniel Palmer, of Makefield Twp., Bucks Co. (11 Sept.)

OWEN, Dr. Edward, a physician of Phila. - died there 16 Sept. (18 Sept.)

BURNET, Gov. of Massachusetts - died last Tuesday in Boston in his 42nd year - Boston item of 8 Sept. (18 Sept.)

HARRY, David - has taken over the business of Samuel Keimer, who plans to leave Pennsylvania, at Keimer's late dwelling in Second St., Phila. (18 Sept.); Harry has declined, and the business will be taken over by Benjamin Franklin and H. Meredith (25 Sept.)

LONG, Capt., commander of a man-of-war - took up 6 convict runaway servants who had seized a ship; they confessed; 2 were reprieved and the others executed (2 Oct.)

DANCER, Clifford, merchant lately arrived from Liverpool - when he was coming in a long-boat from Chester River to Annapolis last Friday se'night, was overset in the bay and drowned, together with John Moll, of Newtown, Kent Co., and 2 sailors - Annapolis item of 16 Sept. (2 Oct.)

SMITH, James - was sentenced to death Thursday last at Supreme Court in Phila. for burglary and felony (2 Oct.); he was to be executed Saturday next (9 Oct.) but was reprieved (16 Oct.)

The following were elected 1 Oct. for Phila. Co.: - for Assembly--John Swift, Job Goodson, Edward Horne, William Monington, Jonathan Robinson, David Potts, John Cadwalader and Thomas Rutter; for commissioner--Isaac Leech; for assessors--John Pawlin, William Corker, Andrew Robinson, William Fisher, Evan Thomas and James Bingham; for sheriffs--Charles Read and Nicholas Scull; for coroners--Owen Owen and Mirick Davis; for city burgesses--Thomas Kearsly and Thomas Tresse; for city assessors--Thomas Nixon, Timothy Stevenson, William Chancellor, John Rutter, John Harrison and Joseph Trotter (2 Oct.)

The following were elected 1 Oct. for Chester Co. - for Assembly--Caleb Copelar, Richard Hayes, Joseph Brinton, Thomas Chandler, William Webb, Samuel Gilpin, James James and Joseph Penock (2 Oct.)

CALVERT, Benedict Leonard, Gov. of Maryland, who for some
days visited the Gov. of Pennsylvania in Phila. - set
out Tuesday last to return home (2 Oct.)

MARTIN, John, servant of a brewer of Phila. - Monday last,
being about to put a cask of beer on board the ship of
Capt. Annis, fell and was drowned in the river (2 Oct.)

EANON, Mr., the conterfeiter of the 18d. bills of New
Jersey, who died in passage from Dublin to Phila. - his
associates are all apprehended, according to report
from Amboy (2 Oct.)

CRESSWEL, John, servant - runaway from Richard Prichard,
of Whiteland, Chester Co. (2 Oct.)

ARNOLD, Melchizedeck, servant - runaway from William Dewes,
of Germantown Twp., Phila. Co. (2 Oct.)

LE, John, whose shop is in Market St., over against the
Presbyterian Meeting-house in Phila. - has for sale imported goods (2 Oct.)

AMBLER, John - was tried last week for the murder of his
Negro boy and was found guilty of manslaughter -
Portsmouth, N. H., item of 26 Sept. (9 Oct.)

The following were elected last week as representatives
for Lancaster Co.: Thomas Edwards, John Wright, James
Mitchel and Thomas Reed (9 Oct.)

GRIFFITHS, Thomas, Esq. - Tuesday last was elected Mayor
of Phila. (9 Oct.)

DUMMER, W., Gov. of Massachusetts - his speech was brought
on 17 Sept. to the Massachusetts Assembly by Secretary
Willard (16 Oct.)

MARTIN, Thomas, captain of a 38-ton schooner - 14 July
last was taken captive by Indians when he was 3 days
out of Canso and his vessel ran aground on the east
side of the Island of St. John's - Boston item of 6
Oct. (16 Oct.)

PORTER, Israel, of Salem, Mass. - died there Monday last -
Boston item of 6 Oct. (16 Oct.)

PRICE, Rev. Mr. - was voted 8 pounds a week by the congregation of the King's Chapel in Boston - Boston item of 6
Oct. (16 Oct.), but the amount was presently raised to
10 pounds a week - Boston item of 27 Oct. (10 Nov.)

JOHNSON, Rev. Mr., late of St. Andrews, Holborn - succeeds
Rev. Mr. Gordon in the Rectory of Bridgtown, Barbadoes
- Boston item of 6 Oct. (16 Oct.)

BORDEN, Joseph, Esq., Treasurer of Rhode Island - died
Wednesday last - Rhode Island item of 3 Oct. (16 Oct.)

WYAT, Ebenezer, master of sloop Friendship from Curracoa -
upon his arrival at New York on 6 Oct. reported that on
22 Sept. he had sighted an overturned sloop - New York
item of 13 Oct. (16 Oct.)

LONDONDERRY, Lord, General of the Leeward Island - died 17
Sept., according to report brought by the sloop Exchange
to New York in 16 days from Antigua - New York item of
13 Oct. (16 Oct.)

NORWOOD, Capt., from Phila. - arrived 23 Sept. at Antiqua
- New York item of 13 Oct. (16 Oct.)

OVERY, Capt., who arrived this week at New York from London - reports the conclusion of a truce with Spain -
New York item of 13 Oct. (16 Oct.)

LINDSEY, Alexander, of Phila. - last Saturday se'nnight,
when going down the river in a boat with several men,
fell overboard near Red Bank and was drowned (16 Oct.)

PILES, Mr., a fiddler - sometime last week his canoe overset near Newtown Creek, and his wife was drowned (16
Oct.)

HAMILTON, Andrew, Esq. - was chosen Speaker of the House
of Representatives (16 Oct.)

HARRIS, Rev. Henry, fellow of Jesus College, Oxford, and
one of the ministers of King's Chapel in Boston - died
Monday last in Boston in his 42nd year - Boston item
of 13 Oct. (23 Oct.)

OLDHANS, Cunrad - Tuesday last, when riding in his cart
on road at Towmenson, Phila. Co., by plantation of
Daniel Williams, his cart overset and he was killed by
wheel falling on his head (27 Oct.)

MORGAN, Benjamin, in King St., Phila. - one may treat with
him at his house or with the master of the 60-ton
brigantine Ann & Elizabeth, at Robert Ellis's wharf,
in regard to freight (27 Oct.)

SEARLE, John, at house of Benjamin Morgan, wine-cooper in
King St. - has choice maidservants to be disposed of

(27 Oct.)

GORDON, Patrick, Lt.-Gov. of Pennsylvania and the 3 counties on Delaware - address on 23 Oct. of House in reply
to Governor's address of 21 Oct. (30 Oct.)

WELLINGTON, Capt. - his large ship, belonging to Bristol
and bound for Boston from Lisbon with cargo of salt, on
10 Oct. ran ashore on Marshfield Beach near Scituate
and broke to pieces - Boston dispatch of 20 Oct. (30
Oct.)

BIGGELOW, Capt., master of a Connecticut sloop - 10 Oct.
his sloop ran ashore at Plymouth, Mass. - Boston dispatch of 20 Oct. (30 Oct.)

FITCH, Joseph, a young man of Boston - died there Thursday last on night he was to have been married - Boston
dispatch of 20 Oct. (30 Oct.)

Gov. of Pennsylvania - returned to Phila. 27 Oct. from
Newcastle (30 Oct.)

GLENTWORTH, Capt. - arrived in Phila. last week from
Madiera (30 Oct.)

House and tract of about 1,000 acres, on South River, a-
about 4 miles from Brunswick and 8 miles from Amboy,
is for sale - apply to Gabriel Steelea, Esq., at Perth
Amboy, or Dr. Brown near Burlington (30 Oct.)

MURPHY, Richard, master of the ship Jenny Galley, of Dublin, Ireland - sailed about 25 July from Londonderry
bound to Newcastle upon Delaware; on 14 Sept. the captain tried to take ship to Virginia; passengers and
mates refused; William Kinley, first mate, took over
ship but reached Sandy Hook by mistake; Capt. Long, of
H.M.S. Shorham enquired into matter as did Governor and
Council; mates, supercargo and passengers were discharged but are detained by captain till matter is settled in court - New York dispatch of 27 Oct. (3 Nov.)

DUMMER, Jeremiah, Esq., late agent for New England - his
letter concerning dispute between Governor and people
(6 Nov.)

ADAMSON, Capt. Anthony - convicted 9 Oct. for counterfeiting - Perth Amboy dispatch of 1 Nov. (6 Nov.)

SCOT, William - same as above

SLEST, Matthias, of Kingston, Ulster Co., N. Y. - on 26

Oct. his brew and malt-house there destroyed by fire
(6 Nov.)

CURREN, George, Irish servant, age c. 21 - runaway from
David Davies, of Goshen, Chester Co., Pa. (10 Nov.)

LEEDS, Titan, of Burlington - charges that William Bradford, of New York, has forged an almanac in his name
(10 Nov.); reply of William Bradford; Felix Leeds's,
Titan Leeds's and William Birket's almanacks are to be
sold by William Bradford in New York and Andrew Bradford in Phila. (13 Nov.)

READ, Charles - offers for sale 300 acres in Bucks Co., 2
miles from the courthouse and also 76 acres, bounding
on Cobb's Creek, within 6 miles of Phila. (10 Nov.)

ALDSEWORTH/ALDSWORTH, Mr., late keeper of the Sun Tavern
in Burlington - supposed drowned 2 or 3 miles from
town (13 Nov.); his dead body found last week on
Jersey shore (19 Mar.)

OWEN, Owen - has returned to his former house, the Indian
King in Market St., Phila. (13 Nov.)

LOTHROP, Capt. - in October last, in his passage from
Boston to Martha's Vineyard, off Monimoy sighted a
vessel in distress, bound from Ireland to Phila., and
put ashore such people as had not starved to death
(20 Nov.)

WRIGHT, Capt., of schooner John, cleared out of Boston,
laden with wheat - overset in the bay after the pilot
left her (24 Nov.); the above report is found false
(9 Dec.)

ATKINS, Capt., of a sloop belonging to Boston - his crew
mutinied off coast of Guinea, threw him overboard; when
in Antigua, they were betrayed by some Negroes aboard,
arrested, tried and convicted of piracy - New York dispatch of 24 Nov. (27 Nov.)

WALLIS, Capt., of the Watts Galley - is arrived in the
river at Phila. in 8 weeks passage from England (27
Nov.)

ALLEN, William, of Phila., merchant - is returned in the
Watts (27 Nov.)

MERCER, Capt., of the ship Drogheda Merchant - tried Friday last in Phila. at a Court of Admiralty (Gov. Patrick Gordon, president; John Wells, John Hugg, Peter

Bard and John Moore, commissioners; Thomas Lawrence, Samuel Hazel, Capt. John Hopkins and Capt. Thomas Bourn, assistants) for murder of Thomas Flory on passage from Ireland to Pennsylvania; Flory, who confessed he stole 100 guineas from a Mr. Steward, was allegedly tortured and died on board; a passenger, Mr. Moneypenny, was considered prejudiced and was not allowed to testify at the trial; Capt. Mercer was acquitted (1 Dec.)

CLAYPOLE, George, of Phila. - offers red clover seed for sale (1 Dec.)

HORNE, Edward, lately removed to his plantation about 3 miles from Phila. - people owing him are to pay debts to William Rawle, of Phila., merchant, who sells cloth, stationery, sealing wax, paper (4 Dec.)

STEPHENS, Capt., master of a schooner which arrived in New York 26 Nov. in 28 days from Curacoa - reports that Capt. Garret was cast away last summer on passage to New York from Jamaica (9 Dec.)

GEDDES, Capt. - supposed to have perished in storm in coming through the Windward Passage (9 Dec.)

HUME, Capt. - same as above

COCKRAM, Capt. - supposed lost in a storm (9 Dec.)

ANTRUM, John, of Burlington Co. - on 15 Nov. shot a horse in his cornfield, mistaking the beast for a deer (9 Dec.)

SEVERN, John, of Trenton - his stable there was burnt to the ground on 5 Dec. (16 Dec.)

PHILIPS, George, of Byberry, Phila. Co. - 9 Dec. was accidently killed when felling trees (16 Dec.)

Servant men and boys, just imported from London in the ship Boneta, Thomas Reed master - are to be sold by William Rawle and Edward Horne (16 Dec.)

SCARTH, Timothy, at house of Widow Stacey in Phila., tanner - offers reward for recovery of saddle stolen from back of a horse at the George Inn in Second St. (16 Dec.)

EGLESTON, Mrs., of Boston, only child of, age between 2 and 3 - about a fortnight ago accidently burned to death at Newton, where it had been put out to board - Boston dispatch of 1 Dec. (23 Dec.)

BROWN, Capt. Abraham, of Watertown, Mass. - found dead
in his bed morning of Wednesday last - Boston dispatch
of 1 Dec. (23 Dec.)

MILES, Samuel, of New Haven, Conn. - gives account of re-
markable preservation of himself and part of his company on voyage from New London to Antigua in Sept.
1728; after shipwreck they were rescued by sloop of
Robert Gardner, from Rhode Island, bound to Antigua; 3
of Miles's passengers were James Westbury, his son William and daughter Anne, and crew members were Hackalier
Thomas and James Tuthil, all of New England (23 Dec.)

PROUSE, James, a servant - was charged last week at court
in Phila. with entering house of Mr. Sheed, of Front St.,
Phila., barber, to which he was admitted by a servant
of Mr. Sheed, and there stealing (23 Dec.); according to
his confession, he was born at town of Brentford, Middlesex Co., England; his father was a corporal in the late
Lord Oxford's Regt. of Horse; James was for a time in
the care of an uncle at Eling; in his 12th year he came
to Phila.; he is now about 19 years of age; he was induced to steal from his master by one John Greyer; he
claims that James Mitchel is innocent; he was pardoned
at the gallows (20 Jan. 1730)

MITCHEL, James, who, like Prouse, broke prison and was retaken at Amboy - was charged with waiting to watch while
Prouse was in Sheed's house; both criminals were sentenced to death but Mitchel was directed to apply to
the Governor for mercy (23 Dec.); execution of Prouse
and Mitchel set for 14 Jan. (13 Jan. 1730); according
to his confession, he was born at Antrim, Ireland; at
age of 13 was apprenticed to a bookbinder, whom he
served 4 years; he then went to England, where he was
pressed on board the man-of-war Berwick, George Gordon
commander; he returned to England in Oct. 1728 and then
came to America as a servant; he was arrested on charge
of robbing George Sheed, but is innocent. He was pardoned at the gallows (20 Jan. 1730)

CALAGHAN, Charles - was tried in Phila. for rape on a
girl under age of 10; he was acquitted of rape but will
be prosecuted for an assault, with intent to ravish (23
Dec.); was whipped around town at cart's tail on Friday
last (13 Jan. 1730)

HERNE, Lawrence, servant, age c. 22 - runaway from Nicholas
Scull, of Phila., innholder (23 Dec.)

MACKCLANEN, Jane, servant, age c. 23 - runaway from Moses
Hewes, of Phila. (30 Dec.)

FETTERLY, Johannes, Dutch servant, age <u>c</u>. 34, who speaks
very little English and has been a trooper in the
Emperor's service - runaway from John Naglee, of Germantown, Phila. Co., butcher (30 Dec.)

1730

STEWART, Admiral - reported that he arrived in Jamaica
with 2 men-of-war - New York dispatch of 29 Dec. (6 Jan.)

SARLY, Capt., of brigt. <u>Hope</u> - has arrived from New York
in London - New York dispatch of 29 Dec. (6 Jan.)

BRADWAY, Mary, a noted midwife, born New Year's Day,
1629/30 - died in Phila., 2 Jan. 1729/30 and was interred 5 Jan. (6 Jan.); an elegy on death of Mrs. Mary
Broadwell is sold by David Harry, printer in Phila.,
and William Heurtin in New York (27 Jan.)

WESTCOTT, Stephen, servant - runaway from Thomas Hynson
Wright, of Queen Ann's Co., Md. (6 Jan.)

WESTCOTT, James, servant - runaway from Thomas Wilkinson,
of Queen Ann's Co., Md. (6 Jan.)

MARGATROYD, Michael,. servant - runaway from William Gough,
of Queen Ann's Co., Md.; he and the other 2 runaways
pretend to be sailors leaving Capt. Stringfellow in
Maryland; reward will be paid by owners for their recovery or by W. Crossthwaite, periwig-maker in Phila.
(6 Jan.)

Owner asked to claim dark bay horse left in stable of
George Shoemaker, innholder at the Lion, in Elbow Lane
near Market St. (6 Jan.)

Titan Leed's, Felix Leed's, John Jerman's, William Birkett's
and the New York almanacks for 1730 are for sale by the
printers (6 Jan.)

HASTINGS, Samuel shipwright at Phila. - poem appeared in
the <u>Maryland</u> <u>Gazette</u> of 30 Dec. about his launching the
<u>Maryland</u> <u>Merchant</u>, built at Annapolis (13 Jan.)

FROST, John, stay-maker and children's coat-maker, lately
from London - lives at Evan Morgan's, near the market
in Phila. (13 Jan.)

WINKLEY, Capt., who about 3 months ago sailed from Boston

in a brigantine for Jamaica - he arrived Saturday last
from Rhode Island in Boston and told how he and his
passengers, Mr. Rogers and Mr. Wille, were captured and
abused by pirates - Boston dispatch of 22 Dec. (20 Jan.)

KENSEY, Matthew - offers reward for recovery of a large
   Church Bible, stolen from his house in Upper Merion (20
   Jan.)

GORDON, Gov. Patrick - his speech is printed as is the
   reply of the General Assembly (27 Jan.)

BOURNE, Joseph - on 26 Nov. was ordained pastor of church
   in Boston; the elders convened on this occasion were
   the Rev. Mr. Lord, of Chatham, and 2 Indian pastors from
   Martha's Vineyard (27 Jan.)

PEABODY, Rev. Oliver, pastor of the English and Indian
   Church at Natick - was ordained 17 Dec. at Cambridge,
   Mass.; prayer was by Rev. Mr. Appleton, of Cambridge;
   Rev. Mr. Sewall, of Boston, preached; Rev. Mr. Baxter,
   of Medfield, gave the charge; Rev. Mr. Williams, of
   Weston, gave the right hand of fellowship (27 Jan.)

FRANCISCUS, Christopher - some time since at Conestogoe
   caught a wolf near his sheep-pen and with his daughter's help killed the beast (27 Jan.)

PEGG, Daniel - offers for sale his great brick house at
   the north end of Phila. (27 Jan.)

SEWALL, Judge - died in Boston 1 Jan. in his 78th year
   (3 Feb.)

SLAUGHTER, Capt. - Monday last his vessel, coming from the
   bay to Boston, ran aground on the south side of Martha's
   Vineyard - Boston dispatch of 5 Jan. (3 Feb.)

FITCH, Rev. Mr. - preached a Christmas sermon in Portsmouth, N. H. (3 Feb.)

GEARFIELD, Mrs., born at Watertown, Mass. - died 11 Dec.
   at Marlborough, Mass., aged 90 (3 Feb.)

WARD, Samuel, born at Sudbury, Mass. - died 15 Nov. at
   Marlborough, Mass., in his 89th year (3 Feb.)

JOHNSON, Mrs. Mary, born at Sudbury, Mass. - died at
   Marlborough, Mass., within space of a year, in her
   85th year (3 Feb.)

DAVIES, W., next door to A. Hamilton, Esq., in Chestnut

St., Phila. - offers books for sale (3 Feb.)

CELL, Luke, _alias_ John Dodson - on 19 Dec. last left a 14-
year-old Negro boy named Jack at the house of Thomas
Carty, at Manhatawny, Phila. Co.; Jack says he was apprenticed to Cell by his master, James Wood, near Williamsburgh in Virginia (3 Feb.)

JONES, Evan, chymist - is removed from Second St. to the
Paracelsus' Head in High St., _alias_ Market St., over
against the prison (3 Feb.)

STURGIS, Mr. - Saturday last, because of a difference with
his wife, jumped into the river near Carpenter's wharf
in Phila., but was taken out again (10 Feb.)

BEVAN, Evan, master of the sloop _Morning Star_ - his ship
foundered at sea in Oct. last; the people in the boat
were saved and arrived at Antigua in about 3 days (19
Feb.)

One Johnson has been appointed Governor of South Carolina
and Jonathan Belcher has been appointed Governor in
place of Gov. William Burnet (19 Feb.)

SMITH, Robert, master of the sloop _Swan_, now at Burlington
wharf - will agree with persons desiring to transport
themselves or goods (19 Feb.)

REES, Thomas - offers for sale his plantation on the River
Schuylkill, on the Chester Co. side, about a mile above
Thomas Miller's mill (19 Feb.)

READ, Charles - offers for sale 2 tracts of land, late the
estate of Jonathan Dickinson, Esq., dec'd; one is to
south of Phila., on east side of the Schuylkill; the
other is on east side of the King's Highway, adjoining
lands lately belonging to Richard Hill, Esq., dec'd
(19 Feb.)

BROCKDEN, Charles - offers reward for arrest of person or
persons who stole fencing rails from his lot on Society
Hill, next Third St., in Phila., and from his plantation at Moyamensing (19 Feb.)

SARLY, Capt., in brigantine _Hope_ - reported put up in London for New York in Nov. last - New York dispatch of
14 Feb. (19 Feb.)

DOWNING, Capt., in ship _Alexander_ - reported to have arrived in London 19 Oct. from Port of New York - New
York dispatch of 14 Feb. (19 Feb.)

FORBES, Lord - reported to have been appointed Gov. of the Leeward Islands (19 Feb.)

CLEVELAND, Capt. - his ship Ostins, bound from Boston to Barbadoes, was lost 19 Jan. on the back side of Cape Cod; all men escaped except one who froze to death - Boston dispatch of 1 Feb. (24 Feb.)

HARRIS, John, first made of Capt. Winslow - on 19 Jan. fell between ship and wharf and was drowned - Boston dispatch of 2 Feb. (24 Feb.)

KEIMER, Rob., master of ship George and Anne - acquitted Friday last of charge of murdering Edw. Norris on board ship in her passage from Dublin to New England - Boston dispatch of 2 Feb. (24 Feb.)

SEAVER, Subael, of Roxbury, Mass. - died there Friday last in his 93rd year; he left brother in his 89th year and a sister in her 86th year, all born in Roxbury; this brother is a twin; the other twin reached 70 - Roxbury dispatch of 22 Jan. (24 Feb.)

WAINWRIGHT, John, of Oley, age c. 22 - on 16 Feb. made a eunuch of himself (24 Feb.)

BALL, John, living in house formerly Thomas Chalkley's, in Laetitia Court - teaches writing, arithmetic and French (24 Feb.)

GRIFFIN, Mr., who keeps the ferry between Bradford and Haverhil - within 11 days lost his mother and 5 of his 8 children from fever - Boston dispatch of 2 Feb. (5 Mar.)

BELCHER, Gov. Jonathan - plans to embark in Capt. Carey for Massachusetts about middle of March - Boston dispatch of 9 Feb. (5 Mar.)

CALUPLON, ___, a Frenchman by birth - his son was captured and killed last fall by the Catawbies, who inhabit the land southwestward of Virginia (5 Mar.)

MORGAN, John, of Milnehouses, Durham Co., England - seeks his son John, who left England about 24 years ago, as he is now heir, since all his brethren have died without issue (5 Mar.)

WHITE and Taylor, of Phila. - offer red clover seed for sale (5 Mar.)

SCULL, Nicholas - offers reward for recovery of black mare stolen from stable of the Bear Inn in Phila. (5 Mar.)

ORPWOOD, Edward, late of Oxford Twp., dec'd - demands on his estate are to apply to Francis Knowles or Thomas Gilpin, his executors (5 Mar.)

TEAGUE, Elizabeth, late of Phila., dec'd - persons with demands on her estate are to apply to Henry Hodge or Francis Knowles (5 Mar.)

NORRIS, Benjamin - convicted 25 Jan. by a court of admiralty at Portsmouth, N. H., of having cut down a white pine tree of about 36 inches in diameter, fit for making a mast for the Royal Navy - Portsmouth, N. H., dispatch of 25 Jan. (13 Mar.)

VUNICE, Paul - Thursday last convicted at Superior Court in Boston of counterfeiting Rhode Island bills (13 Mar.)

SHAW, Capt. Richard, of East-Hampton, Long Island - on 7 Jan. his house was burnt down and his wife, aged c. 20, and 3 Negroes were burnt to death (13 Mar.)

KELSEY, William - executed Saturday last at Newcastle for burglary and burning the county goal; in his speech he says his father died when he was young; he stole and was transported from England; he was servant to Edward Mayne in Kent Co. and stole from him and from William Melliner; then at Christiana he broke into John Garretson's house and stole; being apprehended, he was committed to the prison, to which he set fire; he lied when he said that William Scott was with him in breaking into Garretson's house - Newcastle dispatch of 9 Mar. (13 Mar.)

RUTTER, Thomas, Sr., who was the first to erect an iron-works in Pennsylvania - died Sunday last in Phila. (13 Mar.)

SHANNAN, Agnes, administratrix of estate of Jeremiah Shannan, late of Newcastle Co., dec'd - at her house near Christiana Bridge will be sold by vendue a 250-acre tract belonging to the estate, on White Clay Creek, near Samuel Johnson's mill and bounding on James Hermitage, Esq., and the Rev. George Gatasbey (13 Mar.)

NAYLOR, Robert, servant, age c. 20 - runaway from John Parker, joiner, at William Biles's in Bucks Co. (13 Mar.) John Parker, of Bristol (20 Aug.)

DOWNING, Anstis, alias Agnes MacDaniel, Irish servant, age c. 23 - runaway (with George Welsby, who lately married her and has a Maryland pass signed Charles Markland) from John Clark, of Bucks Co. (13 Mar.)

Copy of the memorial of the General Assembly in New England, sent home by Jonathan Belcher against the proceedings of the then Gov. Burnet (19 Mar.)

HILL, Capt. Thomas, master of sloop **Ann** - on 17 Feb. met
a pink belonging to Boston, John Kint, captain, coming
from Bay of Honduras, bound for Boston but blown off
her course and forced for Island of Jamaica - New York
dispatch of 16 Mar. (19 Mar.)

Dead whale, about 50 feet long - came ashore 5 Mar. about
20 miles eastward of Cape May (19 Mar.)

JAMES, Isaac, of Montgomery Twp., Phila. Co. - his house
burnt to the ground Tuesday last when he was absent
(26 Mar.)

PARIS, Austin, of Phila., founder - died last night (26
Mar.); poem on his death (9 Apr.)

MACGUIRE, John, Irish servant - runaway from John Philips,
of Kent Co., Md. - reward offered if he is brought to
his master or to Enoch Jenkins on Bohemia Manor in
Cecil Co., Md., or to William Evans of London Tract in
Newcastle Co. (26 Mar.)

The following engage at Phila. after 15 Jan. to accept in
payments one-fourth in paper money of the Lower Counties
on Delaware: Andrew Hamilton, Isaac Norris, James Logan,
Samuel Preston, William Fishbourn, Clement Plumstead,
Thomas Lawrence, William Allen, Isaac Norris, Jr., Peter
Lloyd, Samuel Hasel, White and Taylor, Thomas Sober,
Joseph Turner, Patrick Greeme, Joseph Growden, Jr.,
James Hume, John Richmond, Thomas Hatton, Avent Hassart,
Benjamin Godeffroy, Alexander Woodrop, Loes and Pearson,
William Atwood, George Macall, Anthony Morris, Thomas
Willing, Thomas Sharp, William Rabley, John Hopkins,
Cassel & Maugridge, John Hyat, George Claypole, John
Bringhurst, George Emden, John Cadwalader, Henry Hodge,
Thomas Bourn, Mark Joyce, Thomas Griffitts, Charles
Read, Ralph Asheton, William Rawle, William Masters,
James Parrock, John Bowyers, Arnold Cassel, Thomas
Asheton, Charles West, Michael Hulings, Richard Allen,
Samuel Cooper, Francis Knowles, Joshua Maddox, Thomas
Leech, William Corker, William Chancellor, Edward
Roberts, Robert Worthington, John Mason, John Warder,
Simon Edgell, Paul Preston, John Stamper, Joseph Lyn,
Thomas Chase, John Roberts, Joseph Pennock, John Bell,
John Wright, Samuel Gilpin, George Rice Jones, Thomas
Holloway, John Heathcoat, Zachary Hutchins, John Kay,
Daniel Hyberd, Joseph Hinchman, John Renshaw, Mathias
Aspdin, Jacob Shute, William Tidmarsh, Benjamin Shoe-

maker, John Buley, Norton Pryor, Blacston Ingeldew, William Williams, William Carter, Jeremiah Langhorne, William Biles, Thomas Canby, Thomas Watson, Joseph Kirkbride, Jr., John Hall, Nathan Watson, Benjamin Jones, Thomas Yardley, William Paxson, Thomas Biles, Simon Butler, Timothy Smith, Matthew Hughes, Abraham Chapman, Isaac Penington, Christian Vanhorn, Jr., Abr. Denormandie, John Baker, George Clough, Samuel Baker, Jonathan Palmer, Thomas Marriot, John Watson, Paul Blakir, Robert Edwards, Richard Sands, John Claves, Niel Grant (2 Apr.)

FISHBOURN, W. - states that the Trustees of the General Loan-Office of Pennsylvania will receive the bills of credit of the 3 Lower Counties in amount not exceeding one-fourth part of the annual quotas to be paid in (2 Apr.)

WROE, Joshua, of Boston, merchant - died Wednesday last and body was interred Saturday - Boston dispatch of 23 Mar. (9 Apr.)

MEDCALFE, Joseph, a farmer, in 73rd year - married 10 Mar. in Medfield, Mass., Mrs. Hannah Fisher, in her 75th year (9 Apr.)

ATKINS, Robert, of Perth Amboy, merchant - died Tuesday last - Perth Amboy dispatch of 4 Apr. (9 Apr.)

RAWLE, William, in behalf of Edward Horne - on 5 May, at house of Widow Hoskins in Chester, will be sold by auction a plantation on Brandywine Creek, formerly taken in execution by Sheriff of Chester Co. and sold for payment of debt due from Joseph Cloud to E. Horne (16 Apr.)

Account of pirate off east end of Long Island - New York dispatch of 13 Apr. (16 Apr.)

TALIFERO, John, alias Luke Cell, alias John Dodson, servant - runaway from Stephen Hollingsworth, of Phila., cordwainer (16 Apr.)

A grist mill at Salisbury Town, upon head of Duck Creek, Kent Co., on Delaware, 37 miles from Newcastle, offered for sale -- apply to William Rawle in Phila. or Joseph Rawle in town of Salisbury (16 Apr.)

GARONO, Isaac, French servant, age c. 25 - runaway from Abraham Wood, of Bucks Co. (23 Apr.)

BREWER, Henry, Irish servant, age c. 30 - runaway from Nicholas Parker, of Bucks Co. (23 Apr.)

CUMMINS, Joseph, Irish servant, age c. 22 - runaway from
Isaac Walker, of Tredyffryn, Chester Co. (23 Apr.)

SMITH, George, servant, age 21 - runaway from John Baldwin of Kennet, Chester Co. (23 Apr.)

SEARLE, John, at house of Benjamin Morgan in King St. -
enquire of him to let to freight his brigantine Anne
and Elizabeth (23 Apr.)

CORTLAND, Philip, Esq. - Thursday last was sworn as member
of Council of New York - New York dispatch of 24 Apr.
(30 Apr.)

SPOTSWOOD, Col., Postmaster General - has arrived in Virginia (30 Apr.)

DICKINSON, J. - his house, other houses and a store near
Fishbourn's Wharf were destroyed by fire Friday last
(30 Apr.)

Grist mill and 70 acres of land about 3 miles from a good
landing on Susquehannah River are offered for sale by
John Everitt, of West Nottingham, Chester Co. - apply
to Everitt or to John Piggot (30 Apr.)

BOWEN, Richard, servant, age 22 - runaway from Samuel
Worthington of Manor of Moreland, Phila. Co. (30 Apr.)

PURNEL, James, servant, age 30 - same as above (30 Apr.)

PHILIPS, Abel, age 24 - runaway from Henry Comeley, of
Manor of Moreland, Phila. Co. (30 Apr.)

KELLEY, Peter, Irish servant, who speaks good French -
runaway from Thomas Duffell, of Manor of Moreland,
Phila. Co. (30 Apr.)

HUGHS, Samuel, a West Country servant, who has served some
time in Frankford and looks to be 30 years old but says
he is but 25 - runaway from John Wallace in Derby (30
Apr.)

HYNDSHAW, John, at the Sign of the Two Bibles in Market
St., over against the Presbyterian Meeting-house in
Phila. - binds and sells books (7 May)

FROST, John, servant, age c. 30, tailor and staymaker by
trade - runaway from Evan Morgan of Phila. (7 May)

DUNNING, Thomas - offers reward for recovery of horse stolen
from stable of George Inn in Second St., Phila. (7 May)

MONTGOMERIE, Gov. John - text is given of his speech to the New Jersey Assembly at Amboy on 7 May (14 May)

HEDFORD, John, servant - runaway from White & Taylor (14 May)

CORNSDALE, Thomas - offers reward for recovery of roan gelding strayed or stolen from pasture of Benjamin Wright in Bristol, Bucks Co.; apply to Wright or to Evan Harris (14 May)

A still will be sold Saturday next at Jonathan Fisher's, opposite to the Market House in Phila. (14 May)

PETERS, Thomas, shopkeeper - has removed to his new house right opposite to the Three Tuns in Chestnut St., Phila. (14 May)

BERRY, Benjamin, servant - runaway from Samuel Eves, near Newcastle on Delaware, sadler (14 May)

MURPHEY, Lawrence, Irish servant, who has worked as weaver, hatter and schoolmaster - runaway from Jeremiah Clement, of Chester, hatter (14 May)

BURRIDGE, William - sentenced to death at Annapolis for breaking open the store of James Donaldson - Annapolis dispatch of 14 Apr. (21 May)

CLARK, Charles, age c. 16 - sentenced to death at Annapolis for breaking open the house of Mr. Poloke, of Annapolis - Annapolis dispatch of 24 Apr. (21 May)

LLOYD, Eleanor - committed to goal in New York Saturday last on suspicion of murdering her bastard child - New York dispatch of 18 May (21 May)

GRAY, Joseph, at the Middle Ferry, Phila. - a black horse was left at his stable (21 May)

MONTGOMERIE, Gov. John - address to him by order of Speaker of the House, J. Kinsey, Jr., and the governor's reply (28 May)

DUBOIS, Noah, of Providence Twp., Phila. Co. - on 9 May committed suicide by shooting himself (28 May)

Plantation of 85 acres in Whitpin Twp., joining to Whitemarsh for sale - enquire of John Ward, living in Combes's Alley, Phila. (28 May)

A dun mare, accustomed to run in Falconer's Swamp - reward

offered if brought to John Snider's at Whitemarsh (28 May)

KEENHAN, John, of Twp. of Ballymony in Barony of Ballbrit, Kings Co., Ireland, now at house of Thomas Howard, joiner, in Second St., Phila. - offers reward for news of his brother, William Kain, of England's Grove, about 54 miles from Phila., who came to Pennsylvania about 46 years ago and has 3 sons by the wife he first married (28 May)

LONDONDERRY, Lord, dec'd - is to be taken home from Antigua in a leaden coffin on board a man-of-war, accompanied by Lady Londonderry - Antigua dispatch of 5 May (4 June)

LOB, Joseph, carpenter - runaway from the ship Salisbury, Daniel Williams, master; reward for his capture offered by Simon Edgell (4 June)

ROCHET, Emanuel, Scotch sailor - same as above

CRAB, Thomas, sailor, a lad - same as above

SCOT, George, indented servant - same as above

DUBORN, Daniel - teaches French at Mr. Cunningham's, a barber, next door to Mrs. Rogers in Market St., Phila. (4 June)

BOND, Mr., of Boston - in latter part of May died of small pox, as did 5 of his children - Boston dispatch of 1 June (11 June)

FULLER, Mr. - executed at Barnstable, Mass., 20 May for murder of his wife - Boston dispatch of 1 June (11 June)

CRUMP, Mr. - this week was committed to prison in Phila., charged with beating and abusing his wife; a woman is imprisoned with him as accessary (11 June)

NORRIS, John, servant, age c. 24 - runaway (supposedly in company with James Curry, age 19, apprentice to Mrs. Paris, of Phila., brass-founder) from William Smith, of Phila., shoemaker (11 June)

FORD, John, servant, West-Country lad, age c. 17 - runaway from Matthew Hughes, of Buckingham, Bucks Co. (11 June)

Two hundred acres of land on branches of Nespining, in Amwell Twp., Hunterdon Co., West New Jersey - apply to

John Maultsby at Phila. or Joseph Peace at Trenton (11 June)

TYLER, John, servant, age c. 22, hatter by trade - runaway from James Brendly, of Phila. (18 June)

TAMERLANE, Thomas, East Indian servant, rigger by trade, age c. 23 - runaway from Charles Black, at the Sign of the Brigantine in Phila. (18 June)

NEVILL, Thomas - offers sweet almonds for sale at his house in Chestnut St., Phila. (18 June)

CAMPION, George, at the Tun in Water St., Phila. - offers reward for recovery of a silver-hilted sword lost between Frankford and Burlington (18 June)

BELCHER, Gov. Jonathan - will leave next week for Portsmouth, England, to imbark for New England in the man-of-war Blandford, Capt. Protheroe - London dispatch of 25 Apr. (25 June); the Blandford arrived Saturday last in Boston - Boston dispatch of 10 Aug. (20 Aug.)

TAILER, William - has been made Lt.-Gov. of Massachusetts in place of William Dummer (25 June)

BROWN, William, servant, age c. 20 - runaway from John Dexter, of Phila., sadler (25 June)

A person lately from London, at William Crossthwaite's, peruke-maker, opposite to the Pewter-Platter in Front St., Phila. - has ivory, knives and forks for sale (25 June)

NEVETT, Robert, from Wales, at his house, a little below Dr. Jones's, on the roadside in Merion - has merchanize and groceries for sale (2 July)

HUMPHREYS, Owen, in Market St., Phila. - offers reward for recovery of brown bay gelding, supposed gone about Byberry, Frankford, Oxford or Pennypack (2 July)

FIELD, Mr. - on 8 July was arrested in Phila., charged with uttering counterfeit Spanish money (9 July)

FAIRMAN, Benjamin, near Phila. - 2 horses strayed from his pasture; reward will be paid if horses are delivered to Fairman or to Samuel Bustill in Burlington (9 July)

ROGERS, Thomas - offers reward for recovery of mare taken out of a field in Nottingham, Chester Co. (9 July)

Description of terrible storm 13 June at Saybrook, Conn.
(16 July)

EVANS, Richard - 15 July in Phila. received 39 lashes and
was imprisoned for life at hard labor, having been
convicted of bigamy (16 July)

TAILER, William, Lt.-Gov. of Massachusetts - 30 June delivers speech to General Assembly at Cambridge - Boston dispatch of 9 July (23 July)

BOURK, Mr., Irishman lately out of servitude - is in irons
in goal of Chester Co., Pa., charged with stabbing to
death a countryman on the other side of Brandywine -
Chester dispatch of 17 July (23 July); coroner's jury
brings in verdict of wilful murder against him (30
July); convicted of manslaughter and burnt in the hand
(3 Dec.)

WRIGHT, Edward, master of ship Constantine, about to sail
for London - freighters and passengers are to apply to
the master or to Thomas Lawrence (23 July)

RICHARDS, Nathaniel, of Chester Co. - accidentally killed
by fall from his wagon (30 July)

ANNIS, Capt. - Saturday last arrived in Phila. in about 12
weeks from London (30 July)

About 10 days ago a schoolmaster on Staten Island was imprisoned there for counterfeiting New Jersey bills (30
July)

HARWOOD, Rev., minister of church in Burlington - died
there Tuesday last (30 July)

Three men-of-war, the Biddiford, Capt. Wayne, soon to sail
for England, the Solebay, Capt. Warren, bound to New
York, and the Greyhound, Sir Yelverton Payton (who last
came from Havana with a passenger, a Mr. Wyndham) - all
are at Hampton, Virginia (30 July)

FORREST, Thomas, servant, age c. 30, skinner by trade -
runaway from Jonathan Fisher, of Phila., glover.
Forrest is in company with William Varrell, who has
runaway from his creditors (30 July)

LLOYD, Peter, merchant, in Phila. - has for sale one-third
of an undivided 600-acre tract in Willistown, Chester
Co., bounded by the lands of Mr. Yarnel, Michael Jobson, Rees Thomas and Peter Jones (30 July)

Samuel Powell and Samuel Preston, executors of estate of
Esther Shippen, devisee in trust of Edward Shippen, late
of Phila., merchant, dec'd - will sell lot between house
of James Logan and house of Samuel Powell; also a lot
bounded on N. by Dock St., W. by lots of Samuel Powell,
S. by lot of John Thomas and E. by Second St.; also
brick house of Joseph Shippen, of Phila., gent.; also
210 acres of land (6 Aug.)

BELCHER, Jonathan - congratulatory poem to him, dated 31
Mar. 1730, and signed I. Watts, is lately communicated
from London (13 Aug.); is welcomed and entertained in
Boston 9 Aug. (27 Aug.)

EADES, Michael, servant, age 24, shoemaker - runaway from
Joshua Cowpland, of Chester (13 Aug.)

Jack, young Negro - runaway from William Moore, of Moorehall, Chester Co.; reward if brought to his master or
to John Moore, Esq., in Phila. (13 Aug.)

HASSERT, Arent, near William Fishbourn's in Front St.,
Phila. - offers cloth and tea for sale (13 Aug.)

BREINTNALL, John, of Phila. - has taken up a large bay
horse (13 Aug.)

ROBERTS, Miles, of Chester Co. - his wife Rebecca has
eloped from him (13 Aug.)

Newly appointed trustees of the General Loan Office of
Pennsylvania are the following: Andrew Hamilton,
Charles Read, Jeremiah Langhorne and Richard Hayes
(20 Aug.)

HORNE, Edward, at Coffee-House in Phila. - on 14 Sept.
will sell by vendue the following ground-rents (by
deed of trust to him made for the use of the creditors
of Joseph Jones, of Phila.) late Tho. Parsons's now
paid by Elizabeth Hill; late Abraham Hooper's by Anne
Woods; late John Fellows by Edmund Williams at Derby;
Thomas Griffith by John Lock; Frances Little by Joseph
Claypoole; Hannah Delarle by Lloyd Zachary; John Songhurst by Daniel Radly; Joseph Cross by the Widow Shelly;
Robert Tate by Widow Shelly; Rose Plumly by William Allen; Nathan Sikes by Mr. Yeldall's; William Salleway,
the estate of John Carpenter, dec'd, by Isaac Norris,
Sr.; and late Isaac Rikets, the estate of said John Car-
penter by said Isaac Norris; late William Salisbury by
William Bevan; Robert Roberts of North Wales; Jacob
Evans by Richard Waln (20 Aug.)

HODGE, Henry, attorney - warns squatters on "the London Company's Land" to make satisfaction for damage (20 Aug.)

TATEHAM, Mr., at Woodbury Creek - his servant twice hanged himself, once last Sunday and again on Monday but did not die (27 Aug.)

PORTER, Abraham, lately dec'd - his executors, Mahlon Stacy, Jonathan Wright and Thomas Scattergood, of Burlington, offer land in Gloucester Co., West Jersey, for sale (27 Aug.)

DUNBAR, Col. David, Surveyor General of His Majesty's Woods - his letter, dated Boston, 15 Aug. 1730, relating to the new settlements to the eastward and his notice, dated Boston, 22 Aug. 1730, forbidding cutting of white pine trees (3 Sept.)

MONTGOMERIE, J. - his speech on 26 Aug. to the New York Assembly (3 Sept.)

THURKETTLE, Capt. - arrived 25 Aug. in New York in a brigantine 21 days from Jamaica (3 Sept.)

MARSTON, Capt. arrived 20 Aug. in New York in a brigantine from Jamaica (3 Sept.)

Two recent accidents at cider-mills are reported, one in Germantown and the other near Faulkner's Swamp (3 Sept.)

The Governor of Pennsylvania left Phila. Tuesday last for New York (3 Sept.)

FLOWER, Mary, widow, in Water St., near the Crooked Billet, Phila. - has a Negro woman to sell (3 Sept.)

O'DONNOLLY, Owen, Irish servant, age c. 26, who professes to be a brickmaker and mason - runaway from William Anderson, of Whitemarsh, near Justice Farmer's (3 Sept.)

RAWLINGS, Capt., from Jamaica - arrived Tuesday last in Boston and recounted his capture by pirates; when on board the pirate ship he saw an instrument marked "Joseph Gardner," who was supposed to be master of a Rhode Island sloop taken by the pirates about a month before - Boston dispatch of 31 Aug. (10 Sept.)

WOODBERRY, Capt. - on voyage from Boston to Surinam fell overboard and was nearly 3 hours in the sea before he was rescued - Boston dispatch of 31 Aug. (10 Sept.)

GORDON, Gov. - was received in New York Saturday last by

the Governor of New York; Gordon was lodged in the fort;
the ladies were lodged at Col. Gilbert's at the Bowery,
"in the pretty house which Mr. Bickley built" - New York
dispatch of 27 Aug. (10 Sept.)

MARSTON, Capt., who arrived in New York 28 Aug. from Jamaica
- tells of his being chased by a Spanish pirate ship (10
Sept.)

HESON, Capt. - letter of 7 Aug. from Bermudas reports his
arrival there from Providence and that Capt. Philip
Cockram of New York was taken by the Spaniards, who cut
him and most of his men to pieces (10 Sept.)

DALLOWAY, Joseph, servant, age c. 35, blacksmith - runaway
from John Lloyd of Phila. (10 Sept.)

Tony, Negro, age 25 - runaway from Major John Betterfield
of Phila. (10. Sept.)

BELCHER, Gov. Jonathan - dispute with New Hampshire Assembly on question of the Governor's salary (17 Sept.)

RHYDDARCH, Philip, who was born in Caermarthenshire in
South Wales and came to Pennsylvania about 40 years ago
- died Sunday last of a flux at Newtown, Chester Co.,
in his 102nd year, leaving 6 children, 35 grandchildren
and 48 great-grandchildren (17 Sept.)

MAC DONNELL, Nicholas, Irish servant, baker, age c. 23 -
runaway from Nicholas Rogers, of Phila. (17 Sept.)

ROE, John, servant, smith, age c. 24 - runaway from Thomas
Lindley, of Phila. (17. Sept.)

GRIGG, Thomas, servant, mason, age 17 or 18 - runaway from
Thomas Hart of Phila. (17 Sept.)

WOODS, Mark, servant, pretended bricklayer, age c. 24 -
runaway from Esther Lowdon, of Phila. (17 Sept.)

WHITE, Garret, servant, age c. 22 - runaway from John Hart,
of Phila. (17 Sept.)

MOORE, John, Collector of Port of Phila. - offers reward
for discovery of person or persons who damaged the
customhouse boat, lying at Vining's Wharf (17 Sept.)

STEEL, Capt. John, master of the Wilks Frigat, who arrived Saturday last in Boston - relates how his ship
sank in hurricane on 2 Aug. in passage from St.
Christophers to London; those who escaped in the long-

boat were taken up by Capt. Sparks bound from Jamaica to Bristol; some then went on board ship of Capt. Clymer with Palatines bound from Rotterdam to Phila.; from this they met a sloop from North Carolina bound to Boston; they left it at Rhode Island and came by land to Boston - Boston dispatch of 7 Sept. (24 Sept.)

BOULDING, Capt., master of a brigantine of Phila. - reported lost in a hurricane at Barbadoes 15 Aug. (24 Sept.)

PRICE, Evan - offers reward for return of a mare that strayed from Robert Jones's mill at Whitemarsh, Phila. Co. (24 Sept.)

TRAUNTER, William - offers reward for spaniel stolen Saturday last from on board the ship London Hope at Phila. (24 Sept.)

BELCHER, Jonathan - his speech to General Assembly of Massachusetts, address of Council, address of House of Representatives, answer of Governor (1 Oct.)

List of vessels driven ashore at Barbadoes 16 Aug, in hurricane: snow of Liverpool, James Read, master; brigantine of Virginia, Hugh Tringle, master; schooner of Ireland, James Ferguson, master; brigantine of Phila., Bowling, master; sloop of Barbadoes, Edward Nichols, master; sloop of Barbadoes, Capt. Newton, master (1 Oct.)

Jack, Negro, age c. 30, who speaks little or no English - runaway from Abraham Lincoln, of Springfield, Chester Co.; reward will be paid if Jack is brought to his master or to Mordecai Lincoln living among the upper inhabitants on Skuylkill or to William Branson in Phila. (1 Oct.)

GRIFFITS, Thomas - elected Mayor of Phila. on 6 Oct. (8 Oct.)

ALLEN, William - elected alderman of Phila. (8 Oct.)

NORRIS, Isaac, Jr. - same as above

STEEL, James - elected common councilman of Phila. (8 Oct.)

EMLEN, George - same as above

TAYLOR, Abraham - same as above

POWEL, Samuel, Jr. - same as above

MIFFLIN, George - same as above

WHITE, John - same as above

Officials elected for Phila. Co.: Assembly--Jonathan
Robeson, William Monington, Thomas Leech, Job Goodson,
John Cadwalader, William Allen, David Potts and John
White; commissioner--William Fishbourn; assessors--An-
drew Robeson, Evan Thomas, William Corker, John Pawlin,
William Fisher, John Rutter; sheriffs--Charles Read,
Nicholas Scull; coroners--Owen Owen, John Roberts;
city burgesses--John Kearsley, Thomas Tresse; city as-
sessors--Edward Warner, Thomas Peters, Joseph Trotter,
Timothy Stephenson, William Chancellor, James Bingham
(8 Oct.)

Officials elected for Bucks Co.: Assembly--Joseph Kirk-
bride, Jr., William Paxton, Jeremiah Langhorne, Abraham
Chapman, Christopher Vanhorne, Andrew Hamilton, Matthew
Hughes, Thomas Canby; sheriff--Timothy Smith; coroner--
Jonathan Woolston (8 Oct.)

Officers elected for Chester Co.: Assembly--Henry Pierce,
John Taylor, Samuel Lewis, John Parry, Thomas Chandler,
Samuel Gilpin, William Webb, Henry Hayes; sheriffs--
John Owen, John Bennet; coroners--John Wharton, Abraham
Darlington; commissioner--Evan Lewis; assessors--John
Davis, William Paschal, James Stacey, Charles Corsley,
Philip Taylor.(8 Oct.)

Officers elected for Lancaster Co.: Assembly--John Wright,
George Stuart, Thomas Edwards, John Musgrove; sheriffs--
John Galbreth, David Jones; coroners--Joshua Lowe, John
Mitchel; commissioner--John Davis; assessors--Gabriel
Davis, Emanuel Carpenter, John Caldwell, Joshua Lowe,
Thomas Wilkins, Walter Deney (8 Oct.)

Officials elected for Newcastle Co.: Representatives--An-
drew Peterson, Samuel James, Joseph Robinson, John
M'Cool, Robert Gordon, Thomas Noxon; sheriff--William
Read; coroner--Abraham Gooding (8 Oct.)

Officials elected for Kent Co.: Representatives--John
Tilton, William Rodeney, George Newel, John Newel, James
Morris, Thomas Dixon; sheriff--John Hall; coroner--
Samuel Perry.

Officials elected for Sussex Co._ Representatives--William
Till, Richard Hinman, Jacob Kollock, John Rhodes, Henry
Brook, Thomas Davis; sheriff--John Hall; coroner--
Cornelius Whitbank (8 Oct.)

TAFT, John, servant, weaver, age c. 35 - runaway from Samuel Bunting, of Bucks Co., near Joseph Kirkbride's
(8 Oct.)

WICKS, John, servant - runaway from Duncan Mackenzie, of
Phila. (8 Oct.)

WOORE, Joseph, servant - runaway from Joseph Flower, of
Phila., joiner (8 Oct.)

A servant man - runaway from Armstrong Smith, of Phila.,
shipwright (8 Oct.)

WILLIS, Robert, servant, shoemaker - runaway from John
Jones, of Phila. (8 Oct.)

FITZGERALD, James, servant, age 18 - runaway from Jonathan
Fisher, glover, of Phila. (8 Oct.)

HAMILTON, A., Esq. - last night chosen Speaker of the House
of Representatives (15 Oct.)

Account of trial of persons accused of witchcraft Saturday last at Mount Holly - Burlington dispatch of 12
Oct. (22 Oct.)

COWMAN, Capt. - reported arrived at Bristol from Phila.
in about 5 weeks passage (22 Oct.)

Report of Negro conspiracy in South Carolina to destroy
the English there - letter dated 28 Aug. (22 Oct.)

Hurricane in South Carolina on 27 Aug. (22 Oct.)

SPEARE, John - Sunday last fell into the river between a
flat and a ship at Phila. and was drowned (22 Oct.)

CUNNINGHAM, William, age c. 24 - broke out of Gloucester
Goal in New Jersey; reward offered for his delivery to
Samuel Harrison, Sheriff (22 Oct.)

GREY, Richard, a West-country man, butcher, age c. 40 or
45 - same as above

GORDON, Patrick, Lt.-Gov. - speech 21 Oct. to Representatives of the Counties on Delaware and the reply to
him on 22 Oct. (29 Oct.)

List of vessels in Port of Charlestown, S. C., at time of
the hurricane on 27 Aug.: ship Union, William Burrish.
master, for London; ship Adventure, of London, Stewart
Powel, master; ship Joseph and Isaac, of London, Valen-

tine Burden, master; brigantine <u>Katharine & Elizabeth</u>, of Phila., Samuel Farra, master; brigantine <u>Groton</u>, of Boston, Samuel Waterhouse, master; sloop <u>Two Sisters</u>, of Bermudas, William Gibbs, master; sloop <u>Endeavour</u>, of Antigua, bound to Holland, Samuel Parsons, master; schooner <u>Manatee</u>, of Bahama, Samuel Fox, master; all the above were lost or went ashore; the following rode out the storm: 3 men-of-war; ship, Hemming, captain, for London; ship <u>Sarah</u>, Henry Basset, master, for London; ship <u>Sea Nymph</u>, of London, Richard Forster, master; sloop <u>Albany</u>, of Boston, Mindert Wimple, master; sloop, of Bermudas (29 Oct.)

CAR, James, of Phila. - Thursday last fell from top of load of hay and died of injury next day (29 Oct.)

FISHBOURN, William, late a trustee of Loan Office - Sunday night his house was broken open and 2,000 pounds of public money stolen (29 Oct.)

BURLEIGH, Joseph - offers for sale his plantation of some 200 acres in East New Jersey, 20 miles from Brunswick and 10 from Trenton, bounded upon Benjamin Clark, Sarah Worth and Edmund Bainbridge (29 Oct.)

MORGAN, John, at Radnor Twp., Chester Co. - has a stray mare (29 Oct.)

Message 16 Oct. of Gov. J. Belcher to Massachusetts House of Representatives (5 Nov.)

Report of discovery of Negro conspiracy to kill the whites in South Carolina on 15 Aug.; in the whole province there are about 28,000 Negroes and 3,000 whites (5 Nov.)

BRADLEY, Mr. - being in liquor on Monday night fell into a ditch at upper end of Market St., Phila., and drowned in less than 6 inches of water (5 Nov.)

JONES, Griffith - 4 Nov. stood an hour in pillory in Phila. and then was whipped round the term at cart's tail for assault with intent to ravish a girl of 6 years (5 Nov.)

Glascow, an Indian - 4 Nov. stood an hour in pillory in Phila. and was whipped round the term for assault with intent to ravish a young woman (5 Nov.)

WILKINSON, John, from London, brushmaker, living at Robert Steel's, within 2 doors of the Plume of Feathers in Front St., Phila. - desires to buy hogs bristles (5 Nov.)

Brilliant Aurora Borealis observed at Newport, R. I.,
Boston and New Hampshire on 22 Oct. (12 Nov.)

BROOKE, H., Speaker of House of Assembly of the 3 Counties
on Delaware - asks holders of old bills of credit to
turn them in (12 Nov.)

MITCHEL, James, servant, cooper, age c. 28 - runaway from
John Orr, near Skuylkill, Phila. (12 Nov.)

HALL, Richard, Irish servant, age c. 22 - runaway from
John Armitage, Esq., of Newcastle Co. on Delaware (19
Nov.)

LEVETT, Charles, Irish servant boy, age c. 18 - runaway
from Widow Watson, of Newcastle Co. on Delaware (19 Nov.)

Sloop belonging to John Donelson, of Maryland, bound for
North Carolina, was lost 9 Sept. on Cape Henry - Williamsburg dispatch of 3 Oct. (19 Nov.)

Negro uprising feared in Virginia and activity of the
Militia to prevent the same - Williamsburg dispatch of
3 Oct. (19 Nov.)

Disastrous fires in Newport, R. I., and near the
Market in New York City (19 Nov.)

THOMAS, Elizabeth, age c. 13 - tried at court in Newtown,
Bucks Co., Pa., for murder of infant of 18 months and
found guilty of manslaughter (19 Nov.)

James Dyer, Joseph Dyer and wife Deborah were indicted for
murder of child aged one year; James Dyer did not appear; the other 2 were acquitted (19 Nov.)

POTTS, David, member of Pennsylvania Assembly - died
Monday last (19 Nov.)

About a fortnight ago a small child at Little Choptank fell
into the fire and died (19 Nov.)

Nicholas Toop and Hannah Newman, who were to have been
married Tuesday evening in Charlestown, Mass., died
Wednesday last of smallpox - Charlestown, Mass., dispatch of 23 Oct. (26 Nov.)

HAMMERDEN, Capt., from London - reports that the ship Great
Caesar, of Portsmouth, bound from Cadiz to Portsmouth,
foundered upon the Banks of Newfoundland; ship's company was taken up from their boat by a ship bound from
Nevis to London, Capt. Hicks, commander, and taken to

the Downs - Boston dispatch of 16 Nov. (26 Nov.)

JUMP, Capt., of Boston - reported to have been murdered, along with his company, off the coast of Guinea by the Negroes on board (26 Nov.)

GLEAVES, Thomas, of New York, 18-month-old child of, accidentally burnt to death on Wednesday last - New York dispatch of 23 Nov. (26 Nov.)

BOULDER, Capt., in ship _Arent_ - arrived Sunday last during storm at New York in 5 weeks from Bristol (26 Nov.)

CROSSTHWAITE, William, peruke-maker, over against the Pewter Platter in Front St., Phila. - will pay a good price for clear white horsehair and for good light or grey human hair (3 Dec.)

PORTER, Abraham, dec'd - 2,500 acres, belonging to his estate, on both sides of Gloucester River (commonly called Timber Creek) in West Jersey, 12 miles from Phila., are for sale; apply to Mahlon Stacey, Jonathan Wright and Thomas Scattergood in Burlington, trustees of said estate, or to Isaac Porter at John Sherborn's in Phila. (3 Dec.)

LAMB, Anthony, mathematical instrument-maker, from London, now living in New York, near the New Dock, at the Sign of the Compass and Quadrant - sells instruments for sea and land (3 Dec.)

WILLING, Thomas, late of Phila., merchant - persons indebted to him are to settle accounts with Charles Willing or Joseph Shippen, Jr. (3 Dec.)

WILLIS, Capt., of the _Amity_ - reports that as he was coming from Virginia he found a Negro stowaway; the Negro said he was going ambassador from the Negroes to King George; said Negro was put ashore and whipped through every county to the place whence he came (8 Dec.)

Report from Jamaica, July 5, that 100 white men sent after runaway slaves were all destroyed by the Negroes; report also that, from 24 Mar. 1729 to 24 June 1730, 11,421 hogsheads of sugar were exported from the island and 4,631 Negroes imported from the coast of Africa (8 Dec.)

CROCKER, Capt. - arrived Monday last in Boston from London, bringing with him Capt. Wier of Charleston and his company; Wier's ship had sprung a leak on passage from the West Indies to London - Boston dispatch of 23 Nov. (8 Dec.)

FORTESCUE, Alexander - last Saturday was found dead in his bed on board a shallop at Phila. (15 Dec.)

PEMBERTON, John - reported in May last to have killed a buffalo on Shunadore River that weighed, when dressed, 1,400 pounds (15 Dec.)

SANDIFORD, Ralph, being bound for England - has printed a second impression of his Negroe Treatise, to be distributed gratis by him or by Matthias Aspdin his attorney (22 Dec.)

GRAVES, Mrs. Grace, widow, one of the first female English children born in Boston - died Thursday last in Ipswich, Mass., in her 99th year - Ipswich dispatch of 27 Nov. (29 Dec.)

SMITH, Elnathan, master of a sloop belonging to Killingsworth - his sloop overset 14 Dec.; 2 men were drowned but Smith, clinging to the wreck, was finally taken off by a ship and brought to New London (29 Dec.)

1731

Article on trade between England and Pa. (5 Jan.)

FRYER, John, servant, formerly servant to Col. French, dec'd - runaway from Abraham Gudding, coroner of New-Castle Co.; he had been sold out of prison by the sheriff; he had been tried for breaking open the store of John Read and stealing goods (5 Jan.)

FALCONAR, John, opposite to the Sign of the Scales, near Walnut St. wharf, Phila. - offers reward for discovery of person or persons who broke open his home and stole his goods (5 Jan.)

TUTHILL, Christopher, goldsmith, next door to the Star and Garter in Front St., Phila. - his shop was broken into and robbed of the following items: part of a silver skellet (wt. 10 oz.), bar of silver (wt. 12 oz.), ebony snuff box with silver hinges, a silver toothpick case marked on the bottom A. D. with a crown over it, 10 yards of silver wire rolled up (5 Jan.)

GORDON, Patrick - speech to Representatives in Phila. and their address to him (12 Jan.)

Digest of Gov. Belcher's speech to the Massachusetts Assembly (12 Jan.)

ASHTON, Benjamin, of Lower Dublin, Phila. Co. - his wife
Ann/Anne has eloped from him (12 Jan.); wife claims
Benjamin promised to put away his red-haired girl, but
locked himself up with her instead and shut his pregnant wife (Anne) into the kitchen to lie by the fire
(26 Jan.)

Corporation of St. Anns, Burlington, R. Ellis clerk --of-
fers for sale 260-acre tract of land in Somerset Co.,
N.J., formerly belonging to Richard Stockton and afterwards to Thomas Leicester, dec'd; apply to Abraham
Hewlings and William Cutler at Burlington (12 Jan.)

KENSEY, John - was chosen 18 Jan. to serve in the Assembly
for Phila. Co. in place of David Potts, dec'd (19 Jan.)

READING, Capt., master of ship Katharine, belonging to New
York - his ship arrived in Bristol but he and 5 of his
men were washed overboard and lost (26 Jan.)

Digest of a second speech by Gov. Belcher to the Massachusetts Assembly (26 Jan.)

PEIRCE, Edward, Esq., Attorney General of the Jersies -
19 Jan. at Burlington married Mrs. Catherine Talbot,
widow of Robert Talbot (26 Jan.)

SKUYLER, Mr., Esq., proprietor of the great copper mine
at York - lately died there (26 Jan.)

HILL, Richard, Esq., dec'd - persons indebted to his estate are to settle with his executors at Phila., Lloyd
Zachary and Mordecai Lloyd (26 Jan.)

BERRY, Benjamin, servant - runaway from Samuel Eves, near
New-Castle, sadler; another servant ran away with
Berry (26 Jan.)

GARDNER, Peter, of Blockley Twp. - offers reward for recovery of horse that strayed from his barn
(26 Jan.)

Tract of 500 acres, part in Little Creek Hundred and part
in Dover Hundred, in Kent Co. on Delaware (the northerly part is about 3 miles from Fast Landing at Duck
Creek, the middle part about 2 miles from the landing
at Little Creek and the southerly part about 2 miles
from the landing at Jones's Creek; apply to Charles
Read, of Phila., or Hugh Durborow, Jr., in Kent Co.
(2 Feb.)

HORSLEY, Joseph, servant, age c. 25 - runaway from John

Wallace of Chester, smith (2 Feb.)

Among recent laws, dated 6 Feb. are an"Act for the Relief
of Benjamin Mayne, with Respect to the Imprisonment of
his Person" and an "Act to disable William Fishbourn
from holding any Office of Trust or Profit within this
Province" (9 Feb.)

KELLY, Cornelius, and Edward Greagin, both Irish servants,
aged c. 20 - runaways from Nathan Dix and James Portell,
both of Octerara in Nottingham Twp., Chester Co. (9 Feb.)

Answer of Massachusetts House of Representatives to their
Governor's speech (16 Feb.)

HUGG, John, J. P. and member of the King's Council in the
Jersies - Saturday last when riding home was taken ill
and died that night (16 Feb.)

Society of Ancient Britons - on Mar. 1, St. David's Day,
will meet at Owen Owen's, the Indian King in Market
St., Phila. (16 Feb.)

ROBERTS, John, dec'd - accounts with his estate to be settled with the executors, John White and John Cadwalader (16 Feb.)

BROWNE, Dr. - plantation of 230 acres, where he now lives,
between the River Delaware and York Road, about 9 miles
from Burlington, is to be sold; apply to Dr. Browne before 30 Mar., when it will be sold by vendue at Micajah
How's, 9 miles from Burlington (23 Feb.)

Ancient Britons Society after dinner on Monday last proceeded to Wickaco to attend launching of Capt. Bromage's
ship; the stewards chosen for the ensuing year are Rowland Rice, Joseph Howel, Capt. Samuel Bromage and William Major (4 Mar.)

Inoculation for smallpox is increasing; J. Growdon, Esq.,
the first patient of note that led the way, is now upon
the recovery (4 Mar.)

Tract of about 6,000 acres in Hunterdon Co., West New Jersey, about 22 miles from Brunswick and near the same
distance from Elizabeth Town, is for sale; apply to
the owner, Joseph Kirkbride, of Bucks Co., Pa. (4 Mar.)

Tract of land of about 350 acres, about 4 miles from the
great meeting house in Nottingham, Chester Co., Pa., is
for sale; apply to the owner, David Fristane, or to
John Browne, living on Ellis's wharf, Phila. (4 Mar.)

Jack, elderly Negro, carpenter by trade, who has a wife
in New-Castle Co. and who formerly belonged to Sir William Keith at his works in New-Castle Co. - runaway from
John England and Company, at Principio Iron Works (4
Mar.)

Governor Belcher speaks to the Massachusetts General Assembly of 10 Feb. (11 Mar.)

TADLOCK, Edward, who came from Kent Co. - 10 Feb. was found
dead in the woods near Swattarrow Creek in Lancaster Co.
(11 Mar.)

HENDRICKS, James, Jr. - accidentally shot in the woods near
Sasquehanah 26 Feb., when his father's gun went off, and
died at once; another brother who was with them had 3
years before accidentally shot and killed his cousin, a
young man (11 Mar.)

HOYLE, Michael, servant - at Manhatawny, despairing of cutting down a great tree which his master ordered him to
fell, he cut his throat with a razor; it is thought he
will live (11 Mar.); Hoyle has died (1 Apr.)

BLOWDEN, John, servant, shoemaker - runaway from Arthur
Wells, of Phila. (11 Mar.)

BENJAMIN, Capt., who some time since sailed from Boston
for Jamaica - was cast away near Island of Bermudas but
the men were saved - Boston dispatch of 8 Mar. (18 Mar.)

Gov. Johnson has safely arrived in South Carolina (18 Mar.)

LINDSEY, Lawrence or Luke, Irish servant, age c. 17 - runaway from Samuel White, of Caecil Co., near Nottingham
(18 Mar.)

Irish servant, age c. 16 - runaway from John Patton, of
Caecil Co., near Nottingham (18 Mar.)

BURREL, Mr., of Phila., pilot - reported to be drowned
in Virginia (25 Mar.)

Ship Prince William, Mavrick Thomas, commander, now at Burlington wharf, about to sail for Liverpool and Dublin -
apply for transport to Thomas Hendry, of Burlington,
merchant (25 Mar.)

NORRIS, Isaac, of Fairhill, near Phila. - offers reward for
recovery of horse strayed or stolen (1 Apr.)

MC AULAY, Alexander, at Messers. Reddish and Paxton's,

sadlers, opposite to the Great Meeting-House in Phila.
- has a Negro boy for sale (1 Apr.)

OWEN, O. - informs that horse about 3 weeks ago was left
at the Sign of the Indian King in Phila. (1 Apr.)

CALLEHAN, Charles, servant, age c. 20 - runaway from William
Biddle, of Phila. (1 Apr.)

Lord and Lady Baltimore are preparing to go from England
to Maryland (8 Apr.)

BEAUCLERK, Lord Vere, brother to the Duke of St. Albans -
is appointed governor of a large tract of land in New
England (8 Apr.)

O HAROE, James, Lord Tyrawley - is appointed Governor of
Barbados - Boston dispatch of 29 Mar. (8 Apr.)

LLOYD, David, Chief Judge of Pa. - died Monday last at
Chester at an advanced age (8 Apr.)

GROOME, Mr., who kept the ferry at Indian River - was
drowned 20 Mar., with his son and various passengers
according to an account from Lewis Town (8 Apr.)

JONES, Owen, Welsh servant, age c. 25 - runaway from Edward
Thomas, of Red Lion Hundred, New-Castle Co. (8 Apr.)

GRACE, Robert - persons indebted to him are to pay his attorney, Charles Read in Phila. (15 Apr.)

GRAY, Elizabeth, in Wallace's Alley, in Front St., near the
Sign of the Pewter Platter - washes linens (15 Apr.)

NORRIS, Isaac, Esq. - is made Chief Judge of Pa. in place
of Judge Lloyd, dec'd (15 Apr.)

PENN, Springet, Esq. - has died in Ireland (22 Apr.)

CHARLES, Robert, Esq. - married last Wed. to Miss Philadelphia Gordon, the governor's oldest daughter (22 Apr.)

The May Fair next, for health reasons, prohibited to be
kept in Burlington by the Petty Sessions of the Peace
for Burlington Co. (22 Apr.)

Furniture, chariot and horses for sale and a dwelling,
coach house, stable and pasture to be let by Rebecca
Palmer in Arch St., Phila. (22 Apr.)

Tract of 407 acres in Northern Liberties of Phila., between

Phila. and Frankford, about 3½ miles from Phila., bounded to west above a mile oh Frankford Creek; apply to William Rawle in Phila. - (22 Apr.)

BARCLAY, John, Postmaster at Amboy, brother of Robert Barclay - died last week in Amboy (29 Apr.)

PARIS, Ferdinando John, Esq. - chosen by the Pennsylvania Assembly to be agent for Pa. at the Court of Great Britain (29 Apr.)

ORANGE, Robert, pilot of Boston - on 9 Apr. was accidentally crushed to death in Boston; in Feb. and Mar. 2 other pilots, Kerton of New York and Burrel also met violent deaths (29 Apr.)

TOMSON, Jacob (alias Ham), New England born, an Indian - runaway from John Owen, sheriff of Chester, Pa. (29 Apr.)

Account of Cape Fear (6 May and 13 May)

Saturday last Gov. of Massachusetts dissolved the Assembly and will leave 27 Apr. for New Hampshire - Boston dispatch of 26 Apr. (6 May)

HANMORE, Capt., master of sloop bound from the east end of Long Island to Boston - sloop was cast away on the point of Cape Codd; the men escaped (6 May)

SCOT, Capt. George, of Rhode Island - when returning with cargo of slaves from Guinea, the Negroes rose and killed 3 of his man on watch, John Harris, doctor, Jonathan Ebens, cooper, and Thomas Ham, sailor; another member of the company was Thomas Dickinson; Capt. Scot and a boy alone escaped and made their way back to Rhode Island; after escape, they refreshed themselves on sloop of Monserat, James Collingwood master (6 and 13 May)

SMITH, Capt., master of the Beaver - left London 18 Mar. and arrived in New York 26 Apr.; he reported that one of the Annis's was to sail in a day or 2 for Phila. (6 May)

MACLANE, Alexander, Irish servant, age c. 20 - runaway from James English, of Freehold, Monmouth Co., N.J. (6 May)

MORRIS, John, of Montgomery Twp. - 28 Apr., when he was felling a tree, his wife was accidentally struck by the tree and killed (13 May)

A bear weighing upwards of 300 lbs. was lately killed near Mount Holly (13 May)

GREEN, William, servant, age c. 20 - runaway from John
Comely of the Manor of Moreland (13 May)

BAYNTON, Peter, at lower end of Front St. - sells sugar,
oil and sundry European and West India goods (13 May)

BURRINGTON, Gov. - has arrived in North Carolina (27 May)

ROGERS, T., master of the sloop Humbird - arrived 8 May in
Rhode Island, from Jamaica; he had been taken 26 Apr.
by a Spanish pirate but later got off with his sloop
(27 May)

EWER, Matthew - at his store on Chestnut St. wharf in
Phila. sells rum, molasses, sugar, cotton, lime juice
and dry goods (27 May)

WILLIAMS, John, age c. 17 - runaway from David Potts, at
Socken, above the Great Swamp; reward will be paid if
the runaway is secured and notice given to George Shoemaker, innkeeper in Phila. (27 May)

LEES & PEARSON, late of Phila. - all persons indebted to
the firm are to pay debts to Willing & Shippen, Peter
Evans (3 June)

HULL, Joseph, Esq., Collector of Customs at Burlington,
N. J. - is removed to post of Collector at New London,
Conn., in place of John Shackmaple, Esq., dec'd (10
June)

Ship John and Frances, John Ellwood master, new at Master's
wharf, Phila. - will sail by 3 July or sooner to St.
Christopher's (10 June)

JORDAN, Robert, a preacher among the Friends - married last
Thursday se'nnight to Mrs. Mary Hill, widow of Richard
Hill, Esq. (17 June)

EVERSON, Richard, of Thornbury, Chester Co., Pa. - 3 or 4
weeks ago a servant lad belonging to Everson hanged
himself in a swamp near his master's house (17 June)

HALL, Joseph, tanner, near Frankfort - died suddenly this
week (17 June)

FORLINDEY, Jendey, Irish servant, weaver, age c. 30 -
runaway from Richard Stanley, of Phila., potter (17
June)

RAWLINGSON, Job - has removed from his store on Fishbourn's
wharf in Phila. to store next to Dickenson's burnt

houses in Water St. (17 June)

Brigantine <u>Dolphin</u>, William Hill master, now at Carpenter's wharf, Phila. - will sail by 10 July for Cork; for freight or passage apply to John Beard or master in Front St. (17 June)

BEVAN, Henry, of Newcastle Co., age <u>c</u>. 60 - recently murdered by his wife, age <u>c</u>. 50, and a man servant (24 June); the wife, Catherine, has been tried, convicted and sentenced to be burnt alive; the man servant, David Murphy, has been condemned to be hanged (2 Sept.); name of servant given as Peter Murphy in account of execution on 10 Sept. (23 Sept.)

TAYLOR, Capt., master of a schooner - arrived a few days ago at Phila. from Jamaica and related how his ship had been stopped and plundered by a Spanish sloop from Havana (24 June)

SUNDERLAND, Edward, master of a sloop belonging to Boston - on passage from Phila. to Newfoundland his sloop was struck by lightning and sank; the captain and crew made land in their boat and arrived a few days ago in Phila. (24 June); wreck of the sloop came ashore in Accomack Co., Va; the Collector stopped looting and recovered some objects taken by local people (2 Sept.)

WALTER, Robert, Esq., first of H.M.'s Council in New York and Second Judge - died last week in New York and was interred Saturday last - New York dispatch of 21 June (24 June)

Letters from London of 14 Apr. via Boston bring news that a bill to prohibit the northern colonies from exporting horses and lumber to foreign plantations and importing from them sugars, rum and molasses is likely to pass (24 June)

GORDON, Mary, shopkeeper in Front St., Phila. - has for sale Bohea tea and Jamaica pepper (24 June)

The Sign of the Plough in Rodner Twp., Chester Co., where David Evans kept a public house, is to be let by said Evans (24 June)

DAVIS, Mary, servant - runaway from Evan Morgan of Phila., shopkeeper (1 July)

BOLTON, Robert, of Phila. - offers for sale anchovies, capers, olives, and sweet oil, all imported from London (1 July)

MAYNARD, Joseph, master of the <u>Bristol</u> <u>Merchant</u>, now at
William Fishbourn's wharf in Phila. - will soon sail for
Bristol; apply for passage or freight to the master or
to Simon Edgell (1 July)

CHAMPION, William - persons indebted to him are to settle
account or expect trouble from his attornies, Simon
Edgell and David Bush, of Phila. (1 July)

Speech of Gov. Belcher to Massachusetts Council and House
(8 July)

CLOUGH, James, and his apprentice John Potter, founder,
both of Boston, and M. Pierce of Wooburn - Friday last,
when trying to get at a copper mine in Wooburn by using
powder, the powder ignited, and Clough lost a hand and
an arm, Potter his right arm and Pierce was wounded in
the face, so that he still remains blind - Boston dispatch of 17 June (8 July)

SERJEANT, Joseph, of Almsbury, Mass., who about 2 months
ago married a widow who lived at Salisbury - last Sunday afternoon at Almsbury a boy of hers (age <u>c</u>. 10) and
a girl of his were playing with a loaded gun; the boy
accidentally shot the girl to death (8 July)

CHANNING, John, who kept the <u>Union</u> <u>Flag</u> at Newport, R. I.
- died there suddenly last week - Boston dispatch of
28 June (8 July)

MONTGOMERY, John, Gov. of New York - died there Thursday
last and was buried in the King's Chapel Friday evening
- New York dispatch of 5 July (8 July)

VAN DAM, Rip, Pres. of the Council of New York - 1 July
issued proclamation for continuance of all officers -
New York dispatch of 5 July (8 July)

LEGRANGE, Johannes - lately died about 26 miles above Albany, aged 106 - New York dispatch of 5 July (8 July)

WILLIAMS, William, born in Wales, blacksmith - runaway from
Capt. Robert Anderson, commander of ship <u>Robert</u> <u>and</u>
<u>Mary</u>, lying in Sassafras River, Md. (8 July)

PARKER, John, servant, age <u>c</u>. 20 - runaway from Thomas
Green, of Caln, Chester Co., Pa. (8 July)

GREENWICH, Giles, servant - runaway from Moses White, Jr.,
of Caln, Chester Co. (8 July); the servant was captured and confined in Burlington Jail (31 July 1732)

DAMSEL, Henry, servant - runaway from William Nichols, of Caln, Chester Co. (8 July)

The following plantations are to be sold for ready money or security, with payment of interest for 12 months to John England, of Principio, Md.: one of 250 acres on Christiana Creek, formerly Henry James's; one of 370 acres, late Mr. Nichols's; one of 200 acres, late John Kyle's (8 July)

OLDMAN, Joseph, of Phila. - offers reward for recovery of a mare that strayed away (8 July)

MARRIOTT, Thomas, of Bristol - offers reward for recovery of a mare stolen from his stable (8 July)

Paper drawn up by Agents of the Northern Colonies entitled "The Case of the British Northern Colonies" (15 July)

HENMAN, John, master of a sloop from the Bay of Honduras - reports a ship from England, commanded by Roger Groves (late of New York City, feltmaker) was taken in the Bay of Honduras by a small Spanish sloop - New York dispatch of 12 July (15 July)

PALMER, Nathaniel, in Walnut St., Phila. - makes and sells starch and starch powder (15 July)

EMMERY, John, cabinet-maker, who went from England in 1725 to the West Indies and thence to some of the northern colonies - if he will apply to the printer he will hear something to his advantage (15 July)

MEGEE, George, nailer, at corner of Front St., in Arch St., by the Arch wharf, Phila. - makes and sells all sorts of nails (22 July)

HUDSON, John, master of brigantine Patience - arrived 14 July in New York from Bristol, whence he sailed 26 May - New York dispatch of 16 July (29 July)

VATER, Capt. - arrived in brigantine at New York from Dover in passage of 12 weeks (29 July)

PAYTON, Capt. - arrived in brigantine at New York from Dover, whence he sailed 29 May (29 July)

BURNIRON, Michael, of Phila., who was delirious with fever - Saturday last left his house and was found drowned in the Delaware (29 July)

WRIGHT, Robert, seaman on the ship Three Batchelors -

Tuesday last fell from the main topmast head and died about 2 hours after (29 July)

DELANCEY, Mr., merchant of New York, one of the daughters of - is lately married to the captain of the man-of-war <u>Shoreham</u>, stationed in New York (29 July)

Mr. Read's mare Polley and Mr. Chancellor's Now or Never tomorrow are to run again on Passayunk Road for 20 pounds a side (29 July)

THOMAS, Capt., master of the ship <u>Succession</u>, who sailed from Lisbon 14 June, old style - arrived 1 Aug. in New York (5 Aug.)

CLIFTON, John, near upper end of Third St., Phila. - sells starch (5 Aug.)

HARDING, John, servant, butcher, age <u>c</u>. 30 - runaway from the Widow Wragg of Phila. (5 Aug.)

HOW, Lt. Samuel, of Framingham, Mass. - died 18 July in his pew in church (12 Aug.)

LE PART, Capt., master of a French sloop from Cape Francois to Cape Breton - Tuesday last put in at Boston; in their passage they had been plundered by a Spanish pirate - Boston dispatch of 2 Aug. (12 Aug.)

RICHARDSON, Benjamin, of Leicester, Mass., butcher - last week in his sleep killed his little daughter - Boston dispatch of 2 Aug. (12 Aug.)

CONDON, James, Irish servant, weaver, age <u>c</u>. 25 - runaway from Jonathan Park, of Bradford Twp., Chester Co., Pa. (12 Aug.)

MASTERS, Capt. - arrived Monday last in Boston in about 8 weeks from Seville - Boston dispatch of 5 Aug. (19 Aug.)

Eight-year-old son of a farmer at Suncook was devoured by a bear - Boston dispatch of 5 Aug. (19 Aug.)

THOMPSON, Cornelius, age 40 - broke out of Phila. Goal night of Aug. 18; reward for his capture will be paid by Charles Read, sheriff (19 Aug.)

WALKER, John, stonecutter - same as above

FLOWER, John, seaman - same as above

JONES, Griffith, Welshman, skinner, age <u>c</u>. 40 - same

LEWIS, James, in Front St., Phila. - will sell servant
maid's time of 2 years (19 Aug.)

Proclamation of Lt. Gov. Patrick Gordon (26 Aug.)

Statistics of burials in Boston from 1700 to 1731 (20 Aug.)

Proclamation of Gov. of Massachusetts, publishing 5th and
6th articles of treaty of peace (Nov. 1686) between
Great Britain and France (26 Aug.)

Grist mill, house, store and cooper's shop, with about 60
acres of land at Salisbury Town, at head of Duck Creek
on Delaware, 37 miles from New-Castle are for sale -
apply to William Rawle in Phila. or Joseph Rawle in
Salisbury (26 Aug.)

WRIGHT, Edward, master of ship **Constantine** - will sail middle of Oct. for London; for freight or passage apply to
the master or Thomas Lawrence, of Phila. (2 Sept.)

REEVE, John, master of ship **Elizabeth and Dorothy**, now lying at William Fishbourn's wharf, will sail for London
- for freight or passage apply to the master or to Matthias Aspdin in Market St., Phila. (2 Sept.)

HENZEY, John, dec'd - his executor, Thomas Gray, has advertised for sale a 260-acre tract in White Clay Creek
Hundred, in Newcastle Co.; John Coats and Samuel Hale
warn that they have a right to the land (2 Sept.)

INGLIS, John, at Mr. Moss's in Chestnut St., Phila. - offers for sale tools, cloth, etc. (2 Sept.)

RICE, Capt. - arrived Friday last at Phila. in a schooner
from South Carolina; on 20 Aug., during a storm, one
Hoskins, a passenger, became light-headed and died; 6
days later they met a New England sloop, **Beaufort**,
James Royers captain, which had lost its mast (9 Sept.)

AMYET, John, of Bristol, Bucks Co., Pa. - his wife Jane
has eloped from him (9 Sept.)

WEAR, Hugh, servant, age c. 22, spinner and worker in
linen, who lately was servant to James Mackay in Phila.
- runaway from Patrick Carrigan (9 Sept.)

WILLIAMS, Capt., of Phila. - Thursday last his ship, bound
from the West Indies to Virginia, came into Phila.,
having lost her master in the great storm of 20 Aug.
(23 Sept.)

Letter from Barbados, dated 16 Aug., describes hurricane of
13 Aug. and tells of a duel between Major Mason and Col.
Edward Chearnly (23 Sept.)

FITZGERALD, James, servant, age c. 19, leather-dresser and
breeches-maker and glover - runaway from Isaac Corin, at
the Center (23 Sept.)

BRIAN, Daniel, Irish servant, age c. 18 - runaway from
Caleb Ranstead (23 Sept.)

READ, Widow - has removed from the upper end of High St.
to the new printing office near the market; she continues to make and sell her well-known ointment for the
itch (23 Sept.)

Smallpox, flux and fever prevail very much in New York
City - New York dispatch of 27 Sept. (30 Sept.)

MOORHOUSE, Peter, Englishman, tinker - broke out of Chester Goal; reward for his capture offered by John Owen,
sheriff (30 Sept.)

MACK, William, Irishman - same as above

CAIN, William, Irishman - same as above

Plantation of 130 acres adjoining to the town of Trenton
to be sold and another plantation, 3 miles above Trenton, near the ferry above the falls, one mile from
Yardley's old mill, to be let - enquire of Capt. James
Goould at Trenton (30 Sept.)

HASEL, Samuel - Tuesday last was elected Major of Phila.
for year ensuing (7 Oct.)

Elections on Friday last for Phila. Co.: Representatives
--William Allen, Esq., Jonathan Robinson, Thomas Leech,
John Kensey, John Cadwalader, William Monington, Job
Goodson, Edward Farmer, Esq.; burgesses--John Kearsly,
Israel Pemberton; sheriffs--Charles Read, James Bing-
ham; coroners--Owen Owen, John Roberts; commissioner--
Edward Warner; assessors--Andrew Robeson, John Pawlin,
William Corker, John Rutter, Evan Thomas, Thomas Peters;
city assessors--Joseph Paschal, Joseph Trotter, Timothy
Stephenson, John Dilwin, William Chancellor, Benjamin
Morgan (7 Oct.)

Elections on Friday last for Chester Co.: Representatives
--Joseph Harvey, John Parry, Esq., Samuel Lewis, Caleb
Cowpland, Esq., John Taylor, Henry Pierce, Esq.;
sheriffs--John Owen, William Smith; coroners--John

Wharton, Benjamin Davis; commissioner--Jacob Howel;
assessors--Jeremiah Star, John Davis, Charles Crosley,
William Paschel, Thomas Green, Thomas Marshal (7 Oct.)
Add as representatives Joseph Brinton and Evan Lewis
(14 Oct.)

Elections Friday last for Bucks Co.: Representatives--
Joseph Kirkbride, Jr., Jeremiah Langhorne, Esq., Wil-
liam Paxton, Esq., Christian Vanhorne, Esq., Abraham
Chapman, Esq., Andrew Hamilton, Esq., Matthew Hughes,
Esq., Benjamin Jones, Esq. (7 Oct.)

Elections Friday last for Lancaster Co.: Representatives
--John Kyle, Andrew Galbreth, John Musgrove, Thomas
Edwards, Esq.; sheriffs--John Galbreth, David Jones;
coroners--Joshua Lowe, Edward Smout; commissioner--
Andrew Cornish, Esq.; assessors--Walter Deney, Gabriel
Davis, Thomas Wilkins, Emanuel Carpenter, Daniel Ferey,
Thomas Baldwin (7 Oct.)

Elections for New-Castle Co.: Representatives--Andrew
Peterson, Esq., Robert Gordon, Esq., Thomas Noxon, John
Richardson, Esq., John M'Coole, Samuel James; sheriff--
John Gooding; coroner--Robert Robertson (7 Oct.)

Elections Friday last for Kent Co.: Representatives--
Andrew Hamilton, Esq., David French, Esq., Mark Man-
love, Esq., John Tilton, Esq., Hugh Durborough, Esq.,
Daniel Rodeney (7 Oct.)

Elections Friday last for Sussex Co.: Representatives--
William Till, Esq., Henry Brooke, Esq., Richard Hin-
man, Esq., John Roades, Esq., Jacob Kollock, Esq.,
John May; sheriff--Simon Kollock; coroner--John
Clowes (7 Oct.)

WRIGHT, Richard, of Ireland, who lately kept a school at
Perth Amboy - is notified that his brother, Joseph
Wright, is arrived in these parts and cannot learn
whither he is removed (7 Oct.)

Report from New York that the French have built a fort at
Crown Point and about French plans for next spring
(7 Oct.)

MAYNARD, Capt. - on 3 Oct. his ship, Bristol Merchant,
was driven ashore upon our Cape, near Lewes (14 Oct.)

BECKFORD, Col., of Island of Jamaica - was lately killed
there in a duel by a colonel (14 Oct.)

FINNEY, Lawrence, Irish servant - broke out of the workhouse at Chester; Nathan Worley offers reward for his capture (14 Oct.)

BIDDLE, James, servant, chimney-sweeper - runaway from Thomas Hart, bricklayer (14 Oct.)

EDWARDS, John, servant, bookbinder - runaway from William Davies (14 Oct.)

MANKIN, Mrs., near Arch St., Phila. - has for sale Madera wine (14 Oct.)

TIMOTHEE, Louis, dwelling in Front St., next door to Dr. Kearsley, in Phila. - will keep a French school (14 Oct.)

REYNOLDS, Lawrence - offers reward for recovery of 2 brass kettles that were stolen Friday last (14 Oct.)

BORANCE, William, of Kingston, Ulster Co., N. Y. - his grist mill, with several thousand bushels of wheat, has been burnt down - New York dispatch of 18 Oct. (21 Oct.)

SIPKINS, Capt. - brings advice from Curacoa that 2 sloops of that island took a Spanish guard la coast that attacked them - New York dispatch of 18 Oct. (21 Oct.)

MACFERSON, Capt., and 4 others - tried at Phila. Friday last for piracy by Court of Admiralty, consisting of Patrick Gordon (president), James Smith (Secretary of the Jersies), Alexander Keith (Collector of New Castle) and (commissioners) Andrew Hamilton, Esq., Samuel Hazel, Esq., Clement Plumstead, Esq., Capt. Richmond, Capt. Grocock and Capt. Wallace; the pirates were convicted and sentenced to be hanged (21 Oct.)

ADAMS, Mr., a young man of Kent Co. - some days ago was struck overboard by the boom in a shallop bound down the river and drowned near Chester (21 Oct.)

HASTINGS, Samuel - when a ship built by him was being launched last Tuesday at Back Creek in Maryland, 2 men were accidentally killed and several persons injured (21 Oct.)

GORDON, Patrick - his speech to General Assembly at New-Castle and address of representatives to him (28 Oct.)

HOMANS, Capt. - brings news from London that Gov. of Massachusetts will have orders to accept the salary offered him last year by the Assembly (28 Oct.)

H.M.S. **Lowestaff**, Capt. Norris, from South Carolina, ar-

rived in New York and the Solebay, Capt. Warren, goes
to the station at South Carolina - New York dispatch
of 25 Oct. (28 Oct.)

WOOD, John, servant, born at Birmingham, Eng., carpenter
and sawyer, age c. 22, who came a servant from Bristol
in 1730 - runaway from Isaac Norris of Fairhill (28 Oct.)

BRINGHURST, John, of Phila. - offers reward for recovery
of horse that strayed or was stolen (28 Oct.)

Ship Rebecca, Mark Joyce commander - will sail in 3 weeks
for Barbados - for freight or passage apply to him at
his store in Water St., Phila. (4 Nov.)

PARKHOUSE, Robert - offers for sale English cider on board
the Swift at Mr. Fishbourn's wharf in Phila. (4 Nov.)

GALBRETH, John, sheriff of Lancaster Co. - offers reward
for capture of John Brown, alias Robinson, who escaped
from him (4 Nov.)

OGLE, Samuel, who had a command in a regiment in the Irish
Establishment - is preparing to embark for Maryland;
Lord Baltimore had appointed him governor in place of
his lordship's brother, Benedict Leonard Calvert, who
is returning home for his health - London dispatch of
20 Aug. (11 Nov.)

LLOYD, John - keeps a night school in Water St., opposite
to Mr. Lawrence's store in Phila. (11 Nov.)

FISHER, Joseph, master of the snow Lowther, lying at Israel Pemberton's wharf in Phila. - his snow will sail
in a fortnight for Dublin; he gives notice to the
Palatines who came with him in the snow that they are
to pay at once for passage (11 Nov.)

ORMSTON, Rev., formerly minister in Phila., lately minister in Cecil Co., Md. - died lately in Cecil Co. (18
Nov.)

WISHART, Peter - has rosemary for sale (18 Nov.)

GORDON, Patrick - his speech 22 Nov. in Phila. to Representatives and their address to him (27 Nov.)

HUTCHINS, William - 15 Nov., about midnight, going on
board the ship Diligence, to which he belonged, fell
off the wharf at Phila., and was drowned (27 Nov.)

CONNOR, Patrick, servant, currier, age c. 27 - runaway

from William Plywell, of Phila., tanner (27 Nov.)

HORNE, Edward, who lives near Fairhill - offers for sale
one-eighth part of the Abington Furnace, on Christiana
Creek; apply to Horne or to William Rawles, merchant,
in Phila. (27 Nov.)

MATTY, Robert, next door to Mr. Rakestraw's in Third St.,
Phila. - offers for sale 3 years' time of a servant
man, a distiller (27 Nov.)

SMITH, Capt. Thomas, master of the ship Beaver, who sailed
from Gravesend, Eng., 4 Oct., and arrived in New York
29 Nov. - reports that news of Gov. Montgomery's death
reached London the latter end of August; it is said
that the government of New Jersey will be separated and
that Col. Paget will have New York and Sir William
Keith New Jersey; also Col. Cosby is applying for
governorship of New York - New York dispatch of 29 Nov.
(2 Dec.)

A house about 4 miles back of Benjamin Wood's, on the
other side of the river, was burnt to the ground a few
days ago, according to Phila. item (2 Dec.)

HUMPHRIES, Peter, servant, age c. 26 - runaway from John
Fruin, baker (2 Dec.)

CALAHAN, Charles, servant, age c. 22 - runaway from William
Biddle, of Phila. (2 Dec.)

Tavern and 250 acres of land, about midway between
Glocester and Salem, now in the possession of Christopher Taylor - is offered for sale; apply to William Plywell, tanner, in Phila. (2 Dec.)

GUEST, John, mathematician - within a few days will sail
for the West Indies to discover longitude at sea by an
instrument he has invented (14 Dec.)

BELCHER, Gov., of Massachusetts - at meeting in Cambridge
of Overseers of Harvard on 1 Nov. produced 3 diplomas
from University of Glasgow, conferring degree of D.D.
on Rev. Benjamin Colman and Mr. Joseph Sewall, ministers in Boston, and degree of M.A. on Mr. Mather, chap-
lain of his majesty's Castle William - Cambridge dispatch of 1 Nov. (21 Dec.)

An Apology for the True Christian Divinity, written in
Latin and English by Robert Barclay, printed by J.
Franklin - is for sale at the New Printing Office near
the Market, Phila. (21 Dec.)

WILLING & SHIPPEN, at their store on Carpenter's wharf,
    Phila. - offer for sale servants lately imported from
    Bristol in the <u>Jane Galley</u> (21 Dec.)

NORRIS, Isaac, Jr. - offers for sale a young Negro man and
    a Negro woman (28 Dec.)

The brigantine <u>Swallow</u>, John Plasket master - will sail in
    10 days for Bristol; for freight or passage apply to
    Simon Edgel or David Bush, merchants in Phila. (28 Dec.)

<u>1732</u>

MAKENZIE, Duncan, late gunsmith of Phila. - Alexander M'-
    Kenzie, attorney for said Duncan, bids those who left
    guns to be repaired with Duncan to take them to shop
    of John Lee in Second St., over against Andrew Brad-
    ford's, next door to Nathaniel Edgecome's (4 Jan.)

FUSSUL, Solomon - now lives in Second St., next door to
    Geo. Wilson, joyner, almost opposite to the Church,
    Phila.; he works woolen cloth (4 Jan.)

REDDY, John, Irish servant, who works at husbandry, has
    been among the Indians and pretends to be a Quaker -
    runaway from Jonathan Tatnall, near Phila. (4 Jan.)

JERVAS, Richard, shipwright - offers for sale a brigantine
    now on the stocks near Trenton (4 Jan.)

Instruction (13 Aug. 1731) to Gov. Belcher of Massachu-
    setts and Belcher's speech to the Assembly (11 Jan.)

VICARS, William, at Mr. Croan's in Front St., Phila. -
    cures epilepsy and fits (11 Jan.)

GRAHAM, Dr. Hugh, late of Phila., dec'd - accounts due es-
    tate for physic or surgery to be settled with Patrick
    Baird, who has been impowered by executors; other ac-
    counts to be settled with George M'Call, executor (18
    Jan.)

WILLIS, William, servant, age <u>c</u>. 24 - runaway from David
    Bacon, of Chesterfield Twp., Burlington Co. (18 Jan.)

FREEMAN, Samuel, servant, age <u>c</u>. 25 - same as above

Counterfeit dollars circulating in New York City (25 Jan.)

Much inoculation against smallpox on at Jamaica, Long
    Island, where of those inoculated only one, Foster

Waters, died, and at Amboy, New Brunswick and adjacent places (25 Jan.)

WELLS, Abraham, apprentice, age c. 18 - runaway from Robert Shewell, cooper, at Judge Langhorne's mill in Middletown near Bristol in Bucks Co. (25 Jan.)

The sloop Happy, lying at Chichester, for sale - apply to Prudence Moulder or Joseph Wheldon at Chichester (25 Jan.)

Speech of Gov. of Massachusetts to the House of Representatives and reply of J. Quincy, Speaker (1 Feb.)

ELLICOT, Andrew - persons indebted to him are to bring their payments to Joanna Kelley's in Front St., Phila. (1 Feb.)

MILLER, William, servant, who formerly kept the Upper (commonly called Roach's)Ferry, age c. 45 - runaway from Andrews and Postlethwaite of Phila. (1 Feb.)

BOUD, Thomas, of Phila, - has for sale brewing vessels (1 Feb.)

HIDE, Sam., an Indian - died 5 Jan. in Dedham, Mass., in his 106th year (8 Feb.)

Account of great number of Palatines who starved to death on voyage from Rotterdam to Martha's Vineyard (8 Feb.)

JONES, Evan, chemist, and Dr. Matthew Hooper - persons indebted to them are to settle accounts; persons indebted for sums under 40 shillings may pay Charles Snow (8 Feb.)

GRAY, Joseph, keeper of the High St. Ferry, Phila. - asks owners of teams to be careful (15 Feb.)

Remonstrance of the Massachusetts House of Representatives which Major Brattle, Major Epes, Mr. Jacob, Capt. Alden and Capt. Gould are ordered to present to the Governor (22 Feb.)

GREEN, Jonathan, of Newtown in New England - his house was burnt to the ground the night of 22 Jan. (22 Feb.)

TUTHIL, Mrs. Sarah, widow - died at Ipswich, Mass., 24 Jan. in her 86th year; she had 13 children, by 7 of whom she had 177 grandchildren and great-grandchildren (22 Feb.)

Letter of Gov. of Pennsylvania to Gov. of Massachusetts in
behalf of the distressed Palatines on Martha's Vineyard (22 Feb.)

Land near Horsham and lots in Bucks Co. are offered for
sale by William Fishbourn (22 Feb.)

Tract of 500 acres of land in Sussex Co., about 12 miles
from Lewes Town - to be let; apply to Josiah Rolfe at
Messieurs White & Taylor in Phila. (29 Feb.)

O'NEAL, Charles (supposed to now call himself Thomas
Davis), servant - runaway from James Yates, Jr., of
Newtown, Bucks Co., Pa. (29 Feb.)

A Negro Barbadian wench and a Negro girl are for sale -
enquire of W. King, next door but one to the Plume and
Feathers in Front St., Phila. (29 Feb.)

Brigantine <u>Britannia</u>, Isaac Beauchamp commander, from Rhode
Island - burned last Wednesday night at Charlestown,
S. C., according to the <u>South-Carolina</u> <u>Gazette</u> of 8
Jan. (7 Mar.)

Northernmost buoy put down near the Charlestown, S.C.,
bar by the direction of Mr. Eveliegh - was dislodged by
a strong wind - item in <u>South-Carolina</u> <u>Gazette</u> of 29
Jan. (7 Mar.)

Friday last 6 Cheroquee Indians, come to Charlestown,
were presented to the Governor by John Herbert, Esq.,
Commissioner for Indian Affairs. J. Savy was the interpreter; the Governor ordered the Treasurer, Col.
Parris, to give some ammunition and paint and saw that
they obtained some conch shells -<u>South-Carolina</u> <u>Gazette</u>
of 29 Jan. (7 Mar.)

The snow <u>Alice</u> <u>and</u> <u>Elizabeth</u>, John Pain master, in passage
from Jamaica to Charlestown - on 9 Dec. was stopped off
the Bahama Banks by a sloop with French and Spaniards
aboard; Christopher French, mate of the <u>Alice</u> <u>and</u> <u>Eliza-</u>
<u>beth</u>, spoke in French with the captain of the sloop;
after it was robbed, the snow was permitted to proceed
- <u>South-Carolina</u> <u>Gazette</u> of 29 Jan. (7 Mar.)

JONES, Charles - last week was pursuing a runaway Negro
who resisted him; Jones killed the Negro and reported
the fact to a Justice, who ordered him to cut off the
Negro's head and set it up on a pole in a crossroad
near Ashley Ferry - <u>South-Carolina</u> <u>Gazette</u> of 29 Jan.
(7 Mar.)

VALENTINE, George, Surgeon to H.M.S. Fox - last Saturday
in the presence of all the surgeons of His Majesty's
ship in Charlestown, tapped for dropsy on Richard Evans,
a sailor of the Fox - Charlestown, S. C., dispatch of
5 Feb. (7 Mar.)

ABBOT, Mr., who was confined in the New London, Conn.,
prison for counterfeiting - was visited Monday last by
his wife, who exchanged clothes with him, so that he
escaped thus disguised - Boston dispatch of 14 Feb. (7
Mar.)

OWEN, Dr. Griffith, young man - died Thursday last in
Phila. (7 Mar.)

HODGE, Henry, merchant, of Phila. - died in Phila. last
Saturday (7 Mar.)

CARPENTER, Samuel of Phila., brewer - wishes all accounts
to be settled with him (7 Mar.)

HOMER, John, servant, shoemaker - runaway from Thomas
Wills, of Middletown, Chester Co. (7 Mar.)

LAMPLUGH, Nathaniel - his wife Abigail has eloped from
him and gone into Phila. (7 Mar.)

Last week a stranger passing through Burlington passed
counterfeit bills; he was purused and taken in a boat
going to Trenton and committed to Burlington Goal
(10 Mar.)

M'FARSON, John, in Goal of City of Phila., being captain
of a crew condemned for piracy - escaped from Goal;
Gov. of Pennsylvania offers 20 pounds reward for his
capture (16 Mar.)

PEGG, Daniel - will let or sell the great house at the
north end of Phila. and also sell a Negro woman (16 Mar.)

Spanish Indian woman, age c. 20, is for sale - enquire at
Capt. Thomas James's in Second St., Phila. (16 Mar.)

Land and tenement in Walnut St. now in the improvement of
Edward Robinson is for sale - enquire of Peter Evans
or Michael Jobson (16 Mar.)

RAMMAGE, Mr., of New-Castle Co. - about 2 weeks ago his
store there accidentally caught fire and burnt to the
ground (23 Mar.)

Persons indebted to late partners, John Postlethwaite

and Ephraim Andrews, are to settle accounts with them (23 Mar.)

Thirty acres in Northern Liberties of Phila., near Edward Horn's plantation, for sale - enquire of George Bringhurst at Germantown (23 Mar.)

STILES, Mr., was arrested in New Hampshire 21 Feb. for counterfeiting, along with John M'Vicker and one Brian (scribe of M'Vicker) - Portsmouth, N. H., dispatch of 22 Feb. (30 Mar.)

TOWNSEND, Richard, a very ancient preacher among the Friends - interred 30 Mar. in Phila. (30 Mar.)

COLEMAN, William, late of Phila., carpenter, dec'd --accounts to be settled with his widow and administrator (30 Mar.)

EVANS, David, of Tredyffryn, Pa. - his book, A Help for Parents and Heads of Families, is printed and sold by B. Franklin (30 Mar.)

ANSEL, Capt., master of the snow Experiment - taken near the Colorados, to the westward of Cuba, by a Spanish guard la coast - Charlestown, S. C., dispatch of 19 Feb. (6 Apr.)

BAKER, Capt., who lately came from Jamaica to Charlestown tells of 6 vessels taken going to or from that island - Charlestown, S.C., dispatch of 19 Feb. (6 Apr.)

GOUGH, Mr. - killed one day this week by an insane man - Charlestown, S.C., dispatch of 19 Feb. (6 Apr.)

COREY, David, of Southold, Long Island - 27 Feb. his small son was stamped to death by a frightened horse - Boston dispatch of 27 Mar. (6 Apr.)

CLARKE, John, late of Bucks Co., dec'd - those indebted to his estate are to settle with his executors, Rachel Clarke, Solomon Warder and Joseph Kirkbride, Jr. (6 Apr.)

BURGAN, Patrick, servant, age c. 23 - runaway from Jacob Wright of the Great Valley, Chester Co., Pa. (6 Apr.)

A young man, who was rescued when a child from the Indians by a Frenchman - being in New Hampshire last Tuesday by a resemblance was judged to be of the Hutchins family of Kittery, taken from Spruce Creek about 24 years ago; his mother recognized him - Boston dispatch of 3 Apr. (13 Apr.)

BONNER, Capt. - arrived 3 Apr. in Boston in about 7 weeks from London - Boston dispatch of 3 Apr. (13 Apr.)

WORTHINGTON, Samuel, of Byberry - Friday last his house was burnt to the ground (13 Apr.)

KEITH, Sir W. - reported to be made Surveyor General of the Customs of the Northern District in America (13 Apr.)

FITZWATER, George, of Phila. - has red clover seed for sale (13 Apr.)

BICKLEY, Abraham, dec'd - 7 tracts of land belonging to his estate in West Jersey are offered for sale by his executors, William Hudson, James Steel, George Fitzwater and Samuel Bickley (20 Apr.)

OSWALD, Capt., from London and Madeira - arrived in Phila. (27 Apr.)

WRIGHT, Capt., from London - arrived in Phila. in about 6 weeks (27 Apr.)

ROBERTS, John, late of Phila., dec'd - debts to estate to be paid to the executors, John White and John Cadwalader (27 Apr.)

COLE, William, servant, age c. 24 - runaway from Richard Wright, of Phila. (27 Apr.)

EDWARDS, Henry, servant, a West countryman, wool-comber - runaway from John Riley, near Chester; he was seen the night he ran away at Mr. Dunning's the George Inn (27 Apr.)

VAN BEBBER, Hendrick, doctor of physic - has removed to Phila. and lives in Laetitia Court, in same house with Arent Hassert, merchant, in Phila. (27 Apr.)

CRANLEY, John, some years ago of the City of Winton, upholsterer, age c. 40, who served his apprenticeship in London - 5 guineas reward will be paid by Samuel Smith, draper in Winchester, to person who informs him where Cranley now lives (27 Apr.)

A mulatto, Andrew Scoto, leader of an insurrection - defeated a large force of Biscayners, according to letters from Caracas - Barbados dispatch of 3 Mar. (4 May)

READ, William, Esq., one of the trustees of the Loan Office - died Monday last at New-Castle (4 May)

BADCOCK, Mr., of Phila. - his brewhouse was burned down
Sunday last during afternoon service (4 May)

ROE, John, servant, age c. 25 - runaway from Thomas Lindley, of Phila., smith (4 May)

Ship John & Anna, James Shirley master - will sale for Barbados; for freight or passage apply to John Reynell at his
store in Water St. or to the master on board at W. Fishbourn's wharf (11 May)

Tract of 407 acres with good stone quarry in Northern
Liberties about 3½ miles from Phila., between Phila.
and Frankfort, bounded to westward above a mile upon
Frankford Creek; to buy, apply to William Rawle (11 May)

HARRIS, Francis, apprentice to Capt. Richmond - Friday
last fell overboard into the river at Phila. and was
drowned (18 May)

WHITFIN, William - Monday last hanged himself in a sap-
ling near Whitemarsh (18 May)

Young lad (son of Samuel Burroughs), who last Jan. fell
through the ice near Phila. - his body came ashore
Thursday last at the landing belonging to their plantation (18 May)

HASKINS, Capt., master of the sloop Tace, which sailed
1 Feb. from Carolina bound for Phila. - a letter from
Rhode Island, dated 1 May, tells of storms, shortage
of food, help from Capt. Pearson of Whitehaven, who
gave them a cask of beef, water and some bread; they
finally made Rhode Island (18 May)

Two noblemen arrived at Boston in the station ship, a son
of the Duke of Grafton and a son of Lord Townsend (25
May)

KINMAN, Samuel, living in Cheltonham Twp. - offers reward
for recovery of strayed brown horse (28 May)

CAMBRIDGE, Sarah (widow and executrix of Giles Cambridge,
late of Phila., shipkeeper, dec'd) - persons owing her
are to pay debts to Alexander Woodrof, Peter Lloyd or
Samuel Powell, Jr., whom the widow has impowered to
receive sums due her (25 May)

SMITH, Henry, formerly hostler at the Black Horse Inn, in
Phila. - recently in Kent Co., in a struggle, Smith
drew a knife and murdered William Halfpenny; Smith is
now in Dover Prison (1 June)

MACKENZY, John, Scotch servant, age c. 30, who was a soldier in Flanders - runaway from Peter Cuff (1 June)

REEVES, Capt. - arrived in Phila. last night in 11 weeks from London (8 June)

JONES, John, servant, age c. 22 - runaway from Jacob Scuten, of Blockley Twp., near Roche's Ferry, in Phila. Co. (8 June)

Brigantine John, Benjamin Haskins master, now lying at Capt. Bourn's wharf - will sail for South Carolina; for freight or passage agree with Capt. Anthony Peele or the master (8 June)

HIGGINS, John, servant, worsted-comber - runaway from Michael M'guire, of Birmingham, Chester Co., Pa. (8 June)

A mast ship, William Hills master, on 26 May finished loading trees for his majesty's navy at Falmouth in Casco Bay; one tree is 40½ inches in diameter and its tongue is almost 29 yards in length (15 June)

BURGAIN, Patrick, Irish servant, age c. 20 - runaway from Jacob Wright and Richard Anderson, of Whiteland Twp., Chester Co., Pa. (15 June)

FLUD, John, Irish servant, age c. 20 - same as above

Speech of Gov. Belcher to Massachusetts General Assembly on 1 June (19 June)

At Boston on 1 June John Quincy, Esq., was chosen Speaker of the Massachusetts House of Representatives and J. Wainwright, Esq., clerk; the sermon was preached by Rev. John Swift of Framingham (19 June)

ANDERSON, Enoch, at the Falls Ferry - has had in his possession since November last a stray mare (19 June)

BRADLEY, Edward, glasier, near the Post Office in Front St., Phila. - has for sale glasier's diamonds, window glass and silvered looking glasses (19 June)

GOOCH, William, Gov. of Virginia - his speech on 18 May to Council and House of Burgesses (26 June)

Masonic Society met Saturday last in Phila. at the Sun Tavern in Water St.; W. Allen, Esq., was chosen Grand Master of Pa., William Pringle, Deputy Master, and Thomas Bonds and Benjamin Franklin, Wardens (26 June)

Dr. Godfrey's General Cordial - sold by Samuel Emlen near
the Market in Phila., by Thomas Mariot at Bristol, by
Joseph Read at Trentown, Elizabeth Johnson at Burlington, Thomas Mason at Salem, Ann Hogg at New-Castle and
Anthony Shaw at Chester (26 June)

Addresses of Council and House of Burgesses to Gov. William Gooch of Virginia on 20 May (3 July)

Schooner Charming Molly, John Field master, bound from
Charlestown, S. C., to Providence - was lost off one of
the Bahama Islands, but the master and crew were saved
- Charlestown dispatch of 20 May (3 July)

COPPIN, Thomas, age 14 - was accidentally killed in St.
John's Parish- Charlestown dispatch of 27 May (3 July)

BARR, John, a tanner, lately come to South Carolina from
Pa. - drowned 18 May when his canoe overset in Ashley
River - Charlestown, S. C., dispatch of 27 May (3 July)

DENNIS, Christopher, of North Edisto - Wednesday last was
killed by 2 men lately come from Cape Fear, a Mr. Robinson and Michael Cavino; Capt. Rawlins has sent a hue and
cry after them - Charlestown dispatch of 27 May (3 July)

GOLDING, John (servant to Mr. Gregory Haines) - reported
lost between the Cherokees and Congorees - Charlestown
dispatch of 27 May (3 July)

GLOVER, Col. Charlesworth - on Thursday last brought dele-
gation of Indian chiefs, who, on orders of Col. Glover,
were met by Col. Prioleau and troop of horse; then, at
the Bowling-Green, they were received by Col. Parris and
foot companies and so escorted to the Council Chamber,
where they were received by the Governor and Council -
Charlestown dispatch of 3 June (3 July)

HAYS, Mrs., of Barbados - was buried Monday last; she was
murdered by her husband who has been convicted of wilful murder - Barbados dispatch of 8 Apr. (3 July)

NEALSON, Alexander, servant, age c. 24 - runaway (in company with a servant man belonging to William Hudson,
Jr.) from Edmund Farrel, of Phila., skinner and tanner
(3 July)

Samuel and Molly, Capt. Pearson master - arrived at Charlestown, S. C., 22 June from Bay of Campeachy - Charlestown
dispatch of 24 June (10 July)

ROGERS, James - Tuesday last his house in Allentown was

struck by lightning (10 July)

HALL, William, Esq., late of Salem, Salem Co., N.J., dec'd
- by act of Assembly lands, etc., of estate in West New
Jersey (except grist and fulling mills) became vested
in Sarah Hall (widow of William Hall), Clement Plumstead, of Phila., merchant, John Kay, of Gloucester Co.,
gent., and Israel Pemberton, of Phila., merchant; on
7 Aug. some of estate of William Hall will be sold at
house of George Satterthwaite in Town of Burlington,
N.J. (10 July)

SANDIMONT, Joseph, servant, glover, age c. 19 or 20 - runaway from Joseph Hayes of Haverford, Chester Co. (10
July)

Articles of friendship and commerce between Gov. Robert
Johnson of South Carolina and Indian chiefs

Observations of Col. Dunbar, Surveyor General of His
Majesty's Woods, Jeremiah Dunbar, Deputy Surveyor of
the Woods, and Thomas Coram on trade matters in New
England (17 July)

Exchange of messages between Gov. Belcher of Massachusetts
and his House of Representatives (19 July)

PARSTOW, Stephen, English servant, blacksmith, age c. 21 -
runaway from William Cox, of Brunswick - reward for
Parstow's capture will be paid by Cox or by Simon Edgel
in Phila. (17 July)

DENIM, William, servant, tailor - runaway from the plantation at Hopewell belonging to Joseph Reed, merchant
in Trenton (17 July)

BUTWELL, Thomas, from England, at his shop in Phila. under
the new Printing Office - makes stays and children's
coats (17 July)

Answer of Massachusetts House of Representatives to their
Governor's speech (24 July)

TAILER, Col. William, lately dec'd - House of Representatives has made grant of lands to his family in recog-
nition of his services (24 July)

COSBY, Col., Gov. of New York - reported to be at Madera
on way to New York - New York dispatch of 24 July (31
July)

FARRA, Capt., master of the Eagle from Phila. - arrived

62

at Dover about 14 May (31 July)

LANGFORD, John, born in England, who lately has followed
butchering in and about Allenstown and Trenton - broke
out of goal of Trenton 26 July; reward for capture offered by Enoch Anderson, Jr., sub. sheriff (31 July)

BUTLER, Edward, who pretends to be a shoemaker and turner
and has lived on Long Island - same as above

BARR, Warren, middle-aged Irishman, who formerly kept the
ferry next above Delaware Falls, on the Jersey side -
same as above

Servant, who pretends to be a Quaker - runaway from Joseph
Jackson, of Bristol (31 July)

OLIVER, Hon. Daniel, Esq. - died 23 July about noon in
Boston (7 Aug.)

HILL, James, pretending to be dumb - for some weeks has
been traveling about, making profit from the charity
and credulity of the people (7 Aug.)

Plantation - for sale - in Byberry Twp., Phila. Co.,
about 12 miles from Phila. and 1 mile from the River
Delaware; enquire of Nathaniel Walton, Sr. (7 Aug.)

PENN, Thomas - has arrived at Chester; address of Andrew
Hamilton, the Recorder, to Mr. Penn (14 Aug.)

COSBY, William, Gov. of New York - arrived Tuesday last
at Sandy Hook in H.M.S. _Seaford_, Capt. Long commander,
in 7 weeks from Great Britain - New York dispatch of
7 Aug. (14 Aug.)

FITZSYMONS, Norris, of Ireland, dec'd - his son Maynard
Fitzsymons, supposed to be in Pennsylvania, is to apply
to the printer; he is heir to a considerable estate
(14 Aug.)

POWEL, Evan, at the Blue Ball in Chestnut St., Phila. -
offers for sale geese feathers (14 Aug.)

Address of House of Representatives of Pennsylvania to
Thomas Penn and the Proprietor's answer (21 Aug.)

Address of New York officials to Gov. W. Cosby and Cosby's
Speech (21 Aug.)

Arrival Saturday last at Boston from the eastward of the
Gov. of Massachusetts in H.M.S. _Scarborough_ (21 Aug.)

Extract of letter from Capt. Fitche, commander of H.M.S. Sheerness at Canso to Capt. Durell, commander of H.M.S. Scarborough - he states that the French are going to carry Jews to settle the Island of St. John's in the Gut of Canso; Monsieur Ovide, Gov. of Cape Breton, and several officers are going there from Lewisburgh to settle the boundaries (21 Aug.)

HUGHS, Philip, of Uwchland, Chester Co., 2½-year-old son of - 22 Aug. lost in the woods but found safe some days later (28 Aug.)

Plantation of 630 acres, in the Forks of Neshaminey, adjoining Dr. Rodman's land in Bucks Co., about 18 miles from Phila., is for sale - apply to Benjamin and Joseph Walton (28 Aug.)

Allen and Turner have for sale a parcel of Negro boys and girls just arrived from St. Christopher's (28 Aug.)

CLEMENTS, Richard, supposed to live in Maryland - will hear something to his advantage by applying to the printer (28 Aug.)

Address of the minister, church wardens and vestry of Christ Church, Phila., to Thomas Penn and the proprietor's answer (7 Sept.)

Some Indian chiefs, who have been in Phila. and have made a treaty, left on Saturday (7 Sept.)

NEAL, Dennis, Irish servant, age c. 19 - runaway from Daniel Walker, of Chester Co. (7 Sept.)

RICHARDSON, Joseph, Irish servant, age c. 18 - runaway from Philip Yarnal, of Edgmont, Chester Co. (7 Sept.)

HENDERSON, W., practitioner in physic and chirurgery, who lodges over against Henry Badcock's in Second St., Phila. - soon will embark for Europe (7 Sept.)

JENKINS, Nath., at the Boot in Front St., Phila., near the Coffee House - has for sale window glass just imported from England (7 Sept.)

SINCLAIR, Robert - his white servant man on 29 June committed suicide by drowning himself in Black River - Charlestown, S.C., dispatch of 15 July (12 Sept.)

BONNER, Capt. - arrived yesterday in Boston from Newcastle - Boston dispatch of 4 Sept. (18 Sept.)

Address of Presbyterian Ministers of Synod to Thomas
Penn and his answer (26 Sept.)

Address of Representatives of the 3 Lower Counties on Delaware to Thomas Penn and his answer (26 Sept.)

SMITH, Thomas, shopkeeper at New-Castle - offers reward for
capture of runaway servant man (26 Sept.)

KING, John, servant, weaver, a Devonshire man - runaway
from Ralph Sandiford (26 Sept.)

The Minister of Christ, and the Duties of His Flock, by
David Evans, minister at Tredyffryn - has just been
published by B. Franklin (26 Sept.)

HOLLIS, Mr. (nephew of the late Thomas Hollis, Esq., of
London) - from him Harvard has just received a micro-
scope, an armillary sphere and an orrery - Cambridge,
Mass., dispatch of 9 Sept. (5 Oct.)

GRANT, Mr., at the ferry, about 1 mile from Marblehead,
Mass. - Wednesday last his house burnt to the ground
- Marblehead dispatch of 16 Sept. (5 Oct.)

Address of the Baptists to Thomas Penn and his answer;
signers of the address are Nathaniel Jenkins, Jenkin
Jones, Owen Thomas, Joseph Eaton, John Davis and John
Evans (5 Oct.)

Address of a body of freeholders of Phila. to Thomas Penn
and his answer (5 Oct.)

READ, Charles, high sheriff of Phila. Co. - makes speech
at opening of elections for Phila. Co. (5 Oct.)

Persons elected for Phila. Co.: Representatives--Jonath.
Robeson, Tho. Leech, John Kensey, W. Allen, Robt. James,
Job Goodson, W. Monington, John Cadwalader; burgesses--
John Kearsley, Israel Pemberton; sheriffs--Septimus
Robeson, Robert Ellis; coroners--Owen Owen, John Roberts;
commissioner--William Coates; assessors--W. Corker, Tho.
Peters, Evan Thomas, J. Jones, Hugh Evans, Jacob Leech;
city assessors--Jos. Paschal, Tim. Stephenson, Benj.
Morgan, Joseph Trotter, W. Chancellor, Nath. Allen
(5 Oct.)

Persons elected for Chester Co.: Representatives--Caleb
Cowpland, Jos. Harvey, Jos. Brinton, Thos. Thomas. W.
Webb, Jos. Penock, John Davis, W. Hewes; sheriffs--John
Parry, W. Smith; coroners--Anthony Shaw, John Wharton;
commissioner--Samuel Lewis (5 Oct.)

Persons elected for Bucks Co.: Representatives--Jos. Kirkbride, Jr., Jer. Langhorne, W. Paxton, Abr. Chapman, Christian Vanhorne, And. Hamilton, W. Biles, Nath. Hughes; sheriffs--Isaac Pennington, John Hart; coroners--W. Atkinson, Joseph Wildman; commissioner--W. Paxton (5 Oct.)

Persons elected for Lancaster Co.: Representatives--George Stuart, Samuel Blunston, Tho. Edwards, And. Galbreth; sheriffs--John Galbreth, Rob. Bohenan; coroners--Joshua Lowe and ___ ___; commissioner--James Paterson (5 Oct.)

Schooner Ann, John Rice Master - will sail in 12 to 14 days to South Carolina; for freight or passage apply to the master at the King George in Water St., Phila., or on board the schooner near the Market wharf (5 Oct.)

HALL, Hugh, Esq., member of his majesty's Council for Island of Barbados - died 20 Sept. at Cambridge, Mass. (9 Oct.)

SHALCROSS, J., Jr. - 9 Oct., when going with his team between Phila. and Frankford, fell down and wheel passed over him so that he died in about 3 hours (9 Oct.)

WALBANK, Edward, at his stores under W. Fishbourn's new house, the lower end of Water ,St., Phila. - offers many goods for sale; he intends within 6 weeks to go to the West Indies (9 Oct.)

PATTISON, Thomas, of Darby - people indebted to him are desired to pay him at once (9 Oct.)

WRIGHT, Anthony, near Bristol - has taken up a roan mare (9 Oct.)

GIBBS, Capt. - Sunday last arrived in Newport from Jamaica with the report that Capt. Peters, commander of one of the Party Companies in Jamaica, had taken a large Negro town - Newport dispatch of 4 Oct. (26 Oct.)

HAMMET, Thomas, under sentence of death for the murder of Katherine Cook - 10 Oct., dressed in his wife's clothes, escaped from the Newport prison - Newport dispatch of 11 Oct. (26 Oct.)

SMITH, James, member of his majesty's Council and Secretary of the Province of New Jersey - died 15 Oct. of a fever - Burlington dispatch of 11 Oct. (26 Oct.)

KOFFMAN, Jacob - 24 Oct., when driving through Germantown, accidentally fell down, a wheel passed over his head, and he died immediately (26 Oct.)

McGUIRE, William, Irish servant, shoemaker - runaway from
Joseph Reyner, of Chester (26 Oct.)

Sloop Dove, Henry Davis master, lying at the Market wharf
in Phila. - will sail for South Carolina in a few days
(26 Oct.)

BARBER, Joseph, of Phila. - offers reward for recovery of
a black horse strayed away (26 Oct.)

HUSSEY, John, in West Nottingham - offers reward for recovery of a mare strayed away (26 Oct.)

A turner, lately arrived in Phila. from London - works at
the shop of William Morgan over against the Three Tuns,
Chestnut St. (26 Oct.)

CROSWEL, James, servant, age c. 30, shoemaker - runaway
from Jacob Johnson near Mount Holly (26 Oct.)

PEAGRUM, John, Esq., Surveyor General of his majesty's
Customs for North-America - arrived Monday last in
ship Cambridge, John Crocker commander, from London -
Boston dispatch of 23 Oct. (2 Nov.)

CORNEY, Capt., who left Oran 9 Aug. - arrived Sat. last
in Boston with news of Oran - Boston dispatch of 23
Oct. (2 Nov.)

PERKINS, Hannah, age 91 - died of cold and cough 16 Oct.
at Ipswich, Mass. (2 Nov.)

FULLER, Mary, age 85 - same as above

SMITH, Priscilla, age 86 - same as above

WOOD, Abigal, age 67 - same as above

DOW, Mary, a maiden, age 91 - same as above

ALKIN, Capt., from Providence, at Newport, R. I. - reports
that near Cape Maez, in the Windward Passage, he met
7 English men-of-war (2 Nov.)

Ship Mary, Robert Abbot master - will sail for London in
14 days; for freight or passage agree with the master
or Thomas Ashton, shipwright in Phila. (2 Nov.)

Some people on the balcony of the Bunch of Grapes Tavern
in King St., Boston, watching fireworks on Wednesday

last were injured when the balcony collapsed - Boston
dispatch of 16 Oct. (9 Nov.)

BERKLEY, Rev. Geo., Dean of Londonderry - has given his
farm, worth about 3,000 pounds, to Yale College in
Conn. (9 Nov.)

PERKINS, Capt., late commander of a sloop from Guinea -
was killed 7 Apr. by Negroes - Newport dispatch of 25
Oct. (9 Nov.)

FITZROY, Lord Augustus (son of Charles, Duke of Grafton)
- 23 Oct. in New York was presented with the copy of
his freedom, to which was annexed the city seal, in a
gold box engraved with the arms of the city (9 Nov.)

About 12 or 13 acres of land in Allentown, East Jersey,
are for sale - apply to Peter Van Tilburgh, of Allentown (9 Nov.)

HARPE, Peter, a Palatine, age c. 40 - escaped from Goal
of Phila.; J. Robinson, sheriff, offers reward for his
capture (16 Nov.)

M'GINNIS, Francis - same as above

MIDDLETON, Aaron, servant, clockmaker, age c. 26 - runaway
from Isaac Pearson of Burlington (16 Nov.)

COLLINS, William, of Francony, Phila. Co. - 19 Nov., returning from visit to a neighbor ½-mile away, died in
the snow, probably as result of violence of the
weather (30 Nov.)

Lord and Lady Baltimore arrived in Maryland 10 Nov. (30
Nov.)

SENTRY, Robert, alias PERKINS, servant - runaway from Daniel Cook, of Back Creek at the head of Bohemia Manor
(30 Nov.)

MOORE, John, Esq., who had been Collector of Customs for
Port of Phila. for above 30 years - died Saturday
morning in Phila. in his 74th year (30 Nov.)

FARRA, Samuel, mariner, of Phila. - his wife Ann has
eloped from him (7 Dec.)

TURNER, Mr., of Pembroke, Plymouth Co., Mass. - Saturday
last his house burned; 2 daughters, one aged 15 and
the other 12, perished; Turner, his wife and 2 children narrowly escaped - Boston dispatch of 9 Nov. (12
Dec.)

DOTIN, J. - his corn destroyed by 10 or 12 persons from
Christ Church Parish in Barbados - letter dated 20
Sept. from Boston (12 Dec.)

MARTYN, Mr., of Bridgetown - narrowly escaped with his
life from a gang on Barbados (12 Dec.)

ANDREWS, Mrs. Ruth (born in Duxbury, Mass.), the relict of
Capt. Thomas Andrews (who died of smallpox in Boston on
his return from Canada) - died at Hingham, Mass., on 23
Oct. in her 99th year, leaving 2 daughters and 2 sons,
one of whom is Rev. Jedidiah Andrews, paster of a church
in Phila. (12 Dec.)

Speech of Gov. Belcher to Massachusetts Assembly (12 Dec.)

BROCKDEN, R., Keeper of the Indian Prince Tavern in Phila.,
had a man arrested, on orders of A. Hamilton, Esq., for
passing a counterfeit bill; the man (who had a sister
with counterfeits in her possession) confessed the bad
money was brought from Ireland by one Grindal, who came
from there this summer with Capt. Blair; another con-
federate was a certain Watts, or Watt, who was at Eastown
in Chester; Watts, too, was then arrested (19 Dec.);
10 Jan. Watt was whipped, pilloried and cropt; Grindal
was taken in the Jerseys but escaped (11 Jan. 1733)

The following vessels bound for Phila. are at Lewes but
must wait till the river opens up: ship Diamond, Sam-
uel Flower master, from Barbados; ship Ruby Galley,
Joseph Arthur master, from Antigua; snow Lovely Hannah,
J. Wilcocks master, from Newfoundland; brigantine
Thistle, Thomas Glentworth master, from Jamaica; a brig-
antine, Lawrence Anderson, master, from Jamaica; snow
Speedy, Thomas Ramsey master, from St. Kts; ship John,
Edward Jones master, from London; a ship, Capt. Tole
master, from Jamaica; 2 sloops from Boston (19 Dec.)

Ship John is ashore upon a shoal, about 10 miles from
Lewes (19 Dec.)

Brigantine Prosperity, Capt. Blair master, having lost
both anchors, put out to sea (19 Dec.)

CHARLTON, Thomas - last week at dinner was suddenly taken
speechless and died in about ½ hour (19 Dec.)

ROUSE, Capt., who left Bristol 26 Sept. and arrived in
Boston 1 Dec. - reports that the ship Virgin, of Bristol,
Capt. Story King master, laden with sugar from Jamaica,
was cast away in a storm going up the Bristol Channel
and all hands were drowned - Boston dispatch of 4 Dec.
(28 Dec.)

The Massachusetts Assembly voted 22 Nov. that Mr. Wells,
Mr. Cooke, Major Brattle, Col. Savage, Capt. Goddard,
Mr. Cushing and Col. Alden be a committee to prepare an
address to the British House of Commons; it was also
ordered that the Speaker, Mr. Welles, Mr. Cushing, Col.
Savage and Major Brattle prepare a draft of a letter to
be sent to Agent Wilks; also answer to the governor's
speech (28 Dec.)

Tract of 1,000 acres of land on Little Creek, Kent Co. upon
Delaware, distant 5 miles from Dover and about 2 miles
from Duck Creek and Little Creek Landing, for sale -
apply to Laetitia Hall, widow, or Timothy Hanson in Kent
Co. (28 Dec.)

Poor Richard; An Almanack for 1733 - printed and sold by
B. Franklin (28 Dec.)

1733

Addresses presented to Charles, Lord Baron of Baltimore,
by the Catholics, Quakers and Church of England Clergy
of Maryland - Annapolis dispatch of 3 Dec. (4 Jan.)

LYDIUS, Mr. - Saturday last came by land from Albany to
Boston and brought news from a relation at Montreal in
Canada - Boston dispatch of 4 Dec. (4 Jan.)

Sloop, John Buckland master, bound from Boston to Connecticut, on 17 Dec. was cast ashore on Sandy Point -
Boston dispatch of 4 Dec. (4 Jan.)

HUGHES, Rev. - got ashore, with 2 sailors, from the ship
John which is ashore in the Bay; he died from cold and
hardship soon after reaching Lewes (4 Jan.)

BREINTNAL, David, late of Phila., shopkeeper, dec'd - accounts with estate to be settled with John Breintnal in
Chestnut St. (11 Jan.)

HOLT, Thomas, servant, age c. 21 - runaway from Stephen
Armit of Phila. (11 Jan.)

Ferry passing from Boston to Winnisimit, with 7 passengers
and a man and Negro who plied the boat, overset Monday
last near Moulton's Point - eventually all died save a
young man of Boston, John Belcher, some of whose fingers were frozen; those who died were Withers Berry
(member of the House of Representatives for Kittery),
John Horton (a young cooper of Boston), Mr. Rindge of
Block Island, W. Ridgle (a butcher of Boston), Samuel

Marshall (a glazier), John Thomas, the Negro ferryman, and one other - Boston dispatch of 14 Dec. (18 Jan.)

During late storm in the Bay 2 ships put out to sea, the snow <u>Lovely Hannah</u>, John Willcox master, and a sloop from Boston, laden with salt (18 Jan.)

CLARKE, Valentine, Irish servant, age <u>c</u>. 19 - runaway from Samuel Hurfoot, near Frankfort (18 Jan.)

JONES, Henry, lately dec'd - accounts to be settled with his widow Eleanor Jones and his son, Isaac Jones, executors (18 Jan.)

COOPER, James, of Phila., lately dec'd - accounts to be settled with executors, Samuel Cooper and John Cadwalader (18 Jan.)

McBEAN, Locklin, of Tesakey in the Indian country in South Carolina - 2 Sept. 1732 in a storm 2 hailstones came through 3 lays of bark, 2 lays of clapboards, a clay floor and a lay of poles into his store (25 Jan.)

Three vessels arrived 1 Dec. in Charlestown, S. C., H.M.S. <u>Squirrel</u> from cruizing, Capt. Snelling from Boston and Capt. Hart from London; it is reported that Capt. Edwards is coming with 50 Palatines (25 Jan.)

Address of the Swedish clergy to Thomas Penn and Penn's answer (25 Jan.)

PHIPPS, Thomas, of Phila., schoolmaster - intends to leave off keeping school 30 Apr. next (25 Jan.)

Virginia assembly amended the Tobacco Law and have given John Randolph, Esq., 2,200 pounds to go home to get tobacco under an excise and to get repealed a Law made in last Parliament to secure payment of debts in the plantations to the merchants of England; an annual salary of 100 pounds was settled on William Parks, printer, for printing their laws, journals, etc. (1 Feb.)

SULLIVAN, Mary, servant maid in Phila. - died 16 Jan. a few hours after drinking a large quantity of rum (1 Feb.)

A Swede, mate of a vessel in Christine Creek, who lately came over in the ship <u>John</u> and was cast away when entering the Bay - drowned last week when he fell through the ice (1 Feb.)

POWEL, William, cooper, lately dec'd - persons indebted to the estate are to settle with John Armit, executor (1 Feb.)

CASH, Caleb, Jr., heel- and last-maker - has removed from Chestnut St., in Phila. to the foot of Market St., in the house where Widow Appleton lately lived (1 Feb.)

GARVI, Malachi, Irish servant, age c. 34 - runaway from Samuel Worthington, of Manor of Moreland (1 Feb.)

SALTER, Capt. Malachi, who sometime since sailed for North Carolina - is put ashore by the ice at Sandy Point - Boston dispatch of 4 Jan. (1 Feb.)

WILKS, Fra., agent for Massachusetts in London - his letter of 23 Oct. 1732; he wrote that his last was per Capt. Snelling, and copy per Capt. Webster (8 Feb.)

BELL, Capt. - arrived at Newport, R. I., Monday last from Curracoa, from which he sailed 20 Oct.; he related how a Spanish pirate sloop (which had aboard 1,500 pieces of eight and 2 gold chains) was captured by 2 sloops and brought to Curracoa - Newport dispatch of 28 Dec. (8 Feb.)

ALMY, William, 10-year-old son of last week at Newport, as he was walking over the Cove, fell through the ice and was drowned - Newport dispatch of 28 Dec. (8 Feb.)

By a ship that arrived at Newport Sunday last in 7 weeks from Barbados, it is reported that Capt. Lanclet, who built a brig at Newbury and sailed from Boston in her last summer, fitted her out at one of the Leeward Islands with design "to go a pyrating" on the Spanish Coast - Newport dispatch of 28 Dec. (8 Feb.)

HAMILTON, A., Esq., plaintiff - 20 Jan. in Phila. at Court of Common Pleas recovered 500 pounds from Robert Gregory and Mary his wife, who conspired to charge him with unnatural abuse of the body of said Mary (8 Feb.)

HILL, John and Thomas - have lately erected at their still-house in Boston, by advice of Rowland Houghton, a water-engine, drawn by a horse, which delivers a large quantity of water 12 feet above the ground (15 Feb.)

ALDEN, Capt., arrived in Boston - brings news that Parliament was prorogued to 17 Jan. - Boston dispatch of 17 Jan. (15 Feb.)

THORNTON, Richard - last Thursday night slept in an open outhouse and was found there dead, killed by the cold - Phila. item (15 Feb.)

CORKER, W., lately dec'd - accounts with estate to be settled with the executors, Mary Corker and Edward Waters; house in Chesnut St. where Thomas Skelton lives is for sale (15 Feb.)

PRINCE, Capt. - last week his sloop, which sometime since was thought to be lost, came to Boston - Boston dispatch of 15 Jan. (22 Feb.)

GREY, Joseph - Sunday last water was nearly 2½ feet high on the ground floor of his house at the Middle Ferry at Phila. (22 Feb.)

ATKINS, Capt. - June last saw Greenland bear (whose skin is 12 feet in length) on a cake of ice and shot her and captured her cub, which is now on display in a cage at the south side of Clark's wharf at the north end of Boston (28 Feb.)

TAYLOR, Abraham, considerable merchant of Phila. - Saturday last married one of the governor's daughters (28 Feb.)

Plantation within 1½ miles from Amboy and 2 from Woodbridge, owned by John Vail, who lately lived there - is to be sold; apply to John Vail, now living at the Blew Hills about 10 miles from Woodbridge, or to Thomas Gage, at the foot of Strawberry Hill in Woodbridge, who also will show the premises (28 Feb.)

ONION, Stephen - his house on Susquehanah has suffered much by the ice (8 Mar.)

DOW, Mrs. Mary - 21 Jan. died at Hampton, N.H., in her 95th year; she was born at Newbury, daughter of Christopher Hussey, Esq.; she first married Thomas Page and after him Henry Dow, Esq.; her father and last 2 husbands were members of his majesty's Council; by one of her daughters, Mrs. Robie, now living, she has left 65 issue, 7 of which are of the fifth generation (15 Mar.)

JARVIS, Capt. Elias, master of the brigantine Two Brothers - arrived last week at Boston in 8 weeks from Lisbon (15 Mar.)

Many Newenglanders have arrived at St. Christopher's, including one MacFeathers, who was bound from London to Boston (15 Mar.)

PAXTON, Capt., in his voyage from Boston to Jamaica, touched at Antigua, where he found the following blown

off the coast: Captains Sears, Searl, Wallington and
Hodges; Capt. Viscount from Cayan, going to Antigua,
lost his sloop - Boston dispatch of 19 Feb. (15 Mar.)

SACHEVERELL, John, who engraves or carves metals - has just
arrived from London and sells pewter and other ware at
Mr. Stone's, next door to Samuel Par's in Front St.,
Phila. (15 Mar.)

The following Palatines who came passengers from Rotterdam in the ship John and William, Constable Tymberton
commander, are to make speedy payment or give good security to George M'Call, merchant in Phila.: Hans
Emick, Stephen Matz, Friedrich Kuhler, Michael Blum-
hauer, Hans Peter Brechbiel, Philip Melchioner, Nico-
laus Paschon, George Adam Sties, Abraham Thiebo,
Matthias Manser, Hans Riel, Caspar Willaar, Philip
Melchior Meyer, Johan George Wahnzodel (15 Mar.)

NELSON, Alexander, Irish servant, age c. 24 - runaway from
Edmund Farrel, tanner; the runaway has the old inden-
tures and pass of one James MacDaniel, out of Maryland,
now free (15 Mar.)

BLOWDEN, John, age c. 25, formerly servant to Arthur
Wells of Phila. - runaway from William Smith of
Phila. (15 Mar.)

KNIGHT, Joseph, servant - runaway from Thomas Moore, of
Brandewyne Hundred in New-Castle Co. (22 Mar.)

Address of Gov. to House of Representatives of Pennsylvania
and reply to Gov. (29 Mar.)

LOW, Robert, servant, age c. 24 - runaway from ship Swift,
David Russan master (29 Mar.)

IDDENS, John - 11 Mar. at upper part of the French Creek
killed a bear with his ax (29 Mar.)

MERREWETHER, James, of Town of New-Castle - offers for
sale a house, tan-house and tanyard in the said town
(29 Mar.)

KUHL, Mark, baker, near the prison in Phila. - offers reward for recovery of a lost dark gelding (29 Mar.)

SUTTON, Robert, a fisherman - died of exposure Tuesday
last when a schooner ran upon a rock called the Whales
Back and sank - Newcastle, N.H., dispatch of 16 Feb.
(5 Apr.)

HIEDEN, John, a baker - same as above

PROBERT, Thomas, Welsh servant - runaway from Peter Cuff, brewer of Phila. (5 Apr.)

HOW, Lord, Gov. of Barbados - is expected there shortly from England (12 Apr.)

FOULK, Stephen - will let for 7 years his sawmill upon Redclay Creek in Kennet, Chester Co., Pa. (12 Apr.)

PACKOM, Timothy, servant, blacksmith - runaway from Evan Jones in Kent upon Delaware (12 Apr.)

DURELL, Capt. Thomas, commander of H.M.S. Scarborough from Saltertuda arrived Monday last at Salem and Wednesday last at Boston - reported that 2 Spanish men-of-war on 13 Mar. captured the following English vessels: ship Katharine, Andrew Woodbury master, brig Hopewell, brig Two Sisters and brig Three Brothers - Boston dispatch of 16 Apr. (26 Apr.)

WHITE, John, English servant, age c. 30 - runaway from Thomas Shoemaker (26 Apr.)

WILLIAMS, Charles, in Front St., Phila. - offers for sale 3 years and 4 months time of a servant, tailor by trade (26 Apr.)

BREINTNAL, Joseph, Secretary of the Library Company of Philadelphia - meeting will be held 7 May at house of Louis Timothee, where the library is kept, in the alley next the Boar's Head tavern (26 Apr.)

DUTCH, Capt., who arrived in Boston 8 Apr. - reports that Capt. Butler and Capt. Littleton, both bound to the Bay of Honduras, December last were cast away upon Glover's Reach and that the Spaniards took 4 vessels, 2 of which were commanded by Captains Hinman and Braden - Boston dispatch of 16 Apr. (3 May)

SAVAGE, Habijah, J. P. for Suffolk Co., Mass. - Saturday last committed to prison an imposter, John Hill, and his wife Rachel Hill alias Fig; Hill picked up the woman at Roxbury and they were married by the town clerk of Westown (3 May)

PARKE, Thomas, late of Burlington Co., West New Jersey - on 20 Apr. assigned all his debts and demands to Thomas Lawrence, Alexander Woodrop, Israel Pemberton, White & Taylor, William Attwood, William Rawle and Samuel Mickle, all of Phila., merchants (3 May)

Plantation of about 300 acres in Bybury Twp., Phila. Co.,
about a mile from the Delaware River and 12 miles east
of Phila., late property of Nathanael Walton, dec'd,
for sale - enquire of Nathanael Walton, schoolmaster
at Frankfort, and Malachi Walton, executors (3 May)

EVAN, David, at the Crown, Phila. - sells Rhenish wine
and Holland geneva (3 May)

Gov. of Pennsylvania - set out 10 May to visit Gov. Cosby,
Gov. of New York and New Jersey, at Burling (10 May)

Account, from the South-Carolina Gazette of 31 Mar., of
the progress of the first colony sent to Georgia (17 May)

BROWN, William, alias William Dorrell, servant, age 21 -
runaway from Joseph Richardson of Perkiomy in New
Providence Twp., Phila. Co.; reward offered if he is
returned to his master or to George Emlen in Phila.
(17 May)

INGRAM, Thomas, cutler, next door to the Three Tuns in
Chesnut St., Phila. - makes and sells cutlery (17 May)

Account, from the South-Carolina Gazette of 31 Mar., of a
voyage to and remarks made at Georgia (24 May)

Dick, Negro slave, age c. 25 or 30 - runaway from Samuel
Hasell, of Phila. (24 May)

George, Negro slave, age c. 25 - runaway from Thomas
Griffitts, of Phila.; both Dick and George have been
seen in the Northern Libertys, near the Vineyard and
Jacob Dubery's (24 May)

WATHEL, Thomas, late of Borough of Bristol, Bucks Co.,
dec'd - accounts with estate to be settled with executor, Joseph Peace (24 May)

CHAMLIT, Rebecca, who lived at north part of Boston with
Mr. John Adams - Friday last was committed to prison
by Justice Savage on charge that she murdered her
bastard child - Boston dispatch of 14 May (31 May)

AYRES, Capt. - arrived Thursday last at Marblehead, Mass.,
in about 6 weeks from London - Boston dispatch of 21
May (31 May)

SPITSBURY, Thomas - drowned a few days since in the Skuylkill, according to report from New Providence, Phila.
Co., when trying to escape from a constable (31 May)

BROWN, Philip, servant, age c. 21, who talks West Country dialect - runaway from John Ogden, of Phila., tanner (31 May)

WHITE, William, a young man who attended at the granary on the Boston Common - was committed to goal in Boston Saturday last for breaking open the granary and stealing; Mary Frank, his sweetheart, had been given stolen goods by him - Boston dispatch of 21 May (7 June)

Last week a great ship coming up the Bay to Phila. to some merchants who had purchased her struck upon a shoal below Bumbo Hook and went to pieces (7 June)

WILKINSON, John, brush-maker - has lately returned from Europe and lives, as formerly, in Front St., near the Sign of the Plume of Feathers in Phila. (7 June)

CUFF, Peter, of Phila., brewer - asks return of a set of gold weights and scale that had been borrowed (14 June)

WATT, Joseph, age c. 40 - broke out of Phila. goal where he was under sentence for counterfeiting Pennsylvania bills of credit (14 June)

Speech of Gov. of Massachusetts to his Assembly and votes of the Assembly (21 June)

FLEXNEY, Thomas, merchant, dec'd - accounts with estate to be settled with executors, Clement Plumsted or Samuel Powel (21 June)

WILKINSON, Gabriel, lately dec'd - accounts with estate to be settled with Anthony Wilkinson, executor (21 June)

Proposal to set up markets in Boston - voted affirmatively Monday last - Boston dispatch of 31 May (28 June)

TEMPLE, Mr. - had 6 sheep and lambs killed in a thunder storm 7 June - Boston dispatch of 11 June (28 June)

MURRAY, Humphry, Esq. - Monday last elected Grand Master at a Masonic meeting held at the Tun Tavern in Water St., Phila.; he appointed Thomas Hart his deputy; Peter Cuff and James Bingham were chosen wardens (28 June)

JACKSON, Elizabeth (wife of Marmaduke Jackson), both elderly, of Richland, Bucks Co. - 15 June was found dead in her field (28 June)

Letter, dated 13 Apr., from Cork advises that Captains

Barwick, Dun, Wilcocks and Stedman were arrived there; it was reported that Capt. Nickolson, bound to Phila., had sailed from Cork 7 weeks before (28 June)

Lands above or to the north of Rarington River within the East and West Divisions of New Jersey, belonging to the Proprietors of Pennsylvania, are for sale - apply to John Budd, of Hanover Twp., N.J. (28 June)

BINGHAM, James, in Phila. - offers for sale the following lands in New Jersey belonging to John Budd: 50 acres near head of Allaways Creek in Salem Co.; 50 acres in Gloucester Co. by the north branch of Raccoone Creek and 69 adjoining them; 500 acres near the same on Quohockon Road, about 13 miles from Gloucester; 230 acres a little above Stephen Jones's, about 13 miles from Gloucester (28 June)

House and lot in Market St., Phila., now occupied by John Bryant, baker, are for sale; apply to Capt. Samuel Harwood or his attorney, Charles Hughes, at the Great Last in Arch St. (28 June)

Ship _Dolphin_, Constant Hughes master, will sail for Cape Fear; for freight or passage apply to Edward Nichols, turner, in Chesnut St., Phila. (28 June)

OGLETHORPE, James - 1 May left Savannah and 4 May arrived at Charlestown, S.C., bringing with him Tomochichee Mico (chief of Yammacraw) and 2 nephews, the eldest of whom is Tooanouchee; Oglethorpe left Charlestown 14 May and lay at Col. Bull's house on Ashley River; Rev. Guy, Rector of St. John's waited on him there; the 15th he was at Capt. Bull's; the 16th he embarked at Daho and rested at Mr. Cochran's Island; the 17th he dined at Lt. Watt's at Beaufort; the 18th he landed at Savannah, where he found Mr. Whiggan, interpreter, and the chiefs of the Lower Creek Nation; among the Indians were Yahou-Lakee, Essoboo (son of old Breen), Cusseta, Tatchiquatchi, Ogeese, Neathlouthko, Ougachi, Outhletchoa, Thlauthlo-thlukee, Figeer, Sootamilla, Chutabecche, Robin (bred among the English), Gillatee, Oueckachumpa, Coowoo, Tomaumi; speech of an Indian was interpreted by Mr. Wiggan and Mr. Musgrove; other Indians mentioned were Stimoiche and Illispelle; when a peace was concluded, care of the people was recommended to James St. Julian and Mr. Scott; Oglethorpe left the Savannah Monday the 21st and dined at Mr. Bullock's at Willtown the 22nd - Charlestown dispatch of 12 May (5 July)

Letters that reached Capt. Kenwood at Topsham, after his

departure from London, inform that the Sugar, Rum and Melasses Act passed the House of Lords on 3 May - Boston dispatch of 25 June (5 July)

KYLY, John, Irish servant from Waterford, age c. 32 - runaway from Martin Howard, of Newport, R.I. (5 July)

Brick house and lot in Bristol for sale - apply to William Hope at his plantation in Bensalem or Joseph Jackson in Bristol (5 July)

WARDER, John, hatter, in Second St., Phila. - has 2 Negroes for sale (5 July)

The James, Capt. Yoakley master, from London with passengers and stores for Georgia - sailed 8 May from Port Royal and arrived 14 May at Savannah; Lt. Watts with the garrison boat arrested mutineers on the James - Port Royal dispatch of 21 May (12 July)

Message of Gov. Belcher of Massachusetts to his House of Representatives - Boston dispatch of 21 June (12 July)

Ordered 19 June by Massachusetts House of Representatives that Mr. Cooke, Mr. Cushing, Mr. Welles, Major Brattle and Mr. Thatcher be a committee to prepare a vote for the reception of James Oglethorp on his way to London; Mr. Agent Wilks has advised of the many good offices of Oglethorp for Massachusetts - Boston dispatch of 21 June (12 July)

BERKELEY, Rev. Dean - has employed Henry Hewman to purchase an organ to present to the church at Newport, R.I.; Berkeley also plans to present collection of books to Harvard - Boston dispatch of 28 June (12 July)

Complaint was made to House of Commons that the Massachusetts House of Representatives had censured Jeremiah Dunbar, Esq., for giving evidence in relation to the trade of the sugar colonies (12 July)

PARKER, William, of Phila. - offers reward for recovery of strayed horse (12 July)

Brigantine Beaver, Benjamin Christian master, lying at Mr. Drury's wharf in Phila. - will sail for St. Christophers; for freight or passage apply to the master on board or to Evan Bevan in Second St. (12 July)

WILLIAMS, John, keeper of Goal of Monmouth Co., East New Jersey - offers reward for capture of Simon Gillman, West Country man, fuller by trade, who has run away from the goal (12 July)

Speech of Robert Wright, Chief Justice, in Council of
South Carolina on 28 Apr. and protest of the House of
Assembly (signed by I. Amyand) that Wright has violated
the privileges of the House by granting 2 writs upon an
action of debt, one at the suit of James Greeme, the
other at the suit of Rouland Vaugham against John Brown,
messenger of the House; and by signing a rule of court
to Robert Hall, Esq., the Provost Marshal, to make a
return in 2 days of a writ on an action of debt at the
suit of Thomas Cooper against the said Brown (19 July)

WELCH, Joseph, dec'd - real estate in Burlington to be
sold by the executors, Samuel Lovett, Richard Smith,
Jr., and Caleb Raper (19 July)

In Georgia Mr. Oglethorp, with Capt. Macpherson and a
troop of Rangers, have selected a place where a forti-
fication, to be called Ft. Argyle, will be erected -
Savannah dispatch of 25 June (26 July)

In Georgia King Timo Chi Chi calms an uproar of the Indians - Savannah dispatch of 25 June (26 July)

Schooner **Christiana**, George Stewart master - will sail for
North Carolina; for freight or passage apply to the
master or to William Parker in Water St., Phila. (26
July)

WOOD, William, servant, age c. 18 - runaway from Thomas
Postgate, of Salem Co., in Maninton Twp. (26 July)

Speech of James Oglethorp to Assembly of South Carolina
(2 Aug.)

DIXY, Mr., at Marblehead, Mass., Ferry - sudden gust of
wind Thursday last took the roof off his house - Boston
dispatch of 16 July (2 Aug.)

SLAUGHTER, Capt., of Boston, late master of the schooner
Dolphin - 1 Nov., when he was on shore at Island of
Bonavisto, his mate, John Tenny, with Tho. Gosling,
John Martin and a boy named Joseph Cohagen, slipt or
cut the vessel's cables and made off with her - Boston
dispatch of 23 July (9 Aug.)

DUNNING, Thomas, at the George Inn in Second St., Phila.
- offers for sale an engine loomb (9 Aug.)

General Assembly of Barbados have settled an annual salary
of 3,000 pounds on their governor, Lord Viscount How -

Boston dispatch of 30 July (16 Aug.)

HARDING, Amaziah, of Eastham on Cape Cod - has been arrested for the murder of his wife and committed to
Barnstable Goal - Boston dispatch of 30 July (16 Aug.)

MARSHAL, John, of Placentia in Newfoundland, merchant -
17 May his store there was burnt down, as were all the
houses of Mr. Stignac's plantation - Boston dispatch of
30 July (16 Aug.)

DOWSE, Capt. - Friday last arrived at Newport, R.I., in
a brigantine from New-Castle - Boston dispatch of 30
July (16 Aug.)

COSBY, Hon. Major - arrived 19 July in New York (16 Aug.)

OGLETHORP, Mr. - will take passage to Great Britain from
New York (16 Aug.)

A sloop that arrived in Boston 29 July spoke on 21 July
with Capt. Durell of H.M.S. Scarborough (16 Aug.)

Epitaph from tombstone of Col. Byfield, lately dec'd (16
Aug.)

MORRIS, John, of Skippack, Phila. Co. - offers reward for
news of his brother, Daniel Morris, of Skippack, who
about 2 years ago went to the Lower Counties and has
not been heard of since (16 Aug.)

GILL, Capt. - Thursday last arrived at Boston in 6 weeks
from Gibraltar - Boston dispatch of 13 Aug. (23 Aug.)

Account from St. Christophers with a list of vessels and
how they fared in the hurricane of 30 June; ships at
St. Christophers: Fane Frigat of London, Capt. Samuel
Marshall; sloop Mary of Rhode Island, Capt. Natha.
Potter; a snow of Liverpool, Capt. Parr; sloop Mary,
of Rhode Island, Capt. Jos. Sanford; brigantine Robert
of Boston, Capt. Wm. Dowrick; brigantine Sally of Phila.,
Capt. David Burch; ship Friendship of Boston, Capt. Moses
Prince; snow Honest Endeavour of London, Capt. John
Levitt; brigantine Dispatch of Boston, Capt. Nath. How-
land; ship Nassau of Bristol, Capt. Samuel Jennings;
ship Stapleton of Bristol, Capt. Tho. Easton; ship Mary
of London, Capt. John Gray; ship Dorsett of London, Capt.
Arthur Ellis; ship Prince of Wales of Liverpool, Capt.
Joseph Davis; brigantine Antient Britain of Bristol,
Capt. Thomas Tennatt; ship St. Andrew of Scotland, Capt.
John Brown; snow Paddington of Bristol; Capt. Bedgood.
Vessels at Old Road: Capt. Conwany in a ship for Hull;

Capt. Williams in a sloop for the Spanish coast; Capt.
Carruthers in a sloop St. May, loaded for Boston. At
Sandy Point: James Wright in the Eagle of Rhode Island;
Capt. Crispin in a sloop of St. Kitts for Rhode Island;
Capt. Dunbar in a sloop of and for Rhode Island; Capt.
Benson in a snow for London; Capt. Richardson in a ship
for London. At Deep Bay: Capt. Richards in a brigan-
tine of North Carolina for London; Capt. Mathews in the
Potomoke of Boston; Capt. Kinslow in a brigantine of
St. Kitts for Boston. At Mountserat: Capt. Belcher of
Boston; Capt. Sears of Connecticut. At Nevis: Capt.
Payne in a snow from Guiny for London; Capt. Cussens in
a brigantine from Boston for London. At Spanish Town:
the Phenix of New York for Holland. To leeward of
Sabia: Capt. Wingfield of Boston for London (30 Aug.)

Books of value are come in Alden, a present from Rev. Dean
Berkley, consigned to Mr. Belcher (son of the governor)
for Harvard College and Yale College - Boston dispatch
of 13 Aug. (30 Aug.)

SAWYER, Caleb, of Lancaster, Pa. - with some friends recently fished up from a spring a bottle of milk he had
dropped there 8 years before (30 Aug.)

BEWLY, John, about 20 miles from Phila. - offers reward for
recovery of 2 strayed bullocks (30 Aug.)

The Temporal Interest of North-America - has been printed
and is sold by B. Franklin (30 Aug.)

CHILCOTT, Thomas, of Phila. - his wife Esther has eloped
from him (30 Aug.)

Ship Constantine, Edward Wright commander - will sail for
London; for passage apply to the captain or to Mr.
Lawrence (30 Aug.)

Speech of Gov. Belcher to the Assembly of Massachusetts
(7 Sept.)

PEGG, Sarah, living at upper end of Phila. - offers for
sale a cart, 3 horses and a cider-mill (14 Sept.)

HOPKINS, David - 26 Aug. went away from Nathaniel Poole,
shipwright in Phila.; reward will be paid if intelligence of him is brought to Reece Jones at the White
House in Market St. or to Robert Davis at the Queen's
Head in Water St. (14 Sept.)

Address of Justices of the Peace at Dover, Kent Co., on
Delaware on 13 Sept. to Thomas Penn and his reply (21
Sept.)

Address of Gov. Belcher to the Massachusetts Assembly Wednesday last - Boston dispatch of 20 Aug. (21 Sept.)

Vote of Massachusetts Council about a fast day brought down by Seth Williams, Esq., and Mr. Hall was ordered to go up with a message to the Board (21 Sept.)

Discussion 25 Aug. in Massachusetts House of Representatives of Fredericks Fort built by Col. Dunbar at Pemaquid (21 Sept.)

HOMANS, Capt. John - arrived Tuesday last in Boston and Capt. Croker the next day, both from London - Boston dispatch of 10 Sept. (21 Sept.)

NEWINHAM, John, apothecary, lately arrived from Ireland - keeps shop at John Richardson's in Front St., Phila. (21 Sept.)

SHEPARDSON, Capt., from London in about 8 weeks and thence in 5 weeks from Land's End - arrived 30 Sept. in Boston (11 Oct.)

Gloster, Negro man - runaway from Justice Farmer of Whitemarsh (11 Oct.)

Negro man and woman - runaways from John Petty, Indian trader (11 Oct.)

Corke, Negro man - runaway from John Baily, of Phila., shoemaker (11 Oct.)

A Negro man - runaway from the Widow Bird of Phila. (11 Oct.)

Bristor, Negro man - runaway from John Noble of Phila. (11 Oct.)

Order, signed by Andrew Hamilton, Charles Read, Jeremiah Langhorne, Richard Hayes and John Wright, for all mortgagers in arrears to pay the Loan Office forthwith (11 Oct.)

All persons indebted to Willing and Shippen at Phila. are desired to settle accounts (11 Oct.)

Brigantine Mary, John Maynard master - will sail for Bristol; for freight or passage apply to Simon Edgell or to the master at William Fishbourn's wharf in Phila. (11 Oct.)

Ship Hope, Daniel Read commander - will sail for South

Carolina; for freight or passage agree with the master or Benjamin Shoemaker in High St., Phila. (11 Oct.)

BLOWDEN, John, who formerly belonged to Arthur Wells, of Phila., dec'd - runaway from William Smith, of Phila., cordwainer (11 Oct.)

UNDERWOOD, Joshua, master of brigantine Success from Bay of Honduras - arrived Saturday last at Boston and brought news that the following ships were cast away 4 Aug. on the southern Fore Keys: ship Phaenix, Capt. Stupart; the ship Plaisance, Capt. Ratsey; the sloop St. Jago, Capt. Harrison - Boston dispatch of 8 Oct. (18 Oct.)

CUSHING, Matthew (servant to Mr. Fatherly), who some months ago broke out of Bridewell - Monday night broke into house of Joseph Cooke, shoemaker, and robbed him; Cushing was caught next day and committed to prison by Justice Savage - Boston dispatch of 8 Oct. (18 Oct.)

LANGHORNE, Jeremiah - Monday last was chosen Speaker of the Pennsylvania House of Representatives (18 Oct.)

READ, Charles, one of the trustees of the Loan Office of Pennsylvania - married 17 Oct. to widow of Joseph Harwood, Gent. (18 Oct.)

NORRIS, John (eldest son of Isaac Norris, Esq.) - died week before last in Phila. (18 Oct.)

CROW, Capt. of sloop belonging to Rhode Island - sloop was overset 5 Aug. off the Bermudas; after 19 days they were rescued by Capt. Jonathan Remington of Rhode Island, bound for Antigua; 4 days later Capt. Leppington from Surranam took aboard Capt. Crow, his mate and boy and brought them to Boston - Boston dispatch of 4 Oct. (25 Oct.)

A son of Mr. Bouteneaus of Boston accidentally chopped off 3 fingers of a brother - Boston dispatch of 4 Oct. (25 Oct.)

GRIFFIS, Michael, sailor - runaway from the ship Diligence, Samuel Wood master (25 Oct.)

Tuesday last the officials in Phila. celebrated the King's birthday (1 Nov.)

HOPKINS, John, servant, cook by trade - belonging to George Fleming - runaway from the Bristol Hope, Arthur Tough master - reward will be paid by Tho. Campbel in

Second St. if the runaway is delivered to the Workhouse in Phila. (1 Nov.)

Schooner <u>Anne</u>, John Rice master, now lying at Crane
wharf in Phila. - will sail for Cape Fear; for freight
or passage apply to the master or to John Grainger in
Water St. (1 Nov.)

Lands in Willistown and Goshen Twp. in Chester Co., belonging to John Trent (son and heir of William Trent,
late of Phila., merchant, dec'd) - are taken in execution at the suit of Samuel Preston and Samuel Powel
and will be sold by John Parry, sheriff (8 Nov.)

BASEENER, Andreas, Dutch servant, age <u>c</u>. 25 - runaway
from Joseph Gray at the Middle Ferry on Skuylkil (16
Nov.)

EISMAN, Hans Wulf, Dutch servant, tailor, age <u>c</u>. 22 - runaway from Christian Grassholt (16 Nov.)

Reward offered for recovery of an old fashioned silver
spoon with a flat flowered handle marked I.C., the
bottom of the bowl also flowered, and a silver snuffbox marked M.C. (16 Nov.)

REEVES, Capt., from London - arrived 21 Nov. in Phila.
with news from Europe (22 Nov.)

HAMMERDEN, Capt. - arrived 18 Nov. at Boston from London
(22 Nov.)

MEAKINS, Thomas, an "ancient" man, who had taught school
in Phila. - Monday evening last fell off a wharf into
the Delaware and was drowned (29 Nov.)

FLOWER, Widow, of Phila. - Monday last her house in
Second St. was consumed by fire (29 Nov.)

RUBBEL, John, of Lancaster Co. - his wife Christiana has
eloped, deserting him and 5 young children (29 Nov.)

BRADSTREET, Moses - 14 Nov. went hunting to Plumb Island;
there he found wild geese so fatigued by a storm that
they could not fly; he killed 60 with a club and shot
others - Boston dispatch of 23 Nov. (6 Dec.)

HAYNES, George, servant, a cooper, age <u>c</u>. 28 - runaway
from ship <u>Vigor</u>, William Harris master, lately arrived
at Phila. from Bristol (6 Dec.)

WOOD, Samuel, servant, who has been formerly in Virginia -
same as above

WILLIAMS, John, servant - same as above

Gov. of New York last week allowed a French sloop from
Cape Breton to load provisions for the garrison at
Lewisburgh, where it is said the people are starving
because crops failed - Boston dispatch of 29 Nov. (13
Dec.)

Sloop bound from Jamaica to Boston, Benj. Kent master -
last Monday evening drove upon the rocks near Scituate,
Mass. - Boston dispatch of 29 Nov. (13 Dec.)

GALE, Capt. - is arrived at Marblehead from Newfoundland,
bringing crew belonging to a French ship, Mancmein of
Rochell, Bartholomew Adiere master, which foundered
100 leagues east of Newfoundland - Boston dispatch of
29 Nov. (13 Dec.)

Some sailors, going from Boston to New London to go aboard
the Don Carlos, when passing through Providence made
such noise with a drum on the Lord's Day that they were
arrested, fined 25s. each and 25 pounds costs - Boston
dispatch of 29 Nov. (13 Dec.)

A poor crop of rice in South Carolina (13 Dec.)

Address of magistrates, William Till, president, of
Sussex Co. to Thomas Penn and Penn's reply (13 Dec.)

DURFEY, Capt. - last week arrived at Newport, R.I., from
the Havanna with a great quantity of pieces of eight -
Boston dispatch of 3 Dec. (20 Dec.)

CASTEEN, Monsieur Bonas - arrived 6 Nov. at Pemaquid and
reported that his brother arrived from Canada about 10
days ago with orders to apprehend any Frenchman or
Indian molesting any English trader or fisherman (20
Dec.)

Speech of Lt.-Gov. Patrick Gordon to Representatives in
Phila. on 18 Dec. (20 Dec.)

Iron hoops for sale - enquire at Widow Gordon's in Front
St., Phila. (20 Dec.)

Sloop Albany, John Davis master - arrived 13 Dec. at New
York in 21 days from St. Christophers with news that
the Negroes on Island of St. John's have massacred all
the white people on that island (31 Dec.)

Address of General Assembly of Pennsylvania to Lt.-Gov.
Gordon (31 Dec.)

GRIFFITS, Thomas, Mayor of Phila. - asks persons capable of cording wood and also any person disposed to take charge of the almshouse in Phila. to apply to him (31 Dec.)

Brick house in the Market St. in Burlington, N.J., is offered for sale by John Parsons (31 Dec.)

1734

JOHNSON, Robert, Gov. of South Carolina - his speech to Assembly of that Province (8 Jan.)

The Laws of the Province of New Jersey and The Indian Tale - are printed and sold by B. Franklin (8 Jan.)

CAEESAY, James, of Marcus Hook - his wife Sarah has eloped from him (8 Jan.)

BYLES, Thomas, late of Phila., dec'd - accounts with estate to be settled with Samuel Byles, administrator, or with his trustee and attorney, Evan Morgan in Market St. (8 Jan.)

FROST, John, staymaker (late servant of Evan Morgan) - lives in Second St., Phila., over against Doctor Hooper's, in partnership with Thomas Carter (8 Jan.)

Time of a young boy and of a young woman to be disposed of by Thomas Parry and Isaac Williams, Overseers of the Poor for Phila. (8 Jan.)

House, barn and 300 acres in Haverford Twp., Chester Co., are offered for sale by Rice Price, of Merion (8 Jan.)

WEBSTER, Col. - died 23 Dec. 1733 in Boston at house of Mr. Barnes, where he lodged since he came from Barbados to recover his health (16 Jan.)

REDISH, Capt., of Barbados Stationship - brings account from Martineco that French are preparing for war - extract of letter from Barbados dated 22 Oct. 1733 (16 Jan.)

DRYSKYL, William, Irish servant, tailor, age c. 17 - runaway from Ralph Lees, of Phila. (23 Jan.)

Speech of Gov. Belcher at Portsmouth, N.H., to General Assembly of New Hampshire (30 Jan.)

PALMER, Madam, a West India gentlewoman who has resided

some years in Phila. - died Sunday last in Phila. (7 Feb.)

Feb. 6 arrived in Phila. Captains Glentworth and Walmesly from the West Indies (7 Feb.)

Society of Ancient Britons will meet 1 Mar. at Owen Owen's, the Sign of the Indian King in Market St., Phila. (7 Feb.)

Persons indebted to Evan Jones, chymist, and Dr. Matthew Hooper are to pay debts before March Court next (13 Feb.)

Message of people of Burlington, N.J., to Gov. William Cosby; they inform him that they have sent to Joseph Warrell, attorney general, a rough draft of a charter for Burlington; Cosby's reply (20 Feb.)

ALLEN, William, Esq., one of principal merchants of Phila. - Sunday last married Mrs. Margaret Hamilton (only daughter of Andrew Hamilton, Esq.) (20 Feb.)

Notice of J. Steel, Receiver General, with regard to quit rents (20 Feb.)

Speech of Gov. Jonathan Belcher to Massachusetts General Assembly (27 Feb.)

Gov. Cosby promises to fortify New York (27 Feb.)

BAIRD, Pat., vendue master - will sell goods at store of Capt. Stevenson at end of Bourn's wharf in Phila.; Stevenson intends for Europe (27 Feb.)

BENTLY, Tho., servant, age 18 - runaway, in company with Wm. Mark, a hired man to Henry Smith, from Henry Smith's plantation above Tulpehocken (27 Feb.)

JAMES, Capt. - arrived 15 Feb. at Charlestown, S.C., from Bristol in 10 weeks, with European news (6 Mar.)

At Meeting of Society of Ancient Britons Friday last in Phila. a sermon in Welch was preached by Rev. Hughes at Christ Church and feast was held at Owen Owen's (6 Mar.)

A right to take up about 600 acres of land in West New Jersey is offered for sale by Samuel Bustill at Burlington (6 Mar.)

Speech of Gov. Belcher to Assembly of Massachusetts (13 Mar.)

Two Frenchmen, Michael Sheguien and William Holyday, deserters from Ft. St. Peters at Martineco, were arrested in Boston last week on suspicion of being spies; Paul Dudley and Joseph Wadsworth, members of Council, examined them and dismissed them - Boston dispatch of 16 Feb. (13 Mar.)

Massachusetts law relating to firearms (13 Mar.)

Small shallop offered for sale by William Patterson or William Danforth at Christine Bridge, or when in town, at the Widow Campions in Water St. (13 Mar.)

DUNN, Martin, belonging to H.M.S. Alborough - 23 Feb., when with Benjamin Story in his periauger in northern branch of Store River, stuck at an alligator, fell overboard and perished - Charlestown, S.C., dispatch of 2 Mar. (21 Mar.)

Petition of 16 maids to Gov. Johnson of South Carolina (21 Mar.)

FARMER, Capt., of the ship Catharine - arrived 6 Mar. in New York from Madera (21 Mar.)

BURROW, Capt., master of a sloop - arrived 11 Mar. in 14 days from Bermuda (21 Mar.)

DRAPER, Capt. - lately arrived at Newport, R.I., in about 7 weeks passage from Lisbon (21 Mar.)

ANNIS, Capt. - reported, by way of Maryland, that he has arrived in London (21 Mar.)

EDWARDS, John, servant - runaway from James Boyd, of Sudsbury Twp., Chester Co. (21 Mar.)

Schooner Christiana - will sail for South Carolina; for freight or passage apply to William Parker in Water St., Phila. (21 Mar.)

PEGG, Daniel, dec'd - 20 acres of land and mansion there, joining on road leading to Frankfort, belonging to his estate, are offered for sale by Septimus Robinson, sheriff (21 Mar.)

Speech of Gov. Patrick Gordon to Assembly at New Castle and reply of the Representatives (28 Mar.)

Account (in letter from Savannah, dated 16 Feb.) of trip taken by Mr. Oglethorpe 23 Jan. in row boat commanded by Capt. Ferguson; Oglethorp named an island Jekyll

Island after Sir Joseph Jekyll, Master of the Rolls;
he visited fortifications built by Capt. Mackpherson
and encountered gentleman who on the eastern coast on
Ossabow found the wreck of Mr. Evleigh's perriauger
(28 Mar.)

Town meeting in Boston on 22 Feb. elected Thomas Fitch,
Esq., moderator, and presented memorial about defence
of the town to the Governor; the following were appointed to make repairs on Castle William: Spencer
Phipps, Speaker of the House, John Quincey, Esq., and
Benj. Bird, member of the House - Boston dispatch of
28 Feb. (28 Mar.)

White bear, brought about a year ago from Greenland to
Boston by Capt. Atkins - 27 Feb. was shipped aboard
Capt. Walker, bound for London (28 Mar.)

Dying words of Terence Rogers, a Roman Catholic, age c.
33, who was executed 13 Mar. for murder at Chester,
Pa. (28 Mar.)

McDERMOT, Michael, servant, age c. 25 - runaway from
Daniel Quigley of Burlington (28 Mar.)

FULLER, Capt. - arrived Tuesday last at Boston from Madera via Barbados, with news that many planters at
Barbados are discouraged and intend to leave and
settle at Cape Fear - Boston dispatch of 11 Mar. (4
Apr.)

Negroes rise on Island of St. John and attempt rising at
St. Kit's - extract of a letter from Antigua dated 11
Jan. (4 Apr.)

MORINO, Charles, mate of a sloop belonging to Boston -
arrived 14 Mar. at Rhode Island from Havana; Edward
Morss, master of said sloop, died of fever 3 days before
sloop was cast away (18 Dec.) on the Martiers in the
Gulf of Florida; Capt. Thomas Wells of New York, Capt.
Richard Cupit, Samuel Trip and Aaron Griet of Newport
made land in a canoe but were killed by Indians - (4
Apr.)

Ship Newbury, Capt. Green, belonging to Phila. is lost
on Island of Bermuda but all the people saved (4 Apr.)

Plantation of 400 acres in Plymouth Twp., Phila. Co.,
about 14 miles from Phila., and other land offered
for sale by Mary, John and Thomas Davis (4 Apr.)

RINGO, Philip - offers for sale real estate in Trenton,

N.J., apply to Philip Ringo in Amwall or Cornelius Ringo in Trenton (4 Apr.)

MASTERS, T. - at his store house at his wharf in Phila. has cloth, tobacco pipes, tea, sugar for sale (4 Apr.)

Voted at Boston town meeting that the following be a committee for mounting cannon: Jacob Wendell, Esq., James Bowdoin, Esq., Col. Estes Hatch, Messers Isaac White, John Checkley, Thomas Lee and Samuel Clark (11 Apr.)

GORHAM, Capt., who sailed from Connecticut for Charlestown, S.C., about a month since - arrived at Marblehead but himself and most of his men froze (11 Apr.)

WOODBURY, Capt. - a few days since arrived at Boston from Maryland - Boston dispatch of 2 Apr. (11 Apr.)

Masonic Grand Lodge, with Gov. Belcher present, met Friday last at Mr. Lutwytche's long room in King St. Boston - Boston dispatch of 1 Apr. (18 Apr.)

HOWARD, Capt. - made report 15 Feb. to the Massachusetts House of Representatives (18 Apr.)

FAIRCHILD, Mr., a butcher of Rhode Island - 26 Feb. accidentally fell from his horse when passing through Norwich, Conn., and died from wounds (18 Apr.)

BOGUE, Richard, of Haddam, who went out to cut wood on 25 Feb. - was found dead the next day as result of an accident (18 Apr.)

PIKE, Capt., who has loaded at Marblehead, Mass. - has been captured by the Salleeteens (18 Apr.)

FLAGG, John, of Watertown, Mass. - Thursday last was found dead at bottom of a hill in Newtown, presumably from a fall from his cart; he has left a widow and several children - Boston dispatch of 1 Apr. (18 Apr.)

COLEWELL, William - at a training at Stoughton put too much powder in his gun, so that the barrel split and caused the powder in a powder horn in his pocket to explode; another man was also wounded; both men probably will not live - Boston item of 2 Apr. (18 Apr.)

A large wood boat belonging to Francis West of Stonington on Monday last overset off Point Judah; the 2 men aboard were saved but one Saray Merry, born at Dartmouth, was drowned - Rhode Island item of 28 Mar. (18 Apr.)

Ship <u>Vinyard</u>, William Richmond captain - 2 Apr. arrived
at New York from Lisbon (18 Apr.)

BULKLEY, Capt., who left Gibralter 7 Feb. - arrived 8
Apr. at Boston (18 Apr.)

A bad fire raged in Phila. Monday last but was brought
under control by use of the engines (18 Apr.)

BREINTNAL, J., Secretary - gives notice that on 6 May
subscribers to the Library in Phila. will elect directors and a treasurer at house of John Roberts in High
St. near the market (25 Apr.)

SMITH, Richard, engineer in Second St., near the dock in
Phila. - offers reward for recovery of watch (with
"R. ARNOLD, Providence" engraved on the dial) lost in
removing goods at the late fire (25 Apr.)

Brigantine <u>William</u>, Robert Hall master - will sail for
Barbados - for freight or passage apply to the master
at Fishbourn's wharf (25 Apr.)

MILLWATER, Joseph, <u>alias</u> Grimes, servant, age <u>c</u>. 40 -
runaway from Daniel Dairs of Chichester (or Marcus
Hook), sawyer (25 Apr.)

WATERHOUSE, Capt., who sailed 11 Feb. from Portsmouth,
N.H., for Antigua - on 14 Feb. lightning killed one of
his crew and on 18 Feb. he met with a "prodigious sea"
(2 May)

Brigantine <u>Recovery</u>, of which Capt. Braddick was lately
commander - arrived in Boston Tuesday last from St.
Christophers with news that an Indian named Witness
and a boy, his accomplice, were hanged 23 Feb. at
Barbados for murder of Capt. Braddick - Boston item of
18 Apr. (2 May)

Portersfield, plantation of 1,800 acres of the late Major
Porter in Gloucester Co., West New Jersey - will be
sold by his executors, Jonathan Wright and Mahlon
Stacy (2 May)

Snow <u>Swift</u>, Samuel Jennings master - will sail in 30 days
for Bristol; for freight or passage apply to the master or to Simon Edgell, who sells window glass (1 May)

Saltzburghers, who arrived in Georgia with Capt. Fry in
ship <u>Purrysburg</u>, (esp. Mr. Von Reck, then commissary,
Mr. Gronau, their minister, and Mr. Zwilfler, their
doctor), together with Mr. Oglethorpe and Paul Jenys

(Speaker of the House of South Carolina) go by water as far as Mr. Musgrove's cowpen and then by land to choose site for settlement - Charlestown, S.C., item of 30 Mar. (9 May)

MAHANY, Cornelius, tailor and staymaker - works in Second St., Phila., in a shop of Evan Morgan (9 and 16 May)

Dying confession of Ziggey John Witness, age 25 in May, born on Long Island, who sailed with Capt. Braddick from Boston in 1733 to Madera; on way to Island of Sall, Witness, John Smith, John Main (a caulking master) and Thomas Parker (a boy) mutined and killed the captain and first mate; Henry Peck, second mate, had not part in the mutiny; Main turned evidence for the King; Witness and Parker were executed at Barbados (9 May)

Dying confession of Thomas Parker, born at Cannock, Stafford Co., in 1717, son of a farmer; one uncle, William Parker, is an attorney-at-law within half a mile of Stafford Town; another uncle, John Parker (eldest brother of Thomas's father), is a cheesemonger in London; Thomas served on 2 men-of-war, the Windsor and the Namure; then on the brigantine Anne and Elizabeth, John Hurst master, from London to Lisbon; next on the ship Albany, William Maxwell master, from Lisbon to Madera; finally with Capt. Braddick (9 May)

Tract of 130 acres of land on Swan Creek, Baltimore Co., for sale - apply to Thomas Hughs of Nottingham, innkeeper, who lives on the road to said land, 14 miles from it (16 May)

Schooner Anne, John Rice master - will sail from Phila. for Cape Fear and South Carolina or New Georgia; for freight or passage apply to the master or to Joshua Granger (16 May)

Brigantine Eglinton, Capt. Atkinson, arrived 18 May at New York from Louisburgh, Cape Breton, in 4 weeks - in a storm they were blown off the coast to Martinique, and a sloop, Le Caesar, to St. Thomas (23 May)

HUNTER, Gov. of Jamaica - died there 31 Mar. (23 May)

LAWS, Lt.-Gov. of Jamaica - died there some time before Gov. Hunter (23 May)

There is a Negro rebellion on Jamaica and a force of 1,000 is raised to suppress it (23 May)

Fire broke out 22 May in a building behind Dr. Jones's in

Market St., Phila., but was soon extinguished (23 May)

MARTIN, James, of Phila., mariner - his wife Elizabeth has
   eloped from him (23 May)

SMITH, Thomas, of New-Castle - notifies he will sue debtors
   who do not pay balance by 1 July (23 May)

Fox's Acts and Monuments and Salmon's Herbal are for sale
   by John Ingram in Third St., Phila. (23 May)

A Sermon printed in London by J. Peele is for sale by B.
   Franklin in Phila. (23 May)

CHEW, Mrs. (wife of Dr. Chew of Phila.) - died in Phila.
   Sunday last (30 May)

LEA, Anthony, servant, born in Lancaster, Eng. - runaway
   from John Leacock from Pool Forge (30 May)

ESINGTON, James, servant, born in London, age 14 or 15 -
   same as above; Lea and Esington ran away in company
   with a servant of Samuel Brown (30 May)

Ship Three Batchelors, William Spafford master, now lying
   at Carpenter's wharf, Phila. - will sail for London;
   for freight or passage apply to the master or Thomas
   Sober (30 May)

HOY, Ralph, of New-Castle - fell out of boat in sight of
   Phila. and was drowned (6 June)

LLOYD, Capt. Thomas, of Phila. - 5 June married at Fairhill Mrs. Susannah Owen (6 June)

ATKINSON, Charles, master of brigantine Eglinton - gave
   affidavit in New York 31 May before Robert Lurting,
   Major, that when he arrived 24 Mar. at Lewisburgh he
   found population almost starving and quickly unloaded
   his cargo to relieve them; Robert Frost, mate, George
   Montgomery, boatswain, and Miles Reilly, linguister,
   of said brigantine depose to same effect (13 June)

Fresh drugs imported from London are for sale in Phila. at
   shop of Samuel Chew and Thomas Bond in High St. near
   the Market (13 June)

Two Negro men, country born, and also 50 acres of good
   grass within 2 miles of Phila. are offered for sale by
   Capt. Palmer (13 June)

WARNER, Thomas, schoolmaster, who served his time in the

lower parts of Virginia, pretends to be a watchmaker -
he came to Darby, Pa., in June 1733, kept school, got
a woman with child and had to marry her about 29 May -
has run away, abandoning wife and child (13 June)

MATTHEWS, Capt., young son of, from Boston - recently
drowned in Pennsylvania (20 June)

PAIN, Edward, servant, potter, age c. 26 - runaway from
Samuel Hale, of Phila., potter (20 June)

NICHOLSON, John, servant, age c. 27, who pretends to be
a chair-carver - runaway from Anthony Wilkinson, of
Phila., carver (20 June)

HAVERSACK, John, Palatine servant, age c. 40, who has
traveled with armies in France, Spain, Germany, Italy,
Turkey, England and Scotland and speaks their languages
- runaway from Francis Smith of Evesham, Burlington
Co. (20 June)

Plantation and ferry, called Ferry Point, of 400 acres,
about 4 miles below Burlington - for sale; apply to
Joseph Fennimore in Burlington Co. or Bartholomew Horner
in Gloucester Co. (20 June)

CLAYTON, Asher, dec'd - plantation of 500 acres within a
mile of Christine Bridge is offered for sale by his
executors, Mary Clayton and Samuel Bickley (20 June)

Sale of Negroes, rum, sugar, molasses, cotton, etc., will
be held Friday morning at house of John Inglis in
Second St., opposite to the Post-House in Phila. (20
June)

ROE, James, servant, born in Dublin, age c. 18 - runaway
from Owen Owen, of Phila. (20 June)

The King of the Nauchees on Monday last asked leave of
the governor to settle with all his people at Savannah
- Charlestown, S.C., item of 27 Apr. (27 June)

H.M.S. Alborough sailed Tuesday last from Charlestown for
London, having on board James Oglethorpe, Esq., and 8
Creek Indians, with Tomo-chi-chi their chief - Charles-
town item of 11 May (27 June)

Masonic Grand Lodge of Pennsylvania met Monday last at the
Tun Tavern in Water St., Phila. - Benjamin Franklin was
elected Grand Master and he appointed John Crap his
deputy; James Hamilton, Esq., and Thomas Hopkinson,
gent., were chosen wardens (27 June)

Counterfeit Jersey bills have been uttered at Burlington (27 June)

Rose, Negro slave, age <u>c</u>. 16 or 18, branded N.R. on the breast - runaway from house of John Richardson, shoe-maker in Phila.; reward offered for her return to her master or to B. Franklin, printer (27 June)

Plantation of about 1,100 acres at Horsham, Phila. Co., 18 miles from Phila., offered for sale; apply to C. Brockden of Phila. (27 June)

ALDER, Edmund, who accidentally fell into the river from a shallop on 28 May and was drowned - his body was found Monday last (4 July)

Chairs made and repaired by Nicholas Gale, next to the Sign of the Pewter Platter in Front St., Phila. (4 July)

CAVENAUGH, James, Irish servant - runaway from George Aston of East-Caln Twp., Chester Co., Pa. (4 July)

WILTSHIRE, Thomas, English servant, sadler - same as above

COASHER, Josiah, hired man, born in New England - same as above

Letter (dated Savannah 6 Apr. 1734) from Tho. Christie, Recorder of Savannah, to James Oglethorpe - Christie related how Job Wiggin, who worked at Musgrove's cowpen, was accused of adultery with wife of an Indian named Defatige by Capt. Skee and his lieutenant Istiche; the court sent for Justice Musgrove's Indian servant and Francis to interpret; one of the Indians at the trial was Talihomme; Wiggin was convicted, put in irons and is to be whipped; Christie mentions arrival and de-parture of Mr. Colleton and his brother, the coming down of the Tybe people, arrival of the Happy, man-of-war, and things mentioned in Mr. Causton's letter; Mr. Del-mass, very ill with a fistula, was brought to house of Mr. Christie in town and is almost cured and will soon return to Skidoway (11 July)

At Groton, Conn., on 1 June a drunken Indian beat his son so that the child died; the father has fled - Boston Item of 20 June (11 July)

DAVENPORT, Samuel, of Shrewsbury, Mass., age <u>c</u>. 25 - at training on 5 June his ancle was accidentally shattered and leg had to be amputated (11 July)

HARDING, Maziah, in his 63rd year - 5 June at Barnstable,

Mass., was executed for murder of his wife (11 July)

FRASIER, Mrs., of Phila. - died suddenly Saturday last, leaving 9 children, most of them small (11 July)

WORTHINGTON, James, of Byberry - Saturday last dropped dead when reaping (11 July)

A person lately arrived at Phila. from Bristol with Capt. Tough - was accidentally drowned when swimming in the river (11 July)

LEE, Jacob, a gardiner - Tuesday died when clipping a hedge (11 July)

GOFORTH, Aaron, daughter of - died Tuesday from the heat (11 July)

Ship *Jane*, John Richmond master, now at Fishbourn's wharf - will sail from Phila. for London; for freight or passage apply to the master or to White and Taylor (11 July)

Tract of 740 acres near Christine Bridge and a water lot in Town of New-Castle adjoining the Free wharf - to be sold by Widow Battel, executrix of W. Battel, late of New-Castle, dec'd (11 July)

HOBART, John, late keeper of the Sun Tavern in Water St., Phila. - has removed to the Sign of the Conestogoe Waggon in Market St. (11 July)

MORRIS, John - will let a fulling-mill in Whitemarsh Twp. - (11 July)

Extract from a late account of Holland - seasonable admonition to Philadelphia (18 July)

BEARD, Mrs., lately brought to bed - died 7 July in Boston, probably from the excessive heat (18 July)

THOMAS, John, the Western Rider - a few days ago a person coming part way with him lost his horse in about 6 hours of riding because of the heat - Boston item of 8 July (18 July)

Plantation in Nottingham, Burlington Co., about 4 miles from Trenton, is for sale - apply to Mahlon Kirkbride in Pa. about 2 miles above the Falls Ferry (18 July)

HUNT, John, staymaker - is removed from Second St. into Front St. over against the corner of Market St., at the house of Robert Read in Phila. (18 July)

GREW, Theophilus, in Second St. over against the Sign of the Bible in Phila. - teaches mathematics (25 July)

DANBY, John, in Third St., Phila. - has for sale a Negro woman, a mill and a screen for cleaning malt (25 July)

PARSTOW, Stephen, English servant, age c. 22, blacksmith - runaway from William Cox of New Brunswick (25 July)

CHRISTIAN, Capt. Benjamin, in Water St., Phila - has 2 Negro girls for sale (25 July)

Ship Tartar Pink, Capt. Norris - arrived in New York 26 July to be the Station Ship (1 Aug.)

Negro man belonging to Capt. Richmond on Aug. 1 at Phila. fell between a ship and the wharf and was drowned (1 Aug.)

ENGLAND, Joseph, late of Phila., dec'd - accounts with estate to be settled with Harmanus Alrichs of Phila. (1 Aug.)

Brigantine Worcester, George Stewart master, now at Parker's wharf, Phila. - will sail' for Boston; for freight or passage apply to the master or to Mr. Parker in Water St. (1 Aug.)

Mare, formerly belonging to William Harper, of Buckingham Twp. - strayed from keeping of George Wilson at Skuylkill Ferry; a sorrel horse strayed from Phila.; Thomas Hodgkin offers reward for bringing the horse or mare to George Shoemaker in Phila. (1 Aug.)

RUSSEL, Capt. - brought letter from London to gentleman in Boston (8 Aug.)

Franklin prints 2 letters sent to him (8 Aug.)

HAMILTON, A., at Phila. - calls attention to counterfeit 20s. bills of Pennsylvania (8 Aug.)

WHITE, John, surviving executor of estate of John Roberts, dec'd, being bound for England - asks that debts to the estate be paid to Benjamin Morgan or Thomas Edwards of Phila. or Humphry Jones at North Wales (8 Aug.)

DAVIS, William, Welchman, age about 30 or 40, who pretends to be a great miner - runaway from Jacob Lightfoot of Chester (8 Aug.)

OLDHAM, Robert, age c. 17 or 18, who says he served his time with Charles Gross near Justice Gatchel's in Nottingham, Chester Co., and that he has been 7 years in the country - 22 July arrested on suspicion of being a runaway and put into the goal at Burlington (8 Aug.)

DALTON, Capt., just arrived at Boston from Canso - brought an affidavit of Francis Drake, skipper of the schooner Susannah of Canso, made 3 July before Mr. Kilby, a justice of Canso; Drake swore when he was at the Island of St. John's in the Gulf of St. Lawrence an inhabitant told him that 2,500 Indians were going to Canso to surprise it; the Indians had applied to Gov. Pensans, who would not give them liberty or assistance; they were waiting for the arrival of Gov. St. Ovid from Lewesburg (15 Aug.)

CUSSENS, Capt., of Boston - 27 June in a gale at St. Christophers lost his vessel (15 Aug.)

SHIPPEN, William, chymist, over against the prison in Market St., at the Sign of the Paracelsus Head (where Evan Jones, chymist, lately dwelt) - sells chemical preparations (15 Aug.)

Party sent against rebellious Negroes in Jamaica defeated them (22 Aug.)

WILLARD, Josiah, of Gilford, Conn. - reports that on 7 July lightning struck Nathanael Fernum at Killingsworth and his son, aged 7; Mr. Fernum survived but his son died about 16 hours after (22 Aug.)

Snow Helen of Liverpool, Samuel Wallace master, lying near Chesnut St. wharf - will sail for Virginia; for freight or passage apply to the master on board or at the London Coffee-House (22 Aug.)

Ship Elizabeth and Dorothy, John Reeve master, now lying at Samuel Powel's wharf in Phila. - will sail for London; for freight or passage apply to the master or to Mathias Aspdin (22 Aug.)

Reward offered for return of a watch, lost Saturday last, with name Fletcher, London, on the dial plate, to Capt. William Wallace's in Phila. (22 Aug.)

WADE, Robert, late of Chester Co., Pa., dec'd - devised to Robert Wade his nephew and Lydia his wife the plantation called Essex House in Chester; from the yield he ordered that 5 pounds be paid annually towards the maintenance of a free school in Phila.; the overseers

of said school insist on such payments and payments of
all arrears (22 Aug.)

Itinerary of Gov. of Massachusetts on board H.M.S. Scarborough, Capt. Durell commander, to the north and east
(29 Aug.)

It is reported that 23 July some Indians came to Capt.
Giles at George's and told him how some Indians killed
a white man about Mount Desart; Capt. Giles sent the
account to Capt. Woodside at Pemaquid, who delivered it
to the governor (29 Aug.)

WINNET, Capt. - Thursday last arrived at Boston from
Annapolis Royal with news - Boston item of 5 Aug. (29
Aug.)

Schooner Dolphin, James Lusk master - will sail for South
Carolina; for freight or passage apply to the master
or to Tho. Shute or Anthony Morris (29 Aug.)

New sloop at Marcus Hook is for sale - apply to William
Haly at the Hook aforesaid (29 Aug.)

STEEGLITZ, Dr. Nicholas, late of Whitemarsh, dec'd - debts
to his estate are to be paid to Thomas Steeglitz at
Whitemarsh (29 Aug.)

Ship Constantine, Edward Wright commander - will sail for
London; for freight or passage apply to the commander
or to Mr. Lawrence (29 Aug.)

At beginning of last week a Negro raped a young woman of
Boston who was on her way to visit a friend at Dedham
- Boston item of 19 Aug. (5 Sept.)

Brigantine Success, Henry Stocks master - his ship was so
injured by a hurricane that it put back to Boston -
Boston item of 19 Aug. (5 Sept.)

ORMESBY, John, alias Ormeby - Friday last at a court in
Boston was found guilty of the murder of Thomas Bell
- Boston item of 19 Aug. (5 Sept.)

POTHECARY, Mrs. Elizabeth (wife of Edward Pothecary,
Master of Arms on board H.M.S. Scarborough), aged 68 -
died Tuesday last and Thursday was interred at Roxbury,
Mass. - Boston item of 26 Aug. (5 Sept.)

JACKSON, Daniel, fuller, of Bristol - notifies those who
come to the yearly meeting at Burlington that he has a
16-acre pasture at the town's end where horses may be
put (5 Sept.)

ELLIS, Capt. Edward - arrived Saturday last at Boston in about 8 weeks from Bristol and Cork with European news (12 Sept.)

TODD, Capt. Edward - his ship was wrecked 27 Aug. and his brother (the mate) and 2 sailors were drowned; Capt. Todd, one sailor and 2 Negroes were picked up 1 Sept. by Capt. Wilson and brought to New York (12 Sept.)

LEA, Anthony, servant born in Lancashire, age c. 20 - runaway (in company with a young woman named Elizabeth) from John Leacock at Pool Forge (12 Sept.)

BANTOFT, William, late of Phila., dec'd - persons indebted to estate are to settle with the administrators, White & Taylor or William Chancellor (12 Sept.)

JONES, David, Welch servant - runaway from John Mickel, near Gloucester in Gloucester Co. (12 Sept.)

HARROW, Isaac, an English smith - has lately set up a plateing and blade mill at Trenton, N.J.; his wares may be obtained from him or from George Howell, lastmaker in Chesnut St., Phila. (12 Sept.)

LELORI, Joseph, a Spanish carpenter - was tried Wednesday last at Charlestown, S.C., for piracy and stealing the goods of Don Francisco de Heymes, who was murdered; the witnesses were cross-examined by Richard Allen, Esq., council for the prisoner; Lelori was found not guilty - Charlestown item of 2 July (19 Sept.)

Wife of the Governor of Pennsylvania - died Saturday last at his county house near Phila.; she was descended from a family in southern part of Scotland; her brothers became Catholics; the eldest, now dec'd, held high office at the Court of the late Duke of Tuscany; the other is Confessor to his most Catholic Majesty (19 Sept.)

A chased gold watch, on view at John Wood's, watchmaker in Front St., Phila., will be raffled for at Mr. Shubart's London Tavern in Water St. (19 Sept.)

Cheese, sugar, rum, etc., to be sold at store of Richard Sharp in Front St.; Sharp soon plans to go to London (19 Sept.)

WILSON, Capt. J. - arrived 6 Sept. at New York in the brigantine Prince Frederick in 9 weeks from Plymouth, with Palatines (25 Sept.)

Ship Manwaring, John Chubard captain, from Liverpool --

arrived in New York 19 Sept. (25 Sept.)

PENN, John, Esq. - arrived in Pennsylvania from London
with his brother-in-law, Mr. Freame, his lady and
family (25 Sept.)

WELFARE, Michael, one of the Christian philosophers of
Conestogoe - arrived 25 Sept. in Phila., where in full
market he preached against the iniquity of the inhabitants of the city (25 Sept.)

HADEN, Joseph, sailmaker from London - keeps a sail-loft
at Mr. Plumstead's new wharf in Phila. (25 Sept.)

FULKS, John, and his wife Elizabeth - have stolen articles
from shop of Marcus Kuhl in Market St., Phila. (25 Sept.)

GILLMORE, Christopher, lately a Roman Catholic priest - on
14 July at Bridgetown, Barbados, made a public recantation of the errors of the Church of Rome; the following
certify as to the said recantation at the Parish Church
of St. Michael: J. Blenman, Tho. Tunckes, William Duke
(dept. secr.), Howe, William Johnson (rector), Charles
Game, Joseph Young (church warden), Tho. Withers (church
warden), Jos. Brook (curate) and Tho. Harrison (3 Oct.)

JOHNSON, Rev. William, Rector of St. Michael's - Sunday
last preached his farewel sermon, as he was going
northward for his health - Barbados item of 24 July (3
Oct.)

Tuesday last Thomas Lawrence, Esq., was chosen Mayor of
Phila. and the following men were chosen for Phila.
Co.: Representatives--Robert Jones, Thomas Leech,
William Monington, John Kensey, Jonathan Robeson, Wil-
liam Allen, Job Goodson, Isaac Norris; sheriffs--Septi-
mus Robinson, Andrew Robeson; coroners--Owen Owen, John
Roberts; commissioner--Thomas Peters; assessors--Hugh
Evans, John Dillwin, Jacob Leech, Thomas Potts, John
Jones Carpenter, Joseph Noble; burgesses for Phila.
City--Israel Pemberton, John Kearsley; assessors for the
city--Joseph Paschal, Benjamin Morgan, John Nichols,
Edward Bradley, Nathan. Allen, William Pywell (10 Oct.)

Tuesday last were elected for Chester Co.: Representatives
-- Joseph Harvey, Joseph Brinton, Caleb Cowpland, John
Evans, William Webb, William Moore, John Owen, Joseph
Pennock; sheriffs--John Parry, Richard Jones, Robert
Park; coroners--John Wharton, Nathan Worley; commissioner
--John Davis; assessors--John Parry, William Jeffries,
James Jeffries, Edward Brinton, Joseph Hayes, Benjamin
Freed (10 Oct.)

102

Tuesday last elected for Bucks Co. were: Representatives
-- Joseph Kirkbride, Jr., Christian Van Horne, Jeremiah
Langhorne, Abraham Chapman, Andrew Hamilton, William
Biles, Thomas Merrit, Lawrence Growden; sheriffs--
Timothy Smith, John Hall; coroners--William Atkinson,
Jonathan Woolston; commissioner--Joseph Kirkbride; as-
sessors--Benjamin Taylor, Richard Mitchel, Nathan Wat-
son, John Dawson, John Lupton, David Williams (10 Oct.)

Tuesday last were elected for Lancaster Co.: Representa-
tives--James Hamilton, John Emerson, Andrew Galbraith,
John Wright; sheriffs--Robert Buchanan, James Mitchel;
coroners--Joshua Low, Samuel Bethell; commissioner--
Tobias Hendrick; assessors--Samuel Smith, Samuel Eweing,
Conrad Weiser, Thomas Rinick, Andrew Douglas, James
Swafort (10 Oct.)

Tuesday last were elected for New-Castle Co.: Representa-
tives--John M'Coole, Thomas Noxon, Andrew Peterson,
David French, Robert Gordon, Samuel James; sheriffs--
Henry Newton, John Dunning; coroners--Henry Gunn,
Robert Robinson (10 Oct.)

Sloop Pembroke, William Tucker master, at Mr. Plumstead's
wharf, Phila. - will sail for Barbados; for freight or
passage apply to the master or John Inglis (10 Oct.)

Just arrived at Phila. the Britannia from Milford with
servants, whose times are to be disposed of by Simon
Edgel (10 Oct.)

Tract of 600 acres, at head of Chesapeak Bay, within a
mile of Susquehannah River is for sale - enquire of
Humphrey Wells Stokes at Joppa, Baltimore Co., Md.
(10 Oct.)

ASHTON, Richard, servant, age c. 25 - runaway from Thomas
Dunning at the George Inn in Second St., Phila. (10
Oct.)

M'CALLON, Thomas, servant, tailor, age c. 19 - runaway
from Capt. Christopher Postgate (10 Oct.)

HAMILTON, Andrew - Monday last chosen Speaker of the
Pennsylvania Assembly (17 Oct.)

The proprietors of Pennsylvania returned Monday from
Durham (17 Oct.)

Upholsterers work is performed next door to Caleb Ran-
steed's in Market St., Phila. (17 Oct.)

Sloop *Charming Betty*, Thomas Crossthwaite master - will
    sail for South Carolina (17 Oct.)

Speech of Gov. Patrick Gordon at Phila. and reply of the
    Representatives (24 Oct.)

OXNARD, Mr., merchant of Barbados - died when passenger
    on board Capt. King, on passage to Boston - Boston item
    of 16 Sept. (24 Oct.)

At muster held Tuesday last at Watertown, Mass., Capt.
    Edward Durant, with troop of horse, made a handsome ap-
    pearance - Boston item of 16 Sept. (24 Oct.)

PICO, Capt. - arrived last week at Boston from St. Thomas
    after a passage of about 24 days; he told of crushing
    of Negro revolt on Island of St. John's - Boston item
    of 16 Sept. (24 Oct.)

JEKYLL, J., Esq., Collector of the Port of Boston - Sunday
    last married in Phila. Mrs. Margaret Shippen of Mary-
    land (24 Oct.)

CHALKLEY, Capt., from Dublin - brought news of a French
    defeat (24 Oct.)

Brigantine *Pennsylvania Hope*, Charles Palmer master - will
    sail for London; for freight or passage apply to the
    master or John Stamper, merchant, in Water St., Phila.
    (24 Oct.)

Speech of Gov. Patrick Gordon at New-Castle, address of
    the Representatives, answer of the governor, address
    of the Representatives to John Penn and his answer (31
    Oct.)

BAKER, John, late of Phila., shopkeeper, dec'd - accounts
    with estate to be settled with Benjamin Morgan, of
    Phila., one of the executors (31 Oct.)

Speech of Jonathan Belcher to Assembly of New Hampshire
    on 11 Oct. (7 Nov.)

BRYANT, Capt. in ship *Albany*, arrived in New York Wednes-
    day last in about 8 weeks from London - reports that
    the King has confirmed James De Lancey as Chief Justice
    of New York - New York item of 4 Nov. (7 Nov.)

MACKAY, James, merchant in Front St., Phila. - sells West
    India salt (14 Nov.)

DAVIS, Capt. - arrived this week in Phila. from London

with account of a battle in Italy (21 Nov.)

SPENCE, John, late of Phila., dec'd - accounts with estate to be settled with Jacob Duche, of Phila., administrator (21 Nov.)

LUCAS, Robert, of Wellingborrow Twp., Burlington Co. - wishes to keep a ferry; he designs to cut a road from the Red House to the house adjoining the great road next to Leonard Van Degrift's plantation (21 Nov.)

Plantation of 100 acres in Warminster, Bucks Co., upon Upper York Road is for sale - apply to William Howel near the Bank Meeting-House in Phila. (21 Nov.)

Elegy and epitaph on Richard Lewis, late master of the Free School in Annapolis, by W. Byfeild, late of New-Castle upon Tine (5 Dec.)

Two vessels, one commanded by Capt. Hathaway and the other by Capt. Grindal, bound to Boston from North Carolina, collided sometime last month; Hathaway's vessel sank but the men got back to Carolina; nothing has been heard of Grindal or his crew - Boston item of 14 Nov. (5 Dec.)

NELSON, John, Esq., age 84, of a distinguished English family - died at Boston 16 Nov.; he survived his consort but 3 weeks - Boston item of 18 Nov. (5 Dec.)

Sloop belonging to Cape Ann, of which John Higgen was master - overset in the bay last week and 3 of the crew were drowned - Ipswich, Mass., account from Boston under date 18 Nov. (5 Dec.)

Counterfeit money has been found hidden on an island in the middle of a great marsh; the men suspected, Conway and Sherwin, were confined in Salem Goal in the Jerseys but are now admitted to bail (5 Dec.); Conway and Sherwin were sentenced at New-Castle last week (25 Feb. 1735); Thursday last they were whipped, pilloried, cropt and fined (27 Mar. 1735)

NICHOLS, Samuel, late of Phila., bricklayer, dec'd - accounts with estate to be settled with his widow, Mary Nichols (5 Dec.)

Ship Ann, John Stedman master - will sail for London; for freight or passage apply to the master at his store on Fishbourn's wharf (5 Dec.)

CROSTHWAITE, William, of Phila., perukemaker - offers reward for recovery of wigs stolen from his shop (5 Dec.)

RAKESTRAW, William - offers for sale a 3-acre lot, bounding on York Road, about 100 yards from the brickyard
lately belonging to Daniel Pegg, dec'd (5 Dec.)

KERON, Lawrence, Irish servant, age c. 22 - runaway from
Rees Pritchard, of Whiteland, Chester Co. (12 Dec.)

JACKSON, Joseph, of Bristol, Bucks Co. - offers reward for
goods stolen from him by a thief, supposed to be a
Welshman, who pretends to be a tanner and shoemaker,
and for the apprehension of the thief (19 Dec.)

The following, who made an accord with Daniel Flexney,
merchant in London, and were brought to America by
Capt. Johan Ball, are to pay what they owe or be prose-
cuted: Johan Lang, Peter Stocker, Ulrich Ebeguth, Johan
Adam Spach, Johan Coetner, Johan Paul Vogt, Wilhelm
Imler, Nigolas Hetzel; Daniel Flexney lives with Mrs.
Mankin in Market St., Phila. (19 Dec.)

Address of Gov. of Virginia to House of Burgesses (4
Oct.), address of the Council and House to the Governor
and his reply (26 Dec.)

GRAHAM, William, at house where Henry Hodge lately dwelt
in Phila. - sells Antigua rum, St. Kits mellasses,
chocolate, cotton, ginger, pepper (26 Dec.)

HOPKINS, Robert, of Phila. - offers reward for recovery of
strayed or stolen mare (26 Dec.)

1735

Gov. Jonathan Belcher's speech about mast pines to the
Massachusetts Assembly and his proclamation about them
(2 Jan.)

Description of counterfeit bills of Pennsylvania and New-
Castle (2 Jan.)

Gov. of South Carolina 1 Nov. directs Col. Parris, Treasurer of South Carolina, to meet 70 Cherokee Indians
near Charlestown (16 Jan.)

GORDON, Capt., whose ship was in Rebellion Road - fired at
a marshal with a warrant against him at the suit of
Martha Deane for debt; at this Capt. Anson of H.M.S.
Squirrel sent Mr. Barnard, master of the Squirrel, to
assist the marshal; in an exchange of fire Capt. Gordon

106

was shot and killed; his body was brought to the house
of Mr. Baker, merchant in Charlestown and interred -
Charlestown item of 2 Nov. 1734 (16 Jan.)

His Majesty's snow the Happy, much damaged by storms, returned 2 Nov. to Charlestown, S.C., as did the Mary-
Anne, Capt. Shubrick in 7 weeks from London, bringing
Peter Horry, merchant of Charlestown - Charlestown item
of 2 Nov. (16 Jan.)

WARNER, Capt. Daniel, merchant of Portsmouth, N.H. -
Tuesday last his warehouse and other buildings were
burned down - Portsmouth item of 10 Dec. 1734 (16 Jan.)

GORHAM, Capt., bound from North Carolina to Boston - 13
Dec. ran upon the rocks near Scituate - Boston item of
23 Dec. 1734 (16 Jan.)

PARKER, Jacob, of Boston, an ancient man and noted Eastern
Coaster - 13 Dec. ran ashore on spit of land at entrance to harbor; Mr. Parker died Friday last of exposure - Boston item of 23 Dec. 1734 (16 Jan.)

Martial law was proclaimed at Jamaica last week on account of the rebellious Negroes; Col. Brookes to leeward, Major Sweaton and Major Mumbee to northward were
to command 600 militia men to go in quest of the Negroes - letter from Jamaica dated 5 Nov. 1734 (16 Jan.)

Ship Sarum, Capt. Langston, arrived at New York from Cadiz
in less than 8 weeks (16 Jan.)

Ship Sarah, Capt. Wingfield - last week sailed from New
York for London - New York item of 7 Jan. (16 Jan.)

HARRISON, Joseph, carpenter, late of Phila., dec'd - accounts with estate to be settled with John Harrison or
John Leech, executors (16 Jan.)

SMITH, Richard, Jr., of Burlington - offers reward for
recovery of horse stolen from him (16 Jan.)

Plantation of 300 acres in Nantmel Twp., upon French Creek,
about 30 miles from Phila., is for sale; apply to Simon
Meredith, now living on the place (16 Jan.)

SMITH, Samuel, Sr., of Salem, N.J. - his house was burnt
down a few weeks ago (23 Jan.)

SPOTSWOOD, Col., Post-Master General - allows the Pennsylvania Gazette to be sent postage free to all parts
of the Post Road from Virginia to New England (23 Jan.)

Item from Boston, 16 Dec. 1734, about Georgia in general
and the 4 towns already settled there (28 Jan.)

Speech of Gov. Belcher to both houses of the Massachusetts
Assembly (28 Jan.)

WILLIAMS, Mary, in Strawberry Alley, Phila. - has a loom
and shuttles for sale (28 Jan.)

A letter to Franklin about preventing fires in Phila.;
the writer suggests roofs be made more safe to walk
upon by carrying the wall above the eaves as Mr. Turner's house in Front St. or Mr. Nichols's in Chesnut
St. (4 Feb.)

Massachusetts Assembly appointed the following to be a
committee to consider that part of the Governor's speech
of 22 Nov. 1734 relating to private bank or merchants
notes: Elisha Cook, Robert Hale, Job Almy, and Samuel
Danforth, Esqrs., Col. Alden, Charles Church, John
Wainwright, Thomas Tileston and John Bowles, Esqrs.
(4 Feb.)

Massachusetts House of Representatives chose the follow-
ing members to attend the governor on his tour to visit
the western frontiers: Col. John Quincy (Speaker),
Col. William Wainwright, Samuel Wells, Esq., Col.
Tileston, Major Bowles, Col. Epes, Robert Hale, Esq.,
Samuel Danforth, Esq., Col. Prescot, Col. Stoddard,
Capt. Wells, Col. Chandler, Col. Willard, Major Warren,
Elisha Bisby, Esq., Col. Goreham, Col. Church, Col.
Almy, Capt. Hill, Enoch Coffin, Esq., Major John Hol-
man (4 Feb.)

Voted (21 Jan.) by the House of Representatives of Pennsylvania that Lewis Morris, Esq., late Chief Justice of
New York, being gone to Great Britain, should be asked
to work in conjunction with Ferdinand John Paris, Esq.,
(agent of Pennsylvania in London) to work against a
certain resolution of the House of Lords in January
1733 relating to the plantations in America (4 Feb.)

BOUD, Thomas, bricklayer, in Phila. - has seasoned cedar
boards for sale (4 Feb.)

DUPUY, Odran, who served 7 years in London as a watch-
finisher - will open a French school next door to the
Bell in Arch St., Phila. (4 Feb.)

Letter from Capt. Samuel Winder at Mumma-Naney Town, 19
Dec. 1734 to Col. Charles Davis in Kingston, Jamaica;
it gives an account of military operations against the

rebellious Negroes since the troops left Mr. Burnets;
the letter was taken by Mr. Witter; the writer asks
that the contents be communicated to Mr. Pratter (18
Feb.)

A plantation of 100 acres in Warminster, Bucks Co., upon
the upper York Road 18 miles from Phila., now in the
tenure of George Morgan - will be sold at auction at
the Coffee-House in Phila. by Patrick Baird, vendue-
master; the plantation belongs to William Howel near
the Bank Meeting-House in Phila. (18 Feb.)

SNOWDEN, John, tanner, of Phila. - offers for sale 450
acres on Black River (a branch of the Rariton) in
Jersey; nearly 200 acres further up in the last Indian
purchase; 2½ acres joining Judge Leonard's land in
Princeton near the tavern; 200 acres on Ouldman's Creek
in Gloucester Co., part of it being formerly John
Standbank's (18 Feb.)

HIGGINS, Capt. Ephraim - arrived 22 Jan. at Newport, R.
I., from the Bay of Honduras, where about 28 Sept. 1734
his ship was taken by 3 Spanish pettyawgers but re-
taken 3 days later by Capt. Richard Durfey of Rhode
Island, commander of the ship Pappilion; he tells how
Capt. Durfey restored prizes to the proper commanders,
one of whom was Capt. Edmonds of Boston; vessels in the
Bay of Honduras when Higgins sailed were those of Cap-
tains Durfey, Lilly, Heffernand, Sheffield, Crump, Carr,
Lewis and Stoddard (25 Feb.)

A New York item of 17 Jan. gives news of military action
in Jamaica against the rebellious Negroes (25 Feb.)

Warning about Thomas Dershew, alias Denis, alias Maxfield,
who calls himself a joiner of New-Castle but is a
horse thief (25 Feb.)

Warning about a vagrant named John Mitchel, a notorious
cheat, who pretends to be a Dutchman bred somewhere
about Raiton (25 Feb.)

MANSELL, Robert, who about 2 years ago fled from Barbados
on account of his murder of John Gage in the Parish of
St. Philips - has been taken up from on board a sloop
belonging to St. Christophers and has been committed
to goal - Barbados item of 16 Nov. 1734 (4 Mar.)

Negro woman on Island of Barbados on 5 Dec. 1734 gave
birth to 2 boys joined together (4 Mar.)

On 13 Dec. 1734 at Bridgetown, Barbados, sentence of death

was imposed on John Patrick for the murder of Patrick M'Caevock (a constable in the execution of his office) and Robert Mansell for the murder of John Gage; Nathaniel Winter was tried for the murder of Mary Walter but was acquitted (4 Mar.)

CUSHING, Benjamin, of Boston, shipwright - last week in the north part of Boston fell from the stage at his shipyard and died instantly, leaving a wife and 4 young children - Boston item of 5 Feb. (4 Mar.)

SAVAGE, John, a young man of New-Castle - Saturday last, riding very hard to town, struck his head against a tree in the dark and died in a few hours (4 Mar.)

BELDEN, Samuel, of Norwalk, Conn. - on 8 Feb. his shop was broken open and goods were carried off, supposedly by 2 Irishmen, John MacNeil and William MacKeel (4 Mar.)

Speech of Gov. Robert Johnson of South Carolina to the Commons House and the address of the House to him (11 Mar.)

Col. Purry has lately arrived at Purysburg in ship _Simon_, Capt. Cornish, with 260 Swiss Protestants and their minister, Mr. Chiefelle - Charlestown, S.C., item of 16 Nov. 1734 (11 Mar.)

Account from St. Thomas of the crushing of the Negro revolt on St. John's (11 Mar.)

Account of fire last Monday night on a sloop lying at the Long Wharf in Boston - Boston item of 13 Feb. (11 Mar.)

Account of a fire Monday last at a pot-house in Market St., Phila. (11 Mar.)

ARMITT, John, of Phila. - offers reward for recovery of horse strayed or stolen (11 Mar.)

HUNTER, John, lately from England (whose wife is a mantua-maker), at the Widow Lamb's, opposite to the Coffee-House in Front St., Phila. - posts books, draws accounts and will teach mathematics (11 Mar.)

RAKESTRAW, William - sells chestnut posts for fencing (11 Mar.)

PATRIDGE, John, a New England servant, age c. 17 - runaway from Evan Price in Robinson Twp., Lancaster Co., Pa. (11 Mar.)

WILLIAMS, William, of Uwchland - will sell at auction 25 Apr. at Vale Royal his mill at Whiteland, Chester Co. (20 Mar.)

HERBERT, William, of Phila. - offers reward for capture of horse stolen from him and of the supposed thief, John Mitchel (20 Mar.)

Account of what befell ships at Deal, Eng., in a storm in January (27 Mar.)

DURFEY, Capt. - arrived early last week at Rhode Island from the Bay of Honduras - Boston item of 24 Feb. (27 Mar.)

Brigantine Nanticoke, Capt. Thornton, which sailed November last from Phila. for Dublin - supposed to be the vessel in Padstow Harbor bottom upwards (27 Mar.)

House in Strawberry Alley, Phila., was broken open and robbed by 3 servants, who have been taken at Byberry and are now in goal in Phila. (27 Mar.)

Negro man belonging to Widow Cox of Phila. - died suddenly Wednesday last (27 Mar.)

A huge ox, raised and fattened at Shrewsbury, East Jersey, was killed Wednesday last at Phila. by Joseph Stinnard (27 Mar.)

DAVIS, William, removed next door to Thomas Miller in Chesnut St., Phila. - binds books (27 Mar.)

Subscription being made in London for a statue of William III to be sent to New England and erected in King St. in Boston - Boston item of 10 Mar. (3 Apr.)

BROWN, Valentine, next door to Mr. Edward Nichols in Chesnut St., Phila. - offers Negroes for sale (3 Apr.)

Fire broke out Wednesday night in a smith's shop near the prison in Phila. (10 Apr.)

BOGG, Samuel, of Alleways Creek - about a week ago his house burnt to the ground (10 Apr.)

HEMPHILL, Rev. - will be tried Thursday next in Phila. by a commission of the Presbyterian Synod on a charge of heterodoxy (10 Apr.)

DERING, Mr., dancing master in Phila. - gives notice of his division of his school (10 Apr.)

REYNOLDS, Lawrence, in Chestnut St., Phila. - sells cow-
skin whips (10 Apr.)

PATTISON, Thomas, late of Darby, Chester Co., innholder -
Samuel Lewis, John Davis and Samuel Bunting, all of
Chester Co., yeomen, have been directed by court order
to audit Pattison's accounts (10 Apr.)

Tuesday last in Phila., at a court of Oyer and Terminer,
2 men, Fitzgerald and Obrian, were found guilty of
burglary and were sentenced to death (17 Apr.)

Last week at Chester Co. at an auction, when a man was un-
reasonably abusive to his wife, the women formed themselves into a court, tried the man, found him guilty,
had him ducked 3 times in a pond and had half of his
hair and beard cut off (17 Apr.)

Brigantine Worcester, Robert Hall commander - will sail
from Phila. to Barbados; for freight or passage apply
to the commander at William Parker's wharf (17 Apr.)

Schooner Ann, Joshua Grainger, Jr., master, now lying at
the Crane wharf in Phila. - will sail for North and
South Carolina; for freight or passage apply to the
master or to Joshua Grainger, Sr. (17 Apr.)

Ship Garland, Robert Knowland master - arrived Sunday last
at Charlestown, S.C., from Bristol in 7 weeks and 3
days (24 Apr.)

BRIENTNAL, Joseph, Sec. - gives notice of meeting of subscribers to the library in Phila. at house of John
Roberts in High St. (24 Apr.)

Ship St. George, John Staples master, will sail for London;
for freight or passage apply to Peter Baynton or the
master at Dickinson's wharf (24 Apr.)

Ship Fraeme Gally, John Green master, will sail for London;
for freight or passage apply to the master at Master's
wharf in Phila. or Isaac Norris, Jr. (24 Apr.)

ELFRETH, Caleb, in Third St., Phila. - sells pickled
sturgeon (1 May)

POWELL, Tho. - will sell above year and a half's time of
a servant lad, age c. 18, shoemaker by trade (8 May)

MORRIS, Isaac, late of Whitemarsh Twp., Phila. Co., dec'd
- his plantation, containing 324 acres, will be sold at
auction by Sarah and Mordecai Morris, executors (8 May)

BRYANT, Capt., of ship <u>Albany</u>, which arrived at New York 5 May from London - reports that the brigantine <u>Joanna</u>, Capt. Stephens, and the ship <u>Beaver</u>, Capt. Thomas Smith, sailed from London some days before him, as did Capt. Shepherdson for Boston - New York item of 12 May (15 May)

PARKER, Peter, late of Bucks Co., labourer - admits before Robert Collyer, Henry Paull and M. Davies, witnesses, that the scandalous reports he spread about Edward Wells of Cheltenham, Phila. Co., husbandman and victualler, are totally unfounded (15 May)

TURPIN, Capt. Matthew, master of sloop <u>Sweet</u> <u>Nelly</u>, which sailed from Barbados 8 Feb. - arrived this week at Charlestown, S.C.; Turpin's sloop, being left behind the fleet conveyed by Capt. Brand, was taken on 16 Feb. by a Spanish sloop, which later put in at west of Hispaniola at a place called Orcanes; when some of the Spaniards went ashore for water and provisions, the French commander there seized the Spaniards, examined the sloop and, finding Turpin and his crew confined in the hold, released them and let them go - Charlestown item of 3 May (22 May)

The following have arrived at New York: on 12 May Capt. Holloway in a brigantine from Holland and Capt. Teach from Madeira; on 16 May Capt. Skinner from Holland; on 18 May Capt. Waters from Holland - New York item of 19 May (22 May)

JOHNSTON, Gov., of South Carolina - reported to have died - New York item of 19 May (22 May)

EDGEL, Simon, a servant of - was drowned Sunday last when a boat overset about a mile this side of Gloucester (22 May)

RANSTEAD, Caleb, of Phila. - offers reward for recovery of piece of silk lost from one of the stalls in the fair (22 May)

STEADMAN, David, Irish servant, age <u>c</u>. 35 - runaway from Armstrong Smith, shipwright, of Phila. (22 May)

COWLEY, Matthew, skinner on Society Hill - offers reward for bay gelding strayed or stolen (22 May)

FLOWER, Henry, late Postmaster of Pennsylvania - persons indebted to him are desired to pay him at the old coffee-house in Phila. (29 May)

RENAUDET, James, next door to Owen Owen's in Market St.,
Phila. - sells European goods, black pepper and indigo
(29 May)

NORRIS, Isaac, of Fairhill, Esq., many years a member of
Council and often representative in the Assembly - died
Wednesday morning at Germantown Meeting of an apoplec-
tic fit (5 June)

PENN, John, Esq. - Address of the Library Company of
Phila. to him and his answer (5 June)

Grist mill on a stream dividing New-Castle and Kent Counties, about 25 miles from New-Castle, and a house, store
and cooper's shop are for sale - apply to Nathaniel
French and William Rawle of Phila. or Joseph Rawle at
said mill in Kent (5 June)

REDDISH, Nicholas - asks that geographical dictionary he
lent may be returned to him (5 June)

MAKIN, Mrs., in Market St., Phila. - has Florence oil for
sale (5 June)

Barr & Carroll at the Crooked Billet in Front St., Phila.
- have snuff and tobacco for sale (12 June)

Speech of Gov. Jonathan Belcher to the Massachusetts Assembly (19 June)

TWELLS, Rachel, of Phila. - died Sunday last from too
much strong drink (19 June)

Schooner _Christiana_ will sail for North Carolina - for
freight or passage apply to William Parker in Water
St., Phila. (19 June)

CARRIER, Thomas, of Colchester, Conn. - lately died there
in his 110th year, leaving 5 children, 39 grandchildren and 28 great-grandchildren - Boston item of 16
June (26 June)

WARD, Owen, Irish servant, age c. 23, who professes to be
a husbandman and miner - runaway from Thomas Ustick of
Second River in Newark, East Jersey; reward offered if
he is brought to his master or to Thomas Dunning, at
the George Inn, Phila. (26 June)

Account of the murder on or about 2 Jan. of Capt. Christopher Brooks, commander of the ship _Haswell_ of London,
and of his first and second mates on the passage from
Madera to Virginia; Robert Anderson, boatswain, and

some of the crew committed the deed; on 31 Jan. killed one Francis Hudson and threw him overboard; when they put into the French island called Mari-gallent, James Hill, a passenger, wrote a note in French and slipped it into the governor's hand; Anderson and 5 others were convicted and broken alive upon the wheel and 3 of the crew were strangled (3 July)

The Masonic Lodge on 24 June met at the Indian King in Market St., Phila., when James Hamilton was chosen Grand Master for Pennsylvania; he appointed Thomas Hopkinson, gent., his deputy; William Plumstead and Joseph Shippen were chosen Grand Wardens (3 July)

Brigantine Mary, James Marshal master - will sail for Dublin; for freight or passage apply to the master or Peter Baynton (3 July)

WHARTON, Joseph - sells rum, sugar, wine and salt (3 July)

Reward for return of a brown horse, strayed or stolen from the Common at Phila., will be paid by William Sommerset or Samuel Holt (3 July)

ROBERTS, Thomas, Welsh servant, age c. 22, branded T.R. on his right hand - runaway from Widow Ann Amos at Poqueston (3 July)

WINDHAM, Capt., brewer of Charlestown, S.C. - Tuesday night last 3 Negroes broke into and stole from his brew-house; Windham caught one Negro, a slave of Mr. David Hext; constables are sent after the other 2 Negroes - Charlestown item of 21 June (10 July)

Some Negroes belonging to James Crokatt, of Charlestown, merchant, on Thursday were found to have stolen goods of value, above 2,000 pounds - Charlestown, S.C., item of 21 June (10 July)

BARDINE, Capt., who arrived 28 June at Boston from the north side of Jamaica - reported that a force of Whites and Blacks from the Parishes of St. Ann's and St. James's in Jamaica had defeated a party of rebellious Negroes (10 July)

LURTING, Col. Robert, Mayor of New York City - died there 3 July and Paul Richard, merchant, is appointed in his place (10 July)

DENT, Commodore - has arrived in Jamaica from England (10 July)

Bay horse will be raffled for at the house of Owen Owen, the Sign of the Indian King in Market St., Phila. (10 July)

Medicines are for sale by Dr. Peter Sonmans over against the Baptist Meeting House in Second St., Phila. (10 July)

Three tracts of land situated on Georges Road in New Brunswick Twp., Middlesex Co., East New Jersey: one, called Saplin Ridge, well watered by Lawrence's Brook and sundry springs, adjoins William Cox's sawmill; another is in the Great Swamp; the third, called "The Small Windfalls," is bounded eastward by Thomas Lawrence's land, westerly by John Nevil's lands, southerly and northerly by Robert Davis's land; to purchase apply to Peter Sonmans in Phila. or Benjamin Clark, Jr., of Stonybrook or Barefoot Brinton of Milstone (10 July)

Resolution 25 June in the Massachusetts House of Representative concerning Samuel Fiske (late pastor of the First Church in Salem, who is deposed by his church) (17 July)

A Spanish pirate on 27 Feb. forced a sloop belonging to Spanish Town, commanded by Lewis Soire, ashore on the Island of Saba; General Matthew fitted out a sloop to look for the pirate - extract of a letter from St. Christophers, dated 17 Mar. (17 July)

About 6 weeks ago a sloop owned by Messers Augustus Boyd and Anthony Wharton was carried off from St. Christophers by some white men and 17 Negroes, who carried her to Porto Rico; there the governor sold her and the Negroes and pocketed the money - letter of 17 Mar. from St. Christophers (17 July)

Notice is given for persons indebted to the estates of Thomas Chase, dec'd, or Mrs. Mary Appleton, dec'd, to pay their debts; John Leacock and Charles Read are executors of Chase and said Read and Caleb Cash, Jr., of Mrs. Appleton (17 July)

Some Observations on the Proceedings Against the Reverend Mr. Hemphill is printed and sold by B. Franklin (17 July)

On 16 July at New York the governor named the new battery on Whitehall Rocks "George Augustus's Royal Battery"; after a round of firing the last cannon burst, killing the following 3 persons: John Symes (High Sheriff), Miss Courtlandt (only daughter of Col. Courtlandt) and a son-in-law of Alderman Romur (24 July)

BARNES, Martha, servant, age c. 36 - runaway from David
    Heldreth, of Middletown, Monmouth Co., East New Jersey
    (24 July)

Person who borrowed B. Franklin's Law Book of Pennsylvania
    is desired to return it (24 July)

MORRIS, Lt., of Brigadier Jones's Regiment - died a few
    weeks since at Jamaica - London item of 13 May (31 July)

HEMPHILL, Rev. (lately suspended by the Commission of the
    Synod) - Sunday last preached twice in Phila. at the
    house where the Assembly used to meet (31 July)

ROBINSON, Richard, servant, tailor by trade - runaway (in
    company with a sailor named Tom) from Dr. Patrick Sim,
    of Prince George Co. in Maryland; reward will be paid
    if he is brought to his master or to Charles Browne at
    Annapolis (31 July)

A few weeks ago the house of Mr. Johnson in Woodbury,
    Conn., caught fire; his wife was burned to death but
    his 4 children were saved - Boston item of 28 July (7
    Aug.)

GEORGES, John, Secr. - gives notice at Phila. concerning
    lottery for 100,000 acres of land in Pennsylvania (7
    Aug.)

RONANE, William, servant, age c. 24 - runaway from Joseph
    Hargrave at Point Nopoint (7 Aug.)

EDEY, Ebenezer, servant, born in New England, ship-carpen-
    ter - runaway from Thomas Croasdale of Burlington (7
    Aug.)

HAMBLETON, Robert, servant, age c. 21, formerly servant to
    John Elfreth, shipwright in Phila. - runaway from Jo-
    seph Burleigh at the Sign of the Crown in New Bristol
    (7 Aug.)

Brick house and lot in the High St., Burlington, near the
    Town wharf is for sale; apply to Simon Nightingale,
    living in said house (7 Aug.)

MERRET, Capt., who sailed from Boston some time since in
    a brigantine for Cape Fare - was attacked by a number
    of Negroes in a small sloop; the Negroes were overcome
    by the people in the brigantine and some were hanged as
    examples - Boston item of 30 June (14 Aug.)

Commencement at Harvard in Cambridge, Mass., on Friday

last - Boston item of 7 July (14 Aug.)

GOULD, Mr. - Friday last, when drawing a bucket of water
from a well in the Arms House in Boston, fell into the
well; a bucket was let down and, when he put his arm
through the handle, he was drawn up uninjured - Boston
item of 7 July (14 Aug.)

French deserters from New Orleans get to Albany, whence 3
go to Philadelphia and 2 to Boston; 6 French deserters
came from Canada to Boston (14 Aug.)

Friday last a mariner of Boston, absent 10 or 11 years on
a man-of-war and then a prisoner in Sallee, returned to
Boston and found his wife about to marry a shoemaker
that evening; the shoemaker quitted all pretentions
to the woman - Boston item of 14 July (14 Aug.)

CLIFTON, John - offers reward for return of a gold chain
lost between Phila. and Brunswick (14 Aug.)

EVANS, William - Welsh servant, age c. 28, who calls himself a carpenter, sawyer and shoemaker - runaway from
Edward Man Sherwood of Talbot Co. (14 Aug.)

CLAYPOOLE, James - offers reward for recovery of horse
supposed to have been stolen by an Irishman named John
Hopkins, who was seen going up Wisahickan Road toward
Patomock (14 Aug.)

Earthquake at Antigua on 16 July (21 Aug.)

Tuesday last 2 Negroes, a man named Yaw and a boy named
Caesar, attempted to poison their master, Humphrey Scar-
let of Boston, victualler, his wife and 2 children with
arsenic or ratsbane, placed in a skillet of chocolate;
Caesar finally admitted he got the poison from a Negro
slave of Capt. Whiting of Bristol; prompt action by a
physician has probably saved the lives of the poisoned
family; the Negroes are committed to goal - Boston item
of 4 Aug. (21 Aug.)

Young servant woman, age c. 19, of Providence, Phila. Co.
- is confined for concealing the birth of her bastard
child (21 Aug.)

EVANS, David - desires return of a barbicuing iron he lent
and also offers reward for recovery of a strayed colt
(21 Aug.)

Account of terrible storm in Connecticut on 18 July from
Windham to the sea - Boston item of 31 July (18 Aug.)

Two French deserters from Mississippi and a man, half
French, half Indian, arrived Wednesday last at Phila.
(28 Aug.)

DOWTHEL, James - found murdered and scalped about 300
miles northward of Phila.; William Balden, who went with
him, is missing (28 Aug.)

Report of a distemper, which begins with swelling in the
throat, that is prevalent in several towns in New Hampshire and has killed many persons - Boston item of 4
Aug. (4 Sept.)

MASON, Samson, of Rehoboth, a batchellor, in his 85th
year - married 14 July by Rev. David Turner of Rehoboth
to Mrs. Abigail Farris, a widow aged about 45, of Rehoboth; she has a child aged about 3 years - Boston
item of 4 Aug. (4 Sept.)

FOSTER, Capt. - is daily expected at Boston from London -
New York item of 1 Sept. (4 Sept.)

INGRAM, John, bricklayer - will dispose of time of a servant man for 5 years (4 Sept.)

EDGELL, Simon of Phila. - persons who do not settle accounts with him will be sued (11 Sept.)

FITZGERALD, William, Irish servant, age c. 25 - who pretends to be something of a sailor - runaway from Timothy Dargen, of Prince William Co. in Virginia (11 Sept.)

MULHALL, John, Irish servant, middle-aged man - same as
above

MEREDITH, Reese (whose store is on Wm. Fishbourn's wharf
in Phila.) - plans to leave Pennsylvania in 4 weeks
and wishes to settle all accounts (18 Sept.)

STRICKLAND, Miles in Market St., Phila. - sells Dr. Bateman's pectoral drops (18 Sept.)

Brigantine Prince Frederick, Capt. Wilson from Holland -
arrived 15 Sept. at New York with between 40 and 50
Palatines (25 Sept.)

PENN, Hon. John - Sunday last left Phila. for New-Castle
to embark on Capt. Budden's ship for London (25 Sept.)

DOWNS, Richard - offers for sale a fulling-mill at Fishing Creek, Cape May Co. (25 Sept.)

ASSON, John, at Lewistown - offers reward for recovery of
2 horses strayed or stolen from Daniel Rodney's pasture
at Dover (25 Sept.)

The following were elected 1 Oct. for Phila. Co.: Repre-
sentatives--Thomas Leech, Robert Jones, John Kinsey,
Job Goodson, Edward Warner, William Allen, Isaac Norris,
John Jones Carpenter; sheriffs--Joseph Breintnal, John
Roberts; coroners--Owen Owen, David Evans; commissioner
--Jacob Leech; assessors for the county--John Dillwin,
Hugh Evans, Thomas Potts, Joseph Noble, John Bartholo-
mew, James Jones; burgesses for the city--John Kears-
ley, Israel Pemberton; assessors for the city--Joseph
Paschal, Edward Bradley, Nathaniel Allen, James Parrock,
Benjamin Morgan, Moses Hughes (2 Oct.)

The following were elected for Chester Co.: Representa-
tives--Joseph Harvey, William Pennock, Joseph Pennock,
Caleb Cowpland, John Evans, John Parry, Joseph Brinton,
Thomas Cummins; sheriffs--John Owen, Benjamin Davis;
coroners--John Wharton, Henry Lewis; commissioner--
Richard Jones; assessors--John Parry, Jr., Benjamin
Freed, Edward Brinton, James Jeffries, Joseph Hayes,
William Jeffries (2 Oct.)

The following were elected 1 Oct. for Bucks Co.: Repre-
sentatives--Joseph Kirkbride, Jeremiah Langhorne,
Christian Van Horne, William Biles, Andrew Hamilton,
Lawrence Crowden, Matthew Hughes, Benjamin Jones;
sheriffs--Timothy Smith, John Hall (2 Oct.)

BEEN, Thomas, or William Crossthwaite of Phila. - will pay
reward for capture of William Dillin, barber, of Newtown, Md., and return of a horse, who Dillon hired of
Been to go to New-Castle; Dillin, however, went off
towards New York (2 Oct.)

FRENCH, Nathaniel in Second St., Phila. - sells rum, historical chimney tiles and iron chimney backs (2 Oct.)

Tuesday last William Allen was elected Mayor of Phila.
(9 Oct.)

The following were elected for Lancaster Co.: Represen-
tatives--James Hamilton, Thomas Edwards, Andrew Galbraith, Thomas Armstrong; sheriffs--Samuel Smith, James
Mitchel; coroners--James Armstrong, William Cadwell (9
Oct.)

The following were elected for New-Castle Co.: Represen-
tatives--David French, Andrew Peterson, John Richardson,
Thomas Noxon, John M'Cool, Jehu Curtis; sheriffs--Henry

Newton, John Goodwin; coroners--Henry Gunn, James Hamilton, tanner (9 Oct.)

The following were elected for Kent Co.: Representatives --Andrew Hamilton, James Morris, John Holiday, William Barnes, Henry Molliston, Roger Train; sheriffs--Daniel Rodney, Caesar Rodney; coroners--Nicholas Lockerman, Samuel Berry (9 Oct.)

The following were elected for Sussex Co.: Representatives --Simon Kollock, William Till, Jabez Fisher, Jacob Kollock, Richard Hinman, Rives Holt; sheriffs--Cornelius Woolbank, John Shanklin; coroners--Daniel Nunis, William Sultridge (9 Oct.)

MURRY, Humphry, late of Phila., dec'd - accounts with estate to be settled with William Allen and Edward Shippen, executors; real estate they offer for sale is as follows: 2 houses and lots at lower end of Front St. in Phila. near the drawbridge where the Widow Crap now dwells; a plantation (where Moses Marshal now lives) at Neshaminy, containing 150 acres; 500 acres in Limerick Twp., Pa.; 625 acres on Loakoling (a branch of the Delaware), part of the Lotting Purchase No. 57 in Amwel Twp. in Hunterdon Co., West New Jersey; 1,420 acres near Whipany on both sides of Rohaway River (9 Oct.)

Proprietors of Pennsylvania filed a bill 21 June in H.M.'s High Court of Chancery against Lord Baltimore in connection with boundaries between Maryland and Pennsylvania (16 Oct.)

HUGHES, Thomas, innkeeper at Patapsco Ferry - Friday last his house burned down; there were 7 gentlemen in bed above stairs; Capt. Reynolds (commander of a ship from England), Mr. Tidmarsh of Newtown on Chester River, William Waltham, Peter Overy of Annapolis, John Lee of Patapsco, Capt. Morgan and Mr. Newland; the last 2 escaped, as did the innkeeper and his family, but the other gentlemen perished (6 Nov.)

Jacob Tylor's, John Jerman's and Poor Richard's Almanacs are now in the press and will soon be printed and sold by B. Franklin (6 Nov.)

WHITE, Robert - is presumed drowned, as Saturday last his flat was found adrift with his coat on it - Phila. item of 13 Nov. (13 Nov.)

HENDRY, John, Irish servant, age c. 22, shoemaker - runaway from George House of Phila. (20 Nov.)

BLOWDEN, John, hired servant, formerly servant to Arthur Wells and afterwards to William Smith, both of Phila. - runaway from James Norrel of Oley, Phila. Co. (20 Nov.)

Brigantine Worcester, James Lowrey master, lying at William Parker's woodyard - sailing for London; for freight or passage apply to Thomas Lawrence (20 Nov.)

AINSWORTH, William, servant, age c. 29 - runaway from William Perkins (20 Nov.)

Account of celebration 5 Nov. in Boston of anniversary of the Gunpowder Plot (27 Nov.)

Petition (22 Oct.), signed by William and Elizabeth Alexander and others, to the Assembly of New York with regard to the lands lately taken out of Connecticut and added to New York (4 Dec.)

WILKINS, Thomas, who kept a sawmill - last week was found dead by the roadside without marks of violence (4 Dec.)

ARMITAGE, Benjamin, of Phila. Co., old and feeble - Friday night last missed his way in the dark and sank so deep in mud and water in a meadow that he could not get out and was found there dead (4 Dec.)

Account of 2 hunting accidents, one at Egg Harbour and one near Frankford (4 Dec.)

BAIRD, Patrick - prints notice about lottery for 100,000 acres of land (4 Dec.)

WHITE, Andrew - if he enquires of William Allen, Esq., or the printer, he will hear something to his advantage (4 Dec.)

PAWLIN, Henry, Jr. - since March a mare branded ST has been at his plantation in Perkiomun (4 Dec.)

Speech of Gov. Belcher of Massachusetts to his Assembly on 19 Nov. (11 Dec.)

SEABURY, Mr., saddler - Thursday se'nnight his shop near Groton Ferry was burnt to ashes- Boston item of 1 Dec. (11 Dec.)

PALMER, William, living near the Falls of Schuylkill - offers reward for recovery of a horse strayed or stolen from Schuylkill Mill; horse is to be brought to the owner or to Stephen Beasley, blockmaker in Phila. (11 Dec.)

CROSHERY, William, _alias_ M'Clauskey, Irish servant, age c. 22, tailor - runaway from James Mackey (18 Dec.)

Owner of a strayed horse that has been running about the west side of the River Skuylkil is desired to repair to Joseph Grey at the Middle Ferry on Skuylkil (18 Dec.)

Letter to Mr. Franklin about article in Bradford's _Mercury_ (24 Dec.)

READ, John - his storehouse in New Munster near the head of Elk River was robbed by 2 transients who go by the names of John Smith and James Duddley (24 Dec.)

GRAINGER, Joshua, offers for sale a new sawmill up Timber Creek, 10 or 11 miles from Gloucester, being nearest to Phila. (24 Dec.)

Brigantine _Dispatch_, Benjamin Christian master, now at Mr. Clymer's wharf - will sail for Jamaica; for freight or passage apply to the master or Capt. Anthony Peel at his house in Arch St., Phila. (24 Dec.)

CARR, Capt. - last Tuesday arrived at Boston from the Old River in the Bay of Honduras in 28 days; he reports that 2 Spanish petiaugers took Capt. Bond of Boston, Capt. Smith of Jamaica and Capt. Wickham and Capt. Pitman of Rhode Island, but Col. Cranston of Rhode Island pursued them and rescued Capt. Wickham and his vessel - Boston item of 15 Dec. (30 Dec.)

At house of George Brownell in Second St., Phila. (formerly house of John Knight, dec'd) reading, writing, etc., are taught (30 Dec.)

1736

Sundry redemptioners who came in the ship _Hopewell_, Anthony Fauset, master, the brigantine _Lawson_, Benj. Lowes master, the snow _Frodsham_, James Aspinal master, are to pay what they owe to James Mackey in Phila. or be prosecuted (6 Jan.)

MOOR, Thomas at Naaman's Creek, offers reward for person who secures in goal John Jones, a Welshman, who stole a mare from John Strickland (6 Jan.)

ROBERTS, John, dec'd - debtors to his estate are to settle accounts with John Danby in Third St., Phila., or Rowland Roberts of North Wales (who are both authorized by John White, executor, to collect debts) (6 Jan.)

Brigantine <u>Princess</u> <u>Anne</u> (whereof John Young was master,
who died at sea upon the coast) - arrived Saturday last
at New York from Jamaica in 28 days - New York item of
6 Jan. (15 Jan.)

Sloop, Capt. Higgs master, belonging to Mr. Dinwiddie, Collector of Bermuda, bound to New York - was cast away at
Rockaway Rocks on Long Island; 3 of the crew froze to
death and the master is ill - New York item of 6 Jan.
(15 Jan.)

CRANSTON, Col., Commodore of the Bay Fleet - arrived 8 Dec.
at Newport, Rhode Island (22 Jan.)

CURTIS, Capt., of the Bay Fleet - is ashore at the Vineyard but will save all the cargo and furniture of his
vessel - Boston item of 16 Dec. (22 Jan.)

HOUGHTON, Rowland - Massachusetts House of Representatives
has voted him the sole privilege for 10 years of making
and vending his new <u>theodolite</u> - Boston item of 16 Dec.
(22 Jan.)

The French language is taught at the house of Lawrence Reynolds in Chesnut St., Phila. (22 Jan.)

STEVENSON, Thomas at the Falls Ferry, Schuylkil - offers
reward for recovery of 3 horses that strayed from him
if they are brought to him at said ferry or to John
Stevenson in Bethlehem, Hunterdon Co., West Jersey
(22 Jan.)

RATSEY, Capt. - arrived at New York 7 Jan. from Madera,
whence H. E. Henry Cunningham, Gov. of Jamaica, sailed
in November last - New York item of 19 Jan. (29 Jan.)

COOK, Mr., living near Andrew Peterson's in Cecil Co. -
26 Jan. Cook's house burnt to the ground when he and
his wife were visiting a neighbor; 2 of his children
were burned to death but a servant girl and another of
his children escaped (29 Jan.)

RAKESTRAW, William - will let a store near the Pennypot
Houses (29 Jan.)

REDDISH, Nicholas - member of his family has been cured of
the dropsey by an elixir made by Edward Jones of Phila.,
gent. (29 Jan.)

ASSHETON, Ralph - will lease 23 lots of land about a mile
from Phila. on the highroads to Conestogoe, Merion and
Haverford; draughts of said lots may be seen at the

houses of Owen Owen, Thomas Dunning and James Bainbridge in Phila., of David Cowpland and John West in Chester, of Joseph Burleigh at Bristol and also at the 3 lower ferries on Schuylkill; good stone is for sale at Ralph Asheton's Ferry (29 Jan.)

GRISCOM, Sarah, of Phila., who sells stays and cider - warns that persons indebted to her are to settle accounts (29 Jan.)

Reprint of item on the new distemper in New England, published in the Boston Gazette of 6 Oct. 1735 (5 Feb.)

Speech of Gov. Belcher to the Massachusetts General Assembly (5 Feb.)

PLAISTED, Thomas, of London, now residing in Boston - has petitioned the Massachusetts Great and General Court to be allowed proper encouragement to manufacture potash (5 Feb.)

JESSON, Robert, late merchant of Phila. - claims to have been cured of dropsey by elixir made by Edward Jones (5 Feb.)

ASPDEN, Matthias - will go to England from Phila. in about 2 months and wishes to settle all accounts (5 Feb.)

In a letter from London (8 Nov. 1735) from Messrs. Stark and Gainsborough to Robert Livingston, merchant of New York, is reference to the affair of Col. Morris with the Gov. of New York; the Committee of Council expressed that the governor's reasons for removing Morris were not sufficient - New York item of 2 Feb. (11 Feb.)

BROOKE, Henry, Esq., Collector of Customs for Port of Lewes Town and sometime Speaker of the Assembly in the Lower Counties - died last week in Phila. (11 Feb.)

KNOWLES, Mrs. Sarah, a preacher among the Friends at Phila. - Sunday last was taken ill in the Meeting and expired a few hours later (11 Feb.)

BOYNTON, Mr., of Newbury Falls - has buried another child, the seventh, dead of the distemper - Boston item of 15 Jan. (11 Feb.)

Reading, writing, dancing, etc., are taught at house of William Dering in Mulberry St., Phila (11 Feb.)

French is taught at house of Hermanus Alrichs in Second St., Phila. (11 Feb.)

FLEXNEY, Daniel, of Phila. - intends to leave for England
in 20 days and wishes to settle all accounts (19 Feb.)

Sloop Speedwell, William Richardson master, at James Morris's wharf - will sail for Barbados (19 Feb.)

HASTINGS, Samuel, shipwright in Phila. - will pay reward
for recovery of a mare strayed from Richard Sands in
Bucks Co., Pa. (19 Feb.)

Ship George, William Mirick commander - 22 Jan. arrived at
Boston from London (25 Feb.)

FITZ ROY, Lady (daughter of Gov. Cosby of New York) is
brought to bed of her second son - New York item of 17
Feb. (25 Feb.)

Brigantine Grace, Thomas Thompson master, at Fishbourn's
Dock - will sail for Barbados; for freight or passage
apply to the master at Robert Ellis's in Phila. (25
Feb.)

MEREDITH, Reese, late of Phila., merchant, departed - persons indebted to him are requested to settle accounts
with Samuel Neave, who is impowered to receive payments
(4 Mar.)

Mansion, late of John Songhurst, dec'd, between the Proprietor's Arms Tavern and the house of Stephen Armit,
with an alley into William Carter's great alley, is to
be sold by Isaac Williams, next door to the Boar's Head
in Second St., Phila. (4 Mar.)

BREINTNALL, John, walebone-cutter - sells wool and tow
cards (4 Mar.)

Partnership of Nicholas Reddish and Alexander Paxton, sadlers in Phila., is broken up (4 Mar.)

PARKER, Thomas (who broke out of Lancaster Goal in August
last) - is now in prison in Burlington (4 Mar.)

BLOWDEN, John (after whom James Norrel of Oley sometime
since had advertisements printed) - is now imprisoned
in Burlington (4 Mar.)

DELAGE, Peter, sugar-baker, at house of John Dillwyn, at
upper end of Second St., Phila. - sells sugar, molasses,
candy and tea (4 Mar.)

TURNBULL, Capt. James, late master of the brigantine Fal-
conburg, who sailed 29 Nov. last from North Carolina for

Boston - arrived Friday last in Boston and gave account of suffering at sea; he and his crew were 1 Jan. taken on board the schooner of Capt. Avery, bound from Gibraltar to Portsmouth, N.H. - Boston item of 3 Feb. (11 Mar.)

BICKFORD, Mr., of Portsmouth, N.H. - his 3 children died of distemper - Portsmouth item of 6 Feb. (11 Mar.)

BOYNTON, Mr., of Newbury Falls - has buried his eighth child dead of distemper (11 Mar.)

JEFFERS, Thomas - Wednesday last died of apoplexy and Friday last his wife also died - New York item of 1 Mar. (11 Mar.)

BUDDEN, Capt., from Phila. passed Gravesend yesterday - London item of 2 Dec. 1735 (11 Mar.)

The Penn Gally, Capt. Kirk master, from Phila. - parted her anchors and drove on the North Bull - item in the Dublin Post of 25 Nov. 1735 (11 Mar.)

Sloop St. Andrew, Israel Cornuck master, which sailed from Phila. for St. Christophers 12 Dec. 1735 - foundered in January; the ship's company got safe to one of the Virgin Islands (11 Mar.)

Large schooner from Perth Amboy, bound to Cape Fear, Richard Hartshorn master, foundered 4 Feb.; the company in a boat were taken up by Capt. Wyatt, bound for St. Augustine; after 4 days they took to their boat again and got ashore at Otter's Island (between Georgia and South Carolina) and thence to Charlestown, where they took passage in Capt. James Lusk for Phila. (11 Mar.)

BROWN, William, of St. Mary's Co. in Maryland - his house accidentally burnt to the ground 28 Dec. 1735 (11 Mar.)

BOWMAN, Peter, who lived near the mill at Chester River, going home somewhat in liquor from Queens Tavern on 14 Feb. - fell from his horse and perished from the cold (11 Mar.)

WOOD, John, of Woodberry Creek - his house accidentally burnt down Friday last (11 Mar.)

Young man belonging to Capt. Trenchard - Sunday last fell overboard and was drowned (11 Mar.)

Warning that a Negro called America, who pretends to be free, is slave of William Morgan, turner, in Second

St. Phila. (11 Mar.)

COOPER, Ichabod, of Southampton, L.I., only daughter of,
age c. 12 - perished 30 Jan. in a snowstorm at Coagg,
about 12 miles from Southampton - Newport, R.I., item
of 19 Feb. (18 Mar.)

JESUP, Henry, of Southampton, L.I., 6-year-old daughter of
- same as above

CARTER, Capt., from Barbados but last from Antigua - has
arrived in Boston and reports crops turn out miserably
on both islands - Boston item of 1 Mar. (18 Mar.)

Ship Amsterdam, belonging to Col. Wendell, coming from New-
Castle to Barbados - was blown off this coast - Boston
item of 1 Mar. (18 Mar.)

MONRO, Capt. Hugh (a lieutenant of the company of Fuzileers
in New York City, whereof Richard Riggs is captain) -
died 9 Mar. in New York (18 Mar.)

COSBY, William, Gov. of New York - died 10 Mar. in New
York (18 Mar.)

CLARKE, George, Sec. of Province of New York - 10 Mar.
was sworn President of the Council and Commander in
Chief of New York (18 Mar.)

MILLER, John, of Cohansey - when cutting wood a few days
since with his son fell over and presently died (18 Mar.)

Two whales were killed at Cape May 25 Feb. (18 Mar.)

HORNE, Edward, dec'd - his plantation between Phila. and
Germantown, on main road, about 3½ miles from Phila.,
is offered for sale by his executrix, Elizabeth Horne
(18 Mar.)

MORRIS, Anthony, Jr., of Phila. - sells rice, turpentine
and leather (18 Mar.)

WOODBURY, Capt. - was taken by the Spaniards but he rose
upon them and killed several; his vessel is since cast
away - Boston item of 15 Mar. (1 Apr.)

GIBBS, Capt. - arrived Saturday last at Boston in 6 weeks
from Anguilla - Boston item of 15 Mar. (1 Apr.)

WHITE, Thomas, of Boston, engraver - Friday evening, when
2 of his children were left alone, one of them, aged
c. 19 months, was burnt to death when its clothes caught

fire - Boston item of 15 Mar. (1 Apr.)

BARNS, Capt. from Georgia - reports that Capt. Richard
Hartshorne, in passage from Charlestown to Cape Fear in
a boat, overset at the mouth of Clarendon River; he and
4 of his crew (one was Richard Smith, son of Capt. Smith
of New Jersey) were drowned - New York item of 26 Mar.
(1 Apr.)

BOYD, Capt. William - arrived Saturday last at New York
from Barbados, bringing with him as a passenger Capt.
Abraham Skinner, who sailed from New York 26 Jan. in
brigantine Jolly, with cargo of wheat for Gibraltar;
ship was damaged in 2 gales and on 10 Feb. they were
taken up by Capt. William Cross of Virginia and taken
to Barbados - New York item of 29 Mar. (1 Apr.)

BARNS, Thomas, master of a sloop arrived at New York 25
Mar. from South Carolina - reports that James Oglethorpe had arrived from London with 400 persons to settle on an island between Georgia and St. Augustine -
New York item of 29 Mar. (1 Apr.)

WOLF, Capt., of New York, master and sole owner of a
sloop - was taken by a Spanish pirate off Madeira; he
and his men were put ashore on the Rocus's - New York
item of 29 Mar. (1 Apr.)

ALEXANDER, James, member of Council of New York (who was
served with a protest by Rip Van Dam, Esq.) - denies he
advised or consented to George Clarke's taking over the
administration of the government of New York - New York
item of 24 Mar. (1 Apr.)

ANDERSON, Hon. Col., President of the Council of the Jerseys - died Saturday last at Amboy and Col. Hamilton is
now become President of Council - New York item of 29
Mar. (1 Apr.)

Report of Committee of both houses of Massachusetts Assembly about fixing value of bills of credit brought
down by Benjamin Lynde, Paul Dudley, Samuel Thaxter and
Josiah Willard; Thomas Hutchinson signs the report -
Boston item of 3 Feb. (8 Apr.)

MAYO, Capt. - arrived 17 Mar. at Boston from North Carolina; one of his passengers reported that Capt. Ball of
Piscataqua on passage to North Carolia sighted a sloop
belonging to Mr. Carnes of Boston (whereof Capt. Lumman
had been master); in a storm Capt. Lumman was lost overboard; Capt. Ball took the crew and some of the money
from the ship and put in at North Carolina; the crew of

Mr. Carnes's sloop hastened into the country and were suspected of guilt, so that a hue and cry issued out for apprehending them (8 Apr.)

SCOTT, Robert, of Chester Co. - on 20 Mar., going over Susquehannah at John Williams's Ferry, was drowned, with a lad belonging to Williams, when the boat sank (8 Apr.)

BUSH, William, servant, age <u>c</u>. 18 or 19 - runaway from Jacob Lippincut of Burlington (8 Apr.)

KLIN, Valentine, of Germantown - his wife Christiana has eloped from him (8 Apr.)

PERKINSON, Robert, servant, age <u>c</u>. 30, weaver - runaway from Richard Baily, of Phila., weaver (8 Apr.)

DICKENSON, Jonathan - his <u>God's</u> <u>Protecting</u> <u>Providence</u> (2nd edit.) is published and sold by B. Franklin (8 Apr.)

CUNNINGHAM, Col., Gov. of Jamaica = died there of fever 6 weeks after his arrival; his sister, age <u>c</u>. 16, daily expected from England, was voted 2,000 pounds by the government of Jamaica (15 Apr.)

BROWN, Mr., heretofore of Phila. - is appointed Collector for the ports of Salem and Marblehead, vacant by the death of Benjamin Vining (15 Apr.)

SIPPLE, Mr., of Kent Co. - has lost upwards of 100 cattle (15 Apr.)

These persons received death sentence for house breaking at court of Oyer & Terminer in Phila., namely John Watnal, Michael MacDermot and Catherine Connor, <u>alias</u> Smith (15 Apr.)

LLOYD, David, Esq., dec'd - his plantation on River Delaware, adjoining Town of Chester, is offered for sale by Grace Lloyd, living upon said plantation (15 Apr.)

<u>Sea-Horse</u>, man-of-war, Capt. Compton - arrived 18 Apr. at New York, bringing letter from Robert Hunter Morris, who refers to petition of Rip Van Dam, his own father's hearing, and complaints against Mr. Cosby (22 Apr.)

Ship <u>Elizabeth</u> <u>and</u> <u>Dorothy</u>, William Sutton master - will sail for London; for freight or passage apply to Matthias Aspdin, near the Courthouse or the master on the ship at William Fishbourn's wharf (22 Apr.)

Charge delivered by James Logan, Esq., Chief Judge of

Pennsylvania, to the Grand Inquest 13 Apr. will be
printed and sold by B. Franklin (22 Apr.)

Arrival of Mr. Oglethorpe 4 Feb. at the Road with the
Simond, Capt. Cornish, and the London Merchant, Capt.
Thomas, with 300 passengers; on 6 Feb. he arrived at
Savannah and Tomo Chaci and his nephew, Tooanabowi came
to welcome him; on 7 Feb. Hector Berenger de Beaufain,
Capt. Holzindorff, Mr. Tfisslly Dechillon (a Patrician
of Bern) and other Swiss from Purrysburg waited on Oglethorpe; on 8 Feb. Baron Von Rech and the 2 Saltzburg
ministers waited on Oglethorpe; on 8 Feb. Oglethorpe
went by water to Sir Francis Bathurst's house, 6 miles
above Savannah, passed by the sawmill set up by Mr.
Augustin; he went on to Col. Purry's house and the next
day returned to Savannah - Savannah item of 13 Feb.
(29 Apr.)

PARRIS, Alexander, Esq. - died Wednesday last at Charlestown, S.C., at age of 74 wanting a few days; he was one
of oldest settlers in South Carolina, where he had been
45 years; he had been 41 years married to his wife (who
died nearly 2 years since) and from her had 53 children
and grandchildren - Charlestown item of 13 Mar. (29 Apr.)

Report of a sea monster seen at Bermuda (29 Apr..)

MORGAN, Evan, at the Sign of the Two Sugar Loaves in the
corner shop, against the courthouse stairs, in Market
St., Phila. - sells cloth, spices, salt, oil, logwood,
etc. (29 Apr.)

GALLOWAY, John, English servant, age c. 22, belonging to
Cornelius Tobit - escaped from William Tufft, sub-sheriff
of Salem Co. (29 Apr.)

Schooner Isaac and Murray, Duncan Murray master, at Fishbourn's wharf - will sail for Boston (29 Apr.)

Five horses will be sold at auction at house of Thomas
Shoemaker in Fourth St., Phila. (29 Apr.)

LARKINS, Capt., master of the ship John and Margaret, at
Falmouth, on way to South Carolina; ship caught fire
and blew up Tuesday last, so that Larkins was killed -
London item of 17 Feb. (6 May)

Woman who nursed Lord Fitz-Roy's child at New York was
convicted 24 Mar. of stealing coined gold and other
valuables from Madam Cosby's cabinet and was setenced
to death; she was reprieved until first Tuesday in October because she was pregnant - New York item of 3 May
(6 May)

Three tenements in Water St., Phila., on Bickley's wharf, over against the Turk's Head, are offered for sale by Joshua Grainger (6 May)

CLAYPOOLE, James - reports that a shoulder of mutton was stolen off the cutler's window over against the shambles on Saturday last and a pump-handle was lately stolen from his pump (6 May)

DERING, William of Phila. - offers reward for recovery of a horse strayed from plantation late of Aaron Goforth, dec'd (6 May)

Several Negroes, just arrived from Barbados, are to be sold by Alexander Woodrop, William Allen and Joseph Turner (13 May)

Ship London Merchant, Capt. Thomas, and ship Simond, Capt. Cornish, both from Georgia - arrived 19 Mar. at Charlestown, S.C.; Mr. Oglethorpe went up Allatamaha River to Barnwell's Bluff and went into the woods with Capt. Dunbar, where he slept the night; the Spanish Court sent with Mr. Oglethorpe from England a Mr. Dimsky, who has gone to St. Augustine to settle the boundaries between Georgia and that government; Major Richards went to St. Augustine on that account 3 weeks ago - Charlestown item of 20 Mar. (20 May).

REED, Capt. - Tuesday last arrived in Boston from London; he met a schooner, John Sander master, bound to Maryland from North Carolina, having been 6 weeks and 4 days at sea; crew was almost starved; Capt. Reed gave them food and took with him a woman and 6 children and brought them to Boston (20 May)

McCOUN, Thomas, servant, born in Dublin, age c. 22, weaver - runaway from Thomas Wynne, of Blockley Twp. (20 May)

STEEL, James - offers reward for return of a mare strayed or stolen from the Hon. Proprietors (20 May)

MUSGRAVE, James - offers reward for return of a mare strayed or stolen from his plantation in Strasberry Twp., Lancaster Co. (20 May)

Ship Loretta, John Lithered master, now lying at Mr. M'Call's wharf - will sail for Barbados from Phila. (27 May)

SHEWEN, Tobias, indented servant, age c. 23 - runaway from service of the Hon. Proprietary; person who takes up the runaway will be rewarded by James Steel (27 May)

MILLER, Grissel, Scotch servant maid, age <u>c</u>. 20 - runaway
   from Edmund Peers of New York; reward will be paid if
   she is brought to Henry Hartley at the Compass and
   Horseshoe in Strawberry Alley, Phila. (27 May)

ROBERTS, Robert, age 30, and his 2 sons, Daniel (the eld-
   est) and John, all servants - runaways from Richard
   James of Kent Co. on Delaware; Robert lives with his
   wife and sons on the Widow Newberry's plantation, near
   Benjamin Moor's at Ancocus Creek, Burlington Co. (27
   May)

MITCHEL, Mr., of Annapolis Royal in Nova Scotia, a Deputy
   Surveyor of the Woods - lately sent the following relation in a letter to Col. David Dunbar, Lt.-Gov. of New
   Hampshire: on 1 May at the harbor of the Pobomcoumps
   Mitchel met Mrs. Butler, who told this story: on 7 Oct.
   last she sailed with her husband, Andrew Butler of Ireland, for Annapolis, Md., in a brigantine belonging to
   her husband; in December they arrived at Tiboge, where
   a maid and a Negro boy were sent ashore in the ship's
   boat; they never returned; the ship's company had little
   water to drink for 2 months and were forced to drink
   mixed rum, salt water and lime juice; Mr. Butler died;
   4 Apr. some Indians came aboard, found cherry brandy,
   became drunk, plundered the vessel, took Mrs. Butler
   ashore; after some days some Frenchmen came and took her
   to their own houses - Boston item of 24 May (3 June)

FLOWER, Henry, lately dec'd - accounts with estate are to
   be settled with the executors, Thomas and Enoch Flower
   (3 June)

HALL, John, English servant, age <u>c</u>. 19 - runaway from John
   Ingram, bricklayer (3 June)

Schooner <u>Speedwell</u>, lately belonging to William Pettit and
   Nathan Merrow, which was attached to answer a debt due
   to John Flower - will be sold at auction 6 Aug. at
   Goshen Landing, Cape May Co. (3 June)

FLANAGAN, Hugh, living near the Wall-Kills, about 25 miles
   from Esopes - offers reward for recovery of a black
   stallion stolen from him near Prince-Town, Sommerset
   Co., N.J., by one John Brown, who lately stole 9 pounds
   1 shilling from Thomas M'Gee's pocket at the house of
   Owen Owen in Market St., Phila. (3 June)

Third part of Manatawny iron-forge and other real estate
   belonging to the estate of John Rutter, dec'd - offered
   for sale by Samuel Nutt and Mary Rutter, executors
   (10 June)

CROKER, John - offers reward for recovery of a mare colt
(which was wintered on Jacob Dubre's plantation) that
strayed off the Commons in Phila. (10 June)

SALOMON, John, from Paris - will teach Latin and French
in Phila., adjoining to Thomas Hind's, shopkeeper in
Market St. (17 June)

MACHON, Thomas, servant, age c. 24, weaver - runaway from
William Harrison of New Hanover, Burlington Co. (17 June)

Speech of Patrick Gordon to Assembly of the Three Lower
Counties and their address to him (24 June)

Lengthy account, dated 12 Apr. 1736, from Frederica, Ga.,
with news of Mr. Oglethorpe, who has hired men to build
a fort; Capt. McPherson, Lt. Hugh Mackay and Mr. Augustine have come from Savannah to Darien; Tomachichi Mico
and his nephew Tooanahowi brought in many deer; Major
Richards returned from escorting the Spanish gentleman
to St. Augustine; 2 ships, the James, Capt. John Yoakley, and the Peter and James, Capt. Geo. Dymond, are
riding close under the fort; on 13 Apr. a detachment of
30 men arrived at Frederica under command of Ensign
Delegall (24 June)

HOUSTOUN, Mr. - brings account from Frederica that Creek
Indians have cut off a Spanish garrison opposite to St.
Juan's (24 June)

LOWNDES, Charles (separated from his wife) - last Saturday shot himself through the head and instantly died;
he left several writings, directed to Arthur Middleton,
Ralph Izard, Col. Blake, Nath. Broughton and John Colleton - Charlestown item of 29 May (24 June)

SONMANS, Peter, Esq., of Perth Amboy, Middlesex Co., N.J.
dec'd - the lands, tenements and real estate bequeathed
to his wife Sarah Sonmans are now vested in Samuel
Neirl, of London, Eng., gent. (eldest brother and heir
at law of the said Sarah), John Nevil, of Perth Amboy,
gent., and Peter Sonmans, of Phila., Doctor of Physic
(24 June)

Schooner Catherine, John Rice master, now at Mr. Powel's
wharf - will sail for Charlestown; for passage apply to
William Parker near the drawbridge in Phila. (24 June)

Letter dated 27 Mar. 1736 from New Providence gives an ac-
count of a mutiny of some 42 soldiers in the fort on 17
Mar.; the governor, Mr. Fitzwilliam, aided by Mr.
Stewart (his Surgeon), Capt. Charles Walder and Mr.

Samuel Lawford seize a sloop in which the mutineers were trying to flee; 12 mutineers and their French pilot were executed; Lt. Howel, the only lieutenant present at the time of the mutiny, who was suffering from gout, was saved by being carried from his house (1 July)

DAVIS, John, of Springfield Manor, Phila. Co., husbandman - his wife Katherine has eloped from him (1 July)

BROCKWAY, Capt. Richard - arrived 27 May at New London, Conn., whence he had sailed 30 June 1735 for Nevis; he described their many sufferings from weather, a leaky ship and lack of food; he mentioned help from one Philip Goold, a Frenchman (who had been a privateer on the coast of Connecticut many years ago) - New London item of 27 May (8 July)

THAYER, David, Jr., 3-year-old daughter of - died 20 June at Mendon, Mass., from bite of a rattlesnake - Boston item of 28 June (8 July)

CANBEY, Thomas - will dispose of time of a servant, who has 3 years to serve from 20 May last; the servant is a sawyer but wants to be a hostler or drive a team (8 July)

PALMER, Joseph, young lad - Thursday last was kicked in the head by a mare and died on Monday (8 July)

Grand Masonic Lodge met in Phila. 24 June; Thomas Hopkinson, who was chosen Grand Master of Pennsylvania, nominated William Plumstead his deputy; Joseph Shippen and Henry Prat were chosen Grand Wardens (8 July)

Notice is given for any persons who have orders from John Petticrew or Thomas Findly, merchants in Dublin, to apply to John Echlin in Phila., owner of the snow John and Margaret, which will sail for Dublin (8 July)

Reward will be paid for recovery of 3 Bibles (stolen out of Baptist Meeting Houses) by Rees Jones, near the Iron Works in the Welch Tract, or Jenkin Jones in Phila., or Benjamin Griffith in Montgomery; 2 Bibles were stolen from the meetinghouse on Christiana, near the Iron Works in the Welsh Tract in New-Castle Co., one in English, the other in Welsh (having name of Lewis Jones in it); the third Bible, stolen from the meetinghouse in London Tract in Chester Co., has the name of John Evans in it (8 July)

POINCE, Michael, late of Phila., dec'd - accounts with estate to be settled with George Ashbridge, Jr., or David Davis of Goshen in Chester Co. (executors to the estate)

or William Burge or Samuel Power, Jr., in Phila. (8
July)

DARLINGTON, William, English servant (formerly servant to
Jacob Metcalf, opposite to Phila., and afterwards to
George Hargrave, back of Burlington), age c. 30 - run-
away from William Beeks of New-Castle (15 July)

CLARK, Patrick, Scots servant, age c. 20 - runaway from
Joseph M'Forland of Cecil Co., Md. (15 July)

CLERK, Valentine, Irish servant, age c. 24 - runaway from
Lawrence Reynolds of Phila., currier (15 July)

DEWEES, William, of Whitemarsh - has taken up a brown mare
(15 July)

Indians are questioned by Mr. Oglethorpe about clashes with
the Spaniards; 1 May Capt. Ferguson with the Carolina
scout-boat brought an account of Major Richards and Mr.
Horton and about men under the command of Capt. Herms-
dorf - item from Frederica, Ga., of 10 May (22 July)

Translation of last will and testament (dated 9 Sept. 1735)
of an Indian, Peter Oquanhut, of Gay Head upon Martha's
Vineyard, minister; he makes bequests to his wife and
his daughter, Dorcas Amos; witnesses were Josiah Homit,
of Gay Head, and Zachariah Honoit, Gay Head Justice -
Boston item of 12 July (22 July)

MILLS, Hezekiah, servant, age c. 14, who worked as a tailor
in England but in America as shipwright - runaway from
Robert Toms of Phila. (22 July)

HORNE, Edward, dec'd - at the plantation lately belonging
to him, near Phila., household goods, horses and cattle
will be sold at auction (22 July)

A brick house at upper end of Market St., commonly called
High St., in Burlington is for sale - apply to John Ro-
berdes at the Sign of the Hat, near Market St. wharf,
Phila., or Isaac Decow in Burlington (22 July)

SCOTT, Capt. - arrived Friday last at Boston in about 8
weeks from London - Boston item of 19 July (2 Aug.)

KEITH, Sir William - reported in London that he stands best
chance of being appointed Governor of New Jersey (2 Aug.)

WATKINSON, Paul, of Burlington - offers reward for recovery
of a horse stolen from him (2 Aug.)

Plantation of 1,000 acres in Twp. of Richlands, commonly called the Great Swamp, in Bucks Co. and also about 80 acres of land lying between Joseph Jones's and Richard Waln's plantations in the Northern Liberties of Phila., about 4 miles from the city - offered for sale by Lawrence Growdon, at Joseph Richardson's, silversmith in Front St. (2 Aug.)

Sloop _Hannah_ - will sail for Cape Fear; for freight or passage apply to Joseph Grainger in Water St., Phila. (2 Aug.)

GOLDEN, Joseph, an English inhabitant at Cape May - 16 July a coroner's jury found his killing of a drunken Indian in a quarrel; Isaiah Stites gave evidence (7 Aug.)

GORDON, Patrick - Lt. Gov. of Pennsylvania and the Counties on Delaware - died Thursday last in his 73rd year; he had arrived in Pennsylvania in June 1726 (7 Aug.)

SPROGLE, John Henry, Jr., in New Hanover, Phila. Co. - has taken up a mare about 2 miles below Manatwany on Phila. Road (7 Aug.)

Speech of James Logan, President of the Council, to Representatives of Pennsylvania and Counties on Delaware and address of the representatives (12 Aug.)

Negro girls and boys for sale by Messers Allen and Turner (12 Aug.)

Negro girls and boys for sale by Robert Ellis (12 Aug.)

SULIVAN, Daniel, servant, age c. 25 - runaway from Mahlon Stacy of Mount Holly, Burlington Co. (12 Aug.)

MERRATTY, James, Irish servant, age c. 40 - runaway from Daniel Kelly of Manor of Moreland, Phila. Co. (12 Aug.)

Plantation, commonly called Ferry Point, now in occupation of Henry Dell, in Wellinborough Twp. - offered for sale by Joseph Fenimore and James Wills, of Burlington (12 Aug.)

The story of Mrs. Buckler, printed last May, is repeated with the following addition: from the houses of the French she was taken by Mr. Mitchel to Annapolis Royal, where she was entertained by Col. Armstrong, Lt.-Gov. of Nova Scotia, who sent her on to Boston, whence she sailed for London with Capt. Bennet; it turns out that she was a Miss Mathews (or Dowdy), under sentence of death for theft, reputed a common strumpet in Dublin.

Miss Mathews impersonated Mrs. Mary Buckler in Bridgetown, Barbados, to defraud the deceased's real widow;
it is believed that Miss Mathews and the crew killed
Mr. Buckler (2 Sept.)

Governor of St. Augustine has embargoed all Carolina vessels; Capt. of the Charming Betty and Capt. Parsons are
held in the harbor of St. Augustine, and someone from
the Charming Betty sent word of the situation to Phila.
by Capt. Kipp via New York (2 Sept.)

BOOTH, Thomas, Irish servant, age c. 21 - runaway from
Thomas Edwards of Lancaster Co. (2 Sept.)

NEAVE, Samuel, whose store is on Fishbourn's wharf in
Phila. - intends to go to London (2 Sept.)

Ship Jane, John Richmond master, will sail for Barbados;
for freight or passage apply to White and Taylor or to
the master on board the vessel at Fishbourn's wharf (3
Sept.)

Reward for return of a mare strayed from the stable of
George Shoemaker will be paid by James Hammer; mare is
to be taken to said Shoemaker in Phila. or to Thomas
Dunning in Phila. (2 Sept.)

JACKSON, Joseph, of Bristol, fuller - offers reward for
cloth stolen from his shop (9 Sept.)

Mr. Vane and Nolens have been again to Tiboge and brought
back the long boat and tokens of Dowdy's (the cheat who
pretended to be Capt. Buckler's widow) - Letter of 3
Aug. from Annapolis Royal to friend in Boston - Boston
item of 6 Sept. (16 Sept.)

Reward offered by B. Franklin for items belonging to the
press that were either left on the wharf at Burlington
or dropped off the dray between the waterside and the
market in Phila. (16 Sept.)

Plantation called "Traveskan," a Negro man and his wife, a
coach and horses are offered for sale by Robert Charles
and Abraham Taylor, executors of the late Gov. Gordon
(16 Sept.)

Two bolting mills, weights, scales, etc. - offered for
sale by Thomas Beasley, bolter in Third St., Phila.;
enquire of said Beasley at Margaret Nichols's or Evan
Jones's, Doctor of Physic in Market St., Phila. (16
Sept.)

ELDERTON, John, born in Parish of Bow near London - will hear something to his advantage if he will apply to the printer (16 Sept.)

RICHARDSON, Francis, goldsmith, at corner of Letitia Court in Market St., Phila. - makes, sells and mends clocks and jacks (16 Sept.)

POWEL, Evan, at the Sign of the Thistle and Crown, opposite to the State House in Chesnut St., Phila. - sells geese feathers (16 Sept.)

O'LOUG, Dennis, servant - runaway from Archibald Beard of Mill Creek Hundred, New-Castle Co. (16 Sept.)

Part of Colebrookdale Furnace and rights of land ajoining, being the estate of John Rutter, dec'd, will be sold at auction by Mary Rutter and Samuel Nutt, executors of John Rutter, at the Coffee House in Phila. (16 Sept.)

Sloop Winyaw, Richard Painter master - will sail for South Carolina; for freight or passage apply to Robert Ellis or to said master at Robert Ellis's wharf (16 Sept.)

Proclamation of J. Logan, President, and the Council of Pennsylvania, also signed by R. Charles, Secr. (23 Sept.)

MORRIS, Hon. Lewis, Esq., and his son Robert Morris - arrived 18 Sept. at Boston after passage of 7 weeks and 2 days (23 Sept.)

FINLOW, John - killed Monday last by a falling limb at Horsham as he was cutting down a tree (23 Sept.)

SHEPHERD, Thomas - Tuesday his body was found in the river; he probably fell overboard from the ship Princess Augusta to which he belonged (23 Sept.)

Two copper stills are for sale at Robert Bolton's, shopkeeper in Market St., Phila. (23 Sept.)

Sloop Hopewell, John Hughes master - will sail for North Carolina; for freight or passage apply to Edward Nichols, turner, in Chesnut St., Phila. (23 Sept.)

A hand is wanted in business of weaving haircloth - apply to Widow Rakestraw at upper end of Front St., Phila. (23 Sept.)

SPOTSWOOD, Col., according to order of House of Burgesses of Virginia, in August 1732 directed Robert Cary (his correspondent in London) to purchase Arms for Brunswick

Co.; Sir John Randolph, Clerk of the House of Burgesses
in 1733 told Mr. Cary there was no need as yet to send
the arms; in May last Mr. Cary wrote he had forgotten
how many arms were to be sent and wrote Mr. Gooch it
was his (Cary's) fault they were not sent; the House
could not be dissuaded from passing a resolve to start
action against Col. Spotswood - vote of House of Burgesses 30 Aug. 1736 (30 Sept.)

M'MANUS, Brian, servant, age c̲. 36 - runaway from Joseph
Thomson of Ridley Twp., Chester Co. (30 Sept.)

Snow Charming Molly - will sail for Dublin or Belfast; for
freight or passage apply to James Chalmers at his house
in New-Castle or James Finney on board said snow at
Wellings-Town on Christine Creek (30 Sept.)

MELLICHAMP, Thomas, found guilty of forging South Carolina
bills - was arrested 4 Aug.; his mother and family, who
were concerned in the crime, are expelled from the
colony (7 Oct.)

At New York City in elections held 29 Sept. all magistrates
of the last year were re-elected without opposition except in the Dock Ward, where 2 good men stood candidates
for common councilmen, Gerrard Beekman and Wessel Wes-
sels; Beekman was elected - New York item of 30 Sept.
(7 Oct.)

Before the election in New York Rip Van Dam informed the
aldermen that he would appoint the mayor and other officers which are yearly in the appointment of the commander in chief; George Clarke, Esq., claimed the same;
aldermen were advised by their electors to accept a
mayor etc. from Mr. Van Dam; appointed by Mr. Clarke
were the following: Mayor--Paul Richards; recorder--
Daniel Horsemanden; sheriff--William Cosby; coroner--
Richard Nichols; appointed by Mr. Van Dam were the
following: Mayor--Cornelius Vanhorne; recorder--William
Smith; sheriff--Richard Ashfield; coroner--Richard
Nichols; Mr. Van Dam the day after Gov. Cosby's death
forbade people to act with Mr. Clarke and on 29 Sept.
Clarke forbade people to act with Van Dam (7 Oct.)

Friday last the following were chosen for Phila. Co.:
Representatives--Thomas Leech, John Kinsey, Robert
Jones, Edward Warner, William Allen, Job Goodson, Jona-
than Robinson, Septimus Robinson; sheriffs--Joseph
Breintnal, Isaac Leech; coroners--Owen Owen, David
Evans; commissioner--George House; assessors for the
county--Thomas Fletcher, John Dillwin, James Jones,
Thomas Potts, Samuel Norris, miller, Joseph Trotter;

burgesses for the city--John Kearsley, Israel Pemberton; assessors for the city--Benjamin Morgan, Joseph Wharton, John Ogden, Benjamin Shoemaker, William Plywell, Samuel Ashton (7 Oct.)

Friday last the following were chosen for Chester Co.: Representatives--Joseph Harvey, Thomas Cummings, John Evans, Caleb Cowpland, William Webb, William Moore, Thomas Chandler, John Parry; sheriffs--John Owen, Benjamin Davis; coroners--John Wharton, Robert Park; commissioner--Samuel Lightfoot; assessors--Joseph Hayes, James Jefferies, John Parry, Jr., Joshua Thomson, Benjamin Fredd, Edward Brinton (7 Oct.)

Friday last the following were chosen for Bucks Co.: Representatives--Joseph Kirkbride, Jr., Jeremiah Langhorne, Christian Vanhorne, Andrew Hamilton, William Biles, Matthew Hughes, Benjamin Jones; sheriff--Timothy Smith; coroner--Jonathan Woollstone (7 Oct.)

Friday last the following were elected for Lancaster Co.: Representatives--James Hamilton, Andrew Galbraith, Thomas Armstrong, Thomas Edwards; sheriff-Samuel Smith; coroner--Joshua Lowe (7 Oct.)

Friday last the following were elected for New Castle Co.: Representatives--David French, John M'Coole, Thomas Noxon, Andrew Peterson, Jehu Curtis, Samuel Clemens; sheriffs--Henry Newton, Thomas Grey; coroners--Henry Gun, Richard Few (7 Oct.)

Friday last the following were elected for Kent Co.: Representatives--Mark Manlove, Andrew Hamilton, John Holiday, William Pharsons, John Housman, James Morris; sheriffs--Daniel Robinson, Jehosaphat Highland; coroners--Richard James, Martin Ashburn (7 Oct.)

Friday last the following were elected for Sussex Co.: Representatives--William Till, Rives Holt, Simon Kollock, Jabez Maud Fisher, Abraham Wynekoop, Jacob Kollock; sheriffs--John Shankland, Cornelius Wellbank; coroners--Daniel Nunes, P. Clewes (7 Oct.)

COWMAN, Capt. Nathan, of Phila. - drowned at Jamaica along with boatswain and 2 hands, when the longboat overset (7 Oct.)

PLUMSTEAD, Clement, Esq. - Tuesday last chosen Mayor of Phila. by the aldermen of the Common Council (7 Oct.)

DULANY, D., of Annapolis - issues a warning about Moses Rainey (sometime a practicing attorney in Cecil Co.)

who hired himself as a clerk in Sept. 1735 to Dulany
but has run off (7 Oct.)

ROBINS, John, in Walnut St., Phila. - sells cordage and
spike nails (7 Oct.)

MORRIS, Lewis, Esq. - Friday last arrived at New York, was
met at Fresh Water by Rip Van Dam and was given a sup-
per at house of John De Honneur in New York City - New
York item of 11 Oct. (14 Oct.)

MORRIS, Robert Hunter - states that Mr. Bradford in his
Gazette misrepresented his conversation in Boston, regarding Mr. Van Dam and Mr. Clark (14 Oct.)

FOGO, Capt. - Monday last his body was taken up near Eagle
Point (14 Oct.)

Indians in Phila. confirm purchase of lands lying upon
Susquehannah made by Col. Dongan (14 Oct.)

Ship Townshend, Thomas Thompson commander, will sail for
South Carolina; for freight or passage apply to Simon
Edgell in Phila. (14 Oct.)

GORDON, Robert, at New-Castle - gives notice of horses
left in his care (14 Oct.)

About 6 weeks ago some Cutaboes killed 2 Tuscorora Indians
to obtain the premium offered by the government of
South Carolina - Charlestown item of 3 July (21 Oct.)

Speech of Indian King Opayhatchoo to the Governor and
Council of South Carolina, with reference to building
of a fort by Mr. McCoy; robbery of the chief man of
the Cutaboes - Charlestown item of 10 July (21 Oct.)

BLAKELY, John - some weeks ago in Goose Creek Road knocked
down a pedlar and robbed him; later the pedlar pointed
out his assailant and Blakely is committed to goal -
Charlestown item of 10 July (21 Oct.)

WELSH, Mr., storekeeper at Wiltown - on 8 July his house
was accidentally blown up when 2 barrels of powder ignited and Welsh and a boy were killed - Charlestown item
of 17 July (21 Oct.)

A committee of both houses has been sent from South Carolina to Mr. Oglethorpe to treat with him on measures
to preserve the peace between both provinces; when they
reached Savannah they were received by Mr. Causton in
the absence of Mr. Oglethorpe; a petition was sent from

South Carolina to London by Capt. Baker - Charlestown items of 24 July, 7 and 14 Aug. (21 Oct.)

DONE, Elijah, a farmer of Bucks Co. - rode to Bristol and sent rum homewards to entertain people who were at his house helping in husking Indian corn; he then rode to Burlington where he rode over a cow, broke an arm, languished for 2 days and then died (21 Oct.)

GORDON, Alexander, master of the brigantine Diligence, now at Fishbourne's wharf - has the time of Scotch servant men to dispose of (21 Oct.)

PETTS, George, of Perkiomun - Saturday last found dead in his bed (28 Oct.)

EDDY, Ebenezer, servant, who lately came to Phila. in the brigantine John, Capt. Frazier, under the name of Matthew Bond, ship-carpenter by trade - runaway from Thomas Croasdale at Burlington (28 Oct.)

CHARD, Martin, English servant, weaver, who lately arrived from Bristol with Capt. Bromadge - runaway from William Watson of Phila., shipwright (28 Oct.)

PRITCHARD, Rees, of Whiteland, Chester Co. - offers 500 acres of land for sale (28 Oct.)

EVANS, Thomas, of Chester Co. - warns people not to take an assignment of the promissary note he gave to Samuel Bromadge, as he was deceived in the consideration for which the note was given (28 Oct.)

SHIPPEN, Joseph in Front St., Phila. - sells tea, coffee and sugar (28 Oct.)

FINNEY, George (son of George Finney of Wolverhampton), supposed to have been in this country about 7 years - will hear something to his advantage by applying to William Veer of Phila. (28 Oct.)

BORDEN, Joseph, of Tiverton - 14 days ago was accidentally killed by the pounder of a fulling mill - Rhode Island item of 15 Oct. (4 Nov.)

WILLSTON, Ichabod, of Little Compton - 11 Oct. accidentally killed at his cider mill when the uppermost great beam fell on his head (4 Nov.)

ENMAN, Mr., of Smithfield, R.I. - on 5 Oct. a large beam of his cider press fell on him and killed him (4 Nov.)

WAISCOAT, Mr., of Providence, R.I. - accidentally killed
Friday last when beam of his cider press fell on him -
Boston item of 18 Oct. (4 Nov.)

CLARKE, George - received commission appointing him Lt.-
Gov. of New York by Capt. Bryant who arrived 29 Oct.
(4 Nov.)

STENNARD, Joseph - on 18 Nov., the third day of the fair,
an ox will be roasted whole for the entertainment of
the country at his house in the Northern Liberties of
Phila. (4 Nov.)

LEONARD, John, Irish servant, tailor, who lived some time
with the Dutch tailor at Germantown - runaway from John
Croker of Phila. (4 Nov.)

House of late Philip Johns, dec'd, near the Swede's Church
at Wicaco, a pleasant walk from Phila. - is offered to
let; apply to Widow Johns, now living in the house, or
William Crossthwaite in Front St., Phila. (4 Nov.)

A woman seeks household work or to be employed as a nurse
- enquire at Capt. Norwood's in Phila. (4 Nov.)

Ship Tryal, William Grieves master, at Powel's wharf,
Phila. - will sail for London; for freight or passage
agree with Clement or William Plumstead or Samuel Powel
(11 Nov.)

HASSERT, Arent, living at Laetitia Court, Phila. - intends
to go to London and Holland (11 Nov.)

Plantation of 370 acres in Lancaster Co., about 60 miles
from Phila. and 2 miles from Town of Lancaster is offered for sale - enquire of James Logan at Stenton near
Germantown or of Edward Shippen in Phila. (11 Nov.)

WILKINSON, John, brushmaker in Second St., Phila., opposite to the Postoffice - will buy hogs' bristles if
brought to him or Thomas Shreeve of Burlington or
Thomas Hutton or William Atley, merchants in Trenton
(18 Nov.)

GRIFFITTS, Thomas in Phila. - sells Lisbon salt (18 Nov.)

EDWARDS, William, Welsh servant, age c. 35, who professes
to be a miller and a sailor - runaway from Nathanael
Grub, of Willistown, Chester Co. (18 Nov.)

SEMBLER, Sarah, English servant, age 25 - same as
above

CROSSTHWAITE, Capt. Thomas - arrived last week in Boston from St. Augustine and reports that disputes between the English at Georgia and Spanish at St. Augustine are accommodated by Mr. Oglethorpe and the Spanish governor - Boston item of 9 Nov. (25 Nov.)

Negro plot to destroy their masters on Antigua has been discovered (25 Nov.)

SMITH, Samuel, sheriff of Lancaster - one of 4 Pennsylvania men named by the Gov. of Maryland to be arrested; a reward of 100 pounds per head is offered (25 Nov.)

BASDON, William, over against the Coffee House in Front St., Phila. - offers for sale a Negro woman and a boy (25 Nov.)

HAVERD, Elizabeth (daughter of William Haverd, of Twp. of Merion, Phila. Co.; who clandestinely made a bill of sale to his brother John Haverd of the Twp. of Haverford, Chester Co., of a young Negro named Tom, belonging to Capt. George Roche of Antigua, and left the Negro with Elizabeth his daughter) - gives notice that she has no power to sell the Negro and no one should try to purchase him (2 Dec.)

GOODWIN, John, shopkeeper, who formerly lived in Chesnut St. - is removed into Front St., Phila., next door to Messrs. Willing and Shippen, at the Sign of the Sugar-Loaf (2 Dec.)

Improvements, implements and utensils of the brew-house in Water St., Phila., now directed by William Cundell, adjoining the Sun Tavern - to be sold at auction; Patrick Baird is vendue-master (2 Dec.)

Ship _Charming Nancy_, John Steadman master - will sail for London; for freight or passage apply to said master at Fishbourn's store in Water St., Phila. (2 Dec.)

WHARTON, Joseph - sells sack at 8s. per gallon (2 Dec.)

Sugar is sold by Peter Delage at house of John Dillwin at upper send of Second St., Phila. (2 Dec.)

Among leaders of a Negro plot at Antigua the following were executied: Mr. Kerby's Court, Tho. Hanson, Jr.'s Tomboy and John Christopher's Hercules (all 3 racked to death in the market place), Mrs. Lodg's Fortune (a fidler), Phillip Darby's Jack, Thomas Steven's Frank and Anth. Garret's Venture (a carpenter) (all 4 burnt alive in the pasture of Major Otter's) - extract of a letter from a gentleman in Antigua to a friend in Boston, dated 18 Oct. 1736 (9 Dec.)

Details of Negro plot on Antigua: Tomboy (Negro of Thomas Hanston), Hercules (Negro of John Christophers) were to plant gunpowder in Mr. Christopher Dunbar's new house and blow it up; at the same time King Court, Tomboy and Hercules were to head a party of 400 men each, one from the east end of town, one from Otter's pasture and one from Morgan's pasture; all whites were to be slain; King Court on 20 Oct. was broken on the wheel, as were Tomboy and Hercules later, while 4 other Negroes were burnt alive - extract from St. John's, Antigua, dated 24 Oct. 1736 (9 Dec.)

POLUCK, Johannes, servant, born in Switzerland, age $\underline{c}$. 20, who came over from Holland in the brigantine <u>Prince Frederick</u>, Joseph Willson, master, to New York about middle of Sept. - runaway from Mathew Clarkson in New York; reward will be paid if servant is put in goal and notice is given to Arent Hassert in Phila., Gerardus De Peyster at New Brunswick or Mathew Clarkson in New York (9 Dec.)

WILLIAMS, Thomas - sells cloth at his store of Fishbourn's wharf, Phila. (9 Dec.)

Negotiations between Mr. Oglethorpe and Don Antonio de Arredondo (the Spanish Commissary); after departure of the Spaniard, when Mr. Oglethorpe was at Darien, Capt. Macpherson arrived with a drove of cattle brought over-land from South Carolina - item from Frederica, Ga., 20 Sept. (16 Dec.)

Haircloth and hairlines are made by Widow Rakestraw at upper end of Front St., Phila.; she has 2 large rooms with fireplaces to let (16 Dec.)

Observations on the reasons given by Mr. Hamilton's ad-visers for his detaining the seals of the Province of New Jersey after the demand made of them by Lewis Morris, Esq., President of the Council and Commander in Chief of the Province of New Jersey; mentioned are Gov. Montgomerie, Lord Cornbury, Mr. Hunter, Col. Pin-horn, Col. Dudley, Col. Slaughter, Earl of Bellomont, Lt.-Gov. Nanfan, Col. Smith (30 Dec. 1736 and 6 Jan. 1737)

WILLER, Peter Michael, Dutch boy aged $\underline{c}$. 7 - Thursday last his dead body was found in the woods near Schuylkill (30 Dec.)

HOPKINSON, Thomas, in Chesnut St., Phila. - sells coffee
(30 Dec.)

PARSONS, William, in Second St., Phila. - sells canary wine
(30 Dec.)

1737

McQUATTY, David, Scotch servant, hammerman and refiner, who
formerly followed shalloping up and down the bay to Egg
Harbour - runaway from Samuel Nutt, of French Creek Iron
Works, Chester Co. (6 Jan.)

SCULL, Joseph, of Phila. - offers to sell or let a 10-acre
pasture on Passyunk Road, adjoining the land of William
Tidmarsh, about 1 mile from Phila. (6 Jan.)

INGLIS, John, at his house below the Drawbridge in Front
St., Phila. - sells cloth, pewter, wine, rum, sugar (6
Jan.)

BRADBURY, Thomas, English convict servant - runaway from
James Baxter at the Principio Iron Work in Maryland (6
Jan.)

CRONE, Nicholas, of Phila. - offers reward for recovery of
horse strayed or stolen from the Commons near Phila.
(6 Jan.)

/The Drinkers Dictionary/- (13 Jan.)

CHAUNCEY, Rev., Minister of Hadley, Mass., son of - something more than a week ago - died when an outhouse was
consumed by fire - Boston item of 9 Dec. 1736 (13 Jan.)

HOW, Mark, of Ipswich, Mass. - some days ago buried his
eighth child dead of the throat distemper - Boston item
of 9 Dec. (13 Jan.)

ABBOT, John, of Ipswich, Mass., neighbor of Mark How - has
lately buried 8 children, soon after which Mr. Abbot's
father, aged c. 90, died of the distemper - Boston item
of 9 Dec. 1736 (13 Jan.)

BEAN, Capt. - arrived at beginning of this week at Boston
from Antigua, but last from Coracoa; Spaniards took
Bean on the passage, shot his mate dead and took his
ship to Porto Rico, where, after 6 days, he was released - Boston item of 9 Dec. 1736 (13 Jan.)

READ, Charles, of Phila., several times mayor and sheriff

of Phila. and a representative for Phila. Co., Judge of
the Vice Admiralty, member of Council, a commissioner
of the loan office, all in Pennsylvania, and likewise
Collector of the Port of Burlington in New Jersey - died
Thursday last in Phila. in his 51st year (13 Jan.)

WILLIAMS, Capt., of Salem, Mass. - Tuesday last sen'night
was drowned off Cape Ann - Boston item of 16 Dec. 1736
(20 Jan.)

COLMAN, Rev. Dr. - Friday last preached sermon for day of
fasting and prayer in Massachusetts - Boston item of
16 Dec. 1736 (20 Jan.)

EBRING, Isaac, of New York - Saturday last a lad belonging
to him fell from a wagon and had bones broken when
wheels passed over his legs - New York item of 20 Dec.
1736 (20 Jan.)

SMITH, Thomas, of New York - Saturday last, when driving a
cart along a street in Smiths Fly, was dashed against a
porch, his scull was fractured and he died 19 Dec. -
New York item of 20 Dec. 1736 (20 Jan.)

GRAEME, William, who lived in the northern liberties of
Phila. - on 19 Jan. was found frozen dead in the road
to Frankford, about 2 miles from Phila. (20 Jan.)

LINDSEY, Capt., in ship **St. George,** arrived from London at
the Capes - cannot come up because of the ice (20 Jan.)

Pamphlets lately printed in London - are to be sold by
Martin Jervas, 3 doors below the Post Office in Second
St., Phila., or by Miles Strickland in Market St. (20
Jan.)

TREAT, Rev. - lately persuaded a number of Moheags and some
that belonged to Farmington and Middletown to withdraw
from an Indian dance and frolic at Middletown, Conn. -
Boston item of 23 Dec. 1736 (27 Jan.)

MATTAWAN, John, a Christian Indian youth at Farmington,
Conn., upon the advice of Gov. Tallcott at Hartford,
went with other young Indians to a gathering of Indians
from New Milford, Patatuk, and other places and abated
their drunken frolic - Boston item of 23 Dec. 1736 (27
Jan.)

DEWING, Nathanael, living in south part of Weston, Mass. -
at beginning of December 1736 lost 4 children of the
distemper - Boston item of 23 Dec. 1736 (27 Jan.)

AYRES, Joseph - Tuesday evening last in Bucks Co. was frozen to death on the road (29 Jan.)

HIGINBOTHAM, Charles, of Baltimore Co. - sends letter dated 4 Jan. 1737 to John Ross of Lancaster Co., and Ross sends a reply dated Lancaster Co., 11 Jan. 1737. The problem is one of the boundaries between Maryland and Pennsylvania and violence in the dispute, such as the burning down of Capt. Creasap's house; among persons mentioned are Lord Baltimore, Mr. Penn, Sheriff Samuel Smith, Mr. Charlton, Messers Lee and Lugg (Lugg defendant), Knolls Daunt (murdered by Creasap), Col. Rigby, Laughlan Maloan (one of Creasap's men), Michael Rysner (one of Creasap's men), Mr. Fitzgerald (3 Feb.)

GREY, Joseph - water Sunday last was near 6 feet high on the ground floor of his house at Middle Ferry when the ice in the Schuylkill broke up (3 Feb.)

SHERRARD, Francis and Alexander Percy, attornies-at-law in Phila. - were drowned Sunday last when trying to ford Brandywine Creek (3 Feb.)

A new Congregational Church was gathered in the westerly part of Boston on afternoon of Monday last. Rev. Mr. Prince was the moderator; Mr. Foxcroft made the closing prayer - Boston item of 10 Jan. (17 Feb.)

VASSEL, Leonard, of Boston - Wednesday night last his house in Summer St. caught fire through carelessness of a Negro servant - Boston item of 10 Jan. (17 Feb.)

Persons indebted to estate of Gasper Stoneburner, late of Phila., shopkeeper, dec'd, are to make payments to Gaspar Wistar of Phila. or Frederick Ox of Germantown (17 Feb.)

DAVIES, Capt. - arrived Tuesday last at New York from Antigua; he reported 60 Negroes had been executed for their conspiracy and revolt and 9 were executed during his stay; the day Capt. Davies departed from Antigua about 40 Negroes were confined on Capt. Sutlif's vessel for want of prison-room - New York item of 7 Feb. (23 Feb.)

BODIN, Capt. - arrived Friday last at New York in 6 weeks from Lisbon - New York item of 7 Feb. (23 Feb.)

Plantation in Bristol Twp., Phila. Co., bounding on Tacony Creek, about 6 miles from Phila. - offered for sale by James Dilworth (23 Feb.)

It is reported from Middlesex Co. that smallpox was caught
by a slave of Christopher Robinson's family when the
slave had run away and was confined in Phila. goal; when
he was brought home, he died of the disease and it
spread to the family and to still others - Williamsburg
item of 7 Jan. (3 Mar.)

EMLEN, Samuel, near the Market in Phila. - sells Dr. Bateman's Pectoral Drops, English bitters and Dr. Godfrey's
cordials just imported in Capt. Lindsey from London
(3 Mar.)

LOGAN, James, President, and the Council of Pennsylvania -
issues a proclamation forbidding providing any supplies
to the Spaniards, since Lt.-Gov. Thomas Broughton of
South Carolina reports he has received advice from Commodore Dent at Jamaica that the Spaniards at Havana are
preparing to send ships and troops to St. Augustine to
attack Georgia and South Carolina; R. Charles, Secr.,
signed the proclamation (10 Mar.)

BRIAN, Mr., carpenter of Charlestown, the wife of - coming
home 1 Jan. she had a fit, fell into the fire and was
burnt to death - Charlestown item of 1 Jan. (10 Mar.)

WILLIAMS, Mr., a tailor in St. John's Parish, S.C. - because he was unhappy with his wife, shot himself through
the head - Charlestown item of 1 Jan. (10 Mar.)

H.M. sloop Drake, Capt. Fox commander, dispatched by Commodore Dent from Jamaica - arrived Thursday at Charlestown
- Charlestown item of 5 Feb. (10 Mar.)

Saturday last an act was ratified empowering Lt.-Gov.
Thomas Broughton to embargo ships from sailing and to
impress ship, men, ammunition, etc. - Charlestown item
of 12 Feb. (10 Mar.)

Tuesday last a bounty offered in South Carolina to anyone
who enlist under Col. Hext to go to Port Royal; 25
Switzers, lately arrived with Col. Dunbarr, enlisted,
who, with 25 men more under Lt. Chevillette are going
to embark for Port Royal - Charlestown item of 12 Feb.
(10 Mar.)

Saturday last arrived at Charlestown the Baltick Merchant,
Capt. Mackenzie from Bristol in 32 days - item from
South-Carolina Gazette of 19 Feb. (10 Mar.)

Saturday last an act for establishing and regulating pa-
trols was passed in South Carolina - Charlestown item
of 19 Feb. (10 Mar.)

EVERETT, Capt., who arrived at Boston about 12 days ago -
saw a brigantine lying upon her side - Boston item of
7 Feb. (10 Mar.)

Account of Negro plot on Antigua; leaders were Court, _alias_
Tackey, Caromantee slave of Thomas Kersby, and Tomboy,
a Creole, born in Antigua, master carpenter, belonging
to Thomas Hanson; Court was brought to Antigua as a
slave about 10 years ago and was executed when about 45;
other principals who joined them were Hercules (slave
of John Christophers), Jack and Scipio (slaves of Philip
Darby), Ned (slave of Col. Jacob Morgan), Fortune (slave
of Mrs. Johanna Lodge) and Toney (slave of Col. Samuel
Martin), all Creoles, except Fortune; the most active
incendiaries under Tomboy were Freeman's Secundi and Sir
William Codrington's Jaco, both Creoles; Martin's Jemmy,
being made drunk at Treblin's, took oath as one of the
conspirators; Court held a show and dance 3 Oct. at Mrs.
Dunbar Parke's pasture; Court had no umbrella, since
Emanuel (faithful slave of Mr. Gregory) had refused to
make it; Court's officials were as follows: Hawe's
Gift was his brassoo, Gregory's Ammoo his marshal,
Gregory's Quashee his asseng; Tomboy, Hercules, Fortune
and Darby's Jack were his generals; the plot was discovered by a magistrate much owing to the confessions
of Emanuel, Robin (Coromantee slave of Col. John Gun-
thorp) and Cuffee (Coromantee slave of Walter Nugent);
said Cuffee overheard an important conversation at Mr.
Kerby's back door; further evidence came from Philida
(sister of Tomboy) and her brother Jemmy, who both told
of meetings by night at house of Tremblin (slave of Samuel Morgan); other slaves admitted as evidence were
Langford's Billy, Col. Martin's Jemmy, Lynch's Tom, Mr.
Stephen's Dick, Major Martin's Quamino and Col. Fry's
Quomino; oath of the conspirators was administered at
the following places: the grave near the point, at
Treblin's house, at Secundi's house, at the house of
John Sabby, at his master Mr. Pace's plantation, at a
great feast at Mr. French's estate, at the house of
Langford's Billy, at Targate's house and at Mr. Lind-
sey's; Seeundi had called to his assistance a Negro
Obia man or wizzard; some conspiators were executed and
others banished (17 Mar.)

This week arrived in York River the ship _Burwell_, Capt.
Waff, the ship _John_, Capt. Seabrooke and the ship _Timo-
thy and Jacob_, Capt. Belcher, and in James River a ship
commanded by Capt. Wigg, all from London; Capt. Seabrooke reports he saw a yacht founder, in which were
Mr. Walpole's servants and baggage - Williamsburg item
of 11 Feb. (17 Mar.)

Last night arrived at York the ship <u>Gooch</u>, Capt. William
   Harding from London; he saw 2 ships go into James
   River, one of them the <u>Mary</u>, Capt. Stephen Read from
   London - Williamburg item of 18 Feb. (17 Mar.)

PRICHARD, Rees - offers for sale 300-acre plantation, on
   which he lives, in the Great Valley, Chester Co. (17 Mar.)

MORRIS, Anthony in Water St., Phila. - sells pitch and tar
   (17 Mar.)

SHIPPEN, William, chemist, at the Sign of the Paracelsus-
   Head in Market St., Phila. - sells medicines, tar,
   spices, tea, sugar (17 Mar.)

Plantation of 155 acres in Lower Merion, about 10 miles
   from Phila. - enquire of Rees Lloyd, carpenter, in Phila.
   (17 Mar.)

Remainder of report on Negro plot in Antigua: 2 slaves
   have fled from justice, Davy (a driver, belonging to the
   estate of Col. George Thomas) and Old Tom (a Coromantee
   driver, belonging to the estate of the late Edward
   Byam, dec'd; a person called Mullatto Jack claims he
   was free born in Ireland, stolen from there 15 or 16
   years since and sold as a slave in Antigua, an account
   which seems correct; a free Negro named John Corteen
   and a free Mullatto called Tom were released, being free,
   but they are too dangerous to remain in Antigua; it is
   suggested the following informers be rewarded: Cuffee
   (slave of Major Walter Nugent), Robin (slave of Col. John
   Gunthorpe), Emanuel (slave of Edward Gregory) and Philida (slave of Thomas Hansen); the following constables
   should be rewarded: James Hanson, John Bolen, Gustavus
   Christian, John Libert, Hugh Shewcraft, Mr. Davison and
   Richard Jackson; the report, dated Antigua 30 Dec. 1736,
   is signed by John Vernon, Ashton Warner, Nath. Gilbert
   and Robert Arbuthnot; there follows the list of slaves
   executed for the late conspiracy: Kerby's Court, Hanson's Tomboy, Christopher's Hercules, Lodge's Fortune,
   Darby's Jack, Stephen's Frank, Hodge's Cudjo, John
   Harve's Gift, Gregory's Quashy, Garret's Venture, Mor-
   gan's Green, Tudway's Littlee Cuffee, Hoskin's Quashy,
   Morgan's Nedd, Gamble's Coley, Jos. Martin's Charles,
   Morgan's Jack, Codrington's Jacko, Codrington's Glode,
   F. Freeman's Secundi, Painter's Anthony, Dunbar's Tan-
   gaw, Col. Martin's Toney, Col. Thomas's Geoffrey, Tom-
   linson's Cuffee, Tomlinson's Billy, Redwood's Oliver,
   Redwood's Scipio, Col. Martin's Scipio, Ned Otto's
   Colon, Ned Otto's Jean, Nevil's Bristol, Rodeney's Nel-
   sen, Kerby's Quacoo, Wyne's Samson, Goble's Billy,
   Goble's Oliver, Capt. Byam's Cudjo, Sydeserfe's Sabby,

Freeman's Natty, Yeoman's Quashy Cooms, Wickham's Primus, Darby's Scipio, Minahan's Only, Chester's Frank; the following fled from justice: the late Mr. Byam's Old Tom, Col. Thomas's Davy; free Negroes in prison for the conspiracy: John Corteen, Mullatto Tom, Mullatto Jack, Free Simon; list of slaves proposed to be banished: Morgan's Newport, Skerit's Billy, Langford's Robin, Boudinot's Dick, Tomlinson's Barry-Man, Lavington's Samson, Monk's Minger, Byam's Quaw, Sydeserfe's Robin, Goble's English Dick, Douglasses' little Dick, Ned Otto's Tom, Roach's Talgate, Hanson's Quash, Rodney's Ned Chester, Col. Thomas's Crumwell, Col. Cockran's Prince, Col. Cockran's Jack, Col. Fry's Phillip, Goble's London, Elmes's sen. Jack, Elmes's jun. Quamina, Osborn's Cobbino, Delap's Tom, Delap's Robin, Standrett's Babtist, Sanderson's Toney, Pare's Quacoo, Pare's Cesar, Pare's John Sabby, jun., Pare's Digo, F. Freeman's Troulus, R. Ash's jun. George, R. Ash's, jun. Okao, Wm. Hunt's Quacoo, Wm. Hunt's Cuffee, Lutton's Tom, P. Brown's Primus, Monk's Natty, Lynche's Delamoure, Lindsey's Quash, Codrington's Sacky, Godsell's Charles; witnesses to be sent off: Morgan's Trebling, Martin's Jemmy, Jos. Martin's Quamina, Lynche's Tom, Col. Fry's Quamina, Langford's Billy, Stephens's Dick; Robert Arbuthnot, Esq., is to be praised for his strict orders to peace officers and, as a magistrate of St. John's, for his severe punishment of delinquents; the report, dated Antigua, 30 Dec. 1736, is signed by John Vernon, Ashton Warner, Nath. Gilbert (17 and 24 Mar.)

Meteor observed in the sky last Saturday sen-ninght - Boston item of 7 Feb. (24 Mar.)

Piéce of land below Armstrong Smith's on Delaware River (lately belonging to Swan Bankson) is to be let - apply to Ebenezer Tomlinson, carpenter, in Water St., Phila. (24 Mar.)

Geese feathers are for sale at house of John Boyd at upper end of Market St., Phila. (24 Mar.)

SCATTERGOOD, S., Clerk of the Council of Proprietors of the Western Division of New Jersey - directs that persons that have rights to take up a fifth dividend of land meet the council at the house of William Bickley in Burlington (24 Mar.)

Sloop Two Brothers, Gabriel Wayne master - will sail for South Carolina and Cape Fear; for freight or passage apply to the master at his house in Fourth St., Phila., or with Rees Lloyd (24 Mar.)

WILLIAMS, Ennion, of Bristol, Bucks Co. - his bakehouse
lately burned down because of defect in the oven (7
Apr.)

ASHETON, Ralph - Sunday last his house on Schuylkil
burned down (7 Apr.)

Negro man and Negro girl, age c. 5, are for sale - enquire
at house of Widow Vangiezel in Water St., New-Castle
(7 Apr.)

HUTCHINSON, James, who lately lived at Whiteclay Creek -
has removed to Willingtown; he will transport goods between that place and Phila. or from Phila. to Willingtown (7 Apr.)

MALLABE, Thomas, staymaker from London, now living at the
Sign of the Stays and Child's Coat, over against the
Post Office in Second St., Phila. - makes stays and
coats, backboards and collars (7 Apr.)

MEGEE, George, nailer, opposite to the Bank Meeting-House
in Front St., Phila. - makes and sells nails, wholesale
or retail (7 Apr.)

SWEAT, Benjamin, of Truro - last Saturday night his house
was consumed by fire; he escaped with wife and children, all unharmed - New England item of 25 Feb. (14
Apr.)

Farm house at Woodstock (belonging to Col. Chandler of
Worcester, the same in which he formerly lived) - a
few days ago burned to the ground; the woman of the
house escaped but her child and a Negro were burnt to
death - Boston item of 21 Mar. (14 Apr.)

WADSWORTH, Rev. Benjamin, aged President of Harvard College - died Thursday last at Cambridge - Boston item of
21 Mar. (14 Apr.)

Saturday last a lad in Mr. Lee's shipyard in North part of
Boston was killed by a spar which fell on him - Boston
item of 21 Mar. (14 Apr.)

At Northampton on 13 Mar. the front gallery of the Meeting-
house collapsed and many persons were injured - Boston
item of 21 Mar. (14 Apr.)

PORTER, Capt. - arrived yesterday at Boston from Barbados
in 35 days - brought news of a Guinea ship that sank at
sea - Boston item of 21 Mar. (14 Apr.)

SOAPER, Capt., who arrived at Boston last week from North Carolina - informed that on his voyage to North Carolina he rescued Capt. Ebenezer Welch, his mate and 4 men in a Moses boat about 6 leagues east of Cape Hatteras; their sloop, bound from Maryland to Antigua, sank about 6 days before - Boston item of 21 Mar. (14 Apr.)

WARREN, Capt., commander of H.M.S. Squirrel at Boston - intends to join warship at New York, commanded by Capt. Norris, in order to proceed to South Carolina and Georgia to protect those places from the Spaniards - Boston item of 28 Mar. (14 Apr.)

ALLEN, Alice, age c. 11 (daughter of Ralph Allen of Portsmouth) - Monday last was found dead in the well of John Easton in Newport, R.I.; it was discovered that a Mulatto woman had murdered the child - Newport item of 31 Mar. (14 Apr.)

McGRAGH, John, servant, country born, age c. 24 - runaway from William Rumsey of Cecil Co., Md. (14 Apr.)

HENDERSON, Samuel, Irish servant, tailor, age c. 20 - runaway from James Bennet of Aston, Chester Co. (14 Apr.)

Ship Catherine, Capt. Farmer, arrived 12 Apr. in New York from London (21 Apr.)

Ship Carolina, Capt. Gill, arrived at New York 13 Apr. from London (21 Apr.)

WILLIAMS, Moses, servant (his father was an Indian and his mother a white woman) - runaway from Mary Wilson in Queen Ann's Co., near Choptank River (21 Apr.)

BENNET, John, West Country servant, butcher, age c. 25 - runaway from Mary Wilson in Queen Ann's Co., near Choptank River; reward for capture of Williams or Bennet will be paid by Mary Wilson or Thomas Dunning, innkeeper in Phila. (21 Apr.)

CUFF, Widow, dec'd - persons with demands on her estate are to apply to the administrators, Thomas Holland and James Bingham (21 Apr.)

TRESSE, Thomas - is removed from High St. to his house in Front St., next door to the Sign of the Boot and Shoes; he sells rum, sugar, molasses, salt, rice, oils and English goods (21 Apr.)

Yesterday arrived at Boston Capt. Long from Portsmouth and Capt. Orrick from Bristol in passage of 7 weeks -

Boston item of 17 Apr. (28 Apr.)

CORNEY, Capt. - arrived at Boston last night from London,
    which he left 23 Feb. - Boston item of 17 Apr. (28 Apr.)

BIGGER, Peacock, brazier, in Market St., Phila., near the
    Sign of the Indian King - sells copper ware (5 May)

Ship <u>Dragon</u>, Charles Hargrave master, lying at Arch St.
    wharf in Phila. - will sail for Jamaica; for freight or
    passage apply to the master or Simon Edgel in Market
    St. (5 May)

RICHARDSON, Francis, goldsmith, in Market St., Phila. -
    sells clocks, brass jacks, handles and escutchions,
    tea-table bolts and desk hinges (5 May)

Reward offered for return of a quart silver tankard,
    marked I.^{R}·E. and the maker's mark CLR, stolen from the
    house of Lawrence Reynolds, tanner, in Chesnut St.,
    Phila. (5 May)

HANEY, Thomas, Irish servant, age <u>c</u>. 18 - runaway from
    Joseph Durborow, shipwright (5 May)

Snow <u>Prince</u> <u>of</u> <u>Orange</u>, William Devonshire master, now at
    Fishbourn's wharf - will sail for Bristol; for freight
    or passage agree with William Hellier or the master
    (12 May)

VALENTINE, John, in William Fishbourn's store in Water St.
    - sells goods just imported from England (12 May)

HULINGS, Michael, shipwright, at upper end of Front St.,
    Phila. - offers reward for recovery of mare, strayed
    or stolen from the Common (12 May)

CHEW, Dr. Samuel - persons indebted to him are to make
    payment to his attorney, Thomas Hopkinson in Chesnut
    St., Phila. (12 May)

Cattle to be sold at auction at Carpenter's Island by or-
    der of Joseph Richards and John Inglis, administrators
    (12 May)

THOMAS, Col., of Antigua - private letters from London
    mention his appointment as Governor of this province
    (19 Mary)

At Court of Oyer and Terminer for Phila. Co. on Friday
    last 3 persons were sentenced to death: Henry Wildman
    for burglary, Isaac Brandford for robbery and Catherine

Connor for burglary (19 May)

BROWNE, Dr. John, surgeon - died 11 May in Burlington Co. of a stoppage of his urine (19 May)

New house near Dr. Francis Naff's in Germantown - offered for sale by Theobald Endt, sadler in Germantown (19 May)

BAGG, Thomas, Irish servant, age c. 30 --runaway from Blakeston Ingledew, of Phila., butcher (19 May)

Negro man, age 22, is for sale - enquire of Henry Lewis in Haverford, Chester Co., or Joseph Grey at the Middle Ferry on Schuylkill (19 May)

STRETCH, Peter, watchmaker in Phila. - offers reward for recovery of a stolen watch, made by Stroud of London (19 May)

Parcel of young servants, just imported in ship Mary and Hannah, Henry Savage master, from London - offered for sale; apply to the master on board the ship lying off Market St., Phila., or John Reynell in Front St. (19 May)

BARBER, Elizabeth, alias Rugstone, alias Burroughs, English servant, age c. 21 - runaway from Thomas Godfrey, of Phila., glazier (19 May)

FORBUSH, William, servant, shoemaker, age c. 20 - runaway from Micajah How of Burlington (19 May)

Plantation of 460 acres in Chesterfield Twp., Burlington Co., West New Jersey, is for sale - apply to Daniel Bacon who lives thereon (26 May)

Auction of cloth, hats, etc., will be held at store apposite to Reese Meredith's in Water St. (26 May)

HOGG, Capt. - arrived at Phila. Sunday night from Barbados with news that the Spaniards had taken the Bay of Honduras and all vessels there, including the ship Harle, Capt. Ralph Harle; the captain and both mates were killed (2 June)

Ship Lancashire, Capt. Corbin master, at Powel's wharf, Phila. - caught fire Monday last but blaze was quickly extinguished (2 June)

FARRA, Capt. - arrived Monday last at Phila. - on voyage from Jamaica he had been castaway at Palachee Bay within Cape Florida; Indians and Spaniards helped to get him to St. Augustine, where Capt. Farra hired a Rhode Island sloop and came to Phila. (2 June)

GRIEVES, Capt. - arrived 1 June at Phila. from London (2 June)

Plantation, late in possession of Samuel Lukens, dec'd, in Bristol Twp., Phila. Co., about 7 or 8 miles from Phila., is for sale - apply to Morris Morris or Benjamin Lay of Abington or to the printer (2 June)

MORRIS, Anthony, of Phila. - offers reward for recovery of mare strayed or stolen from the Common (2 June)

NICHOLS, Widow, in Third St., Phila. - offers for sale 2 carts and horses (2 June)

CLARK, Joseph, baker in Second St., Phila. - plans to leave the province by 1 Aug. (2 June)

H.M.S. Sea-Horse, Capt. Compton, arrived at Charlestown Wednesday last from Virginia and Capt. Norris and Capt. Warren are daily expected from New York and Boston - Charlestown item of 23 Apr. (9 June)

On 2 June Garrit Van Horn, James Alexander, John Walter and John Johnson were chosen to serve in the General Assembly of New York - New York item of 6 June (9 June)

Candidates and votes received at Jamaica, Queens Co., N.Y., on 2 June were as follows: Col. Isaac Hicks (432), David Jones, Esq. (390), Capt. Benjamin Hicks (342) and Thomas Alsop, Esq. (217); the first 2 were elected - New York item of 6 June (9 June)

Representatives chosen for Suffolk Co., N.Y., were Major Ebenetus Platt and Mr. Pierson - New York item of 6 June (9 June)

BOYD, John, in Market St., Phila. - has to let a house in Market St., convenient for shopkeeper, merchant or innkeeper (9 June)

GRACE, Robert, of Phila., merchant - desires accounts to be settled with him; he has to let the house in which Mr. Tresse lately dwelt, with the stores next the alley (9 June)

MORGAN, John, a Pembrokeshire servant, age c. 24 - runaway from Owen Evans of North Wales, Phila. Co. (9 June)

Brick granary or storehouse in Borough of Chester is for

sale - apply to George Ashbridge in Chester (9 June)

BOLTON, Robert, shopkeeper in Phila. - desires to settle accounts as he plans to leave the province (9 June)

DROUGHERTY, John, Irish servant - Monday last fell out of a boat into the river and was drowned (16 June)

Monday night some persons pretending to be free Masons, under pretence of making a young man a Mason, so injured him that he died; in behalf of all members of St. John's Lodge at Phila., Thomas Hopkinson, Will. Plumsted, Joseph Pratt and Henry Pratt signed a statement disclaiming any connection with the affair (16 June)

HAMILTON, A., offers reward for detection of counterfeiters of Pennsylvania 5 shillings bills; an Irishman (just arrived at Phila. from New England, who claims he came from Ireland August last) was taken up with some of the counterfeits which are signed John Parry, Abraham Chapman, Edward Horne and Thomas Tresse (16 June)

DAVID, John, of Kent Co. on Delaware Bay - his wife has eloped from him (16 June)

SOMERS, Timothy, Irish servant, age c. 27 - runwaway from William Watson of Phila., shipwright (16 June)

RICHARDSON, John (son of John Richardson, of New-Castle Co., Esq.) - Saturday last at the raising of a house at Willington was so injured when a piece of timber fell on him that he died within half an hour (23 June)

Brigantine Bristol Hope, Capt. Arthur Tough, bound to Phila. from Antigua - last week struck a shoal called the Crossledge in coming up the bay and is lot; men and part of the cargo were saved (23 June)

BLAKE, Mark, who has been a bricklayer's labourer for several years - Saturday last his body was found hanging from a tree a small distance from Phila. (23 June)

Ship Mary and Hannah, Henry Savage master - will sail for London; for freight or passage apply to the master at Clymer's wharf or to John Reynell in Front St. (23 June)

LOYD, Thomas, Welsh servant, age c. 22, who pretends to be a sailor - runaway from Philip Thomas of Vincent Twp., Chester Co. (23 June)

BROWN, John - offers for sale a case of drawers and chamber table (23 June)

GROWDON, Joseph, late of Bucks Co., gentl., dec'd - demands on estate to be presented to his son, Joseph Growdon, administrator (23 June)

HEWES, Moses, in Chesnut St., Phila. - sells canary (23 June)

CHACE, Thomas, of Phila., dec'd - accounts with estate to be settled with John Leacock, of Phila. (surviving executor) or Jonathan Beere of Phila. (23 June)

Friday last at the Indian King in Phila. the Grand Lodge chose William Plumstead Grand Master of Pennsylvania; he appointed Joseph Shippen, Jr., deputy; Henry Pratt and Philip Syng were chosen Grand Wardens (30 June)

ESDAILE, James, at Mr. Dering's in Front St., or at his store on Carpenter's wharf, Phila. - offers for sale a young Negro (30 June)

ROULT, James, Irish servant, age c. 15, who pretends to be a linen-weaver - runaway from David Davis of Goshen, Chester Co. (30 June)

General Court of Massachusetts has granted 200 pounds to the Rev. Mr. Holyoke for his support this year as President of Harvard College and 140 pounds to be paid to the Society in Marblehead to which he now stands in a pastoral relation (7 July)

WILDMAN, Henry, a Shropshire man, age 53, nailor by trade - was executed Saturday last at Phila. for burglary (7 July)

SMITH, Catherine, alias Connor (formerly transported from Ireland to Virginia) - was executed Saturday last at Phila. for burglary; she left a small child (7 July)

BRANDFORD, Mr., who had been condemned for robbery - was reprieved (7 July)

BEVEN, Thomas (who had been transported from England to Maryland) - was executed Saturday last at Chester for firing and robbing a house (7 July)

WOOLLEY, Edmund - offers reward for recovery of a horse (bred and sold by Thomas Miller at Crosswicks and sold to Nathaniel Wilkinson of Burlington and then sold by Wilkinson to Woolley) that strayed or was stolen from the Commons at the upper end of Phila. (7 July)

Enquire at Mrs. Connolly's in Water St., Phila. - to buy

a Negro wench, Creole born, age 18 (7 July)

EDGELL, Simon, of Phila. - intends to depart from Pennsylvania in ship <u>Constantine</u>, Edward Wright commander, so
desires to settle accounts (7 July)

M'QUATTY, David, Scotch servant, hammerman and refiner -
runaway from Samuel Nutt at the French Creek Iron Works,
Chester Co. (7 July)

BROWN, Michael, silk-dyer from London - continues to live
next door to Joshua Emlen, tanner, in Chesnut St.,
Phila. (7 July)

ELLIS, Robert, in Water St., Phila. - has for sale Negroes
just imported in the snow <u>Martha</u>, Cornelius Kollock
master (7 July)

Ship <u>Lancashire Gally</u>, Angel Corbin master, now at Samuel
Powell's wharf in Phila. - will sail for London; for
freight or passage agree with the master or Michael
Aspden in Market St. (7 July)

CREIGHTON, John, servant, age <u>c</u>. 25, by trade a penknife
haft-maker, who served his time at Sheffield and has
been a soldier - runaway from Benjamin Paschall, of
Phila., cutler (7 July)

DUCHE, Anthony, at upper end of Chesnut St., Phila., near
the State-House, offers for sale a house and lot and
utensils belonging to the potter's business (7 July)

Ship <u>Neptune</u>, Capt. Andrew Sim master, of Phila., bound
from Phila. to Newfoundland - in the night ran ashore
at Liscomb's Harbor, about 20 leagues west of Canso -
Salem report, Boston item of 4 July (14 July)

Still-house of Messers Bayard and Co. in New York - was in
danger when a hogshead caught fire Thursday last but
the blaze was promptly extinguished - New York item of
4 July (14 July)

BIRMINGHAM, James, distiller, of Merion - died there Friday last (14 July)

BUTLER, Michael, belonging to the brigantine <u>Hampshire</u> -
Saturday last fell overboard into the river and was
drowned (14 July)

Lease (13½ years) of a lot in Market St., just below the
prison in Phila., with a wheelwright's shop, for sale -
enquire of Samuel Langley, wheelwright, living on the

premises (14 July)

Brigantine <u>Debby</u>, George Stewart master, now at Anthony
Morris's wharf - will sail for South Carolina; for
freight and passage agree with the master on board or
with Anthony Morris in Water St., Phila. (14 July)

MAC KILRONAN, Matthew (born in Co. of Cavan in Parish of
Templefort, near Belterfort in Ireland), weaver, who
has been in this country about 3 years - if he applies
to John Clifton, weaver, in Third St., Phila., he will
hear something to his advantage sent him from his sister in Ireland (14 July)

Persons who borrowed books from Charles Read, Esq., dec'd,
are asked to return them (14 July)

BOND, Thomas, who shortly intends a voyage to sea - wishes
to settle accounts; he may be met with at the corner of
Market St., in Phila., opposite to Charles Read's house,
where he has removed his shop (14 July)

THOMPSON, John, an aged man, living in Salem, N.J. - 3
July, when drunk and angry with his wife, declared he
would go to Carolina but when getting into a canoe fell
into the water and was drowned; his son was drowned
near same place about 2 years ago, also when drunk (21
July)

CLEMENS, Mr., of Hattonfield, over the river - on Sunday
last was struck by lightning; he recovered but his barn
was burnt down (21 July)

BARRET, Richard, Irish servant, age c. 20 - runaway from
Nathaniel Grubb of Willistown, Chester Co. (21 July)

HARTLEY, William, at Matthias Aspden's in Market St.,
Phila. - will sell times of servants lately arrived in
Phila. from Newry in North of Ireland in ship <u>Diamond</u>,
Robert Asher master (21 July)

MAJOR, Edward, servant (born in England and bred to garden-
ing) - runaway from Richard Pearne, at Skuylkil in
Blockley Twp., Phila. Co. (21 July)

McDANIEL, John, Scotch servant, age c. 24 - runaway from
William Roe, of New-Garden in Chester Co. (28 July)

MACALL, Philip, native Irishman, servant age c. 24 - runaway from Robert Holiday, of New Garden in Chester Co.
(28 July)

TOMMINS, Patrick, born in Dublin, age <u>c</u>. 18, servant - same as above

ASH, Thomas, formerly of Burlington Co. but late of Bucks Co., dec'd - accounts with estate to be settled with Eleanor Ash, executrix (4 Aug.)

DUNNING, Thomas, at the George in Second St., Phila. - has for sale a chariot of London make, to be seen at Thomas Montgomery's coach-maker in Chesnut St. (4 Aug.)

Grist and boulting mill in the Great Valley in Whiteland Twp., Chester Co., near Isaac Malin's - offered for sale; half is owned by David Evans, half by Thomas Lloyd (4 Aug.)

Meeting of creditors of estate of Joseph Growdon, late of Bucks Co., gent., will be held by his son Joseph (administrator) at house of David Evans in Market St., Phila. (4 Aug.)

The following representatives to serve in General Assembly of New York were chosen: For the city and county of New York--Capt. Garrit Van Horne, James Alexander, Esq., John Walter, Esq., Simon Johnson, Esq.; for Suffolk Co.--Major Epenetus Plat, Mr. David Peirson; for Orange Co.--Col. Vincent Matthews, Mr. Cornelius Cuyper; for the Manor of Courtland--Philip Verplank, Esq.; for the Co. of Westchester--Col. Lewis Morris, Col. Frederick Philipse; for Queens Co.--Col. Isaac Hicks; for Ulster Co.--Col. Abraham Gaasbeck Chambers; for Richmond Co.--John Le Count, Esq., Mr. Adam Mott; for the Borough of Westchester--Col. Lewis Morris, Jr. (11 Aug.)

Speech of Lt.-Gov. George Clark to Assembly of New York; address of the House by its Speaker, Lewis Morris, Jr. (11 Aug.)

SIDI, Schick, age <u>c</u>. 45, a Christian from Barut near Mt. Libanus in Syria, who fled Turkish prosecution and lived in Russia and England - came passenger with Capt. Jones to Boston from Bristol - Boston item of 25 July (11 Aug.); he went to Newport and plans then to visit New York, Phila. and Jamaica and then return to London - Boston item of 22 Aug. (1 Sept.)

Sloop <u>Frederica</u>, Capt. Goodwin, supposed lost - has arrived in Georgia (11 Aug.)

TONKIN, Charles, sub-sheriff of Burlington - offers reward for capture of John Crues, weaver by trade, who pretends to be a Quaker preacher and who broke out of Burlington Goal (11 Aug.)

FINNEY, George (son of George Finney of Wolverhampton), supposed to have been in the country about 8 years - will hear something to his advantage by applying to William Vere of Phila. (11 Aug.)

BAGNALL, Benjamin, Jr. (eldest son of Benjamin Bagnall of Boston, merchant) - Thursday last, in Quaker manner, married in the Prebyterian Meeting-House Miss Ann Hawden (daughter of James Hawden, of Boston, merchant); among the guests was the governor - Boston item of 8 Aug. (11 Aug.)

Lords Commissioners of Trade, on 26 May, after a hearing on petition of Lord Baltimore against Col. Thomas's being appointed Governor of the Three Lower Counties, reported in favor of the Proprietors of Pennsylvania (18 Aug.)

SHIPPEN, Joseph, Jr., of Phila., who intends for London in ship _Constantine_, Edward Wright commander - wishes to settle accounts; his shop is in Front St., opposite to the Sign of the Scales (18 Aug.)

SONMANS, Peter, chemist - is removed from Second St. to Market St. in Phila., near Bickley's Corner (18 Aug.)

LISTER, John, servant - runaway from James Williamson, Rector of All Saints in Calvert Co., Md. (18 Aug.)

ROGERS, Robert, servant, house-carpenter - same as above

BALFORD, Joseph, Irish servant, age c. 19 - runaway from Amos Austin of Evesham, Burlington Co. (18 Aug.)

REED, Jonathan, Irish servant, age c. 32, lately come from Dublin, currier by trade but can work at the shoemaker's and brushmaker's trades - runaway (in company with John McCarrol, attorney-at-law) from Edward Williams of Boston, currier (18 Aug.)

Ship _Sarah_ of Ramsgate, John Moses master - Saturday last entered York River from London and Cadiz - Williamsburg item of 5 Aug. (25 Aug.)

JENYS, Paul, Esq., eminent merchant of Charlestown and late Speaker of the House of Assembly of South Carolina - died Wednesday last at his plantation on John's Island - Charlestown item of 23 July (25 Aug.)

ABBOT, John, of Little River in Craven Co. - not long since
embarked in a boat with his wife, a blacksmith and his
daughter and 10 Negroes to go to South Carolina and defraud his creditors; at the mouth of the New River in
North Carolina the boat filled and all were drowned except 4 Negroes, who were seized, and Abbot, who escaped
- Charlestown item of 23 July (25 Aug.)

Saturday last arrived at New York the pink Crawley, Robert
Clark master, in 8 weeks from London; he brings news
that the Lord Delawar is appointed Governor of New York
and New Jersey and that Sir Orlando Bridgman is appointed
Governor of Barbados - New York item of 22 Aug. (25 Aug.)

ROBINS, William - teaches writing, arithmetic, book-keeping
and mathematics over against the George Inn (25 Aug.)

House wherein Frederick Elvershat lately dwelt, in High
St., opposite the prison in Phila. - is offered for
sale; enquire of Thomas Sober, Israel Pemberton or
Charles Willing (25 Aug.)

Two last sermons preached at Christ's Church, Phila., by
Richard Peters - are printed and sold by B. Franklin
(25 Aub.)

GRIFFITH, Timothy - in Chesnut St., Phila., opposite to
the head of Strawbery Alley, teaches Latin, Greek and
other subjects (25 Aug.)

The snow Catherine, of Workington in Ireland, Robert Walker
commander, and Messers Adam McNeal and David Thompson,
freighters - sailed 4 June from North Rush in Ireland
bound to Boston; on 17 July the vessel was driven in a
reef of sand at the east end of the Isle of Sable and
98 persons perished, including Messers. Archibald and
Charles McNeal and their wives, Mrs. Margaret Snell;
some people patched the long boat and got to Canso,
where Gov. Cosby sent Capt. Richards in a schooner,
who brought off the survivors from the Isle of Sable -
Boston item of 18 Aug. (1 Sept.)

Sampson, a Negro - Monday last was sentenced to death in
Phila. for burning the house near the President's
country seat (1 Sept.)

PERCY, Capt. - arrived Monday last at Phila. with 300
Germans from Holland (1 Sept.)

INGLE, Frederick of Middletown in Chester Co. - 28 Aug.
died when he fell and cart wheel passed over him (1
Sept.)

WILLIAMS, John, West Country servant, age c̲. 37, clockmaker - runaway from Isaac Pearson, of Burlington,
West New Jersey (1 Sept.)

PHILIPS, Josias, age c̲. 21 - was executed 8 July at
Bridgetown, Barbados, for the murder of Judge Corner
by shooting him off his horse (1 Sept.)

WELLS, Thomas, age c̲. 23 - executed 8 July at Bridgetown,
Barbados, for murder of his wife (1 Sept.)

OGLETHORPE, James, Esq. - will be appointed general of
H.M.'s forces in South Carolina and Georgia - London
item of 18 June (8 Sept.)

H.M.S. Sea Horse, Capt. Compton - arrived Monday last in
James River in less than 48 hours from New York - Williamsburg item of 19 Aug. (8 Sept.)

This summer a cucumber of the Turkey or Morocco kind,
which measured a yard in length and nearly 14 inches
round the thickest part of it, grew in the garden of
Daniel Parke Custis in New Kent Co. - Williamsburg item
of 19 Aug. (8 Sept.)

Ship Hawker-Gally, Charles Heyman master - will sail for
Jamaica; for freight or passage agree with the master
on the ship at Fishbourn's wharf or with Thomas Sober
(8 Sept.)

HALL, Robert - has Negroes for sale (8 Sept.)

Speech of Gov. George Clarke to the General Assembly of
New York (15 Sept.)

DELAGE, Peter, sugar baker - is removed to a house over
against James Steele's in Phila. (15 Sept.)

Tract of land on east side of Susquehannah River, at
mouth of Sickasalongoe Creek, in the lower part of
Donegal Twp., is for sale - enquire of John Ross,
living near said place (15 Sept.)

BARNES, John, under sentence of death for murder - Tuesday
night last again escaped from prison in Boston - Boston
item of 5 Sept. (22 Sept.)

NOBLE, Abel - Monday last preached from the Courthouse
stairs to a large congregation in the Market place in
Phila. (22 Sept.)

A Treaty of Friendship held with the Chiefs of the Six

<u>Nations</u>, at <u>Philadelphia</u>, <u>in</u> <u>September</u> and <u>October</u> 1736 - has just been published by B. Franklin (22 Sept.)

A year and three-quarters time of a servant, a good workman at the skinners and breeches-makers trade - enquire of Thomas Grace in Chesnut St., Phila., or the printer (22 Sept.)

CROFTS, Dudley, at his store on Mr. Bourn's wharf - sells nails, locks, hinges, files etc. (22 Sept.)

Persons indebted to estate of Charles Read, Esq., dec'd, who do not pay before 16 Nov. will be sued by Sarah Read, administratrix (22 Sept.)

House and lot in Market St., Phila., lately in possession of John Rutter, dec'd, and 138 acres of land between Colebrookdale Furnace and Pine Forge - will be sold by Mary Rutter and Samuel Nutt, executors (22 Sept.)

Address of General Assembly of New York in reply to the Speech of Lt.-Gov. George Clarke (29 Sept.)

Ship <u>Sarah</u>, Capt. Green - arrived Monday last at Boston from London - New York item of 26 Sept. (29 Sept.)

Capts. Gill and Farmer from New York - have arrived in London (29 Sept.)

MORGAN, Evan, at the Sign of the Two Sugar Loaves in Market St., near the Courthouse, in Phila. - sells gunpowder, wine, rum, tea, sugar etc. (29 Sept.)

Saturday last the following persons were elected for Phila. Co.: For representatives--Robert Jones, John Kinsey, Thomas Leech, Jonathan Robeson, Edward Warner, William Allen, Isaac Norris, William Monington; for burgesses for the city--Israel Pemberton, John Kearsley; for sheriffs--Joseph Breintnall, Isaac Leech; for coroners-- Owen Owen, David Evans; for commissioner--Joseph Trotter; for assessors for the county--John Dillwyn, Samuel Morris, miller, Thomas Potts, James Jones, Samuel Lane, Joseph Noble; assessors for the city--William Rawle, James Morris, Richard Parker, Jeremiah Elfreth, Philip Hillier, George Mifflin (6 Oct.)

Saturday last the following persons were elected for Chester Co.: Representatives--Thomas Chandler, Joseph Harvey, John Evans, Thomas Cummings, William Moore, James Gibbons, William Hewes, Richard Hayes; for sheriffs-- John Owen, John Wharton; for coroners--Stephen Hoskins, Evan Ellis; for commissioner--John Parry, Jr.; for as-

sessors: Joshua Thompson, James Jeffreys, Benjamin
Fred, Edward Brinton, William Jeffreys, David Stephens
(6 Oct.)

Saturday last the following persons were elected for Bucks
Co.: For representatives--Joseph Kirkbride, Jr.,
Jeremiah Langhorne, Christian Vanhorne, Andrew Hamilton,
Lawrence Growdon, William Biles, Matthew Hughes, Benjamin Jones; for sheriffs--John Hart, Charles Biles; for
coroners--William Atkinson, Jonathan Woolaston; for
commissioner--Jeremiah Langhorne (6 Oct.)

Saturday last the following persons were elected for Lan-
caster Co.: Representatives--James Hamilton, Andrew
Galbraith, John Wright, Samuel Smith; for sheriffs--
Samuel Smith, James Mitchell; for coroners--Michael Mc-
Clery, William Caldwell; for commissioner--Gordon
Howard (6 Oct.)

Saturday last the following persons were elected for New
Castle Co.: Representatives--John McCool, Andrew Peter-
son, David French, Thomas Noxon, Jehu Curtis, John
Finney; sheriffs--Henry Newton, John Gooding; coroners--
John Dunning, Henry Gonne (6 Oct.)

Saturday last the following persons were elected for Sussex Co.: Representatives--William Till, Rives Holt,
Simon Kollock, Jacob Kollock, Abraham Wynkoop, Jabez
Maud Fisher; sheriffs--John Shankland, Cornelius Whill-
bank; coroners--Daniel Nunez, Peter Clowes (6 Oct.)

Tuesday last the Aldermen and Common Council of Phila.
chose Thomas Griffitts, Esq., Mayor (6 Oct.)

PLUMSTED, Clement, Esq., late Mayor of Phila. - Thursday
last gave a feast for nearly 150 persons (6 Oct.)

Snow Seneca, John Jones master - will sail for Barbados;
for freight or passage agree with the master at William
Fishbourn's wharf or with Thomas Sharp at his store in
Water St., Phila. (6 Oct.)

Sloop Charming Betty, Thomas Crossthwaite master, at Mr.
Bourn's wharf - will sail for South Carolina (6 Oct.)

HEWES, William, living at Marcus Hook - offers reward for
recovery of mare stolen from Cordwell's plantation in
Kennet Twp., Chester Co. (6 Oct.)

Choice parcel of servants just imported from Dublin in the
snow Prince of Orange, William Rankin master, lying
opposite the Drawbridge - for sale by Emerson and

Graydon (6 Oct.)

RIDGELY, Nicholas, near Salem Town in Salem Co. - offers
for sale 3 lots of land in Marcus Hook in Chichester
Town, Chester Co.; one is where Capt. William Welding
now lives; the second adjoins the churchground and
yard; the third consists of 2 acres of woodland (6 Oct.)

SHERRADON, Patrick, native Irish servant, age c̲. 26 -
runaway from Caleb Cowpland of Chester, Pa. (6 Oct.)

WOORE, Joseph, servant joiner, age c̲. 34 - runaway from
Samuel Austin, of Phila. (6 Oct.)

DAVIES, William, English servant, age c̲. 25 - runaway from
Benjamin Smith of Trentown, West New Jersey (6 Oct.)

HOLLOND, Arthur, Irish servant, age c̲. 30 - runaway from
Richard Noland of Trentown, West New Jersey (6 Oct.)

WHITE, Thomas, Irish servant, age c̲. 18 - runaway from
Peter Saunders of Phila., shoemaker (6 Oct.)

HAMILTON, John, age c̲. 25 - runaway from sloop _Dolphin_ of
Boston, Nathaniel Welsh master; he stole clothing from
John Bryan and William Tally on board the sloop (6 Oct.)

WILKINSON, Anthony of Tacony - a quantity of lead was
stolen from his plantation (6 Oct.)

VERE, William of Phila., who designs to depart from the
province - desires payment of all debts due him (6 Oct.)

HARTLEY, William of Phila., who designs to depart for England and Ireland - all persons indebted to him are to
make speedy payment (6 Oct.)

A ship (owned by Capt. Cheevers), Capt. Harris master,
bound from Cales to Boston - last week ran ashore on the
back of Cape Cod; all the men were saved - Boston item
of 26 Sept. (13 Oct.)

Persons elected for Kent Co. are the following: Represen-
tatives--Mark Manlove, William Farson, John Houseman,
William Barns, John Holiday, James Morris; sheriffs--
Daniel Robinson, Jonathan Raymond (13 Oct.)

BARD, Peter - intends to leave Pennsylvania by beginning
of next month (13 Oct.)

BRAME, John - has removed from his store on Fishbourn's
wharf to a store on Bickley's wharf, next to Market St.

wharf in Phila. (13 Oct.)

MORGAN, William (late Sexton of Phila.), designing to leave
Pennsylvania - desires persons indebted to him to make
speedy payment (13 Oct.)

Billinder **Townshend**, Thomas Thomson commander - will sail
for Cork and Bristol; for freight or passage agree with
Simon Edgell, who intends to depart for London in ship
Constantine, Edward Wright commander (13 Oct.)

KNOWLES, John, living at the Boar's Head in Market St.,
Phila. - Saturday last received by mistake a bill of
considerable value for a bill of 18¢ (20 Oct.)

HOOPER, John, English servant, age <u>c</u>. 21 - runaway from
John Jones of Worcester Twp., Phila. Co.; reward for
capture of the runaway will be paid by Owen Owen at the
Indian King in Phila. or by John Jones (20 Oct.)

Sloop **Hopewell**, Bristow Brown master, at Bourn's wharf in
Phila. - will sail for Bermudas (20 Oct.)

Ship **Virtuous Grace** - will sail for South Carolina; for
freight or passage agree with the master at the Sign
of the Ship Aground or with Benjamin Shoemaker in
Market St., Phila. (20 Oct.)

Negro fellow and Barbados tar for sale - enquire at the
Widow Young's in Chesnut St., Phila. (20 Oct.)

Ship **Catherine**, Jasper Farmer commander - arrived Saturday last at New York in 7 weeks from London, with news
that Lord Delawar will set out for New York in the
spring, that Capt. Gill sailed through the Downs for
New York and that Capt. Bryant was to sail in 3 or 4
days - New York item of 24 Oct. (27 Oct.)

REES, Thomas, of Roxbury near Phila., 10-year-old son of -
on 26 Oct. fell from cart and died instantly (27 Oct.)

<u>Every Man his own Doctor</u> - has been printed by B. Franklin
(27 Oct.)

MILLS, John, servant, age <u>c</u>. 18 - runaway from William
Crossthwaite of Phila., peruke-maker (27 Oct.)

WOOLEY, Edmund, of Phila. - offers reward for recovery of
horse strayed or stolen from the Commons at upper end
of Phila. (27 Oct.)

Letter from New York, directed to Rev. Baptist Boyd in

North of Ireland, near Aughnacloy, Co. of Tyrone, from
James Murray, who extolls life in America and urges
people to come; especially named are the Rev. Boyd's
sons, Samuel and James, James Gibson, James Broon, of
Drumern; letters for Murry are to be directed to him
in care of the Rev. John Pemberton in New York (3 Nov.)

GILL, Capt. - arrived at New York last week from London,
Nealson in a brigantine from Dover, and Saturday last
the ship Albany, Capt. Bryant, from London - New York
item of 31 Oct. (3 Nov.)

PITT, Gov. of Bermuda and his family are embarked for
London on a ship of Phila. - New York item of 31 Oct.
(3 Nov.)

Saturday last Thomas Crow (second mate of the snow George
and Henry, William Allison master), accidentally fell
into the river at Phila. and was drowned (3 Nov.)

A Negro woman and a Negro boy (age 12), both Barbados-born
- are to be sold at John Fruin's, in Arch St., Phila.
(3 Nov.)

MILLS, John, servant, age c. 18 - runaway from William
Crossthwaite, of Phila., peruke-maker (3 Nov.)

WOOLEY, Edmund, at Phila. - offers reward for recovery of
a horse strayed or stolen from the Commons, at the upper
end of Phila. (3 Nov.)

Sadlery ware is sold by Nicholas Raddish, sadler, over
against the Great Meeting-house in Second St., Phila.
(3 Nov.)

Snow Seneca, John Jones master - will sail for Barbados;
for freight or passage agree with the master at William
Fishbourn's wharf or with Thomas Sharp, at his store in
Water St., Phila. (3 Nov.)

Sloop Charming Betty, Thomas Crossthwaite master, now at
Mr. Bourn's wharf - will sail for South Carolina (3
Nov.)

Ship Virtuous Grace, John Bull master - will sail for South
Carolina; for freight or passage agree with the master
at the Sign of the Ship-aground or with Benjamin Shoemaker in Market St. (3 Nov.)

Ship Constantine, Edward Wright master - will sail for
London; for freight or passage apply to Messrs. Edgell
& Sons or the master on board, now lying at Thomas

Griffitt's wharf (3 Nov.)

NEAVE, Samuel, at his store near Fishbourn's wharf in Water St., Phila. - sells cloth, thread, laces, cutlery, etc. (10 Nov.)

MORGAN, Evan, cooper, over against Mr. Turner's in Front St. and opposite to the Still and Blue Ball in King St., commonly called Water St. (10 Nov.); sells canary or sack (28 Feb. 1738)

OGDEN, John, tanner, in Chesnut St., Phila. - has Negroes for sale (10 Nov.)

PARR, Samuel - offers reward for recovery of a 15-foot yawl taken away from the snow Warren at Thomas Austin's wharf (10 Nov.)

DELAGE, Peter, sugar baker, who has removed to a house over against James Steele's - sells sugar and tea (10 Nov.)

READ, Charles, Esq., dec'd - accounts with estate to be settled with Sarah Read, administratrix (10 Nov.)

WELCH, William of Phila., porter - drowned 9 Nov. when his canoe overset off against Billinsport (17 Nov.)

BRIENTNALL, John, in Chesnut St., Phila. - sells tenterhooks for fullers, spectacles and pocket compasses (17 Nov.)

BICKLEY, William, of Burlington - desires debts due him to be paid promptly (17 Nov.)

RENAUDET, James, in High St., Phila., next door to Owen Owen's - sells wine, chocolate, spices (17 Nov.)

ATTWOOD, William, in Front St., Phila. - has a Negro man for sale (17 Nov.)

OWEN, Owen - offers reward for recovery of mare strayed or stolen from the Indian King, in Market St. (17 Nov.)

HAGEN, James, Irish servant, age c. 35 - runaway from Peter Rose, of Burlington (24 Nov.)

IMPTY, John, age c. 22 - runaway from Henry Smith, of Tulpahocken, in Lancaster Co. (24 Nov.)

BUTLER, James, English servant, house-carpenter, who came to Phila. last year from Bristol with Capt. Bromadge (24 Nov.)

172

QUIGLEY, Matthew - found Monday last near his master's door and quickly died (1 Dec.)

Stable belonging to Joseph Turner in Phila. caught fire Monday last and was consumed with the hay in it (1 Dec.)

DEVERILL, John, master of the ship _Bacchus_, from Bristol - has for sale a parcel of servants on board the ship at William Fishbourn's wharf (1 Dec.)

FINLY, David, Irish servant, blacksmith - runaway from John Shankland, living in Sussex Co. (1 Dec.)

BOYD, John, in Market St., Phila. - has for sale geese feathers (1 Dec.)

SORSBY, William, schoolmaster - offers reward for capture of thief and goods he stole from the schoolhouse on the plantation of Edward Kimble in Springfield, Burlington Co. (1 Dec.)

A Brief Narrative of the Case and Tryal of John Peter Zenger - to be sold by Benjamin Franklin (8 Dec.)

SANSOM, Samuel, at his store in Norris's Alley, Phila. - sells blankets, cloth, tea, chinaware (8 Dec.)

KIER, Archibald, Scotch servant, age c. 24 - runaway from Mr. Warrell, at Trenton, West New Jersey (8 Dec.)

Ship _Charming Nancy_, John Steadman master - will sail for London; for freight or passage agree with the master at his store in Water St., opposite to Thomas Sharp's (8 Dec.)

Thursday last the _Eastern Prince_, Capt. Loftus, left Phila., bound for Barbados (15 Dec.)

Peter Heckie and Brian Conner, murderers - were executed in Virginia on 18 Nov. (15 Dec.)

CLAYTON, John, Esq., Attorney General and Judge of the Court of Vice Admiralty of Pennsylvania - died 18 Nov. (15 Dec.)

German book, _Die Weissheit Gottes_, published and sold by Benjamin Franklin and Johannes Wüster in Phila. (15 Dec.)

HARRISON, Henry - has removed from his store at the Scales to a store the fourth door below the Sign of the Pewter Platter (15 Dec.)

ASHMORE, Richard, of Phila., shopkeeper - has surrendered
all his effects to his creditors, who have appointed
John Reynell, Capt. Hellier and John Armit to act for
them (15 Dec.)

MITCHEL, John, servant - runaway from Robert Story of
North East (15 Dec.)

GILDER, Tobit, servant - same as above

Speech of Jonathan Belcher to the Assembly of Massachusetts (22 Dec.)

GEORGES, John, Esq., F.R.S., late Secretary to the Proprietor - died Sunday last in Phila. (22 Dec.)

JEFFREYS, William, of Bucks Co., blacksmith - last week
was found dead in the woods, having been crushed by a
falling tree (22 Dec.)

Sloop William and Elizabeth, Stephen Williams master - will
sail from Phila. to South Carolina; for freight or
passage agree with William Crossthwaite or the master
on board at Bickley's wharf (22 Dec.)

McCLANNON, Samuel, shoemaker in Phila. or Nicholas Gale,
at Wickacoe - will pay reward for recovery of a horse
strayed or stolen from Wickacoe (22 Dec.)

A hog, weighing about 900 pounds, is on view at the third
house below Owen Owen's in Market St., Phila. (22 Dec.)

LEVY, Nathan and Isaac, of Phila. - have a young Negro
man to be sold (22 Dec.)

MOORE, William, servant, age c. 20 - runaway from John
Park, of Fallowfield, Chester Co. (22 Dec.)

INGLIS, John, at his house below the drawbridge in Phila.
- sells rum, molasses, sugar, cocoa   (29 Dec.)

1738

Ship Tryal, William Grieves master - will sail for Dublin;
for freight or passage agree with John Erwin at Mrs.
Richardson's in Front St., Phila., or with the master
on board at Plumsted's wharf (3 Jan.)

Proclamation by President and Council of Pennsylvania,
signed James Logan and Robert Charles, Sec. (10 Jan.)

BINGHAM, James, late of Phila., dec'd - accounts with estate to be settled with Anne Bingham, executrix (10 Jan.)

O'NEAL, Ferdinando, servant, age c. 30 - runaway from Joshua Baker, of Phila. (10 Jan.)

GULSTONE, Thomas, supposed to be living in Pennsylvania - a package of goods directed to him from London is in the hands of Robert Grace, merchant, in Phila. (10 Jan.)

MINSHALL, Widow, in Providence, Chester Co. - has taken up 2 mares (10 Jan.)

TUCKER, Capt., from South Carolina, arrived at New York, brings news that Mr. Oglethorp is Gov. of Carolina and Col. Halsey Lt.-Gov. and that Gov. Broughton and his nephew, Nathaniel Johnson, Esq., both died in South Carolina just before Capt. Tucker sailed (17 Jan.)

KIP, Capt., in a sloop from St. Augustine - reports that many Indians in Mexico have died of a plague - New York item of 24 Dec. (17 Jan.)

BODDISCURTE, John, servant, age c. 25, shipwright - runaway from Joseph Lynn, shipwright, of Phila. (17 Jan.)

LLOYD, Edward, at his store on Samuel Powell's wharf, Phila. - sells cloth (17 Jan.)

KINNICUT, Hezekiah, servant, age c. 24, joiner - runaway from Thomas Stevenson, of Prince Town, N.J. (17 Jan.)

McNELLEOUS, Alexander, baker, in Second St., Phila. - has about 5 years of a servant lad's time to sell (17 Jan.)

Tract of 800 acres, known as Lamaconick, about 25 miles from Brunswick, on a branch of Rariton River, and a tract of 300 acres, on a branch of Rariton River, known by Indian name of Mansaloky, are for sale; enquire of Fretwell Wright in Burlington (17 Jan.)

Two houses in Fifth St., on south side of Walnut St., Phila., are for sale, as is a corner house in Chesnut St., opposite to Peter Stretch's; enquire of Edward Nichols, living in the house last mentioned (17 Jan.)

Three tenements and lots on west side of lower end of Front St., near the drawbridge in Phila., late the estate of William Parker, dec'd; apply to his widow and executrix Esther Parker, who has impowered Samuel Kirk, of Phila., to receive payments of debts due the estate (24 Jan.)

FARMER, Edward, of Whitemarsh, and his son, Samuel Farmer -
accounts with them are to be settled with James Macky,
merchant, in Phila.; among tracts of land to be sold by
Edward Farmer or James Macky are a plantation in Springfield Twp., a tract in Upper Dublin, 110 acres in Nar-
rington Twp., 120 acres in Whitemarsh, a 100-acre plantation next adjoining Isaac Norris's, the plantation
next adjoining (now in possession of John McCallister),
another adjoining in the tenor of Robert Renolds, a
plantation in the tenor of John Anderson, another plantation in the tenor of William Dewees, Jr., a plantation upon Schuylkill, a small island, one-tenth part of
the furnace at Coolbrook-Dale, one-third part of Rutter's Forge (24 Jan.)

Ship Mineva, Capt. Nicholson, arrived yesterday at barr in
sight of Charlestown from London, struck ground but was
gotten off; the goods were sold at low rates; among
passengers was Robert Johnson, Esq. (son of H. E. Robert
Johnson, Esq., dec'd, late Gov. of South Carolina) -
Charlestown item of 8 Dec. (24 Jan.)

SHOEMAKER, Jacob, spinning wheel-maker, in Market St.,
Phila. - will pay 1s. a pound for horse tails (31 Jan.)

CREELY, Peter, Irish labourer, who some time since went
away from Salem, West New Jersey - John King, of Salem
Co., offers a reward for tidings of Creely but a postscript notes that King is in the Salem Goal on suspicion of having murdered Creely (31 Jan.)

HOGG, Capt. Robert - persons indebted to him in redemption
or otherwise are desired to pay the same to William
Shaw, Esq., at Newcastle, or James Mackey, merchant, at
Phila. (31 Jan.)

At Court of Oyer and Terminer, which ended Friday last
at Phila., John Wood, labourer, was sentenced to death
for breaking into the house of John Cox at Passayunk
Twp. and stealing pieces of pewter (7 Feb.)

A detailed account is given of the mock initiation into
Free Masonry of an apprentice of Dr. Evan Jones, of
Phila., who was found guilty of manslaughter; the case
for the Crown was plead by Mr. Growdon, the King's
Attorney-General; Dr. Jones was burnt in the hand as
punishment (7 Feb.)

GOESCH, John Henry - at Court of Oyer and Terminer was
indicted for setting fire to the Sugar House but was
acquitted (7 Feb.)

SIRON, Simon, shopkeeper in Second St., Phila., who keeps
a store at Plymouth Meeting-House - desires settlement
of all accounts, as he designs to remove out of Phila.
in April (7 Feb.)

A stage wagon will set out from William Atlee's and Thomas
Hooton's in Trenton on Monday, 21 Mar., and continue
going from Trenton every Monday and Thursday, returning
Tuesday and Friday from Brunswick (7 Feb.)

A group of Negroes, regaling themselves at a warehouse on
Wentworth's wharf in Boston, accidentally set the roof
on fire; the blaze was extinguished but each Negro was
given 50 lashes - Boston item of 16 Jan. (15 Feb.)

Friday last a fire broke out at the Sign of the Drum in
Boston but the blaze was extinguished - Boston item of
16 Jan. (15 Feb.)

Saturday last the house of Mr. Imms of Dedham, Mass.,
caught fire and was wholly consumed - Boston item of
16 Jan. (15 Feb.)

On 14 Jan. the house of John Ruggles, of Brantrey, Mass.,
was consumed by fire (15 Feb.)

On 15 Jan., according to a letter from Capt. Joseph Kellogg, of Fort Dummer, to the Gov. of Massachusetts, the
fort caught fire, the powder room blew up and the whole
fort was destroyed (15 Feb.)

Friday night a fire broke out in a store near Mr. Fishbourn's wharf in Phila., but was quickly extinguished
(15 Feb.)

A letter, dated Charlestown, S.C., 19 Jan., from a gentleman in London to a friend at Cowes, on board Capt.
Ayres, for Charlestown, tells of the death of the Queen
(15 Feb.)

Benjamin Franklin gives his own defense against charges
that he encouraged the tragic hoax played on Dr. Jones's
apprentice (one Daniel R...s); John Danby and Harmanus
Alriths swear to the truth of Franklin's account; Danby,
Alriths and Franklin were met, as auditors in an affair between Dr. Jones and Armstrong Smith, in a tavern
in Market St., when they first heard from Dr. Jones and
a Mr. R...n about their deception of Jones's apprentice
(15 Feb.)

Tract of 600 acres in Bucks Co., on Neshameneh Creek, and
4 acres of pasture on Society Hill are for sale; en-

quire of Joseph Claypole in Walnut St., Phila. (15 Feb.)

DUNNING, Thomas, late of Phila., innholder, dec'd - accounts with estate to be settled with Martha Dunning, executrix (15 Feb.); she continues to keep the George Inn (21 Feb.)

ALTON, William, English servant, brickmaker - runaway from Capt. James Chalmers, of Willingtown, Newcastle Co. upon Delaware; adv. is signed by Jenet Chalmers (15 Feb.)

This week arrived in Charlestown, S.C., from the Bay of Honduras Capt. John Busley in the sloop Three Friends belonging to Boston; he relates that the Spaniards took the following English vessels in the Bay: a sloop from Jamaica, John Thomas owner; a sloop of Charlestown, Maxey Dowse commander; 2 vessels of Capt. Busley; the Spaniards also took William Reeves, living in the Bay, with 2 of his Negroes; Capt. Stephen Eastwick, in a schooner from Jamaica, drove off some Spaniards who attacked him; among English vessels in the Bay when Capt. Busley came out were the following: the Eagle, Capt. Cathcard; the Torrington, Capt. Sampson; the Agatha, Capt. Merchant; the Carena, Capt. Doubt; the Vine, Capt. Hall; Three Brothers, Capt. Sam. Carr; the Elizabeth, Capt. Thomas; the Honduras, Capt. Linning; the sloop Marlborough, Capt. Warren - Charlestown item of 17 Nov. (21 Feb.)

Tuesday last the Masons in Phila. met at Mr. Seaman's (Master of Solomon's Lodge), whence they proceeded to wait on John Graeme, Esq., Provincial Grand Master; they then went to the courtroom at Charles Shepheard's house; James Graeme was re-elected Grand Master, and he appointed James Wright, D.G.M., Maurice Lewis, S.G.W., John Crookshanks J.G.W., James Michie G.T. and James Gordon G.S.; James Crockatt was unanimously chosen master of Solomon's Lodge (21 Feb.)

It is reported that Col. Horsey will be made Governor of South Carolina (21 Feb.)

Saturday last at New York David Provoost, Jr., Master of the Masonic Lodge, gave an elegant dinner at the Black Horse and resigned, as he was about to leave the province; Matthew Norris, Senior Warden, who was chosen Master, appointed John Saint, who was Junior Warden, to be Senior Warden and Henry Holt to be Junior Warden - New York item of 24 Jan. (21 Feb.)

Seventy-two Christian slaves of the Bashaw of Tangier in
Nov. escaped from the castle; their boat, however, was
leaky, so that they tried to go aboard a brigantine
then in the bay; the master, an Irishman named Burne,
fired upon them and all were killed or captured - extract of a letter from Malaga, 27 Nov. N.S. (21 Feb.)

STEEL, J., Rec. Gen. - sets times and places for payment
of quit-rents (21 Feb.)

RICHARDSON, Francis, at the house of Joseph Richardson,
goldsmith, in Front St., Phila. - sells chinaware and
cloth (21 Feb.)

In Oct. Ontaussoogoe and 4 other delegates of the Cagnawaga
Indian tribe met with the 5 Commissioners of Massachu-
setts, John Stoddard, Eleazer Porter, Thomas Wells,
Joseph Kellogg and Israel Williams (28 Feb.)

Account of goods exported and imported from 1 Nov. 1736 to
1 Nov. 1737 at Ports of Charlestown, Georgetown and Port
Royal, S.C. (28 Feb.)

Speech of William Bull to General Assembly of South Carolina and address to Gov. Bull of Charles Pinckney,
Speaker of the House (28 Feb.)

Ship Charming Nancy, John Stedman master, now at Mr. Fishbourn's wharf in Phila. - will sail for London; for
freight or passage agree with the master at his store
in Water St., opposite to Thomas Sharp's (28 Feb.)

BARR, George, tobacconist - has removed from his house in
Chesnut St., to a house on the north side of Market St.,
opposite to the Market House in Phila. (28 Feb.)

CORNISH, James, Welsh servant, age c. 21 - runaway from
Nicholas Castle, in Phila. (28 Feb.)

Stays and coats are made by Robert Miller and John Frost
at the house of Robert Miller, over against the Widow
Gordon's in Front St., Phila. (28 Feb.)

Manager is sought for a fulling-mill; apply to George Adam
Weidner, at Oley, in Manhatawny Creek, who has lately
built a fulling-mill there (28 Feb.)

DOYLING, John, Irish servant, age c. 17 or 18 - runaway
from William Tateham, of Woodberry Creek, Gloucester Co.,
West New Jersey (28 Feb.)

An English servant man has run away from Moses Ward, of

Woodberry Creek, Gloucester Co., West New Jersey (28 Feb.)

An almost new chaise is for sale at Mr. Montgomery's, chaise-maker, in Chesnut St., Phila. (28 Feb.)

In Cecil Co., Md., a young woman, granddaughter of Matthias Vanbebber, was accidentally burnt to death (7 Mar.)

Two Negroes were imprisoned at Trenton last week when they tried to persuade another Negro to poison his master and when they told him that Mr. Trent and 2 of his sons and Mr. Lambert and 2 of his wives had been kiled with poison by their slaves (7 Mar.)

A house in Mulberry St. (commonly called Arch St.), near the Quaker's Burying-Ground, and another in the same Street, opposite to the Sign of the George, are for sale; apply to Elinor and Isaac Jones (executors of Henry Jones, dec'd), living in Mulberry St., opposite to the George Inn, in Phila. (7 Mar.)

McCLENNY, Margaret, Irish servant, age c. 40 - runaway from Henry Clark, at the Sign of the Coach and Horses in Chesnut St., opposite the State House in Phila. (7 Mar.)

RENSHAW, Richard - keeps the ferry over Delaware River from Wiccaco to Gloucester (7 Mar.)

Two sloops that arrived 7 Mar. at New York from South Carolina bring news that Capt. Matthew Norris is appointed Commissioner of Plymouth (7 Mar.)

It is feared that Capt. Green, of Phila., is lost at Newfoundland (7 Mar.)

FREEMAN, Thomas, Esq. (son-in-law of the late Gov. Cosby) - died Saturday last at Trenton (7 Mar.)

PEEL, Anthony, living in Arch St., Phila. - has for sale 2 Negroes and sundry sorts of merchandize (7 Mar.)

A great coat was left in September last upon Samuel Powel's wharf in Phila. (7 Mar.)

Plantation in Darby, on navigable part of Darby Creek, is for sale; enquire of Joseph Bonnsall in Darby or Owen Owen in Phila. (7 Mar.)

List of unclaimed letters brought into the Post Office at Phila. since 29 Sept. 1737, with Franklin's abbreviations as follows: pen = Pennsylvania, phi. = Phila.,

180

bu = Bucks, ch = Chester, lan. = Lancaster, co. =
county (21 Mar.): ABERNETHY, William, in Northampton,
bu co.; ADAMS, John, in Horsham Twp.; ADAMS, John, bu.
co.; ALISON, Rev. Francis, at New London, pen.; ATT-
WOOD, Faith, phi.;

BAKER, James, in phi.; BANFIELD, Lewis, commander of
the Jenny snow; BARLOW, William, in phi.; BARNET, Robert,
of Salisbury, lan. co.; BARSONS, Grace, in phi.; BIGAR,
Robert, to the care of Margaret Chambers; BLUNDER, Polly,
at William Moor's, Wapping, new phi.; BOLLANS, Richard,
mate of the Amity, phi.; BOURK, Richard, to the care of
John Emerson, phi.; BOUTCHER, William, shipmaster, phi.;
BRAYNON, John, living with Joseph Cooper, Jerseys;
BROCKENRIDGE, Joseph, in pen.; BROWN, John, hatter, ch.
co.; BROWN, Robert, mate of Capt. Richmond; BUNN, William, phi.; BURGESS, John, phi.;

CADWELL, John, at John Holland's, phi.; CAR, James,
porter, phi.; CARLILE, Rev. Hugh, Newtown; CLELAND, John,
to the care of the Rev. Mr. Tenant; COLLINS, William,
to the care of Francis Knowles; COTTON, Samuel, Esq.,
Cohansie; COUPER, John, to the care of John Care, phi.;
COX, William, merchant, North-East; CULLEN, Catherine,
8 miles from phi.;

DAVIS, Ambrose, with Robert Miller, at Caln, ch. co.;
DAVIS, Elizabeth, at Northampton, bu. co.; DAVIS, James,
at Montgomery Twp.; DEARMON, Sarah; DERKINDEREN, Eliza-
beth, at Mr. Peter Baynton's, phi.; DOBBS, William, with
Moses Coats, ch. co.; DONALDSON, Isaac, at phi.;
DORATHY, William, Newtown (2 letters); DYER, Roger, at
Leacock, pen.;

EDWARDS, John, of Shiptown, near phi.; ELLIS, William,
ropemaker, phi.; ELMER, Daniel, at Cohansey; EMERSON,
William, to the care of John Lowls, phi.; ESLIK, Mary,
in Water St., phi.; EUSTACE, Robert, blockmaker, phi.;

FALCONER, David, phi.; FINNEY, Capt. James, of the
Charming Molly, phi.; FITZPATRICK, Terence, phi.; FLIN,
William, in West Jersey, Gloucester co.; FOSTER, David,
Donnegal, lan. co.; FULLERTOWN, William Pequay, to the
care of Adam Boyd, minister;

GARCELON, Peter, phi.; GARRET, ____, in-the-heaven,
Skippack Road; GIBBENS, Jane, in Westown; GILBARD, Joanna, at John Cattel's, phi.; GRAHAM, Archibald, hat-
maker, phi.; GREGORY, Robert, phi.;

HALL, Samuel, mariner, in Chesnut St., phi.; HANLON,
Patrick, mercht., phi.; HARRISON, John, near phi.; HAR-
RUP, Thomas, an English sawyer, phi.; HAWTHORN, James,
of Cape May near Eggharbor; HAYTER, Abraham, near Buck-
ingham Meeting-House; HEIR, Mrs., shopkeeper, phi.;
HENOCK, Henrick, phi.; HERINGTON, William, in West Jersey;
HOCK, Christel, duische Kledermaker, tot phi.;
HODGKINSON, Peter Aris, phi.; HOLDER, John, directed to
be left at the post office, phi.; HOMES, William, near

phi.; HOUEY, Joseph, to the care of John Cross, phi.; HUDSON, William, in Piscataway near phi.; HUGHES, James, at Ilkwater, to the care of Mr. Crayhead; HUSBANDS, Robert, at Samuel Hall's, bricklayer, phi.; HUSSEY, John, mercht., phi. (2 letters);

ISDAILL, Mary, living with Thomas Small, gunsmith, phi.;

JACKSON, John, Front St., phi.; JAMISON, John, at Milford, bu. co.; JOBE, James, with Alexander Moore, phi.; JOHNSON, Joseph, directed to be left at the post office, phi.; JOHNSON, Matthew, Derry Twp.; JOHNSON, William, on board the Charming Molly; JOLLINS, Elizabeth, to be left at Widow Fisher's, phi.; JONES, Hugh, tanner, North Wales; Jones, Thomas, Abington, phi. co.; Jones, William, carpenter, in Charlestown, near Skuylkill;

KENNEDY, David, and James Cockran, at Fog's Mannor, pen.; KILPATRICK, James, Octorara;

LANCASTER, Thomas, carpenter, in phi.; LARKIN, Comick, in Donnegall; LAWRENCE, John, near the Market, phi.; LEARD, James, taylor, for Thomas Gray, near phi. (2 letters); LEGET, Michael, near phi.; LESTER, John, in bu. co.; LEWIS, John, surgeon;

McCADDAN, Hugh, Donnegall; McCAY, Jane, pen.; McCORD, John, in Octorara, lan. co.; McDUFF, James, to the care of Samuel Rees, pen.; McGAA, Martha, pen.; McGUIGAN, Neal, tailor, phi.; McLEAN, Joseph, bu. co.; McMORERY, John, near phi.; McNEAL, Neal, phi.; McREAIGHT, William, to the care of Samuel Rees, pen.; McREE, John, lan. co.; MADDEN, James, in Mutton Lane; MANWARING, Robert, at Joseph Large's in Buckingham; MAY, Moses, Whitestown, to the care of Mr. Baker; MEAR, Alexander, Upper Dublin; MILLER, John, in Hopking, pen.; MILLER, William, New Garden, ch. co.; MILLER, William, near Newgarden, in ch. co.; MITCHEL, James, Donnegall; MITCHEL, William, to the care of Mr. Anderson, Donnegall; MONTGOMERY, Thomas, phi.; MORRISH, Thomas, to be left with Henry Pawling in New Providence, phi. co.; MOUER, John, phi.;

PALMER, Capt. Charles, phi.; PARSONS, Capt. Samuel, phi.; PEARSOR, Benjamin, at Darby, pen.; POPE, Thomas, phi.; PORT, Elizabeth, pen.; POUGE, James, near phi.; POULTNEY, John, living with Henry Shepherd, phi.;

QUEN, William, to the care of George Walters, phi.;

REA, John, near Thunder Hill, pen.; READER, William, to be left at Cornelius Empson's, phi.; RICKEY, Alexander, bu. co.; RICKEY, John; ROBERTS, Isaac, phi. (2 letters); ROGERS, Andrew, near phi.; ROSS, John, Fog's Mannor, pen.; RUSH, Dick, phi.;

SASHLOE, William, phi.; SAWYER, William, at Mrs. Compton's, phi.; SCHIDIT, His Highness Prince; SCORES, James, at Milford, bu. co.; SCOT, Andrew, near phi.; SHARPLES, Eleanor, phi.; SIDDAL, George, on board the

Carolina Merchant; SIGOURNEY, Daniel, phi.; SIMPSON, Peter, at Ralph Perkenson's, phi.; SLOANE, Henry, or Elizabeth Wylie, to the care of Rev. Mr. Tenent; SMITH, Capt. Alexander, phi.; SMITH, John, near Tho. Williams, tanner, North Wales; SMITH, Thomas, to the care of Mr. James, phi.; SPENCER, George, mercht., phi.; STOREY, Eleanor, at Katey Davis's, phi.; SYM, Capt. Andrew, phi.;

THOMAS, John, phi.; THOMPSON, William, at Society Hill, phi.; TILLY, Richard, shoemaker, phi. (2 letters), TOPP, Ann, Walnut St., phi.; TOUGH, Arthur, phi.; TURNER, John, carpenter, on board the Mary;

VALENTINE, John, mercht., phi.; VANDERPOOLE, Isaac, in phi.; VINCENT, John, at Byberry, pen.;

WIGHT, William, at David Wilson's, Shaminey, bu. co.; WILLIAMS, James, to the care of James Elder, phi.; WILLIAMS, Richard, phi.; WILLIAMS, Walter, to the care of Capt. James Foster, phi.; WILLIAMSON, James, pen.; WILSON, James, mercht. in America; WOOD, Richard, phi. near Shaminey; WRIGHT, Jonathan, carpenter, pen. (2 letters) (21 Mar.)

STRETTELL, Robert, merchant, in Phila. - will sell the following tracts of land in New Jersey: 1,250 acres at Persipeny, 1,250 acres near the head of Pessiack River, 625 acres in Glocester Co., 1,875 acres in Pilesgrove (21 Mar.)

BURROWS, Stephen, master of the sloop Delight, at Mr. Allen's wharf in Phila. - has for sale a Bermudian Negro woman (21 Mar.)

MILLER, George, joiner, in Chesnut St., next door to the Dolphin in Phila. - is about to leave off his trade (21 Mar.)

The following have arrived at New York from London: Capts. Farmer, Ratsey, Langdon - New York item of 22 Mar. (30 Mar.)

MORRIS, Robert, Esq. (son of Col. Morris) - is appointed Judge of the Admiralty for New York, the Jerseys and Connecticut and one of the Council for the Jerseys - New York item of 22 Mary. (30 Mar.)

MORRIS, Col. - reported to have been appointed Gov. of New Jersey (30 Mar.)

TURNER, William, noted robber, store-breaker and horse-stealer - has been arrested at Dover, Kent Co. on Delaware, and taken to Maryland (30 Mar.)

The Rain-Bow, Capt. Christian, of Phila. - reported to have
been driven on the North Bull by a storm, according to
word from Dublin (30 Mar.)

GREEN, Capt., of Phila. - has safely arrived at London
(30 Mar.)

JONES, Rees, surgeon, of Christiana Bridge - offers reward for recovery of a mare and colt stolen or strayed
from him; colt and mare may be taken to him at Uchland,
Chester Co., or to Thomas Edwards, Esq., in Lancaster,
or to Rees Jones at Christiana Bridge (30 Mar.)

BURROWS, Stephen, master of the sloop Delight, lying at
Allen's wharf in Phila. - has a Bermudian Negro woman
for sale (30 Mar.)

A letter to Franklin, signed "Y.P." mentions Zenger and
Mr. Hamilton, as does "The Craftsman" (6 Apr.)

A Brief Narrative of the Case and Tryal of John Peter
Zenger - has been published by B. Franklin (6 Apr.)

DOWNING, James, Irish servant (formerly servant to Joseph
Thomas of Pencader Hundred in Newcastle Co.; he afterwards went to Ireland and came back last fall as servant to James Johnson) - runaway from John Read, at
Christiana Bridge (6 Apr.)

BOLTON, Robert, late of Phila. but now of Maryland, merchant - has impowered John Ross, of Phila., attorney-
at-law, to collect debts due him (6 Apr.)

A servant, shoemaker by trade - his time of more than 3
years will be sold by Thomas Powell in Chesnut St.,
Phila. (6 Apr.)

MACHAN, Archibald, who lately sailed out of New York -
if living, he is to apply to Margaret Berwick, at the
Sign of the 3 Mariners, Front St., Phila., to hear something to his advantage (6 Apr.)

REED, William, at his store in Thomas Master's corner
house in Market, Phila. - sells cloth, cutler, etc. (6
Apr.)

COUCH, William, son of - was drowned 4 Apr. in Skuylkill
when his canoe overset (13 Apr.)

ADAMS, Abraham - was drowned 5 Apr. in Perkiomun Creek
when his canoe overset (13 Apr.)

THOMAS, Col. - is appointed Gov. of Pennsylvania and the Three Lower Counties (13 Apr.)

Schooner Good-Intent, William Rigby master - will sail from Phila. for Cape Fear; for freight or passage agree with David Bevan or the master at Mr. Robert Davis, at the Queen's Head in Water St., Phila. (13 Apr.)

PARSONS, William, in Second St., Phila. - sells linseed oil (13 Apr.)

MACCOLLOUGH, Capt., from St. Jago de Cuba wrote to Henry Crawford, of Jamaica, about Spanish preparations to take Georgia and Carolina; Capt. Dent, of the Kingsale man-of-war had sent his lieutenant, Mr. Watson, on shore at Havana but Watson was confined; Mr. Fox, factor at St. Jago, has confirmed what Capt. Macclough wrote to Mr. Crawford - Boston item of 3 Apr. (20 Apr.)

COMELY, Walter, of Bybery - last week his farm burnt down (20 Apr.)

ALOAN, Mary, Irish servant, age c. 26 - runaway from David Niven of Mill Creek Hundred in Newcastle Co. (20 Apr.)

BREINTNALL, Joseph, Secretary of the Library in Phila. - gives notice that there will be a meeting of subscribers at the house of John Roberts in High St. (20 Apr.)

Charles, Negro, age c. 24, who pretends to be a tanner - runaway from Amos Strickland, of Newtown, Bucks Co. (20 Apr.)

Lot in Front St. in Phila., bounded westward with part of Paul Preston's lot and northward with a lot now of Isaac Norris's, is for sale; enquire of William Cathcart or Nicholas Castle (20 Apr.)

Parcel of servants, just imported in the brigantine Charming Sally, is to be sold by John Mathers at Chester and Robert Barton, opposite to the Post Office in Phila. (20 Apr.)

Ship Agnus & Betty, John Brame commander - will sail for London; for freight or passage agree with the master on board at Fishbourn's wharf or at his store on Bickley's wharf (20 Apr.)

As Lord Baltimore has withdrawn objection, the King has approved appointment of Col. Thomas as Gov. of Pennsylvania and the Three Lower Counties (27 Apr.)

YATES, James, English servant, engaged to teach school -
runaway from Cornelius Vanhorne and others of Upper
Freehold, Monmouth Co., N.J. (27 Apr.)

PERRY, Elizabeth, English servant, age c. 20 - runaway,
with James Yates, from Cornelius Vanhorne (27 Apr.)

FLEXNEY, Daniel, of London - proposes settlement by arbi-
tration of differences between him and Thomas Jones, of
London St. near Ratcliff Cross, late master of the
Elizabeth, mariner (27 Apr.)

Boulting-cloths, imported in the ship Mary and Hannah,
Henry Savage master - are offered for sale by Arent
Hassart in Letitia Court, Phila. (27 Apr.)

LEDRU, Noel, in Letitia Court, during summer will teach
writing, arithmetic and pattern-drawing (27 Apr.)

KENARD, Samuel, of Frankfort, miller - desires persons indebted to him to make prompt payment (27 Apr.)

Parcel of English servants, just arrived in Ship Mary and
Hannah, Henry Savage master - will be sold by John Rey-
nell in Front St., Phila., or the master on board at
Fishbourn's wharf (27 Apr.)

New House on west side of Fifth St., near Walnut St.,
Phila., lately belonging to Edward Nichols, turner, is
to be sold by Edward Shippen (27 Apr.)

Parcel of servants, just imported - their times to be disposed of by John Stamper, in Water St., Phila. (27 Apr.)

Persons indebted to James Johnson are to pay their debts
to William Shaw, Esq., in Newcastle (27 Apr.)

Lot, wharf, stores, house, at Willing Town on Christine
Creek, are for sale; enquire of James Hutchinson,
living at said place (4 May postscript)

JONES, Thomas, who in Nov. 1735 was appointed master of
the ship Elizabeth at the Port of London by Daniel
Flaxney, Sr., answers adv. of Daniel Flaxney, formerly
an apothecary living in Bishops-Gate St. near Clarks
Alley, who precipitously went to Jamaica about 5 years
since (4 May postscript)

List of letters brought to the Post Office at Phila. since
21 Apr. last and remain unredeemed: ANDERSON, Thomas,
to the care of Peter Hunt, phi.;
BAGGS, Samuel, near Hattonfield; BROOK, Jonathan,

phi.; BRUMFIELD, Thomas, in Amity Twp.;

CALLAGHANE, Daniel, drawer, phi.; CAREY, John, in Plumstead Twp.; CARTER, John; CAWOOD, Richard, Wrights-Town; CLARK, Daniel, Ancocus Creek; CLAYTON, Aaron, Allens-Town; COOK, Andrew, to the care of Timothy Greer;

DAVIS, Joseph, to the care of Henry Hayes, ch. co.;

EATON, Simon, clothier, phi.; EDWARDS, Thomas, Esq., lan. co.; EVANS, John, North Wales;

FISHER, Joseph, Darby; FORKISON, Thomas, French Creek; FOX, Robert, Falls Twp., bu. co.; FRASER, William, gold-smith, phi.; FRYER, Anthony, to the care of Tho. Hooton, Evesham, bu. co.;

GARTRILL, John, schoolmaster, ch. co.; GIBBON, Nicholas or Leonard, at Greenwich (2 letters); GLADING, Mary; GREER, Timothy, phi.;

HALL, Thomas, Blockley, pen.; HAWLEY, Joseph, pen.; HEELY, Nicholas, at John McCollow's, pen.; HENDERSON, John, at New-London, near Whiteclay Creek; HODGE, Thomas, horpresser, phi.;

JACKSON, William, merchant, phi.; JOBSON, Joseph, phi.; JOHNSON, John, near phi.;

KEEF, Dennis, to the care of Capt. Edgar; KING, Charles, at John Holliday's, near Duck Creek; KINSON, Edward, ch. co.;

LANGTRY, John, merchant, phi.; LEE, Abraham; LEYLY, Bryan, to the care of Simon Hadley; LEVIS, Samuel, at Springfield; LIGHTWOOD, Capt. Edward; LOVELACE, John, with Joseph Wader, in Falls Twp.;

MINSHALL, Joshua, ch. co.; MOORE, George, Marl-borough, ch. co.; MOORE, William, Christine Creek; MORGAN, John, Radnor;

PEARSON, Francis, Eastown, ch. co.; PENNINGTON, Re-becca, Walnut St., phi.; PILES, Thomas, Water St., phi.; POMEL, Henry, wine-cooper, phi.; POTTS, Thomas, butcher, Germantown; POWEL, Samuel, Bristol Twp.;

QUALE, Robert, phi.;

RATHMELL, Buckingham; REYNOLD, Patrick, Mount Holly; RYAN, Mary, to the care of Juddy Fitzgerald; RYAN, Timothy, merchant, phi.;

SCOTT, Abraham, at Rochom, bu. co.; SHEPHARD, Henry, bricklayer, phi.; SKETCHLEY, John, at Ridley, ch. co.; SLACK, John, phi.; SMITH, John, to be left at the Post Office; SMITH, John, at Joseph Lynn's, phi.; SMITH, William, to be left at the Post Office; STEADMAN, James, at John Haines, Goshen; STEWART, James, Marpleton, pen.; STIRK, George, at Pennypack;

TAMPELAN, Samuel, French Creek; TAYLOR, Sarah, to the care of Joseph Miller, ch. co.; THOMSON, John, preacher,to the care of William McCullock; TILBURY, Thomas, at Hugh Evans's, Merion; TUCWOOD, Thomas, at the Blackmore's Head, phi.; TURNER, Thomas, at Samuel Lane's, in Providence, pen.;

WARR, Henry, phi.; WILLIAMS, George, in Shrewsbury,
N.J.; WILSON, John, Birmingham, ch. co., to the care of
Tho. Williams; WITT, Christopher, Germantown;
YETTS, Robert, Newtown, bu. co. (11 May)

PARKER, William, dec'd - 2 houses belonging to his estate,
near the drawbridge in Phila. will be sold by the sheriff
at the house of Widow Johns, a tavern hard by (11 May)

COUGH, William, Irish servant - runaway from Samuel Butt,
of Plumsted Twp., Bucks Co. (11 May)

Counterfeit 5s Pennsylvania bills, signed Abraham Chapman,
John Parry and Edward Horne have been uttered; reward
for apprehension of the passer is offered by Jer. Langhorne and A. Hamilton (11 May)

NEAVE, Samuel, at his store in Water St., near Fishbourn's
wharf, Phila. - sells cloth and other items (11 May)

SCULL, Joseph, at the Workhouse in Phila. - sells bedcords,
braces, halters, rope, hemp, flax, etc. (11 May)

WRAGG, James, at his store, next to the Scales, in Front
St., Phila. - sells gunpowder, shot, ironmongery (11 May)

KINGSLEAH, John, on 14 Nov. writes a letter from Havana
to his uncle, Peter Luce, merchant in Boston; John
Kingsleah and Capt. Henry Ware of Bristol are being
kept prisoners on board the Dispatch, Capt. Philip Dela-
motte; John writes that his man, Thomas Proving, is
going to Cadiz; John sends a certificate to his uncle
Peter Luce and to Uncle Piron - Boston item of 1 May
(18 May)

Snow John and William, William Devonshire master, will
sail for Bristol; for freight or passage agree with
the master or William Hellier in Market St., Phila.
(18 May)

Sloop Sarah, Arthur Burrows master, will sail for St.
Christophers; for freight or passage agree with William
Hellier in Market St. (18 May)

REDDISH, Nicholas, in Second St., Phila. - sells iron (18
May)

CALLENDER, Ephraim, servant, American born, age c. 30 -
runaway from George Stroud, of East Bradford, Chester
Co. (18 May)

Sloop Dove, Peter Albouy master, now at Bickley's wharf -

will sail for Jamaica; for freight or passage agree with
the master on board or with Capt. Bell at Powel's wharf
(18 May)

At Court of Oyer and Terminer at Burlington on 11 May, before Robert Lettice Hooper, Chief Justice of New Jersey, the following were convicted: Martha Cash of petty
larceny, sentenced to be whipped 2 market days; John
Simmonds of felony, in breaking open a schoolhouse and
chest and stealing property of William Sorsby, for which
he was burnt in the hand; Robert Murrey, of grand larceny, for which he was burnt in the hand; Timothy Denison, of burglary, for which he is to be executed 2 June
(25 May)

GROWDEN, Joseph, Attorney-General for Pennsylvania - died
Monday last in Phila. (25 May)

MORRIS, Col., whose commission for government of New Jersey has passed the seals, will be ready to come in
Capt. Pearce to New York (25 May)

BROWN, John, of Limerick - was found dead in the woods on
Sunday last (25 May)

STRETTEL, Robert, whose store is in Water St., facing Fishbourn's wharf, has for sale 5,000 acres of land in West
New Jersey (25 May)

NICHOLS, William, servant, age c. 34, brickmaker, who
lately came with Capt. Chads from Bristol - runaway
from John Parry, of Chester Co. (25 May)

CLAYPOOLE, Joseph, joiner, has left off his business, which
has been taken over by his son Josiah; Josiah has removed from the shop in Walnut St. to the Joyners Arms
in Second St. (25 May)

KIRKBRIDE, Joseph, late of Bucks Co., dec'd - accounts
will be settled with Mary and John Kirkbride, executors
(25 May)

Robert Ellis and John Ryan - have for sale at said Ellis's
house in Water St., Phila., a parcel of Negro slaves
(25 May)

GRIFFIN, William, Welsh servant - runaway from William
Hamilton, of Doe Run, Chester Co. (25 May)

SMITH, Robert, constable of Oley Twp. - offers reward
for capture of Thomas Gray (who was committed to Phila.
Goal for horse-stealing), who escaped from said

Constable Smith (25 May)

Cuffy, Negro, age c. 40 - runaway from Henry Pawling, of
Perkiomun, Phila. Co. (25 May)

NICKERSON, Deborah (wife of Nehemiah Nickerson and granddaughter of John Scull) of Absecum on Egg Harbour -
was drowned 7 May at Absecum (1 June)

THOMAS, Col. George, Gov. of Pennsylvania - arrived at
Phila. 1 June in Capt. Arthur from Antigua (1 June)

EMERSON, Lambert, joiner and looking-glass-maker, at the
Sign of the Looking-Glass in Front St., Phila. - also
sells locks, brasses, coffin handles, etc. (1 June)

Reward offered if oval pearl snuff box, set in silver,
lost between house of John Leech and Bickley's Corner,
is brought to the printer (1 June)

ONIONS, Thomas, English servant, bellows-maker - runaway
from Samuel Yarnal, of Edgmont, Chester Co. (1 June)

COLLINS, Edward, gardner, near Phila. - offers reward for
recovery of his horse (bred by Francis Holland in Baltimore Co., Md.), strayed or stolen; horse may be
brought to owner or to Owen Owen at the Indian King in
Phila. (1 June)

ROUTH, Christopher, late dec'd - accounts with estate to
be settled with Hannah Pearson, his executrix, at the
Sign of the Pewter Platter in Front St., Phila. (1 June)

Proclamation of Lt. Gov. George Thomas of Pennsylvania
and the Three Lower Counties on Delaware (8 June)

Ship, built for the Hon. Charles Windham, Esq., Capt. of
H.M.S. Rose, was launched Tuesday last at Charlestown,
S.C., and named the Duke of Cumberland - Charlestown
item of 27 Apr. (8 June)

On Monday last the Mayor and Commonalty of Phila. wait on
the governor and A. Hamilton, Esq., Recorder, con-
gratulates him (8 June)

Lot of ground in Town of Chester, adjoining to a lot of
Thomas Comings on the west and a lot of George Simsons
on the east, is to be sold or let; enquire of Isaac
Williams in Phila. (8 June)

Ship Constantine, Edward Wright master, now at Thomas
Griffitts's wharf in Phila. - will sail for London;

for freight or passage agree with master on board or
Messers. Shippen and Edgell (8 June)

LOWNDES, James, in Passayunk, has taken up a black mare
(8 June)

READ, Charles, in Phila. - sells rum, sugar, molasses and
slaves (8 June)

BOND, James, West country servant, sawyer - runaway from
Joseph Lynn, of Phila., shipwright (15 June)

SYMS, Capt. - his ship was taken by the Spaniards; he got
to the Virgin Islands in his boat and thence to Antigua and Maryland (15 June)

DEAN, Joshua, London convict, age c. 40, transported to
the plantations for life, servant of Alexander Spotswood - runaway from his master at Germanna, Virginia
(15 June)

Reward offered for recovery of a dog, lost or stolen, with
name of Samuel Jenkins engraved on the collar (15 June)

Schoolmaster seeks a position; apply to David Evans at
the Crown, near the market in Phila. (15 June)

All persons from the Pfalz who came over from Amsterdam
in the ship Townsend, Capt. Thomas Thomson - are to pay
their passage money due (15 June)

Ship Neptune, John Reeve master - will sail for London;
for freight or passage agree with the master on board
at Mr. Hamilton's wharf or with Messers White and
Taylor (15 June)

TOMLINS, John, servant, age c. 26, imported June last in
the brigantine Priscilla - runaway from John Lewis, of
Gloucester Co., Virginia (15 June)

MAYNARD, John, age c. 26, plaisterer, imported June last
in the brigantine Priscilla - same as above

LEE, Thomas, convict servant, imported March last in ship
York into York River, age c. 50, joiner - same as above

BARRY, George, convict servant, age c. 16 or 17, barber,
imported March last in ship York into York River -
same as above

WATERS, William, convict servant, age c. 20 or 22, joiner
or chair-maker, imported March last in ship York into

York River - runaway (in company with the 4 servants of John Lewis) from the Rev. Thomas Hughs, of Gloucester Co., Virginia (15 June)

McDANIEL, Randal, Irish servant, tanner, age c. 50 - runaway from Timothy Scarth, of the Northern Liberties, tanner (15 June)

EAGEN, John, Irish servant, tanner, who has been a hatter, age c. 20 - same as above

FRUIN, John, late of Phila., baker, now removed to Willington - has impowered Samuel Kirk, of Phila., to receive payments due him (15 June)

TURNER, Enoch, of New Haven, Conn. - reported to weigh 46 pounds at age of 18 months - Boston item of 29 May (22 June)

JARVIS, Capt., who arrived at Boston last week in a brigantine from Jamaica - recounted his escape from a Spanish pickeroon - Boston item of 5 June (22 June)

Tracts of land in Bucks Co., all belonging to estate of Joseph Growden, Sr., dec'd - will be sold at auction at the Coffee House in Phila. by Samuel Hasell, Samuel Bulkley and Hannah Growden (22 June)

Brigantine Sally, John Seymour master, now at Capt. Bourn's wharf - will sail for London; for freight or passage agree with the master on board or at Thomas Stapleford's in Second St., Phila. (22 June)

Tenement (lately belonging to Edward Nichols, turner) on west side of Fifth St., near Walnut St. in Phila. - will be sold at auction at the Proprietor's Arms in Second St. (22 June)

MAGARAGILL, John (alias John Farrel, alias John Dixon), Irish servant, age c. 25, tailor - runaway from Isaac Smith, of Accomack Co., Va. (22 June)

Part of a letter from J. J. Huber, dated 1 June, directed to Dr. Samuel Chew and an answer thereto (22 June postscript)

Speech of Gov. Jonathan Belcher to the Massachusetts General Assembly (29 June)

ROUSE, Capt. - arrived 18 June at Boston from Bristol (29 June)

POOLE, Peter, of Maxatawny - on 13 June accidentally shot
and killed his mother, Anna Sophia Poole, who was
cleaning fish among some bushes; he shot in the belief
that it was a deer (29 June)

RICHMOND, Capt. - arrived 28 June at Phila. from Lisbon
(29 June)

HOWARD, Thomas, of Phila. - offers reward for recovery of
a silver quart-tankard stolen from his house; it is
marked R D on the handle and the maker's stamp is P S
(29 June)

LANCISCUS, Thomas, apprentice, age $\underline{c}$. 19 - runaway from
Michael Hillegas, of Phila., potter (29 June)

CAVANNAH, Garret, Irish servant, age $\underline{c}$. 26 - runaway from
Joshua Baker, in Lancaster Co., near Newtown (29 June)

BRADY, Richard, Irish servant, age $\underline{c}$. 22, miller - same as
above

REYNOLDS, Patrick, Irish servant, age $\underline{c}$. 30 - same as
above

McDERMOT, Terence, Irish servant, age between 30 and 40,
distiller - same as above

HARDMAN, John, from North of Ireland, who about 2 years
since came to Pennsylvania from Antigua - printer has
a letter for him, with proposals to his advantage (29
June)

KENNY, Lazarus (whose father is a Molatto and his mother
a white woman) - runaway from Joseph James, of Cohansey
(29 June)

KINSEY, John - offers for sale tracts of land in the
eastern division of New Jersey, late part of the estate of William Dockwra, dec'd, and now belonging to
Margaret Bowles (29 June)

HOURE, John, English servant, age $\underline{c}$. 20 - runaway from
Nathan Lewis, of Newtown, Chester Co. (29 June)

DEVEREL, Capt. John, at Capt. Pritchard's in Market St.,
Phila. - sells gunpowder (29 June)

Reward will be paid by Philip King, of Charlestown, Chester Co., innkeeper, for return of his horse, stolen
from the stable of Michael Hillegas, in Phila.; Hillegas will also pay the reward (29 June)

SANSOM, Samuel, who intends for London this fall, is now removed over against the workhouse in Third St.; he sells cloth articles there or at Rees Meredith's store on William Fishbourn's wharf (29 June)

Parcel of English and Irish servants imported in the snow Hercules - to be disposed of by William Hartly, Thomas Robinson or Lawrence Anderson, on board said snow, now lying off opposite to Market St. wharf (29 June)

On Saturday, 24 June, at the Indian King in Phila. Joseph Shippen was chosen Grand Master of Pennsylvania; he appointed Philip Syng his deputy. Dr. Thomas Cadwalader and Thomas Boude were chosen Grand Wardens (6 July)

BROWNELL, Madam (wife of George Brownell), respected for her method of educating young ladies - died 5 July in Phila. (6 July)

BROWN, Thomas - 5 July fell out of a boat and was drowned (6 July)

GROVES, Alexander, practitioner in physic and chirurgery, who arrived about a week ago from Cadiz in the schooner Speedwell, William Weldon commander - Saturday last was seized with a fit and fell from his horse and died (6 July)

FISHLY, William, from Lancaster Co. - at Bristol, Bucks Co., when attempting to swim with his horse across the mouth of the mill creek, was drowned (6 July)

Mollatto Jemm, alias James Earl, Mulatto - runaway from Edward Farmer, of Whitemarsh (6 July)

MORDOX, James, Irish servant, age c. 60, smith - runaway from Henry Sparks, of Gloscester Twp., West New Jersey (6 July)

FISHBOURN, William, of Phila. - forbids anyone to detain, entertain, trust or employ Morris Kerril, his indented Irish servant, house-plaisterer (6 July)

GROWDON , Joseph, Esq., dec'd - accounts with estate to be settled with the executrix, Hannah Growdon, who wishes to sell her late husband's library, to be seen at the house of Samuel Hazel, Esq., in Front St., Phila. (6 July)

Item signed by Benjamin Walker about rattlesnake-root, which was addressed to Mr. Parks of the Virginia Gazette of 16 June (13 July)

WYER, Capt. Nathaniel - arrived last week at Boston from
the West Indies - his ship had been struck by lightning
off Bermuda - Boston item of 3 July (13 July)

MUCKLEWAIN, John and wife, suspected pickpockets, on Thursday last were committed to Bridewell in Boston by Mr.
Justice Adams, and Saturday last Peter Hambleton and
his wife, Mucklewain's friends, were committed to prison
for picking a pocket - Boston item of 3 July (13 July)

COLEMAN, Capt. - arrived Saturday last at Boston from
Cadiz - Boston item of 3 July (13 July)

BENNET, Capt. - arrived last Tuesday at Boston from Cork -
Boston item of 3 July (13 July)

BOLTON, Robert - is expected to return and open a dancing
school in Phila. (13 July)

BROWNELL, George, of Phila. - desires to settle accounts,
as he designs to leave Pennsylvania (13 July)

BUTLER, Mrs. Anne, if still living - by applying to Capt.
Daniel Cheston in Phila. she may hear of her husband
and something to her advantage (13 July)

HUMPHREY, George, English servant, age c. 19 - runaway in
a boat on the Potomack River from John Heard, Thomas
Brook, Abraham Barns and Robert Ford, all in St. Mary's
Co., Md. (13 July)

HIGGINS, Barnaby, Irish servant, age c. 25, joiner or carpenter - same as above

MARA, Michael, Irish servant, age c. 25, turner - same as
above

MAINE, John, English servant, bred to the sea, middle-aged
- same as above

MORE, John, Irish servant, middle-aged, labourer - same
as above

Peter, Negro, age c.. 25, country born - same as above

FRUIN, John, late of Phila. but now of Willington - persons
indebted to him are desired to make payment to Joseph
Peace of Bristol or John Ross, of Phila. (attorney to
Peace) (13 July)

Reward offered for recovery of a carnelian seal set in
gold, lost on the road from William Allen's fishing

place to Pensbury or from Pensbury to Phila. (13 July)

HAMBLETON, Peter and wife, convicted Monday last before
Justice Adams of picking William Greenleaf's pocketbook, for which they were whipped 10 stripes each and
committed to prison to be tried at Quarter Sessions for
stealing stockings out of shop of George Tilley - Boston item of 10 July (20 July)

TEMPLAR, Capt. - Saturday last arrived at Marblehead from
Lisbon - Boston item of 10 July (20 July)

List of letters brought into Phila. Post Office since 11
May and remaining unclaimed: ADAMS, Walter, Frankford;
ANNELY, Edward, phi.; ANTHONY, Capt. Richard, phi.;
ARCHIBALD, Anne; ASH, Thomas, phi; ASTON, Nicholas,
Abington;
    BATEMAN, Daniel, at Jonathan Fisher's, phi.; BEALE,
William, Whiteland Twp., ch. co.; BEVAN, Evan, merchant,
phi.; BLACKLEY, Thomas, mariner, phi.; BOUCHER, Matthew,
ch. co. (2 letters); BOYER, James, in the care of Widow
Sprogle; BOYER, Stephen, at Perkiomang, phi. co.; BROWN,
James, near Abington Meeting-house; BURN, Christopher,
bu. co.; BURN, Patrick, Springfield Manor; BURNINHAM,
John D., ch. co. (2 letters);
    CAMPBELL, Andrew, near phi.; CAMPBELL, William,
mariner, to the care of George Gray; CARLISLE, Jonathan,
Plumsted Twp.; CARROLL, Catherine; CARVER, Frank, to the
care of Mr. Greaten; CARY, Samuel, merchant, Newtown,
bu. co.; CAUELL, John, near phi.; CLEMENS, Catherine,
at Joseph Kirkbride's; COX, William, to the care of
Capt. Annis; CRALY, Henry, phi.;
    DAVIS, Robert, phi.; DAWSON, Daniel, phi.; DAY, John,
ch. co. (2 letters); DEAL, Michael, Springfield Manor;
DEAN, John, near phi.; DELL, Thomas, Ridley, ch. co.;
DENMARK, John, phi.; DIXON, Charles, at Mr. Mather's,
phi.; DOBBS, William, Charlestown, ch. co.; DOOGAN,
John, shipwright; DOWNING, Thomas, Willingstown; DWAR-
RYHOUS, William, phi.;
    EDWARDS, Poole, pen.; EYRE, Ann, to the care of Mr.
Henry Dixon, phi.;
    FILLPOT, William, Newtown, bu. co.; FLOWER, John,
at William Robinson's, pen.;
    GALAGHER, John, phi.; GLEAVE, John, Springfield,
ch. co.; GREEN, Thomas, pen.; GREW, Mrs. Betty, phi.;
GRISTON, Thomas, phi.;
    HAMTON, Simon, ch. co.; HANSON, Timothy, Esq., Kent
Co.; HART, John, in Warminster, bu. co.; HEWIT, Benj.,
Commander of the Three Sisters (2 letters); HUTCHINSON,
Thomas, at Lancelot Martin's;
    INGRAHAM, Job, phi.;
    Landlady at the Queen's-Head, in Lord st., phi.;

LANG, Alexander, at Newport, pen.; LAWRENCE, John,
Hopewell Twp., Cony-cut-chegg; LEAFRTY, Widow, near
Wilby Creek, pen.; LEE, Abraham, living with Henry
Williamson, ropemaker; LEWELLYN, David, Harford, near
phi.; LILLY, Samuel, Goshen, ch. co.; LINDSEY, Rev.
John, minister, pen.;

McGUIRE, Michael, at John Rennets; MARSHALL, David,
Duck Creek; MAYS, Sarah, to the care of Hugh Knight;
MENDINGHALL, Benjamin, Concord, ch. co.; MORRISON,
John, next the Bull's-Head Alehouse, pen.; MUSGROVE,
Abraham, Haverford, ch. co.;

NEWMAN, Richard, Northampton, N. J.; PARKER, John,
Birmingham, ch. co.; PARKER, Martha, Darby; PARKINS,
Hannah, phi. or Brunswick; PASTMORE, John, Kennet, ch.
co.; PETERSON, William, Racoon Creek, Goucester Co.;
PIPON, John, Jesey /sic!/; PUGH, Rev. Mr., Apoquinimink;

RICHARDSON, Capt. Joseph, phi.; RIDGELY, Nicholas,
Salem, West Jersey; ROBINSON, William, at Mount Pleasant, near phi.; ROGERS, Andrew, at Samuel Greave's,
at the Center Meeting-House, near phi.; ROSS, Mr.,
peruke-maker;

SATTERTHWAITE, William, bu. co.; SEYMOUR, William,
at John Taylor's, Thornbury; SHEPHERD, Charles, at Cornelius Hooper's, phi.; SMITH, John, to the care of R.
Stephens, Newtown, near Glocester; SMITH, Ralph, phi.;
SMITH, Thomas, Nottingham; SOCKERMAN, Hester, at Nicholas Sockerman's, Kent Co.;

TANNER, John, at Mary Stockdale's, phi.; TANTUM,
John, Nottingham, West Jersey; TAYLOR, Thomas, Middle-
town, ch. co.; TELFORD, Charles, to be left at Thomas
Carrel's, mason; THOMAS, Robert, Montgomery Twp.;

WALLIS, Phillip or Robert, N. J.; WHERLEY, Caleb, to
the care of Capt. Brown; WILLIAMS, Joseph, miller,
Merion; WILLIAMS, Thomas, Monmouth Co., N. J.; WILSON,
William, to the care of William Todd, Whitemarsh;
WOLFINGTON, Matthew, to be left with James Miller, N.
Garden; WRIGHT, William, to the care of Christopher
Bryant (20 July)

MALONE, JAMES, Irish servant, age c. 18 - runaway from
Thomas Willcox, of Chester Co., paper-maker (20 July)

MEGLOUGHIN, Neal, age c. 40, who served his time about 15
years ago at Crosswicks - runaway from Nathaniel Ring,
of Chester Co. (20 July)

BURN, Hugh, Irish servant - runaway from Edward Richards,
of Chester Co. (20 July)

PLUMLEY, George - recuts sickles (20 July)

Household goods are sold at the Widow Sharp's, next door

to Mr. James Steel's, in Second St., Phila. (20 July)

PRINCE, Capt. - arrived 12 July at Boston from London (27 July)

H.M.S. Rose, Capt. Wyndham, arrived last week at New York from Carolina - New York item of 24 July (27 July)

Gin seng, of which an account is given in Chambers's Dictionary and Pere du Halde's account of China, has been found growing near Susquehannah in Pennsylvania (27 July)

Brigantine Anna, Henry Tisdale master, will sail for South Carolina; for freight or passage agree with master on board at Samuel Powel's wharf or Francis Richardson, in Front St., Phila. (27 July)

House between William Chancellor's and James Steele's in Second St., Phila., is to be let (27 July)

SALEVAN, John, who came from Co. Killdare, Ireland, and is supposed to be at house of Mr. Hunter on River Delaware, merchant - is desired to apply to William Harper in Second St., Phila., to hear something to his advantage (27 July)

HARPER, William - offers reward for recovery of horse, stolen or strayed from the Commons of Phila. (27 July)

Plantation to be let by Christopher Taylor, of Tenicom Island; enquire of William Pyewell, in Front St., Phila., or said Taylor at said island (27 July)

FORD, Benjamin, of Brandywine Hundred, Newcastle Co. - offers reward for apprehension of the thief (supposedly John Kelly, an Irishman) who broke open and robbed his house (27 July)

First term of lease of brewhouse back of the Tunn Tavern, in Water St., Phila., will expire, and Isaac Norris, Esq., has given notice to leave; place is to let; enquire of John Danby, in Third St. (3 Aug.)

Subscriptions are being taken for A Treatise on the Diseases of Virginia and the Neighbouring Colonies, by John Tennent (3 Aug.)

MURREY, Roger, servant, age c. 28 - runaway from Patrick Reynolds, of Edge Pillick, Burlington Co. (3 Aug.)

Hannah, Negro, age c. 22 - runaway from Thomas Lawrence, of Phila. (3 Aug.)

Lots of ground on north side of the house late of Paul
Preston in Front St., Phila., having one brick and one
wooden tenement thereon, now in possession of William
Cathcart - will be sold at auction at the Crooked Billet in Phila. (3 Aug.)

PAYNE, John, merchant, dec'd - accounts with estate to be
settled with the administrators, Edmund Iliffe and
James Day, at the dec'd's late store (at Robert Moore's,
shopkeeper, near the Court House, in Phila.) (3 Aug.)

BOLTON, Mr. - plans to open a school in September next,
where children may board as usual with Mr. Brownell (3
Aug.)

Parcel of English and Irish servants, just arrived from
Dublin in the snow Jolly Bacchus, Peter Cullen commander, to be disposed of by Thomas Walker, butcher, or
Samuel Walker or John Beaumont or said master on board
the snow (3 Aug.)

BIGGER, Peacock, brazier, in Market St., Phila., near the
Sign of the Indian King - sells all sorts of copper
work (3 Aug.)

Yesterday was se'nnight, in New Kent Co., Va., a bridge
belonging to Col. Basset's milldam broke and Major
Philip Roots, Capt. Robert Whiting and Capt. Charles
Friend all fell 12 feet but were not injured - Williamsburg item of 21 July (10 Aug.)

BRUIT, Mr., of Carolina Co., Va. - lately committed suicide - Williamsburg item of 21 July (10 Aug.)

DOWRICK, Capt., of Boston - lately lost his vessel on the
coast of Ireland - Boston item of 31 July (10 Aug.)

The Rose, of London, Capt. Croak commander, which on 3
Aug. arrived at Phila., on 17 June took aboard 61 persons from the Speedwell, of which William Stockdale had
been master, which was sinking; Stockdale had sailed
from the Island of St. Michael's for Lisbon on board
one Capt. Gillegan (10 Aug.)

Cloth, nails and Bristol steel are for sale - by Lawrence
Growdon at Joseph Richardson's in Front St., Phila.
(10 Aug.)

GARDNER, Thomas - offers reward for recovery of a mare
strayed or stolen from the Commons of Phila.; mare may
be brought to Owen Owen in Market St. (10 Aug.)

Time of a servant lad, age c. 15, is to be disposed of; enquire of Thomas Nesmith, at Richard Martin's mill in Cheltenham, Phila. Co., or Isaac Williams, in Phila. (10 Aug.)

JONES, John, servant, age c. 21, who came in lately with Capt. Chads from Bristol - runaway from Lewis Lewis, of Richland, in the great swamp, Bucks Co. (10 Aug.)

Tenement and lot on north side of Mulberry St. (commonly called Arch St.), opposite to the Sign of the George, now in the tenure of Rebecca Robins, to be sold at auction at the Crooked Billet in Phila.; as to tile, inquire of the Widow Jones, living next door to the said tenement (10 Aug.)

LLOYD, Thomas, who has taken the brewhouse near the Tun Tavern, will remove it to a more convenient place; he is removed to the Sign of the Golden Mortar and Pestle, the house where Andrew Bradford formerly lived in Second St., where he sells drugs and medicines (10 Aug.)

Speech of Lt.-Gov. George Thomas to the Pennsylvania Assembly and reply by A. Hamilton, Speaker, for the Assembly (17 Aug.)

TURNER, T., at Rappahanock River in Virginia, sends account of Mr. Huber's proposals for purchase of tobacco by Edward Barradall, of Williamsburgh, Va., and Philip Thomas, of Anne Arundel Co., Md., for the Farmers General of France; the following will deliver tobacco: William Byrd, John Robinson, John Grymes, John Tayloe, Philip Lightfoot, Thomas Lee, Robert Bolling, Henry Fitzhugh, William Fairfax, Joseph Ball, Matthew Kemp, Benjamin Walker, John Mercer (17 Aug.)

LAY, Benjamin - copies of his book against slave-keeping will be left for sale with Benjamin Franklin (17 Aug.)

Ship Constantine, Edward Wright master, will sail for London; for freight or passage agree with Messers Shippen and Edgell or with the master on board at Thomas Griffitts's wharf (17 Aug.)

MIFFLIN, Jonathan - sells wine, sugar, glass, hardware (17 Aug.)

GROWDON, Lawrence - has taken up a horse at his plantation at Bensalem (17 Aug.)

CARAWAN, John, Irish servant, age c. 18, who lately came in the brigantine Hannah, William Tiffin master, from

Dublin - runaway from Samuel Davis, of Worcester Twp., Phila. Co. (17 Aug.)

PRITCHARD, Rees, servant, age c. 30 - runaway from Anthony Cunrad, of Worcester Twp., Phila. Co. (17 Aug.)

Barbados born Negro lad, age c. 17, is for sale; enquire of John Luke at William Calender's in Second St., Phila., near Peter Stretch's (17 Aug.)

PEARCE, Mary - her creditors are desired to meet at the Crooked Billet in Phila. (24 Aug.)

Sloop George and Elizabeth, George Bishopp master - will sail for Carolina or Antigua; for freight or passage apply to Weldon Simmons, shipwright, next door to the Bank Meeting House or to the master on board (24 Aug.)

WELCH, James, Irish servant, age c. 23 - runaway from Joseph Talbott, of Middletown, Chester Co. (24 Aug.)

KELLY, Cornelius, servant, age c. 21 - runaway from Mahlon Stacy at the Mount Holley Ironworks in Burlington Co. (24 Aug.)

REYNELL, John - has for sale salt just imported from Lisbon in the ship Dispatch, Elias Guilliot master (24 Aug.)

Friday last arrived at New York Capt. Pearce in H.M.S. Flamborough, bringing commission for Lewis Morris as Governor of New Jersey (31 Aug.)

DUNNING, Thomas, dec'd - accounts with estate to be settled with Martha Dunning, executrix (31 Aug.)

Parcel of servants, just arrived from London in the brigantine Pennsylvania Packet, Henry Harley master, now at Pemberton's wharf, will be sold by Nathan and Isaac Levy or by the master (31 Aug.)

PULLEN, William, servant, who talks West-Country, age c. 21 - runaway from John White, of Phila. (31 Aug.)

HACKETT, Theobald, dancing-master, from England and Ireland - has opened a dancing-school in Phila. at the house where Mr. Brownell lately lived, in Second St. (31 Aug.)

Proclamation of Lt.-Gov. George Thomas (7 Sept.)

Spaniards have violated their agreement with Mr. Oglethorpe - New York item of 4 Sept. (7 Sept.)

Commission of Lewis Morris as Governor of New Jersey was published Tuesday last at Amboy (7 Sept.)

RICE, John, indented servant belonging to the brigantine Pennsylvania Packet - Saturday last fell overboard into the river and was drowned (7 Sept.)

Tuesday last arrived at Phila. the ship Winter Gally, Edward Paynter commander, with 360 Palatines (7 Sept.)

Brick house in Market St., between George Mifflin's and Wm. Paschal's, is to be sold; enquire of Simon Edgell (7 Sept.)

HEWES, Moses, in Chesnut St., Phila. - has for sale Canary and Madera wine (7 Sept.)

SUNDERLAND, William, servant, a Londoner, age c. 20 - runaway from John Bunting, of Chesterfield, Burlington Co. (7 Sept.)

PIGGOTT, John - offers reward for recovery of mare, strayed or stolen from the dwelling place late of John Piggott, dec'd, near Nottingham, in Chester Co. (7 Sept.)

Message of Gov. George Thomas to the Pennsylvania Assembly (14 Sept.)

Lately arrived at Phila. the ship Two Sisters, James Marshall commander, the ship Glasgow Gally, Walter Sterling master, the ship Robert and Alice, Walter Goodman master, with 1,003 Palatines, the ship William and Mary, William Blair master, and the snow Jane, John Andrews master, with 130 passengers and servants from Ireland (14 Sept.)

Attempts were made 9 Sept. to break into Loan Office, joining to the State House in Phila., under care of Andrew Hamilton (14 Sept.)

CLIFTON, John - has for sale a Negro boy and a Negro girl (14 Sept.)

BARR, George, tobacconist, living over against the Court House in Phila. - sells snuff and tobacco (14 Sept.)

Lot and house on west side of the lower part of Front St., Phila., between the lots of John Bayly and Matthew Cowley, belonging to James Kirk, are to be sold; enquire of Philip Syng, Jr., silversmith, in Front St. (14 Sept.)

SEARLE, John, master of the brigantine <u>Laurel</u> - offers reward for capture of runaway Irish servant man, age <u>c</u>. 22 or 23, who was brought up to cloth-shearing in Bristol (14 Sept.)

Lately arrived at Phila. are the ship <u>Nancy</u>, William Wallace master, and the ship <u>Queen</u> <u>Elizabeth</u>, Alexander Hope master, with 440 Palatines (21 Sept.)

MAC HAFEE, John, Irish servant, age <u>c</u>. 20 - runaway from Lancelot Martin, near Bristol, Bucks Co. (21 Sept.)

MORGAN, Evan, cooper, in Front St., Phila., over against Mr. Turner's, sells Canary and Vidonia wines (21 Sept.)

Reward will be paid to person who brings to J. Logan's plantation near Germantown one John Brewer, a young servant from Warwickshire, who has absented himself "by Means of Liquor" (21 Sept.)

HARRIS, John, Welsh servant - runaway from Humphrey Brooke, in King William Co., Virginia (21 Sept.)

Abraham, Negro, Virginia born, age 25, shoemaker, belonging to Col. George Braxton, of King and Queen Co., Va., has run away (21 Sept.)

Windsor, Negro, age <u>c</u>. 20, Virginia born - runaway from George Braxton, Jr., who will pay reward of 2 pistoles each for capture of the above 3 runaways (21 Sept.)

FISHBOURN, William - offers for sale houses and land in Phila., including woods opposite to Clement Plumsted's place (21 Sept.)

Speech of Lt.-Gov. George Clarke to New York Assembly (28 Sept.)

Proclamation of Gov. Lewis Morris of New Jersey and addresses to him from corporations of Perth Amboy, Burlington and New Brunswick (28 Sept.)

Arrived at New York on 23 Sept. the brigantine <u>Prince Frederick</u>, Capt. Neilson, from Bristol (28 Sept.)

Ship <u>Amsterdam</u>, Capt. Willson, is daily expected at New York from Plymouth, with 300 Palatines (28 Sept.)

Capts. Bryant, Farmar and Langdon all arrived in England from New York (28 Sept.)

ELKINS, Capt. John, who arrived at Marblehead on 13 Sept.

- brought news from Europe (28 Sept.)

PEARCE, Mary - her creditors are to bring their accounts
to Reese Meredith and William Hellier (28 Sept.)

Address of Justices and Freeholders of Monmouth Co. to
Lewis Morris and answer of the governor (5 Oct.)

Sunday last the sloop <u>Dolphin</u>, Adam Decheseau commander,
from Cape Francois, arrived at Block Island; on 3 Sept.
Peter Legrand and 2 others of the French murdered the
captain and an Englishman named Edward and threw their
bodies overboard; then Legrand and one of the company
named Frank forced 2 passengers, Thomas Davis (resident
of Block Island) and John Merchant (resident of Martha's Vineyard), to throw overboard a boy, Stephen
Decheseau (nephew of the captain); Monday the sloop was
driven on the rocks; the persons brought in on Tuesday;
Peter Legrand, Peter Jesseau, Francis Bowdoin, John
Couprey and the 2 English passengers were all imprisoned on a charge of murder - Newport item of 22 Sept.
(5 Oct.)

Arrivals at Boston on 24 Sept. were Capt. Tanner from New-
castle and Capt. White from London; it is reported that
Capt. Morris was to sail for Boston about 1 Aug. -
Boston item of 25 Sept. (5 Oct.)

Monday last the following were elected for Phila. Co.:
Representatives--Edward Warner, William Monington,
Thomas Leech, John Kinsey, Jonathan Robeson, William
Allen, Job Goodson, Morris Morris; sheriffs--Septimus
Robinson, Isaac Leech; coroners--Owen Owen, David Evans;
commissioner--Andrew Robeson; assessors--John Dillwyn,
Samuel Morris, miller, Edward Williams, Owen Evans,
William Paschal, Abednego Thomas; burgesses--John
Kearsley, Israel Pemberton; city assessors--William
Rawle, Philip Hillier, Samuel Austin, Philip Syng,
Nathaniel Allen, James Morris (5 Oct.)

Monday last the following were elected for Bucks Co.:
Representatives--Jeremiah Langhorne, Joseph Kirkbride,
Abraham Chapman, Andrew Hamilton, John Watson, Benjamin
Field, Thomas Marriot, Thomas Canby; sheriffs--John
Hart, Enoch Anderson; coroners--William Atkinson, James
Shaw; commissioner--Abraham Chapman; assessors--Bar-
tholomew Longstreth, John Hutchenson, Abraham Grif-
fiths, Robert Smith, Cephas Child, John Dawson (5 Oct.)

Monday last the following were elected for Chester Co.:
Representatives--William Moore, James Gibbins, Thomas
Chamdler, Joseph Harvey, John Owen, William Hewes,

Thomas Tatnal, Jeremiah Starr; sheriffs--Benjamin Davis,
John Parry; coroners--Aubrey Bevan, Evan Ellis; com-
missioner--Joshua Thomson; assessors--William Jeffrys,
John Allen, Daniel Walker, John Yarnal, James Jeffrys,
David Stephens (5 Oct.)

Monday last the following were elected for Lancaster Co.:
Representatives--James Hamilton, Andrew Galbraith,
Samuel Smith, John Wright; sheriffs--Robert Buchanan,
James Galbraith; coroners--Joshua Low, William Caldwell;
commissioner--Andrew Douglas (5 Oct.)

Monday last the following were elected for Newcastle Co.:
Representatives--Andrew Peterson, Thomas Noxon, John
McCabe, David French, John Curtis, John Finney; sheriffs
--Henry Newton, John Gooding; coroners--John Duning,
Thomas Downing (5 Oct.)

Tuesday last Anthony Morris, Esq., was chosen Mayor of
Phila. by the Aldermen and Common Council (5 Oct.)

Saturday last Thomas Griffitts, late Mayor of Phila., made
a great feast for his citizens (5 Oct.)

Monday last James Anderson mariner, fell into the river
at Phila. and drowned (5 Oct.)

Ship _Delaware_, David Davis master, now at Mr. Powel's
wharf - will sail for Bristol (5 Oct.)

Ship _Winter Gally_, Edward Paynter master, now at Mr.
Austin's wharf - will sail for South Carolina; for
freight or passage agree with the master on board or
with Benjamin Shoemaker, merchant, in Market St.,
Phila. (5 Oct.)

BENEZET, J. Stephen - has tea for sale (5 Oct.)

BISPHAM, Joshua, sadler, lately arrived from England -
is next door to the Post Office in Phila. (5 Oct.)

Dwelling-house in Water St. (joining to Abraham Bickley's
on the north side and the alley by Robert Hopkins on
the south side, over against the Turks-Head and near
the market wharf) is to be let by Evan Morgan in Market
St. (5 Oct.)

KEMBLE, John, living near Richard Murray's plantation
near Whitemarsh, offers reward for recovery of strayed
colt (5 Oct.)

Indian slave man - has runaway from George Dasheil, of

Somerset Co., Md. (5 Oct.)

Warning against buying watches stolen from chest brought
to Phila. from London in the brigantine Pennsylvania
Packet, Henry Harley master (5 Oct.)

COWLEY, Capt. - arrived at Boston Tuesday last from Antigua; he recounted much suffering on that island from
smallpox, a fever and hurricane; a ship belonging to
Piscataqua, Capt. Papoone commander, was stove to
pieces (12 Oct.)

On 10 Oct. John Emley and Benjamin Smith, Esqrs., were
elected to serve in the assembly for Hunterdon Co.
(12 Oct.)

Indigo, oil, iron pots, psalters, rum etc. - sold by Ambrose Vincent and Company at their store on Fishbourne's
wharf, Phila. (12 Oct.)

STAPLEFORD, Thomas, of Phila. - offers reward for recovery
of a brass kettle stolen from his kitchen (12 Oct.)

WHARTON, Joseph, of Phila. - offers reward for recovery
of a mare strayed or stolen from the Commons near
Phila. (12 Oct.)

Reward for recovery of 2 horses strayed from Capt. Woodrop's
plantation will be paid by Robert Ellis in Phila. (12
Oct.)

ROBINSON, Daniel - offers reward for capture of the following, who broke out of the goal at Dover, Kent Co.:
Thomas Johnson, Irishman, a blacksmith; William Spencer,
a joiner (12 Oct.)

VERE, William, of Phila., who intends to leave Pennsylvania - desires that all persons indebted to him make
payment (12 Oct.)

Monday last arrived at Phila. the brigantine Fox, Charles
Ware master, from Cowes, with 153 Palatines (19 Oct.)

Brew-house in Water St., adjoining the Tun Tavern, will
be sold at auction at the Coffee House in Phila. by
Patrick Baird, vendue-master (19 Oct.)

SHARP, Thomas, at his store on Fishbourn's wharf - sells
cloth, rum, sugar, etc. (19 Oct.)

MEREDITH, Reese, who intends for England next spring - at
his store on William Fishbourn's wharf sells goods

lately imported in the ship <u>Elizabeth</u>, James Allan master (19 Oct.)

Snow <u>Two Sisters</u>, James Marshall master - will sail for South Carolina; for freight or passage agree with the master on board at John Parrot's wharf (19 Oct.)

Ship, Alexander Hope master, will sail for South Carolina; for freight or passage agree with Benjamin Shoemaker, merchant, in Market St., Phila., or master on board ship at Bickley's wharf (19 Oct.)

WRAGG, James, who is designing for England - sells iron-mongery at his store, next to the Scales, in Front St., Phila. (19 Oct.)

A horse, supposed stolen, was left at the Sign of the Indian King in Newcastle by a Welshman who had a pass from Elisha Gatchel, Esq. (19 Oct.)

KINDLEY, Peter, Irish servant, age <u>c</u>. 30, tailor - runaway from William Miller, of Middletown Twp., Chester Co. (19 Oct.)

A piece of woolen cloth was left at house of Jacob Shoemaker, wheel-maker, in Market St., Phila. - owner is desired to claim it (19 Oct.)

Persons indebted to Messers William Masters, Thomas Robinson and William Heartley for servants bought from the snow <u>Hercules</u> of Phila. are to make payment at Nathaniel Allen's, cooper, in Front St., Phila. (19 Oct.)

Caesar, Negro, age <u>c</u>. 24 - runaway from Alexander Morgan, of Waterford Twp., Gloucester Co., West New Jersey; 2 white men are supposed to have gone with him, Thomas Powell and Henry Watkins (19 Oct.)

DOWEN, Philip, Irish servant, age <u>c</u>. 20 - runaway from Thomas Wills, of Middletown, Chester Co. (19 Oct.)

WELCH, James, Irish servant, age <u>c</u>. 23 - runaway from Joseph Talbot, of Middletown, Chester Co. (19 Oct.)

BENN, John, Irish servant, age <u>c</u>. 20 - runaway from Alexander Hunter, of Middletown, Chester Co. (19 Oct.)

At Court of Admiralty, opened at Newport, R.I., on 5 Oct. Thomas Davis, Peter Legrand, Peter Jesseau and Francis Baudoine were sentenced to be executed 3 Nov., but John Merchant and John Couprey were acquitted (26 Oct.)

HANDLIN, Capt., who arrived at New York Monday last from
St. Thomas - reports that there had been a terrible
storm there: Capt. Pinder of St. Eustatia lost his
vessel and people at Crabbe Island; the ship _Prince_
Frederick foundered at sea; Capt. Stephen Paynter, in
the sloop _Unity_, suffered from a hurricane but made
Bermuda and while he was there arrived Capt. Conyers
from Phila., who had 3 of his men washed overboard -
New York item of 22 Oct. (26 Oct.)

TINGLE, Capt., who arrived at New York 21 Oct. from
Georgia, reports that General Oglethorpe is arrived
there with 4 men-of-war and about 400 soldiers (26 Oct.)

Sunday last arrived at Phila. the ship _Davy_ from Holland;
the captain, both mates and 160 Palatines died on the
passage, and the carpenter brought in the ship (26 Oct.)

Sloop _Speedwell_, Jeremiah Baker master, from North Carolina,
bound to Boston, was stove to pieces on the beach at
Barnagat; the people were all saved (26 Oct.)

LOGAN, J. - offers reward for recovery of a French book,
Jugemens Des Savans, Tom. VII, taken or dropped out of
a chaise in Phila. or in road to Germantown; it may be
brought to the owner or to Edward Shippen in Phila.
(26 Oct.)

STRETTELL, Robert - has removed his store from Water St.,
facing Fishbourn's wharf, to the house late Henry
Flower's in Front St., 4 doors from Chesnut St. (26 Oct.)

JOHNSON, Thomas, of Perth Amboy, barber - offers reward
for recovery of a case containing 6 razors, lost or
mislaid (26 Oct.)

GREW, Theophilus, mathematician - will teach school this
winter over against James Steel's in Second St., Phila.
(26 Oct.)

LLOYD, Thomas, at his house in Second St., Phila. - sells
tea, hats, gloves, gunpowder, raisins, pickled salmon,
etc. (26 Oct.)

RACHFORD, John, English servant - runaway from John Housman, of Kent Co. on Delaware; runaway may be taken to
keeper of the King's Goal at Dover (26 Oct.)

CLAY (or CLAYTOWN), Joseph, English servant - same as above

Speech of Lt.-Gov. of New York to the New York Assembly
(2 Nov.)

List of letters brought to Post Office at Phila. since 20
July past and remaining unredeemed: ALLASON, Capt. William, of the <u>George</u> <u>and</u> <u>Henry</u> snow, phi. (2 letters);
ALLEN, Robert, in pen.; ANDREW, Capt. John, of the ship
<u>Jane</u>, phi.; APRUNTEY, Bryan, at Robert Jones's, Merion;
ARCHER, Oliver, on board the <u>Pennsylvania</u> <u>Pacquet</u> (2
letters);
 BALLARD, William, at Nicholas Custer, smith, phi.
co.; BARTLET, John, phi.; BAYLIS, George, at Amwell;
BEATON, Daniel, to the care of James Anderson, ch. co.;
BELL, Hamilton, Neshaminy; BELL, Joseph, to the care of
John Bools, in Plumsted, bu. co.; BELL, Thomas, in
Swaterraraw near John McCowns; BEST, John, house-carpenter, ch. co.; BLAKE, William, phi.; BOYD, James,
Middletown, ch. co.; BREAUNO, John, in phi.; BRODRICK,
Francis, to the care of John Griffin, America; BROWN,
Coling, to the care of John Thomson, Sadsbury; BROWN,
Samuel, near Delaware Falls; BROWN, Zechariah, phi. (2
letters); BROXTON, Edgmont, to the care of Joseph Pratt;
BULLOCK, Robert, phi.; BUM, Christopher, with Thomas
Forster, bu. co.;
 CAMPBELL, Isaac, phi.; CARR, James, to the care of
James Johnston, phi.; CARRUTH, Walter, to the care of
Rev. Bartram, pen.; CAUEL, Thomas, near Phi.; CAVEN,
Samuel, preacher, pen.; CHANDLER, Mary, to the care of
Sam. Rutcliff, Conestogo; COOMBES, Joseph, Plumsted
Twp., bu. co.; CORAY, John, at A. Robinson's, near phi.;
CORREN, George, at Gabriel Walker's, ch. Road; CORRY,
George, N. London Twp., pen.; CRAWLY, Henry, phi.;
CREAGHTON, John, to the care of the Rev. Mr. Tennent;
CRISSON, Solomon, turner, phi.; CROFTS, Dudley, merchant,
phi.; CUMINE, Joseph or Samuel Robinson, pen.;
 DAUGHERTY, John, pen.; DAVIS, John, on board the
<u>Bristol</u> brigt., phi.; DAVIS, Sam., bu. co.; DAVISON,
Alexander, Wrights-town; DAYSERT, John and James, Marlborough, pen.; DENS, Richard, wodcoller; DIAS, Moses,
near the Gap, pen.; DIGHT, Abraham, Darby, ch. co.;
DODD, Gabriel, or his wife; DODD, Thomas, Pennepack;
DOWTHWAITE, Sam., at Ro. Davis's; DOYLE, Philip, West
New Jersey, near phi.; DRACK, Francis, living in Broad
St., phi.;
 EDDY, Thomas, New Providence, near Schuylkil; EDMUNDSON, William, Lancaster Town; EDWARD, Isaac, phi. co.;
EGAN, John, with David Owens, Limrick, phi. co.; EGERLY,
Simon; EGGER, Robert, to the care of Archibald Marshon;
ELLIS, George, Jersey; ESSPY, John, Lebanon, Donnegal,
pen.; EZZD, Christian, Morris's River, in Salem co.;
 FARMER, Francis, phi.; FINLY, William, to the care
of Jeremiah Allen, soap-boiler, phi.; FISHER, George,
at Sam. Eastburn's, bu. co.; FISHER, William, at Robert
Davis's, phi.; FLECK, James, Northampton, bu. co.;
FLEEMAN, John, in middle Octorara; FORD, Standish, phi.

co.; FOX, Elizabeth, at Joseph Large's, Buckingham;
FOY, William, to the care of Edward Richardson, Woodbury Creek; FREEK, William, to be left with Thomas
Clifford, Bristol; FRISTAN, David, Pilesgrove, Salem
Co., N.J.;

GARFATT, George, Goshen, ch. co.; GATTS, Mary, to
be left at Thomas Dell's, pen.; GIBBON, Nicholas or
Leonard, at Greenwich, in New Jersey; GIBSON, Alexander,
to the care of Rev. Mr. Allison; GILBERT, Alexander,
phi.; GLADING, Mary; GRAHAM, James, phi.; GRAHAM, John,
to the care of Rev. Mr. Bertram; GREDEN, John, New-Garden; GULDIN, Samuel, Germantown; GULLIFORD, William,
phi.;

HAMILTON, John, East Sadsbury, ch. co.; HAMILTON,
Wm., Dromore; HARAH, Isaac, phi.; HARRIS, Evan, Bethlehem, pen.; HARRIS, Hector, tailor, phi.; HARRIS, Sarah,
phi.; HASILLWOOD, Wm., Esq., phi.; HAVART, David, ch.
co.; HAWLEY, Joseph, pen.; HEMPHIL, James, pen.; HERD,
John, with Wm. Gretcham, Arch St., phi.; HESKET, John,
at Capt. Anderson's; HOLDSWORTH, Stephen, Westgate,
Wakefield, pen.; HOPKIN, David, Octorara; HOTHAM, Richard, Evesham, Burlington co.; HOWEL, Thomas, Charlestown, ch. co.; HUGHES, Catherine, Maxfield, bu. co.;
HUMPHREY, Benjamin, Merion (2 letters); HUMPHREY, John,
Merion; HUNTER, Agnes, Swateraarow, pen.; HUTCHISON,
John, Eastown, to the care of James Kirk, Society Hill;

IFTONS, Simon, Duck Creek;

JACKSON, Jonathan, at John Jones's, London, Britain;
JOHNSTON, Hugh, Londonderry; JONES, Abraham, upholsterer,
phi.; JONES, John, Duck Creek; JONES, John, Lancaster
co.; JONES, Mary, to the care of Susanna Bond; JONES,
Thomas, phi.; JONES, Thomas, to the care of Robert Ellis;

KELSE, Archibald, bu. co.; KENDAL, Benjamin, ch. co.;
KERGAN, Hugh, at Richard Buffin's, ch. co.; KILL, Joseph,
to the care of Allan Delap;

LAUGHLIN, Elizabeth, with Mr. Wm. Shiply, ch. co.;
LEE, Joseph, shipwright, phi.; LEVIS, Samuel, or Josiah Hibbert, Springfield; LEWIS, John, baker, phi.;
LEWIS, John, surgeon, phi.; LOREY, Robert and John,
Nottingham; LOUGHRAN, Joseph, to the care of John
Alexander; LOVELESS, John, with Joseph Warder, Falls
Twp.; LOW, Oliver, belonging to the Charming Sally (2
letters); LOWDER, William, to care of James Whitehill,
pen.;

McCALA, John, lan. co.; McCALL, Alex., Sadsbury,
lan. co.; McCAVER, Arabel, pen.; McCREIGHEN, Henry,
these with care; McDONNEL, Randal, merchant, phi.; Mc-
DOUGH, Wm., tailor, Chesnut St.; McDOWEL, Wm., phi.;
McEOUN, Daniel, joiner, phi.; McFALL, Neal, bu. co.;
McFERSON, John, Octorara; McMINE, John, ch. co.; MADDEN,
James, Motton Lane; MALONE, Daniel, carpenter, phi.;

MARIS, Terence, to the care of Wm. Passmore, ch. co.;
MARSHAL, James, Arch St., phi.; MARTIN, John, Manta
Creek, Gloucester co.; MASTERS, Edward, pen.; MASTERS,
Wm., phi.; MEABREY, John, pen.; MERES, Alex., pen.;
MESTAYER, Daniel, Salem, N.J.; MILLER, Robert, Caln,
ch. co.; MITCHEL, Robert, pen.; MOOR, Adam, Donnegal;
MOOR, Wm., Donnegal; MORREY, Richard, phi.; MOWBERRY,
Susanna, phi.; MURREY, Wm., smith, Octorara;

NELSON, John, to care of Thomas Hus; NEWMAN, Richard,
Northampton, Jersey; NICKINSON, John, Blockly, Pen.
(2 letters); NILLY, Thomas, to care of John Elison, Donnegal; NIXON, James, to care of Wm. Long; NIXON, Wm.,
Milford, pen.;

OLIVER, John, at the Spread Eagle, phi.;

PATTERSON, Wm., Gloucester co.; PERKINS, Abraham,
Ancocas; PETTIGREW, Wm., Whitley Creek; PHILIPS, John
(2 letters); PINDAR, Mary, phi.; PINKERTON, David,
Pequay, lan. co.; PORTER, John, phi.; POWEL, Alice,
Springfield; POWEL, Nicholas, phi.; POWEL, Sam., Bris-
tol Twp., phi.; POYL, Ann, Byberry; PULLIN, Peter, phi.;

READ, James, to care of Robert Smith, Coldspring,
pen.; REISEL, Hans Jonas, phi.; REYNOLDS, John, Wrightstown, bu. co.; RICHARDSON, Capt. Joseph, phi.; RICHARD-
SON, Wm., at the head of Pequa; RIET, Lenert, Tulpehocken, pen.; ROBINS, Rebecca, phi.; ROSS, George,
peruque-maker, phi.; ROY, Alex., rope-maker, phi.; RUD-
DER, John, Nottingham, pen.; RUTTER, John, smith, ch.
co.;

SALE, Adam, ship-carpenter, phi.; SAUNDERS, Joseph,
phi.; SHANNON, John, to care of George Ducker, phi.;
SHARP, Dr. James, Salem; SHEMAN, James, Octorara, to
the care of James Garner; SHEPHARD, Charles, at Dunks's
Ferry; SHEPTO, John, Evesham, Burlington co.; SIDWEL,
John, Nottingham, ch. co.; SIMPSON, Alex., at Widow
Jones's, phi.; SMITH, Francis, Evesham, Burlington co.;
SMITH, Michael, phi.; STEPHENSON, John, Second St.;
STEVENS, Robert, Newtown; STEVENS, Susanna, to care of
John Gilbert, barber; STEWART, Thomas, ch. co.; STUART,
Alex., London Tract;

TAYLOR, James, New London Twp., pen.; THOMAS, David,
on board the Bristol brig., phi.; THOMPSON, Daniel,
cooper, phi.; THOMSON, John, Sadsbury, pen. (3 letters);
TORQUITT, James, phi.; TURBET, James, to the care of
Alex. McClain or the Rev. Mr. Boyd, Minister of the
Gospel in Octorara, in ch. co., near Newcastle in pen.,
to be left with Mrs. Ann McCoole in Newcastle, or Mr..
Griffes, baker, in phi. and given to Mr. Hugh O'Neill,
tailor in phi. This to the care of Capt. Cross and Mr.
Andrew McCoard; Please gentlemen to forward this to
James Turbet in the Great Valley;

WALKER, John, and Jo. Taylor, ch. co.; WALKLY, John,
at Ob. Johnston's, Darby; WANE, Anthony, Eastown, ch.

co.; WEST, Richard, West Jersey; WEST, Thomas, Concord,
ch. co.; WHITE, Henry, phi.; WHITESIDE, Wm., lan. co.;
WILDS, Ruth, Duck Creek; WILLIAMS, John, at Thomas
Williams, tanner, North Wales; WILSON, Anthony, Middle-
town, bu. co.; WILSON, James, near the cop. mines; WIT-
MAN, Christoffel, church-warden of the Lutheran Con-
gregation, pen.; WOOD, Thomas, pen.; WORSTAL, John,
Buckingham; WRIGHT, Deborah, phi. (2 Nov.)

One Whitesides, lately come from Ireland in Capt. Grieves,
has been imprisoned at Newcastle for passing counterfeit 20s. bills (2 Nov.)

Reward will be paid for recovery of a horse strayed away
from Burlington if it is delivered to Thomas Croasdale
of Frankford or John Milner of Burlington (2 Nov.)

STEEL, James - offers reward for recovery of a gelding
strayed or stolen from his pasture near Phila. (2 Nov.)

KINSEY, John (Clerk of the Yearly Meeting held at Burling-
ton for New Jersey and Pennsylvania), by order of the
Meeting expresses disapproval of the book All Slave-
Keepers, etc. (2 Nov.)

DEXTER, Henry - offers for sale the plantation where he
now lives at the Lower Ferry, opposite to George Gray's
(2 Nov.)

PAR, Samuel - wishes all accounts with him to be settled
as he intends to leave the province (2 Nov.)

MORGAN, Alexander, of Waterford Twp., Glocester Co. - offers reward for apprehension of Thomas Powel and Henry
Watkins, who came from Virginia but last from North
Carolina, both of whom claim to be sawyers; Watkins has
been taken up for stealing from Thomas Spicer, Esq.,
but escaped; the 2 men persuaded a Negro of Morgan's to
steal gold from his master and they then received the
gold (2 Nov.)

Speech of Lt.-Gov. George Thomas to General Assembly of
the Three Lower Counties and their address (David
French speaker) to him (9 Nov.)

OGLETHORPE, General - arrived 17 Sept. at Frederica with
600 persons - Charlestown item of 5 Oct. (9 Nov.)

Corporation and gentlemen of Perth Amboy on 30 Oct. waited
on Gov. Lewis Morris and celebrated the King's birthday
(9 Nov.)

Brigantine <u>Anna</u>, Henry Tisdale master, now at Mr. Fishbourn's wharf, will sail for South Carolina; for freight
or passage agree with said master or with Reese Meredith
(9 Nov.)

Several plantations are offered for sale by Lawrence Growdon at his house in Bensalem, Bucks Co., or at Joseph
Richardson's in Front St., Phila.; one item is a tract
in the Northern Liberties of Phila., between the plantations of Ralph Asheton and Richard Waln (9 Nov.)

PENROSE, Bartholomew - sells Rhode Island cheese and cider
(9 Nov.)

Sloop <u>Samuel</u> and <u>Mary</u>, Constantine Hughes master, will
sail for Virginia; for freight or passage agree with
William Hudson, Jr., in Chesnut St. (9 Nov.)

LEWIS, Samuel, at his plantation in Hartford, Chester Co.,
has taken up a sorrel horse (9 Nov.)

WHITE, William, at his plantation in Kennet Twp., Chester
Co., has taken up a bay horse (9 Nov.)

Ship <u>Tryal</u>, Patrick Crump commander - will sail for Ireland; for passage agree with Messers Thomas Robinson
and John Erwin, at Mr. Lambert Emerson's, looking-
glass-maker, in Front St., Phila. (9 Nov.)

At Newport, R.I., Thomas Davis hanged himself on 3 Nov.
and later the same day Peter Legrand, Peter Jesseau
and Francis Bowdoin were executed at Bulls Point -
Newport item of 3 Nov. (16 Nov.)

Reward will be paid for recovery of a mourning ring (in-
scribed with the name of the late Gov. Gordon) if same
is brought to the printer (16 Nov.)

A stray mare has been taken up at Walter Clark's in Kennet Twp., Chester Co. (16 Nov.)

ALRICHS, Hermanus - offers reward for recovery of a mare
strayed or stolen from the Commons (16 Nov.)

PARSONS, William - sells linseed oil (24 Nov.)

Time of an English servant man is for sale; enquire of
John Kirkbride or Israel Pemberton (24 Nov.)

ROUTH, Christopher, dec'd - accounts with his estate to
be settled with Hannah Routh, executrix (24 Nov.)

213

VICKERY, Capt., who arrived at Boston about a week ago
from Antigua, reported the following vessels lost as
the result of 2 hurricanes: Capts. Couzens, Sleigh,
Martin, Papoon and Owen - Boston item of 13 Nov. (30
Nov.)

DORBY, Capt., at Boston refitting, who was at Nevis during
the August storm; on 18 Aug. he put out from Nevis in
company with the following: ship Grenadier, Capt. Bur-
roughs; ship Glocester, Capt. Berwick; ship Sea Nymph,
Capt. Barnes; brigantine Sarah, Capt. Sears; Capt.
Corey from Rhode Island; Capt. Elkins from Salem; Capt.
Astin from Boston; Capt. Edwards and Capt. Monford,
from New London; on the 22 Aug. Capt. Dorby reached St.
Thomas, where he found the following disabled vessels:
Grenadier, Capt. Burroughs; ship Lydia, Capt. Ladd;
ship Charming Molley, Capt. Pike; the John pink, Capt.
Paul; the Gloster, Capt. Berwick; Capt. Soames; Capt.
Corey's ship was overset; Capt. Nevin abandoned his
ship; ship Frederick, Capt. Whitwood, was overset -
Boston item of 13 Nov. (30 Nov.)

A letter from Kingston, Jamaica, dated 20 Sept., gives the
following news: John Gilbert was taken on south side
of Hispaniola; Capts. Bedlow and Bennet are probably
taken; Capt. Deal, of Port Royal, who had 160 Negroes
on board, and Moses Mendos, a Jew, are taken and put
in goal; Capt. Russel has taken a Spanish ship (30 Nov.)

CHICKERING, Capt. - brings news from Jamaica - Boston item
of 13 Nov. (30 Nov.)

Fire broke out 30 Nov. at Mr. Clark's near Black Horse
Alley, Phila., from some brands left in the dancing
school fireplace, but was soon extinguished (30 Nov.)

BAMBRIDGE, James, at the Three Tons in Chesnut St., Phila.
- offers reward for lost red leather pocketbook (30
Nov.)

BOND, Capt. - is expected every tide from Bristol with
servants, whose time will be sold by Simon Edgell (30
Nov.)

Speech of Gov. Lewis Morris to the New Jersey Assembly (6
Dec.)

RAWLINSON, Robert, of Phila., baker, intending to leave
Pennsylvania - wishes to settle all accounts (6 Dec.)

Brigantine Britannia, John Bond master, lying at Thomas
Griffitts's wharf - will sail for Jamaica; for freight

or passage agree with the master or Simon Edgell (6 Dec.)

MOORE, Joseph, in store on Fishbourn's wharf - sells onions (6 Dec.)

KETTSENDORFF, William, Dutch servant, age c. 18 - runaway from Nathan Lewis, of Newtown, Chester Co. (6 Dec.)

Ship Elizabeth, James Allan master - will sail for London; for freight or passage apply to the master or to John Reynell, merchant, in Front St., Phila. (14 Dec.)

House of Burgesses of Virginia elects a Speaker on Wednesday last; Mr. Harrison moved that Mr. Robinson take the chair and his motion was supported by Mr. Moscoe, Mr. McCarty and Mr. Blair; Henry Fitzhugh, Esq., was recommended for Speaker by Mr. Corbin, and his motion was supported by Mr. Carter, Mr. Willis and Mr. Hedgman; Mr. Curtis moved for electing Mr. Conway and was seconded by Mr. Embry; Mr. Robinson was chosen Speaker - Williamsburgh item of 3 Nov. (21 Dec.)

Addresses of Council and House to Gov. William Gooch of Virginia and his answers - Williamsburgh item of 3 Nov. (21 Dec.)

Petition of the Quakers in Virginia to the House of Burgesses, signed by the following: John Cheadle, Abraham Ricks, Wike Hunicut, William Lad, Armiger Trotter, Peter Benford, William Denson, William Outland, John Murdaugh, Edmund Jourdan, Thomas Pleasants, Matthew Jourdan, Thomas Newby, Thomas Trotter, Robert Ellyson, John Crew, John Pleasants, Samuel Sebrel, Samuel Jourdan, John Denson - Williamsburgh item of 17 Nov. (21 Dec.)

DITTOAD, Anthony Francis - was executed 24 Nov. for the murder of Mr. Evans the coach-maker; John Davis was reprieved (21 Dec.)

Thursday or Friday last in Glocester Co. the son, aged 14 or 15, of a Mrs. Cozens, who lived within 4 or 5 miles of Glocester Town, was murdered and linen and other valuable goods were stolen (21 Dec.)

Confession of John Barnes, alias John Greenwood, alias John Thompson, alias George Brown, executed at Newark, Essex Co., N.J., on 17 Nov.; born in Lancashire, bound out to age of 24, stole frequently, at Liverpool bound as a servant for 4 years to Maryland; in West Jersey stole cloth from John Brown, a fuller; worked for John

Deen; together with one John Price stole a silver
tankard and spoons; together with Roger James stole
sheep; stole also from the following: Mr. Van Bruck,
Hendrick Van Wee, Philip Harris, Mr. Cresap in Maryland, Mr. Wileman at the Highlands, Thomas Coleman,
Philip Arnel, William Salter in Pennsylvania, Mr. Eag,
John Smith of Burlington, Joseph Fowler, Thomas Baily
(21 Dec.)

JACKSON, Stephen, on Skuylkill, near Joseph Gray's ferry -
has a young Negro man for sale (21 Dec.)

BRETT, Richard, deputy Postmaster at Potomack - offers
reward if lost horse is taken to William Vernell's (21
Dec.)

MARTIN, Samuel, on 4 Oct. last in Virginia, signed a note
to one Thomas Clark; as he received no consideration
for the note, Martin warns people not to take an assignment of the note (21 Dec.)

KELLEY, Dennis, Irish servant, age c. 22 - runaway from
Daniel Jones of Blockley Twp., Phila. Co. (21 Dec.)

SHIELS, Robert, English convict servant, age c. 26, gardner - runaway from Peter Presly, of Northumberland Co.,
Va.; reward will be paid if he is returned to his master or to B. Franklin, in Phila. (21 Dec.)

ROBERTS, William, English convict servant, age c. 23,
shoemaker, who also goes by the name of William Simmons - same as above

BRAGGS, Ann, of Portsmouth, R.I., when drunk lost her way
and froze to death on 24 Nov. (28 Dec.)

OTIS, Solomon, of Barnstable, Mass. - his daughter, age c.
12, fell down when the house caught fire a few weeks
ago and died in a few minutes - Boston item of 11 Dec.
(28 Dec.)

WILSON, John, of Andover, Mass., recently buried 8 children, who all died of the throat distemper - Boston
item of 11 Dec. (28 Dec.)

1739

ENGELBRECKT, Anthony, stone-cutter, next door to the horse-
mill, in Market St., Phila. - does marblework (4 Jan.)

BEARD, John, in Pequay - has taken up a mare and colt (4
Jan.)

The following persons have unclaimed letters at the Post Office in Phila. since 2 Nov. past: ADARE, Joseph, cooper, phi.; ALL, Richard, Upper Providence, ch. co.; ARCHER, Oliver, on board the <u>Pennsylvania</u> <u>Pacquet</u> (2 letters);

BALL, Charles, phi.; BATEMAN, Daniel, merchant, phi.; BEATLEY, Samuel, ch. co.; BELL, Joseph, to the care of John Boyle, Plumsted, bu. co.; BIRES, David, Donnegal, to the care of the Rev. Mr. Adam Boyd, Octarara; BISHOP, William, shoemaker, phi.; BOX, Nathaniel, Pilesgrove, Salem co., to be left with Alexander Woodrup, phi.; BROOKS, George, on board the <u>Prince</u> <u>Augustus</u>, phi.; BUYARS, William, Donnegal, to the care of Wm. Karr, phi.;

CAINE, Christopher, phi.; CARROL, Patrick, phi.; CATRINEAGEN, Mrs., phi.; CHAMRON, William, to be left at Joseph Paul's, phi. co.; CLOAK, Peter, Wrights Town, bu. co.; COLLSON, Ann, to be left at Mr. Willin's, phi.; COOPER, Heely, phi.; CORNET, George, phi., for Simon Edgerly;

DALRUMPLE, George, to the care of John Hutchinson, phi.; DAVIES, Hugh, near Newtown, pen.; DAVIS, Samuel, bu. co., pen.; DAY, John, Birmingham, ch. co.; DEANE, Clement, on board the <u>Dragon</u>, phi.; DITCHERTS, William, at the Black Horse, phi.; DODMEAD, James, Merion, phi. co.; DUNLOP, James, Salem, West Jersey;

EDGER, Moses, lan. co.; EDMONSTON, Archibal, near phi. (2 letters); EDWARDS, Mary, to be left at Capt. Anderson's, New Jersey; ELLIOT, Robert, to the care of George Stewart, lan. co. (2 letters); ERWIN, James, phi.; EVAN, John, to be left at White and Taylor's, merchants, phi.; EVANS, John, Whitemarsh;

FLOOD, Patrick, phi.; FORBES, Thomas, pen.;

GALT, Matthew, in Swaterraraw; GREGG, Thomas, at John Price's, blacksmith, phi.;

HALLAHAN, John, phi.; HANNA, James, shoemaker, pen.; HARBUTT, William pen.; HARDING, Elizabeth, pen.; HOLELER, John, pen.;

IRWIN, George, New Jersey; IRWIN, Henry, to the care of Moses Edger, lan. co.;

JAMES, Charles, to be left at James Stell's, phi.;

KEAN, Nicholes, bu. co.; KENDAL, Benjamin, ch., pen. (2 letters); KINSON, William, ch. co.; KYDE, William, merchant, phi.;

LE CORNU, James, phi.; LEE, John, phi.; LEWIS, John, surgeon, bu. co.; LINN, Andrew, Bethlehem, N.J.;

McCAFFERY, Hugh, to be left with Elias Dehart, Skuylkil; McGREE, John, pen.; McINTYRE, Dugald, nigh phi.; MAHIGAN, Charles, merchant, phi.; MARTIN, Richard, Abington; MILBOURN, John, on board the <u>Dragon</u>, phi.; MISSING, William, commander of the <u>Adventure</u>, phi. (2 letters); MORA, William, to the care of John Carnahan, Octorara; MORGAN, David, schoolmaster, to be left at

David Evans's, phi.;

NEATE, Capt., commander of the <u>Dragon</u>, phi.; NORRIS,
John, near Phi.;

PAINCOAT, John, Mansfield, near Burlington; PARFIT,
John, at Cooper's Ferry; PASSMORE, John, Birmingham,
ch. co.; POPKINS, Evan, bu. co., to be left with Jenkin
Jones, phi.; POWES, Peter, Cohansey, to the care of
William Cooper, phi.;

REYNOLDS, Mary, ch. co.; RIVIER, John, phi.; ROBERTS,
Thomas, Milford, bu. co.; ROBERTS, William, near phi.;
RUSH, Joseph;

SEYMOUR, William, at John Taylor's, Thornbury, bu.
co.;SMITH, Daniel, Octorara;

WELCH, Edward, rope-maker, on Society Hill, phi.;
WHITE, Christopher, to be left with William Peacock,
Marlborough, ch. co.; WHITE, John, to be left at Wm.
Johnson's, phi.; WILKS, Francis, Buckingham, bu. co.;
WILLSON, Anthony, Middletown, bu. co. (4 Jan.)

ALRIHS, Hermanus - house where he now lives in Second St.,
Phila., is to be let (4 Jan.)

MAULL, Joseph, in store on Fishbourn's wharf - has onions
for sale (4 Jan.)

Speech of Lt.-Gov. George Thomas and address to him (signed
A. Hamilton, Speaker) (11 Jan.)

MORRIS, Anthony, mayor - instructs constables to enforce
law against tippling in taverns on Sunday (11 Jan.)

FARQUHAR, Alexander, of Kent Co. on Delaware - offers reward for apprehension of Moses Lewis, New England born,
carpenter by trade, who stole 2 horses from Farquhar's
plantation (11 Jan.)

CARPENTER, Samuel, dec'd - brew-house belonging to his estate is offered for lease by Joseph Richards and John
Inglis (11 Jan.)

FRANKLIN, Benjamin, printer - is removed from the house
where he lately lived, 4 doors nearer the river, on
the same side of the street (11 Jan.)

O'NEAL, Brian - his creditors are desired to bring their
accounts to J. Stephen Benezet or John Reynell (11 Jan.)

Address of Council to Gov. Lewis Morris of New Jersey and
his answer (18 Jan.)

Negro man of Robert Hooper, Esq., of Rocky Hill, Sommerset Co., N.J., murdered the little son of the overseer's

wife and set fire to Mr. Hooper's barn; the Negro was
tried and executed for his crimes (18 Jan.)

BOWLS, John, servant, shoemaker - runaway from Joseph Decow, of Trenton, Hunterdon Co., West New Jersey (18 Jan.)

LLOYD, Edward, an Englishman, age c. 22, who hired himself
out for a month to Samuel Wheeler at Miamensin, near
Phila. - has gone away (18 Jan.)

BOOD, John, of Carpenter's Island - will pay reward if
horse strayed or stolen from him is brought to him or
to John Rouse, smith, in Phila. (18 Jan.)

Messages, instructions, etc., with respect to reprinting,
exchanging and re-emitting the bills of credit of Pennsylvania - mentioned Gov. George Thomas, Thomas Lawrie
(secretary) and A. Hamilton (Speaker) (25 Jan.)

Tuesday last John Winthrop (second son of Adam Winthrop,
Esq., of Boston) was installed as Hollisian Professor
of Mathematics and Philosophy at Harvard; prayers were
said by Pres. Holyoke, Rev. Dr. Wigglesworth and Rev.
Dr. Sewall; Henry Flynt, Esq., Senior Fellow, administered the oaths of allegiance - Boston item of 2 Jan.
(1 Feb.)

A letter from Block Island, dated 1 Jan., to Gov. John
Wanton, informs that a ship from Rotterdam, commanded
by George Long, with 400 passengers and servants bound
for Phil., was cast away 26 Dec. on Block Island; Capt.
Long and nearly 200 Palatines died on the passage and
but 105 were landed on Block Island where some 30 more
died; Peter Baise was sent to inspect the affairs of
the Palatines at Block Island - Newport item of 13 Jan.
(8 Feb.)

Notice about quit-rents due is signed by James Steel, at
Phila. (8 Feb.)

BAYNTON, Peter, at his store at lower end of Front St. -
sells wine, rum, iron, etc. (8 Feb.)

LLOYD, Mordecai, almost opposite the Baptist Meeting house
in Phila. - has for sale thread, hose, lats, brushes,
pipes, cutlery and Dutch servants (8 Feb.)

Votes of the Pennsylvania Assembly and speech of the
Governor (15 Feb.)

YELDHALL, Susanna - has to let the house where she lives
at the upper end of Walnut St., at the corner of Fifth

St., Phila.; enquire of her or B. Franklin (15 Feb.)

Sunday last arrived at York River the ship <u>Bobby</u>, Capt.
Crane, from Jekyl Sound, Ga., who reports that on 18
Sept. last the <u>Blandford</u> man-of-war, Capt. Burrish, with
General Oglethorpe, arrived in Georgia; in revolt of
troops Capt. Mackaw shot a soldier; another soldier
tried to shoot Capt. Debrisay but gun did not go off;
6 ringleaders were put prisoners on board the <u>Blandford</u>;
one mutineer said he would shoot the colonel or Capt.
Herring - Williamsburgh item of 8 Dec. 1738 (22 Feb.)

Speech of Mr. Conway in the House of Burgesses against the
inspecting law - Williamsburgh item of 9 Dec. 1738 (22
Feb.)

Governor of Virginia assented to resolve that 100 pounds
be paid John Tennent for publishing his <u>Discovery</u> <u>of</u> <u>the</u>
<u>Use</u> <u>of</u> <u>the</u> <u>Seneca</u> <u>Rattlesnake-root</u> and that an additional
salary of 80 pounds be paid William Parks, printer -
Williamsburgh item of 22 Dec. 1738 (22 Feb.)

LLOYD, William, Irishman, age <u>c</u>. 30, who has been a
schoolmaster - has stolen clothing from the house of
Benjamin Franklin (22 Feb.)

ANNELY, Edward, late of Phila., dec'd - accounts with estate to be settled with Simon Edgell, administrator
(22 Feb.)

PARKHOUSE, Richard - absconded from his bail (Simon Edgell) and from the brigantine <u>Britannia</u>, John Bond commander, bound for Jamaica; Parkhouse was late mate of
said brigantine (22 Feb.)

DELAGE, Peter, over against James Steele's, in Second St.,
Phila. - sells sugar, candy, tea (22 Feb.)

GARLAND, William Irish servant - runaway from Thomas Blair,
of Bucks Co., near Derham Ironworks (22 Feb.)

Gov. Jonathan Belcher refuses assent to bill of Massachusetts Assembly for emitting 60,000 pounds in bills of
credit; address of Assembly is signed by John Quincy,
Speaker, and sent to the governor - Boston item of 29
Jan. (1 Mar.)

On Thursday the body of Robert Lettice Hooper, who for 17
years was Chief Justice of New Jersey, was interred at
New York - New York item of 19 Feb. (1 Mar.)

Report that Joseph Scattergood, master of the brigantine

Katherine and Mary, abused John Fisher, Jr. (son of one of the owners of the vessel), is declared false by John Carson, James Smart and William Oram in a sworn statement before William Allen, and by John Assheton, who was a passenger on said brigantine (1 Mar.)

JONES, Daniel, of Blockley Twp. - has to let a fishing place in Schuylkill (1 Mar.)

A curious piece of clockwork is to be seen at the house of Henry Clark, at the Sign of the Coach and Horses, opposite to the State House, in Chesnut St., Phila. (1 Mar.)

Accounts with estates of Thomas and Martha Dunning, dec'd, are to be settled with Samuel Dunning, executor of Martha Dunning (1 Mar.)

MORRIS, Owen, of Parish of Kennis in Montgomeryshire in Wales, left there about 40 years ago and was not heard of till 1736, when he wrote his brother Richard Morris; he asked that a relative might come to him to be heir to his estate; he gave as his address the White Hart in Boston; Ann Roberts (daughter of a newphew, Owen Morris, Jr.) came to America but cannot find Owen Morris, the Elder, now nearly 80 years of age; Ann Roberts, now in Phila., at Edward Nicholls's, will pay a reward for news of Owen Morris, the Elder (8 Mar.)

McCARTER, Charles, a Highlandman servant, age between 35 and 40 - runaway from Thomas Thomas, of Welch Tract, Newcastle Co. upon Delaware; reward will be paid if servant is returned to his master or to Owen Owen at the Indian King in Phila. (8 Mar.)

HUGHES, Constantine, about a league without the Cape - has taken up a cable and anchor (8 Mar.)

EMBLEN, Samuel, at the Sign of the Heart, opposite to the New Market, in Phila. - gives away An Abstract of a Short Treatise on Dr. Bateman's Pectoral Drops (8 Mar.)

TAILER, Isaac, English servant who speaks West Country and who was imported about 2 years since into Virginia, afterwards put into Dover Goal, sold to Richard Manwarring; Tailer ran away and was put into Phila. Goal and then sold to John Burr; he has now run away from John Burr of Burlington Co. (8 Mar.)

HAZARD, Mrs. Mary, born in Rhode Island (widow of Robert Hazard of South Kingston and grandmother of the dec'd George Hazard, late Deputy Governor of Rhode Island) - died 28 Jan. last in her 100th year (15 Mar.)

Brigantine **Elizabeth** **and** **Mary**, Bristow Brown master, now
at Bickley's wharf in Phila. - will sail for Barbados
(15 Mar.)

Hannah, Negro, Barbados born - runaway from Thomas Lawrence, of Phila., merchant (15 Mar.)

DITCHETT, William, English servant, age c. 24 - runaway
from Thomas Croasdale, of Frankford, near Phila. (15
Mar.)

Message from Gov. Belcher to the Mssachusetts Assembly and
reply of the House, with reference to salary of Gov.
Burnet and Gov. Shute (22 Mar.)

In a storm on 25 Feb. the houses of Mr. and Mrs. Nathaniel
Langley and Mr. and Mrs. Heyman, both in Dorchester,
Mass., were struck by lightning; Mrs. Langley was
struck down but recovered; one of her legs was scorched;
Mr. Heyman's house is about 60 rods south of Langley's
(22 Mar.)

KABAR, John, Irish servant, age c. 24 - runaway from Evan
Ellis, of East-Town, Chester Co. (22 Mar.)

Ned, Negro, age c. 27, who speaks Dutch very well - runaway from Andrew Robeson, of Rocksborough, near Phila.
(22 Mar.)

WHITE, Henry, woolcomber, who came from Bristol with Capt.
Nathan Cowman about 4 years ago - by applying to the
printer may hear something to his advantage (22 Mar.)

Ship with 300 Protestant Switzers was lately wrecked and
only about 90 survived, among them a daughter of Col.
Brown, chief of the group - Williamsburg items of 12 and
19 Jan. (29 Mar.)

GRINAWAY, Prudence (wife of Henry Grinaway and granddaughter of William Lea, late of Phila., shopkeeper) -
warns people not to purchase messuages and lots to
which she is entitled from John Robinson, of Phila.,
attorney-at-law; she had signed a deed, as did her husband, which was witnessed by one Garland (a brother-in-
law of Robinson) and a Capt. Knowlman (29 Mar.)

KOYLE, Michael, in Front St., Phila. - offers reward for
recovery of a lost silver watch (maker's name Thomas),
chain and seal (29 Mar.)

Country seat, about 15 miles from Phila. and near Horsham,
is offered for sale by Standish Ford, living on the

premises; apply to him or to Benjamin Franklin (29 Mar.)

Tract of 600 acres, formerly called James Morris's land, near Lewistown, Sussex Co. on Delaware, is to be sold; apply to Martin Jervis, in Second St., Phila., or William Pim, in Chester Co. (29 Mar.)

A few days ago several men on board a sloop at the north end of Boston, firing at a mark on the dock, accidently hit a Mrs. Morberly but her life was saved when the bullet lodged in several thicknesses of cloth upon which she was working; Mr. Morberly narrowly escaped with his life - Boston item of 26 Feb. (5 Apr.)

A child of Capt. Thomas Homans in the western part of Boston, near Hooper's Meeting, was killed and Mrs. Homans and some other women were severely burnt when some powder caught fire Wednesday last - Boston item of 26 Feb. (5 Apr.)

MONTGOMERY, Capt., from the Bay of Honduras - reports that Capt. Gwynn from Boston was taken by the Spaniards and also that Capt. Darby recovered from the wreck of a Spanish sloop about 7,000 pieces of eight, 500 pistoles and articles of gold and silver - Boston item of 12 Mar. (5 Apr.)

BOWEN, Henry, servant, age c. 17 - runaway from James Sharples of Lower Providence, Chester Co. (5 Apr.)

PUNCH, David, Irish servant, weaver - runaway from Isaac Rees of Upper Merion, Phila. Co. (5 Apr.)

McGUIRE, Nicholas, Irish servant, age c. 40, who formerly belonged to Samuel Harrison, Esq., of Glocester, West New Jersey - runaway from Caleb Perkins of Brandywine Hundred in Newcastle Co. (5 Apr.)

On 13 Mar. was held an election for the Assembly in New York, presided over by David Provoost, merchant, of New York; at 11 at night the poll stood thus: John Moore 510, Adolph Philipse 415, William Rome 411, David Clarkson 403, C. Van Horne 396, J. Alexander 381. The 4 elected invited Van Horne and Alexander to drink a glass with them at Mr. Ingliss's - New York item of 14 Mar. (12 Apr.)

Speech of Lt.-Gov. George Clarke of New York to the Assembly (12 Apr.)

COLLIS, John, at Pensoken - so overcome with remorse for suing a debtor who could not pay that on 1 Apr. he drowned himself (12 Apr.)

OWEN, Edward, Irish servant, age <u>c</u>. 17 - runaway from
Robert Roberts of Lower Merion, malster (12 Apr.).
Owen's body on Monday last was found floating in the
Schuylkill (19 Apr.)

ASSHETON, William - comments on the advertisement signed
Prudence Grinaway with regard to Mr. John Robinson (12
Apr.); further comment by Assheton (16 Apr.)

READ, Charles, late of Phila., dec'd - house and lot belonging to his estate, situated on High and Front Sts.,
will be sold at auction at the Coffee House in Front
St. by Sarah Read, administratrix (12 Apr.)

LAY, Abraham, English servant, age <u>c</u>. 30, who pretends to
be a carpenter - runaway from Lewis Howell, at Christiana Bridge (12 Apr.)

KITCHINGMAN, William, English convict servant, a linen-
printer - runaway from Col. Henry Willis, of Fredericksburgh, Va. (12 Apr.)

BARNET, William Cole, English convict servant, wig-maker -
runaway from James Boyd, of Fredericksburgh, Va.;
Kitchingman and Barnet stole 2 horses, belonging to
Nicholas Bantin and Adam Reed, (12 Apr.)

Speech of Gov. Lewis Morris to House of Representatives
of New Jersey (19 Apr.)

Speech of George Clarke to General Assembly of New York
(19 Apr.)

It is reported from London that Capt. Norris, commander
of the late station ship at New York, is dead (19 Apr.)

Meeting of subscribers to the library in Phila. will be
held at the house of John Roberts in Second St. (19
Apr.)

Palatines whose notes and bonds are due for freight in
the following ships are to make payment to Benjamin
Shoemaker, in High St., Phila.: ship <u>Hope</u>, Daniel Reed
commander; ship <u>Samuel</u>, Hugh Percy commander; ship
<u>Mercury</u>, William Willson commander; ship <u>Princess
Augusta</u>, Samuel Marchant commander; ship <u>Virtuous</u> <u>Grace</u>,
John Bull commander; ship <u>Harle</u>, Ralph Harle commander;
ship <u>Winter Gally</u>, Edward Painter commander; ship <u>Queen
Elizabeth</u>, Alexander Hope commander; ship <u>Glascow</u>, Walter
Sterling commander; ship <u>Friendship,</u> Henry Beech com-
mander (19 Apr.)

GUBBY, John, English servant, age c. 35, who pretends to
be a waterman - runaway from Edward Collings, of Cheltenham Twp., Phila Co. (19 Apr.)

LEE, John, of Hanover Twp., Burlington Co. - his wife Joan
has eloped, leaving him with 4 small children; since she
left him she has had a child by another man (19 Apr.)

Sunday last a Negro man, who belonged to John Penn but was
put to live with his master's brother, Benjamin Penn,
near the fork of Patuxon in Maryland, murdered a white
child and a Negro wench and then hanged himself - Annapolis item of 15 Apr. (26 Apr.)

SMITH, Mrs. Mary, of Willingstown - Saturday last was
found drowned with her horse near the long bridge in
the Northern Liberties of Phila. (26 Apr.)

COX, Daniel, one of the justices of the Supreme Court of
New Jersey - died 25 Apr. at Trenton (26 Apr.)

Two tracts of land of 500 acres each, belonging to the estate of John Georges, dec'd, on the branches of Mana-
kasey Creek, are to be sold by Thomas Grame, administrator (26 Apr.)

October last a hoard of gold and silver coins of Queen
Elizabeth, James I and Charles I was found in the
ruins of a house in Isle of Wight Co., Va., where Col.
Bridger formerly lived - Williamsburg item of 6 Apr.
(3 May)

WATSON, Hugh, servant, a tinker - runaway from Nathan
Rigbie, of Baltimore Co., Md. (3 May)

HERPIN, Abraham, of Oley, Phila. Co. - his wife Mary has
eloped from him (3 May)

SPURSTEW, John, servant, age c. 30, refiner in copper, who
came from Bristol in the brigantine Britannia, John
Bond master - runaway from Simon Edgell, of Phila.,
pewterer (10 May)

The Art of Preaching - is published and sold by B. Franklin (10 May)

BROWN, Michael, silk-dyer, from London - continues to live
next door to Joshua Emlen, tanner, in Chesnut St.,
Phila. (10 May)

HAYES, Richard, of Haverford, Chester Co. - has for sale a
tract of 284 acres in Plymouth Twp., Phila. Co. (10 May)

LANCASTER, Sarah, sive-weaver, who lived in Market St. - has removed to Arch St., a little up from Second St., Phila. (10 May)

ROBERTS, Hugh, in Second St., Phila. - sells canary wine, sweet oil, lime juice and salt (10 May)

REDDISH, Nicholas, late of Phila., sadler - accounts with him are to be settled with John Webb, of Phila. (10 May)

CAMBELL, Charles, Irish servant, age c. 24 - runaway (in company with one Martha Bostuck) from Henry Huddelston, of Plumsted Twp., Bucks Co. (10 May)

Speech of Samuel Ogle, Gov. of Maryland, to House of Assembly and address of the Upper House (17 May)

JUSTICE, Morton, Jr., a young man, near Christiana, in Newcastle Co. - on 10 May in his father's house was struck and killed by lightning (17 May)

MADDOCK, Henry - on 14 May fell off a wharf into the river at Phila. and was drowned (17 May)

SCULL, Joseph, at the Workhouse in Phila. - sells cards, lines, twine, oakum, hemp, tow (17 May)

BROWN, Philip, West-County servant, age c. 24 - runaway from John Parry, of Haverford Twp., Chester Co. (17 May)

Snow Pennsbury will sail for London; for freight or passage agree with William Hellier, at his house in Market St., Phila. (17 May)

Plantation at Billingsport, Glocester Co., N.J., about 12 miles from Phila., is for sale; enquire of Nicholas Dahlberg, who lives on said place (17 May)

Negroes, lately imported from South Carolina, are for sale; apply to John Billiald, at the Widow Connoly's in King St. or William Crosthwaite, peruke-maker, in Front St., Phila. (17 May)

In 1734 Andrew Justice and Thomas Willing, of Willings Town, gave a lot in the town for a public market; Thomas Willing and his wife deeded to Samuel Kirk a lot butting on the market place and Kirk conveyed this to Thomas Shiply (son of William Shiply); Thomas Tatnall bought a lot in Second St. that butted on said Market Square; Simon Edgell bought a lot on Market St., bounded on Thomas Tatnall's piece and next to William Shiply's (17 May)

WARNER, Edward, of Phila. - offers reward for recovery of strayed horse (17 May)

Address of House of Delegates to Gov. Samuel Ogle of Maryland (24 May)

Ship Mary Ann, Charles Hargrave commander, will sail for London; for freight or passage agree with the commander or Thomas Annis in Phila. (24 May)

Caesar, Negro - runaway from Thomas Emson, at Duck Creek, Kent Co. on Delaware (24 May)

SMITH, John - offers reward for recovery of gelding strayed from him at plantation of Isaac Norris on Frankford Road, near Phila. (24 May)

PARVIN, Silas, who has purchased Egg Island and beach from Fortescue Island to Dividend Creek - forbids taking of sand from either place without his permission (24 May)

Answer of Gov. Samuel Ogle of Maryland to the address of the Lower House (31 May)

Elected at Rhode Island in May 1739 were the following: John Wanton, governor; Daniel Abbot, deputy-governor; assistants--John Chipman, Peter Bourse, Ezekiel Warner, Joseph Fenner, George Cornel, Gideon Cornel, James Arnold, Philip Arnold, Jeremiah Gould, Rouse Helm; secretary--James Martin; attorney general--James Honyman, Jr.; general treasurer--Gideon Wanton; sheriff--Jonathan Nichols - Rhode Island item of 4 May (31 May)

At meeting of freeholders and inhabitants of Boston on 2 May, presided over by John Jeffries (one of the Selectmen), the following 4 representatives were elected: Thomas Cushing, Jr., Edward Bromfield, James Allen and Christopher Kilby; Thomas Cushing, Jr., was chosen moderator; the following were chosen as a committee to draw up instructions for the 4 representatives: Capt. Nathanael Cunningham, Hugh Vans, Samuel Adams, Capt. Benjamin Pollard, Middlecot Cooke; copy of the above records was certified by Samuel Gerrish, town clerk - Boston item of 7 May (31 May)

JOHNSON, James - on 30 May seized a man who had robbed him; the highwayman escaped but soon was caught and committed to prison at Phila. (31 May)

Jack, Negro (who formerly belonged to the estate of Joseph England and was taken at the suit of Thomas Stretch for a debt of said England's widow), age c. 21 - was stolen from on board the snow <u>Drake</u>, James White master, at Phila.; reward for his capture will be paid by Edward Bradley and Company, owners of the snow (31 May)

Parcel of English and Irish servants, just arrived from Dublin in the brigantine <u>Hannah</u>, William Tiffin commander, will be disposed of by John Stamper, merchant, in Water St., Thomas Walker, butcher, in Walnut St., or John Beaumont and Samuel Walker, merchants, on board said brigantine, opposite Market St. (31 May)

Record of proceedings of the Assembly of Pennsylvania upon the paper money bill: John Kinsey, John Kearsley, Thomas Marriot, James Gibbins and Samuel Smith were ordered to wait upon the governor with the bill; vote on making the proprietors an allowance was as follows: for the affirmative--William Monington, Thomas Leech, William Allen, Job Goodsonn, Jonathan Robeson, Morris Morris, John Kearsley, Israel Pemberton, Jeremiah Langhorne, Joseph Kirkbride, Abraham Chapman, Benjamin Field, Thomas Mariott, Thomas Canby, James Hamilton, Samuel Smith, John Wright; for the negative--Edward Warner, John Watson, James Gibbons, Thomas Chandler, Joseph Harvey, John Owen, Thomas Tatnal, William Hewes and Jeremiah Star (7 June)

PEEL, Anthony, who intends to leave the country - wishes to settle all accounts (7 June)

LASANT, Jacob, Dutch Palatine servant, age $\underline{c}$. 20, who speaks very good French and pretends to be a butcher - runaway from Herman Richman, of Piles Grove, Salem Co. (7 June)

Address of Samuel Ogle to Maryland Assembly and of Assembly to Ogle (14 June)

Speech of Jonathan Belcher to Massachusetts Assembly (14 June)

TURNER, William - sentenced to death in Maryland for horse-stealing - Annapolis item of 28 May (14 June)

GYANTS, Richard, convicted in Queen Anne's Co. of murder - has escaped from prison - Annapolis item of 28 May (14 June)

WILLDEAR, Thomas, Irish servant - runaway from Samuel Hastings, of Phila., shipwright (14 June)

CURRY, Edward, Irish servant, age $\underline{c}$. 26, who served a time in Chester Co. and was some time in Chester Goal,

belonging to John Mackintosh - runaway from Abraham
Bryan, of Burlington Co., West New Jersey (14 June)

DOLIN, John, Irish servant, age c. 18 - runaway (in com-
pany with Dennis McGlaugh) in a wherry belonging to
John Ladd, Jr., from William Tateham, of Gloucester Co.,
West New Jersey (14 June)

TATEHAM, William, Esq., late High Sheriff of Gloucester
Co. - died 19 June at Deptford, Gloucester Co., West
New Jersey (21 June)

Brigantine Debby, George Stewart master, at Anthony Morris's wharf - will sail for South Carolina; for freight
or passage agree with Anthony Morris, Jr., or the master on board (21 June)

A riding coat has been taken up on the road between Phila.
and Germantown - apply to Thomas Armstrong on James
Logan's plantation (21 June)

Rice by the barrel is for sale at Anthony Duche's in Front
St., Phila. (21 June)

English and Welsh servants, just imported in the ship
Delaware, David Davis master, from Bristol, are to be
disposed of on board, just opposite to Fishbourn's
wharf in Phila. (21 June)

BRETT, Richard - offers reward for recovery of horse
strayed or stolen from Mrs. Mary Hase's, at Patapsco
Ferry; horse is to be brought to said ferry (21 June)

LEDREW, Henry, age c. 8 or 9 - was drowned Friday last
near the Market wharf in Phila. (28 June)

ANNER, Hans (servant to the Widow Dungworth, of the Manor
of Moreland) - was drowned Saturday last when bathing
in the mill-dam (28 June)

Snow Pennsbury, William Hellier master - will sail for
London; for passage agree with the master at his house
in Market St., Phila. (28 June)

McKENNEY, Charles, Irish servant, age c. 24 - runaway from
Thomas Marshall, of Concord, Chester Co. (28 June)

BANKSON, Swan, late of Wicaco, dec'd - accounts with estate to be settled with Daniel or Peter Bankson, administrators (28 June)

TRAVATT, John Christian, Palatine servant, who came in

Capt. Stedman's ship last fall - runaway from David
Bush, of Willings Town (28 June)

List of letters brought to the Post Office at Phila. since
4 Jan. and remain unredeemed: ALLASON, Capt. William,
phi.; ALLEN, Thomas, phi.; AMONT, Mary, phi.; ARCHER,
Oliver; ARNAUD, Stephen, phi.; ATKINGS, John, near
Frankfort;
     BANCROFT, Ambrose, Solebury, bu. co.; BARLOW, Wil-
liam, phi.; BATEMAN, Clement, Northampton, bu. co.;
BICKNEL, Elizabeth, phi.; BLADES, Margaret, phi.; BOR-
LAND, Andrew, pen.; BOWER, Henry, at Samuel Parr's,
phi.; BOX, Nathanael, Pilesgrove; BOYD, William, London
Grove; BREAUNO, John, phi.; BRODRICK, Ann, phi.; BROOCK-
SON, George, phi.; BROOKS, William, Timbercreek; BROWNE,
Thomas, Plumsted Twp., bu. co.; BUCKLEY, Samuel, phi.
(2 letters); BURGES, John, phi;
     CAINE, Christopher, phi.; CAMPBELL, Jonas, pen.;
CAMPBELL, William, mariner, phi.; CANWOOD, Richard,
Wrightstown, bu. co.; CARTER, Robin, sawyer, phi.;
CHARLTON, Thomas, phi.; COATS, Moses, French Creek, pen.;
COLLINS, John, to the care of Edward Pleadwell, phi.;
COOPER, Bethel, anchor smith, phi.; COX, John, phi.;
CROFTS, Henry, chair-maker, phi.; CROFTS, William, on
board the Thistle, phi.; CUNNINGHAM, Moses, in American
land;
     DAGWORTHY, James, phi.; DALTON, Robert, phi.; DAVEN-
PORT, Ann; DAVIS, Samuel, bu. co.; DAWSON, John, Manor
of Moorland, pen.; DEAVES, Clement, on board the Dragon,
phi.; DERKINDER, Elizabeth, phi.; DEVERELL, Capt. John,
phi.; DOUGLAS, James, Octorara; DRUMMOND, Seth (2 letters); DUNSCOMB, Tadding, phi.;
     EARLE, Elizabeth, Springfield; EDWARDS, John, Ship-
town, near phi.; ELLICOTT, Andrew, Jr., Solesbury;
ELLIS, Capt. William, phi.;
     FERGUSON, Thomas, French Creek; FITZGERALD, Thomas,
phi.; FRENCH, Alexander;
     GARDNER, Theophilus, merchant, phi.; GARRISON,
Charles, at Arris Shouter's, bu. co.; GARTRIL, John,
Nottingham, ch. co. (2 letters); GIBBERT, Alexander,
phi.; GILES, John, ship-carpenter, phi.; GREEN, Godfrey, at Capt. Attwoods, phi.; GREGG, James, bu. co.,
to the care of Joseph Kirkbride; GRIFFINE, Thomas, North
Wales;
     HAINES, Robert, Chesnut St., phi.; HALL, Samuel,
Third St., phi.; HAMILTON, Archibald, Clam Hall, Salem,
(2 letters); HAMMATT, William, Walnut St., phi.; HAN-
NINGTON, Bernhard, merchant, phi.; HAWKINS, Elizabeth,
phi.; HERD, John, with William Gretcham, Arch St., phi.;
HIRST, John, Solesbury, bu. co.; HODGE, Thomas, hot-
presser, phi.; HOOPES, Daniel, Westown, ch. co. (2
letters); HUNTER, Robert, on board the Glasgow, phi.;

HUTCHINSON, John, Fall Twp., bu. co.; HUTCHISON, John, to the care of James Kirk, Society Hill (2 letters);
INGRAM, Samuel, at Knockbroon;
JACOBSON, John, from Norway, mariner, phi.; JEN-KING/S?/, Elizabeth, phi.; JENKINS, Nathanael, Cohansey; JESSE, Walter, Marple, near phi.; JONES, John, in the Gap; JONES, William, phi.;
KASEBEER, Christian, phi.; KEAN, Nicholas, mason, near the great Savana, bu. co.; KINGSLEY, Elinor, glove-washer, phi.; KINGSTON, Thomas, at Thomas Evans, Northampton, bu. co.;
LEAMY, Mathias, tailor, phi.; LeCORNU, James, phi.; LIMOUS, William, phi. (2 letters); LOVELESS, John, with Joseph Warder, Falls Twp., bu. co.; LUPTON, Mary, Solebury, bu. co.; LYON, Robert, of the ship Thistle,
McCARMICK, William, baker; McCLURE, Charles, lan. co.; MACFERRAN, John, to the care of John Kernahan, Octorara; McLEISTER, Capt. Neal, phi.; MACHON, Archibald, phi.; MARSHAL, Alexander, at Robert Toms's, phi.; MARSSEY, Widow, phi.; MARTIN, Richard, of Maurice River, Salem co.; MONIC, William, clothier, pen.; MONTGOMERY, David, cooper, lan. co.; MOORE, Charles, Marple Twp., near phi.; MORGAN, Charles, at the Stays, phi.; MORGAN, Thomas, Carnarvan, lan. co.; MORPHY, Patrick, phi.; MURIEL, Robert, Newtown, ch. co.; MURRAY, William, smith, Octorara;
NORE, Michael, phi.;
OLIPHANT, Thomas, phi.;
PACE, Mary, at Jonathan Cogshall's, phi.; PAINTER, Paul, phi.; PALMER, Sarah; PARRY, John, cutler, phi.; PATISON, Edward, at William Hudson's, phi.; PAYELL, William, phi.; PHILIP, Nathanael, phi.; POWES, Peter, Greenwich, Cohansey; PRINGLE, Andrew, phi.;
QUISOCK, Alexander, Londonderry, pen.;
REECE, Thomas, Newtown; REED, John, Octorara; REY-NOLDS, Henry, Nottingham; RICHARDSON, Thomas, to the care of Simon Egerly; ROBINSON, Samuel, Suetara; ROBI-SON, John, lan. co.; ROOTARMEL, Anna Margarita;
SCHULTZ, John George, phi.; SLEIGH, Joseph, to the care of George Howel, phi.; SMALL, John, Ancocus Creek; STEPHENS, Henry, Deerfield, pen.; STEVENS, Joseph, stone-cutter; STEWART, Robert, phi.; STICH, John, phi.; STOCK-DALE, Joseph, phi.; SUTHEREN, Benjamin, bu. co.;
VEALE, Nehemiah, Cohansey;
WALKER, Alexander, to the care of Tho. Shenon, Soles-bury; WALKER, John, Shaminey; WEBSTER, John, Abington; WEIR, John, smith, phi.; WELLS, Capt. Thomas, phi.; WESTFIELD, Mary, at Capt. Grave's, phi.; WHITE, Edward, Bristol Twp.; WILBRAHAM, Thomas, to the care of James Bary /?/, phi.; WILSON, John; WOTTON, Mary, at Capt. Philip's, Walnut St., phi. (2 letters); WRIGHT, William, to the care of Rev. William Becket, Lewes (28 June)

MOSELY, Charles, servant, butcher - runaway from Ralph
Perkenson (28 June)

FLING, Cornelius, age c. 40, butcher - runaway from Thomas
Walker, of Phila., butcher (28 June)

HARPER, William, at the Ship-a-Ground, near Chesnut St.
wharf, in Phila. - has servants to dispose of who have
just arrived in the ship Rebecca, David Sterling commander (28 June)

ROSE, Joseph, at the New Printing Office in Market St. -
intends to collect and print the poems of his dec'd
father, Aquila Rose (28 June)

HAXLY, David, Welsh servant, age near 40 - runaway from
Perkiomun Copper Works - reward will be paid if he is
brought to Joseph Wharton at Phila. (28 June)

COMPTON, Richard, of Upper Freehold, Monmouth Co. - his
wife Lydia has eloped (28 June)

YOUNG, Rebecca - offers for sale a brick house; joining
on the east Mr. Chapman's and on the west Edward
Nichols's, on the south side of Chesnut St. near Second
St., in Phila. (28 June)

Speech of Samuel Ogle to the Maryland Assembly (5 July)

BAILIE, John (son of John Bailie), of Warwick, Providence
Co., R. I., age 10 - was ill for 50 days, taking almost
no food, until about middle of May, when he died (5
July)

Resolution of Governor, Council and Justices at Newport,
desiring prayers that smallpox epidemic be halted; it
is signed by John Wanton, Samuel Collens, Charles Borden, James Sheffield, Henry Bull, Peter Bourse, John
Gardner, Benjamin Ellery, Samuel Wickham - Boston item
of 25 June (5 July)

VAN VOORHEES, Garrit, who arrived 21 June at New York in
the snow Eagle, Jacobus Kierstead master - Saturday
last was committed to goal in New York for uttering
counterfeit bills - New York item of 25 June (5 July)

BUFFINGTON, Richard, Sr., from Great Mark upon the Thames
in Buckinghamshire, England, age c. 85 - on 30 May at
his house in Chester Co. his 115 children, grandchildren and great-grandchildren met, together with his 9
sons and daughters-in-law and 12 great-grandchildren-
in-law; his eldest son, now in his 60th year, is the

first born of English descent in Pa. (5 July)

GOODIN, Mary, who lately arrived from Ireland - died Saturday last in Phila. (5 July)

CHESTON, Daniel, at John Biddle's, next door to the Indian King in Market St., Phila. - sells snuff, cutlery, shot, etc. (5 July)

FRANCIS, Tench, at his house in Second St., Phila., where Mr. Delage lately lived - sells cloth, hardware, etc. (12 July)

COLEMAN, Christopher, at Henry Hartley's, at the Sign of the White Horse, in Elbow Lane, Phila. - has for sale a parcel of servants (12 July)

PENNEROY, Bennett, who left Phila. about 12 years ago for Virginia or Maryland - will hear something to his advantage if he will apply to Edward Evans, cordwainer, in Front St., Phila. (12 July)

TUB, William, servant, age c. 20, tailor - runaway from John Williams, of Phila., tailor (12 July)

SPRAGGS, William, English servant, age c. 33 - runaway from Thomas Williams, of Phila., hatter (12 July)

The Memorial and Remonstrance of John Tennent, practitioner in physic (19 and 26 July, 2 Aug.)

HILL, Richard, Esq., dec'd - accounts with estate to be settled with Lloyd Zachary and Mordecai Lloyd (19 July)

Reward is offered for pocketbook, with papers, lost between Benjamin Ford's of Brandywine Hundred and Chester if said book and papers are returned to Thomas Gray, of Whiteclay Creek, David Bush, of Willingstown, the said Benjamin Ford, James Mathers, of Chester, or the printer in Phila. (19 July)

COMBS, Mr. (eldest son of Elizabeth Combs, which said Elizabeth was born in Beckington in Somersetshire, whose father was formerly a wine-cooper in Bristol), who is supposed to live somewhere in **Bucks** Co. - if he applies to Isaac Jones, living opposite to the George Inn, in Arch St., Phila., he will hear something to his advantage (19 July)

GRIFFITTS, Philip, West Country servant, age c. 30 - runaway from Richard Ashton, near Paxton, Lancaster Co.; reward will be paid if servant is returned to his master or to Edward Shippen, in Phila. (19 July)

BOND, Thomas, in Paris, writes to his brother, Phineas
Bond and cites Mr. Jussien, physician and professor of
botany to the King, concerning Seneca Snake-root, in
confirmation of its character as set forth by Dr. Tennent (26 July)

The History of Joseph - is printed and sold by B. Franklin
(26 July)

JONES, William, merchant, of Birmingham, Chester Co. - offers reward for information about Richard Gibbert (who
was an apprentice to Mrs. Leventhorp, horner, in London
and about 4 years ago came as a servant to Phila., where
his time was bought by an Indian trader); Gibbert has
inherited an estate yielding 100 pounds sterling annually and also houses and money (26 July)

WOOD, John, West Country servant, age c. 40, who has been
in this country 10 or 11 years and has worked in Chester
Co., Phila. Co. and New Jersey - runaway from Francis
Smith, of Burlington, N. J. (26 July)

BROWN, John, servant, age c. 21 - runaway from James Paul
Heath, in Cecil Co., Md. (26 July)

Plantation of Traveskan, late the estate of Gov. Gordon,
dec'd, on Passyunk Rd., within 1½ miles of Phila. -
will be sold at auction by Patrick Baird, vendue-master,
at the Coffee House in Front St., Phila. (26 July)

WARD, John, near Anchocas - on 26 July, when hunting deer,
accidentally shot and killed a neighbor, James Sherrin
(2 Aug.)

ALLEN, Ulrich, of Phila. - will pay no debts contracted
in future by his wife Eve (2 Aug.)

STOCKDALE, Joseph, living at the house of Andrew Edge,
next door but one to the Baptist Meeting-house in
Second St., Phila. - does all sorts of upholsterer's
work (2 Aug.)

FLEESON, Plunket, lately from London and Dublin, upholsterer
- works at the Sign of the Easy Chair, near Mr. Hamilton's, in Chesnut St., Phila. (2 Aug.)

CHARLES, Robert, intending to leave Pennsylvania and go
to Britain - wishes to settle all accounts (9 Aug.)

MEREDITH, Rees, designing for Europe very soon - desires

all persons indebted to him to make payment at once to Stephen Dayton or Thomas Williams (9 Aug.)

ESDAILE, James, at his store on Carpenter's wharf - sells molasses and rum (9 Aug.)

SONMANS, Peter, in Market St., Phila. - will dispose of the time of a Welsh maid (9 Aug.)

McDONNEL, Bryan, servant, age c. 20 - runaway from Robert Carr, of Hopewell Twp., West New Jersey (9 Aug.)

LIPSCOMB, John, servant, age c. 18 - runaway from John Eastburn, of Norrington Twp., Phila. Co. (9 Aug.)

Sloop _Charming Betty_, Thomas Crosthwait master, at Capt. Bourn's wharf - will sail for South Carolina; for freight or passage agree with William Crosthwait, peruke-maker, in Front St., Phila., or with the master on board (9 Aug.)

BARTON, Robert, near the Post Office in Phila. - makes and sells chairs, couches, tables (9 Aug.)

DOUGHERTY, Keziah (granddaughter of Ambrose Farmer), who left Dublin about 10 years ago at age of about 13 aboard a ship belonging to James Stevenson of Dublin, bound for Phila. - is desired to enquire of William Reynolds in Charlestown on Pickering Creek, Chester Co., or Patrick Reynolds at Whitemarsh, at the plantation of Jonathan Robeson in Phila. Co., or George Jones at the Sign of the Black Horse in Black Horse Alley, Phila., or Dominick Kavanagh, merchant in Phila. (9 Aug.)

The government of South Carolina has granted a bounty of 200 pounds to Daniel James on building a water mill and the same to Jacob Buchholts for building another mill (16 Aug.)

All persons indebted to Messers. William Masters, Thomas Robinson and William Hartley on account of servants bought from on board the snow _Hercules_ in 1738 are to apply to said Robinson at his house in Second St. or to William Hartley at his lodgings at George Magee's in Front St. (16 Aug.)

SIMMONS, James, who pretends to be an Indian trader and was tried in the Jerseys for burglary and burnt in the hand - stole a silver watch from the house of Joseph Webb in Birmingham, Chester Co. (16 Aug.)

235

SKELTON, Thomas and Hannah, late of Phila., dec'd - accounts with their estates to be settled with Edward Bradley or Wight Massey, administrators (16 Aug.)

FAREE, Daniel, of Lancaster Co., near Pequa Creek - offers reward for recovery of 3 horses, strayed or stolen (16 Aug.)

HOLLAND, William, mason, lately from London - has a shop next door to Stephen Beezley's in Phila. (16 Aug.)

A Negro man will be auctioned off at Mr. Owen's, the Sign of the Indian King, in Market St., Phila. (16 Aug.)

BOONE, George, of Oley - has taken up a number of horses (16 Aug.)

Proclamation of Gov. George Thomas (23 Aug.)

A Negro, carpenter and sawyer - runaway from Antill Deaver in Baltimore Co., Md. (23 Aug.)

A white servant, cooper by trade, and a Negro (who formerly belonged to Dr. Richard Hill) - runaways from Thomas Shea and Richard More, of Baltimore Co., Md. (23 Aug.)

A Negro - runaway from Samuel Webster, of Baltimore Co., Md. (23 Aug.)

Proposal about tanyards in Phila., signed by William Hudson, Jr., Samuel Morris, John Ogden, John Howell, William Smith and John Snowdon, tanners (30 Aug.)

PORTER, Andrew - killed at Octorara Friday last when struck against a tree by his horse in a race (30 Aug.)

HULBEART, Philip, at the Boatswain and Call, near the drawbridge in Phila. - offers reward for recovery of a silver watch (marked Stevenson's Make, London) lost in Phila. or on road to Chester (30 Aug.)

WELCH, Thomas, English convict servant - runaway (with a freeman named John Smith) from on board a schooner, Thomas Betson skipper, lying in Principio Creek; they broke open the skipper's chest and stole money and other items; reward for their capture will be paid by James Baxter, at Principio Iron Works (30 Aug.)

GRIFFITHS, John, servant, age c. 20 - runaway from Edward Wyatt, of Phila., tailor (30 Aug.)

POET, Benjamin, Dutch apprentice, age c. 16 - same as above

CHAMBERS, Jonathan, servant, age c. 19 - runaway from Henry
   Norwood, of Phila.; the above 3 runaways are supposed to
   be in company with Edmond Howard, who belongs to Jacob
   Casdorp, of Phila., shipwright (30 Aug.)

The grist mills at Trenton and 2 small tenements, now in
   the tenure of Joseph Peace, are to be let; apply to said
   Peace or to Thomas Sober, merchant, in Phila. (30 Aug.)

The Squirrel man-of-war, Peter Warren commander, and the
   Tartar, George Townshend commander, sailed Sunday last
   from Boston against the Spaniards - Boston item of 21
   Aug. (6 Sept.)

Capts. Stoddard (from Newcastle) and Tilden (from Jamaica)
   have arrived with news at Boston - Boston item of 27
   Aug. (6 Sept.)

DUMARESQUE, Capt. Philip, of Boston, has been granted a
   commission to cruise against the Spaniards (6 Sept.)

McNEAL, Capt. - sailed 27 Aug. from Boston for the West
   Indies with a letter of marque (6 Sept.)

BARON, John - has for sale Vidonia wines at Thomas Lawrence's, Esq. (6 Sept.)

Brigantine Betsey, Walter Spurrier master, at Fishbourn's
   wharf - will sail for Antigua - for freight or passage
   apply to master at Mrs. Andrew's or Thomas Lloyd at the
   Sign of the Golden Mortar in Second St., Phila. (6 Sept.)

BLEWET, Capt. - arrived 31 July at St. John's in Newfoundland from Lisbon (13 Sept.)

JONES, Isaac - has removed from his store opposite the
   George in Arch St., to his store at the corner of Mc-
   Comb's Alley, in Second St., opposite to the Baptist
   Meeting-house (13 Sept.)

BEDDES, Richard, servant, age c. 17 - runaway from Thomas
   Rees, of Heydelburg Twp., Lancaster Co. (13 Sept.)

COLTIS, James, servant, age c. 27, who pretends to be a
   carpenter - runaway from French Creek Iron Work, Chester Co.; reward for his capture will be paid by Samuel
   Savage (13 Sept.)

INDICOTT, Joseph, living near Mount Holly - he has attached
   shingles to recover debt owned him by Isaac Howell;

William Sharp, Levi Shinn and William Garret have been appointed auditors by the County Court at Burlington (13 Sept.)

SHARP, Thomas, late of Phila., merchant, dec'd - accounts with estate to be settled with administrators, John Hopkins and John Inglis (13 Sept.)

MILLHOLLAND, Arthur, servant, age c. 30, who has been an Indian trader - runaway from James Adams, of Londongove, Chester Co. (13 Sept.)

The following ships, belonging to Newport, R. I., are to sail as privateers against the Spaniards: sloop Revenge, James Allen captain, owned by Capt. John Bowne, merchant; sloop Virgin Queen, Charles Hall master, owned by Capt. George Wanton & Co.; sloop Charming Betty, Benjamin Wickham commander, belonging to Capt. Godfrey Malbone - Newport item of 7 Sept. (20 Sept.)

Lately arrived at Portsmouth, N. H., are Capts. Baldwin (from Cork) and Pearson (from Lisbon) - Boston item of 10 Sept. (20 Sept.)

MATSON, John - Saturday last at Gloucester Co., N. J., was killed when his cart overset (20 Sept.)

JOHNSON, John, servant, age between 20 and 30, Birmingham-born, barber - runaway from William Crosthwaite (20 Sept.)

MORTON, John, servant, lately from Scotland, age c. 24 - runaway from John Richey, of Makefield, Bucks Co. (20 Sept.)

DRAPER, Stephen, servant, age c. 27 - runaway from Anthony Bright, of Phila., silversmith (20 Sept.)

NEWMAN, Margaret, late of Phila., widow, dec'd - accounts with estate to be settled with John Newman, executor, at his house in Second St. (20 Sept.)

CARY, Sampson, late of Bristol, Bucks Co., dec'd - accounts with estate to be settled with Sam. Cary, executor, at Newtown, Bucks Co. (20 Sept.)

SHERWIN, James, late of Chester Twp., Burlington Co., who was shot and killed - the undersigned neighbors (an asterisk indicates those on the coroner's inquest) state that the person who shot and killed him had never before shot at him: Edward Hollinshead, Jonathan Borden, Hugh Sharp, *Joseph Claypoole, William Hollinshead, John

238

Hollinshead, Jr., Nehemiah Hains, Thomas Moore, John
King, Joseph Bray, Francis Dudley, Nathan Middleton,
*Arthur Borradaill, *Edward Clemens, Joseph Fennimore,
William Hooton, *John Hollinshead, *Samuel Atkinson,
Joseph Budden, Samuel Hollinshead, Joshua Wright, Jacob
Taylor, John Seeds, *Matthew Allen, Robert Bishop, *Henry
Warrington, *John Millbourn, Peter Philips, Ezekiel
Harden, *Andrew Cortro /or Contro?/, Richard Bordon,
William Sharp, Benjamin Allen, Hugh Hollinshead (20
Sept.)

Speech of Lt.-Gov. George Clarke, of New York (27 Sept.)

Towards the end of July a young man (who falsely claims to
be a son of the late Gov. Burnet) at Speights Town,
Barbados, at the wedding of a young Jew (whose father
is named Lopus), on complaining of a headache, was told
by Lopus to go to his (Lopus's) house and lie down;
half an hour later Lopus, with 5 or 6 companions stripped
the young man and beat him, charging him with stealing
money; the young man is bound over for trial but is
suing the Jew in 2 actions of 10,000 pounds; a mob has
driven the Jews out of town and pulled down their syna-
gogue; the Jews, who have assembled at Bridgetown, resolve to have satisfaction; it is reported they are
"generally pretty rich" and will be protected by one
of the greatest men of the island (27 Sept.)

ALLEN, Capt. Christopher, of South Kingsdon, came 16 Sept.
to Boston to have his will drawn; he dined at Capt.
Almy's and when both men were riding into town Allen
fell dead from his horse; he had no children; he was
carried to William Clagget's house and was there placed
in a coffin and carried to his seat in South Kingston
(27 Sept.)

CROW, Capt. Samuel, who arrived a few days ago at Boston
from the Bay of Honduras reported that on the coast of
Florida he saw a wreck and on the shore on the mast of
a pinnace the inscription: "The May, Thomas Gladman
Commander, from Jamaica, bound to London, was lost
June 10th, Anno Domini, 1738. John Saunders Mate, and
Samuel Hogsflesh, Carpenter." - Boston item of 17 Sept.
(27 Sept.)

Declaration of Andrew Hamilton, Speaker of the Assembly,
declining to serve further as a representative (27 Sept.)

COXE, Daniel, dec'd - 2 of his executors, John Coxe of
Trenton and Samuel Bustill of Burlington, are to be seen
by all in possession of land in Hopewell or Maidenhead in Hunterdon Co. who did not purchase or lease

said land of Daniel Coxe (27 Sept.)

Brigantine <u>Lydia</u>, James Hasleton commander, lying at Mr.
Plumstead's wharf - will sail for Dublin and Newry;
for freight or passage agree with Thomas Clark at the
house of Owen Owen, Esq., at the Indian King in Phila.
or with the master (27 Sept.)

BARD, Peter, intending for South Carolina - desires that
all accounts with him be settled (27 Sept.)

KERSLAKE, Abraham, servant, age c. 30, born at Tiverton in
the west of England - runaway (in company with an Englishman named William Green, age c. 23) from Stephen
Onion's plantation at Conijohah, 4 miles below Mr.
Wright's Ferry over Susquehannah River (27 Sept.)

PARKE, Thomas - offers reward for recovery of a horse and
a mare from pasture of Caleb Cowpland, Esq., near
Chester (27 Sept.)

CLAY, Slator, at Robert Bolton's in Second St., Phila. -
has for sale a copper still (27 Sept.)

HILL, Capt. - has brought to Boston letters and passengers
with European news (4 Oct.)

SCHUYLER, Col. - communicated to the New York Assembly a
letter from commissioners appointed to erect a stone
fort at Albany (4 Oct.)

Letter from Lt.-Gov. George Clarke to Adolph Philipse,
Esq., speaker of the New York Assembly (4 Oct.)

Sum of 600 pounds was voted by the New York Assembly to
build a fort in the Mohawks Country; those who voted
500 pounds were Messers Cornell, Jones, Hardenbergh,
Haesbrook, Nicholl, J. Lott, LeCaint, Purdy, Stillwell,
Ludlow and Gale; voters for 600 pounds were the Speaker,
Messers Winne, Livingston, Clarkson, Terbos, Bradt,
Roome and Cols. Ranslaer, Schuyler, Beekman, Moore and
Philipse (4 Oct.)

Monday last the following were elected for Phila. Co. -
Representatives: Robert Jones, Edward Warner, John
Kinsey, Isaac Norris, Owen Evans, Joseph Trotter, Thomas
Leech, James Morris; sheriffs: Septimus Robinson, Isaac
Leech; coroners: Owen Owen, David Evans; commissioner:
Thomas Peters; assessors: Samuel Lane, James Jones,
Evan Thomas, Jeremiah Elfreth, Joseph Noble, Samuel
Morris (4 Oct.)

Monday last the following were elected for Bucks Co. -
representatives: John Watson, Mark Watson, Thomas
Canby, Jr., Jeremiah Langhorne, Joseph Kirkbride, Abra-
ham Chapman, Benjamin Field, Benjamin Jones; sheriffs:
John Hart, Francis Hague; coroners: William Atkinson,
Benjamin Taylor; commissioner: Timothy Smith; assessors:
Abraham Griffith, Cephas Child, Robert Smith, John
Hutchinson, Bartholomew Langstreth, Garrit Vansandt
(4 Oct.)

Monday last the following were elected for Chester Co. -
representatives: James Gibbins, Thomas Chandler, Joseph
Harvey, William Hughes, Jeremiah Starr, William Moore,
Samuel Levis, John Owen; sheriffs: Benjamin Davis, John
Parry; coroners: Aubrey Bevan, Evan Ellis; commissioner:
John Davies; assessors: John Allen, John Yarnall, Daniel
Walker, David Stephens, James Jeffreys, Thomas Morgan
(4 Oct.)

Monday last the following were elected for Lancaster Co. -
representatives: John Wright, Thomas Ewing, Thomas
Linley, Thomas Edwards; sheriffs: James Mitchel, Robert
Buchanan; coroners: Joshua Lowe, James Reddy; com-
missioner: James Whitehill; assessors: Wm. Allison,
Andrew Work, Wm. Renicks, Robert Barber, John Morgan,
David Jones (4 Oct.)

Tuesday last the following burgesses were chosen: John
Kearsley, Israel Pemberton; city assessors elected were
Philip Syng, Richard Parker, Joseph Oldman, William
Rawle, Edward Bradley, John Ogden; Edward Roberts was
chosen Mayor; Anthony Morris, late Mayor, gave a feast
for his citizens on Friday last (4 Oct.)

DEWEES, William, Jr., has taken up at his paper-mill in
Cresham Twp., Phila. Co., a brown horse (4 Oct.)

SHELLY, Abraham, thread-maker and tape-weaver - lives next
door to Charles Williams, tailor, at the Sign of the
Adam and Eve in Arch St., Phila. (4 Oct.)

Snow Southall, Thomas Richardson master - will sail for
Bristol; for freight or passage agree with Reese Mere-
dith or master at Capt. John Reeves's or on board (4
Oct.)

Owners of a horse and mare may obtain them from Evan Jones
and Henry Cary at the plantation of Joseph Todd in Warminster, Bucks Co. (4 Oct.)

Tract of 89 acres in Kingsessing Twp., Phila. Co., about
one mile from Lower Ferry on Skuylkil is for sale -

enquire of Nathan Gibson (4 Oct.)

PRICE, William, of Chesterfield, Burlington Co. - offers reward for recovery of strayed or stolen roan gelding (4 Oct.)

FIELD, Mrs. John, of Tolland, Conn. - on 1 Sept. was accidentally shot and killed by a person hunting bees who took Mrs. Field for a bear - Boston item of 24 Sept. (11 Oct.)

Messages of Lt.-Gov. Belcher to the Massachusetts Assembly (11 Oct.)

On 1 Oct. the following were elected for Newcastle Co. - representatives: Andrew Peterson, David French, John McCoole, Thomas Noxon, Jeremiah Woolaston, Jehu Curtis; sheriff: John Goodwin; coroner: John Downing (11 Oct.)

On 1 Oct. the following were elected for Kent Co. - representatives: James Gorrel, William Farson, Thomas Skidmore, Mark Manlove, James Morris, William Barns; sheriff: David Robinson; coroner: Thomas Tarrant (11 Oct.)

On 1 Oct. the following were elected for Sussex Co. - representatives: Jabez Fisher, William Till, Jacob Kollock, Abraham Wyncoop, John Shanklin, Simon Kollock; sheriff: Cornelius Whiltbanck; coroner: John Wyncoop (11 Oct.)

KOLB, Jacob, of Skippack - on 4 Oct., when pressing cider, was struck by the beam of the press and died within half an hour (11 Oct.)

FARMAR, Richard, "Professor of Physick, Surgery, Chymistry and Pharmacy," lately come to Phila. - has settled next door but one to Owen Owen's in Market St. (11 Oct.)

Ship **Loyal Judith**, Edward Paynter commander, now at Arch St. wharf - will sail for South Carolina; for freight or passage agree with the commander on board or at Samuel Austin's (11 Oct.)

WILKINSON, Anthony - has choice onions for sale (11 Oct.)

Pompey, an Indian, age c. 24, who has been whipped in Barbados - runaway (in company with a Negro woman named Pegg, age c. 22, this country-born) from Richard Ruff, near the head of Bush River in Baltimore Co., Md. (11 Oct.)

ASHETON, William, late of Phila., attorney-at-law, dec'd -

debts due his estate are to be settled with William Asheton (11 Oct.)

Tract of 1,250 acres in Hunterdon Co., on both sides of Rockaway River, a branch of Passaic River, about 18 miles from Newark, for sale; to see it, apply to Gasha Mott, of Whipany; a buyer may agree with George Miranda, shopkeeper, over against the Sign of the George, in Second St., Phila. (11 Oct.)

KINSEY, John - Monday last was chosen Speaker of the Pennylsvania House (18 Oct.)

Speech of George Thomas to the Pennsylvania Assembly, reply of the House by Messers Robert Jones, Edward Warner, Joseph Kirkbride, Joseph Harvey and John Wright, and answer of the Governor (18 Oct.)

DORST, Herman, of Germantown Twp., an ancient man - on 14 Oct. was found dead in his bed (18 Oct.)

READ, Charles, late of Phila., merchant, dec'd - part of Iron Works at Derham, Bucks Co., belonging to estate of the dec'd, is to be sold by Sarah Read, administratrix (18 Oct.)

McCULOUGH, Mrs. Margaret, next door but one to the Adam and Eve in Arch St., Phila. - has rice for sale (18 Oct.)

O'NEIL, Hugh, age c. 30, native Irish servant - runaway from John Huey, of Mill Creek Hundred, Newcastle Co. (18 Oct.)

CUSHING, Mr., of committee of the Massachusetts House, reports and message is sent to the Governor; Thomas Cushing, Jr., is chosen to serve as agent in Great Britain, or, if he declines, Christopher Kilby is to serve (25 Oct.)

BRACKBILL, Willmouth, a Palatine - on 20 Oct., driving on Conestogo Rd., slipped and was accidentally killed (25 Oct.)

MILLER, Jonathan, a tailor, who lived many years in Phila. - accidentally fell out of an upper door of a house in the Manor of Moreland a few days ago and died in a few days (25 Oct.)

OWEN, Owen, of Phila. - offers reward for recovery of a horse strayed or stolen (25 Oct.)

Brigantine Sally, Slater Clay master, at Samuel Powel's

wharf - will sail for London (25 Oct.)

FRANCIS, Tench, at his house in Second St., Phila., where Robert Charles lately lived - sells cloth, hardware, lead (25 Oct.)

READ, John, of Christiana Bridge - offers reward for recovery of 2 mares strayed or stolen (25 Oct.)

FARQUAR, Alexander, dec'd - his executors, James Gorrell and Mary his wife, offer for sale a grist mill and a bolting mill, situated 2 miles from Dover and 1 mile from the Forest Landing on Lt. Jones's Creek in Kent Co. on Delaware (25 Oct.)

A lot of ground in Bridge Town, at Mount Holly in West New Jersey, adjoining Thomas Shinn's, will be sold - apply to Evan Morgan, cooper, in Phila. (25 Oct.)

Speech of Lt.-Gov. George Thomas to General Assembly of the Three Lower Counties on Delaware, their address to him and appointment of David French, Andrew Peterson, John Curtis, Thomas Noxon, Richard Grafton and John Finney as committee to consider means for defense of Town of Newcastle (1 Nov.)

Sloop **Samuel** **and** **Mary**, John Dunn master - will sail for Cape Fear - for freight or passage agree with John Hyatt, merchant, in Front St., Phila. (1 Nov.)

STANDLEY, Richard, of Phila. - offers reward for recovery of a stolen or strayed horse (1 Nov.)

SULAVAN, John, Irish servant - runaway from Stephen Hoopes, of Westown, Chester Co. (1 Nov.)

WILLIAMS, James, age 22 - absconded from his bail, Robert Basil, in Kent Co. on Delaware, taking with him horse belonging to Daniel Rodney (1 Nov.)

MORGAN, William, English servant, age c. 29 - runaway from William Williams, of Whitemarsh, Phila. Co. (1 Nov.)

SWIFT, John, dec'd - accounts with estate to be settled with Samuel Swift, executor (1 Nov.)

WILKS, Francis, Agent of Massachusetts in London - his letter to Gov. Belcher on report of the Lords of Trade about bill to emit paper money is read to the Assembly (8 Nov.)

WHITEFIELD, Rev. - landed last week from London at Lewes-

Town in Suffolk Co.; various goods contributed by charitable people England are to be sold in Phila. at Mr. Whitefield's house in Second St. in which Capt. Blair lately dwelt (8 Nov.)

BROWN, Charity, late of Phila., shopkeeper, dec'd - accounts with estate to be settled with Owen Owen, house-carpenter, administrator (8 Nov.)

SANSOM, Samuel, next door to Peter Stretch's in Second St., Phila. - sells cloth, cutlery and linen goods, just arrived per Capt. Stephenson from London (8 Nov.)

BRIENTNALL, John, in Chesnut St., Phila. - sells tenter-hooks (8 Nov.)

EMBLEN, Samuel, at the Sign of the Heart, opposite the New Market in Phila. - will lend abstract of a treatise of Dr. Bateman's Pectoral Drops (8 Nov.)

CAREY, Capt. - arrived 28 Oct. at Boston with news from London (15 Nov.)

The Augustine Packet boat has been taken by Capt. Warren in the Squirrel man-of-war and Capt. Laws in the Spence - Charlestown item of 5 Nov. (15 Nov.)

SHARPAS, William, for about 46 years Town Clerk of New York - died there Sunday morning last in his 70th year, leaving a daughter - New York item of 12 Nov. (15 Nov.)

WHITEFIELD, Rev. - Thursday last began to preach from the Court House gallery in Phila.; on 26 Nov. he leaves for New York; B. Franklin will print copies of his journals and sermons (15 Nov.)

The following real estate is offered for sale by Elizabeth Biles and Thomas Cadwalader at Trenton: 1,500 acres near Piles Grove, Salem Co., N.J.; 1,200 acres in Amwell Twp., Hunterdon Co.; a 200-acre plantation (where Neill Grant now lives) in Bucks Co., near Thomas Yardley's; one-sixteenth part of the forge at Trenton; a 250-acre plantation (where Peter Lott now lives) (15 Nov.)

ROSE, Joseph, intending to leave his master - desires to collect and print poetry of his dec'd father, Aquila Rose (15 Nov.)

TOWN, Benjamin, living on the premises in Bristol Twp., Bucks Co., opposite to Dr. Rodman's old mill on Neshaminy Creek - will let a stone back-house, a cooper's shop and a boulting-mill (15 Nov.)

Sloop Speedwell, John Miers master, now at Master's wharf
in Phila. - will sail for Cape Fear or North Carolina
(15 Nov.)

HILLBORN, John, living in Frankford, near Phila. - offers
for sale a 220-acre plantation in Wrights Town, Bucks
Co. (15 Nov.)

Subscriptions are being taken for Magnus Falconar's col-
lection of divinity by Andrew Bradford and Benjamin
Franklin in Phila., William Bradford in New York and
Messers Kneeland and Green in Boston (15 Nov.)

LE FEVRE, Capt., who arrived at Boston last week from
Jamaica - brought news of naval activities in the West
Indies - Boston item of 5 Nov. (22 Nov.)

DUMARESQUE, Capt. Philip - sailed Friday last from Boston
in a sloop upon a cruise against the Spaniards - Boston
item of 5 Nov. (22 Nov.)

JORDAN, Capt. James - arrived Friday last at Newport, R.I.,
from Jamaica, with news of capture of 3 Spanish vessels
- Newport item of 9 Nov. (22 Nov.)

HOLLAND,William, mason, whose shop is in Water St., Phila.,
next door to Stephen Beezley's; during the next 2 weeks,
while he is working in New York, his place is being
taken in Phila. by Anthony Wilkinson, ship-carver (22
Nov.)

McKENNAN, Charles, Irish servant, age $\underline{c}$. 24 - runaway from
Thomas Marshall, of Concord, Chester Co. (22 Nov.)

HOLT, John, servant, age $\underline{c}$. 23 - runaway from John Thomas,
of Charlestown, Chester Co. (22 Nov.)

JONES, John, owner of the sloop Young Eagle, Capt. Dumaresque commander - Thursday last at Marblehead induced the
captain to forego having 3 mutinous sailors flogged;
the 3 were sent ashore - Marblehead item of 9 Nov. (29
Nov.)

HUBBEL, Mr., of Stratfield, near Strafford, Conn. - last
Monday, when hunting, accidentally shot and killed an
older brother, recently married, who left a widow with
child - Boston item of 13 Nov. (29 Nov.)

WHITEFIELD, Rev. - account of his preaching in New Jersey
(29 Nov.)

HYATT, James - offers reward for recovery of pocketbook

lost near the church in Phila.; it contained a note
from Arnold Hancock to James Hyatt and an account of 14
hides from John Snowdon (29 Nov.)

CREIGHEAD, John, living at the head of Pequey - offers reward for recovery of 2 strayed geldings (29 Nov.)

POOCK, John, of Warwick Twp., near Neshaminey Meeting-house
in Bucks Co. - offers reward for recovery of a mare (29
Nov.)

Ship Dragon, Capt. William Neate - arrived 5 Dec. at Phila.
from London, with European news (6 Dec.)

Letter from Charlestown, S.C., relates that a captured
Spanish vessel had flour and butter bought from Capt.
Kip of New York - Boston item of 26 Nov. (6 Dec.)

WHITEFIELD, Rev. - left Phila. Thursday last (6 Dec.)

Poor Richard's Almanac for 1740 contains a letter to the
author from Titan Leeds, dec'd (6 Dec.)

Plantation of 400 acres in Buckingham Twp., Bucks Co., is
offered for sale by Enoch Pearson, living on said plantation (6 Dec.)

PROWEL, James, of Vincent Twp., Chester Co. - has taken up
a stray horse (6 Dec.)

UNDERWOOD, Capt., who has arrived at Boston from the Bay
of Honduras - met with Capt. Serjeant of Boston not far
from Havana - Boston item of 26 Nov. (13 Dec.)

SPENCER, Joseph, English convict servant, age c. 30 - runaway from James Baxter at the Principio Iron Works
(with a convict servant named John Mathews) (13 Dec.)

ALLAN, Capt. James, of ship Lydia, on passage from London
to Phila. - on 21 Nov. spoke with a New England schooner
commanded by Capt. Randolph from the Bay of Honduras
(20 Dec.)

STEDMAN, Capt., in the Charming Nancy, on passage from
Plymouth to Phila. - on 23 Nov. spoke with Capt. John
Hadaway in the brigantine Phenix of Rhode Island from
the Bay of Honduras and on 30 Nov. with Capt. John
Cullen, in the ship Francis of Boston, also from the
Bay of Honduras (20 Dec.)

BERCLEY, John, carpenter of the ship Dragon - Tuesday last
when going aboard on a plank from the wharf, fell into

the water and was drowned (20 Dec.)

ALLEN, William, and Edward Shippen, executors of estate of
Humphrey Murrey, dec'd - offer for sale the following
tracts of land belonging to the estate: tract of 625
acres called Leoglan in Amwel Twp., Hunterdon Co., West
New Jersey, near John Reading, Esq.; 1,420 acres near
Whipany, Hunterdon Co., near John Budd, Esq.; 500 acres
in Limerick Twp., Phila. Co., about 30 miles from Phila.
(20 Dec.)

BRIDGES, Edward, at the Scales, in Front St., corner of
Walnut St., Phila. - sells West Indian and European
goods (20 Dec.)

INGLIS, John - has for sale times of some West Country-born
men-servants, just imported in the ship Nelly from
Bristol (20 Dec.)

Ship Catherine. John McKnight master, now at Plumsted's
wharf, will sail for Dublin; for freight or passage
agree with Davy and Carson, at their house over the
drawbridge in Front St., Phila., or with the master (20
Dec.)

BRADFORD, Mrs. Dorcas (wife of Andrew Bradford, printer) -
died Thursday last in Phila. (27 Dec.)

SEDIMON, John, Dutch servant, age c. 17 - runaway from
Lodowick Debler, of Amity Twp., Phila. Co. (27 Dec.)

OLIVER, Christopher, English servant, age c. 20, weaver -
runaway from Samuel Osborne, of Westown, Chester Co.
(27 Dec.)

1740

Speech of Lt.-Gov. William Bull to the South Carolina Assembly and address of the House (3 Jan.)

WHITAKER, Benjamin - on Tuesday last was appointed Chief
Justice of South Carolina - Charlestown item of 17 Nov.
1739 (3 Jan.)

ARROWSMITH, Capt., who sailed from New York with Capt.
Lush - arrived Saturday last at Charlestown in command
of a prize taken by Capt. Lush, who had also taken 2
other prizes from the Spaniards - Charlestown item of
17 Nov. 1739 (3 Jan.)

GLYN, James, Esq., lately appointed Governor of South

Carolina, is expected at Charlestown about Christmas in H.M.S. Greenwich, Capt. Windham commander - Charlestown item of 17 Nov. 1739 (3 Jan.)

MURRAY, Capt. John, who arrived at Charlestown last week from Providence - reported that Capt. Fraser arrived at Providence from Jamaica - Charlestown item of 17 Nov. 1739 (3 Jan.)

WICKHAM, Capt. Benjamin, commander of a privateer (owned by Capt. Godfrey Malbone of Newport, R. I.) - is reported to have taken 2 Spanish ships - Newport item of 14 Dec. 1739 (3 Jan.)

It is reported from New London that a ship from Phila. commanded by Benjamin Jenkins had been abandoned because it had sprung a leak - extract of a letter from New London dated 6 Dec. 1739 (3 Jan.)

SNOW, Capt. - arrived last week at Boston from South Carolina - Boston item of 10 Dec. 1739 (3 Jan.)

BOYDELL, John, Esq., late publisher of the Boston Gazette and Deputy Postmaster in Massachusetts and other governments - died Tuesday last at Boston in his 49th year - Boston item of 17 Dec. 1739 (3 Jan.)

Account of Thomas Newton, quartermaster of Capt. Hill /or Hall?/, of the capture, plundering and burning of the town Port of Plate at Hispaniola - extract of letter from a gentleman in Newport dated 10 Dec. 1739 (3 Jan.; see also 29 Jan.)

DOWRICK, Capt. - arrived some days past at Boston from Jamaica - Boston item of 10 Dec. 1739 (3 Jan.)

SHAHAN, Matthias, of Manor of Moreland, Phila. Co., tailor - died there some days since (3 Jan.)

GRAEME, Patrick, intending for Britain - desires to settle all accounts (3 Jan.)

Address of the General Assembly of the Three Lower Counties on Delaware to Lt.-Gov. George Thomas (10 Jan.)

HARRISON, William - offers reward for capture of thief or thieves who broke open and stole from his house on Passyunk Road near Phila. (10 Jan.)

Tract of 2,237 acres at Paquaess in Hunterdon Co., West New Jersey, bounded on north by John Reading's land, on east by Daniel Cox's, and on west by Joseph Kelby's,

is for sale - apply to Thomas Glentworth, near the Post
Office in Phila. (10 Jan.)

MAHANY, John, servant, age c. 22 - runaway from John
Pricket, who had purchased him the day before from
Capt. Atwood of Phila. (10 Jan.)

Message of Lt.-Gov. George Thomas to the House of Representatives of Pennsylvania (15 Jan.)

Account of action by Capt. Mackey (in command at Ft. St.
Andrews), Adjutant Hugh Mackey and General Oglethorpe
against Spaniards who landed on Island of Amelia - item
from Frederica, Ga., 30 Nov. 1739 (15 Jan.)

WOODFORD, Capt., who arrived Saturday last at New York
from Madeira - reports war was proclaimed in England
against Spain - New York item of 31 Dec. 1739 (15 Jan.)

O'DONALLY, James, servant, age 18 or 19 - runaway from
William Blair of Middleton, Chester Co. (15 Jan.)

Message of House of Representatives of Pennsylvania to
the Governor (22 Jan.)

Tract of 1,250 acres (formerly Nathan Stanbury's) in the
Great Swamp, West Jersey (Morris Co.), adjoining land
late William Biddle's, now Samuel Johnson's, and also
a tract on west side of Muskonetung River, bounding
north on John Bowlsby's line, are for sale - apply to
Robert Jordan in Phila., to Isaac Decow in Burlington
or to Edward Rockhill, living near the premises (22
Jan.)

Message of Gov. George Thomas to the Pennsylvania House
of Representatives and their reply (29 Jan.)

MELLEN, Capt. - arrived Tuesday last at Boston from New
Providence with news that Capt. Hall had taken 3 Spanish
prizes - Boston item of 7 Jan. (29 Jan.)

REDDISH, Nicholas, late of Phila., sadler, dec'd - accounts
with estate to be settled with William Cox, in Phila.,
administrator (29 Jan.)

HUGIN, Rose, mulatto, age c. 26 - runaway from Valentine
Robinson, of Brandewyne Hundred, Newcastle Co.; reward
will be paid if she is brought to Owen Owen in Phila.
(29 Jan.)

NICHOLAS, Edward, in Chesnut St., Phila., administator of
the estate of Susannah Morris, dec'd - demands surrender

to him of a watch and chain and papers belonging to the estate, including a bill of sale from Isaac Tenacliff and 2 bonds of John Jones (29 Jan.)

HALL, Charity (daughter of Thomas Hall, of City of Dublin), who came to Pennsylvania some years ago and lived upon Brandewyne Creek, Chester Co. - will hear something to her advantage by applying to William Reynolds, of Charlestown, near Moor Hall, Chester Co. (29 Jan.)

TOOLE, Terence, Irish servant, butcher - runaway from George Rice Jones, of Phila., butcher (7 Feb.)

WILDEER, Thomas, Irish servant, age c. 25 - runaway from Samuel Hastings, of Phila., shipwright (7 Feb.)

BERRY, Michael, Irish servant, carpenter - runaway from Thomas Sugar, of Phila., carpenter (7 Feb.)

PAYNE, Ianna, of Woodbridge, N.J. - has for sale a 240-acre tract on west side of Rahaway River in Essex Co., 2 lots on Strawberry Hill in Woodbridge and 4 more lots in Woodbridge (7 Feb.)

The following passengers imported last year in the snow Enterprize, Lyonel Wood commander, and the bilander London, Joshua Pipon commander, from London, are to pay their obligations speedily: Johann Richter, Hans Recker, Friederich Recker, Jacob Kistenholtz, Johann Lang, Henrich Lang, Caspar Weider, Henrich Ortley and Vincent Briler (7 Feb.)

RHODES, Capt. - arrived last week at Boston from Holland but last from Plymouth, with European news - Boston item of 21 Jan. (13 Feb.)

MILLER, Mr., of Wrights Town, Bucks Co. - last Thursday se'nnight his house burned down and a child of 4 was burnt to death (13 Feb.)

LOCKHART, Andrew, of Bensalem, Bucks Co. - Friday last his house was destroyed by fire (13 Feb.)

SOBER, Thomas - has to let a dwelling and stable on corner of Chesnut St. and Fourth St. in Phila. (13 Feb.)

LAWRENCE, Joshua - offers reward for recovery of a mare stolen from Phila. (13 Feb.)

DUNSTAR, Charles, dec'd - his executors, Michael Kearney and James Alexander, plan to sell at auction at house of Widow Hay in Perth Amboy the following real estate:

property in East Jersey purchased by Dunstar from James
Lord Drummond; land in East Jersey purchased by Dunstar
from Archibald Campbell and James Blackwood; half of
the estate formerly Joseph Ormston's in New Jersey; 600
acres in East Jersey conveyed to Dunstar by James Armour
(13 Feb.)

TINGLEY, Capt. - arrived Thursday last at New York from
Georgia with account of General Oglethorpe's expedition
against the Spaniards in Florida; the general used forces under Capts. Heron, Mackay and Desbrisay, Lts.
Demeri and Horton and Ensigns Mace, Lemon, Hogan, Sutherland, Cadogan and Steuart and Indians under Hillespelli
and Phance Mico; Lt. Dunbar was sent to search the River
St. John - New York item of 28 Jan. (21 Feb.)

WHITEFIELD, Rev. - arrived Friday last at Williamsburg from
Annapolis - Williamsburg item of 16 Dec. 1739 and arrived at Edenton, N. C., on 20 Dec. (21 Feb.)

DAWSON, Robert, lately from London, now living at the
Reed and Shuttle in Third St., opposite to the Quaker
burying-ground in Phila. - does all sorts of weaving
(21 Feb.)

Land is for sale in Hopewell, Hunterdon Co., N.J., now or
late in possession of the following: Thomas Houghton
(240 acres), George Woolsey (220 acres), Thomas Curtis
(160 acres), James Melvin (350 acres), David Price (220
acres), Daniel Ganns (245 acres), William Scritchfield
(300 acres), Francis Ganns (150 acres), James Richards
(300 acres), Joseph Hart (210 acres); apply to John
Reading, of Amwell, or Thomas Clarke and Joseph Peace,
of Trenton (21 Feb.)

Tract of 500 acres in Phila. Co., within a mile of Pawlin's
Mill, bounding on land that was Nathaniel Puckle's and
with the line of Limerick Twp., is for sale; apply to
John Pike, at Dr. Richard Farmer's, next door but one
to Owen Owen's in Market St., Phila. (21 Feb.)

JACOBI, John Owen, organist of Trinity Church in Newport,
R. I. - died there Wednesday last - Newport item of 25
Jan. (28 Feb.)

Steer weighing 1,533 pounds, bred on Capt. Godfrey Malbone's
farm near Newport - was killed there Wednesday last -
Newport item of 25 Jan. (28 Feb.)

WHITEFIELD, Rev. - arrived at Georgia about 20 Jan. (28
Feb.)

HAY, John, native Irishman - is supposed to have stolen a
bay gelding from Job Harvey, of Darby, Chester Co.,
clothier, and a saddle and bridle from William Hay, of
Chester, innholder (28 Feb.)

Ship Morshaid, John Vivian master, now at Plumsted's wharf
in Phila. - will sail for Cork (28 Feb.)

WILLARD, Henry, late of gloucester Co., N.J., dec'd - accounts with estate to be settled with James Willard,
administrator (28 Feb.)

WHITEFIELD, Rev. George - arrived 11 Jan. at Savannah and
has sent his journal and a letter concerning Arch-
bishop Tillotson to London and Phila. to be printed -
Charlestown item of 19 Jan. (6 Mar.)

MURRAY, Capt. John, who arrived at Charlestown Saturday
last from Providence - reports capture of Spanish vessels by Capt. Charles Hall in the sloop Virgin Queen,
belonging to Rhode Island - Charlestown item of 19 Jan.
(6 Mar.)

Spanish prize sloop, taken off Hispaniola by the sloop
Sea-Nymph, under command of Capt. Joseph Prew - arrived
last week at Charlestown - Charlestown item of 19 Jan.
(6 Mar.)

ROME, Capt., of brigantine Lawrie, reports that Capt.
Bayard in a privateer has taken 2 Spanish vessels worth
10,000 pounds - Williamsburg item of 25 Jan. (6 Mar.)

GALT, Capt., in a snow belonging to Phila., has been taken
and towed into Vigo (6 Mar.)

JONES, Isaac, of Phila., intending for London, desires that
all accounts be settled (6 Mar.)

Persons indebted to Reese Meredith or Samuel Neave are desired to make payment, as Neave is leaving for Europe
(6 Mar.)

READ, John, at Christiana Bridge, Newcastle Co. - offers
reward for recovery of 2 strayed mares (6 Mar.)

MATHAS, Joseph, servant, born in East Jersey, age c. 24,
weaver - runaway from Joseph Kelley, of Upper Freehold,
Monmouth Co., N.J. (6 Mar.)

McDANIEL, Matthew, Irish servant, age c. 21, who has served
a time in Arundel Co., Md., and was taken out of Burlington Jail - runaway from Margaret Jackson, of Bur-

lington, West New Jersey (6 Mar.)

JOHNSON, John, servant, born in Birmingham or thereabouts, age c. 30, barber - runaway from William Crosthwaite (6 Mar.)

HOPKINS, Peter, mariner, dec'd - accounts with his estate to be settled with his widow, Mary Hopkins, now lodging at George Parker's, in Front St., Phila.; she designs for New England in a few days (6 Mar.)

BIRD, Bartholomew, convict servant, age c. 26, shoemaker - runaway from John Senhouse, of Annapolis, Md. (6 Mar.)

Snow <u>Mediterranean</u>, Capt. Bond from Bristol - arrived at Phila. Friday last (12 Mar.)

COUGHRAN, William, of Chester Co. - lately killed when a tree fell on him (12 Mar.)

SKIRRET, Benjamin, of Lancaster Co. - lately died when his horse fell down a steep rocky hill (12 Mar.)

JONES, David, of Lancaster - his house lately was consumed to ashes (12 Mar.)

TODD, Capt. - arrived 12 Mar. at Phila. from Bermudas (12 Mar.)

WINTER, John, painter, from London - works at the Sign of the Easy Chair in Chesnut St., Phila. (12 Mar.)

McSWINE, Thomas (<u>alias</u> Thomas McGill), servant, age c. 20 - runaway from William Wright, of Lancaster Co. (12 Mar.)

WENN, Thomas, servant, age c. 40, barber - runaway from William Crosthwaite (12 Mar.)

CARTER, George, age c. 40, born in White Parish, 11 miles from New Sarum, Wiltshire, baker, who about 1722 boarded a ship at Bristol for Pennsylvania - is desired to return to England or give notice of where he lives to John Atkinson, at the White Lyon Tavern, on Cornhill, London, or to Israel Pemberton at Phila.; if he is deceased, information as to when and where he died is requested and also knowledge of any children (12 Mar.)

GREW, Theophilus - his goods, taken by attachment, are to be sold; auditors are Peter Robertson and William Coleman (12 Mar.)

EVANS, Thomas, of Northampton, about 3 miles from Newtown, Bucks Co. - has for sale a tract of land and house (12 Mar.)

NOXON, Thomas, at Appoquinimy - seeks a fuller (12 Mar.)

McCALL, George, late of Phila., merchant, dec'd - accounts with estate to be settled with executors, Ann McCall, Samuel McCall, Samuel McCall, Jr., and others; Ann lives below the drawbridge in Phila. (12 Mar.)

DUMARESQ, Capt., a Boston privateer, has put into Madeira to refit - Boston item of 3 Mar. (27 Mar.)

OGLETHORPE, General - plans to attack St. Augustine - Charlestown item of 6 Feb. (27 Mar.)

BOYD, Capt., who arrived 5 Feb. at Charlestown, brings news of the war in the West Indies; he left Capt. Lush at Jamaica and reports Spanish prizes have been taken by Capt. Welch and Capt. Steward - Charlestown item of 6 Feb. (27 Mar.)

DEHART, Capt. of a sloop from New York, bound to Rhode Island - Tuesday last sloop was overset at Mt. Misery on Long Island; Thomas Carry alone was not drowned but both legs were frozen; those drowned were Dehart (master), Godf. Sweet (mate), Hancock (foremastman) and 5 passengers, Capt. Seabrook, Co. Mallone, Dan. Still-well, William _____ (blacksmith) and William _____ - Brookhaven, L.I., item of 15 Mar. (27 Mar.)

Privateer St. George, Capt. Axon commander, fitted out at Phila. - in Feb. took a Spanish sloop (27 Mar.)

REID, James, Scotch servant, who speaks very good Dutch, fuller - runaway from Samuel Faires, of Warwick Twp., Bucks Co. (27 Mar.)

SHAW, Samuel - offers reward for recovery of horse, mare and colt strayed from him; Shaw lives at Maiden Creek, Phila. Co.; creatures may be brought to him or to William Nixon, of Milford Twp., Bucks Co. (27 Mar.)

ROACH, Catherine, servant, age 22, a Roman Catholic - runaway from Charles Moor, of Phila., hatter (27 Mar.)

Tract of land, late the estate of Dr. Edward Jones, dec'd, in Merion, Phila. Co., about 7 miles from Phila. and within ¼ miles of Merion Meeting-house is for sale; apply to John Jones on the premises (27 Mar.)

MELVIN, Jame and David Price - warn against purchase of

real estate in Hopewell as advertising in the Pa.
Gazette of 6 Mar. (27 Mar.)

RYAN, John, at one of Mr. Fishbourne's new stores in Water
St., Phila. - sells rice, mahogany, cloth, glass (27
Mar.)

Persons who are debtors or creditors of Robert Grace, of
Phila., merchant, are desired to settle accounts (27
Mar.)

NORWOOD, Eliz., of Phila. - offers for sale a pilot-boat
(27 Mar.)

PRICE, Elizabeth, Irish servant, age c. 23 - runaway from
Joseph Thackery, of Newtown, Gloucester Co., West
Jersey (27 Mar.)

HENDERSON, William, servant, born in Somerset Co., Md. -
runaway (in company with William Turner) from Nathaniel
Waller, Jr., of Somerset Co., Md.; Henderson had been
taken up with Turner and jailed; he turned King's evidence against Turner (27 Mar.); Henderson has changed
his name to William McClemmen; reward will be paid by
Nathaniel Waller, Jr., or George Harding, if servant is
delivered to George Harding, glover, in Market St.,
near the Court House in Phila. (3 Apr.)

Fine new buildings (unfinished) of Mr. Hamilton, near the
bridge in Phila., were consumed by fire Saturday last
(3 Apr.)

WEAVER, Henry, of Maiden Creek, Phila. - his house was
burnt down and one child perished (3 Apr.)

CRANE, George, near Maiden Creek, Phila. Co. - his house
was destroyed by fire and 2 children burnt to death
(3 Apr.)

HUNTER, Elizabeth, in Chesnut St., near corner of Front St.,
Phila. - makes gloves, mittens, stockings (3 Apr.)

FOLWELL, George - gives notice that fairs will be held on
28 and 29 Apr. and 24 and 25 Oct. at Willingtown (3 Apr.)

SHARP, Widow, at Dr. Diemer's, opposite to the Sign of the
George in Second St., Phila. - sells Bermuda platt,
strings, indigo, some drugs and a box of surgical instruments (3 Apr.)

ROBESON, Andrew - offers reward for recovery of a horse
that strayed away (3 Apr.)

MARSHALL, Abraham, Jr., of West Bradford, Chester Co. - offers reward for recovery of strayed or stolen horse (3 Apr.)

WHITEFIELD, Rev. - his letter, dated Savannah 18 Jan., to a friend in London mentions John Wesly, Archibishop Tillotson, Luther and the Rev. Edwards of Cambridge (10 Apr.)

ROGERS, Capt., from Barbados - informs that Thomas Bell (who claimed to be Gilbert Burnet, son of Gov. Burnet, late of Boston) was pilloried and whipped at the latter end of December in Barbados; he had been also sentenced to be branded with "R" on each cheek "for his misdemeanor and wicked Actions" but Gov. Byng released him from this part of his punishment - Newport item of 7 Mar. (10 Apr.)

JOHNSON, Capt. Elisha - arrived at Newport last Sabbath from Jamaica; he cited Capt. James Collins with regard to the success of Capt. Charles Hall; Johnson reports that 2 Spanish privateers have taken the Island of Commanda and taken to the value of 3,000 pounds from a Mr. Thompson there; Capt. Hall's owners design to have a marble statue made of him - Newport item of 21 Mar. (10 Apr.)

LOW, Ned, well-known for his piracies - served as a gunner in a Spanish fort - Boston item of 24 Mar. (10 Apr.)

The Johanna, Capt. Payton, from Madeira - on Friday last was shipwrecked on south side of Long Island, near Hamstead; the captain, mate, 2 sailors and John Bayeux, Jr., were lost; 2 men and a boy got safely ashore - New York item of 31 Mar. (10 Apr.)

TUCKNESS, Capt. - sailed for New York 13 weeks since and Capt. Vatar 11 (10 Apr.)

HANTWERK, Nicholas, a Palatine - on 26 Mar. in Bucks Co. killed one Patrick McQuire after a quarrel and is confined in the County Goal (10 Apr.)

AXON, Capt. - is reported to have taken 2 prizes and sent them to Curacoa (10 Apr.)

Stage will be operated between Trenton and Brunswick by William Atlee and Joseph Yeates (10 Apr.)

Jo, Negro, age c. 22, born in Bermuda - runaway from George Smith, in Arch St., Phila. (10 Apr.)

Letter from Rev. George Whitefield to inhabitants of Maryland, Virginia and the Carolinas (17 Apr.)

Proclamation by Lt.-Gov. George Thomas; troops raised in North America are to be commanded by Col. Spotswood; Col. Blakeney is appointed Adjutant-General (17 Apr.)

Schedule of preaching by Rev. Whitefield (17 Apr.)

STAMPER, Thomas, of Phila. - will not pay debts contracted in future by wife Dinah (17 Apr.)

Persons desiring to inlist for the expedition against the Spanish West Indies are to repair to the following: in Phila. Co.: Capt. Palmer, Thomas Lawrence, Alexander Woodrop, James Hamilton, Samuel Lane at Perkiomen, Marcus Huling at Manatamy, Owen Evan of Limerick; in Chester Co.: Henry Hockley, James Mather, Robert Finney, Lazarus Finney at Flying Hill; in Lancaster Co.: Thomas Cookson, Andrew Galbraith, Thomas Edwards, Samuel Smith late sheriff; in Bucks Co.: Jeremiah Langhorn, Benjamin Jones, Nathanael Irish, Mathew Hughes, Thomas Clarke; in Newcastle Co.: William Shaw, Jehu Curtis, Abraham Goodin, Jacob Goodin at Apoquinimy; in Kent Co.: Charles Hellier, Nicholas Ridgely, John Housman; in Sussex Co.: Abraham Wyncoop, Rives Holt (17 Apr.)

WILKINSON, Gabriel, dec'd - lot on Fifth St. in Phila. will be sold by his executors, Anthony and Gabriel Wilkinson (17 Apr.)

OWEN, Peter, of Concord Twp., Chester Co. - will not pay debts contracted in future by his wife Mary, who has eloped from him and now lives in Phila. and goes by the name of Morris (17 Apr.)

Second letter from Rev. Whitefield to a friend in London (24 Apr.)

SHEAF, Mr., of Charlestown, who came to Antigua on 8 Mar. from Madera - gives account of 3 prizes taken by Capt. Dumaresque - Boston item of 14 Apr. (24 Apr.)

Account of activity of Rev. Whitefield; contributions for him may be sent to Stephen Benezet, in Second St., Phila.; Whitefield is said to have taken up 5,000 acres on the Forks of Delaware to erect a Negro school (24 Apr.)

SOBER, Thomas, merchant, of Phila. - died Sunday last (24 Apr.)

PIEREY, Capt. - arrived last week at Amboy from Madeira, with news about Spain (24 Apr.)

SEYMOUR, John, at house of Widow Stapleford, in Second St., Phila. - sells looking-glasses, teakettles, candle-sticks, cloth, etc. (24 Apr.)

STEEPLES, Thomas, of Springfield, Burlington Co. - offers reward for recovery of stolen horse (24 Apr.)

POWEL, Samuel, cooper, in Phila. - offers reward for re-covery of horse strayed or stolen from the Commons in Phila. (24 Apr.)

KENARD, John, of Manor of Moreland - his wife Margaret has eloped from him (24 Apr.)

Persons indebted to Messrs. Thomas Robinson and Samuel Combs, merchants, for servants bought - are to make prompt payment (24 Apr.)

Tract of 500 acres in Hunterdon Co., West New Jersey, will be sold at auction at the Coffee House in Phila.; it borders on land of John Reading, dec'd, "being land sur-veyed unto Jonathan Wilson deceased, in Right of Mary his Wife, one of the Daughters of Henry Stacy deceased, since intermarried with George Mason, and by the said George and Mary his Wife, conveyed to Clement Pumstead and Thomas Hatton, in Trust to sell, as by the Writings in the Hands of Charles Brockden at Philadelphia may appear." (24 Apr.)

WHITEFIELD, George - remainder of his letter begun in last number (1 May)

VAN DUSSEN, Alexander - is appointed colonel of forces voted by the Assembly of South Carolina to be sent to aid General Oglethorpe; Capt. Richard Wright is com-missioned to head volunteers - Charlestown item of 3 Apr. (1 May); name is given as Alexander Vander Dussen in appointment by James Oglethorpe (15 May)

HALL, Capt., of the privateer Virgin Queen, arrived at Newport, R.I., Tuesday last; Capt. Wickham arrived there last week; Capt. Allen has taken 3 Spanish prizes - Boston item of 21 Apr. (1 May)

Saturday last arrived at New York Capt. Wilson from Am-sterdam and also the New York privateer Capt. Lush, with 2 rich prizes - New York item of 28 Apr. (1 May)

Extensive account of Rev. George Whitefield's preaching

in New Jersey and Pennsylvania (1 May)

HART, Thomas, bricklayer, next door to William Parsons in
Second St., Phila. - has a parcel of salted herrings
for sale (1 May)

Plantation of 217 acres in Buckingham Twp., Bucks Co., is
for sale; apply to Alexander Beal (1 May)

Mr. Franklin publishes a letter critical of the conduct of
William Seward (an intimate companion of Rev. Whitefield) in having the dancing and concert rooms closed
even though the owner, Mr. Bolton, told him they belonged to members of the concert (8 May)

LONEY, Capt. - arrived Sunday last in Rappahannock River
from London with European news - Williamsburg item of
11 Apr. (8 May)

Gov. Gabriel Johnstone, of North Carolina, and Col. Spotswood were expected at Williamsburg on 11 Apr. to confer
with the Governor of Virginia (8 May)

Proclamation of Gov. William Gooch to encourage men to
inlist - Williamsburg item of 11 Apr. (8 May)

WHITEFIELD, Rev. - his schedule of preaching and plans for
travel (8 May)

DAVIS, Capt. David - has time of servant girl for sale
(8 May)

SHOAT, Reuben, servant, a Londoner, age c. 22 - runaway
from Menasses Woods, of Maxfield Twp., Bucks Co. (8 May)

QUE, William, Irish servant - same as above

PEARSE, Vincent, commander of H.M.S. Flamborough - offers
pardon and back pay to deserters who return to service
(15 May)

ALLEN, Capt., in a Newport privateer has taken 50 tons of
gunpowder (15 May)

LATHROP, Capt., from Jamaica - arrived Thursday last at
Boston and gave news of the West Indies from one Capt.
Burn (15 May)

A New York item of 5 May contains news of Capt. Cunningham
(a Jamaica privateer), Capt. Bayard of New York, Capt.
Bedford, who arrived at New York from Georgia Wednesday
last and Capt. Lush (15 May)

JACKSON, Joseph, of Borough of Bristol, Bucks Co. - has
    for sale a plantation of 130 acres within a mile of the
    borough and to let a brick house in the borough (15 May)

IRESON, William, of Phila., skinner - offers reward for
    recovery of a strayed or stolen mare (15 May)

MORGAN, Evan, cooper - is removed to Peter Baynton's house,
    near the dock, in Front St., Phila. (15 May)

Voorbidding ein ieder Christen's Plicht is sold by J. P.
    Zenger in New York and B. Franklin in Phila. (15 May)

Saturday last arrived at New York Capts. Hall, Spafford
    and Bayard - New York item of 19 May (22 May)

OWEN, Owen, at the Sign of the Indian King in Phila. - has
    on display a camel (22 May)

HOLLINSHEAD, William, sheriff, offers reward for capture
    of the following 4 men who broke out of the Somerset
    Co., N.J., Goal: Gilbert Miller, Irishman, age c. 50,
    shoemaker; Edward Hoper, born on Long Island, black-
    smith; Edward Bonnel, born in New Jersey, blacksmith;
    Evan Harry, born in Pennsylvania, sadler (22 May)

WHITEFIELD, Rev. - went on board sloop at Newcastle on
    15 May to sail for Georgia (22 May)

OGLETHORPE, General - arrived 11 Apr. at Uebee Indian Town
    to meet Mr. Eyre, Capt. Brown and Capt. Holmes, with a
    large party of Cherokee Indians (29 May)

On 3 May they beat up at Charlestown for volunteers to go
    on board the prize schooner Pearl, Richard Tyrrel com-
    mander, to go against St. Augustine (29 May)

GRACE, Robert, of Phila. - Monday last at French Creek in
    Chester Co. married Mrs. Rebecca Nutt, a young lady with
    a fortune of 10,000 pounds (29 May)

Plantation of 1,050 acres in Nantmel Twp., Chester Co.,
    late belonging to Ann Roberts, dec'd, about one mile
    from Reading Furnace and 3 from Warwick Furnace, will
    be sold at auction by Awbrey Roberts, executor (29 May)

GRAEME, Patrick - is removed from his house in Market St.
    into Front St., the house adjoining to Dickinson's
    burnt house and next door to Mr. Willing's (29 May)

BYLES, Thomas, pewterer, in Phila. - offers reward for re-
    covery of horse strayed from William Ball's plantation
    (29 May)

EVANS, David, in Tredyffrin, in the Great Valley, Chester
Co., near the Welch Presbyterian Meeting-house - will
sell the houses and land whereon he dwells and his half
part of Thomas Lloyd's grist mills (29 May)

NORWOOD, Elizabeth (widow of Henry Norwood, dec'd) - has
for sale a pilot boat (29 May)

RICHARDSON, Francis, at the house of Joseph Richardson in
Front St., Phila. - sells rice, pitch and tea (29 May)

BERWICK, John, of Phila. - will not pay debts contracted
in future by his wife Elizabeth (29 May)

OGLE, Gov. Samuel, of Maryland - speech to the Maryland
Assembly (5 June)

Subscribers to a course of philosophical lectures and experiments by Mr. Greenwood are desired to meet in the
chamber adjoining the library at the State House (5 June)

CULFORD, Patrick, servant, carpenter - runaway from Nutts
Ironworks in Chester Co. (5 June)

READING, Matthew, servant - same as above

MORGAN, Edward, servant, tailor - same as above

Thomas Smiley, George Caldwell, Henry Robinson and James
Henderson, who came passengers from Ireland with Capt.
James Aspinall in the snow _Frodsham_ in 1735 - are to pay
immediately what they owe to James Mackey in Phila.
(5 June)

BRECHBEL, John Vendel - offers reward for return of gelding
strayed or stolen from Mr. Ball's plantation near Phila.
(5 June)

Mr. Finley's Letter, concerning Mr. Whitefield, Messers.
Tennents, etc. - sold by B. Franklin (5 June)

For sale in New Brunswick, N.J., are the house wherein
Francis Costigan lately lived and that where Samuel
Belknap now lives; apply to Benjamin Price, attorney-at-
law in New Brunswick (5 June)

BOURNE, Patrick, Irish servant - runaway from Andrew
Zelefio, of Cecil Co., Md. (5 June)

HODGE, Henry, late of Phila., merchant, dec'd - his house
on north side of High St. (the lot continues through to
Jones's Alley), a house on another lot in said alley

and a lot on the east side of Capt. Atwood's orchard
are for sale; apply to Wm. Rawle, of Phila., John
Paschal, of Darby, and Thomas Hodge (5 June)

RANKIN, John, fuller, on Whiteclay Creek - offers reward
for recovery of a strayed horse (5 June)

CARNEE, James, Irish servant, age c. 30 - runaway from
Jacob Giles, near Susquehannah Ferry, Md. (5 June)

BOODE, John, or the Widow Fisher, at Kingsess - will sell
herrings in barrels (5 June)

OGDEN, John - has for sale a Negro girl, age c. 11 (5 June)

RHYMES, Capt. - arrived 1 June at Boston from London,
with European news (12 June)

PHENIX, Capt. - arrived 8 June in ship Lequina from Jamaica,
with news from the West Indies (12 June)

SPOTSWOOD, Alexander - died Saturday last at Annapolis,
Md., at an advanced age (12 June)

At the Presbyterian Synod, which began 28 May, sermons
were preached on Society Hill by Rev. Messers Tennents,
Davenport, Rowland and Blair (12 June)

Sunday last Rev. Gilbert Tennent preached several times in
Phila. (12 June)

DENORMANDIE, John Abraham, living in Borough of Bristol,
Bucks Co. - offers for rent a malt-house, brew-house
and dwelling in said borough; enquire of Peter Bard in
Phila. (12 June)

WOODS, Glowd, Irish servant - runaway from Thomas Cummings,
of Chester, shoemaker; Cummings warns that those who
divide or share rum are accounted to be retailing (12
June)

A pleasure boat is to be raffled; it may be seen by applying to William Cunningham, living at the upper end
of Front St.; those wishing to raffle may agree with
William Harris, at the Crown and Scepter in Front St.,
Phila. (12 June)

ALLEN, Capt. - arrived Saturday last at Newport, R.I., in
the privateer Revenge; he is fitting out for another
cruize, as are Capt. James Collingwood in the sloop
Charming Betty and Capt. Charles Davidson in the sloop
St. Andrew - Newport item of 30 May (19 June)

DUMARESQUE, Capt., of a privateer of Boston - has gone to
Gibraltar to have his prizes condemned - Boston item
of 3 June (19 June)

FRANKLIN, B. - has printed and sells Rev. Gilbert Tennent's
Sermon on the Danger of an Unconverted Ministry, Sir
Matthew Hale's Sum of Religion and Some Observations on
the Rev. Mr. Whitefield and His Opposers (19 June)

HOLLAND, William, mason, at his shop in Market St., Phila.
- seeks an apprentice (19 June)

INGLEDEW, Blackston, dec'd - lot on Sassafrass St. and a
house in Front St. are for sale; William Tidmarsh and
Joshua Emlen are administrators (19 June)

SCULL, Joseph, at the Workhouse in Phila. or William Pyewell in Second St., Phila. - will pay reward for recovery of a horse that strayed or was let out of George
Rice Jones's pasture, over against the Half Moon on
Passyunk Rd.; it is thought to have gone towards Dunk's
or Neshamaney Ferry, being lately bought from Thomas
Croasdale, of Frankford (19 June)

OLDMAN, Joseph, of Phila., blacksmith - offers reward for
recovery of a strayed or stolen gelding (19 June)

Proclamation by Lt.-Gov. William Bull of South Carolina
of 28 May as a day of fasting (26 June)

Saturday last it is reported that General Oglethorpe had
taken Ft. St. Diego and was close to St. Augustine -
Charlestown item of 7 June (26 June)

GLAZE, Capt. Malachy, captain of a company of volunteers -
lately died of the flux in camp before St. Augustine -
Charlestown item of 7 June (26 June)

GILL, Capt. - arrived Thursday last at New York from
London, with European news, and on Friday the Catharine,
Jasper Farman captain, from London - New York item of
13 June (26 June)

Saturday last arrived at New York H.M.S. Ludlow Castle,
Capt. Cuzock, with Col. Blakeney on board; also the
ship King George, Capt. Allen, from London, and the
brigantine Rebecca, Capt. Woodford from London - New
York item of 13 June (26 June)

Sunday last arrived at New York the brigantine William,
Charles Cornwell captain, from Ireland - New York item
of 13 June (26 June)

GREGORY, Joseph, late of Salem, West Jersey - on 7 June at
St. Georges, in Newcastle Co., was accidentally thrown
from his horse and killed (26 June)

COOLEY, Christian, a young woman of Upper Dublin, Phila.
Co. - Tuesday last visited a neighbor, leaned her arm
and head on a table and died in a few minutes (26 June)

JONES, Edward, in Norris's Alley, Phila. - has for sale a
parcel of Negroes (26 June)

DODD, Thomas, near George Gray's ferry - seeks news of his
brother Gabriel, who was born in London and served his
apprenticeship with Anthony Furnace, a ship-joiner in
Phila.; it is said that Gabriel went to South Carolina
and died there (26 June)

FARMER, Edward - a horse has been taken up at his mill in
Whitemarsh Twp., Phila. Co. (26 June)

Charles, Negro, age c. 28 or 30 - runaway from Darby Hernly
and John Fuller, in Baltimore Co., Md. (26 July)

McCORNET, James, Scotch servant, age c. 26 - runaway from
John Fuller, of Baltimore Co.

KING, Charles, Scotch servant, age c. 23 - same as above

MORRIS, Lewis, Gov. of New Jersey, by Mr. Home, on 26 June
1740 commands attendance of the House in the Council
Chamber; the House orders that Mr. Stacy and Mr. Van-
boskerk wait on the governor with message from the House;
the governor then replies, stating that Col. Blakeney
carries with him 3,000 arms and that Lord Cathcart will
carry with him spare arms and cloathing; on 30 June the
House resolved that Col. Farmer, Mr. Leaming, Mr. Leonard, Mr. Low and Mr. Hude be a committee to introduce
a bill for victualling and transporting New Jersey
troops to be raised for the expedition to the West Indies (3 July)

GALE, Capt. - arrived Thursday last at Boston in 7 weeks
from Swanzey in Wales (3 July)

VERNON, Admiral - arrived last week at Kingston, Jamaica,
from the Main - letter from Kingston dated 9 May (3 July)

GOOCH, General - arrived Monday last, together with his
wife, in Phila. from Virginia and Wednesday will set
out for New York to have an interview with Col.
Blakeney (3 July)

HUNLOKE, Mr., of Burlington - on 25 June lightning killed a man sitting at his (Hunloke's) door (3 July)

SMITH, J. - his sermon on Rev. George Whitefield, preached in Charlestown, S.C., is printed and sold by B. Franklin (3 July)

RYAN, John, native Irish servant, age c. 18 - runaway from John Williamson, fuller, at Nottingham, Chester Co. (3 July)

BOND, Phineas - sells medicines at the Sign of the Golden Mortar, a few doors below the Quaker meeting-house in Second St., Phila., the shop that lately belonged to Thomas Lloyd (3 July)

BALL, William - announces that 3 lots on Gunners Row, beginning at Kensington Dam, will be sold by auction at the house of Charles Stow, at the Half-Moon in Market St. (3 July)

OKEY, Benjamin, of London, patentee - appoints Samuel Emlen of Phila. his only salesman there for vending Dr. Bateman's Pectoral Drops (3 July)

GREW, Theophilus, in Market St., Phila. - will sell a shallop now at Mr. Powel's wharf (3 July)

House on Front St. near Sassafrass St. and lot on Sassafrass St. in Phila., estate of Blackston Ingledew, dec'd - will be sold by the administrators, William Tidmarsh and Joshua Emlen, by auction at the Crown in Market St. (3 July)

JACKSON, Joseph, of Borough of Bristol, Bucks Co. - offers real estate for sale in that borough (3 July)

Advertisment of Abraham Shelley, thread throwster, living next door to the Adam and Eve in Arch St., Phila. (3 July)

HOLLAND, William, mason, lately from London - sells tombs, hearths, tables, etc. at his shop in Market St., Phila., next door to Capt. Holland's (3 July)

Speech of Lt.-Gov. George Thomas of Pennsylvania to the Assembly (Postscript to Pa. Gazette of 3 July)

Proclamation of Lt.-Gov. Thomas on 9 July (10 July)

At St. Christophers 5 English men-of-war were sighted, supposed to be those under command of Commodore Lestock on the way to join Admiral Vernon at Jamaica (10 July)

FOWLE, Capt. - arrived Tuesday last at New York from
Curacoa with news that the Spaniards have fitted out 2
privateer sloops - New York item of 7 July (10 July)

Sloop arrived 10 July at Phila. in 30 days from Jamaica
with news of activities of British squadron (10 July)

Item from the Boston Evening Post about Town of Chagre,
lately taken by Admiral Vernon, and the castle there
which was taken in 1670 by Capt. Morgan (10 July)

GRAY, Joseph - has taken up a horse at the Middle Ferry
in Schuylkill (10 July)

House and lot on east side of Second St., Phila., now in
possession of Adam Klamper, late the estate of Jane
Jones, dec'd - will be sold by Edward and Susannah
Jones, administrators (10 July)

Proceedings in late session of the Pennsylvania Assembly
on affair of raising money and men for the expedition
against the Spanish West Indies; mentioned are Lt.-Gov.
George Thomas, Sec. Thomas Lawrie, B. Franklin (Clerk
of Assembly), J. Kinsey (Speaker of the House), Robert
Jones, John Wright and James Gibbins (17 July)

SAUNDERS, William, gunsmith - is removed from his house
in Second St., Phila., to the upper end of Market St.,
at the Sign of the Gun, a little above the house of
John Kinsey, Esq. (17 July)

ROSE, Peter, at Burlington - offers 2 Negroes for sale (17
July)

GRAEME, Patrick - is removed from his house in Market St.,
Phila., into Front St., the house adjoining to Dickinson's burnt houses and next door to Mr. Willing's; he
sells European and East India goods (17 July)

Extracts from the votes of the General Assembly of New
Jersey, 1-5 July; mentioned are Mr. Stacy, Col. Farmar,
Mr. Leonard, Mr. Low, Mr. Leaming, Mr. Hude, Mr. Rod-
man, Mr. Morris, Mr. Lyell, Mr. Vandevere, Richard
Smith of Burlington, Mr. Eaton, Mr. Cooper, Mr. Cook,
Mr. Rolph (24 July)

CHEEKE, Capt. - arrived Friday last at Charlestown, S.C.,
from Phila. - Charlestown item of 26 June (24 July)

WHITEFIELD, Rev. - arrived Thursday last at Charlestown

from Georgia - Charlestown item of 5 July (24 July)

Sloop <u>Charming Betty</u> - Tuesday last captured a Spanish ship from Teneriffe near Martha's Vineyard Sound - Newport item of 4 July (24 July)

WICKHAM, Capt. - arrived Saturday last at Boston from Jamaica; he was chased by a privateer sloop near Cape Hatteras - Boston item of 14 July (24 July)

TILDEN, Capt., of Boston - reportedly was boarded by a Spanish privateer sloop - Boston item of 14 July (24 July)

WANTON, John, Governor of Rhode Island - has just died - Boston item of 14 July (24 July)

H.M.S. <u>Flamborough</u> - arrived Saturday last at New York with news that General Oglethorpe had raised seige and that the Spaniards had retaken Fort San Diego - New York item of 21 July (24 July)

MACHER, Capt., who arrived at New York last week from Jamaica - reports he was chased by a Spanish privateer - New York item of 21 July (24 July)

TUCKER, Capt., who arrived at New York last night from Carolina - reports that Capt. Langdon had put in there to refit after engagement with a Spanish privateer off Virginia Capes; Capt. Hall, because of weather, could not help Capt. Langdon - New York item of 21 July (24 July)

AXON, Capt., master of the privateer <u>George</u> of Phila. - arrived Saturday last at Phila., having taken during a cruise goods to value of 4,000 pounds (24 July)

MACARTNEY, Joseph, Irishman, age <u>c</u>. 23, hatter - deserted from Capt. Thomas Fream's Co. of Col. Gooch's Regt. (24 July)

PEARSON, Richard, Irishman, age <u>c</u>. 24, seaman - same as above

SMITH, James, Irishman, age <u>c</u>. 22 - same as above

PEARSE, Simon, Englishman, age <u>c</u>. 24 - same as above

BLACKAL, William, Scotchman, age <u>c</u>. 30 - same as above

BROOK, Martin, born in West of England, age <u>c</u>. 40 - same as above

FITZPATRICK, Thomas, age 29 - deserted from Col. William
Gooch's Regt., Capt. Gordon's Co., quartered at Germantown, Phila. Co. (24 July)

RYAN, Morgan, age 22, painter and glazier - same as above

HUNSMAN, William, born in Upper Dublin Twp., Phila. Co.,
age 21 - same as above

BOUDE, Thomas of Phila. - offers reward for recovery of
strayed horse (24 July)

JONES, Isaac, at his store opposite the Sign of the George
in Arch St., Phila. - sells cloth and other goods (24
July)

MOORE, Charles, of Phila. - offers reward for recovery of
a horse strayed or stolen from the Commons (24 July)

FRANKLIN, B. - has printed and sells sermon preached in
1688 by William Dewsbury (24 July)

SEYMOUR, John, at house of Widow Stapleford in Second St.,
Phila. - sells looking glasses, teakettles, candle-
sticks and many other articles (24 July)

Letter, dated Phila. 15 July 1740, from Ebenezer Kinnersly
to a friend in the country - mention is made of preaching of Rev. Rowland and Rev. Owen (Postscript to Pa.
Gazette of 24 July)

ALLEN, David, of Pemaquid, mariner - makes declaration on
14 July at Boston as to information given him about a
fortnight before at St. John's in Nova Scotia by a Mrs.
Bellisle, a trading woman; she had persuaded the Indians that England was not at war with France - Boston
item of 14 July (31 July)

MESNARD, Stephen, master of the sloop John - arrived Wednesday last at New York from Coracoa and reports he was
chased by a Spanish privateer - New York item of 28
July (31 July)

LANGDON, Capt., privateer of New York, and Capt. Hall -
went on a cruise 11 July; Langdon fought battle with a
Spanish privateer; Capt. Warren of H.M.S. Squirrel is
searching for the privateer - New York item of 28 July
(31 July)

FRANKLIN, B. - has just printed A New and Complete Guide
to the English Tongue (31 July)

CARY, Sanson, late of Bristol, dec'd - his executor,
Samuel Cary, wishes to settle all accounts (31 July)

GILBERT, Mrs. Alexander - is lately arrived in Maryland
from Scotland and is to be found at Madam Hawkins in
Queen Anne's Co., Md.; she seeks her husband, who, from
his letters dated 1734, 1736 and 1737, lodged at one
John Van Boskerk's in Phila. Co. in the Manor of Moreland (31 July)

MOURTON, William, Irish servant, age c. 23 - runaway from
Thomas Barr of Millcreek Hundred, Newcastle Co. (31
July)

TOWNLY, George, servant, carpenter, who speaks broad
Cheshire - runaway from Reese Meredith (31 July)

EVANS, Samuel of Laycock Twp., Lancaster Co. - offers reward for recovery of 3 horses that strayed away; word
of their capture is to be sent to Roger Hunt or John
Miller, tavern-keepers on Lancaster Rd. (31 July)

OGDEN, John - will sell a term of 17 years in the Southern
Moiety of a square of ground, being the first beyond
the turning out of Chesnut St., upon the Lower Ferry
Rd. (31 July)

Messages between Gov. George Thomas and the Assembly of
Pennsylvania; mentioned are Col. Gooch, Col. Blakeney,
Secretary Pat Baird and J. Kinsey (Speaker of the House)
(7 Aug.)

Message to the Assembly from the Proprietor, Thomas Penn
(7 Aug.)

HALLOWEL, Benjamin - is building at Boston a 170-ton
snow for the use of the Province of Massachusetts -
Boston item of 28 July (7 Aug.)

In Boston 3 companies, those of Capts. Goffe, Phillips
and Prescot, are mustered and are ready for the expedition against the West Indies; Col. Blakeney has sent
instructions to complete 10 companies as soon as possible - Boston item of 28 July (7 Aug.)

In Boston on 28 July the companies of Capt. Stuart and
Capt. Richards were reviewed by the governor (7 Aug.)

EVERARD, Capt. - arrived at New York Wednesday last from
London and on Saturday last a brigantine commanded by
Capt. Nelson from Bristol (7 Aug.)

Sloop <u>Dove</u>, Capt. Jauncy - arrived at New York Thursday
last from Caracoa; he reports seeing a black sloop
(probably a Spanish privateer) off Cape May - New York
item of 4 Aug. (7 Aug.)

In New York are 5 complete companies; they are commanded
by Capts. Clarke, Cosby, Provoost, Cuyler and Stevens
- New York item of 4 Aug. (7 Aug.)

Anne (wife of Sir William Keith, formerly Governor of
Pennsylvania) - died Thursday last at Phila., aged 63
(7 Aug.)

DUNN, Daniel, Irish servant, age <u>c</u>. 30 - runaway from
David Ogden of Phila. (7 Aug.)

Brigantine <u>Hannah</u>, William Tiffin master, at Samuel Parr's
wharf in Phila. - will sail for London; for freight or
passage agree with the master or John Stamper (7 Aug.)

Hamilton and Coleman - sell cloth, cutlery, hats, glass,
etc., at their store near Carpenter's wharf in Phila.
(7 Aug.)

DOWNS, Patrick, Irish servant, age <u>c</u>. 25, tailor - runaway
from Richard Porter of Talbott Co., Md. (7 Aug.)

GRIFFITH, David, age 25 - deserted from Capt. Robert
Bishop's Company of Col. Gooch's Regt. (7 Aug.)

REYNOLDS, Humphry, age 30 - same as above

LARIMORE, Hugh, a flat-man, who has gone to Willings-Town
- same as above

PRATT, Henry - offers reward for horse strayed or stolen
from pasture near Phila. (7 Aug.)

MOORE, William, of Moorhall, Chester Co. - offers reward
for return of a Mulatto man slave, age c. 22, who has
run away (7 Aug.)

Message from the House (signed J. Kinsey, Speaker) to the
governor of Pennsylvania; message from Gov. Geo.
Thomas to the Pennsylvania Assembly (he mentions Col.
Blakeney and Lord Cathcart); message to the governor
from the Assembly; address of the Assembly to Thomas
Penn and his answer (14 Aug.)

McNEAL, Capt., with company from Charlestown, S.C., was
reported ready to embark for St. Augustine; by a letter
dated 12 July, however, it is reported that the siege

271

of St. Augustine is raised - Boston item of 4 Aug.
(14 Aug.)

Order, by command of the governor of Virginia, per Benjamin Needler, that no person is to inlist servants in Virginia - item from the Virginia Gazette (14 Aug.)

Petition and remonstrance in the Pennsylvania Assembly is to be drawn up by a committee consisting of Robert Jones, Israel Pemberton, Isaac Norris, Thomas Leech, James Morris and Samuel Levis; it is against inlisting servants (14 Aug.)

The following members of the Church of Christ at Phila. and Pennypack, appointed as a committee, exonerate the Rev. Mr. Jones of charges brought against him by Ebenezer Kinnersly: George Eaton, William Branson, John Hart, William Marshall, Robert Parsons, Thomas Potts and Thomas Dungan (14 Aug.)

BURK, John, merchant, of Bristol, Bucks Co., dec'd - accounts with his estate to be settled with John Abraham Denormandie and Joseph Peace, administrators (14 Aug.)

WALPOLE, Charles, mathematical instrument maker from London - makes, sells and mends instruments at the Sign of the Davis Quadrant at the corner of McCoome's Alley in Front St., near Arch St., Phila. (14 Aug.)

ARTHUR, Joseph in Walnut St., Phila. - sells nails, cloth, hats, gloves (14 Aug.)

A shallop will be sold at Mr. Powell's wharf in Phila. (14 Aug.)

GRANT, James, Irish servant, age c. 21 - runaway from John Coward of Upper Freehold (14 Aug.)

BURROWS, William, servant, age c. 23 - runaway from James Holmes (14 Aug.)

Histoire de Polybe - for sale by B. Franklin (14 Aug.)

WHITEFIELD, Rev. - will preach in Charlestown Saturday and Sunday, Monday at Ashley Ferry and Tuesday at Mr. Bee's at Ponpon - item of 18 July from the South-Carolina Gazette (21 Aug.)

WHITEFIELD, Rev. - arrived at Charlestown 3 July from Georgia; he preached at Mr. Smith's meeting in Charlestown, at Mr. Chanler's Meeting in Dorchester, at Christ Church upon Wando, at the Parish Church on John's Is-

land, at Mrs. Woodward's on James Island - Charlestown
item of 25 July (21 Aug.)

By Capt. Bursly in a brigantine which arrived last week at
Boston from the Bay comes news that Capt. Dunham, in a
schooner of Boston, was attacked in the Bay by a Spanish lanche; Dunham opened fire, put the lanche to
flight and captured the captain, who died after 2 days
in captivity - Boston item of 11 Aug. (21 Aug.)

SMITH, Capt. Josiah - arrived Monday last at New York in
25 days from Jamaica with news that Admiral Vernon had
returned to Jamaica without effecting anything; Capt.
Smith also reported that Capt. Tuckness in a brigantine belonging to New York on her passage to Jamaica
was taken by a Spanish privateer schooner - New York
item of 18 Aug. (21 Aug.)

TINGLEY, Capt. - arrived Thursday last at New York from
Georgia with news that siege of St. Augustine was
raised - New York item of 18 Aug. (21 Aug.)

Assembly of Pennsylvania has voted 3,000 pounds to Thomas
Griffitts, Edward Bradley, John Stamper, Isaac Norris
and Thomas Leech for the King's use (21 Aug.)

BICKERSTAFF, Samuel, an Englishman, age 20, weaver - deserted from Capt. Thomas Freame's company at Darby,
Col. Gooch's Regt. (21 Aug.)

McNEIL, James, Irishman, age 19, husbandman - same as
above

SHARP, Thomas, late of Phila., merchant, dec'd - payments
due the estate are to be made to John Thomas, executor,
living at the house of Jonathan Zane in Second St.,
Phila.; the letters of administration granted to
Messers. Hopkins and Inglis are void (21 Aug.); Hopkins
and Inglis believe the supposed will is a forgery (28
Aug.)

Two tracts of land in West New Jersey are for sale, one
of about 300 acres near Paihaqualy Mountain in Morris
Co., the other of 300 acres on Waweywatah Brook, about
3 miles from Delaware - apply to Isaac Brown in Phila.
(21 Aug.)

Brigantine Catharine and Mary, William Greenway commander,
at Carpenter's wharf, Phila. - will sail for Bristol;
for freight or passage agree with the master on board
or with William Callender in Second St., Phila. (21
Aug.)

McLAUGHLAN, Farrel, Irish servant, age c. 37 - runaway
from Henry Hockley, near Nutt's Iron-Works in Chester
Co. (21 Aug.)

PUNCH, David, Irish servant, c. 20, weaver - runaway from
Isaac Rees, of Upper Merion, Phila. Co. (21 Aug.)

CUFFEEY, John, servant, a Londoner, age c. 30 or 40 -
runaway from Michael Branin of Evesham Twp., Burlington Co. (21 Aug.)

COSWAY, James, servant, age c. 20 - runaway out of Capt.
Jenkins's company at Newcastle from William Berry at
Motherkill in Kent Co. (21 Aug.)

Speech of Gov. George Thomas to the Assembly (28 Aug.)

CRAWFORD, Thomas (alias of a young woman of noble family,
who shipped in the Royal Navy) - when whipped by order
of the commander of H.M.S. Ruby, declared that if Sir
Charles Wager had known how she was used he would
break the commander; her sex was finally detected, she
was put aboard at Maderia and sent home to England -
Boston item of 18 Aug. (28 Aug.)

Brigantine Lucy, John Lindsay master, will sail for South
Carolina; for freight or passage agree with Peter Bard
in Phila. (28 Aug.)

B. Franklin - has printed and sells a collection of Pennsylvania charters (28 Aug.)

WILLING, Charles - intends for England (28 Aug.)

BEAR, Jacob, Sr. - offers reward for recovery of mare
strayed or stolen from his plantation (28 Aug.)

RYAN, John - at his house in upper end of Second St.,
Phila. - has for sale rice imported in the sloop Wil-
liam, Capt. Richard Paynter, from South Carolina (28
Aug.)

INGLIS, John - at his store below the drawbridge in
Phila. sells cloth, gloves, blankets, nails, glass,
sugar, etc. (28 Aug.)

House of Representatives of Pennsylvania (per John Kinsey, Speaker) to the governor (4 Sept.)

PATTERSON, Capt. Richard - arrived 24 Aug. at Boston in
7 weeks from London - Boston item of 25 Aug. (4 Sept.)

BOYD, Capt. - arrived Thursday last at New York from Jamaica; it is reported that Commodore Brown is gone home in Capt. Windham - New York item of 1 Sept. (4 Sept.)

JEFFERYS, Capt. - arrived Saturday last at New York from Antigua - New York item of 1 Sept. (4 Sept.)

JOHNSON, Capt. - arrived Saturday last at New York from Jamaica; he tells how the men of Capt. Bennet killed all Spaniards aboard a snow because the Spaniards had previously captured the snow (which belonged to Jamaica) and killed all the English except the captain and 4 men - New York item of 1 Sept. (4 Sept.); the Spanish captain was a Knight of Malta and his officers and men were all of Don Blase's squadron - New York item of 8 Sept. (11 Sept.)

ELLIS, Robert, in Water St., Phila. - offers for sale Negro boys and girls just arrived in the sloop Charming Sally, David Hall master; said sloop, now at Robert Ellis's wharf, will soon sail for South Carolina and Wynyaw (4 Sept.)

The galley, the Prince of Orange, Capt. Edward Tyng, master, which was built by Benjamin Hallowell for Massachusetts, was launched Wednesday last - Boston item of 1 Sept. (11 Sept.)

STRICKLAND, Miles, in Market St., Phila., near the Court house - sells Dr. Bateman's Pectoral Drops (11 Sept.)

BARTON, Robert, near the postoffice in Phila. - has a servant boy for sale (11 Sept.)

Several tradesmen and husbandmen, servants, are for sale on board the snow Friendship, Patrick Parrott master, lying off Market St. wharf - to purchase apply to the master or to Edward Bridges, at his house commonly called "the Scale." (11 Sept.)

Tract of 200 acres in or near Plymouth Twp., about 16 miles from Phila., is for sale; apply to Hugh Tresse and Mary and Ann Tresse in Second St., near Market St., in Phila. (11 Sept.)

Schooner Two Sisters, Henry Tisdale master, now at Fishbourn's wharf - will sail for South Carolina; for freight or passage agree with the master on board or at the house next door to the Boatswain and Call in Phila. (11 Sept.)

Ship Constantine, Edward Wright master, at Thomas Griffitts's wharf in Phila. - will sail for London; for freight or passage agree with Shippen and Edgell or with the master (11 Sept.)

McCARTHY, Carthy, Irish servant, sailor - runaway from William Bond and William Fell in Maryland (11 Sept.)

TOMLINSON, Thomas, English servant, tailor - same as above

GARDENER, George, English servant, husbandman - same as above

Simon, Negro slave, age 40, can read and write, bleed and draw teeth - runaway from James Leonard, of Kingston, Middlesex Co., East New Jersey (11 Sept.)

TOWNSHEND, Edward, servant, who talks broad West Country and has been in this country about 8 weeks, age 30 - runaway from William and Samuel Pancoost of Mansfield Twp., Burlington Co., West New Jersey (11 Sept.)

LEONARD, John, servant, age c. 18, weaver, who talks board West Country and has been in this country about 8 weeks - same as above

Tract of 2,237 acres in Paquease in Hunterdon Co., West New Jersey, bounded on north by land of John Reading, Esq., on the east by land of Daniel Cox, on the west by land of Joseph Kelby, Esq.; to purchase enquire of Thomas Glentworth at his house in Market St., Phila. (11 Sept.)

A Second Letter from Ebenezer Kinnersley - is just published and is sold by the author near the Sign of the George in Second St., Phila , or by Andrew and William Bradford at the Sign of the George (11 Sept.)

BARNARD, Richard - offers reward for recovery of a horse stolen from his plantation, joining on Marlborough Twp., Chester Co. (11 Sept.)

Tract of 2,511 acres on the branches of Tohockanickon River in Hunterdon Co., now Morris Co., are for sale; apply to White and Taylor in Phila.; a plan of the land is in the hands of Joseph Peace, Esq., of Trenton (11 Sept.)

COMMISSARY, Rev. Mr. - delivered 7 Sept. a discourse at the King's Chapel in Boston to the commissioned officers who are to go on the present expedition (18 Sept.)

BOURDET, Capt., from New York, bound for Georgia - reported to have been taken by a Spanish privateer (18 Sept.)

CLARKE, Capt. - his company of volunteers is to embark 16 Sept. on board H.M.S. _Squirrel_ and _Astrea_ for Jamaica - New York item of 15 Sept. (18 Sept.)

WHITEFIELD, Rev. - sailed 1 Sept. from Charlestown for New England (18 Sept.)

JARRARD, Richard - will carry on malting at the New Malting House at Spring Garden, near Phila. (18 Sept.)

FINNEY, Dr. John, in New Castle - offers reward for recovery of a runaway Negro named Betty, age c. 18, who is supposed to have been taken away by an oyster-shallop, Benjamin Taylor master, bound for Phila. (18 Sept.)

Several servant men, lately imported in the brigantine _Debby_, George Stewart master - are to be sold; enquire of Anthony Morris, Jr., or the said master on the brigantine at Anthony Morriss's wharf (18 Sept.)

HASSART, Anthony, in Laetitia Court, Phila. - sells boulting cloths just imported in the ship _Constantine_ (18 Sept.)

COLLET, John, apprentice, age c. 19 - runaway from Alexander Crukshank of Phila., shoemaker (18 Sept.)

BARD, Dinah, of Burlington - offers for sale a brick house in best part of that city (18 Sept.)

LAWRENCE, Giles, at the Three Legs in Bristol - will have pasture for horses on the Bristol Islands during the Yearly Meeting at Burlington (18 Sept.)

COATES, Samuel - sells cordials, elixirs, spirits at his shop in Market St., Phila. (18 Sept.)

FRANCIS, Tench - sells cloth at his store almost opposite to Peter Stretch's in Phila. (18 Sept.)

Address to Gov. William Gooch by House of Burgesses and the Governor's answer (25 Sept.)

Speech of Gov. Belcher to the Massachusetts Assembly and reply to him (25 Sept.)

LANGDON, Capt. and Capt. Hall arrived Sunday last at Charlestown with 2 prizes - Charlestown item of 6 Sept. (25 Sept.)

CARR, Capt. Benjamin, of Phila. - arrived Tuesday last at
    Newport from Lisbon in 47 days; he reports that on 17
    July the Spaniards took Capt. Green, Capt. Mann and
    Capt. Hamilton, all belonging to Phila. - Newport item
    of 12 Sept. (25 Sept.)

SOUTHERD, Capt. - arrived Friday last at Boston from St.
    Christophers in 15 days; he reports that Lt.-Gen. Flem-
    ming arrived at St. Christophers on 23 Aug. (25 Sept.)

DONELAN, John, Irish servant - runaway from Enoch Ander-
    son of Phila., innkeeper (25 Sept.)

HESSELIUS, Gustavus, from Stockholm, and John Winter, from
    London - paint coats of arms, signs, ships and houses
    and clean and mend pictures (25 Sept.)

SHIPPEN, William, chemist - sells drugs at the Sign of the
    Paracelsus Head and Gally Pot, in Market St., over
    against the Presbyterian Meeting-house in Phila. (25
    Sept.)

ELKINTONG, George, late of Northampton, Burlington Co.,
    N.J. - his heir or heirs, if living, by applying to the
    printer, may hear something to their advantage (25 Sept.)

Sugar, candy, molasses are sold by James Oswald in Front
    St., at the house of Joseph Turner, and by William Wal-
    lace, at the upper end of Second St., Phila. (25 Sept.)

A parcel of servant men - offered for sale by Richard Far-
    mar, lately removed to the Unicorn in Second St., Phila.
    (25 Sept.)

Erskine's Gospel Sonnets - just printed and for sale by B.
    Franklin (25 Sept.)

ROGERS, William, Rector of the Free School in Annapolis,
    Mid. - announces a meeting to choose a master and usher
    (25 Sept.)

Davey & Carson, at their house near Powel's wharf, over
    the Drawbridge - have a parcel of servants for sale
    (25 Sept.)

Parcel of Negro slaves, just imported from South Carolina
    - are to be sold by William Brisbane at Samuel Austin's
    at the lower end of Mulberry St., commonly called Arch
    St., Phila. (25 Sept.)

RYAN, William, servant, an elderly man, shoemaker - run-
    away from on board the Prince of Orange, Robert Wil-

liamson master; reward for his capture will be paid by
Richard Farmar (25 Sept.)

List of books to be sold by Alexander Annand in Second St.,
near the Church, in Phila. (25 Sept.)

Message of Massachusetts Assembly to Gov. Belcher, his
reply and a vote of Assembly appointing committee,
which included Judge Greaves, Edward Hutchinson, Mr.
Cushing, Col. Chandler and Mr. Watts, to consider what
was to be done with regard to the 6 companies raised
by the province for the expedition to the Spanish West
Indies; Samuel Welles, Esq., brought down the committee's report (2 Oct.)

WHITEFIELD, Rev. George - last Sunday arrived at Newport,
R.I., from South Carolina - Newport item of 19 Sept.;
last Thursday he arrived at Boston and the next day in
the forenoon attended prayers in the King's Chapel and
that afternoon preached in Rev. Dr. Coleman's Meeting -
Boston item of 22 Sept. (2 Oct.)

Last week the companies of Capt. Philips and Capt. Stuart
embarked for the expedition against the Spaniards and
22 or 23 Sept. the companies of Capt. Goffe, Capt.
Prescot and Capt. Winslow will embark - Boston item of
22 Sept. (2 Oct.)

The following were elected 1 Oct. for Phila. Co. - repre-
sentatives: Thomas Leech, Robert Jones, John Kinsey,
Isaac Norris, Edward Warner, James Morris, Joseph Trot-
ter, Owen Evans; sheriffs: Mordecai Lloyd, Septimus
Robinson; coroners: Owen Owen, David Evans; commis-
sioner: Edward Bradley; assessors: Samuel Lane, Jacob
Livering, John Dilwyn, Evan Thomas, Jeremiah Elfrith,
James Jones (2 Oct.)

The following were elected 1 Oct. for Bucks Co. - repre-
sentatives: John Hall, Mark Watson, John Watson, Abra-
ham Chapman, Benjamin Field, Thomas Canby, Jr., Mahlon
Kirkbride, Jeremiah Langhorne; sheriffs: Joseph Yates,
Joseph Jackson; coroners: William Atkinson, Benjamin
Taylor; commissioner: John Hutchinson; assessors:
Bartholomew Longstreth, Gurrard Vansand, Cephas Child,
Robert Smith, Adam Harker, Edward Roberts (2 Oct.)

The following were elected 1 Oct. for Chester Co. - representatives: Thomas Chandler, Joseph Harvey, James
Gibbons, William Hughes, Samuel Levis, John Owen, Jeremiah Starr, Thomas Tatnel; sheriffs: Benjamin Davis,
Thomas Marshal; commissioner: William Jefferies; coroners: Awbrey Bevan, Samuel Bittle; assessors: John

Allen, Daniel Walker, John Yarnal, Thomas Morgan, James
Jeffreys, Robert Miller (2 Oct.)

The following were elected 2 Oct. for Phila. City - burgesses: Israel Pemberton, John Kearsley; city assessors: Richard Parker, John Stamper, Edmund Wooley,
Joseph Oldman, Jonathan Zane, Philip Syng (2 Oct.)

PARRY, John, Esq., High Sheriff for Chester Co. - died
Friday last (2 Oct.)

WYNNE, Thomas - last week killed a 200-pound bear in
Blockley Twp. (2 Oct.)

ROBIN, Jeremiah, Indian servant, age c. 30 - runaway from
on board the sloop Triton, James Hodges master (2 Oct.)

ROBIN, Nehemiah, Indian servant, age c. 24 - same as
above

LEVY, Nathan and Isaac, in Front St., Phila. - have raisins for sale (2 Oct.)

Monday last in Mr. Checkley's Meeting-house, where Mr.
Whitefield was to preach, someone said the balcony was
giving way; as a result many persons were injured in
trying to get out; Mrs. Ingersole and a Mrs. Story
died from their injuries in a few minutes, while on
Tuesday last Widow Shepard and Mrs. Ruggles also died
- Mr. Whitefield preached twice a day all last week -
Boston item of 29 Sept. (9 Oct.)

Saturday last all troops raised for the expedition to the
West Indies (except Capt. Winslow's company) sailed
from Nantasket for New York - Boston item of 29 Sept.
(9 Oct.)

HAMMET, Capt. - arrived 29 Sept. in Boston from Newcastle
in about 9 weeks (9 Oct.)

Vessels driven on shore in hurricane at Antigua on 31
Aug. were as follows: ship Catharine of London, George
Monereff master; ship Bethel, Martin Long commander;
snow Nancy, William Lithgo master; snow Neptune, George
Gibbs master; brigantine Friendship, Joseph Forest master; sloop Wheel of Fortune, Ebenezer Dimon master;
schooner Elizabeth and Anne, William Davis master; the
following rode out the storm: the Hull Gally, John
Gorman master; the London Frigat, John Roskel master;
the St. John, John Farril master; the Charming Moll,
William Mason master; the William, Thomas Easton master;
the Ellen, Henry Brown master; the brigantine Liberty,

Henry Simons master; the sloops <u>Mary</u> and <u>Frances</u> got off, as did the schooner <u>Tryal</u>, Tobias Lear master (9 Oct.)

The sloop <u>Adventure</u>, Capt. Tucker, bound for New York, was cast away by Crooked Islands (9 Oct.)

HASEL, Samuel, Esq. - Tuesday last was elected Mayor of Phila. (9 Oct.)

The following were elected 1 Oct. for Lancaster Co. - representatives: Thomas Linly, John Wright, Thomas Ewing, Anthony Shaw; sheriffs: Robert Buchanan, James Mitchel; coroners: Joshua Low, William Caldwell; commissioner: Robert Barber; assessors: James Smith, Andrew Work, James Murrey, Francis Reynolds, Robert Harris, John Reynolds (9 Oct.)

The following were elected 1 Oct. for Newcastle Co. - representatives: Andrew Peterson, David French, John McCoole, Thomas Noxon, Jeremiah Woolaston, Jehu Curtis; sheriffs: John Goodwin, Samuel Bickley (9 Oct.)

The following were elected 1 Oct. for Kent Co. - representatives: James Gorrel, Thomas Skidmore, Mark Manlove, James Morris, William Barnes, Joseph Dowding; sheriffs: Daniel Robinson, Samuel Robinson; coroners: Edmund Badger, Richard James (9 Oct.)

The following were elected 1 Oct. for Sussex Co. - representatives: John Rhodes, Jabez Maud Fisher, John Clowes, Joseph Shanklin, Jacob Kollock, Simon Kollock; sheriffs: Cornelius Whiltbank, Peter Hall; coroners: John Wyncoope, William Sultridge (9 Oct.)

SHELLY, Abraham, thread throwster - lives next door to the Adam and Eve in Arch St., Phila. (9 Oct.)

WELLS, George, next door to the Pewter Platter in Front St., Phila. - has for sale a 19-year-old Bermudas Negro woman (9 Oct.)

TENNENT, Charles - considers Mr. Whitefield to be sound in faith, as does the Rev. Mr. Blair (16 Oct.)

Monday last the levies incamped in Williamsburg, Va., imbarked on board the 4 transports that lay off Col. Burwell's in James River - Williamsburg item of 19 Sept. (16 Oct.)

GOOCH, Gov. William - set out Wednesday last for Williamsburg to Hampton, when he will sail in a few days under convoy of the <u>Wolf</u> man-of-war, Capt. Dandridge; it is said that Sir Yelverton Peyton in the <u>Hector</u> man-of-war will accompany them some distance (16 Oct.)

WHITEFIELD, Rev. - preached at Hampton Wednesday forenoon and at Portsmouth in the afternoon - Piscataqua item of 3 Oct. (16 Oct.)

H.M.S. <u>Ludlow</u> <u>Castle</u>, Capt. Cuzack and transports are fallen down to the Hook, whence they sail to Virginia tomorrow - New York item of 6 Oct. (16 Oct.)

Item from the <u>New-York</u> <u>Gazette</u> of 13 Oct. mentions places where Rev. Whitefield preached, such as Dr. Colman's Meeting-house, Dr. Dewall's, Mr. Foxcroft's, Mr. Webb's, Mr. Gee's, at Harvard College, Mr. Byles's pulpit-window, Mr. Welstead's; he was to have preached at Mr. Checkley's but the panic prevented this (16 Oct.)

KINSEY, John - Tuesday last was chosen Speaker of the Pennsylvania Assembly (16 Oct.)

McCALL, George, a "considerable" merchant of Phila. - died Monday last (16 Oct.)

One-24th part of the iron-works at Derham, Bucks Co., and of 5,900 acres belonging to said works, all belonging to estate of Charles Read, late of Phila., merchant, dec'd - will be sold by Sarah Read, administratrix (16 Oct.)

PARRY, John, Esq., of Chester Co., dec'd — accounts with estate to be settled with the executors, Hannah Parry, widow, William Lewis of Hartford, John Parry, Jr., in the Valley, or Jacob Hall near Frankford (16 Oct.)

SOBER, Thomas, late of Phila., merchant, dec'd - accounts with estate to be settled with John Sober, executor, next door to Mr. Charles Willing's in Front St., Phila. (16 Oct.)

WHITEFIELD, Rev. - is to set out from Boston to Connecticut, New York, etc., on 12 Oct. - Boston item of 13 Oct. (23 Oct.)

ALLEN, Jabez, <u>alias</u> Mead - is in goal in Cambridge, Mass., for horse stealing - Boston item of 13 Oct. (23 Oct.)

LEAR, Capt. - arrived 10 Oct. at Piscataqua in 24 days from Antigua with news of hurricane in the West Indies - Piscataqua item of 10 Oct. (23 Oct.)

LANGDON, Capt. - in a letter dated 11 Sept. he relates how
on 8 Aug. he went up a river on the S. E. part of Cuba,
where he lost 2 men, John Brookman and Andrew Plocknett
(23 Oct.)

HOGG, George, apprentice, age <u>c</u>. 19 - runaway from Joseph
Armit (23 Oct.)

Three years time of a servant man, a hatter, is for sale
- enquire of Charles Moore in Market St. or Joseph
Scull at the Workhouse in Phila. (23 Oct.)

BARTON, Robert, cabinetmaker - is removed from Market St.
to the house in which Capt. Thomas Lloyd lately lived,
opposite to Black Horse Alley in Second St. (23 Oct.)

HINTON, William - offers reward for recovery of a horse
stolen or strayed away from his pasture on Society Hill
(23 Oct.)

DENISON, Timothy, servant, age <u>c</u>. 15 - runaway from the
ship <u>Hanover</u>, Richard Northover commander, now lying
at Capt. William Attwood's wharf (23 Oct.)

MOHEGAN, Daniel, servant, age <u>c</u>. 25 - same as above

WILLIAMS, Samuel, servant, who came over from Bristol with
Capt. Richardson - runaway from William Scot, tailor,
of Phila. (23 Oct.)

MULLINS, Harper, servant lad, painter by trade, who came
over from Bristol with Capt. Richardson - runaway from
Isaac Norris, of Phila., merchant (23 Oct.)

TOWNLEY, George, servant, who pretends to be a carpenter
and who came over from Bristol with Capt. Richardson -
runaway from William Maugridge, of Phila., ship-joiner
(23 Oct.)

DENNIS, John, apprentice, age <u>c</u>. 18 - runaway from Edward
Evans (23 Oct.)

HARDING, George, skinner, in Market St. near the Courthouse in Phila. - offers reward for recovery of horse,
strayed or stolen from off the Commons (23 Oct.)

LAY, Abraham, English servant, age <u>c</u>. 27 - runaway (having
a pocket book with papers belonging to one Elias or
Haley Demerist) from John Gooding, of Reden Island in
Newcastle Co. (23 Oct.)

ALLEN, Capt. - Monday last returned to Newport, R.I., in

the sloop _Revenge_, having taken a prize - Newport item
of 17 Oct. (30 Oct.)

EAGLETON, Capt., at Boston - informs that Capt. Snelling
and other ships of Boston may soon be expected (30 Oct.)

HUNT, Capt. - arrived Friday last at New York in the sloop
Olive Branch from Jamaica; he reports that Capt. Garritson's sloop was taken and carried into St. Jago de Cuba
and that Capt. Rosevelt fell off his mast and was killed
- New York item of 27 Oct. (30 Oct.)

FLOWERS, Capt. - was taken by a Spanish privateer; he was
given a boat by which he got into Providence - New York
item of 27 Oct. (30 Oct.)

RICHARDS, Capt. - arrived at New York from Cork - New York
item of 27 Oct. (30 Oct.)

LANGDON, Capt. - his prize sloop arrived at New York Saturday last from South Carolina; he reported that Capt.
Bennett was drowned - New York item of 27 Oct. (30 Oct.)

WHITEFIELD, Rev. - proposed to be at New York 30 Oct. (30
Oct.)

GODFREY, Thomas - during winter will teach navigation and
astronomy at his house in Second St., Phila. (30 Oct.)

Sloop _Speedwell_, John Miers master - will sail for Virginia;
for freight or passage agree with Joshua Emlen, tanner,
in Chesnut St., Phila. (30 Oct.)

The _William_ and _James_, William Woodlock master, now at
Hamilton's wharf in Phila. - will sail for Belfast; for
freight or passage agree with the master on board or
with James Agnew at Thomas Robinson's in Front St. (30
Oct.)

STEEL, Alexander, Irish servant - runaway from James Agnew, who offers reward if servant is brought to him at
Thomas Robinson's in Front St. or to Capt. William Blair
in Second St. (30 Oct.)

PICKE, Elsa, convict servant, age c. 30 or 40 - runaway
(supposedly with John Manning, a ditcher) from William
Mattingly at Patapsco River (30 Oct.)

HUMPHRYS, Capt. - arrived Saturday last from Plymouth with
news of fleet intended for expedition against the
Spaniards - Boston item of 27 Oct. (6 Nov.)

WHITEFIELD, Rev. - preached Friday, Saturday, and Sunday
in New York - New York item of 3 Nov. (6 Nov.)

KETELTAS, Capt. - arrived at New York just now in 6 weeks
from Dover - New York item of 3 Nov. (6 Nov.)

HARRIS, Edward, attorney-at-law in Queen Ann's Co., Md. -
was murdered 26 Oct. by 2 of his slaves (6 Nov.)

WHITEFIELD, Rev. - proposes to be in Phila. Saturday night;
a letter from him to some Presbyterians will be published Saturday next (6 Nov.)

Poor Richard's and John Jerman's almanacs will be published at the fair (6 Nov.)

CRAGHEAD, Alexander - offers reward for recovery of a mare
that strayed away (6 Nov.)

Usher wanted at the Free-School in Kent Co., Md. - he must
be single, a member of the Church of England and quali-
field to teach grammar; applicants are to apply to the
gentlemen visitors in Chester Town or to Theophilus
Grew in Phila. (6 Nov.)

LEWIS, Amos - offers for sale 208-acre plantation in
Haverford Twp., Chester Co. (6 Nov.)

Parcel of English and Welch servants, just imported from
Bristol - offered for sale by Nathanael Magee on board
the Margaret & Mary, lying off Market St., or at his
house in Arch St., Phila. (6 Nov.)

ROBINSON, Septimus, of Phila. - will have sold at auction
675 acres in Phila. Co., commonly called Carpenter's
Island, lately belonging to Samuel Carpenter, dec'd,
and taken in execution at the suit of Mary Trent (6
Nov.)

YOACUM, Swen, of Kingsess near Phila. - offers reward for
recovery of a mare stolen from him; mare may be taken
to George Gray at the Lower Ferry on Schuylkill (6 Nov.)

DOWEL, Dugel (or Dennis M.), servant, age c. 34 - runaway
from Roger Kirk in West Nottingham (6 Nov.)

Monday last a schooner hired by Major Heron to carry recruits to Georgia was chased by a Spanish privateer
but escaped - Charlestown item of 16 Oct. (13 Nov.)

Hector man-of-war, Sir Yelverton Peyton, commander, is returned to Hampton, where Sunday last the Ludlow Castle

man-of-war arrived from New York with Col. Blakeney;
it is reported that 17 or 18 Spanish men-of-war are
gone to join Don Blass at Carthagena; Admiral Vernon
keeps men-of-war upon the cruise - Williamsburg item
of 24 Oct. (13 Nov.)

Capts. Laws, Bishop, Sears and Perkins have lately arrived at Boston from London - Boston item of 3 Nov.
(13 Nov.)

WHITEFIELD, Rev. - preached 19 Oct. in Northampton, Mass.
(13 Nov.)

KETELTAS, Capt. - arrived last week at New York from Amsterdam via Torbay and Thursday came Capt. Breese from
London; Friday arrived Capt. Wentworth, who reported
he met Capt. Nevin in a privateer owned by gentlemen
of New York who was carrying into Jamaica 2 Dutch vessels and 1 French that were carrying contraband to
Cartagena; one of said vessels was commanded by Capt.
Godet, an Englishman (13 Nov.)

Report of preaching of Rev. Whitefield in Phila. and vi-
cinity; persons wishing to contribute provisions or
other things may take the same to the house of Stephen
Benezet, merchant, in Front St., Phila. (13 Nov.)

DAVID, George - offers reward for recovery of gelding
strayed or stolen from stable of Michael Helegas in
Second St., Phila.; notice of the horse may be given
to John Parry at the Great Valley (13 Nov.)

Two strayed horses are at the plantation of Thomas David
in Goshen Twp., Chester Co. - apply to Samuel Phipps or
Christopher Hicks (13 Nov.)

RYAN, John, at his store at upper end of Second St.,
Phila. - sells English goods (13 Nov.)

Ship Lydia, James Allen master, now at Hamilton's wharf -
will sail for South Carolina; for freight or passage
agree with Stedman and Robinson or with the master at
the Rose and Crown (13 Nov.)

FRANKLIN, B. - will publish and sell The General Magazine
and Historical Chronicle (13 Nov.)

Ship Robert, Lawrence Dent commander, now at Samuel Parr's
wharf - will sail for London; for freight or passage
agree with the master on board or with Edward Bridges
at his house, commonly called the Scales (13 Nov.)

Arrived at Boston on Friday last Capt. Hall from London
and on Saturday last Capt. Hoar from Bristol - Boston
item of 10 Nov. (20 Nov.)

Arrived at New York Saturday last Capt. Ratsy from Dublin
and 16 Nov. Capt. Morgan from South Carolina, who mentions Capt. Phaenix from London bound to New York -
New York item of 17 Nov. (20 Nov.)

MEDCALF, Jacob, Esq. (late High Sheriff of Gloucester Co.,
N.J.), dec'd - debts due him or to his deceased wife,
Hannah Medcalf, are to be paid to Joseph Cooper at
Gloucester; Cooper and William Hudson are executors
(20 Nov.)

GLEAVE, John, of Springfield, Chester Co. - offers reward
for recovery of a stolen or strayed gelding (20 Nov.)

WHITEFIELD, Rev. - on 16 Nov. preached his farewell sermon
in Phila.; he has taken up 5,000 acres on the Forks of
Delaware, Pa., to erect a Negro school; contributions
may be paid to Mr. Benezet, merchant, in Phila., Mr.
Noble at New York, Gilbert Tennent, in New Brunswick, N.
J., or the printer of the Pa. Gazette (27 Nov.)

FRANKLIN, B. - has just published Journal of a Voyage from
Savannah to Philadelphia by William Seward, gent., companion of Rev. Geo. Whitefield, as well as A Continuation of the Rev. Mr. Whitefield's Journal and Poor
Richard's Almanack for the Year 1741 (27 Nov.)

LOGAN, James, near Germantown - offers reward for recovery
of strayed or stolen horse (27 Nov.)

EDGELL, Simon - has indentured servants for sale that have
just been imported from Bristol in the brigantine
Seneca, John Jones master (27 Nov.)

Snow Southall, John Evans commander, now at Carpenter's
wharf in Phila. - will sail from Bristol; for freight
or passage agree with Reese Meredith at his house in
Second St. or the master on board (27 Nov.)

APPLETON, James Wenman, servant, age c. 19 - runaway from
Jonathan Davies, Jr., of Charles Co., Md. (27 Nov.)

Charles, Negro slave, age c. 28 or 30 - runaway from Darbey
Hernley, of the Forks of Gunpowder, Baltimore Co., Md.
(27 Nov.)

Plantation of 500 acres in Chesterfield Twp., Burlington
Co., West New Jersey - offered for sale by Daniel

Bacon, living in Burlington (27 Nov.)

SAUER, Christopher in Germantown - offers reward for recovery of a lost or mislaid box of books brought over in Capt. Allen (27 Nov.)

HILL, Capt. - arrived Wednesday last at New York from Jamaica - New York item of 24 Nov. (4 Dec.)

WHITEFIELD, Rev. George - letter dated Salem 20 Nov. to a friend in New York; he is at Reedy Island about to leave for Georgia; his correspondents are to direct letters for him to James Hutton, bookseller, without Temple Bar, London (4 Dec.)

Letter sent under private seal to William Cosby, sheriff of New York - will soon be printed (4 Dec.)

MARKS, Joseph, at corner of Walnut St. and Second St., Phila. - has for sale a parcel of Negroes, sugars and singer (4 Dec.)

WARNER, Isaac - offers reward for recovery of colt stolen or strayed from his plantation in Blockley Twp., Phila. Co. (4 Dec.)

HANDLIN, Valentine, servant, age c. 30 - runaway from on board the _Diana_, of Dublin, Richard McCarty master; reward for his capture will be paid by William Blair (4 Dec.)

Negro woman with 2 children - offered for sale; enquire of George Harding, skinner, or the printer in Phila. (4 Dec.)

HIGGINBOTHOM, John, servant, age c. 60, a set-work cooper by trade - runaway from Thomas Reed, living in Charles Co., Va., near Newport; the servant stole a mare belonging to Francis Painham (4 Dec.)

WELLS, Susannah, servant, age c. 28, born near Biddeford, England - runaway from Thomas Downing at Wilmington; reward offered for return of servant to her master or to Robert Dixon in Phila.; it is believed she was carried from Newcastle in the ship commanded by Capt. Lawrence Dent, now at Phila. (4 Dec.)

Two tracts of 200 acres each on Manhatawny Road in Plymouth Twp., Phila. Co., about 16 miles from Phila., are for sale - enquire of Aaron Meredith living near said place (4 Dec.)

GIFFORD, Capt.- Saturday last arrived at New York in 29 days from Jamaica; he had come out under convoy of the Falmouth, Capt. Douglas commander; he met Capt. Warren bound to Jamaica - New York item of 4 Dec. (11 Dec.)

HICKS, Capt. - reports that Monday last a ship from Rhode Island was beaten to pieces on the rocks and the sailors and 10 passengers perished - New York item of 4 Dec. (11 Dec.)

OSWALD, James in Front St., Phila., at the house of Joseph Turner, and William Wallace, at the upper end of Second St., sugar-bakers - sell sugar, candy and molasses (11 Dec.)

Ship Loyal Judith, Lovell Paynter commander, now at Samuel Austin's wharf - will sail for South Carolina; for freight or passage agree with the master or with Benjamin Shoemaker, merchant, in High St., Phila. (11 Dec.)

Sloop Swanzey, Robert Goulding master, at Powel's wharf - will sail for North Carolina; for freight or passage agree with Andrew Farrell, tanner, in Chesnut St., Phila., or with the master on board (11 Dec.)

Ship Robert and Ellis, Martley Cusack master, at Hamilton's wharf - will sail for South Carolina; for freight or passage agree with Walter Goodman, at the Widow Coombs's beyond the bridge (11 Dec.)

Snow Margaret and Mary, Alexander Sloan master, at Andrew Hamilton's wharf - will sail for Dublin; for freight or passage agree with John Ervin or Alexander Lang in Martin's Alley or with the master (11 Dec.)

GATHEN, Mary, age c. 11 - absented herself from Joseph Canon of Coventry Twp., Chester Co. (11 Dec.)

Two strayed horses are taken up at the plantation of Jonathan Potts of Whitemarsh (11 Dec.)

TURNER, Peter, whose store is over against the Post Office in Market St., Phila. - sells cloth, nails, shot, lead, tea (11 Dec.)

COMBS, Elizabeth, at her house over the drawbridge in Phila. - sells cloth (11 Dec.)

Benjamin Franklin is accused in the Mercury of depriving that newspaper of the benefit of the post; after a letter from A. Spotswood it is stated by Franklin that he refused to forward any more of Bradford's papers (11 Dec.)

WARREN, Capt. - in letters reports he has taken a Spanish
vessel with 20,000 pounds - New York item of 4 Dec. (11
Dec.)

PHAENIX, Capt. - arrived at New York Monday in about 5
weeks from London - New York item of 24 Nov. (18 Dec.)

HILL, Capt. - arrived last week at New York from Jamaica;
he reports that Admiral Vernon met with Col. Gooch and
returned to Jamaica, where Capt. Warren and Capt.
Clark's company had arrived; Capt. Cusack is expected;
Capt. Nevin's prizes were condemned; Capt. Godet jumped
overboard but was taken and is in chains; Capt. Long
has taken a brigantine going to and from Cartagena -
New York item of 24 Nov. (18 Dec.)

STYLES, Capt. - arrived Thursday last at New York from
Bermuda - New York item of 1 Dec. (18 Dec.)

HINMAN, Capt., and Capt. Harvey were both taken by a
Spanish privateer - New York item of 1 Dec. (18 Dec.)

DAVIS, Capt. - arrived Thursday last at New York in 6
weeks from Bristol - New York item of 1 Dec. (18 Dec.)

SAMPLE, Capt. - arrived at New York Friday last in the ship
William from Bristol in 6 weeks - New York item of 8
Dec. (18 Dec.)

GILBERT, Capt. - arrived at New York Saturday last in 20
days from Curacoa - New York item of 8 Dec. (18 Dec.)

McCALL, George, late of Phila., merchant, dec'd - accounts
with estate to be settled with executors, Ann, Samuel
and Samuel McCall, Jr., and others; Ann McCall's house
is below the drawbridge (18 Dec.)

INGLIS, John, whose store is below the drawbridge in
Front St., Phila. - sells goods imported from London
and Bristol (18 Dec.)

A horse was left at the stable of Joseph Coburn, at the
Three Tuns, in Chesnut St., Phila. (18 Dec.)

CARTER, George, age c. 40, born in White Parish, 6 miles
from New Sarun in Wiltshire, baker by trade, who about
1722 went aboard ship at Bristol bound for Phila. - if
living, is desired to return to England or communicate
with John Atkinson at the White Lyon Tavern, on Cornhill, London, or with Israel Pemberton, Jr., of Phila.
(18 Dec.)

Speech of Gov. Jonathan Belcher to Massachusetts Assembly
(25 Dec.)

JONES, John, of Cymry Twp., Lancaster Co. - offers for sa
sale a tract of 370 acres (25 Dec.)

NOXON, Thomas, at Appoquinimy - seeks to hire a fuller
(25 Dec.)

GREW, Theophilus - his shop goods, lately taken by attachment, will be sold; his creditors are to send accounts
to Peter Robertson and William Coleman, auditors (25
Dec.)

A sorrel horse is at the plantation of Andrew Rambo in
Passiunk Twp., near Phila. (25 Dec.)

1741

KELLER, Capt. and Capt. Fones - in December both arrived
at Boston from London with news from Europe (1 Jan.)

MIRICK, Capt., from the Bay of Honduras - early last week
ran ashore on the back of Cape Cod and the vessel and
4 men were lost - Boston item of 27 Nov. 1740 (1 Jan.)

Men and women servants are offered for sale by Edward
Bridges at his house in Phila., commonly called the
Scales, or by William Harper in Gray's Alley (1 Jan.)

DIMSDALE, Sarah, late of Hattonfield, Gloucester Co., N.
J., widow, dec'd - accounts with estate are to be settled with the executors, Joseph Kaighin and John Dillwyn (1 Jan.)

Tract of 150 acres is offered for sale by Thomas Evans,
of Northampton, about 3 miles from Newtown, Bucks Co.
(1 Jan.)

DUMARESQUE, Capt. - is reported in a letter from Newfoundland to have taken a large French ship into
Gibraltar - Boston item of 30 Oct. 1740 (8 Jan.)

STEVENS, Capt. - arrived Tuesday last at Boston from Lisbon with news that Capt. Seager in a billander of Boston and Capt. Tresse of Phila. have been taken and carried into Lisbon - Boston item of 30 Oct. 1740 (8 Jan.)

DAVIS, Capt. in a Rhode Island privateer - is reported to
have taken 3 prizes - Boston item (8 Jan.)

Pictures of William and Mary, done in London and brought
to Boston by Capt. Fones - have been set up in the
Council Chamber (8 Jan.)

DAVIS, William, late of Phila., bookbinder, dec'd - people
who left any old books with him may have the same by
applying to his widow in Front St. (8 Jan.)

Message from Gov. Thomas to the Pennsylvania Assembly and
message from the Assembly to the governor (15 Jan.)

REMICK, Capt. - arrived Saturday last in Boston in 21 days
from Barbados; he reports that Gov. Byng of Barbados
lately died there - Boston item of 8 Nov. (15 Jan.)

TENNENT, Rev. Mr. - lately preached at the meeting-houses
of Mr. Morehead, Dr. Coleman, Mr. Webb, Rev. Gee and at
the workhouse on the Common - Boston item of 23 Dec.
1740 (15 Jan.)

BROWNE, Capt. Daniel - arrived Tuesday last at Newport,
R.I., in 17 days from Hispaniola - Newport item of 5
Dec. 1740 (15 Jan.)

FRANKLIN, B. - has reprinted and sells Free Grace, a sermon
preached at Bristol by John Wesley (15 Jan.)

List of letters brought to the Post Office at Phila. that
remain unclaimed on 15 Jan. 1741 (the abbreviations
used are as follows: pen. = Pennsylvania; phi. =
Philadelphia; bu. = Bucks; ch. = Chester; lan. = Lancaster; co. = County). ABBOT, Patrick; ALDERIDGE, Thomas,
Haverford; ALEXANDER, John, to the care of Jos. Loughran, pen.; ALLASON, Capt. Wm., phi.; ALL, Richard, Upper
Providence, ch. co.; ALLE, Richard, pen.; ALLEN, Selena,
Phi.; ALLIBONE, Benjamin, to be left at George Shoe-
maker's, phi.; AMENT, Mary, phi.; ANDERSON, Edward, phi.;
ANDREW, John; ARCHIBALD, Anne, to the care of Capt. At-
wood, phi.; ARMITAGE, Benjamin, Bristop Twp.; ARMSTRONG,
Alexander, to be left at Edward Shippen's, phi.; ARM-
STRONG, Samuel, pen.; ARNELL, William, to be left at
the Queen's Head; ASH, John, W. Nottingham, to the care
of Jeremiah Browne; ASHMORE, Anne, to be left at John
Reynell's, phi.; ASHURST, John, Eggharbour; ATKINSON,
John, Newtown, ch. co.;
     BAAR, Zacharias, phi.; BALL, Charles, phi.; BALLARD,
William, living with Nicholas Cutler, phi. co.; BAN-
NIGER, John Jacob, servant to John Marshall, Darby;
BARNARD, Samuel, phi.; BARTHOLOMEW, John, Montgomery;
BARTLET, John, mate on board the Friendship; BARTON,
John, on board the Lucy and Nancy, Capt. Smithson, phi.;
BATEMAN, Arthur, phi.; BAYNUM, Thomas, phi.; BEACH,

Capt. John, of the <u>Penelope</u>, phi.; BEAKENRIDGE, Jos.,
pen.; BEALEY, Hugh, phi.; BEARD, Hannah, phi.; BEASELY,
Mary, phi.; BECHTEL, Johannes, Germantown; BEDFORD,
Eleanor, phi.; BEDFORD, Capt. John, phi.; BEEKE, Thomas,
to be left at John Lewis's, phi.; BEGS, David, ch. co.;
BELL, Arthur, in America, to care of James Bambridge;
BENN, Henry; BENNET, James, ch. co.; BENSON, John, phi.;
BERRAM, Rev. Mr.; BETHEL, William, phi.; BIAGS/?/, Sarah,
at Joseph Reckless's, West Jersey; BISHOP, William, shoe-
maker, pen.; BLACKMAN, Thomas, at Richard Thomas's, Great
Valley; BLACKWOOD, John, phi.; BONNET, Charles, Pidgeon
Run; BOONE, George, Esq., Oley; BOORE, Lawrence, near
phi.; BORDMORE, Henry, phi.; BORELAND, John, to the care
of Roger Kirk, Nottingham; BORLAND, Andrew, pen.; BOULT,
Robert Benedict, at Messrs. Graydon and Emerson, phi.;
BOURN, Mary, phi.; BOURNE, Edmund, at Thomas Forster's,
bu. co.; BOWEN, Elijah, Cohansey, N.J.; BOWMAN, William,
phi.; BOWNE, Alexander, bu. co.; BOX, Nathaniel, Piles
Grove; BOYD, Rev. Mr. Adam; BRAME, Capt. John, to the
care of Capt. Seymour; BRANYON, John, living with Jos.
Cooper, New Jersey; BRAZIER, Richard, Conestogoe Road;
BREAUNO, John, phi.; BREDRICK, Francis, to the care of
John Griffin; BREESE, John, phi.; BRESON, Mary, Northamp-
ton, bu. co.; BRIGHAM, David, Wrightstown; BROOCKS,
George, on board the <u>Prince Augustus</u>; BROWN, Miream, ch.
co.; BROWN, Robert, mate on board Capt. Richmond; BROWNE,
Robert, pen.; BROWNE, William, or Sarah Browne, Piquea;
BROWNE, Zachariah, phi.; BRUSTER, Francis, Cohansey;
BULLOCK, Robert, at Mr. Bruro, block-maker in Front St.,
phi.; BUNN, William; BUNTER, James, ch. co.; BURN, James,
ch. co.; BURNE, Christopher, at Thomas Forster's, bu.
co.; BURROWS, Robert, West Jerseys; BURROWS, Widow, in
the Jerseys; BURT, Bellanger, phi.; BUTLER, Andrew;
BUYARS, William, Donnegall; BYRES, David, Donnegall;
    CAGER, Richard; CAIN, Christopher, phi.; CALAWAY,
Joseph, pen.; CALDWELL, William, in Horseham, phi. co.;
CALEY, Samuel, at John Fawks, Newton, ch. co.; CALHOONE,
William, Duck Creek; CALLISON, James, pen.; CAMERSON,
John, to the care of Richard Mears, Springfield; CAMP-
BELL, Bridget, to the care of George Gray; CAMPBELL,
Bridget, to the care of Mr. Gray at the Lower Ferry;
CAMPBELL, John, at Capt. Davis's, phi.; CAMPBELL, Jo-
siah; CAMPBELL, Nicholas, West Jersey; CARLL, Abiel,
glazier, Salem co.; CARLOW, William; CARMICHAEL, Daniel,
lan. co.; CARROL, Catherine; CARROL, Daniel, gardiner,
near phi.; CARSON, William, West Jersey; CARTER, Pat-
rick, at Whitemarsh; CARTER, Robin, sawyer, pen.;
CASDROP, Herman, to be left at John Postlethwaite, phi.;
CASEY, Thomas, at Timothy Eglington's, Greenwich, glo.
co.; CASHELL, John, to be left at George Shed's, phi.;
CATHCART, Rev. Mr., pen.; CAVEL, Thomas, pen.; CAXON,
Mary, to the care of Tho. Marshal, ch. co.; CHALMERS,

John, phi.; CHAMBERS, William, on board the <u>Eagle</u>,
Capt. Spencer, phi.; CHANLY, Thomas, to be left at the
Flying Horse, phi.; CHARLTON, Agnes, in the Manor of
Moreland, to the care of the Rev. Mr. Treat, Abington;
CHEDDS, John; CHESNUT, Benjamin, bu. co.; CHISALL,
Matthias, phi.; CLAPHAM, Josias, to be left at William
Tidmarsh's; CLARK, Cornelius, phi., at John Butwell's;
COFFE, Edward, phi.; COHANE, William, Duck Creek; COLE,
Walter, at Mr. McGee's, phi.; COLINSON, Robert, at Adam
Harper's, bu. co.; COLLINS, William, to be left at John
Cure's, phi.; COLLISON, William, on board the <u>Salley</u>,
Capt. Seymour, phi.; COLSON, Ann, to be left at Charles
Willings, phi.; COLVELL, Elizabeth, phi.; COMBE, Mr.,
at William Preston's, phi.; CONNER, Edward, at Richard
Martin's, near phi.; CONNER, Michael, ch. co.; COOK,
John, phi.; COOPER, Bethel, anchor smith, phi.; COOPER,
Heely, phi.; COOPER, Capt. Matthew, at Capt. Bell's,
phi.; COOPER, Thomas, New Jersey; COPP, Rebecca, Salem,
West Jersey; CORRY, William, merchant, phi.; COTTYMAN,
Daniel, on board the <u>Lucy</u> & <u>Nancy</u>; COX, Lawrence, Wil-
mington; COYAL, Ann, living in Merion, to be left at Mr.
Thomas Rogers, shoemaker, phi.; CRAIGE, James, to the
care of James Rodgers; CRALY, Henry, phi.; CRAWLEY,
Henry; CRESWELL, George, Marcus Hook; CROKER, William,
phi.; CROSBY, Dennis, at Joseph Taylor's, ch. co.; CROSS,
John, carpenter of the <u>Nancy</u>; CULLIN, Catherine, on York
Road; CULTON, Robert, to the care of James Armstrong,
Elk River; CUMINE, Bishop or Samuel Robinson, in Swe-
tara, to the care of the Rev. Mr. Bertram; CUMMINGS,
Joseph, to the care of Richard Shamkie in the Twp. of
Hanover; CUNDY, William, phi.; CUNNING, James, Whiteclay
Creek; CUNNINGHAM, Moses;

DAGWORTHY, John, phi.; DALRUMPLE, George, to the care
of John Hutchinson, phi.; DALTON, Capt. Robert, phi.;
DARLASTON, John, living with John Harris, lan. co.;
DARLING, James, near Dover, Kent co.; DARLINGTON, Wil-
liam, at Brandewine, ch. co.; DAVIES, Baddam, Upper
Merion; DAVIES, Hugh, near Radnor; DAVIES, James,
Tredyffryn; DAVIES, James, Whiteland; DAVIES, Jonathan,
at Trenton, to be left at Mr. John Fisher's, phi.;
DAVIES, Methusalem, Tredyffryn; DAVIES, Thomas, to be
left with Mr. Richard, phi.; DAVIS, John, Darby; DAVISON,
Archibald, temeswear, to the care of the Rev. Mr. Creag-
head, pen.; DAVISON, George, pen.; DAVISON, Robert;
DEALE, Michael, Springfield Manor, in Justice Farmer's
Square; DEAR, John, on board the privateer; DEARMON,
Sarah; DELANY, William, phi.; DENNIS, Clement, on board
the <u>Dragon</u>; DENS, Richard, at James Logan, Esq.; DERRY,
James, at Apoquinimy; DEVERELL, Capt. John, phi.; DEY-
SERT, John & James, Marlbro'.; DIXON, William, black-
smith, in Durham; DOBBS, William, Charlestown, ch. co.;
DODD, Gabriel, or wife, phi.; DODD, Thomas, Whitemarsh;

DOLLARD, Patrick, hatter, phi.; DONOGAN, David; DOROTHY,
William, to be left at A. Hamilton, phi.; DOUGHTY, Eliza-
beth, near the Swedes Church in Melotan; DOUGLASS, James,
Octorara; DOWGLASS, Archibald, tailor, phi.; DOWTHWAITE,
Samuel, at John Knowle's, phi.; DRAKE, Francis, phi.;
DRAPER, Anne, at Slaughter Neck, Sussex co.; DRAPER,
Stephen, phi.; DRURY, Edward, merchant, phi.; DUFFEY,
Capt. Thomas of the belinda _Charming Molly_, phi.; DUGALL,
Hannah, phi.; DUMBAR, Andrew, bu. co., to the care of
James Crawford; DUNN, John, phi.; DUNSCOMB, Jonathan,
phi.; DYER, Thomas, phi.;
EALOLL, Anthony, at the Sign of the Sloop, phi.; EARL,
Thomas, W. New Jersey; EATON, Simon, clothier, phi.;
EDGER, Moses, lan. co.; EDMUND, John, phi.; EDMUNDSON,
Archibald, pen.; EDMUNDSON, William, Lancaster; EDWARDS,
Isaac, phi. co.; EDWARDS, John, Shiptown, near phi.;
EDWARDS, Thomas, Byberry, phi. co.; EGAN, John, living
with David Owen, Limerick; EGERLY, Simon, phi.; ELMS,
George, ch.; ELMSLY, George, to the care of Mr. Hanne-
son, phi.; ELWALL, Jane, to be left at John Warder's,
phi.; EMERSON, John W., to be left at John Knowl's at
the Boar's Head; ENGLISH, James, at James Allison's, ch.
co.; ENOCH, Henry, Bethlehem, bu. co.; ERSTLAKE, John,
living with Wm. Clare, phi.; ERWIN, James, pen.; ERWIN,
John, phi.; ESSPY, George, Donnegall; EVAN, John, to be
left at White & Taylor's, phi.; EVANS, Edward, Limerick,
phi. co.; EVANS, Sarah, to be left at Samuel Mickel's,
merchant, phi.; EVANSON, John, to the care of Major Copson at Principio Iron-works; EWING, Alexander, lan. co.;
EYRE'S, Samuel, Jr., at Philip Holber's; EZZED, Christian, at Morris' River, Cohansey;
FAIRBROTHER, Thomas, to the care of David Davis,
Charlestown, ch. co.; FARIES, Robert, East Jersey; FARIS,
William, shoemaker, phi.; FARMER, Edward, Esq., White-
marsh; FERGUSON, John, at Wm. Hood's, shoemaker, phi.;
FERGUSON, Samuel, W. Jersey; FIELD, Mary, to the care
of Thomas James, bu. co.; FIELD, William, living with
Thom. David, bu. co.; FIELDING, William, phi.; FILPOT,
William, bu. co.; FINLEY, George; FINNEY, Robert, pen.;
FINNEY, William, Thunderhill, pen.; FISHER, George, to
be left at Jos. Lupton's, Salsbury Twp., bu. co.;
FISHER, John, bu. co.; FISHER, William, to be left at
Robert Davis's, at the Queen's Head, phi.; FITZGERALD,
John, shoemaker, phi.; FITZGERALD, Thomas, phi.; FLEDGER,
James, to the care of Francis Rawl, phi.; FORGNER, Adam,
to the care of James McCullough, pen.; FORISTER, David,
Donnegall; FORROSTAL, Catherine, phi.; FOTTREL, Weldon,
to be left at Andrew Farral's, tanner, phi.; FOURACRE,
Isaac, in Bibery, phi. co.; FOX, Elizabet, living at
Jos. Large, bu. co.; FRAZIER, William, Collector of the
Customs at Nova Cesarea; FREEBORN, Robert, lan. co.;
FRENCH, Alexander, phi.; FRISTAINE, David, to be left

at Israel Pemberton's or William Hudson's, phi.; FRYER, James; FULLERTOWN, David, to the care of Dan. McAserton, phi.; FULLER, Elizabeth, Amwell, Hunterdon Co., N. J.; FURLONG, Nicholas, at Mr. Shuttle's, phi.; FYANCE, John, Springfield, to the care of Henry Hartley, phi.;

GALE, John, blacksmith, bu. co.; GALE, Nicholas, chairmaker, phi.; GAMBLE, John, near Paxton Meeting-house, pen.; GAMPLE, Samuel, phi.; GARRATT, George, Goshen, ch. co.; GARRISON, Charles, bu. co.; GAUDY, Robert, mariner; GAY, Mary, phi.; GEDES, Wm., Northampton, bu. co.; GERRISH, John, at Richard Houghs, Wakefield, bu. co.; GIBBS, Wm., near Thomas Flackert's mill, bu. co.; GIBS, John, ship-carpenter, phi.; GIBSON, Alex., to the care of the Rev. Mr. Allison, New London, ch. co.; GIBSON, Geo., storekeeper, Pequay; GILBERT, Ann, widow, phi.; GILBERT, Robert; GILES, William, at George Wells's, phi.; GILL, John, Abington, phi. co.; GILLIARD, James, phi.; GILPIN, Thomas, ch. co.; GIRVEN, Thomas, Newtown, bu. co.; GLADING, Mary; GOODACYE, John, phi.; GOODMAN, George, butcher, phi.; GORDON, Joseph, near Newtown, bu. co.; GOULD, John, bu. co.; GRAHAM, Archibald, phi.; GRAHAM, James, phi.; GRAHAM, James, London Grove, ch. co.; GRAHAM, John, to the care of the Rev. Wm. Bartram, Sweaterara; GRAY, Capt. John, to the care of Wm. Parratt; GREELAND, Flower, at John Wells's, Sadsbury Ferry, bu. co.; GREGG, Thomas, at Mr. John Price's, phi.; GRIEVES, Wm., commander of the _Tryal_, phi.; GRIFFITH, William, phi.; GRIFFITTS, William, in Amity Twp., phi. co.; GRISTON, Thomas, phi.; GURNEY, Thomas, phi.;

HAGGERSTON, William, at John Norris's, phi.; HALL, Samuel, phi.; HALLIARD, James; HALLIHANE, John, phi.; HAMAN, Richard, to be left at Capt. William Wells's, phi.; HAMILTON, Alexander, to the care of the Widow Wainwright; HAMILTON, Archibald, Salem, West Jersey; HAMILTON, Rebecca, phi.; HAMILTON, William, West Jersey; HAMMAT, William, to be left at Mr. Rosal's, phi.; HAMMON, Capt. John, phi.; HANK, John, phi.; HANNA, James, pen.; HARDING, John, at St. Christopher's Mill, pen.; HARRIS, Hector, tailor, phi.; HARRIS, Sarah, phi.; HARRISON, John, near phi.; HARVEY, William, phi.; HASIL-WOOD, Mr., merchant, phi.; HASILWOOD, William, phi.; HAWLEY, Joseph, Newtown, ch. co.; HAY, David, Norrington Twp.; HAYWARD, John, phi.; HEALY, Darly, phi.; HENDRY, Robert, Brandewyne Hundred; HERD, John, living with William Grettham, phi.; HESKETH, John, at Stephen Beasley's, phi.; HESS, Thomas, phi.; HEWIT, Capt. Benj., of the _Three Sisters_; HIGGS, Aaron, phi.; HIGGS, Capt., of the sloop _Elizabeth_, phi.; HILL, Ambrose, to the care of Robert Smith, Esq., Sussex Co.; HILL, Thomas, at Robert Davis's, at the Queen's Head, phi.; HIR, John, phi.; HODGE, Andrew, to the care of John McCullough, phi.; HODGES, John, to be left at Elizabeth Edgar's,

phi.; HODGKISS, Michael, founder, Mount Holley; HOGG,
Robert, at John Potts's, Mount Pleasant; HOGLAND, Derick,
Southampton, bu. co.; HOLLIDAY, John, Duck Creek, to be
left at Reese Peter's, phi.; HOLLIDGE, John, merchant,
phi.; HOLLOWAY, Thomas, at Mr. Beaks's, Monmouth co.,
to be left at Thomas Howard's, phi.; HOLMES, William,
bu. co.; HOOD, Mr., phi.; HOOD, Thomas, near phi.; HORS-
MAN, Charles, at Joseph Mendenhall, ch. co.; HOUGH,
Elizabeth, Gloucester, N.J.; HOW, John, Pequea; HOWELL,
George, phi.; HUGHES, James, Solebury, lan. co.; HUGHES,
James, to the care of the Rev. Mr. Creaghead, pen.;
HUGHES, John, Upper Merion; HULLFORD, John, to be left
at Adam Buckley's, Marcus Hook; HUMES, David, to the
care of Rob. Allen, N. Castle; HUMPHREY, William, phi.;
HUNT, Mary, phi.; HUNTER, Robert, mate on board the
Glasgow; HUST, Thomas, at William Jones, ch. co.;
HUTCHINSON, John, bu. co.; HUTHAM, Richard, at Timothy
Scarth's; HYLAND, Thomas, at Merchant Reynold's, phi.;
INGRAM, Evan; INGRAM, John, at the Crown and Scepter,
phi.; INSINE, Robert, at Merion, phi. co.; IRWIN, Henry,
to the care of Moses Edgar, lan. co.; IRWIN, William, to
the care of John Mitchel;
JACK, William, to the care of Alexander Dunlope, near
phi.; JACKSON, John, on board the William; JACKSON, Omer,
to the care of James Rodgers; JACOBS, Thomas, Elk River;
JADD, Rowland, Bradford Twp., ch. co.; JAMES, George, at
Trehaydd, in Trediffryn; JAMES, Thomas, millwright; JAMES,
Thomas, at Trehaydd; JAUNCY, James, on board ..pt., John
Painter, phi.; JENKINGS, Elizabeth, phi.; JOB, John, to
the care of Thomas Job, lan. co.; JOBB, James; JOHNSTON,
John, in the Northern Liberties, phi.; JOHNSTON, Joseph,
ch. co.; JOLIFFE, William; JONES, Abraham, upholsterer,
phi.; JONES, Charles, merchant, phi.; JONES, Daniel, on
board Capt. Higgs; JONES, David, shipwright, to be left
at the Sign of the Sloop, phi.; JONES, Henry, to be left
with Nathanael Jenkins, New Garden, ch. co.; JONES,
Oliver, phi.; JONES, Samuel, phi.; JONES, Thomas, Abington; JONES, Thomas, to be left at John Jones's, phi.;
JONES, William, merchant, Birmingham, ch. co.; JORDAN,
Thomas, phi.; JORY, John, to be left at the Post Office,
phi.; JOSLIN, Richard, to be left at Owen Owen's, phi.;
JOSLIN, Richard, to the care of Owen Owen;
KASEBEER, Christian, phi.; KAVENOUGH, George, to be
left with Miles Strickland, phi.; KEAN, Nicholas, mason,
bu. co.; KEEFF, Dennis, to be left at Capt. Edgar's,
phi.; KEER, James, lan. co.; KEITH, James, phi.; KELLY,
Honorey, to be left at Caleb Emerson's, phi.; KELLY,
James, to be left with James Kelly, Tittagam, bu. co.;
KELLY, William, Salem co.; KENDALL, Benjamin, near
Chester; KENEDY, Robert, Plumsted Twp., to the care of
Archibald Campbell, phi.; KENNADY, John, to be for-
warded by William Geer; KENNEY, Augustine, waterman,

phi.; KERNES, Robert, wigmaker, phi.; KILPATRICK, James,
to the care of the Rev. Mr. Adam Boyd, Octarara; KING,
Charles, to be left at John Holiday's, Duck Creek; KING,
John, merchant, phi.; KINGSTON, Thomas, to be left at
Thomas Ewen's, Northampton, bu. co.; KIRK, Samuel or
John, Brandewyne; KOLLOCK, Jacob, Lewistown; KYET,
William, servant to Thomas Macer, phi.;

LAMSLY, Joseph, lan. co.; LAWRENCE, William, phi.;
LAYCOCK, Lucy /?/, at James Parratts, phi.; LEAMING,
William, at Capt. Hopkins's, phi.; LEANING, Widow
Leafrty, near Whiteclay Creek; LE CORNU, James, phi.;
LEWELIN, Morris, to be left at Joseph Gray's; LEWIS,
Elias, Kennet Twp., ch. co.; LEWIS, Dr. John, Amwell;
LEWIS, Lewis, at William Harbor's at the Alms-house,
phi.; LEWIS, Mary, phi.; LIDERL, John, near phi.;
LIMOUS, William, phi.; LINCH, Ann, Bristol, bu. co.;
LINNIHAN, William, blacksmith, living with William
Parker, phi.; LINSEY, Charles, merchant, phi.; LINUS,
Thomas, New Garden; LLOYD, David, to be left at Jos.
Turner's, phi.; LLOYD, John, Robinson Twp., lan. co.;
LLOYD, Philip, merchant, phi.; LOBDELL, Isaac, phi.;
LOFTIS, Capt. Joseph, phi.; LOGAN, Thomas, Freehold;
LORD, Elizabeth, living in Gloucester; LOW, Isaac,
Goshen, ch. co.; LOWDER, William, to the care of James
Whitehill, Pequea; LOWRY, John, ch. co.; LOWRY, Richard,
phi.; LUPTON, Joseph, Solesbury Twp., bu. co.; LYON,
Robert, chief mate of the ship Thistle; LYON, Thomas,
on board the Lucy and Nancy;

McBRIDLE, John, at the Sign of the Fan, phi.; McCAD-
DAM, Hugh, Donnegal; McCALA, John, lan. co., to the care
of Alexander Craghead; McCALL, Alexander, to the care of
John Thompson, Sadsbury Twp.; McCARTHY, Mary, living at
Tho. Hatton's, phi.; McCHESHEY, James, to the care of
Henry Spark, near phi.; McCLEUR, Charles, to the care
of the Rev. Mr. Allison; McCOLLUM, John, phi.; McCOLOUGH,
William, Wrightstown, bu. co.; McCONAL, Thomas; McCONCHY,
Samuel or William, pen.; McCONCHEE, William; McCRACKEN,
William, West Nottingham, ch. co.; McCREIGHAN, Henry;
McCUNN, John, to the care of Archa. Edmundson/?/; McDOAL,
Thomas, pen.; MACKDONNEL, Honora, Thunderhill; McDOWEL,
John, at John Farris's, phi.; McECHERN, Alexander, Horse-
ham; McFALL, Francis, bu. co.; McGALLAND, John, East
Jersey; McGRADY, Samuel, bu. co.; McGREE, Patrick, phi.;
McGUIERA, Patrick, to the care of Thomas Bryne, New
Garden, ch. co.; McGUIRE, James, phi.; McGUIRE, Michael,
at John Bennet's, pen.; McHARRY, John, to the care of
Sam. Dean, bu. co.; McHON, Archibald, to the care of
Richard Berwick, phi.; McKEE, Robert, near phi.; McKIN-
SEY, Joseph, bu. co.; McLAUGHLEN, Dennis, sadler, phi.;
McMASTERS, James, to the care of James Rogers; McMINN,
John, ch. co.; McNEAL, John; McPHILIP, Patrick, phi.;
McREE, John, lan. co.; McWHENEY, John, Forks Manor, ch.

co.; MAHER, Edmund, at the head of Alloway's Creek,
Salem co.; MAHICAN, Charles, phi.; MAIDSON, Anna
Catherine, at Mr. Allan's, soap-maker, phi.; MANY,
Francis, shipwright, phi.; MARKES, Joseph, merchant,
phi.; MARSDEN, Ann, lan. co.; MARSHAL, William, Byberry;
MASSER, Elizabeth; MATHER, Benjamin, phi., or Joseph
Mather, pen.; MATHERS, James, near Thunder Hill; MATTEY,
Robert, merchant, phi.; MATTHEWS, Capt. William, of the
Hopewell; MAY, Moses, in the Jerseys; MAYES, William,
pen.; MAYTER, Sarah, at the Sign of the Ship-a-Ground;
MEASE, Robert, merchant, phi.; MEANS, William, bu. co.;
MEARS, Alexander, at John Hamilton's, U. Dublin; MEN-
DENHALL, George, East Caln, ch. co.; MENDINGHALL, Aaron,
merchant, phi.; MEYER, Daniel, to the care of Jacob
Cardron; MILLBOURN, John, on board the Dragon; MILLER,
James, near Octarara; MILLOT, Daniel, at James Dicken's,
Lower Merion; MILLS, Joseph, near phi., to the care of
William Neely or Robert Watson; MILNER, James, Chris-
tiana Hundred, Newcastle co.; MINCROY, John, near phi.;
MITCHEL, Robert, to the care of John Farris, phi.;
MITCHELL, Thomas, at Capt. John Searl's, phi.; MONFORD,
James, bu. co.; MONTGOMERY, Robert, to the care of Mr.
John Lyell, New Providence; MOONE (or MOORE), Thomas,
phi.; MOORE, Andrew, near Newtown, lan. co.; MOORE,
William or James, Donnegal; MORA, William, to the care
of John Carnaghane, Esq., Octarara; MORRISON, Elizabeth,
Sadsbury in the Great Valley; MORRIS, Tarance, to the
care of W. Passmore, ch. co.; MORRIS, William, bu. co.;
MORRO, Duncan, to the care of Hannah Henderson, phi.;
MOSGROVE, William, to the care of Capt. Rogers; MOULDER,
David, Waterford, in Gloucester Co. in the Jerseys;
MULLETGEN, Issabel, Conestogo; MURRAY, William, smith,
to the care of John Carnaghan, Octarara;
    NEAL, John, Esq., phi.; NEAT, Mrs., phi.; NEATE, Wil-
liam, commander of the Dragon; NEED, Joseph, Darby;
NELE, Robert, of the brigt. Eagle, phi.; NELSON, John,
near Dover, Kent co.; NELSON, John, to the care of
Thomas Huss, pen.; NEVIET, John, to the care of Wm.
Ross, phi.; NEVILE, William, Greenwich, Gloucester co.;
NEWELL, Joshua, ch. co.; NEWMAN, Richard, to be left
at John Bridges, Northampton Twp., bu. co.; NEWMAN, Wil-
liam, to be left at Rob. Shepherd's; NICHOLS, Capt., on
board the Mulbery snow, to be left at Mr. Atwood's, mer-
chant, phi.; NICHOLSON, Clement, on board the Hannah;
NICHOLSON, John, Darby; NITSCHMAN, David, at Dr. Saear's,
Germantown; NIVIAN, John; NIXON, Allen, to be left at
Durham Iron-Works; NIXON, James, to the care of Wm.
Long, pen.; NIXON, William, to be left at Cadwalder
Foulk's; NORE, Michael; NORTON, Philip, to the care of
Capt. Pitt, phi.; NUGENT, John, Whitemarsh; NUTT,
Thomas, phi.;
    ODIORNE, Jonathan, Newcastle; O'MULLIN, Patrick, to

the care of Charles Tennent, Newcastle co.; OSMOND,
John, to be left at the Post Office; OWEN, David, phi.;
PAINE, Thomas, wheelwright, ch. co.; PALMER, Sarah;
PARE, John, to be left at Solomon Fussel's, phi.; PARRY,
David, near Montgomery, ch. co.; PARSONS, Richard, at
James Townshend, ch. co.; PATTERSON, John, phi.; PAYN-
TER, Mary, to be left at Richard Paynter's; PEAKE, Wil-
liam, Piles Grove, Salem co.; PEEL, Anthony, phi.; PEN-
NINGTON, Rebecca, phi.; PERKIN, John, phi.; PERRY, Jo-
seph and John, Pequea; PETIE /?/, Elizabeth, pen.;
PHILIP, Patrick, phi.; PHILPOT, Richard, at John Har-
combe's, phi.; PICKTON, Thomas; PIMROY, George, West
Jersey; PIPON, John, in the Jerseys; PLUMER, John, to
be left at Edward Bridges, merchant, phi.; POLL/?/ILL,
Robert, at St. George's, Newcastle co.; POTTER, Hugh,
near /Che/ster, to be left at John Reynolds's; POWEL,
Mary, at John Angel's, phi.; PRICE, David, schoolmaster,
to be left at William Chancellor's, sailmaker /?/, phi.;
PRICE, David, to the care of Tho. Eatton, pen.; PRICE,
John, tailor, phi.; PRUDENCE /?/, William, Hartford,
ch. co.;
    QUEN, William phi., to the care of Geo. Walter;
QUICK, Robert, phi.; QUICK, William, to be left at Mr.
Nicholas Crones, butcher, phi.; QUISACK, Alexander, to
the care of Mrs. Glen, Newcastle;
    RAMSEY, Joseph, phi.; RANKIN, John, fuller, at Evans's
mill, ch. co.; RAWLINGS, Thomas, at Mr. Ketch/...?/,
phi.; REA, Robert, near Wells's Ferry; READ, James,
Lewistown, to the care of Robert Smith, Cold Spring;
REE, Robert, to the care of John McKollock, phi.; REID,
James, ship-carpenter; REID, John, Solesbury, bu. co.;
RENSEL, John, pen.; REYNOLDS, John, at John Penquits,
Wrightstown, bu. co.; RICE, Benjamin; RICHARDS, John,
phi.; RICHARDSON, Edward, Woodberry Creek; RICHARDSON,
John, and Comp., Christiana; RICHARDSON, Thomas, to the
care of Simon Edgel; RICHEY, /...,/nter, pen.; RICHMOND,
Capt. John, phi.; RISON, Richard, phi.; ROBERTS, Benja-
min, on board Capt. Brown; ROBERTSON, James, merchant,
East Jersey, to the care of John Farris, shoemaker, phi.;
ROBERTSON, John, to be left at W. Shepherd's, phi.;
ROBINS, Alexander; ROBINSON, Edward, to the care of
Henry McColough; ROBINSON, Mary, Kent co., to the care
of James Leard, phi.; ROBINSON, Richard, merchant, phi.;
RODGERS, Andrew, near Sasquehana; ROGERS, Joseph, phi.;
ROSE, Thomas, Germantown; ROSS, John, Forks Manor, ch.
co.; ROSS, Thomas, bu. co., to the care of George Cun-
ningham, phi.; ROWLAND, Morgan, to the care of the
Widow Thomas, phi.; RUS/?/L, Robert, bu. co.; RUSH,
Thomas, phi. co.; RYBURN, Matthew, phi.; RYDER, Richard,
phi.;
    SACRIDER, Mary, phi.; SALE, Adam, ship-carpenter,
phi.; SAMPELL, William, ship-carpenter, phi.; SANDERSON,

Mary, at the Black Horse, phi.; SAUNDERS, John, Gloucester co., N.J.; SCHWEIGHAUSEN, Johan Conrad, phi.;
SCORSE, James, Millford Twp., bu. co.; SCOT, William,
Pennsneck; SCOTT, Andrew, near phi.; SCOTT, George,
tanner, phi.; SCOTT, John, Neshamany, ch. co.; SCOTT,
Dr. John, phi.; SCOTT, Capt. Vincent; SCRIVNER, Benjamin, Byberry; SEAGER, Capt. Reynold, phi.; SELER, Nath.,
phi.; SEMPLE, John, to the care of the Rev. Mr. Jamison; SEWELL, Robert, Solesbury, bu. co.; SHARPLES,
Eleanor, phi.; SHENNON, James, Octorara; SHUTE, William,
at Mr. Wrights, near Gloucester; SIBBALD, John, to the
care of Capt. Oswald, phi.; SITTYMAN, Thomas, East Jersey; SKELTON, Mrs., phi.; SKETCHLY, John, Ridley Twp.,
ch. co.; SKINAR, Robert, phi.; SKINNER, John, on board
the _Elizabeth_; SLIMONS, Thomas, pen.; SMITH, Daniel,
phi.; SMITH, Daniel, Octorara; SMITH, Francis, shoemaker, in the Jerseys; SMITH, Capt. George, phi.; SMITH,
James, to the care of Mr. Gray, leather-dresser, phi.;
SMITH, James, at Mr. Emley's, phi.; SMITH, John, at the
Caladony Copper Mines, to the care of Joseph Lynn,
phi.; SMITH, John, at Tho. Williams's, North Wales;
SMITH, Michael, phi.; SMITH, Richard, Montgomery Twp.;
SMITH, Richard, Montgomery Twp.; SMITH, Robert, near
Shamany Meeting-house; SMITH, Samuel, ship-carpenter,
phi.; SMITH, Simon, Mansfield; SMITH, Thomas, at Thomas
/.../s/?/, bricklayer, phi.; SMITHIES, Sergent, phi.;
SMITHSON, Capt. George; SOMNER, Thomas, to be left at
the Post Office; SPICER, Robert, phi.; SPRINGER, John,
Redclay Creek; STARKEY, Joseph, Sasquehannah; STEEL,
Andrew, at the Forks of Brandewyne; STERLING, James,
phi.; STEVENSON, John, phi.; STEWART, Alexander, to the
care of John Carr; STEWART, Henry, to the care of Isaac
Manypenny, phi.; STEWART, James, merchant, phi.; STEWART,
James, to the care of Joseph Todd, Whitemarsh; STOCKS,
John, Newtown, bu. co.; SUTTON, Mary, West Jersey;
SWANZEY, John, near Sasquehannah;

  TACABERY, Robert, to the care of Mrs. Prichet, phi.;
TANNER, Nicholas, Byberry, to be left at Mr. Taylor's,
merchant, phi.; TANNER/?/, John, on board the _Mary_;
TANTUM, John, Nottingham, West Jersey; TAYLOR, Benja-
min, Kennet Twp., ch. co.; TAYLOR, John, flatman, phi.;
TAYLOR, Joseph, Kennet Twp., ch. co.; TETFORD, Charles,
to the care of Tho. Carroll, phi.; THOMAS, Joseph,
London Britain, ch. co.; THOMAS, Richard, near Owen
Owen's, phi.; THOMAS, Robert, baker, phi.; THOMPSON,
Robert, phi.; THOMSON, Alexander, at Richard Hurdages,
phi.; THOMSON, Isaac, to the care of John Turner; THOM-
SON, James; THOMSON, John, near Upper Dublin; THOMSON,
Tanet, Northampton, bu. co.; THORNLEY, Joseph, Wil-
mington; TILLY, Richard, to the care of John Jones, Jr.;
TITTROY, James, on board the _Sally_; TODD, James, to the
care of Andrew Killpatrick; TODD, Joseph, Warminster,

bu. co.; TOMLINSON, John, Bristol, bu. co.; TOWNSHEND,
Joseph, weaver, phi.; TUCKWOOD, Thomas, phi.;
  UNTHANK, Joseph, to the care of John Reeve, phi.;
VALINTINE, Thomas, to the care of James Steel, phi.;
VANDERHAUL, Mr., goldsmith, phi.; VANDERPOOLE, Isaac,
phi.; VIVIAN, Capt. John, phi.;
  WAKEFIELD, Thomas, to the care of Dr. Jones, at
Christine Bridge; WALKER, Alexander, to the care of
Thomas Shennon, Solesbury; WALKERS, David, to the care
of John McCamly, phi.; WALLIS, Thomas, phi.; WARE,
Thomas, to the care of Jeremiah Beck, phi.; WARR, Henry,
at Mr. John Sparrows, butcher, phi.; WARREN, Mary, to
the care of Capt. Inglis, phi.; WATSON, John, Sr., to
the care of William Alexander, Newcastle co.; WATSON,
Dr. John, Indian River; WATTS, Nicholas, at Abraham
Moss's, phi.; WEBB, Joseph, near phi.; WEBB, Thomas,
blacksmith, Hattonfield; WEBB, William, Kennet Twp., ch.
co.; WEBB, William, Esq., phi.; WEBSTER, Robert, to the
care of Mr. Morris, Wilmington; WEEKS, James, phi.;
WELCH, Thomas, at Edward Waldron's, Darby; WELDON, Capt.,
Marcus Hook; WELK, John, pilot/?/; WELLEY, John, to the
care of Alexander Miller, phi.; WELLS, Wm., phi., to the
care of George Wells; WHITE, Charles, near Duck Creek;
WHITE, Christopher, at Wm. Pencocks, ch. co.; WHITE,
John, to the are of William Johnson, phi.; WHITE, Sarah,
to the care of Joseph Ramsey, phi.; WHITEHILL, James,
Octorara; WHITES, Henry, to be left at William Davis's,
at the Queen's Head; WHITLEY, Anthony, phi.; WHITTAL,
William, phi.; WICKES, Mary, to be left at Lawrence
Boor, Penypack; WILCOCKS, James, on board the Speedwell,
phi.; WILLIAMS, Joseph, Merion; WILLIAMS, Richard, phi.;
WILLIAMS, Theophilus; North Wales Twp., to be left at
Christopher Walliard's, phi.; WILLINGTON, John, phi.;
WILLSON, Sarah, to the care of Robert Greer, phi.;
WILLSON, William; WISER, George, West Marlborough, ch.
co.; WOOD, Edward, to the care of Alex. Quadter, phi.
co.; WOOD, Hannah, phi.; WOOD, Thomas, in the Manor of
Moreland; WOODSTOCK, William; WORLDLY, Nathan, to the
care of Mr. Preston, phi.; WORRELL, Mary, bu. co.;
WRIGHT, Benjamin, phi.; WRIGHT, Hugh, to be left at the
Sign of the Ship, Fishbourn's wharf, phi.; WRIGHT, John,
to the care of Francis Harper, phi.; WRIGHT, Jonathan,
near Shamany; WRIGHT, William, to the care of Christopher Bryant; WRIGHTON, John, bu. co. (2 letters);
  YOURY, Alexander, hatter, phi.; YOAKLY, John, to the
care of Robert Ellis, phi.; (15 Jan.)

DUMARESQUE, Capt. of a privateer belonging to Boston - has
  taken a number of prizes (22 Jan.)

WILLIS, Capt., of a privateer belonging to Boston - on 1
  Oct. 50 of his men, contrary to his opinion, landed on

one of the Canary Islands but did not return (22 Jan.)

TILDEN, Capt., in a sloop from Jamaica - ran ashore Wednesday last near Scituate - Boston item of 22 Dec. 1740
(22 Jan.)

Verses on John Wesley's sermon on Free Grace (22 Jan.)

GROWDEN, Lawrence, at plantation called Trevose offers the
following tracts of land: 80 acres in the Northern
Liberties of Phila., joining to a plantation of Ralph
Asheton, Esq.; 1,000 acres in Richland Twp., Bucks Co.;
190 acres in Bensalem Twp., Bucks Co., adjoining to
William Hoopes; 130 acres adjoining to Jacob Vankirk's
and Abraham Vandegrift's plantations; a 5,000-acre
plantation called Richlieu; 120-acre plantation where
John Breece lives; 100 acres of wood land, joining to
Richlieu, Henry Breeco's and Thomas Tomlinson's plantations; a 200-acre plantation called King's Place; 300
acres of woodland betwen King's Place and Neshaminy
Creek; 200-acre plantation called Belmount and Trevose;
70 acres between William and John Dunkan's plantations;
70 acres of wood land between Richlieu and Samuel Riche's
plantation; a 100-acre plantation where Jonas Keen lately dwelt; half a plantation called Trevose (22 Jan.)

ANDERSON, William, Irish servant, age c. 18, tailor - runaway from John Trimble of Wilmington; it is supposed
that the runaway will enquire for Andrew Love (22 Jan.)

A bay horse has been since November at the plantation of
David Stephens at Nantmel, Chester Co., near French
Creek Forge, under the notice of Wm. Harris (22. Jan.)

Bay mare has been for 2 years at plantation of William
Reynolds in Charlestown, Chester Co. (22 Jan.)

HUSSEY, Capt., in a snow bound to Boston from the Bay of
Honduras - was cast away at the back of Cape Cod -
Boston item of 2 Jan. (29 Jan.)

WEEKS, Capt., from Virginia bound to Boston - is ashore
- Boston item of 2 Jan. (29 Jan.)

JOHNSON, Capt., bound to Virginia - same as above

BARBER, Capt., in sloop belonging to Providence bound from
Boston to Providence - is cast away - Boston item of
2 Jan. (29 Jan.)

MERICK, Capt., from the Bay of Honduras, in distress - was
taken aboard by Capt. Sherburne in a snow bound from

Barbados to New Hampshire; Sherburn, however, on 26
Dec. 1740 was cast away upon the Isle of Sholes and all
aboard was lost - Boston item of 2 Jan. (29 Jan.)

TILDEN, Capt. - his sloop, driven ashore at Scituate, was
stove to pieces - Boston item of 2 Jan. (29 Jan.)

TITCOMB, Capt., in a sloop bound from Boston to Newbury -
narrowly escaped shipwreck upon Nehant Rocks - Boston
item of 2 Jan. (29 Jan.)

WELLS, Capt. - arrived Friday last at New York in 8 days
from Bermudas - New York item of 19 Jan. (29 Jan.)

BOYD, Capt. - arrived Friday last at New York in the
brigantine Jamaica Pacquet from Jamaica; in his passage he met a Spanish privateer, probably the one that
took Capt. Hinman - New York item of 19 Jan. (29 Jan.)

VAUGHAN, Capt. - arrived Friday last at New York in 5
weeks from Jamaica - New York item of 19 Jan. (29 Jan.)

All transports that sailed from North America arrived at
Jamaica 26 Nov. except Capt. Goff's company in a snow
from Boston, Capt. Waterhouse master - New York item of
19 Jan. (29 Jan.)

WARREN, Capt., in H.M.S. Squirrel - took a French sloop
with letters from Don Blass (governor of St. Jago) and
the governor of the Havana to Monsr. De la Nase at
Louganne - New York item of 19 Jan. (29 Jan.)

HINTON, Capt., in a Bermudas sloop from Phila. - his sloop
foundered - 2 men were taken up at sea but the rest
perished - New York item of 19 Jan. (29 Jan.)

DRUMMOND, Capt. Seth, of the privateer George - has taken
a valuable prize and carried it into Port Antonio (29
Jan.)

CATHCART, Lord - died 25 Dec. 1740 at Dominica; his command devolved on General Wentworth (29 Jan.)

Annely, Lewis and Vanderspiegel, at corner of Market St.,
where formerly Charles Read lived - sell cloth and
other goods (29 Jan.)

HUMPHREYS, Joseph, of Haverford, Chester Co. - will let a
plantation in Merion, 8 miles from Phila. (29 Jan.)

THOMSON, Joshua, of Ridley Twp., Chester Co. - offers reward for recovery of a stolen mare and arrest of the

thief named John Blowden, <u>alias</u> John Williams (29 Jan.)

Proclamation of George Clarke, Lt.-Gov. of New York (5 Feb.)

Iron stones are sold by the printer (5 Feb.)

MORRIS, Anthony, Jr. - sells pit coal and sea coal (5 Feb.)

LOGAN, William, and his father, James Logan, as attornies for Laetitia Penn - demand payment of quit-rents due (12 Feb.)

WILLIAMS, Alexander, a labouring man - Tuesday last was found dead at the end of King St. in Boston - Boston item of 12 Jan. (19 Feb.)

ASPINWALL, Capt., in a new sloop bound from Boston to New York - has been cast away; the lives of the men are saved - Boston item of 12 Jan. (19 Feb.)

CUDWORTH, Capt., coming from North Carolina - was lately cast away near Tonington - the captain, mate and pilot perished - Boston item of 12 Jan. (19 Feb.)

EACHARD, Mr. - describes Dominica as one of the best places to water in the West Indies - Boston item of 12 Jan. (19 Feb.)

CHILD, Capt. - Tuesday last his sloop (belonging to Rhode Island) from Antigua was driven upon Fawn Bar and then among the rocks upon Lovel's Island; the ship was lost but the men were saved - Boston item of 12 Jan. (19 Feb.)

GIRDLE, Mr., and Mr. Gidney Clark of Barbados - report at Marblehead, Mass., news from the West Indies, including statement that a ship of Gidney Clark's, Henry Williams of Salem master, was taken by a privateer - Marblehead letter dated 13 Jan. (19 Feb.)

TENNENT, Rev. Mr. - arrived Saturday last at Piscataqua and set out 18 Jan. for Greenland and Hampton, where he preached - Piscataqua item of 19 Jan. (19 Feb.)

KING, Capt., in a sloop from New York bound to Jamaica - was chased by a privateer but escaped - New York item of 26 Jan. (19 Feb.)

GREENHILL, Capt. Thomas - was cast away in a sloop from New York bound for Coracoa - New York item of 26 Jan. (19 Feb.)

DAVIS, Capt. - has brought 4 prizes into Madeira; Capt. Renton and the Torrington, Capt. Knight, have brought 2 prizes into Jamaica; Capt. Cuzack is ordered upon a cruise - New York item of 3 Feb. (19 Feb.)

B. Franklin has printed and sells The 24th Meditation of Dr. John Gerhard, translated from Latin into English, with notes, by the Rev. John Dylander, Minister of the Swedish Church at Wiccaco, near Phila. (19 Feb.)

Persons owing rents for land held of the Trustees of the Congregation Lands in the Burrough of Wilmington are to pay same at the house of Joshua Littler in Wilmington, by order of G. E. Folwell, clerk (19 Feb.)

Letter was read 20 Feb. at Council held in Phila. and attended by George Thomas, Samuel Preston, Clement Plumsted, Thomas Lawrence, Thomas Griffits, Anthony Palmer, Samuel Hasell and Ralph Asheton (26 Feb.)

The snow Francis, Capt. Cox, has arrived at Newcastle from Jamaica (26 Feb.)

Teague's Advertisement, signed A. Bradford, is in verse (26 Feb.)

Account of great fire at Charlestown, S.C., on 18 Nov. 1740; there is reference to house of Col. Brewton (5 Mar.)

BUSH, David, at his store in Wilmington - sells goods imported from London and Liverpool (5 Mar.)

CHANCELLOR, William, of Phila. - offers reward for recovery of a strayed colt (5 Mar.)

McLAUGHLIN, Capt. Henry, dec'd - accounts with estate are to be settled with the administrator, David Bush in Wilmington (5 Mar.)

BROOM, Thomas - has to let a commodious house for entertainment in Market St., Wilmington (5 Mar.)

PARR, Samuel, at his store in Water St., Phila. - sells items just imported from London (12 Mar.)

Accounts with William Atlee and Thomas Hooten, of Trenton, whose partnership was dissolved in December 1739 - are to be settled; William Atlee proposed with John Dagworth, Jr., to continue a store at Trenton (12 Mar.)

WHARTON, Joseph - has hay for sale (12 Mar.)

Sloop _Fanny_ and _Molly_, Robert Goulding master, at the
Walnut St. wharf - will sail for Virginia and Maryland;
for freight or passage agree with Andrew Farrel, tanner,
in Chesnut St., or with the master on board (12 Mar.)

GRISCOM, Sarah, of Phila. - wishes account with her to be
settled; she lives back of Thomas Byles, pewterer, in
Market St., or near the Boar's Head, in Jones's (or
Pewter Platter) Alley (12 Mar.)

Ship _Robert_, Lawrence Dent commander, at Walnut St. wharf
- will sail for London; for freight or passage agree
with Edward Bridges at the Scales or with the master on
board (12 Mar.)

By the brigantine _Swallow_, Capt. Hutchinson, from London
have come prints to 25 Dec. 1740 (19 Mar.)

Ship _Samuel_, George Bere master, at Edward Warner's wharf
- will sail in 10 days for South Carolina; for freight
or passage agree with Benjamin Shoemaker, merchant, in
Market St., Phila., or with the master on board (19
Mar.)

LEWIS, John, of Ridley, Chester Co. - offers for sale a
brick house on east side of Water St., Phila., now in
possession of Robert Hopkins (19 Mar.)

WHITEFIELD, Rev. - 16 Jan. went on board the _Minerva_, Capt.
Meredith master; Saturday last by a warrant he had to
appear before Mr. Whitaker, Chief Justice, for cor-
recting a letter published by Mr. Bryan, wherein he
hinted that the clergy of the Church of England break
their canons daily; Whitefield confessed and was released on bail - Charlestown item of 16 Jan. (26 Mar.)

CLARK, Capt., and Capt. Jefferson - arrived at Newport on
16 and 17 Feb. with news that Lord Cathcart died 24
Dec. at Dominica, that the _Revenge_, Capt. Berry, took
a prize, as did Capt. Davidson; Capt. Powers brought
away 50 Negroes from Oroonoque; Capt. Still, who arrived 19 Feb. at Newport, informs that he met Capt.
Buston from Gibraltar bound to South Carolina - letters from Newport of 19 and 27 Feb. (26 Mar.)

LOGAN, William (eldest son of James Logan, Esq.) - Tuesday last married Mrs. Hannah Emlen at Phila. (26 Mar.)

WRIGHT, Capt. - is arrived in England (26 Mar.)

BUNTING, William, of Montgomery, Phila. Co. - Sunday
evening he and his nephew (age 12) were bound by 2

men; the men knocked down Mr. Bunting, who died in a
few hours, and robbed his store; the murderers are
supposed to be Philip Cane and Lawrence Calaghan, who
were apprehended in Phila.; one Alexander Gregory, a
tailor by trade, is supposed to be concerned in the
crime (26 Mar.); Friday last Philip Cane cut his throat
and died in the prison in Phila. (2 Apr.); Callaghan
was executed 22 Apr. (23 Apr.)

NEAVE, Joel, at Samuel Neave's store, opposite Fishbourn's
wharf, sells goods just imported from London in the
brigantine <u>Swallow</u>, Thomas Hutchinson master (26 Mar.)

BROWN, Michael, silk-dyer from London - lives next door
to Joshua Emlen, tanner, in Chesnut St., Phila. (26
Mar.)

LLOYD, Thomas, opposite to John Dilwyn's in Phila. - will
sell time of parcel of indentured servants from Bristol
(26 Mar.)

OKIL, George - at his store at Israel Pemberton's wharf in
Phila. - sells goods just imported from Liverpool (26
Mar.)

Tract of about 100 acres near Point-No-Point, bounded on
the north with John Oxley's and William Rawle's land,
on the west with Thomas Chalkley's, on the east with
the meadows at Point-No-Point (26 Mar.)

HARRIS, George, servant, West-Countryman, age c. 26 -
runaway from Jonathan Peasley, chocolate-grinder, near
the church, Second St., Phila. (26 Mar.)

MARSHALL, Christopher, next door to the Bird in Hand in
Chesnut St., Phila. - sells glass, paints, lead (26
Mar.)

Parcel of servants imported from Bristol in the brigantine
<u>Catharine</u> <u>and</u> <u>Mary</u>, William Greenaway master, now off
Chesnut St. wharf; enquire of John Fisher, merchant,
in Water St., Phila. (2 Apr.)

JOHNSTON, James, of Alenstown, Monmouth Co., West New
Jersey - offers reward for arrest of John Abbernathy,
age c. 20, who ran away with effects of considerable
value (2 Apr.)

Ship <u>Loyal</u> <u>Judith</u>, John Lemon master, now at Samuel Austin's
wharf - will sail for South Carolina; for freight or
passage agree with the master or with Benjamin Shoemaker, merchant, in Market St., Phila. (2 Apr.)

HICKS, Benjamin, servant, West-Countryman, age <u>c</u>. 26 -
runaway from Henry Smith's plantation at Tulpahocken -
reward if he is brought to Phila. will be paid by his
master or by Edward Shippen of Phila. (2 Apr.)

Ship <u>Concord</u>, Obadiah Browne master, at Thomas Griffits
wharf - will sail for Bristol; for freight or passage
agree with Thomas Griffits at his house in Water St.,
Phila., or with the master on board (2 Apr.)

WILLY, Peter, Irish servant, age <u>c</u>. 20, glover by trade -
runaway from Abraham Emmit; reward will be paid if
servant is brought to his master or to Benjamin Davis,
Esq., in Chester (2 Apr.)

Account of prizes taken by Capt. Drummond, commander of
the <u>George</u>; he fitted out one prize and put it under
the command of Capt. Sibbald (9 Apr.)

SMYTER, Capt., from London - has got safely to South
Carolina (9 Apr.)

The <u>Querists</u>, by Samuel Blair - has been printed and is
sold by B. Franklin (9 Apr.)

<u>Christ Triumphing, and Satan Raging</u>, by Samuel Finley -
will soon be published (9 Apr.)

LEWIS, Amos - will sell 208-acre plantation in Haverford
Twp., Chester Co. (9 Apr.)

REDWITZER, John, tailor, in Plymouth Twp., Phila. Co.,
dec'd - accounts with estate to be settled with Katherine Redwitzer, executrix (9 Apr.)

FOGG, Samuel, at store next to Mr. Bridges in Water St.,
Phila. - sells cloth imported from London (9 Apr.)

BURN, Matthew, native Irish servant - runaway from Wil-
liam Branson's Furnace, called Reading, in Nantmel Twp.,
Chester Co.; reward for his capture will be paid by
Francis McConnal in Phila.; Burn is supposed to have
gone in company with Bryan Kennedy, Irish servant of
George Lion, of Nantmel Twp. (9 Apr.)

DELAGE, Peter, over against James Steel's, in Second St.,
Phila. - sells sugar and tea (9 Apr.)

MOORE, Charles, of Phila. - will not pay debts contracted
in future by his wife Mary (9 Apr.)

MILES, James, of Radnor, Chester Co. - has at his plantation a black mare (9 Apr.)

CALLAHAN, Lawrance - Monday last in Phila. pleaded guilty
    of murder of William Bunting and was sentenced to death
    (16 Apr.)

MORGAN, Evan, shopkeeper, in Market St., Phila. - desires
    persons indebted to him to make payment (16 Apr.)

Reward will be paid at the printer's for return of a pocket
    book lost at Mr. Hays at Kensington; it contained bills
    and an account with Mr. Johnson (16 Apr.)

Plantation of 160 acres in Lower Dublin, Phila. Co., for
    sale; enquire of Joseph Boore at said plantation (16
    Apr.)

BETHEL, Capt. - arrived last week at New York from Jamaica
    - New York item of 20 Apr. (23 Apr.)

CUMMINGS, Rev. Archibald, Commissary of Pennsylvania and
    the Counties on Delaware and Minister of Christ Church,
    Phila. - died Sunday last in Phila. (23 Apr.)

Brigantine Lucy, John Lindsay master, at Samuel Austin's
    wharf - will sail for South Carolina from Phila.; for
    freight or passage agree with Peter Bard or the master
    (23 Apr.)

PROT, William, dec'd - his house at Evesham Twp., Burling-
    ton Co., will be sold at auction (23 Apr.)

ANDERSON, John - will sell a 200-acre tract, within 2
    miles of a mill and 10 acres of marsh in Greenwich Twp.,
    West New Jersey (23 Apr.)

HOLT, Thomas, Irish servant, age c. 28, joiner - runaway
    from James Baldwin, Bristol Twp., Phila. Co. (23 Apr.)

McGLACHON, Charles, servant, Highlandman born (who was
    whipped at Dover for stealing a sheep and listed with
    Capt. Jenkins at Newcastle) - runaway from Charles
    White and Robert Gray (23 Apr.)

OUNGESS, Thomas, servant, Irishman born, who came in
    last fall to Messrs. Davy and Carson - same as above

MURRAY, William, tailor, in Manor of Moreland, 2 miles
    from Fletcher's mill, on road between Phila. and New-
    town - buys rags (23 Apr.)

FARMER, Capt. - arrived Saturday last at New York from

London - New York item of 27 Apr. (30 Apr.)

LEACRAFT, Capt. - arrived 26 Apr. at New York from Jamaica (30 Apr.)

BEACH, Capt. John, some time ago master of a Palatine ship - arrived this winter at St. Christophers; 170 souls died in the passage and those that survived remain at St. Christophers (30 Apr.)

SHEWBART, John - intends next month to remove from the London Coffee House near Carpenter's wharf to the house in Hannover Square, about half a mile from the River Delaware, between Mulbery St. and Sassafras St. in Phila. (30 Apr.)

MORRIS, Samuel - offers to let his fulling-mill in Upper Dublin, Phila. Co., near the great road from North Wales to Phila.; apply to Samuel Morris near said place or to Jonathan Ingham, fuller, in Solebury, Bucks Co. (30 Apr.)

A lot opposite to the Quaker Meeting-house in Germantown and 2 others at the upper end of said town are to be sold at auction; enquire of Dirk Johnson, Thomas Brown, Thomas Rose and John Johnson (30 Apr.)

ROBISON, John, Irish servant, age c. 18, weaver - runaway from Thomas Rogers of Nottingham, Chester Co.; reward will be paid if the servant is brought to his master or to Owen Owen, Esq. (30 Apr.)

SPENCER, William, dec'd - plantation belonging to his estate on the River Delaware, about a mile and a half above Trenton - offered for sale; apply to the executors, Henry Carter and Joseph Yard, living in Trenton (30 Apr.)

School is taught by Charles Fortescue at Chester, Pa.; proposals may be sent to him or to John or James Mather, all of Chester (30 Apr.)

KENNY, William Irish servant, age c. 23 - runaway from John Harvey of Mansfield Twp., Burlington Co., West New Jersey (30 Apr.)

HARMON, Capt. - arrived 26 Apr. at Boston from England (7 May)

The Mercury, a Dutch sloop from Curacoa - arrived at New York last week to get provisions; it had news of Admiral Vernon and Admiral Ogle (7 May)

BRYANT, Capt. - arrived 3 May at New York from London, with news that Capt. Cornel, in a Phila. ship bound to Cork, was cast away off the coast of Ireland and that Capt. Prizgar, in a brigantine belonging to Phila., from Cork, was taken by a Spanish privateer (7 May)

PENISTOR, Capt. - just now arrived at Phila. from Jamaica with news from the West Indies (7 May)

HARTLEY, Charles - sells European goods at one of Mr. Samuel Powel's stores, below the drawbridge in Phila. (7 May)

POTTS, Jonathan - offers reward for recovery of horse stolen from him at Plymouth Twp., Phila. Co. (7 May)

MANSFIELD, James, servant, age c. 18 or 19 - runaway from Stephen Vidal, schoolmaster in Phila. (7 May)

DAMPSEY, Margaret, Irish servant, age c. 18 - runaway from William Hall, living in Chesnut St., Phila. (7 May)

Parcel of English servant men, just imported in the ship Minerva, Capt. Forrest - their times are to be sold by John Inglis, who has removed his store from his house below the drawbridge to the store formerly Mr. Wrag's in Front St., Phila., opposite to Joseph Shippen's (7 May)

SCOTTEN, Samuel, English servant, age c. 20 - runaway from Benjamin Bradford, living at the head of Bohemia, in Caecil Co., Md. (7 May)

ESDAILE, James, at Carpenter's wharf - offers for sale 3 Negroes (7 May)

Cloe, Negro slave - runaway from John Burn in Water St., Phila., near the Tun Tavern (7 May)

HAINS, William, young servant - runaway from Martin Ryerson, of Reading Twp., Hunterdon Co. (7 May)

WILLIAMS, William, Welch servant, age c. 50 - runaway from Joseph Williams, of Merion, Phila. Co.; reward offered for return of servant to his master or to Richard Hughes, innkeeper, Philadelphia Road (7 May)

ASPDIN, Matthias - desires all accounts with him to be settled (7 May)

NORRY, Robert, Irish servant, age c. 20, who may pass for a pewterer - runaway from Robert Mackey; reward will be paid if the servant is brought to James Macky, merchant, in Front St., Phila. (7 May)

Free school of Kent Co. in Chester Town, on Chester River - is taught by Theophilus Grew and James Houston (7 May)

Account of military action at Cartagena (14 May)

BULLOCK, John, of Phila., cooper - Monday last murdered his wife (14 May)

HYATT, John, next door but one to the Sign of the Bible in Front St., Phila. - sells metalwares (14 May)

BRADLEY, Darby, Irish servant, age c. 18 - runaway from Edward Woodward, of Newtown, Chester Co. (14 May)

McGRAY, Nicholas, Irish servant, age c. 26 - runaway from John Dabbin, of Phila., blacksmith (14 May)

DAILY, Andrew, Irish servant - runaway from Joshua Brick, of Salem Co. (14 May)

FRANKS, Moses and David, Phila. - sell green and bohea tea (21 May)

Servant men are to be disposed of on board the brigantine Expedition, George Knight master, near the wharf of Thomas Griffitts in Phila. (21 May)

Swift Galley, Edmund Smyter master, will sail for London - for freight or passage agree with William Till or said master (21 May)

GOVETT, Joseph, of Phila. - offers reward for capture of Warwick Randal, who hired a horse of Govett but has not returned it (21 May)

Since August a brown mare has been at the plantation of Andrew Miller in Lancaster Co., within 3 miles of Newtown by the side of great Conestogo Creek (21 May)

JONES, Isaac, in Arch St., Phila., opposite the Sign of the George - sells cloth and other goods imported from London and Bristol (21 May)

BUSH, David, of Wilmington - will dispose of parcel of servants imported from Cork in the snow Ann and Mary, Samuel Hodson master (21 May)

WILKINSON, Anthony, ship-carver in Water St., Phila., just

above Arch St. - does mason work (21 May)

SHAW, John, at his store on Fishbourn's wharf, Phila. -
sells woolen goods (21 May)

Ship <u>Francis and Elizabeth</u>, Walter Goodman master - will
sail for Corke; for freight or passage agree with the
master at the Ship-a-ground in Front St., Phila. (21
May)

THOMAS, Samuel - offers reward for recovery of a horse
strayed or stolen from the plantation of Abednego
Thomas (21 May)

HAYES, John, Irish servant, age <u>c</u>. 26 - runaway from William Dallam, in Baltimore Co., Md., near Town of Joppa
(21 May)

Plantation of 315 acres, adjoining the Manor of Perkassee,
Bucks Co., about 30 miles from Phila. - will be sold
at auction by Cornelius Bryant (21 May)

POLE, John, at his store opposite to the Tun Tavern in
Water St., Phila. - sells cloth and other items im-
ported in the ship <u>Constantine</u>, Capt. Wright, from
London (21 May)

SPAFFORD, William, in Front St., Phila. - has a Negro for
sale (21 May)

MACANAPPIT, Philip Dennis, supposed to be a runaway, who
says he came from a place called Peach Bottom near Maryland - is taken up and secured in Phila. Goal (21 May)

CUTLER, Capt., who sailed from Virginia last December
with a load of wheat and Indian corn, designed for Boston - was driven out of his course to Madeira; there
the people were nearly starving and bought his cargo
at high prices (21 May)

PITTS, William of Bermuda, a prisoner on board the <u>St.
John</u> privateer sloop, Capt. Lewis commander - reports
that the <u>St. John</u> took the following prizes: the sloop
<u>Dolphin</u>, Solomon Sturges master; the ship <u>Brumsdon</u>,
John Simpson master, from White Haven; the sloop <u>Ranger</u>,
Isaac Johnson of Boston, from Virginia; the ship
<u>America</u>, Robert Kitchin master, from Glascow; the sloop
<u>Minion</u>, of Boston, from North Carolina - New York item
of 25 May (28 May)

Sloop <u>Victory</u>, Capt. Sibbald (the same that Capt. Drummond took from the Spaniards) - arrived Sunday last at

Phila.; he told of engagement with a Spanish ship and
a Spanish sloop, during which James Pearel was shot
and died 7 days later; Robert Wood had a piece of his
hat shot out (28 May)

Bay mare has come to the plantation of George Edges of
Upper Providence Twp., Chester Co. (28 May)

GEOGHEGAN, Edward, at his store at George Claypoole's, near
the Coffee House in Front St., Phila. - sells woolen and
other items imported in the ship Palm Tree from Dublin
and Great Britain (28 May)

ROGERS, Thomas, servant, age c. 21 or 22, tailor - runaway
from the ship Adriatick, Christopher Huddy master; reward will be paid if servant is brought to Thomas
Lloyd (28 May)

Bay mare has come to plantation of William Carpenter, of
New Garden, Chester Co. (28 May)

Parcel of Scotch servants, imported in the brigantine
Blessing, Capt. John Gordon, from Aberdeen - to be
disposed of by John Sober, next door to Charles Willing's
in Front St., Phila., or by Capt. Gordon on board his
vessel off Walnut St. wharf (28 May)

YELDHALL, John, dec'd - house and lot in Sassafras St.,
between Third and Fourth Streets, belonging to his estate are to be sold; apply to Susannah Yeldhall, administratrix, or Richard Pitts, silversmith, in Front
St., Phila. (28 May)

Bard and Lawrence, Jr., at their store in Water St.,
Phila., opposite to Thomas Lawrence's - sell goods just
imported from London in the ship Constantine (28 May)

BENEZET, J. Stephen, at upper end of Second St,, Phila. -
sells tea, cloth, etc. (28 May)

GOODENOUGH, John, English servant - runaway from Thomas
Mullan, of Phila. (28 May)

House, late in occupation of Abel Armstrong, for many
years a tavern, at Christiana Bridge, is for sale -
apply to Dr. Jones (28 May)

HUBBERT, Capt. - arrived Friday last at New York from Jamaica; he met on 6 May at sea Capt. Jenings, who told
him that Cartagena had surrendered; Capt. Hubbert left
Capt. Hill at Jamaica - New York item of 2 June (4 June)

Two Negro men were burnt Saturday last at New York; one confessed he set fire to the governor's house and the other to Mr. Philip's warehouse - New York item of 2 June (4 June)

DUFFIELD, Benjamin, of Phila. - accounts with his estate to be settled with the executors, Joseph Duffield, Edward Bradley, Thomas Whitten (4 June)

ANNAND, Alexander, in Second St., near the church, in Phila. - sells books (4 June)

Plantation of 146 acres in Fallowfield Twp., Chester Co., formerly property of Thomas Cox, taken in execution at the suit of John White and Abraham Taylor - will be sold at auction by Sheriff Benjamin Davis at house of Archibald McNeils in Kennet (4 June)

VINCENT, Ambrose, at Fishbourn's wharf, in Phila. - sells wines, rum, sugar, gunpowder, etc. (4 June)

A Short Reply to Mr. Whitefield's Letter - has just been published by B. Franklin (4 July)

ROBINSON, Charles, of Newcastle Co. - his wife Mary has eloped from him (4 June)

BLEAKLEY, William, at lower corner of Market St., Phila. - sells brown and white linens (4 June)

MORGAN, John, from Bristol, at his store over against the Blue Anchor in Water St., Phila. - sells cloth, glass, earthenware, snuff (4 June)

JOHNSTON, Francis, of New London Twp., Chester Co. - offers reward for recovery of strayed or stolen horse (4 June)

Some Remarks upon the Times - just published and sold by B. Franklin (4 June)

A house and lot in Darby, over the mill-race, are for sale; enquire of Thomas Tatnal (4 June)

McGUIRE, Patrick, Irish servant, age c. 22 - runaway from John Bleakley in Water St., Phila. (4 June)

Vessel belonging to James George, of Posquotank, was taken 13 May by a Spanish privateer - item from Virginia Gazette of 22 May (11 June)

Ship America, Capt. Ricksy, from Glasgow - was taken 11

May off our capes by a Spanish sloop (11 June)

Ship Cumberland, from Whitehaven, escaped a privateer and
   is at Nomini (11 June)

Ship Dragon, Capt. Ticehurst, is arrived in York River
   from South Carolina (11 June)

BLAIR, Hon. President - 21 May received a letter from Gov.
   Johnston of North Carolina concerning Spanish privateers on that coast (11 June)

Spanish prisoner states that St. Augustine is blocked up
   by the Indians on General Oglethorpe's order and that
   since Capt. Knowles took the pay-ship with 200,000
   pieces of eight on board, only small vessels are sent
   out from Havana - Frederica in Georgia item of 16 May
   (11 June)

On 10 May Capt. Richard Norbury, Capt. Albert Desbrisay
   and other officers of General Oglethorpe dined at St.
   Simons; Norbury and Desbrisay quarrelled, fought and
   both were wounded (11 June)

HAMMOND, Capt., in a vessel of Newport, R.I., who sailed
   from Phila. last fall for Jamaica - was cast ashore on
   Hispaniola; Hammond died; Capt. Hall set some of the
   men ashore at Cape Francois - Newport item of 28 May
   (11 June)

WICKHAM, Capt. - Tuesday last sailed in the Colony sloop
   after Spanish privateers - Newport item of 28 May (11
   June)

The Presbyterian Synod in Phila. excluded the Tennents
   and their adherents; Rev. Gilbert Tennent preached 5
   times on 31 May at Phila. (11 June)

On 12 June John Howson, his wife, his daughter and Margaret Cary are to be executed at New York (11 June)

Subscriptions sought for finishing the Charity School and
   House of Public Worship begun last year in Phila. -
   appeal is signed by Edmund Woolley, John Coats, Robert
   Eastburn, Jr., William Price and Edward Evans (11 June)

HOCKLEY, Richard, in Phila., is impowered by the heirs of
   Richard and Robert Vickeris to sell the following tracts
   of land in the counties of Phila. and Bucks: 32 acres
   of Liberty Land on the road from Schuylkill Road to
   Germantown; 250 acres on Wysahecon Creek near Robison's
   mill; 100 acres near the above; 264 acres in the Forks

of Delaware; 775 acres in the Forks, between the lands
of Ferinand John Paris, Esq., and Samuel Mickle; 483
acres between Thomas Jenny's and Samuel Overton's land
near the Fall of Delaware, on which one Tunnicliff is
seated (11 June)

BRYANT, Cornelius - his house and plantation adjoining the
Manor of Perkassee, Bucks Co., about 30 miles from
Phila. - will be sold at auction; for information apply
to James Steel in Phila. (11 June)

REEVE, John, in city of Burlington - sells dry goods, rum,
sugar and molasses (11 June)

Speech of John Wright, Esq., (one of the magistrates of
Lancaster Co.) - has just been published (11 June)

RYAN, John (who lately lived in Second St.) is removed to
Water St., Phila., to the house where Christopher Clymer lately lived (11 June)

Cloth just imported by James Ellis and James Wallace from
Liverpool is for sale at the house of John Barkley,
merchant, in Second St., Phila. (11 June)

A colt is taken up on the plantation of Gwen Ellis, of
Guyneed, Phila. Co. (11 June)

USHER, James, at one of the new buildings of White and
Taylor, between Chesnut and Walnut Sts., Phila. - sells
European goods (11 June)

BARKLEY, John, at the Sign of the Bible in Second St.,
Phila. - sells books and cutlery (11 June)

STANALAND, Thomas, near Bristol, Bucks Co. - offers reward for recovery of 2 geldings strayed or stolen out
of a pasture belonging to Seny Savage at the Free
Stonequary on Schuylkil; horses may be taken to Stanaland or to Thomas Croasdale at Frankford, 5 miles from
Phila. (11 June)

A Protestation to the Synod of Philadelphia - is printed
and sold by B. Franklin (11 June)

ROBINSON, Matthew, in Second St., Phila. - offers reward
for return of a horse strayed or stolen from the Commons of Phila. (11 June)

A Spanish privateer on 25 May took the following 3 vessels: ship Patuxent, John Shaw master, from Maryland
bound to London; the snow Argyle, John McCunn master,

from York River bound to Glasgow; and a New England
fishing boat (11 June)

Deposition made 1 June 1741 before Wilson Carey and Thomas
Mitchel at Elizabeth City by John McCunn, master of the
snow Argyle, and Henry Wadrop and Robert Barclay, seamen, and John Shaw, master of the ship Patuxent; McCunn
and Shaw crave a protest for all losses and damages (18
June)

HEUSTES, John, of New York, his wife and daughter, together with Margaret Cany, alias Newfoundland Peg, alias
Negro Peg, were tried and found guilty of considerating
with Negroes to burn New York and kill the inhabitants;
on Tuesday last Heustes, his wife and their servant
Margaret were executed; the daughter, aged c. 17 or 18,
was reprieved - New York item of 15 June (18 June)

Extract of letter from Capt. George Cunningham, commander
of the Jamaica Pacquet, dated 10 June (18 June)

NOBLE, Roger, English servant, age c. 30 - runaway from
Robert Miller, of Caln Twp., Chester Co. (18 June)

A mare has been some time at plantation of Benjamin Davies,
of Upper Merion, Phila. Co. (18 June)

William Clymer and Company, at Edward Warner's wharf, near
Arch St., Phila. - will sell time of a parcel of servants (18 June)

GOODENOUGH, John, English servant - runaway from Thomas
Mullan, of Phila. (18 June)

Two letters sent to his sister by Capt. Robert Hodshon,
who was appointed commander of the Musquetto Shore by
Gov. Trelawny of Jamaica (25 June)

Sloop Amiable Teresa, brought to Newport, R.I., as a prize
- was confiscated 11 June by a Court of Admiralty held
at Newport by Robert Auchmuty, Esq. (25 June)

An express from Capt. Ray of Block Island came 11 June to
the governor of Rhode Island about a Spanish snow; the
Colony sloop and Capt. Davidson's privateer were sent
in quest of the Spanish vessel (25 June)

Account from the New-England Weekly Journal of 12 May of
the suicide of Thomas Hall, age c. 25, resident with
Dr. Gott, at Marlborough, Mass.; Hall drank laudanum
and took opium pills and informed a neighbor, Mrs. Gore,
he had taken his "death's dose"; he died in a few hours
(25 June)

DAVIDSON, Capt. - defeated and took a French ship of
volunteers - Boston item of 15 June (25 June)

WARREN, Capt. - arrived at New York Saturday last from
Jamaica; he reported that Capt. Stevens and Capt. Cosby
from New York and Capt. Farmer and Capt. Thomas from New
Jersey are well; Capt. Hill was to sail from Jamaica a
few days after Capt. Warren - New York item of 22 June
(25 June)

On 12 June a Negro belonging to John Layer, Esq., of Albany
was executed there for having murdered a child of Conrad
Becker (25 June)

The father and 4 brothers of John Hueston (or Hewson) were
taken up and committed to the goal in Westchester on account of the Negro plot - New York item of 22 June (25
June)

Grand Masonic Lodge of Pennsylvania met 24 June at the Indian King in Phila.; Philip Syng was chosen Grand Master; Thomas Boude was appointed Deputy Grand Master and
Lambert Emerson and Thomas Bond Grand Wardens (25 June)

ROBERTS, Hugh - intends to remove with his Sign of the Pipe
into Market St., Phila., to the house where his father,
Edward Roberts, dec'd, lately dwelt, opposite the end of
the butchers stalls and Presbyterian Meeting-house (25
June)

HICKAY, John, servant, blacksmith - runaway from David Rees
and John Moore, of Radnor, Chester Co. (25 June)

SUTTON, Ashbury, of Annapolis - offers reward for recovery
of 4 silver spoons stolen from him; the silversmith's
mark is PS; three are marked A^{SE} and one M I (25 June)

MORGAN, Evan, shopkeeper, in Market St., Phila. - wishes
to have all accounts with him settled (25 June)

PITTS, David, born in England, servant, nailer - runaway
from on board the snow Ann and Mary, Samuel Hodson
master, at Wilmington; reward for capture of the servant will be paid by Samuel Hodson or David Bush in
Wilmington or Edward Bridges in Phila. (25 June)

The prize snow Princess of Orange will be sold at auction
on Mr. Hamilton's wharf in Phila. (25 June)

British forces before Carthagena have withdrawn (2 July)

TOWNLY, George, English servant, age c. 24 - runaway from

William Maugridge, of Phila., ship-joiner (2 July)

BURK, William, Irish servant, age c. 23 - runaway from
Thomas Stewart, at the head of Back Creek, Caecil Co.,
Md. (2 July)

McGILLAUGHAN, Michael, Irish servant, age c. 20 - same as
above

Dwelling house to be let at Christiana Bridge - enquire
of Francis James on part of the premises or Isaac Janvier, joiner, in Newcastle (2 July)

FALCONAR, Magnus, who teaches navigation in Front St.,
opposite to Pewter-Platter-Alley - has ready for the
press a supplement to Free Grace with a Witness (2
July)

Extracts of letters found on board a French sloop lately
brought into Rhode Island by Capt. Davidson, for exam-
ple from Mr. La Martier, Johair Mortagre and the
Chevalier Du Castet (9 July)

Execution of numerous Negroes in New York (9 July)

Ship Dursley Galley, William Neate commander - will sail
from Phila. as a privateer to Jamaica (9 July)

BOWMAN, Jacob - sundry cows will be sold at his house in
Germantown (9 July)

WHITELOCK, Isaac, at his store at Anthony Duche's in Front
St., Phila. - sells cloth and other items (9 July)

Negroes just imported from Barbados in the brigantine
Vernon, Arthur Burrows commander - are to be sold by
Dennis Leary at the Widow Richardson's in Front St.,
near the corner of Market St., Phila. (9 July)

Negroes, tea, indigo, cinnamon, sugar and capers are to
be sold at Mrs. Stapleford's in Second St., Phila. (9
July)

WRAGG, James, about to depart for London - wishes to sell
or let the house where he now dwells in Fifth St. near
Walnut St., Phila. (9 July)

A parcel of servants, just arrived at Phila. from Cork in
the snow Penguin, Robert Morris master, lying off Market St. wharf - will be sold by said master or Edward
Bridges at the Scales (9 July)

HENDERSON, Samuel, Irish servant, tailor - runaway from
his bail, James Sill, of Chester Co. (9 July)

LEWIS, Susannah, Welsh servant, age c. 20 - runaway from
Belchior Preston, of Phila. - reward will be paid if
she is brought to Joseph Scull in Phila. (9 July)

DRUMMOND, John, at Sassafras Ferry in Maryland - offers
reward for 2 Scots servants who ran away from the ship
Baltimore in Chester River, Maryland; they are named
Thomas Wilson, the other Stewart (alias James Borson)
(9 July)

HARBERT, William - offers reward for recovery of goods
stolen from him from the Almshouse in Phila., supposedly
by James Symmonds (alias Cyrus Symmonds), age above 60,
born in Somersetshire, England; Symmonds has been burnt
in the hand in Burlington and whipped in most towns in
Pennsylvania and the Jerseys (9 July)

MARSHALL, Samuel, dec'd - house, store house and goods of
the estate will be sold at auction by Sarah Marshall,
administratrix, at Newport on Christiana Creek in Newcastle Co. (9 July)

Reward offered by Emerson & Graydon for capture of Spanish
Indian man, age c. 30, a runaway from the snow Lancashire
Witch at Phila. (9 July)

CLARK, David, lately come from Pennypack Mill, who now
lives on Fifth St., near Walnut St., Phila. - as he intends for Europe he wishes all his accounts to be
settled (9 July)

SHERLEY, William - has been appointed Governor of Massachusetts (16 July)

WENTWORTH, Benning - has been appointed Governor of New
Hampshire (16 July)

At New York Hewson's daughter has been reprieved - New York
item of 13 July (16 July)

A Sermon upon Justification by Gilbert Tennent - has just
been published by B. Franklin (16 July)

ROBESON, Andrew - offers reward for recovery of horse
strayed or stolen from his pasture (16 July)

Reward is offered for recovery of a horse strayed or stolen
from Owen Owen's yard, at the Sign of the Indian King in
Phila. - horse may be brought to said Owen or to Owen

Jones, near Merion Meeting-house (16 July)

FARQUHAR, Alexander, dec'd - mill and land belonging to his estate in town of Dover, Kent Co. on Delaware, one mile from landing on St. Jones's Creek - will be sold by the executors, James and Mary Gorrell (16 July)

LONDERGAN, Larke, Irish servant, age c. 18 - runaway from on board James Gorrel's shallop, then at Phila. (16 July)

Land, late estate of Samuel James, commonly called Samuel James's or Arbitinton Iron-works - to be sold at auction at Christiana Bridge, Newcastle Co. upon Delaware (16 July)

CHOATE, John, Esq., of Ipswich - on Wednesday last was chosen Speaker of the House in Massachusetts; the governor, however, disapproved, so John Hobson, Esq., of Rowley, was chosen; Roland Cotton was chosen Clerk; (16 July)

Speech of Jonathan Belcher to the Massachusetts Assembly (23 July)

DAVIDSON, Capt., in the St. Andrew, privateer, is going to join Capt. Norton - Newport item of 9 July (23 July)

SMITH, George, in Arch St., Phila. - has a young Bermudian Negro wench for sale (23 July)

Two young servants, one a worsted-comber, dyer or clothier, the other a sadler, are for sale; enquire of George North or Samuel Burge in Chesnut St., Phila. (23 July)

CHAMPION, John, of Chesnut Hill in German-township - his wife Elizabeth has eloped from him (23 July)

FITZGERRALD, John, servant, age c. 24 - runaway from Samuel Patterson, of Pequa Creek, Lancaster Co., near John Varner, tavernkeeper (23 July)

HOPKINSON, Thomas, in Chesnut St., Phila. - sells sugar (23 July)

JONES, John, attorney, living in Salem, N.J. - has for sale tracts of land in Salem Co. (23 July)

A new ferry is erected at the mouth of Tohickan (23 July)

McCALL, Samuel - has for sale a parcel of Negro boys and girls (23 July)

WHITEHEAD, Edward, servant, age <u>c</u>. 30, fuller - runaway
from Ellis Davies, of Goshen, Chester Co. (23 July)

Sloop <u>Sally</u>, Darlow Marther master, from Madera - arrived
Saturday last at Charlestown, S.C.; he was taken by a
Spanish privateer but retaken by H.M.S. <u>Phaenix</u>, Capt.
Fanshaw; the privateer had also taken Capt. Ford -
Charlestown item of 4 July (30 July)

DUNN, Capt. - has just arrived at Charlestown from Winyaw
- Charlestown item of 4 June (30 July)

This week arrived in York River the snow <u>Seaflower</u>, Capt.
Edwards, from Guinea, with 159 slaves consigned to Col.
Braxton and son - Williamsburgh, Va., item of 10 July -
(30 July)

OGLE, Samuel, governor of Maryland - married 6 July Miss
Anne Tasker, daughter of Benjamin Tasker, President of
the Council of Maryland (30 July)

PEYTON, Sir Yelverton - on 9 July in the <u>Hector</u> man-of-war
returned to Kiquotan - Williamsburgh item of 17 July
(30 July)

Ship <u>Caesar</u>, Capt. Clarke, bound from York River to North
Carolina - about 5 days since was taken about 15 or 20
leagues to the south of Cape Henry - report from Norfolk (30 July)

EAGLETON, Capt. - arrived Saturday last at Boston from the
Bay of Honduras; he picked up at the Island of Aretan
2 of the crew of a sloop lately commanded by Capt. John
Wise; Capt. Eagleston put Capt. Davis in charge of a
sloop to bring it to Boston (30 July)

STURUP, Capt. - arrived Wednesday last at New York from
North Carolina (30 July)

BURCHAL, Capt. - arrived at New York in 25 days from Jamaica (30 July)

HEWSON, John - his daughter was again reprieved - New York
item of 27 July (30 July)

HOWELL, Jacob, of Chester - offers reward for recovery of
horse strayed or stolen (30 July)

TURNER, Peter, at the house lately Mr. William Preston's
in Front St., Phila. - intends for London and wishes
to settle all accounts (30 July)

MACARTY, Dennis, Irish servant, age c. 30 - runaway from
David Linsey, of Northampton Twp., Bucks Co. (30 July)

Tract of 100 acres near Manhatawny, Phila. Co., bounded
north by Manhatawny Rd., east by the manor of Proprietor John Penn, south by Evan Owen's land, northwest by
Evan Owen and John Pott's land (30 July)

WOOD, James, surveyor of Orange Co., living at Opecon, Va.
- has for sale 5,000 acres on south branch of the Potomack River (30 July)

FOX, Capt. G., in the privateer sloop Revenge - arrived 24
July at Newport, R.I.; about 3 weeks ago Capt. Dent
in the Hampton Court sent his lieutenant aboard the
Revenge and informed he was on an expedition with 10
other men-of-war - Newport item of 24 July (6 Aug.)

Colony's sloop, built by James Ward of Middleton, is at
New London, Conn.; she will sail in a few days - extract of letter from New London dated 9 July (6 Aug.)

URY, John, a Romish priest - was convicted Wednesday last
at New York of being concerned in the late conspiracy
- New York item of 3 Aug. (6 Aug.)

LEACRAFT, Capt. - arrived at New York Saturday last from
Jamaica with news from the West Indies - New York item
of 3 Aug. (6 Aug.)

TINGLE, Capt. - arrived 2 Aug. at New York from Georgia
with news that Capt. Rouse in a Boston privateer had
taken off Cape Fear a Spanish privateer (6 Aug.)

HAMILTON, Andrew, Esq. - died 4 Aug. and the next day was
interred at Bush Hill, his country seat - Phila. item
(6 Aug.)

OWEN, Owen, Esq., formerly High Sheriff and for many years
coroner of Phila. City and Co. - died 5 Aug. (6 Aug.)

List of ships taken during the war and carried to St. Jago
de Cuba: ship William, John Annis, from Phila.; sloop
Dispatch, Archibald Lewis from Boston; brigantine Success, James Cashman from Boston; sloop Elizabeth, Nicholas Garritsen from New York; snow George and Henry,
Stephen Seavy from Phila.; brigantine Union, Henry
Totness from New York; sloop Providence, Wm. Corbin
from Phila. - was retaken; sloop Fortune, John Wood from
Boston - extract of a letter from Jamaica dated 10 July
(6 Aug.)

EVANS, David, in Market St., Phila. - desires the return
of a case of drawing instruments taken from his back
room (6 Aug.)

WALDRON, Edward, scyth-maker in Darby, Chester Co. - offers reward for recovery of gelding and arrest of Benjamin Harvey, an Englishman, who stole the horse (6
Aug.)

GORDON, Robert, at Newcastle - offers reward for capture
of Daniel Kelly, age c. 26, who lived in East Jersey
and on 30 July escaped from Newcastle Prison (6 Aug.)

BURK, John, late of Phila., merchant - accounts with his
estate are to be settled with Simon Edgell and George
Dickinson, administrators (6 Aug.)

Remarks upon a Protestation and The Apology of the Presbytery of New Brunswick - both have just been published
by B. Franklin (6 Aug.)

OLIVER, John, Irish servant, age c. 25 - runaway from William Lynch, near the Crooked Billet, on York Rd., Phila.
Co. (6 Aug.)

BAYLY, Widow, in Phila. - has for sale 6 looms (6 Aug.)

GOOCH, Col., governor of Virginia - arrived Monday last
at York in the ship Buchanan, Capt. Crawford, from Jamaica (13 Aug.)

HARRINGTON, John (who had served under Capt. Beers at the
Hadley Fight), of Waltham, Middlesex Co., Mass. - died
there 17 July in his 90th year; his wife Hannah, to
whom he had been married 60 years, died the same day in
her 77th year; they left 11 surviving children and 160
grandchildren - Boston item of 30 July (13 Aug.)

Friday last at Andover, Mass., in the house of Joseph
Robinson, 2 young women were struck by lightning; one
died but the other recovered - Boston item of 28 July
(13 Aug.)

FOX, Capt. - Monday last his prize was condemned in the
Court of Vice Admiralty at Newport, R.I. - Newport item
of 31 July (13 Aug.)

STANTON, Capt. - Wednesday last arrived at Newport from
Jamaica with news from the West Indies - Newport item
of 31 July (13 Aug.)

BOYD, Capt., of the brigantine Jamaica Pacquet - arrived

9 Aug. at New York in 38 days from Bristol (13 Aug.)

Daily _Conversation_ _with_ _God,_ _exemplified_ _in_ _the_ _Holy_ _Life_
_of_ _Armelle_ _Nicholas_ (who died in Bretaigne in 1671) and
also _The_ _Art_ _of_ _Preaching_ - have just been published by
B. Franklin (13 Aug.)

WILKINSON, Anthony, of Phila. - offers reward for recovery
of a strayed mare and colt (13 Aug.)

HART, John, of Plumstead Twp., Bucks Co. - has taken up a
brown horse (13 Aug.)

SMYTON, Benjamin, at Mr. John Shallows near the bridge in
Phila. - has sundry goods for sale (13 Aug.)

ROSE, Aquila - his poems have just been published by his
son, Joseph Rose, at the New Printing Office near the
market in Phila. (13 Aug.)

ANDERSON, Robert, servant, age c. 30 - runaway from Lewis
Williams, of North Wales (13 Aug.)

FRANKLIN, Deborah - desires return of 2 books she lent a
month or 6 weeks ago (13 Aug.)

PENDARVIS, Capt., who arrived in 5 days at Charlestown,
S.C., from Providence - reports that a Spanish privateer near Crooked Island captured a Mr. Bullock and his
sloop - Charlestown item of 11 June (20 Aug.)

Wednesday last Capts. Surrey, Bazely, Winter and Paske
(with rice for the fleet) sailed from Charlestown to
Jamaica - Charlestown item of 11 June (20 Aug.)

DUNBAR, Capt. George, of General Oglethorpe's Regt. -
died at Augusta, Ga. - Charlestown item of 11 June (20
Aug.)

The mate of the _Crawford_, Capt. Ford, and other English
prisoners escaped from St. Augustine and arrived at
Frederica; the privateer that took them also took the
snow of Capt. Gould, bound to Virginia - Charlestown
item of 18 June (20 Aug.)

The Spaniards on the sloop lately re-taken by Capt. Charles
Fanshaw on Tuesday last were examined before Col. Fen-
wicke - Charlestown item of 18 June (20 Aug.)

The _Molly_, Capt. Murray, which sailed from Charlestown for
Providence - was taken 24 Jan. by a Spanish privateer
(20 Aug.)

TINKER, Gov. - has ordered 2 half-galleys for the service of his government - report from Providence, as printed in Charlestown item of 25 June (20 Aug.)

Account of escape of 3 Englishmen from St. Augustine, one of whom, John Lucas, belonged to the Ancona Merchant, taken in November by the Spaniards; it was reported that the privateer that took Capts. Ford, Gould and Marther was preparing to return to Havanna - Charlestown item of 2 July (20 Aug.)

OGLETHORPE, General - has fitted out his guard sloop and 2 privateers, commanded by Capts. Debrisay, Davis and Foster (20 Aug.)

The General Assembly of South Carolina have voted 5 pounds per head for Spaniards that may be taken by Capt. John Rouss, commander of the sloop Speedwell - Charlestown item of 23 July (20 Aug.)

CRAWFORD, John (part owner of the ship Crawford), who escaped with 3 men and a boy from St. Augustine - on 15 June were sent up by the officer of Fort William on Cumberland - Frederica in Georgia item of 13 July (20 Aug.)

Chigeley, Clawbalgee and other Indian chiefs on 10 July had audience of leave with General Oglethorpe (20 Aug.)

Speech of Gov. Belcher to the Massachusetts Assembly (20 Aug.)

On Saturday last H.M.S. Portland, Capt. Hawke commander, arrived at Boston from Barbados and the Province snow, Capt. Tyng commander, arrived at Boston from a cruise - Boston item of 10 Aug. (20 Aug.)

PENN, Hon. Thomas - set out 20 Aug. from Phila. for New York to embark on H.M.S. Squirrel, Capt. Peter Warren, for Great Britain (20 Aug.)

FALCONAR, Capt. Lester - arrived 19 Aug. at Phila. from St. Kitts; he had been taken by a Spanish privateer, as had a Capt. Ewers (20 Aug.)

The Psalms of David, initiated... - has just been published by B. Franklin (20 Aug.)

MARKS, Joseph, at his house in Walnut St., Phila. - has for sale Negroes lately imported from Barbados (20 Aug.)

GREEN, John, Irish servant, age c. 24, barber (of the late

John Gilbert's, barber, dec'd) - runaway from Robert Christie, of Phila. (20 Aug.)

HARPER, William, late of Phila., dec'd - accounts with estate to be settled with Alice Harper, executrix (20 Aug.)

NEDARMARKE, Conrad - has a colt that came to his plantation in Darby Twp., Chester Co. (20 Aug.)

SHERLEY, William, newly appointed Governor of Massachusetts - Friday last walked in procession from his seat in Newbury St. to the Province House, where late Gov. Belcher joined him; they proceeded to the Council Chamber, guarded by a troop of guards and Col. Winslow's Regt. of Militia (27 Aug.)

JAUNCEY, Capt. - arrived last week at New York from Jamaica; he had met the Tilbury, Capt. Long (27 Aug.)

LINDSEY, Capt. - arrived Friday last at Phila. from Providence (27 Aug.)

PARIS, Elizabeth, late of Phila., chandler, dec'd - accounts with estate to be settled with George Okill, executor (27 Aug.)

KOLLOCK, Shepard, of Lewestown, Sussex Co. - among articles stolen from him are a gold chain with a locket marked E. G.; 4 silver spoons marked M. G., the silversmith's mark PD; one ditto with "Hannah Burges" on the handle; one ditto marked I^{B}L.; one ditto marked S^{K}C; a child's spoon marked M.G.; a silver "scissars" chain marked on a heart M G (27 Aug.)

HASELL, Samuel, next door to the Bible in Front St., Phila. - offers reward for recovery of a gelding that strayed away (27 Aug.)

Tract of woodland of 200 acres in or near Plymouth Twp., 16 miles from Phila., bounded partly by the lands and plantations of William Roberts, Daniel Burne and the Widow Williams; apply to Hugh Tresse and Mary and Ann Tresse in Mulberry St. or William Rawle in Water St., Phila. (27 Aug.)

MORGAN, Darby, Irish servant, age c. 18 or 20 - runaway from Robert Lamborn, of London Grove Twp., Chester Co. (27 Aug.)

URY, John, Romish priest - executed Saturday last in New York - New York item of 31 Aug. (3 Sept.)

The following lots and tracts are to be sold or let by
Edward, Joseph and William Shippen: a water lot under
Society Hill, joining to Capt. Woodrop's wharf; a brick
house ¼ mile west from Society Hill; lots in a square
fronting Walnut St. and Fourth St.; about 8 acres on
Passyunk Road, over against William Tidmarsh's barn,
about ¼ mile to the south of Phila.; the Roe-Buck Tavern
in Germantown; 300 acres near Perkiomun, between the
lands of Joseph Pike and Isaac Debayes; 200 acres between Jacob Debayes, John Pauling's and Jacob Merly's
plantations and Bebbey Twp. (3 Sept.)

PAULING, Henry, of Perkiomum - offers reward for recovery
of his mare strayed from the plantation of Anthony
Nise (3 Sept.)

HARRISON, John, over the drawbridge in Phila. - offers for
sale rice, leather, cotton, sugar (3 Sept.)

Saturday last arrived at New York H.M.S. _Seahorse_, Capt.
Allen, with Capts. Hopkins and Winslow of Col. Gooch's
Regt.; they bring instructions from General Wentworth
to raise recruits - New York item of 7 Sept. (10 Sept.)

EVAN, William, age c. 27, who speaks Welch and English -
stole a mare from Jenkin Hugh, of Trediffryn in Chester
Co. (10 Sept.)

JOSEP, Abraham, age c. 24, a Yorkshire man, shoemaker -
runaway from James Hunt and Peter Elliot, of Kingsess,
Phila. Co. (10 Sept.)

Tom, a Negro - same as above

Claus, Negro, age c. 45, who speaks Dutch and English -
runaway from his master, Philip French, of New Brunswick, East New Jersey; reward offered if Negro is returned to his master or to Mr. Vanderspiegel in Phila.
(10 Sept.)

HADAY, Capt. - in a letter dated Cape Fear 7 July reports
his sloop was taken Sunday last, that an English privateer ship, Capt. Walker, has been fitted out; that the
Spaniards have taken a ship commanded by Capt. Dupuy,
bound from Boston to Charlestown - Charlestown item of
6 Aug. (17 Sept.)

PEACOCK, Capt. (who arrived at Cape Fear last week) reported seeing a Spanish privateer, with a schooner
(probably belonging to Capt. Thomas Henning) and a sloop
(probably belonging to Capt. Jonathan Skrine), both of
Winyaw; Capts. Skut and Wellon from Boston are supposed

to have been taken by the Spanish - extract of a letter dated Wilmington 21 July (17 Sept.)

Catherine, Mulatto wench of Francis Varambout, was convicted of setting fire to the house where Moses Mitchell
lives, the corner of Unity Alley fronting Union St., in
Charlestown; Mrs. Mitchell noticed the fire, which was
extinguished - Charlestown item of 6 Aug. (17 Sept.)

MAVERICK, Capt. Benjamin, commander of a schooner belonging to Isaac Mazuck, Esq., of Charlestown - reports how
Monday last he abandoned his vessel when a sloop which
he suspected was an enemy was about to take him -
Charlestown item of 6 Aug. (17 Sept.)

Negro man slave of John Garnier was executed Thursday last
at Charlestown; he, together with Kate, Negro slave of
Francis Varambaut, set fire to the house where Mrs.
Snowden lives; Jenny, an old Negro woman, gave evidence
against the 2 - Charlestown item of 15 Aug. (17 Sept.)

TOWNSHEND, Capt. George, of H.M.S. _Tartar Pink_ took a
Spanish privateer - Charlestown item of 22 Aug. (17
Sept.)

Friday last arrived at Charlestown Capt. Nicholas Legall
in the snow _Elizabeth_, Capt. Nath. Shaw, who relates
that his schooner was taken by the Spaniards, who later
put their captives into the snow _Elizabeth_ - Charlestown item of 22 Aug. (17 Sept.)

DABNEY, John, mathematical instrument maker from London -
has his shop in King St., Boston, Mass. (17 Sept.)

HYNDMARSH, John, of Phila., carpenter, dec'd - accounts
with his estate are to be settled with Elizabeth Hyndmarsh, executrix (17 Sept.)

Spanish privateer on Sunday last took Capt. Clack, Sr.,
near our Capes, in a ship bound from London to James
River, and then a ship bound from Plymouth to Maryland;
Capt. Goodman retook the Plymouth ship - Williamsburg
item of 11 Sept. (24 Sept.)

Capt. Warren and the Hon. Mr. Penn plan to set out Wednesday next from New Hampshire for Boston - Boston item
of 14 Sept. (24 Sept.)

FULLERTON, Capt. - arrived at Boston Friday last in 18 days
from Antigua - Boston item of 14 Sept. (24 Sept.)

The _American Almanack_ by John Jerman - is printed by B.

Franklin (24 Sept.)

COSTEGIN, Francis, of City of New Brunswick - offers reward for recovery of a bay horse (24 Sept.)

Brigantine **Sally**, John Evans master, lying at Mr. Plumsted's wharf - will sail for Barbados; for freight or passage agree with the master or with John Seymour at the Widow Stapleford's in Second St., Phila. (24 Sept.)

Brigantine **Nancy**, David Davis master, at Hamilton's wharf - will sail for Bristol; for freight or passage agree with Richard Hill, Jr., at Charles Willing's or with the master (24 Sept.)

Negro man, age <u>c</u>. 25 or 26 - runaway from Samuel Massey, of Newtown, Kent Co., Md. (24 Sept.)

STORY, Robert, late of Cecil Co., dec'd - real estate and other items belonging to his estate are to be sold or let by Mary Story, administratrix (24 Sept.)

Proclamation of George Thomas, governor of Pennsylvania and the Counties on Delaware: Capt. William Hopkins has been commanded by Brig.-Gen. Wentworth to levy troops in Pennsylvania (1 Oct.)

Connecticut sloop of war, Capt. Philips commander - returned to New London about a fortnight ago - Boston item of 21 Sept. (1 Oct.)

Last week arrived in Boston Capt. Winslow and Lt. Vryling from Cuba to raise recruits - Boston item of 21 Sept. (1 Oct.)

Privateer sloop **Young Eagle**, formerly commanded by Capt. Dumaresq - arrived at Boston Friday last from Gibraltar (1 Oct.)

HASELL, Samuel, Mayor of Phila. - on Tuesday last gave customary feast at the expiration of the mayoralty (1 Oct.)

COWLEY, Mary, on Society Hill (widow and administratrix of Matthew Cowley, skinner, dec'd) - continues to carry on the business of buckskin dressing (1 Oct.)

CULLEN, Mary, servant, age <u>c</u>. 30 - runaway from Alexander Lockhart, of Trenton (1 Oct.)

STENNARD, Joseph, of Northern Liberties of Phila. - offers reward for recovery of a mare (1 Oct.)

SANDS, John, of Bensalem Twp., Bucks Co. - has taken up a
  mare (1 Oct.)

WORMLEY, Henry, late of Phila., baker, dec'd - accounts
  with estate to be settled with Eleanor Wormley, executrix (1 Oct.)

REILY, James, Irish servant, age c. 30, weaver - runaway
  from William Selthridge of Cedar Creek, Sussex Co.;
  the servant stole his indenture, which was assigned
  over to Selthridge by Capt. Pardue, before 3 magistrates, 2 of whom were Mr. Kollock and Mr. Holt of
  Lewestown; one Patrick McClane went with him; they went
  to Muspillion Creek, where they broke the chain or lock
  of John Walton's canoe and took it with them (1 Oct.)

Ten Spanish prisoners brought to Virginia by Capt. Goodman
  are committed to prison in Williamsburg - Williamsburg
  item of 18 Sept. (8 Oct.)

OLIVER, Capt. - arrived at Boston Monday last in a ship
  from Jamaica - Boston item of 28 Sept. (8 Oct.)

Thirty prisoners, among them Capts. Clack and Anter, both
  from London, bound to Virginia - were put ashore Tuesday last on east end of Bermuda by a Spanish privateer;
  said privateer took Capt. North from Barbados - letter
  from Bermuda dated 17 Sept., cited in a New York item
  of 5 Oct. (8 Oct.)

Brigantine Violatta, W. Richards master, from Bristol -
  arrived Saturday last at New York with European news -
  New York item of 5 Oct. (8 Oct.)

On Thursday last the following were elected for Phila. Co.:
  representatives--John Kinsey, Isaac Norris, Robert
  Jones, Thomas Leech, Edward Warner, Joseph Trotter,
  Owen Evans, James Morris; sheriffs--Mordacai Lloyd,
  John Hyatt; coroners--Henry Pratt, John Jones; com-
  missioner--Evan Thomas; assessors--Jacob Livering,
  Jacob Rife, John Dilwyn, Thomas Flatcher, Jeremiah
  Elfrith, James Jones (8 Oct.)

On Thursday last the following were elected for Bucks Co.:
  representatives--John Hall, John Watson, Garret Van-
  sand, Jr., Benjamin Field, Abraham Chapman, Mahlon
  Kirkbride, Joseph Shaw, Mark Watson; sheriffs--Joseph
  Jackson, Joseph Yeates; coroners--John Hart, Abraham
  Chapman (8 Oct.)

On Thursday last the following were elected for Chester
  Co.: representatives--Joseph Harvey, Thomas Chandler,

James Gibbons, John Owen, Thomas Tatnal, Samuel Levis,
William Howes, Jeremiah Starr; sheriffs--Benjamin Davis,
John Davis; coroners--Aubrey Bevan, Samuel Bettle (8
Oct.)

On Thursday the following were elected for Lancaster Co.:
representatives--Thomas Lindley, John Wright, Samuel
Blunston, Anthony Shaw; sheriffs--James Mitchel, John
Galbraith; coroners--Joshua Low, Thomas Rannick (8 Oct.)

On Thursday last the following were elected for Newcastle
Co.: representatives--Thomas Noxon, John McCool, David
French, John Curtis, Benjamin Sweat, Jeremiah Woolaston;
sheriffs--Samuel Bickley, John Gooding; coroners--Henry
Goune, Benjamin Cook (8 Oct.)

On Thursday last the following were elected for Kent Co.:
representatives--James Gorrel, Mark Manlove, Thomas
Skedmore, Joseph Downing, James Morris, William Barnes;
sheriffs--Samuel Robinson, Thomas Green; coroners--Ed-
ward Badger, Benjamin Johnson (8 Oct.)

On Thursday last the following were elected for Sussex Co.:
representatives--Jabez Maud Fisher, John Rhoads, James
Kollock, John Clowes, Joseph Shankland, Abraham Wynkoop;
sheriffs--William Shankland, Peter Hall; coroners--
Peter Clowes, Robert Smith (8 Oct.)

Friday last the following were chosen for Phila. City:
burgesses--Israel Pemberton, Oswald Peel; assessors--
Philip Syng, Richard Parker, Joseph Oldman, John Stamper, Edmund Wodey, Jonathan Zane (8 Oct.)

KEITH, Alexander Henry (son of Sir William Keith, late
Lt.-Gov. of Pennsylvania), for several years Collector
of Customs at Newcastle on Delaware - died Monday last
at the seat of his father-in-law, Anthony Palmer (8 Oct.)

On Tuesday last Clement Plumsted, Esq., was elected Mayor
of Phila.; Robert Strettell, William Parsons, William
Rawle, Thomas Hopkinson, Samuel Rhodes and Andrew Hamilton (son of Andrew Hamilton, Esq., lately dec'd) were
chosen members of the Common Council; the following
were promoted aldermen: William Till, Joseph Turner,
James Hamilton and Benjamin Shoemaker (8 Oct.)

BRIDGES, Edward, late of Phila., merchant, dec'd - accounts
with estate to be settled with Cornelia Bridges, executrix (8 Oct.)

TOMPSON, Hannah, English servant - has run away (8 Oct.)

GATCHELL, Elisha, Jr. - offers reward for recovery of a
mare (8 Oct.)

BROWNE, Isaac - will sell or let about 300 acres on Franck-
ford Rd., 3½ miles from Phila. (8 Oct.)

HOOPES, Nathan, of East Bradford, near the Forks of Brandewyne - offers reward for recovery of his horse, supposed to be stolen by Joseph Jenning, a tailor (8 Oct.)

RICHMOND, Capt. John, for 30 years commander of vessels
from Phila. - died yesterday at Phila. in his 59th
year (15 Oct.)

KINSEY, John, Esq. - yesterday was chosen Speaker of the
Pennsylvania House (15 Oct.)

GUNN, Augustus, Bellman of the City of Cork, Ireland -
procures servants for America (15 Oct.)

Sloop Dolphin, Michael Dumaresque master, at Mr. Fishbourn's wharf; for freight or passage agree with Peter
Baynton at his store in Front St., Phila., or with the
master (15 Oct.)

THOMPSON, Thomas, late of Newcastle, dec'd - a lot of
ground in Newcastle and a smith's shop and stable in
Market St., opposite to the Court House, part of the
estate of the dec'd - to be sold by Francis Janvier
and John McGha, executors (15 Oct.)

Ship Bacchus, Charles Hartley master, at Samuel Powell's
wharf - will sail for Jamaica; for freight or passage
agree with said master at Capt. William Bell's, below
the drawbridge (15 Oct.)

Snow Molly, Cornelius Bowne master - will sail for London;
for freight or passage agree with Thomas Lawrence (15
Oct.)

BRYAN, Michael, Irish servant, age c. 26, a sawyer - runaway from James Casey, of Marcus Hook, Chester Co. (15
Oct.)

By Capt. John Murray, Benjamin Paine and Thomas Poole (one
of the pilots of Charlestown Harbour) comes the information that they, with a boy named William Bridges, concealed on a French sloop commanded by Capt. Declare,
escaped from Havana on 3 Sept.; the sloop sank and they
got into a small boat; on 13 Sept. they saw 2 sails,
Capts. Smith and Chadsey, both from Bristol bound to
Charlestown; Capt. Smith took them up - Charlestown

item of 26 Sept. (22 Oct.)

WAINFORD, Nathaniel - his store in Mill Creek Hundred, Newcastle Co. on Delaware was broken open and many items stolen, including a silver snuffbox, shaped like a book, marked on the inside of the lid with R.R. (22 Oct.)

A white horse was left at the Indian King in Newcastle by John Richardson, who sailed with Capt. Neat for Jamaica (22 Oct.)

CROSTHWAITE, William, peruke-maker in Front St., Phila. - has a horse for sale (22 Oct.)

Ship Marlborough, Thomas Bell, master, now at Samuel Austin's wharf - will sail from Phila. for South Carolina; for freight or passage agree with Benjamin Shoemaker or the master (22 Oct.)

SULLIVAN, Andrew, native Irish servant, age c. 21 - runaway from Lleweling Davis and Job Harvey, both of Charlestown, Chester Co., Pa. (22 Oct.)

LOONEY, Edward, native Irish servant, age c. 16 - same as agove

The New-Jersey Almanack for the Year 1742, by William Ball - is printed by B. Franklin (22 Oct.)

Corner lot in Phila., 17 feet front in Second St., and 70 feet in Mulberry St. - offered for sale by William Ballard in Second St. (22 Oct.)

THOMPSON, Capt., commander of the Success man-of-war - Wednesday last a rich prize he had taken arrived at Boston - Boston item of 19 Oct. (29 Oct.)

Ship Rubie, Thomas Nicholson master, now at Israel Pemberton's wharf in Phila. - will sail for Antigua or Barbados (29 Oct.)

Ship Wilmington, William Stewart master, now at Bush's wharf in Wilmington - will sail for Belfast; for freight or passage agree with David Bush at his house or the master (29 Oct.)

Snow St. Lawrence, William Shagnessy master, now at Mr. Ryan's wharf - will sail for Barbados; for freight or passage agree with Edmund Nihell at Mr. John Ryan's in Water St. or with the master (29 Oct.)

Sloop Samuel and Mary, William Mash master - will sail for

336

Cape Fear; for freight or passage agree with the master
or John Hyatt (29 Oct.)

An Account of the Money received and disbursed for the
Orphan House in Georgia, by the Rev. Mr. George Whitefield - sold by B. Franklin (29 Oct.)

BOND, Dr. Phineas - all persons indebted to him are to make
payments to Thomas Bond, who is removed to the Sign of
the Golden Mortar in Second St., Phila., a little below
the Quaker Meeting-house (29 Oct.)

Three-fourths of the brigantine Globe, William Trimble master, now at Thomas Griffitt's wharf, belonging to the
estate of John Bourk, lately dec'd - to be sold by
George Dickinson and Simon Edgell, administrators (29
Oct.)

KEMP, William, English servant, age c. 27, wool-comber -
runaway from Samuel Hill, of New Garden, Chester Co.
(29 Oct.)

Plantation late of John Moore, Esq., dec'd, in Miamenson -
will be sold by John Dobbins, administrator (29 Oct.)

WAKELY, Robert, at the house of George Claypole, joiner,
next door but one to the Coffee House in Front St.,
Phila. - sells ratteens, frizes, blankets, etc. (29
Oct.)

Brigantine Nancy, David Davis master, at Hamilton's wharf
in Phila. - will sail for Bristol; for freight or passage agree with Richard Hill, Jr., at Charles Willing's
or the master (29 Oct.)

Ship Rundel, Robert Nutt master, now lying in Christiana
Creek - will sail for Londonderry; for freight or passage agree with Messers. Davey and Carson at their
store over the drawbridge in Front St., Phila., or with
the master (29 Oct.)

Speech of Lt.-Gov. George Thomas to General Assembly of
Pennsylvania and the Counties on Delaware and reply to
him (5 Nov.)

TALCOTT, Joseph, Esq., governor of Connecticut for many
years - died on 11 Oct. in Hartford (5 Nov.)

SMITH, Capt., in a brigantine belonging to Boston - on
Friday last arrived at Boston from Barbados; on 17 Sept.
last he was taken by a Spanish privateer but on 26 Sept.
liberated by Capt. Norton in a Rhode Island privateer;

Capt. Smith, however, was taken a second time by a
Spanish ship - Boston item of 26 Oct. (5 Nov.)

WEBB, Joseph, of New Hanover (some years since Minister at
Newark, N.J.) and his son, a student at Yale College -
were drowned early last week in passing over the ferry
at Seabrook - Boston item of 26 Oct. (5 Nov.)

DYLANDER, Rev. John, Pastor of the Swedish Church at Wicaco, near Phila. - died Monday last (5 Nov.)

Mr. Whitefield's Journal - sold by B. Franklin (5 Nov.)

SCHOLEY, John, of New Hanover, Burlington Co., West New
Jersey - offers reward for recovery of a stolen gelding
(5 Nov.)

Imported goods offered for sale by John Ryan and Edmund
Nihell at Ryan's house in Water St., Phila. (5 Nov.)

BULLER, Alexander, at the Public School in Strawberry Alley, Phila. - teaches mathematics, accounting, navigation (5 Nov.)

Ship Concord, Obadiah Bowne master - will sail from Phila.
for Madeira; for freight or passage agree with Thomas
Griffitts and Company or William Till at their houses
in Water St. (5 Nov.)

Brigantine Charming Betsy, Hugh Tresse master, at Thomas
Griffitt's wharf in Phila. - will sail for Barbados;
for freight or passage agree with Simon Edgel or the
master (5 Nov.)

TAYLOR, Abraham (whose partner, John White, has gone to
England), intending for England - offers for sale the
Bank House in which he now lives, opposite to Carpen-
ter's wharf in Phila. (5 Nov.)

Ship William and James, William Woodlock master - will
sail for Belfast; for freight or passage agree with
Patrick Agnew, at Thomas Robinson's, merchant, in
Front St., Phila., or the master (5 Nov.)

Fisher's Island, containing about 300 acres, near the
mouth of Schuylkill - is offered for sale by John and
Jonathan Paschal, executors to John Fisher, dec'd (5
Nov.)

THOMPSON, Capt., of H.M.S. Success - on 23 Oct. met a
sloop, Ebenezer Clark master (owned by Josiah Thompson
of New Haven, Conn.), 80 leagues east of Cape Ann, from

Belfast, Ireland; many on the sloop died of starvation
- Boston item of 2 Nov. (12 Nov.)

McNEAL, Capt. - arrived last week at Boston from the Bay
of Honduras with news that Commodore Anson had taken
Panama City - Boston item of 2 Nov. (12 Nov.)

BULLOCK, John - was executed Saturday last in Phila. for
the murder of his wife (12 Nov.)

Ship Molley, John McKittorick master, at Market St. wharf
in Phila. - will sail for Barbados; for freight or passage agree with master (12 Nov.)

WILLIAMS, Stephen - at his house in Market St., Phila.,
sells goods imported from London in the ship Vernon
(12 Nov.)

HOUSE, George, in Chesnut St., near the Three Tons in
Phila. - sells shoes (12 Nov.)

BYLES, Thomas, pewterer, in Market St., Phila. - has for
sale a still (12 Nov.)

McCALL, Samuel - has removed from his house in Second St.
to that in Water St. next door to William Allen's,
Esq. (12 Nov.)

SKANLON, William, servant from North of Ireland, age c. 20
- runaway from Thomas Clark, of the Welch Tract, near
Mr. Evan's Meeting-house in Newcastle (12 Nov.)

HUTCHESON, John, servant from North of Ireland, age c. 20
- same as above; reward for recovery of the servants
will be paid by James Claxton, next door to the Three
Tons in Chesnut St., Phila. (12 Nov.)

ROBERTS, Edward, late of Phila., dec'd - accounts with estate to be settled with Hugh Roberts, executor (12 Nov.)

HOBART, Widow - has left off business of loaf-bread baking
(12 Nov.)

FARMER, Capt. - arrived Wednesday last at New York from
London with European news - New York item of 16 Nov.
(19 Nov.)

BENNET, Capt. Francis, of the Port-Factor, who sailed a
few weeks past from Charlestown for Lisbon - was murdered on board by 3 Spaniards of his crew - Charlestown
item of 29 Aug. (19 Nov.)

There arrived 12 Oct. at Antigua the son of the Governor
of St. Jago (one of the Cape de Verd Islands), a Negro
(19 Nov.)

House of Representatives voted 3,000 pounds for the use of
the King of England (19 Nov.)

EASTBURN, Benjamin, late of Phila., dec'd - accounts with
estate to be settled with Ann Eastburn, administratrix
(19 Nov.)

Sloop Pasley, Capt. William Houston commander, lately arrived from North Britain and Ireland, now at Mr. Mc-
Call's wharf in Phila. - will sail for Belfast; for
freight or passage agree with William Blair or the
master (19 Nov.)

Capts. William Henry and Thomas Marsden arrived 9 Oct. at
Charlestown from Savannah, Ga.; Marsden, master of the
sloop Martha, of and for Liverpool, had sailed from
Virginia but on 12 July was taken by the Spanish priva-
teer Caesar; this privateer on 18 July took the ship
Polly, Capt. William Henry, and the ship Hawke, of
Biddleford, Richard Williams master, and 23 July the
Squirrel, of Bristol, John Brown master (26 Nov.)

COWTHORN, John, of Phila., a servant - on 12 Nov. hanged
himself (26 Nov.)

KÖSTER, Joseph - on the last night of the fair at Phila.,
in a quarrel was killed by Jacob Evoulkt (or Evolkt),
who was committed to prison (26 Nov.)

DAGG, John - on 20 Nov., being in his shallop, fell into
the river and died (26 Nov.)

Sloop William, Capt. Macnemara, bound from Barbados to
Phila. - was taken 6 Nov. by a privateer (26 Nov.)

STRETTEL, Robert, of Front St., Phila., intending for
London - wishes to settle all accounts (26 Nov.)

Brigantine Sally, Joseph Arthur master - will sail for Jamaica; for freight or passage agree with the master or
Capt. Seymour in Second St., Phila. (26 Nov.)

RAWLINSON, Robert, of Phila., butcher - offers reward for
recovery of strayed or stolen horse (26 Nov.)

STEVENSON, Thomas, of Rocky Hill, Sommerset Co. - his house
was robbed, presumably by Daniel Williams, an Irishman
- reward for capture of Williams will be paid by John

Carle or Thomas Stevenson (26 Nov.)

HOWLAND, Capt. - was taken April last and carried into Havana (3 Dec.)

Ship of Don Rodrigo de Torres - on 1 July was struck by lightning and blew up in harbor of Havana (3 Dec.)

TEMPLER, Capt. - brings European news - Boston item of 16 Nov. (3 Dec.)

BREADING, Capt., who arrived at Boston Friday last from Bristol - brings news of transports to Jamaica - Boston item of 16 Nov. (3 Dec.)

DE LANCEY, Stephen, of New York, merchant - died 18 Nov. in New York in his 78th year (3 Dec.)

BRYAN, Capt., from London - arrived Saturday last at New York, with Count Zinzendorff aboard, who has purchased the land that Mr. Seward bought at the Forks of Delaware - New York item of 23 Nov. (3 Dec.)

SEYMOUR, Capt. - arrived 22 Nov. at New York from Jamaica (3 Dec.)

NEATE, Capt., of Phila. - after a fight with 2 Spanish privateers - has arrived at Jamica - New York item of 23 Nov. (3 Dec.)

ZINZENDORFF, Count - arrived Sunday last at Phila. with some Moravians to be settled at Nazareth (3 Dec.)

The newly invented iron fireplaces - are to be sold at the Post Office in Phila. (3 Dec.)

Poor Richard's Almanack for the Year 1742 - has been printed by B. Franklin (3 Dec.)

RODGERS, Thomas, in Front St., at the Sign of the Boot, in Phila. - has a Negro shoemaker for sale (3 Dec.)

House of Joseph Cattell in Evesham Twp., Burlington Co., is for sale - apply to Jonas Cattell, living in said house (3 Dec.)

NEWTON, Thomas, age c. 35, sailor - runaway from brigantine Lucy, John Lindsay master; reward will be paid if runaway is brought to John Abraham Denormandie at Bristol or John Bard in Phila. (3 Dec.)

DOMINGO, John, a Genoa man, sailor - same as above

HODGES, Capt. - Wednesday last, coming in from North Carolina, ran on the Cohasset Rocks in a fog; vessel and
cargo were lost but the men saved - Boston item of 23
Nov. (10 Dec.)

McNEAL, Capt. - Friday last arrived at Boston from Bristol
- Boston item of 23 Nov. (10 Dec.)

REYNOLDS, Capt. of an English privateer - has sunk a
Spanish privateer off the Canaries - New York item of
7 Dec. (10 Dec.)

The new governor's secretary is arrived at Perth Amboy
with Capt. Farmar from London - Perth Amboy item of
24 Nov. (10 Dec.)

LEACH, Samuel, from London - does all sorts of engraving;
he may be heard of at Samuel Hazard's, merchant, opposite the Baptist Meeting-house in Second St. or at Andrew Farrel's, tanner, in Chesnut St., Phila. (10 Dec.)

MAGEE, Nathanael, in Arch St., next door to the Adam and
Eve - sells cloth and other items just imported from
Bristol (10 Dec.)

JONES, Isaac, in Arch St., Phila. - sells European goods
(10 Dec.)

Sloop _Samuel_ and _Mary_, William March master - will sail
for Cape Fear; for freight or passage agree with the
master or John Hyatt (10 Dec.)

SHOOGLE, Timothy, Irish servant, age c. 16 - runaway from
Joseph Bond, of the Great Swamp (10 Dec.)

WILLIS, Nathanael, Irish servant, age c. 20 - runaway
from William Hopkins, near the 2 branches of Elk River,
Caecil Co., Md. (10 Dec.)

A snow from Londonderry, Ireland, one Rowen master, bound
to Newcastle - ran ashore upon Grand Menan and many
perished - Boston item of 1 Dec. (17 Dec.)

It is reported that Capt. Smyter from Phila. arrived at
London and that Capt. Braeme sailed from Cowes for
Phila. (17 Dec.)

NEAT, Capt. - arrived last week at Phila. from Jamaica (17
Dec.)

Last month 98 privates and 2 cadets embarked at Phila. on
board the _Industry_, Capt. Hogg, and the _Hampshire_, Capt.

Calcott, (17 Dec.)

SMITH, Thomas, servant, currier and tanner - runaway from Joseph Decow, of Trenton, at the Falls of Delaware (17 Dec.)

Bay horse has been taken up at plantation of Griffith John, of Trediffryn Twp., Chester Co. (17 Dec.)

PRICHARD, Joseph, in Chesnut St., Phila. - sells rugs, blankets, etc. (24 Dec.)

Brigantine Delaware, Hugh Hill master - will sail for South Carolina; for freight or passage agree with Peter Baynton in Phila. or Ennion Williams, of Bristol, or the master (24 Dec.)

SCHLEYDORN, Henry, sugar baker - has lately moved into Norris's Alley, Phila. (24 Dec.)

WILEY, Alexander, late of Phila., shoemaker, dec'd - accounts to be settled with executors, Evan Morgan, Jr., and Philip Syng (24 Dec.)

WILLIAM, Ellis, of Goshen, Chester Co. - has taken up a brown mare (24 Dec.)

DAVISON, William, of Merion, Phila. Co. - has taken up a horse (24 Dec.)

WOOLLASTON, Thomas, late of Phila., shoemaker, dec'd - accounts with estate to be settled with Richard Waln, Jr., administrator (24 Dec.)

NORTON, Capt. Benjamin, commander of privateer from Rhode Island - relates that his ship was assisted, when damaged from lightning, by Capt. Frankland, commander of the Rose, man-of-war; that he captured on 26 Sept. a Spanish privateer, Don Francisco Larango commander; among vessels taken by Don Francisco were a sloop, Capt. Stockings; the pink Paxton, John Shaw, bound to London from Virginia; the snow Argyle, John McKeen, from Virginia bound to Dublin; a schooner from New London, Capt. Truman commander, from St. Eustatia; sloop, Capt. Lightwood commander, from Barbados; schooner Sarah, Capt. North, from Maryland; ship Mercury, Capt. Clark, from London bound to Virginia; ship Plymouth, Capt. Anthony, from London to Virginia; brigantine Sarah, Thomas Smith master, bound to Boston from Barbados - Boston item of 30 Nov. (29 Dec.)

Schooner belonging to Mr. Eliery of Cape Ann - arrived

last week at Boston; it was plundered by a Spanish privateer - Boston item of 10 Dec. (29 Dec.)

RENEY, James, at William Murdock's in Chesnut St., Phila. - sells cloth and hardware (29 Dec.)

MURPHY, John, Maryland Post - offers reward for recovery of pocketbook lost between Darby and Chester (29 Dec.)

REAN, James, in Worcester Twp., Phila. Co. - has taken up a bay mare (29 Dec.)

1742

CANNOR, Cornelius (alias Chetbly), Irish servant, age c. 21 - runaway from Moses Coates, of Charlestown, Chester Co. (6 Jan.)

List of books sold by Benjamin Franklin, near the market, Phila. (6 Jan.)

BARKLEY, John, at the Sign of the Bible in Second St., Phila. - intends for England in 2 months (6 Jan.)

Ship Minerva, Thomas Forrest master, at Mr. Plumstead's wharf, Phila. - will sail for Jamaica; for freight or passage agree with John Inglis or the captain (6 Jan.)

Ship Totness, John Deverel master, at Mr. Hamilton's wharf, Phila. - will sail for Barbados (6 Jan.)

WHITE, Townsend, opposite to John Hyatt's in Front St., Phila. - cloth for sale (6 Jan.)

Brigantine Debby, at Anthony Morris's wharf, Phila. - is for sale; enquire of Anthony Morris, Jr. (6 Jan.)

Sloop Tartar, Capt. Benjamin Wickham commander - next week sails from Newport for Cumberland with recruits raised by Capt. Wm. Hopkins - Newport, R.I., item of 11 Dec. 1741 (13 Jan.)

AMERY, Capt. Daniel, commander of a sloop belonging to Newport, R.I., arrived last week at Newport from Fort Royal in Martinico - Newport item of 11 Dec. 1741 (13 Jan.)

AUCHMUTY, Robert, Esq., Judge of the Court of Vice Admiralty at Boston - condemned the ship Grand Juste, which was taken by H.M.S. Success, Capt. Thompson - Boston item of 17 Dec. 1741 (13 Jan.)

Two schooners, Capts. White and James, belonging to Marblehead, bound from Maryland to Marblehead - are cast
away upon the back side of Long Island - Boston item
of 17 Dec. 1741 (13 Jan.)

RICLAY, John, at the Widow Richardson's in Front St.,
Phila. - sells hardware, snuff boxes, necklaces, fans
(13 Jan.)

TROTTER, Joseph, at the Sign of the Sickle and Steelyards,
in Second St., Phila. - sells smith's anvils, vices
and files (13 Jan.)

SPENCE, Capt. John, at his house in Front St. or his store
in Water St., Phila. - has for sale rigging for a
sloop, brigantine or snow, 2 cables and 2 anchors (13
Jan.)

SMITH, George, in Arch St., Phila. - has Negroes for sale
(13 Jan.)

WHITEFIELD, Rev. Mr. - is kindly received in Scotland (20
Jan.)

Train oil and pickled codfish - are for sale on board the
sloop Hum-bird, Samuel Blunt master, at Carpenter's
wharf, Phila. (20 Jan.)

Requests that anyone who knows Daniel Masserly, lately
come to this country to see his brother, Peter Smoke,
to inform said Daniel that his brother lives in Bethlehem, Hunterdon Co., West Jersey (20 Jan.)

Richardson and Eversley, at their store in Water St.,
Phila., where John Stamper lately lived - sell goods
imported from England (20 Jan.)

BROWN, Charity, late of Phila., dec'd - accounts with estate to be settled with Priscilla Owen, widow and administratrix of Owen Owen, house-carpenter and administrator of said Brown's estate (20 Jan.)

BINGHAM, James, late of Phila., dec'd - accounts with estate to be settled with the executors, Ann and James
Bingham (20 Jan.)

HARDING, George, skinner - is removed from next door to
Robert Moore's, in Market St., Phila., to the other
side of said street, near to Bickley's Corner (20 Jan.)

Ship Mary, William Fishbourn, Jr., master - will sail for
London; for freight or passage agree with the master or

John Reynell, in Front St., Phila. (20 Jan.)

William Wallace, at the Sugar House, and James Oswald, at
the house of Joseph Turner, in Phila. - sell sugar,
candy and tea (20 Jan.)

BREINTNAL, John, in Chesnut St., Phila. - sells spectacles,
microscopes, compasses and dials (20 Jan.)

Snow New Susannah, Thomas Landon master, at Mr. Austin's
wharf in Phila. - will sail for Bristol; for freight or
passage agree with Samuel Hazard, in Second St., Phila.,
or the captain (20 Jan.)

LYNEALL, Richard - teaches the small sword - is to be
spoke with at Dr. Richard Farmer's in Second St., Phila.
(20 Jan.)

Messages between the governor and Assembly in January 1742
(27 Jan.)

Account of Commodore Anson's misfortunes - Boston item of
28 Dec. 1741 (27 Jan.)

JAMES, Capt. - arrived 3 Jan. at Boston from Madeira with
account of Capt. Reynolds's brave action in taking a
Spanish privateer off the Canaries (27 Jan.)

H.M.S. Gosport, Capt. Ellis commander - about 10 days ago
arrived at New York - New York item of 19 Jan. (27 Jan.)

FURMAN, Sarah, née Strickland, born at Fairfield, Conn.;
her first husband's name was Roberts, her second husband's name was Furman - she died Friday last at Trenton, a widow, aged about 97; she left 5 children, 61
grandchildren, 182 great-grandchildren and 12 great-
great-grandchildren, in all 160 living (27 Jan.)

Lot of 14 acres (belonging to estate of Samuel Hudson,
dec'd), adjoining to the south side fence of George
Emlen's on Passyunk Rd. - is to be let; apply to Anthony Morris or Joseph Cooper (27 Jan.)

HILLBORN, John, near Frankford, Phila. Co. - has a Negro
man for sale (27 Jan.)

EATON, George, of Lower Dublin Twp. - offers reward for
recovery of strayed or stolen mare; mare is to be
brought to the owner or to Adolphus Yoacas, in Third
St., Phila. (27 Jan.)

WALDRON, Edward, of Darby, scyth-maker - his debtors are

to make payment to his attorney, John Davis, of Darby (27 Jan.)

Votes of the House of Representatives of Pennsylvania; mentioned are Dr. Graeme, Charles Willing, Peter Baynton, Dr. Lloyd Zachary and a resolve submitted by the following: Thomas Leech, Isaac Norris, Israel Pemberton, James Morris, Edward Warner, Samuel Blunston, Abraham Chapman, Jeremiah Starr (3 Feb.)

HARVEY, Augustus, Second Lieutenant of the Superbe man-of-war - was put in command of a prize taken by the Superbe (3 Feb.)

BUDD, John, of Burlington - offers for sale between 300 and 400 acres of land on one of the branches of the Rariton River (3 Feb.)

BRITTON, Grace, late of Phila., baker, dec'd - accounts with estate to be settled with Isaac Jones (3 Feb.)

BOYD, John, of Phila., carpenter, in Market St., opposite the Sign of the Conestogoe Waggon - has for sale door-cases, window-cases, shutters and sashes (3 Feb.)

JONES, Arthur - will sell at the Great Swamp in Bucks Co. a house and 200 acres; enquire of Edward Roberts near said place, or James Delaplaine, Jr., in Germantown, or Arthur Jones at Oxford (3 Feb.)

NEAVE, Samuel, at his store fronting Fisbourne's wharf in Water St. - sells cloth, hardware, etc. (3 Feb.)

Brigantine Vernon, Arthur Burrows master - will sail for Barbados; for freight or passage apply to the master or Joseph Marks (3 Feb.)

Speech of H. E. William Shirley to the Council and House of Massachusetts (10 Feb.)

Colony Sloop Tartar, Capt. Wickham commander, sailed 27 Dec. 1741 for Cuba with recruits for Col. Gooch's Regt. - Newport, R.I., item of 31 Dec. (10 Feb.)

The General Assembly of Massachusetts last Wednesday chose Robert Auchmuty, Esq., and Christopher Kilby to be agents for prosecuting the appeal of Massachusetts from the judgment about the boundary with Rhode Island - Boston item of 11 Jan. (10 Feb.)

BLOWERS, Capt. - arrived last week at Boston from Jamaica - Boston item of 18 Jan. (10 Feb.)

ALLEN, Capt., commander of a Newport, R.I., privateer - last week brought to Newport a Dutch sloop he had taken - Boston item of 18 Jan. (10 Feb.)

ALLEN, Capt. - on 17 Nov. 1741 took a French vessel trading on the Spanish coast which is got into South Carolina (10 Feb.)

NORTON, Capt., commander of a Rhode Island privateer - has retaken and brought into Charlestown, S.C., 2 English ships which had been taken by a Spanish privateer (10 Feb.)

SOUTHER, James - on 12 Jan., when blasting in one of the mines near Newark, was struck by fragments of rock and died - New York item of 25 Jan. (10 Feb.)

HUNT, Thomas, of Westchester - was drowned Tuesday last when a Westchester boat overset not far north of Corlaer's Hook - New York item of 25 Jan. (10 Feb.)

ANNIS, Thomas - accounts with him to be taken to William Annis and William Harrison (10 Feb.)

Teacher of Latin and Greek is sought for King William's School at Annapolis, Md.; John Wilmot, master, at the school will give details to any applicant (10 Feb.)

WALTON, Malachi, innholder, who lately lived at the Sign of the Crown, in Bristol - is removed to the opposite corner house, the new Sign of the Crown (10 Feb); Giles Lawrence, from the Three Legs, has taken over the old Crown Tavern in Bristol, Bucks Co. (17 Mar.)

McDONALD, Arthur, Irish servant, age c. 21 - runaway from Francis Jodon, of Warminster Twp., Bucks Co. (10 Feb.)

BULLER, Alexander, late master of the Publick School in Phila. - accounts with his estate are to be settled with Robert Jordan, administrator (10 Feb.)

Servant shoemaker - his time (about 3½ years) is for sale; enquire of Thomas Powell, shoemaker, in Second St., Phila. (10 Feb.)

THOMPSON, Joseph, in Front St., next to the Ship-a-Ground in Phila. - accounts with him are to be settled, as he intends to leave Phila. (17 Feb.)

The following are to be sold at auction: a lot on north side of High St. and 3 lots in Third St., joining west on a lot of Edward Warner's, north of a lot of Mary

Parker's, and south on the house and alley now occupied by Samuel Preston - enquire of Mary Rutter, widow and executrix of John Rutter, dec'd (17 Feb.)

Lots on Society Hill, Phila. - to be sold or let by Joseph Wharton (17 Feb.)

RAWLE, William, late of Phila., merchant, dec'd - accounts with estate to be settled with the executors, Benjamin Shoemaker, William Cooper, Rebeccah Rawle and Elizabeth Rawle (17 Feb.)

OWEN, Owen, innkeeper, lately dec'd - accounts with estate to be settled with his widow, Ann Owen, executrix, at the Indian King, opposite the butcher's Shambles, Phila.; tract of 100 acres near Neshaminy and North Wales, and bounded near Richard William's land, to be sold, as it also belongs to Owen's estate (17 Feb.)

Plantation of 100 acres, about 5 miles from Chester and 4 from Marcus Hook, is for sale; enquire of Joseph Howel, tanner, in Chesnut St., next door to John Breintnal's, whalebone cutler (17 Feb.)

WELDON, John, late of Chichester, Chester Co., cordwainer, dec'd - accounts with estate to be settled with Elizabeth Weldon, administratrix (17 Feb.)

CALL, Capt. - arrived Tuesday last at Boston in about 8 weeks from Plymouth, England, with European news - Boston item of 1 Feb. (24 Feb.)

ALLEN, Capt., commander of the New Revenge privateer - on 12 Jan. brought into Newport, R.I., as a prize a Bermuda-built sloop (24 Feb.)

BELL, Tom - was committed to goal in Newport, R.I. - Newport item of 13 Jan. (24 Feb.)

ROUSE, Capt., commander of the Young Eagle privateer of Boston - last Tuesday arrived at Newport, R.I. - Newport item of 24 Jan. (24 Feb.)

By letters in Capt. Call is it learned that a Spanish privateer took Capt. Coffin bound from London to Boston - Boston item of 1 Feb. (24 Feb.)

McFALL, Capt. - Thursday last arrived at Boston from the West Indies - Boston item of 1 Feb. (24 Feb.)

DOTY, Capt., who came from New Plymouth to Boston by land last week - arrived at New Plymouth Saturday last from

Port Morant in Jamaica; he brought news of grievous
sickness among land forces in Cuba - Boston item of 1
Feb. (24 Feb.)

DACON, Mr., chaise-maker, at head of School St., Boston -
last Saturday night his shop was consumed by fire -
Boston item of 1 Feb. (24 Feb.)

A sloop was lately sunk near Crab Meadow; it appears that
John Bray was master and there were Germans on board,
for in one book that was found from the wreck was written "Catherina Gaffman van Uberglatt" - New York item
of 8 Feb. (24 Feb.)

BULLOCK, William - on Saturday last was committed to Phila.
Goal, charged with the death of his Negro boy, age 8, by
beating and whipping him at sundry times (24 Feb.)

Tract of 360 acres (formerly belonging to James Dunlap,
in Salem Co., towards the head of Aloes Creek) is for
sale; apply to William Clymer, Jr., in Arch St., Phila.
(24 Feb.)

WOOLLEN, Joseph, late of Germantown Twp., Phila. Co.,
dec'd - persons indebted to his estate are to make payment to Samuel Farmar (24 Feb.)

IRWIN, James, late of North East, innholder, dec'd - accounts with estate to be settled with Francis Maybury,
Jr., administrator (24 Feb.)

BARON, John, of Phila., merchant - accounts with him are
to be settled (24 Feb.)

Snow New **Susannah,** Thomas Landon master, at Mr. Austin's
wharf in Phila. - will sail for Bristol; for freight
or passage agree with Samuel Hazard in Second St.,
Phila., or with the master (24 Feb.)

Six hundred acres of land in Kent Co., Md., about 3½ miles
from Chester Town and about 3½ miles from Worton Creek,
are for sale; enquire of Charles Hynson, of Chester
Town, merchant (24 Feb.)

BLAIR, William, designing 1 Mar. for Great Britain and
Ireland - persons owing him money are to make payment
to his wife, Mary Blair, in Phila. (24 Feb.)

Speech of Gov. Shirley to the Massachusetts General Assembly, extract of the governor's instructions and message
sent up from the House to the governor by Mr. Bromfield,
Capt. Jackson, Col. Minot, Capt. Richmond and Mr. Gardener (3 Mar.)

Appearance of comet on 22 Feb. in Phila. and quotations from Mr. Whiston and Dr. Keill on comets (3 Mar.)

CHEW, Samuel - replies to what he calls a "scurrilous" paper printed against him in Phila. by a Quaker (3 Mar.)

BIGGER, Peacock, opposite the Presbyterian Meeting-house in Phila., brazier - makes stills, Dutch ovens, pots and pans (3 Mar.)

HEAP, George, in Market St., Phila. - makes and mends harnesses and bellows (3 Mar.)

HUNT, John, of Manington - will sell tract of 271 acres in Manington, within 5 miles of Salem (3 Mar.)

Description (in German) of the conference of the German Evangelical religions held on 10, 11, and 12 Feb. in Oley at the house of Johann de Turck (3 Mar.)

BOYD, Ann, Irish servant, age c. 20 - runaway from on board the Rundle Galley, Robert Nutt master; reward will be paid if she is taken up and brought to Redmond Cunningham, at the Widow Harper's, in Gray's Alley, Phila. (3 Mar.)

LYNCH, James, late of the Island of St. Christophers, who intends to depart from Phila. and return to St. Christophers - accounts with him to be settled at his lodgings at the Sign of the Ton in Water St., Phila. (3 Mar.)

Tract of land in East Marlborough, Chester Co., joining to the land of Henry Hayes is for sale by Robert Mickle; at Archibald McNeal's, tavernkeeper, in Kennet Twp., Chester Co. (3 Mar.)

The Rose, man-of-war, Capt. Thomas Frankland commander, is ashore on the North Breaker Head - Charlestown, S. C., item of 2 Jan. (10 Mar.)

OGLETHORP, General - has resolved to besiege St. Augustine - Charlestown item of 2 Jan. (10 Mar.)

NORTON, Capt., in the Revenge privateer - has taken and brought to Charlestown a Spanish prize - Charlestown item of 2 Jan. (10 Mar.)

DAVIDSON, Capt., master of a Rhode Island privateer - account of his capture of a Spanish privateer, a very rich prize - Charlestown item of 5 Jan. (10 Mar.)

FORREST, Capt., from London - arrived at Charlestown Sunday last - Charlestown item of 5 Jan. (10 Mar.)

GOOCH, William, Jr. - Wednesday last was his birthday, as also that of the Prince of Wales - Williamsburg item of 22 Jan. (10 Mar.)

Ship _Virginian_, Capt. Lewis - arrived Saturday last in York River from Bristol - Williamsburg item of 5 Feb. (10 Mar.)

Ship _Duke of Argyle_, Capt. Ludlow - arrived Monday last in York River from Bristol; account of his engagement with a Spanish privateer - Williamsburg item of 5 Feb. (10 Mar.)

WHITEFIELD, Rev. Mr. - has married Mrs. James, a widow, in Abergavenny, Wales (10 Mar.)

Sloop _Albany_, William Bradford master, which sailed November last from New Brunswick, N.J. - sunk at sea but master and men were taken up - New York item of 27 Feb. (10 Mar.)

Last week in New York a woman gave birth to 3 boys, whom she named Abraham, Isaac and John; she already had a son named Jacob - New York item of 27 Feb. (10 Mar.)

TINGLEY, Capt., from Jamaica - gives news of forces at Jamaica - New York item of 27 Feb. (10 Mar.)

Tom, a Negro belonging to Widow Bradt, baker - on 16 Feb. confessed to setting fire to a house near the old Dutch Church in New York; he was condemned to death and 6 accomplices were given 39 lashes each - New York item of 3 Mar. (10 Mar.); Tom was executed Saturday last for setting fire to the house of one Vandewater - New York item of 15 Mar. (17 Mar.)

BERTRAM, John, botanist - subscription is on foot to finance a trip by him through New York, Pennsylvania, New Jersey and Maryland to search for curious vegetables and fossils (10 Mar.)

EVOULKT, Jacob, indicted for the murder of Joseph Koster - Monday last in Phila. was found guilty of manslaughter and burnt in the hand (10 Mar.)

BULLOCK, William - Monday last in Phila. was found guilty of killing his Negro boy (10 Mar.)

GARDINER, George, servant, age c. 40 - runaway from Abraham Merriott, of Springfield Twp., Burlington Co. (10 Mar.)

MARSHAL, William - wishes to let his plantation in the Forks of Brandewyne, Chester Co. (10 Mar.)

NEWMAN, Margaret, dec'd - accounts with estate to be settled with John Newman, opposite to Black Horse Alley, in Second St., Phila. (10 Mar.)

General Oglethorp's privateer sloop - took the Augustine pay-ship - New York item of 15 Mar., citing a private letter from Frederica, Ca., dated 7 Feb. (17 Mar.)

A copy of the subscription paper for the encourage of Mr. John Bartram (17 Mar.)

At the last session of the Court of Common Pleas in Phila. was heard the complaint of Johann Diemer against Jacob Reif in Schippach, who called Diemer and Peter Hellegas church-robbers and thieves; Diemer proved his innocence; Reif was found guilty and sentenced to pay costs (17 Mar.)

STEEL, James, late of Phila., dec'd - accounts with estate to be settled with his executors, Charles Hillyard, Richard Renshaw and Rebeccah Steel (17 Mar.)

BURRASS, Matthew, English servant, baker, age $\underline{c}$. 30 - runaway from Thomas Brown, of Town of Lancaster (17 Mar.)

Plantation of 100 acres in Oxford Twp., lying on the River Delaware - to be let; enquire of Bridget Keen on the premises or John Clifton in Phila. (17 Mar.)

GIBBS, Capt. - Saturday last arrived at Boston from Madeira - Boston item of 8 Mar. (25 Mar.)

POPE, Capt. - Wednesday last arrived at Rhode Island from Antigua - Boston item of 8 Mar. (25 Mar.)

WOODFORD, Capt. - arrived at New York from Lisbon in 7 weeks with European news - New York item of 15 Mar. (25 Mar.)

Tom (the Negro of Widow Bradt), who was executed Saturday last in New York, had implicated Jack Farmers and Philip (Negro slave of Mr. Dyckinck), but he always told a different story so his evidence was of no value - New York item of 16 Mar. (25 Mar.)

Brigantine Abraham and Matthew, Hugh Tress master - on

voyage from New London to Phila., sunk off east end of Long Island - New York item of 22 Mar. (25 Mar.)

LAY, Benjamin - on Monday noon in Phila. in the market place bore testimony against the vanity of tea-drinking by smashing valuable china belonging to his dec'd wife - the populace overthrew him and his box of china and carried off as much as possible (25 Mar.)

BUNTING, Samuel, late of Chesterfield, Burling Co. - his plantation of 285 acres will be sold at auction by his executors, Thomas Miller and Benjamin Fowler (25 Mar.)

FRANKLIN, B. - has published The Government of the Church of Christ and also An Examination and Refutation of Mr. Gilbert Tennent's Remarks (25 Mar.)

SIMS, Joseph, at house where George McCall, dec'd, formerly lived - has for sale a parcel of Negro boys and girls and European goods (25 Mar.)

DUNLAP, James, of Piles Grove, Salem Co., N.J. - his wife Elizabeth has eloped from him (25 Mar.)

ROBINSON, Thomas, of Phila., designing for Europe - wishes accounts with him to be settled with his wife, Sarah Robinson (25 Mar.)

An English servant, age c. 26, a weaver, who came from London about 8 months ago - runaway from Thomas Carr, of Baltimore Co., Md. (25 Mar.)

Boulting mills, chests, scales, weights, etc., will be sold at auction 29 Mar. at the house late of Grace Briton in Third St., Phila. (25 Mar.)

WAINWRIGHT, Samuel, lately dec'd - his plantation at the head of Timber Creek, Gloucester Co., West New Jersey, is for sale; enquire of Samuel McCulloch, living near the premises, or of Jacob Reeder, of Newtown, Queens Co., on Long Island, the executors of the estate (25 Mar.)

BRIDGES, Edward, late of Phila., merchant, dec'd - accounts to be settled with Cornelia Bridges, executrix (25 Mar.)

Sloop Samuel & Mary, William Marsh master, at Market St. wharf, Phila. - will sail for Cape Fear; for freight or passage agree with the master or John Hyatt in Front St. (25 Mar.)

Persons indebted to Clymer & Co. for servants are warned
to pay before next June court (25 Mar.)

SAUER, Christopher, of Germantown - proposes to print a
High Dutch Bible in quarto; subscriptions may be made
with him or with Benjamin Franklin in Phila. (25 Mar.)

Schooner Brilliant, John Andrews master, at Mr. McCall's
wharf - will sail for Barbados; for freight or passage
agree with John Inglis or with the master on board (25
Mar.)

LEEDS, Philo, of Northampton Twp., Burlington Co. - various items to be sold at auction in his house include
the following: plantation of 300 acres now in tenure
of Thomas Budd, farmer; plantation of 400 acres where
Leeds now dwells; plantation of 200 acres where John
Springer now dwells; 200 acres adjoining Leeds's home-
stead; sawmill, lands and tenements now in the possession of Thomas Kemble; ½ of sawmill lately built in
partnership with John Burr; a young Negro man, household goods, wagon, plow (25 Mar.)

An account (in German) of B. Ludewig and also the fourth
general meeting of the church of God from all German
Evangelical religions in Pennsylvania, held at Germantown on the 10, 11 and 12 Mar. at Mr. Ashmead's house
(31 Mar.)

Tract of 400 acres in Nantmel Twp., Chester Co., is to be
sold; enquire of Joseph Hoskins, of Chester (31 Mar.)

The 13th edition of Watt's Psalms - just published by B.
Franklin (31 Mar.)

A notice (in English and German) for volunteers for Col.
William Gooch's Regt. to report to Capt. William Thinn
at Phila. or to Lt. Henry Hodge or Lt. Peter Grung;
also deserters who were enlisted last fall by Lt.
Whiteford will be pardoned if they surrender to Capt.
Thinn (31 Mar.)

BINGHAM, James - has a plantation of 500 acres to let (31
Mar.)

HALL, Edward, living at Cramberry Hall, Baltimore - has
for sale tracts of land: Hall's Park on Swan Creek;
Paradise; Cook's Chance and Hall's Rich Neck, all in
Baltimore Co. (31 Mar.)

PLATT, Nathanael (usher to the late Alexander Buller), at
the Friends School in Strawberry Alley - will give in-

struction in writing and arithmetic (31 Mar.)

FLEMMING, Arthur, an Irishman - has deserted from on board
the brigantine <u>Vernon</u>, Arthur Burrows master; reward
will be paid if Flemming is brought to Thomas Lloyd, of
Phila. (31 Mar.)

DRAKE, Benjamin, a farmer, at Hopewell - accidentally shot
by his little daughter on Thursday last and died the
next day - an account from Maidenhead Twp., New Jersey,
in a Perth Amboy item of 29 Mar. (8 Apr.)

FARMAR, Robert, captain of a company raised in New Jersey
and now in the West Indies - arrived Thursday last at
Perth Amboy, together with Lt. Palmer; they are come to
recruit in New Jersey - Perth Amboy item of 29 Mar.
(8 Apr.)

CLARKE, Edward, Esq. (son of the Hon. George Clarke, Esq.,
Lt.-Gov. of New York) - has been made a major - Perth
Amboy item of 29 Mar) (8 Apr.)

Privateer <u>George</u>, Capt. John Sibbald - arrived Friday last
at Phila. with 2 prizes, English ships which had been
taken by a Spanish privateer commanded by Capt. Louis
Siverio; Capt. Sibbald re-took the vessels (8 Apr.)

KENNY, Timothy, sergt. in raising recruits last fall - is
taken up and committed to Newtown Goal in Bucks Co. on
suspicion of having stolen 70 pounds of new money (8
Apr.)

The Library Company of Philadelphia will meet 3 May by
order of the directors, J. Breintnal, secretary (8
Apr.)

Persons willing to enlist in Col. William Gooch's American Regt. of Foot are to repair to Capt. Robert Farmar
at Brunswick, East Jersey, to Lt. Anthony Palmer in
Burlington, West Jersey, or to Lt. Marshal Davis at
Newark, East Jersey (8 Apr.)

McQUIRE, Thomas, Irish convict servant - runaway from
Peter Worrial in Lancaster Town, Pa.; reward will be
paid if the servant is apprehended and notice given to
Peter Worrial in Lancaster or to John Awbrey at Goose
Creek, Prince William's Co., Va. (8 Apr.)

HERN, Daniel, Irish convict servant, who was lately taken
up at Alexander Osbourn's at Quittipehilla in Lancaster Co., where he had married, and has since made his
escape from Prince William's Co. in Virginia - runaway

from John Awbrey, of Goose Creek in Prince William's Co.; reward if servant is taken up and notice is given to Awbrey or to Peter Worrial in Lancaster (8 Apr.)

HAMILTON, Robert, Irish servant, age 24 - runaway from David Wiley, of New London Twp., Chester Co. (8 Apr.)

WILKINSON, Anthony, in Water St., Phila. - sells pickled sturgeon (8 Apr.)

CORTNEY, John, English servant, age c. 28, shoemaker - runaway from Jeory Tilldine, of Trenton, Hunterdon Co., New Jersey (8 Apr.)

HESS, Henry - claims he was imposed on by Robert Hasle, of Bethlehem, Hunterdon Co., N.J., with respect to a bond (8 Apr.)

STILES, Joseph - at his store in Water St., 2 doors below the Ton Tavern in Phila. - sells cloth and other items (8 Apr.)

SCULL, Joseph, at the Workhouse in Phila. - will sell the time of a Scotchman (8 Apr.)

HOLLOWELL, William, shipwright, at Boston - Thursday last fell into the hold of a new ship at a wharf near Fort Hill and died a few hours after - Boston item of 1 Apr. (15 Apr.)

A Negro woman (servant to Elkanah Leonard, Esq., a member of the Massachusetts House of Representatives) in Middleborough, Mass., on 16 Mar. gave birth to 4 sons, as certified by Hannah Briggs, midwife - Boston item of 1 Apr. (15 Apr.)

TRELAWNEY, Gov. - is going on campaign - extract from letter from a merchant in Kingston, Jamaica (15 Apr.)

By a letter from on board Capt. Benjamin Christian, lying at Cocklea, from Mr. Donnald, a merchant, it is learned that Commodore Anson has taken Paita in Peru - Boston item of 1 Apr. (15 Apr.)

Plantation of Thomas Miller on road from Phila. to North Wales, about 13 miles from Phila., adjoining to Farmer's mill, is for sale; apply to Thomas Miller in Manatawny or Peter Robinson near said place (15 Apr.)

PRIOR, Joseph, servant, born in Pennsylvania, age c. 28 or 30 - runaway (probably with his wife who was born in Ireland) from George Brown, in Joppa, Md. (15 Apr.)

EACHUS, John, in Goshen, Chester Co. - has taken up a bay
    mare (15 Apr.)

Nearly 7 years of a servant boy's time is for sale; en-
    quire of William Crosthwaite, peruke-maker, in Front
    St., Phila. (15 Apr.)

LANDRAM, William, Scotch servant, age c. 28 - runaway
    from Patrick Steward, tailor, of New York; reward will
    be paid if servant is returned to his master or Edward
    Graham in New York or Archibald Campbell in Phila.,
    joiner (15 Apr.)

BRYANT, Capt. - arrived 18 Apr. at New York in 5 weeks
    from London (22 Apr.)

MERREWETHER, James - died Sunday last in Phila. (22 Apr.)

Piece of ground in Phila. between Chesnut and Walnut Sts.,
    bounded east with Front St., west with Second St.,
    north with ground belonging to Mr. Plumstead and others
    and south with a 10-foot alley - to be sold or let; ap-
    ply to Abraham Taylor (22 Apr.)

Parcel of men servants, just imported in the snow Friend-
    ship, Peter Parrett master - to be sold; enquire for
    the master at Mr. Chevalier's, distiller, in Second
    St., Phila., or on board the snow, now lying off Market
    St. wharf (22 Apr.)

HAGEN, John, Irish convict servant, age c. 25, shoemaker
    - runaway from Philip Alexander, living in Stafford
    Co., Va.; he went in company with a sailor belonging
    to Capt. Flood, in Potomack River, Boyd's Hole (22 Apr.)

FORREST, Thomas, master of the Minerva, now at Phila. -
    gives permission to masters of servants secretly en-
    listed by Capt. William Thinn to search the ship for
    them (22 Apr.)

THINN, William, offers reward for apprehension of the
    following deserters: Evan Evans, Timothy Dunn, John
    Robison, William Brock and David Tasker (22 Apr.)

ASHLEMAN, Daniel, of Hemfield Twp., Lancaster Co., Pa. -
    offers reward for recovery of a black horse strayed
    or stolen from his plantation (22 Apr.)

DONNEVAN, Cornelius, Irish servant, age c. 20, who de-
    lights very much in playing hustle-cap - runaway from
    Thomas Yorke of Germantown, Phila. Co. (22 Apr.)

358

Plantation late of Caleb Birchall, dec'd, in Chichester
Twp., and house and lot in Front St., joining to the
estate late of Paul Preston in Phila., are for sale;
enquire of Rebecca Birchall, executrix, living in
Phila. (22 Apr.)

KEPPNER, John Bernard, living on Chesnut Hill, 3 miles
above Germantown, because of the infirmities of his
old age, wishes to sell his plantation of 146 acres
(22 Apr.)

MANKIN, Margaret, dec'd - 2 small messuages on the north
side of Sassafrass St., Phila., are offered for sale
by Catharine and Anne Mankin, administratrix (22 Apr.)

H.M.S. Eltham, Capt. Edward Smith commander, has taken and
sent into Antigua a rich prize (29 Apr.)

ROUSE, Capt. John - arrived 2 Apr. at Charlestown in the
Young Eagle, a Boston privateer, with a large French
sloop taken as a prize (29 Apr.)

Brigantine Elizabeth, Capt. Perdue, of New York - on 2
Apr. arrived at Charlestown from Jamaica; in his passage he fought a running fight with a Spanish privateer (29 Apr.)

The Hawk snow, man-of-war - Capt. Bruce, returned to
Charlestown Tuesday last; he spoke with Capt. Snelling
from Boston, ashore near Cape Roman Shoals (29 Apr.)

SMITH, Thomas - Saturday evening on Society Hill, Phila.,
a man was struck and killed by lightning (29 Apr.)

ROBERTSON, James, a Scotch servant, age c. 25, joiner -
runaway from John Haines, of Phila., joiner (29 Apr.)

McMAHON, John, Irish servant, age c. 25, butcher - runaway from Samuel Boyer, of New York, butcher - reward
will be paid if McMahon is taken up and brought to
John Saunders, huntsman, in Phila., or to said Boyer
(29 Apr.)

The Distinguishing Marks of a Work of the Spirit of God,
by Jonathan Edwards, with a preface by the Rev. Mr.
Cooper of Boston - has just been published by B.
Franklin (29 Apr.)

MALOUGHLAN, Thomas, Irishman - broke out of Chester Goal;
reward for his capture will be paid by Benjamin Davis,
sheriff (29 Apr.)

CARROLL, Charles - offers for sale 5,000 acres at the
head of Tom's Creek and near the head of Monoccasi,
where Capt. John Hanse Steelman lives (29 Apr.)

HUNLOKE, Thomas, Sheriff of Burlington Co. - offers a reward for the capture of the following who broke out of
the Goal of the City of Burlington: Benjamin Farrington, age c. 44, plaisterer; John Tool, age c. 25;
Timothy Ryan, age c. 35; John Lycan, a Swede, age c. 50
(29 Apr.)

DALEY, Daniel, of Phila., mariner - his wife Mary has
eloped from him (29 Apr.)

TURNER, Robert, Irish servant - runaway from James McConoll,
of Solsbury Twp., Lancaster Co. (29 Apr.)

Seven Negroes were sentenced to death in April at the
provincial court held in Annapolis for the murder of
their master, Jeremiah Pattison, about a year ago in
Calvert Co. - Annapolis item of 30 Apr. (5 May)

The following are some of the tracts of land belonging to
the estate of James Steel, dec'd, which are offered for
sale by his executors, Charles Hilyard, of Duck Creek,
or by Richard Renshaw, of Phila.: 16 acres of liberty
land adjoining to Samuel Sellass's plantation, near
Phila.; 310 acres on the west line of James Hamilton's
land on the southwest side of Duck Creek (5 May)

SONMANS, Dr., in Market St., Phila., near Bickley's corner
- has drugs and medicines for sale (5 May)

BRAVEN, Capt. Newcomb, of Lewes Town, Sussex Co. upon
Delaware - on 26 Apr. ran forcibly from the Officers
of the Customs at Port Pocomoke in Maryland in the
sloop Rebeccah (lately belonging to Henry Jaquess, of
Perth Amboy); a counterfeit certificate was left in the
custody of John Scarborough, Deputy Collector (5 May)

EMLEN, Samuel, at the Sign of the Golden Heart, opposite
the market in Phila. - sells Dr. Godfrey's cordials
and Dr. Bateman's Pectoral Drops (5 May)

AXON, Capt. William, intending to leave Phila., wishes to
settle all accounts (5 May)

Account of an engagement near Porto Rico between the man-
of-war Scarborough, Capt. Lisle commander, and a Spanish privateer, which was sunk (13 May)

Sloop Three Sisters, William Tucker master, now at Ingram's

wharf in Phila. - will sale for Barbados; for freight
or passage agree with the master at Thomas Ingram's in
Water St. (13 May)

SANSOM, Samuel, next door to Tench Francis, in Second St.,
Phila. - sells cloth, knives and forks, coffee mills,
pistols, knives, wine (13 May)

DETREVAL, Lewis, a French servant, age c. 24 - runaway from
Charles Brown, living in Queen Anne's Co., near Queen's
Town (13 May)

WEILDING, Samuel, English servant, age c. 28, tailor -
same as above

EVERIST, John, English servant, age c. 22 - same as above

GARNER, Henry, servant, age c. 18 - same as above

MARSHALL, Christopher, next door to the Sign of the Bird-
in-Hand, opposite to end of Strawberry Ally in Chesnut
St., Phila. - sells glass, pictures, paint (13 May)

WEST, William, of Phila., mariner, who was taken by the
Spaniards about 2 years since - his household goods
will be sold at the house in Second St. where John
Longhurst formerly lived; West's indigent wife requests that the charitable and considerate come and bid
(13 May)

Snow Margaret, Francis Shaghnesay master, now lying at
wharf of Thomas Griffitts, Esq. - will sail for Barbados; for freight or passage agree with the master or
with Robert Meade, merchant, at Isaac Norris's Alley
(13 May)

List of vessels taken in March and April 1742 by a Spanish
privateer: a vessel from Barbados bound for South
Carolina, Capt. John Pharow; ship St. Andrew, William
Grigg, of St. Andrews, Scotland, bound from South Caro-
lina to Amsterdam; sloop Prosperity, Michael Stewart,
of Boston; brigantine Success, of Biddeford, Samuel
Shackford, bound from Liverpool to New York; schooner
Hopewell, John Prout, from Maryland; ship Ruth, of
Whitehaven, George Gibson, from Maryland; ship London,
Daniel Russel, bound to London from Maryland (20 May)

MAGWIGIN, Patrick, at the Ironworks in Douglass Twp., in
Phila. Co. - was accidentally killed (20 May)

Sugar, candy, molasses, tea for sale by James Oswald, at
the house of Joseph Turner, and by William Wallace, at

the Sugar-house, sugar bakers, in Phila. (20 May)

SCHLEYDORN, Henry, sugar baker, of Phila. - has lately
moved into Norris's Alley (20 May)

GRIFFIN, Elizabeth, at the Rose and Crown in Water St.,
Phila. - will sell the time of a Dutch servant boy (20
May)

GREW, Theophilus - seeks a single man to teach Latin in
the Publick School of Kent Co. (20 May)

DYLANDER, Eleanor, near the Sweedes Church at Wiccacoa -
has for sale a horse and a harness (20 May)

Plantation late of Wm. Stockdale, dec'd, at Warminster in
Bucks Co., bounded on a large branch of Neshaminy,
within 3 miles of Horsham Meeting-house - to be sold by
Israel Pemberton, Jr., of Phila. (20 May)

Parcels of land in Calvert and Talbot Counties, part of
the estate of the late Col. Henry Mitchell in Maryland
- will be sold at public outcry in Annapolis (20 May)

PELLER, James - has for sale a Negro sail-maker (20 May)

Sailors and others wishing to sign up for a voyage against
the Spaniards on board the schooner George, John Sibbald commander, or the sloop Joseph and Mary, William
Dowell, commander, may do so at the Boatswain-and-Call
in Phila. (20 May)

WILLIAMS, Edward, English convict servant, age c. 30 -
runaway from William Hopper and John Davis, both living
in Queen Anne's Co., Md. (20 May)

DRAPER, Valentine, English convict servant, age c. 40 -
same as above

McGUIRE, Patrick, servant, who lived sometime ago with one
Jones, a shallop-man, at Apoquiminy, age c. 21 - run-
away from James Bennett, near Concord, Chester Co. (20
May)

FOWLER, John, Irish servant, age c. 21, tailor - same as
above

McCOLLISTER, Margaret, servant, age c. 25 - same as above

A plague of caterpillars in Pennsylvania (27 May)

BRADFORD, William, at John Hyatt's in Front St., Phila. -

has for sale a tract of 125 acres in Lancaster Co., a corner of the land of Joshua Hart (27 May)

HOCKLEY, Richard, at his store in Water St., opposite Mr. Fishbourn's wharf in Phila. - sells cloth, paper, china, cutlery, etc. (27 May)

Land belonging to the estate of the late Major John Copson is offered for sale, including the estate where the major lived, near the head of North-East River, Caecil Co., Md., at the head of Chespeak Bay, 100 acres near the mouth of North-East (formerly in the possession of Jacob and John Young), 500 acres near the mouth of Swan Creek, and the plantation at North-East where William Beaks now lives; apply to Capt. Peter Bayard, Col. Thomas Colville and Robert Carmichael on Bohemia (27 May)

NIHELL, Edmund, at the Widow Mason's in Front St., opposite to Norris's Alley, Phila. - has for sale cloth and hardware (27 May)

MEREDITH, Reese, at his store on Carpenter's Wharf, where William Shewbert lived - sells cloth, hardware, maps, pictures, glasses, gunpowder, wine (27 May)

BOWNE, Cornelius - has for sale 3 years of a servant girl's time (27 May)

Message of Gov. George Thomas to the Pennsylvania Assembly and extracts from votes of the House; Jeremiah Star and Joseph Shaw were to carry message from the House to the governor (3 June)

RUSSELL, Capt. - arrived 20 May at Newport from New Providence; he gives account of engagement fought with a Spanish man-of-war by Capt. Charles Davidson, commander of the St. Andrew privateer, and Capt. James Wimble of London; Wimble lost one arm - Newport item of 21 May (3 June)

POWER, Capt., in the privateer Victory - sailed Wednesday last against the Spaniards - Newport item of 21 May (3 June)

WICKHAM, Capt., commander of one country-sloop the Tartar - arrived Monday last at Newport - Newport item of 21 May (3 June)

Province snow of Boston, Capt. Tyng commander - arrived 20 May at Newport (3 June)

It is forbidden to carry off Crum-Creek Scyth-Stones from
the land of Joseph Carter in Ridley Twp., Chester Co.;
such stones may be purchased from John Biddle and
Thomas Peters in Phila.; from Simon Battin in Trenton,
West New Jersey; from Hugh McGarrah in Wilmington; from
John Read at Christiana in Newcastle Co. (3 June)

SAUNDERS, Joseph, at his house next to Job Goodson's in
Chesnut St., Phila. - sells cloth, hardware, snuff (3
June)

CHUBB, Voieall, at Reese Meredith's, merchant, near Carpenter's wharf, Phila. - sells cloth and hardware (3
June)

PETERS, William, attorney-at-law and notary public - his
office is in Walnut St., Phila. (3 June)

THOMAS, Capt. John - arrived 3 Mar. at Jamaica from the
Musqueto Shore; he reports that Gov. Hudson was bound
up the Chagre River, that Capt. William Lee, commander
of the snow Burnator is on the shore and that Capt.
Stupert in a bilander is going down to the River of
Dulce - extract of a letter from Jamaica dated 4 Mar.
(10 June)

Address of the Pennsylvania Assembly to the proprietors,
John, Thomas and Richard Penn (10 June)

TURNER, George - deserted from on board the ship Mary,
George Davis master, bound to London; reward will be
paid if he is taken up and brought to John Reynell in
Phila. (10 June)

QUIN, Michael, Irishman - same as above

BURNE, Dennis, Irishman - same as above

Tea is for sale at the north end of Second St., next door
to Mr. Benezet's (10 June)

BARKER, John, servant, age c. 18, born in London and
brought up in Ireland - runaway from Richard Waln, Jr.,
near Phila. (10 June)

MILLER, Alexander, peruke-maker - has let out the shop belonging to his house and has moved upstairs; Joseph
Goodwin, bookbinder from London, has taken over Miller's shop in Second St. near Black Horse Alley, Phila.
(10 June)

OTTINGER, Christopher, constable of Springfield Precinct -

offers reward for capture of Jacob Ebberman, a German
or Palatine of Germantown Twp., Phila. Co., a butcher,
who counterfeited and altered bills and escaped when
Ottinger was taking him to the Goal of Phila. (10 June)

BLAKELEY, Henry, Irish servant, age <u>c</u>. 17 - runaway from
John McMachin, of Buckingham Twp., Bucks Co. (10 June);
on 4 June John Gooding, sheriff at Newcastle, advertises that he has the runaway in the Goal of Newcastle
(1 July)

PASCHALL, Jonathan - will sell cows, a horse, beef, herring, etc., at auction at the house late of John
Fisher, dec'd, on Fisher's Island (10 June)

VARNALL, Amos, of Willistown, Chester Co. - has taken up
a cow at his plantation (10 June)

DAVIS, John, English servant, age <u>c</u>. 40 - runaway from
Thomas Sligh, of Baltimore Co., Md. (10 June)

HANKER, William, English servant, age <u>c</u>. 30 - same as
above

Sloop <u>Eunice</u>, Joseph Vesey master, now at Ingram's wharf
in Phila. - will sail for Jamaica; for freight or passage agree with the master (10 June)

House, bake-house, cooper's shop, storehouse and wharf in
Bristol, Bucks Co., are for sale; apply to Anthony
Wilson, of Middletown, Bucks Co. (10 June)

The Proprietors Reply to the Address of the Pennsylvania
Assembly (17 June)

Gov. of Jamaica and Messr. Bickfords returned 10 days ago
from Porto Bello with report of the misconduct of the
admiral and general - extract of a letter from Jamaica
dated 26 Apr. (17 June)

The <u>Baltimore</u>, Capt. Biggs, from London - arrived 28 May
at Herring Bay with news that the new governor is to
sail about the middle of July - Annapolis item of 29
May (17 June)

Sloop <u>Endeavour</u>, Thomas Waterman master, now at Ingram's
wharf in Phila. - will sail for Jamaica; for freight or
passage agree with Richard Gilman on board (17 June)

James Friers or James Blacks, at Kensington will pay reward for recovery of a mare strayed or stolen from Robert
Adam's place near Frankford in Phila. Co. (17 June)

The Sign of the Indian King (where Owen Owen, lately
dec'd, lived) in Market St., Phila., is for sale; apply
to said house or Richard Brockden, opposite the Butchers
Shambles in the same street (17 June)

Brigantine **Sally**, Joseph Arthur, Sr., master - will sail
for Jamaica; for freight or passage agree with the
master on board or at his house in Walnut St., Phila.
(17 June)

LOADSMAN, William, Irish servant, joiner - runaway from
Tobias Griscom, living in Queen Ann's Co. (17 June)

GRAFTON, Richard, of Newcastle, who plans to remove to
Phila. - offers real estate for sale (17 June)

CARPENTER, Henry, servant, carpenter by trade - runaway
together with his 13-year-old son, also named Henry,
from Benjamin Mifflin in Phila. (17 June)

GRIGG, John, of Reading Furnace, Nantmel Twp., Chester Co.
- offers reward for strayed or stolen mare (17 June)

Ship **Linnen Draper** is to be sold at auction at Oswald
Peel's wharf in Phila. (17 June)

MAUGRIDGE, William, in Race Place St., Phila. - has pine
plank for sale (17 June)

FRANKLIN, William - offers reward for recovery of a mare
strayed from the Northern Liberties of Phila. (17 June)

BLACKWOOD, Hugh, fuller, of Cohansie, Salem Co., N.J. -
offers reward for recovery of a gelding, supposedly
stolen by an Irishman named William Wahup; reward will
be paid by the owner or by John Blackwood, fuller, at
the head of Timber Creek (17 June)

DUNLAP, Elizabeth - states that threats and abuse from
her husband, James Dunlap, of Piles Grove, Salem Co.,
N.J., caused her to take refuge at her father's; she
will claim her right of dower to her husband's estate
(17 June)

HUNLOKE, Thomas, High Sheriff of Burlington Co. - offers
reward for capture of the following, who broke out of
the goal of Burlington Co.: Hugh Hartley, age c. 35,
collier; James McBridge, age c. 30; Patrick Welch, age
c. 40 (17 June)

HOLTSTYN, Stephen, servant, age c. 33 - runaway from Andrew
Campbell, of Orange Co., Va. (17 June)

366

LEAMING, Aaron, Sr., on Cape May - has taken up a ship's
long-boat about 12 miles without Cape May (17 June)

Letter from Kingston, Jamaica, 29 Apr., recounts failure
of designed march on Panama and speaks favorably of
the assiduity of Capt. Lowther - item from the <u>Virginia
Gazette</u> (24 June)

DAVIS, Henry, age <u>c</u>. 26 or 28, under sentence of death for
the murder of a man in King William Co. - Wednesday
last escaped from prison with the help of 2 criminals,
Thomas Pope and Thomas Hicks, who broke open Mr. Bur-
sett's stable and stole one horse; Pope, Hicks and a
woman accomplice were taken and imprisoned and Davis
came to the prison and surrendered - Williamsburg item
of 28 May (24 June)

HAWES, Capt. - lately come to Boston from the Isle of May;
being chased by a Spanish privateer, he pretended he
was going to attack and the Spaniard fled (24 June)

NEALSON, Capt. John - arrived last week at New York in
the ship <u>Grace</u> from Bristol, with news from England
(24 June)

Saturday last 2 privateers belonging to Phila., the
schooner <u>George</u> and the sloop <u>Joseph</u> <u>and</u> <u>Mary</u>, fell
down the river to proceed against the Spaniards (24
June)

MATHEWSON, William, a Scotchman, who served his apprenticeship to Samuel Parr of New Jersey - absented himself from William Clarke, master of the brigantine
<u>Revolution</u>; if Mathewson is brought to William Clarke
or Edward Durey a reward will be paid (24 June)

ARTHUR, Capt. Joseph, in Walnut St., Phila. - has Negroes
for sale (24 June)

INGLIS, John - has for sale a Negro woman and her daughter (24 June)

BROWN, Michael, silk-dyer from London - continues to live
in Chesnut St., Phila., near Mr. Hamilton's (24 June)

Upon complaint of Capt. Blackleach and William Adams, both
of Stratford, Conn., against disorders caused in their
town by John Davenport and others, the matter was
examined by the General Assembly, which ordered that
Davenport be sent to his place of abode in Southold,
Long Island - Boston item of 14 June (1 July)

COCKS, Capt. Josiah, late commander of the ship <u>Adventure</u>
- arrived at Boston after having run ashore on the Isle
of Sable on 30 Apr.; Mr. James Cox, a passenger, died;
a man and a boy also died on shore as a result of the
hardships they had endured - Boston item of 14 June (1
July)

Thursday afternoon arrived at Charlestown the <u>Wilmington</u>,
Capt. James Howell, from Frederica, with an express
from General Oglethorpe to Capt. Charles Hardy; the
guard schooner of Oglethorpe is the <u>Ranger</u>, commanded
by Capt. Matthew Higginbotham - Charlestown item of 21
June (1 July)

Friday last H.M.S. <u>Rose</u>, Capt. Thomas Frankland commander,
arrived at Charlestown with 4 prizes; Capt. Frankland,
age 22, is a grandson of Oliver Cromwell - Charlestown
item of 21 June (1 July)

ALLEN, Patrick, Irish servant, age <u>c</u>. 30, house-joiner, a
Roman Catholic - runaway from Richard Jerrard, of
Spring Garden, near Phila., wheelwright (1 July)

MORGAN, Evan, living in Market St., Phila. - has some
small printed promisary notes of hand to use in the
present shortage of small change (1 July)

PAWLING, Henry, of Perkiomun, Phila. Co., yeoman - his
wife Mary has eloped from him (1 July)

FULLERTOWN, Capt. - has brought news from Europe - Boston
item of 24 June (8 July)

WILSON, Ebenezer (<u>alias</u> Lloyd) - warning of him is issued,
as he is a thief; last week he was in the Goal of
Phila. for a felony in Chester Co. (8 July)

STRETTELL, Robert, in Front St., Phila. - has for sale
cloth, tea, hardware, wine (8 July)

Chemicals and drugs are for sale at the Apothecary's
Arms, next door but one to Evan Morgan's in Market
St., Phila. (8 July)

MURLEY, Cornelius, Irish servant, age <u>c</u>. 35 - runaway
from William Noble, of Fallowfield Twp., Chester Co.
(8 July)

Cambridge, Negro slave, age <u>c</u>. 38 - runaway from Hannah
Pugh, in Chesnut St., Phila., near Mr. Hamilton's (8
July)

BRADFORD, William, Jr., has set up a new printing office in the house in which Andrew Bradford formerly lived in Second St., Phila. (8 July)

FLING, Edward, Irish servant, age c. 18 - runaway from Thomas Green, near Port Tobacco, Charles Co., Md. (8 July)

HUNTER, Hungerford, convict servant, age c. 26 - runaway from William McAtee, near Port Tobacco, Charles Co., Md. (8 July)

SKADDOCK, Charles (alias Robert Davison), convict servant, age c. 26 - runaway from Samuel Hanson, near Port Tobacco, Charles Co., Md. (8 July)

John Salkeld, in Chester, or Abraham Darlington, in Birmingham will pay reward for recovery of a gelding strayed or stolen from the pasture of John Salkeld in Chester (8 July)

A number of tracts of land in West New Jersey are offered for sale by John Ladd and Edward Shippen, attornies for Col. John Alford, of Charles Town in New England (8 July)

WHITE, Richard, Irishman, age c. 30, a ditcher, who worked lately at the Great Meadows of Mr. George Green - runaway from Jacob Ford, of Hannover Town, Morris Co., East New Jersey (8 July)

COLLINGS, Michael, Irish servant, age c. 24, weaver - runaway from John Scott, of Hannover Town, Morris Co., East New Jersey; reward will be given if he or White is recured and notice given to the above masters or to Manuel Creel at Wells's Ferry or James Johnston at Trenton (8 July)

OLDDIN, John, Jr., of Windsor, Middlesex Co., N.J. - his wife Susannah has eloped from him and left her children (8 July)

McATEE, Thomas, servant, age c. 30, weaver - runaway from David Kennedy, of Londonderry Twp., Chester Co. (8 July)

CROKER, Capt. and Robert Marshall - on Monday last were drowned within 10 feet of the shore at Annapolis when their canoe sank; Croker had a wife and 3 small children near the head of the bay - Annapolis item of 28 June (15 July)

RYMER, Thomas, Englishman, lately inlisted in West Jersey
by Lt. Anthony Palmer - deserted from Regt. of Col.
William Gooch (15 July)

FURY, Thomas, age c. 21, labourer, born in North of Ireland, who worked in Maryland and Chester Co. and lately
in Trenton - deserted from Col. William Gooch's Regt.
(15 July)

DAVIDSON, Capt., commander of a privateer of Rhode Island
- has taken several small Spanish prizes (22 July)

ALLEN, Capt., commander of the Revenge privateer of Newport - has taken a large sloop (22 July)

JACKSON, Capt., late commander of a brigantine belonging
to Boston - last Thursday arrived at Boston; his ship
had been taken by the privateer sloop of Don Francisco
Lewis, who took 36 English vessels, including a brigantine of Boston, commanded by Capt. Dogget and the
brigantine William, John Hauselber master - Boston item
of 12 July (22 July)

GRACE, Robert - will let ¼ part of Coventry Forge in
Chester Co. (22 July)

Sloop Ann, William Hall master, at Market St. wharf,
Phila. - will sail for Jamaica (22 July)

Sugar, candy, molasses and tea - for sale by Mary Oswald
at the house of Joseph Turner, and by William Wallace,
at the Sugar House, sugar baker (22 July)

PITTS, Richard, at his house in Front St., Phila. - sells
sugar, chairs, wool, pitch, etc. (22 July)

PUGH, John, apprentice, age c. 18 - runaway from Benjamin
Betterton, of Phila., cooper (22 July)

BARD, John, whose shop is next door but one to Evan Morgan
in Market St., Phila. - sells chemicals and drugs (22
July)

WALLACE, John, whose store is in Front St., Phila., next
door to Mr. Vanderspiegel's - sells mercery, ironmongery and earthen wares (22 July)

McINTYRE, Henry, of Birmingham, Chester Co. - Saturday
last was assaulted by his Irish servant, Robert Jones,
age c. 20, and was so wounded that he died the next
day (29 July)

ROUKE, Hugh, Irish servant, age c. 18 - runaway from Joseph Grove of Fredrick Twp., Phila. Co. (29 July)

MARSHAL, John, English servant - runaway from Isaac Forman, of Croswicks, West New Jersey (29 July)

HAZARD, Samuel, at his house in Second St., opposite to the Baptist Meeting-house in Phila. - sells cloth, hardware, glass etc. (29 July)

Account of alleged plot of Indians in Kent Co., Md.; an Indian named Toby discovered the plan; many Indians were arrested; Col. Gale seized their magazine - extract of letter from Kent Co., Md., and another from Annapolis (5 Aug.)

HUMPHRYS, Capt. - arrived 26 July at Boston from Holland with European news (5 Aug.)

Four privateers are fitting out at Newport, R.I., Capts. Dyer, Brown, Wentworth and Woolford - Newport item of 23 July (5 Aug.)

It is reported that 1,200 Spaniards have landed on Cumberland Island, where there is a fort and 180 men under Capt. Houghton - extract of a letter from Charlestown, S.C., dated 6 July (5 Aug.)

WARNER, Isaiah, at his office, almost opposite to Charles Brockden's, in Chesnut St., Phila. - does printing (5 Aug.)

GOODING, John, Sheriff - has taken up and holds in the County Goal in Newcastle a certain William Carter, an Irishman, age c. 24, on suspicion of being a runaway servant (5 Aug.)

POTTS, Thomas, late of Burlington Co., tanner, dec'd - accounts with estate to be settled with Sarah Potts, administratrix (5 Aug.)

JACKSON, Joseph, sheriff - will sell at auction at Giles Lawrence's, at the old Crown Tavern, Bristol, Bucks Co., tract of 700 acres, part of tract known as the Mill-land, lately belonging to John Burke, dec'd; it was taken in execution at the suit of Joseph Turner (5 Aug.)

LLOYD, Samuel - offers reward for recovery of a mare and colt; they are to be brought to Benjamin Morgan in Water St., Phila. (5 Aug.)

BARTLESON, Bartle, in Norrington Twp., Phila. Co. - offers reward for recovery of a watch, stolen from him,
it is suspected, by one John Ashbrook (5 Aug.)

Declaration of some pastors in Boston and Charles-Town
with regard to the Rev. James Davenport, of Southold
on Long Island; it is dated 1 July 1742 and is signed
by the following: Benjamin Colman, Thomas Prince,
William Cooper, Samuel Checkley, Joshua Gee, Mather
Byles, Ellis Gray, Joseph Dewall, John Webb, Thomas
Foxcroft, William Welsteed, Hull Abbot, Thomas Prentice, Andrew Eliot (12 Aug.)

Letter from the Rev. G. Tennent, dated New Brunswick, 12
Feb. 1742, to the Rev. Mr. Dickinson's of the Jerseys;
the original was in the hands of the Rev. Mr. Clap,
Rector of Yale College; it is concerned with Mr.
Davenport's conduct (12 Aug.)

A protest to the Synod of Phila. against excluding the
Presbytery of New Brunswick; it is signed by Jonathan
Dickinson, Ebenezer Pemberton, David Elmore, Silas
Leonard, Daniel Whitehead, John Pierson, Simon Horton,
Azariah Horton, Nathaniel Hazard and Timony Whitehead
(12 Aug.)

Ship, the <u>Peggy</u> <u>and Jenny</u>, Martin Long commander, on 24
Feb. took a new from Ostend, which was condemned at
Antigua (12 Aug.)

PATRIDGE, Capt. - arrived at Boston 1 Aug. from Liverpool;
on the passage he spoke with the ship that was Capt.
Fox's, taken by the Spaniards and retaken by the English - Boston item of 2 Aug. (12 Aug.)

FISHBOURN, William, late of Phila., dec'd - accounts with
estate to be settled with Jane Fishbourn, executrix
(12 Aug.)

WOTERING, Johann - warns the public not to lend money on
his bonds to Johann Ludewig Schäffer, since Schäffer is
under arrest (12 Aug.)

BUTLER, Zachariah, of Birmingham Twp., Chester Co. - offers reward for recovery of 2 horses that strayed away
from William Hayes, of Marlborough, Chester Co. (12
Aug.)

WRIGHT, William, servant, age <u>c</u>. 24 - runaway from Obadiah
Hireton, of Springfield Twp., Burlington Co. (12 Aug.)

COES, Anthony, Dutch servant, age <u>c</u>. 16 - runaway from Caspar

Ulrich, of Phila., baker (12 Aug.)

WILLING, Charles, lately returned from England - has a great choice of goods for sale (19 Aug.)

LIGHTFOOT, William - offers reward for recovery of a mare stolen from the plantation of Michael Lightfoot, at Newgarden, Chester Co. (19 Aug.)

PLUMSTED, Clement (surviving trustee of Archibald Hope and Henry Hope) by virtue of a deed from the executors of Jonathan Dickinson, late of Phila., dec'd - will sell property on Society Hill which was formerly in the possession of Abel Tudor and also a parcel of land bounded east by the Delaware, south by land late of Richard Edge, west by King St. and north by land reputed to be Joseph Growden's (19 Aug.)

Message from Gov. George Thomas to the Pennsylvania Assembly and message from the Assembly to the governor (26 Aug.)

FRENCH, David, late Speaker of the Assembly of the Three Lower Counties on Delaware - died at beginning of this week at Newcastle; his body was brought to Chester and interred there (26 Aug.)

PRESTON, Mrs. Margaret, an eminent preacher among the Quakers - died Sunday last in Phila. (26 Aug.)

Brigantine Mary, John Mason master - arrived Monday at Phila. from Holland with 100 Palatines (26 Aug.)

TIFFIN, Capt. - arrived Tuesday at Phila. from Lisbon, with whom came Capts. Green and Hamilton, both of whom had been taken by the Spaniards at the beginning of the war (26 Aug.)

A memorandum of the Rev. Lewis Thurnstein concerning troubles in connection with the Lutheran Church in Phila.; he writes of the Rev. John Christopher Pyrlaeus, a Lutheran divine (26 Aug.)

TURNER, Peter, who intends to leave Pennsylvania with all his family - offers for sale the house late Mr. William Preston's (now in his, Peter Turner's possession) in Front St., 20 feet wide eastward, running between Mr. Robert Strettle and Mr. Joseph Sims (26 Aug.)

Richardson and Eversley will sell many goods in the house where John Stamper lately lived in Water St., Phila. (26 Aug.)

Eight weaving looms - are for sale at the house of Richard Baily, dec'd, on Society Hill (26 Aug.)

KINNERSLEY, Ebenezer, near the George Inn, Phila. - has a Negro woman for sale (26 Aug.)

WEBB, William - offers reward for recovery of mare strayed or stolen from his plantation in Kennet Twp., Chester Co.; the mare may be brought to him or to Benjamin Franklin in Phila. (26 Aug.)

Ship Constantine, Henry Elwes master, now at Mr. Lawrence's wharf in Phila. - will sail for London; for freight or passage agree with Edward Shippen or with the master (26 Aug.)

WISELY, Peter, Irish servant (who was servant to Mr. Postlethwaite about 2½ years ago) - runaway from Daniel Cheston, of Chester Town, Md.; reward will be paid if the servant is brought to his master or to John Wilcocks, merchant, in Phila. (26 Aug.)

STACY, Mahlon, Esq., dec'd - accounts with estate to be settled with Samuel Atkinson and Joshua Wright, administrators (26 Aug.)

GREW, Theophilus - intends to open school in Phila. about the middle of October (26 Aug.)

SAMPSON, Edward, servant, age c. 23, tailor - runaway from Joseph Wright, tailor, of Pequea, Lancaster Co. (26 Aug.)

Message of Gov. George Thomas to the Pennsylvania Assembly and answer of the Assembly (2 Sept.)

Lengthy comment by David Evans, at Piles Grove, on letter of Gilbert Tennent and a letter of Gilbert Tennent to Mr. Franklin, with reference to Mr. Dickinson and Mr. Davenport (2 Sept.)

Letter, signed Britannicus, to David Nitschmann, Bishop of the Moravian Church, now living in Bethlehem in the Forks of Delaware in Pennsylvania, and an answer thereto signed "Angelica" (2 Sept.)

Account of how Capt. Thomas Frankland in the Rose man-of-war took the Spanish privateer sloop commanded by Lewis Severio and also a Dutch snow off the north side of Cuta (2 Sept.)

ROUSE, Capt., commander of a bylander privateer belonging

to Newport, has taken a rich Spanish prize - Boston item of 23 Aug. (2 Sept.)

A prize sloop, taken by Capt. Powers in a Rhode Island privateer, arrived last week at Newport - Boston item of 23 Aug. (2 Sept.)

DAVENPORT, James, of Southold, Suffolk Co., N.Y. - Thursday last was indicted by a Grand Jury of Suffolk Co., Mass., for having made slanderous speeches against ministers, especially those in Boston and Dorchester; as Davenport refused to give bail, he was committed to goal - Boston item of 23 Aug. (2 Sept.)

Ship Loyal Judith, Capt. Cowie, with about 400 Palatines consigned to Robert Strettell, merchant in Front St., Phila. - arrived Wednesday at Phila. (2 Sept.)

VAUGHAN, Thomas, Irish servant, age c. 23 - runaway from James Shields, of New Lynn, Chester Co. (2 Sept.)

SHIELDS, John, Irish servant - runaway (in company with Thomas Vaughan, servant to James Shields) from Samuel McAlbany, of Fallowfield Twp., Chester Co. (2 Sept.)

Persons wishing to serve in Col. William Gooch's Regt. are to repair to Capt. Thomas Clark at Wollard Allen's at the Roll of Tobacco in Second St.,Phila., at Malachi Walton's in Bristol, to the Captain's plantation at the Falls of Delaware, to Lt. Henry Hodge or Lt. Peter Grung, now recruiting; the following are deserters from Capt. Thomas Clark's company: Thomas Upstill, John Price, Luke Maine, Nathaniel Page, Joseph Gilbreth, Alexander Dunche, John Ward, John Murphey, Samuel Meade, Benjamin Port, John Simson (2 Sept.)

WRIGHT, Jonathan, late of Burlington, dec'd - accounts with estate to be settled with the executors, Caleb Raper, Samuel Lovell and Joshua Raper (2 Sept.)

Among tracts of land belonging to the estate of Jonathan Wright, late of Burlington, dec'd, are the following: 250 acres within 3 miles of Burlington, now in the tenure of Benjamin Butterworth; 250 acres at Laomentong, alias Black River, in Morris Co., now in the tenure of Aaron Starke; 50 acres at the half way on the new road from Burlington to Little Egg Harbour, known by the name of Tom Roberts's Meadow - these are to be sold by the executors of the estate (2 Sept.)

CHALMERS, James - has for sale a wharf and stores in Wilmington (2 Sept.)

Bard and Lawrence, Jr., at their store in Water St., Phila., opposite to Thomas Lawrence's - sell cloth, hardware and leather (2 Sept.)

BONE, William, convict servant, age c. 19 - runaway from William and James Dimett, at the Forks of Gunpowder River, Baltimore Co., Md. (2 Sept.)

ARCHDEACON, William, alias Cuddle, convict servant, age c. 49 - same as above

TYNG, Capt., commander of the snow Prince of Orange, of the Province of Massachusetts - has been ordered by the governor of Massachusetts to go in quest of 2 Spanish privateers - Boston item of 30 Aug. (9 Sept.)

BROWN, Capt. - Monday last arrived at Boston in a sloop from Jamaica with news that Col. Cope, governor of Placentia and Lt.-Col. of the America Regt. in the West Indies, died 11 July and that Ensign Brintnal of Chelsea is also dead - Boston item of 30 Aug. (9 Sept.)

Affair of Mr. Davenport, of Long Island, has been put over at the Superiour Court in Boston until Tuesday - Boston item of 30 Aug. (9 Sept.)

McRABBIE, John, Scotchman, who came in a servant for 4 years (2 of which he served with Ephraim McDowel, near Lemington River in East New Jersey) - has been taken up on suspicion of being a runaway by Sheriff Samuel Robinson and has been committed to the Goal of Kent Co. on Delaware (9 Sept.)

BOONE, George, of Exeter, Chief Ranger of Phila. Co. - lists horses that have been taken up (9 Sept.)

Dr. Tennent's Essay on the Pleurisy - for sale by B. Franklin (9 Sept.)

Notice (in German) of a writing against the Herrnhuter, edited by the Dutch clergyman Johann Phillip Boehmen, is sold in Phila. by David Sussholz in Second St., by Johannes Wuster and B. Franklin in Market St., by Henrich Antes in Falckenar Schwamm and George Neisser in Bethlehem (9 Sept.)

JONES, John, late of Phila., bolter, dec'd - accounts with estate are to be settled with the executors, Elizabeth and Charles Jones, Wight Massey and Enoch Flower (9 Sept.)

LAWRENCE, Gyles, states that William Gale, who was committed to goal in Bucks Co. for theft and then escaped, left a mare at the old Crown Tavern in Bristol, Bucks Co. (9 Sept.)

VANSANT, Nicholas, of Kent Co., Md. - offers reward for arrest of James Knox, age c. 30, lately at the head of Elk in Maryland, who sold to Vansant a mare and horse later proved to be the property of Jacob Miller and Mary Dougharty, of Lancaster Co. (9 Sept.)

WHITE, Townsend, opposite to Mr. John Hyatt's in Front St., Phila. - sells goods just imported from London in the ship William, Henry Harrison master (9 Sept.)

NORTON, William, at his store on Mr. Hamilton's wharf in Phila. - sells rum, trainoil, mackrel, pickled lobsters and salmon, chairs, skins, etc. (9 Sept.)

RODGERS, James, at Mrs. Andrews in Water St., next door to the Blue Anchor in Phila. - sells cutlery (9 Sept.)

DAVENPORT, James - Wednesday last at Boston a jury declared him non compos mentis and he was discharged - Boston item of 6 Sept. (16 Sept.)

WIMBLE, Capt. James, of an English privateer, the Revenge - defeated a Spanish privateer in an engagement in the North Straits of Bahama - New York item of 13 Sept. (16 Sept.)

CANNON, Capt., from Boston - arrived 12 Sept. at New York with an extract from a letter giving details of privateering in the West Indies - New York item of 13 Sept. (16 Sept.)

On 6 July arrived at Boston Capts. Rouse, Flowers and Wilkinson in 3 privateers; they had attacked a Spanish fleet off the coast of Florida, had taken 5 Spanish privateers and drove 5 more ashore (16 Sept.)

The following in Phila. on 1 Sept. engaged to accept gold and silver at a fixed rate: Clement Plumsted, Thomas Lawrence, John Inglis, William Allen, Peter Baynton, Samuel McCall, James Hamilton, William Till, John Wallace, Edward Shippen, Charles Willing, Joseph Turner, Peter Kock, Samuel Perry, Abraham Taylor, William Peters, Jaspar McCall, John Yeates, Samuel Powel, Jr., William Bell, Samuel Hasel, Caleb Emerson, Richard Peters, Andrew Hamilton, William Moore, Peter Robertson, George Ellice, Peter Bard, Joseph Sims, Tho. Lawrence, Jr., Nathan Levy, Joseph Shippen, Attwood Shute, Richard Nixon, John Seymour, Richard Hockley,

Robert Wakely, Alexander Graydon, Peter Turner, Annely
& Lewis & Vanderspiegel, Townsend White, John Bleakley,
Samuel Morris, John Harrison, Evan Morgan, Samuel Ha-
zard, William Biddle, John Biddle, David Franks, Pat-
rick Baird, Joseph Redmond, James Boyden, William
Humphreys, Samuel Neave, John Hopkins, Charles West,
William Cooper, Samuel Hastings, Lyn-Ford Laraner,
John Sober, Thomas Hopkinson, James Macky, Benj. Shoe-
maker, Matthias Aspden, Johannes Rush, William Spaf-
ford, John Ryan, Walter Goodman, John Gilleylen, George
Okill, George Entricken, Thomas Bayeux, Davey & Carsan,
John Hyatt (16 Sept.)

MULLOAN, Matthew, servant, native Irishman, age c̲. 20 -
runaway from Jonathan Potts, of Plymouth Twp., Phila.
Co. (16 Sept.)

WISSE, Jacob, on a journey - is desired to come and settle
some needful business at home (16 Sept.)

TEMPLETON, Hugh - taken up by John Hyatt, sheriff, and
committed to Goal of Phila. Co. upon suspicion of being a runaway servant (16 Sept.)

BRIDGES, Edward, late of Phila., merchant, dec'd - his
widow, Cornelia Bridges, intending for Europe, desires
all accounts with the estate to be settled and to let
the house called the Scales (16 Sept.)

NORRINGTON, Thomas, baker, in Second St., Phila., intending to leave Pennsylvania - wishes to have all accounts settled (16 Sept.)

DOUD, Richard, Irish servant, age c̲. 20 - runaway from
Samuel Blair, of Bethlehem Twp., Hunterdon Co., West
New Jersey; it is suspected he has got an indenture
belonging to one John Bath, who served his time in
Lancaster Co. (16 Sept.)

Notice is given that William Philpot, of or near Frankford, and Mary his wife (daughter and one of the heirs
of Richard Wall, the first purchaser of the lots
called Cherry Garden on Society Hill, Phila.) - claim
a right to Cherry Garden, lately advertised to be sold
by Clement Plumsted, Esq. (16 Sept.)

Account of the arrival at Newport, R.I., of Capts. Rouse,
Flower, Wilkinson, of their assistance to Capt. Richardson and their taking of a privateer sloop formerly
taken by Capt. Norton but retaken by the Spaniards;
there is also a relation of General Oglethorpe's defeat
of a Spanish expedition from St. Augustine (23 Sept.)

Among items of real estate to be sold or let by Edward, Joseph and William Shippen are a water lot joining to Mr. Woodrop's wharf, 8 acres on Passyunk Rd., near Tidmarsh's barn, 2 pastures on the road to George Gray's ferry, the house in Germantown called the Roe Buck Tavern (23 Sept.)

FRANKLIN, B. - answers charges that the publication of the minutes of the House had been intentionally delayed (23 Sept.)

Charles, Negro, age c. 30 - runaway from Darby Handly, at the Fork of Gunpowder, Baltimore Co., Md. (23 Sept.)

FLEESON, Plunket, at the Easy Chair, in Chesnut St., Phila. - sells chairs and does upholsterer's work (23 Sept.)

Account of the motions of the Spanish fleet and those of General Oglethorpe; mention is made of the death on 24 May of one man under Lt. Tolson; Capt. William Gray on Cumberland Island saw the Spaniards land there - Charlestown item of 5 July (30 Sept.)

On 27 June the General sent Mr. Mulryne with an express to the Lt.-Gov. and William Smith with another to Capt. Hardy - Charlestown item of 5 July (30 Sept.)

BARRET, Capt. James - will be appointed commander of the Charlestown Row Galley - Charlestown item of 5 July (30 Sept.)

Ship Success, Capt. Thompson - arrived 7 July at Charlestown (30 Sept.)

BEDON, Stephen, Jr., express from Gen. Oglethorpe - arrived 14 July at Charlestown from Frederica to ask for help; Col. Vander Dussen, appointed to command the relief force, begged leave to resign - Charlestown item of 19 July (30 Sept.)

On 7 July the Spaniards killed one Small; Oglethorpe hastened to the spot, and, with some Highlanders, Capt. Grey and Capt. Jones and some Indians charged Capt. Sebastian Saintio and Capt. Mageleeto; Mageleeto was killed; Saintio was taken and the Spaniards were defeated - Frederica item of 9 July (30 Sept.)

Lt. Southerland and Lt. Mackay utterly defeated the Spaniards under Don Antonio Barbaria, who was taken prisoner, mortally wounded - Frederica item of 9 July (30 Sept.)

On 13 July the Spaniards, at sight of English relief ships, hastened on board their vessels in confusion; Col. Beale has been commissioned to fortify Charlestown - Charlestown item of 26 July (30 Sept.)

Within this fortnight Capts. North and Cusack arrived at Phila. from Holland with 900 Palatines (30 Sept.)

PHILPOT, Richard, of Great Egg Harbour, West New Jersey - on Wednesday night was murdered in his own house by Timothy Dennis, age c. 30 or 40, and another man; Dennis is taken and committed to Burlington Goal (30 Sept.)

It is reported by way of New York that Capt. Dowel, in the Joseph and Mary privateer, lately fought an engagement with a Spanish privateer off Porto Rico (30 Sept.)

PARKER, Nicholas - has lately come to America in search for his brother Thomas, who lives in Waterford Twp., Gloucester Co., about 10 miles from Phila. (30 Sept.)

ELLIS, Robert, Jr. - offers reward for recovery of a mare (bred near Perkioman by Grominus Haus), strayed or stolen from a pasture near the road leading from Phila. to the lower ferry (30 Sept.)

Reward will be paid for recovery of 2 geldings, strayed or stolen from the George Inn in Phila., by John Bood, in Phila., or Benjamin Stelle, at Piscataway, East Jersey (30 Sept.)

WORMLY, Henry, late of Phila., baker, dec'd - accounts with estate to be settled with William Hodge, in Walnut St. (30 Sept.)

The Marriage of Cana (sermon preached by Rev. George Whitefield) - just published by William Bradford, Jr., in Second St., Phila. (30 Sept.)

TENNENT, Rev. William, Sr., of Neshameny - wishes to sell the plantation of 100 acres where he now lives in Warminster Twp., on the York Rd., about 18 miles from Phila. (30 Sept.)

LEVY, Nathan, in Front St., Phila. - has a Negro woman for sale (30 Sept.)

BEDDOME, Joseph, at his store in Market St., Phila., behind Mr. Grizley's house - sells cloth and hardware (30 Sept.)

PERRY, Samuel, at his store, the corner of Carpenter's
wharf in Water St., Phila. - sells cloth, cutlery, ironmongery (30 Sept.)

PARKER, Alexander, living almost opposite to the church
burying-ground in Mulberry St., Phila. - offers reward
for recovery of a stolen gelding (30 Sept.)

Monday last the Swift man-of-war, Capt. Bladwell, came
into Charlestown Harbor and on Tuesday H.M.S. Rose,
Capt. Frankland, which received a warm welcome; it is
reported that when Capt. Hardy first sailed for St.
Simon's he met a Rhode Island privateer commanded by
Capt. Allen - Charlestown item of 9 Aug. (7 Oct.)

The South Carolina galley Beauford, Capt. Gibson, put
into Frederica 3 Aug.; Friday last Capt. Frankland,
the Flamborough and Swift, men-of-war, and 4 provincial
vessels (commanded by Capts. Murry, Barrett, Chapman
and Braddock) sailed over the bar to cruise against
the Spaniards - Charlestown item of 16 Aug. (7 Oct.)

Speech of Gov. Thomas Bladen to the Maryland Assembly and
the Address of the House of Delegates to the governor
(7 Oct.)

PHILIPS, Capt. - arrived 26 Sept. at Boston from London
with European news (7 Oct.)

Friday last the following were elected for Phila. Co.:
representatives--Thomas Leech, John Kinsey, Robert
Jones, Isaac Norris, Edward Warner, Owen Evans, James
Morris, Joseph Trotter; sheriffs--John Hyatt, Mordicai
Lloyd; coroners--Henry Pratt, Jacob Duché; commissioner
--John Dylwin; assessors--Jeremiah Elfreth, Moses
Hughes, Thomas Fletcher, Thomas Potts, Jacob Levering,
Evan Jones; burgesses for Phila. City--Israel Pember-
ton, Oswald Peele; city assessors--John Stamper, Rich-
ard Parker, Edmund Wooley, Joseph Oldman, Jonathan
Zane, Thomas Howard (7 Oct.)

Friday last the following were elected for Bucks Co.:
representatives--Mahlon Kirkbride, Mark Watson, John
Watson, Abraham Chapman, John Hall, Benjamin Field,
Joseph Shaw, Garret Vansant; sheriffs--Joseph Jackson,
Timothy Smith; coroners--John Hart, Joseph Chapman;
commissioner--Abraham Chapman; assessors--Barthol.
Longstretch, Cephas Child, Adam Harker, Robert Smith,
John Dennis, John Williamson (7 Oct.)

Friday last the following were elected for Chester Co.:
representatives--James Gibbons, John Owen, Samuel

Levis, Jeremiah Star, Thomas Chandler, Joseph Harvey,
William Hughs, Thomas Tatnal; sheriffs--Benjamin Davis,
John Davis; coroners--Awbrey Bevan, David Cowpland;
commissioner--John Parry; assessors--Daniel Walker,
Joseph Gibbons, John Allen, Robert Millar, Thomas Mor-
gan, Joshua Thompson (7 Oct.)

Friday last the following were elected for Lancaster Co.:
representatives--Samuel Blunston, John Wright, Thomas
Lindley, Anthony Shaw; sheriffs--James Mitchel, James
Galbraith; coroners--John Weems, James Clark; commis-
sioner--John Allison; assessors--Jacob Huber, John
Wright, Jr., Andrew Work, Benjamin Chambers, Hugh Bole,
John Brandon (7 Oct.)

Friday last the following were elected for Newcastle Co.:
representatives--John McCoole, James McMahan, John
Vance, Samuel Clements, William Armstrong, Daniel Corbet; sheriffs--Henry Newton, Samuel Bickley; coroners--
Benjamin Cook, James McMullen (7 Oct.)

Friday last the following were elected for Kent Co.: repre-
sentatives--Mark Manlove, John Robinson, William Farson,
John Tilton, James Gorrel, Abraham Allee; sheriffs--
Samuel Robinson, Thomas Green; coroners--Edmund Badger,
Benjamin Johnson (7 Oct.)

Friday last the following were elected for Sussex Co.:
representatives--John Clowes, Daniel Nunez, Enoch Cummings, Jacob Kollock, Ryves Holt, William Till; sheriffs
--Peter Hall, William Shankland; coroners--Peter Clowes,
Charles Parry (7 Oct.)

TILL, William, Esq. - Tuesday last was chosen Mayor of
Phila. (7 Oct.)

JORDAN, Robert, an eminent preacher among the Quakers -
died Tuesday last in Phila. (7 Oct.)

To be sold or let to freight for Lisbon, Ireland or the
West Indies, by Peter Baynton, a new brigantine, built
at Piscataway in New England, now at Peter Baynton's
wharf (7 Oct.)

BEAUMONT, John, of the Falls Twp., Bucks Co., intending to
depart this province - wishes to settle all accounts
(7 Oct.)

Ship **Phoenix**, William Willson master, now at Oswald Peel's
wharf - will sail for South Carolina; for freight or
passage agree with the master or with Benjamin Shoemaker in Market St., Phila. (7 Oct.)

Lot and tenement in Third St., Phila., nearly against the Work-house, where the Dutch locksmith now lives - for sale; enquire of Abraham Kintzing, the horse-miller, next door to Mr. Hesselius in Market St. (7 Oct.)

BROWN, John, sailer, lately belonging to the ship Hanover Pink, Richard Northover master - escaped from the prison of Phila. - reward for his capture is offered by Thomas Croasdale, Deputy Sheriff (7 Oct.)

SPICER, Jacob, late of Cape May, dec'd - accounts with estate to be settled with John Jacob Spicer, executor (7 Oct.)

On 28 Aug. the following weighed anchor from Charlestown: the Beaufort, Gibson; the Charles-Town, Lyford, the Norfolk, Braddock; the Carolina, Murray; the Kingston, Chapman - Charlestown item of 6 Sept. (14 Oct.)

WATKINS, Lt. Thomas - arrived 24 Sept. at Charlestown from Georgia, having been appointed courier by General Oglethorpe (14 Oct.)

John Jerman's Almanack for the Year 1743 - is printed and sold by William Bradford in Second St., Phila. (14 Oct.)

GREW, Theophilus - teaches school in Phila. in Walnut St. at the house where Joseph Claypole formerly lived (14 Oct.)

GREEN, John, Irish servant, weaver - runaway from John Gill and Samuel Boggs, of Hattonfield, Gloucester Co., West New Jersey (14 Oct.)

McKEW, Katharine, Irish servant - same as above

BLEAKLEY, William, at his shop under John Bleakley's store - sells woolens, checks, Irish linen (14 Oct.)

Letter to Mr. Franklin, signed Philanthropos, with reference to Mr. Tennent and Mr. Davenport (21 Oct.)

WARREN, Capt., of H.M.S. Launceston, at New York - will sail 5 Nov. from there and convoy vessels to Barbados and Antigua (21 Oct.)

Ship Surprize, Joseph Redmond master, now at Mr. Plumstead's wharf in Phila. - will sail for Antigua; for freight or passage agree with the master or William Plumstead (21 Oct.)

Ship <u>Lucea</u>, Thomas Smith commander, at Plumsted's wharf -
will sail for Jamaica - for freight or passage agree
with Charles Willing or the master (21 Oct.)

Tract of land of 86 acres in Bucks Co., lying on Delaware,
adjoining to Dunk's ferry is for sale; enquire of Andrew Hamilton (21 Oct.)

CLYMER, Christopher - has for sale young Negro men (21
Oct.)

AGAR, Philip, at his store on Fishbourn's wharf - sells
cloth, hats, pewter, cutlery (21 Oct.)

LYNEALL, Richard, master of the small-sword - is to be
spoken with at Fredrick Smith's, hatter, at the corner
of Market St. and Front St. (21 Oct.)

Venture, Negro, age <u>c</u>. 20 - runaway from Capt. Charles
Walsh, who offers a reward if the runaway is brought
to Mr. John Parret's, shipwright, in Phila. (21 Oct.)

CARROL, James, of Northampton, Bucks Co. - offers a reward for recovery of a strayed gelding (21 Oct.)

WHITEFIELD, Rev. Mr. - designs to be in Charlestown, with
his wife and child by Christmas - Newport, R.I., item
of 7 Aug. (28 Oct.)

LEEK, John, of Cohansie, West New Jersey - about 2 weeks
ago, after a year's deliverance, made himself a eunuch; he is now in Dr. Johnson's hands (28 Oct.)

BLEAKLY, Henry, <u>alias</u> John Sempell, Irish servant, age <u>c</u>.
18 - runaway from John McMackin, of Buckingham Twp.,
Bucks Co. (28 Oct.)

JONES, William, servant, age <u>c</u>. 30, rug-weaver - runaway
from John Roe, living near Tulley's Neck, Queen Ann's
Co., Md. (28 Oct.)

Ship <u>Francis and Elizabeth</u>, George North commander, now
at Mifflin's wharf, Phila. - will sail for Londonderry;
for freight or passage agree with Walter Goodman, of
Phila., or the master of the ship (28 Oct.)

SIMMS, John, convict servant, age <u>c</u>. 30 - runaway from
John Howard, living at Elk Ridge, Anne-Arundel Co.,
Md. (28 Oct.)

HANDFIELD, Thomas, convict servant, age <u>c</u>. 18 or 20 -
same as above

Jenny, a slim young Negro wench - same as above

WALN, Richard, of Phila. - offers reward for recovery of
a bay horse strayed or stolen from his pasture (28 Oct.)

WRAGG, James, at his store in Water St., near Market St.,
Phila. - sells ironmongry and cutlery (28 Oct.)

Speech of Gov. George Thomas to Assembly of Newcastle,
Kent and Sussex on Delaware and the Assembly's address
to him (signed Rives Holt, Speaker) (4 Nov.)

Last Saturday was sen'night a sloop, Isaac Orr master,
ran upon the rocks off Cape Ann; the men were saved -
Boston item of 7 Oct. (4 Nov.)

Saturday last a sloop, Capt. Webber master, was cast
away in Well Bay near New York; a man, a woman and a
lad of c. 15 were drowned (4 Nov.)

Address presented on 16 Sept. to William Shirley, governor
of Massachusetts, from the Quakers (4 Nov.)

PITTS, Richard - offers reward for recovery of pocketbook
lost last market day in the market place in Phila. (4
Nov.)

Joseph Marks, in Walnut St., Phila., has 2 Negro men and
1 Negro woman for sale (4 Nov.)

RIGHTON, Sarah, in the Church Alley in Phila. - has for
sale a Negro woman (4 Nov.)

BINGHAM, James - has a plantation of 500 acres to let in
Tulpahockin (4 Nov.)

WARREN, Capt., of H.M.S. Launceston, stationed at New
York - offers reward of 5 pounds for capture of any
deserter (4 Nov.)

NORTON, John - offers reward if a horse, strayed or stolen
from his pasture near Phila., is brought to Robert
Couch, at the Pewter Platter in Front St., Phila. (4
Nov.)

Persons indebted to Messrs. White and Taylor are to pay
debts or give security to William Peters, their attorney (4 Nov.)

McCOOLE, Walter, of Windsor, Rockhill Twp., Chief Ranger
of Bucks Co. - has taken up a number of horses (11
Nov.)

Speech of Gov. Lewis Morris to New Jersey Assembly (11 Nov.)

Address of principal inhabitants of Port Royal thanking H. E. James Oglethorpe, who had beaten off the Spaniards - Charlestown item of 30 Aug. (11 Nov.)

Friday last Capt. Dupee arrived at Boston from Jamaica; he tells of plans to assist General Oglethorpe against the Spaniards - Boston item of 11 Oct. (11 Nov.)

Brick house, the Sign of the Swan, formerly belonging to Benjamin Fairman, dec'd, in Kensington, a mile from Phila., is to be sold or let by William Hayes; also a brick house, the Sign of the Three Crowns, belonging to William Hayes, in Kensington is to be sold or let (11 Nov.)

CRELL, Joseph, in Market St., Phila., the fourth house from the Conestogoe Waggon - will teach German or French (11 Nov.)

Tract of 1,150 acres in West Jersey, on a branch of Delaware, called Pohatecung, is for sale; enquire of Abraham Bickley (11 Nov.)

Speech to Gov. Lewis Morris from the New Jersey General Assembly (18 Nov.)

The Catherine, Alexander Phenix commander - was stranded at Barnegat but all lives were saved (18 Nov.)

WATKINS, Lt., courier to General Oglethorpe - arrived Friday last at Phila., having performed his route to Boston (18 Nov.)

HILL, Anthony, servant - runaway from Alexander Higginbottom, of Phila., bricklayer (18 Nov.)

CLAYPOOLE, James, in Walnut St., Phila. - has a Negro woman for sale (18 Nov.)

KASTOR, Arnold, over against the Sign of the Conestogoe Wagon in Market St., Phila. - has for sale hair cloths (18 Nov.)

DAMES, William, at his store in Water St., Phila., opposite the Sign of the Blue Anchor - sells cloth, wigs, fans, gowns, etc. (18 Nov.)

SMITH, William, of North East - offers reward for capture of an Englishman called Henry Yates, who stole a mare from Smith, if the thief or mare are brought to the Three Tuns in Chesnut St., Phila. (18 Nov.)

DUPE, Capt. - arrived Friday last at Boston from Jamaica (25 Nov.)

HAYS, Peter, of Stoneham, Mass., age 85 - was lately married to a widow of 82; she was the gentleman's sixth wife and he was her fifth husband - Boston item of 2 Nov. (25 Nov.)

HILL, Capt., of Phila., who has been missing for some time - has arrived at Charlestown, S.C.; he had been a prisoner of the Spaniards at La Vera Cruz (25 Nov.)

BRADFORD, Andrew, of Phila., printer, member of the Common Council of Phila. - died last night (25 Nov.)

Bilander Lucy, John Lindsay master, now at Edward Warner's wharf - will sail for South Carolina and Georgia; for freight or passage agree with Peter Bard or the master (25 Nov.)

RICKALY, John, dec'd - accounts with estate to be settled with the executors, Dennis Leary and Thomas Ingram (25 Nov.)

GRAY, Joseph - is removed from the Horse and Groom in Strawberry Alley to his house at the Sign of the Conestogoe Stage Waggon in Market St., Phila. (25 Nov.)

Plantation of 190 acres in Chester Twp., Burlington Co., about 9 miles from Phila., is for sale; enquire of Nicholas Toy living on said place (25 Nov.)

NAYLOR, John - offers reward for recovery of John Smith, servant, naylor by trade, who broke out of the Workhouse of Phila. (25 Nov.)

DICKSON, Samuel - has taken up a mare at his plantation in Mastick Twp., Lancaster Co., near Susquehannah (25 Nov.)

A detachment of troops from General Wentworth's forces, under the command of Col. Durour arrived at Charlestown Wednesday last from Jamaica - Charlestown item of 18 Oct. (2 Dec.)

CONYERS, Capt. - arrived Monday last at Phila. from New Providence (2 Dec.)

Taylor's Almanack for the Year 1743 - will shortly be

published by Isaiah Warner, almost opposite to Charles
Brockden's in Chesnut St., Phila.; he has for sale
Spiritual Songs (2 Dec.)

COLAM, Ephraim, servant, age c. 35 - runaway from Richard
Chew, near Timber Creek, West Jersey (2 Dec.)

BRYANT, John, servant, age c. 29 or 30 - runaway from the
ship Lucea, Thomas Smith master, from Jamaica; reward
for his capture will be paid by Charles Willing (2 Dec.)

WILSON, Lewis, Welsh servant, age c. 22, joiner or house-
carpenter - same as above

Snow Margaret and Mary, Nathaniel Magee master, at Edward
Warner's wharf - will sail for Jamaica; for freight or
passage agree with Magee on board or at his house in
Arch St., Phila. (2 Dec.)

GOODWIN, Joseph, bookbinder, at his shop in Second St.,
Phila. - has many books for sale (2 Dec.)

STEEL, Rebecka, in Phila. or William Shute, 4 miles from
Phila. - have for sale a Negro woman, age 28 (2 Dec.)

CONDON, Garrat, Irish servant - runaway from William Rush
in Front St., Phila. (2 Dec.)

SIMSON, William, servant, age c. 30 - runaway from Archibald Home, of Trenton (2 Dec.)

SHELLEY, Abraham, Keeper of the Work-house in Phila. - has
taken up one Daniel Horley, who owns himself to be a
servant of Nathaniel Lightle, of Donnigall Twp. (2
Dec.)

BOONE, George, of Exeter Twp., near Mahanatony - offers
for sale tracts of land, including a plantation of 250
acres on Canadegwinam Creek, about 3 miles from John
Harris's ferry near Susquehannah (2 Dec.)

STEEL, James, late of Phila., dec'd - accounts with estate
to be settled with executors, Charles Hillyard, Richard
Renshaw, Rebecca Steel (2 Dec.)

Tract of 231 acres in West New Jersey on the northeast
side of the west branch of Rariton, in Reading Twp.,
Hunterdon Co., is for sale - enquire of Daniel Seabring
living near the premises, or Thomas Vandike at Shrewsbury (7 Dec.)

Two letters to Mr. Franklin, with regard to Gilbert Ten-

388

nent, one from David Evans and the other from Samuel
Finly (Postscript to the Pa. Gazette, 8 Dec.)

HILL, Capt., who last week returned to Phila. from captivity among the Spaniards - confirms accounts of Commodore Anson's success in the South Seas (14 Dec.)

BERRY, Garrat, Irish servant, age c. 30 - runaway from
Andrew Gardiner, of Salem (14 Dec.)

Lots at Long Point on North East River will be balloted
for, according to Act of Assembly of Maryland - notice
signed by William Knight, register (14 Dec.)

JONES, Evan, of Upper Dublin in Phila. Co. - offers reward for recovery of a mare and colt, strayed or
stolen (14 Dec.)

McDANIEL, John, of Mill Creek Hundred, Newcastle Co. -
offers reward for recovery of a gelding strayed from
his plantation (14 Dec.)

LEADAME, Richard, of Phila. - will not pay debts contracted in future by his wife Mary (14 Dec.); he withdraws his notice on 21 Dec. (21 Dec.)

OGLETHORPE, James - proclaims a thanksgiving to God for
the end of the Spanish invasion of Georgia (21 Dec.)

GARDNER, Capt. - arrived Wednesday at Boston from Curasoe
with news that the Dutch had taken 3 English privateers that were careening at Aruba - Boston item of 29
Nov. (21 Dec.)

Letters from 2 Capts., Sibbald and Dowel, to the owners
of the privateers George and Joseph & Mary, both of
Phila. - give news of prisoner exchange and mention
that Capt. Hog is in Havana (21 Dec.)

MACKY, Capt., from Jamaica - brings news that Admiral
Vernon and General Wentworth sailed for England (21
Dec.)

ELLIS, Lydia - died 8 Dec. at Eastown, Chester Co. in her
84th year; on 10 Dec. she was interred at Haverford
West, by the side of her husband, who left her a widow
with 10 small children 38 years since (21 Dec.)

CORMELY, Robert, Englishman, in Newcastle Goal - Sheriff
Samuel Bickley gives notice that he will be discharged
in one month if his owner does not call or send for
him (21 Dec.)

TYSOR, Emanuel, a Portugese, in Newcastle Goal - same as above

LOVELOCK, Richard, English convict servant, who formerly belonged to John Bowen of Baltimore, Md., now in Newcastle Goal - same as above

A Short Narrative of the Extraordinary Work of God at Cambuslang in Scotland - just published and sold by William Bradford, at the Sign of the Bible, in Second St., Phila. (21 Dec.)

DENNISON, Patrick, Irish servant, age c. 35 - runaway from John Bleakley, of Phila., from on board the sloop Speedwell (21 Dec.)

MORROW, Charles, servant, blacksmith, who came from Ireland in the ship Linnen Draper on 29 May last, age c. 28 - runaway from John Bleakley, of Phila. (21 Dec.)

MORROW, John (brother of Charles), servant, blacksmith, who came from Ireland in ship Linnen Draper on 29 May last, age c. 26 - same as above

Brigantine Mary, Thomas Oliphant master - will sail for Cape Fear; for freight or passage agree with John Sober or the master (21 Dec.)

Edward, Joseph & William Shippen - have real estate for sale, including a water lot joining Woodrop's wharf, a pasture on Passyunk Road, opposite to William Tidmarsh's barn, land in the Northern Liberties near plantation of William Shute and John Renshaw (21 Dec.)

GUILLIOT, Capt. - arrived Sunday last at Phila. with European news (30 Dec.)

HAMILTON, Capt. - arrived at Phila. last night from Boston; he reports that Capt. Stephenson is bound to Phila. (30 Dec.)

Plays will be enacted evenings at 7 at the Sign of the Coach-and-Horses, against the State House, in Chesnut St., Phila. (30 Dec.)

SHELLY, Abraham - will dispose of the time of a servant, a tanner (30 Dec.)

CONARRO, Isaac - offers for sale a house on east side of High St., in Burlington, opposite to the Widow Bickley's and 19 acres about a mile from Burlington, adjoining the plantation of John Rodgers (30 Dec.)

Sheriff Thomas Hunloke has in prison at Burlington a servant of Joseph Briggs (or Boggs), living in or near
Newcastle (30 Dec.)

WILKS, Thomas, convict servant, age c. 40, brick-maker by
trade, who came to Maryland in ship Bladen, Capt. Lawrence commander, in September last - runaway from Patrick Creagh (30 Dec.)

GOTHLEY, George, servant, age c. 30 (who formerly belonged to the Rev. Mr. Hooper, then Mr. Bourdillion
and afterwards Mr. Chase), who last August ran away
and was taken up and put in Lancaster Goal - same as
above

BARRY, Michael, Irish servant, age c. 24, weaver - runaway
from Francis Pearson, of Goshen, Chester Co. (30 Dec.)

1743

GUTTERIDGE, Capt., at Boston - has brought European news
- Boston item of 6 Dec. 1742 (4 Jan.)

Brigantine of Capt. Call, belonging to Boston, was lost
in a hurricane but the men were saved - Boston item of
9 Dec. 1742 (4 Jan.)

HOWLAND, Capt., from Jamaica - reports that the American
Regt. under Col. Gooch is to be reduced - Boston item
of 13 Dec. 1742 (4 Jan.)

SIBBALD, Capt., commander of a Phila. privateer, in a
letter from Providence, dated 9 Dec. 1742, spoke of the
pains of Gov. Tinker and reported that Capt. Dowel and
the Governor's secretary have gone down to Havana; in
a postscript he added that the Rose, man-of-war, Thomas
Frankland captain, had arrived at Providence (4 Jan.)

PURDUE, Capt. - arrived Friday last at New York from Holland and Dover - letter from New York dated 28 Dec.
1742 (4 Jan.)

LYNN, Joseph, late of Phila., shipwright, dec'd - accounts
with estate to be settled with Sarah Lynn, executrix,
and Joseph and John Lynn, executors (4 Jan.)

REECE, Mary, widow, dec'd - demands on estate are to be
brought to the executors, Edward Williams and Evan
Jones (4 Jan.)

FISHBOURN, Jane (widow and executrix of William Fisbourn,

late of Phila., dec'd) - real estate for sale including
the following: 2 brick tenements on the east side of
Water St. (now in the tenure of Stedman & Robinson),
bounded on the north by a house of Mary Andrews, house
on east side of Water St. (now in tenure of John Cross,
at the Sign of the Blue Anchor); a house on east side
of Front St., opposite John McComb; plantation near
Horsham (in tenure of Rebecca Iredel) near the meeting-
house; a ground rent on north side of John McComb's
Alley (in tenure of Mathias Penyard) (4 Jan.)

On 5 Jan. fire broke out the blockmaker's shop in Water
St., Phila., near the Rose and Crown; the buildings of
the following were reduced to ashes: William Clymer
(blockmaker), John Ryan (merchant), Thomas Say (sadler),
Thomas Ingram (tavernkeeper), Robert Hopkins (baker);
Mrs. Till's new house was saved (13 Jan.)

JENNINGS, Capt. - arrived Tuesday last at Phila. from
London, with European news (13 Jan.)

HUNLOKE, Thomas, of Burlington - offers reward for recovery of a small ferry-boat (13 Jan.)

Walker & Griffith, at their store on Fishbourn's wharf, in
Phila. - sell Manchester goods, haberdashery and cloth,
imported in the ship Mary, Capt. Nicholas Stephenson,
from London (13 Jan.)

Tracts of land in Bristol, the estate of John Bourke,
dec'd, taken in execution at the suit of William Whitacre, Esq., will be sold by Joseph Jackson, sheriff, at
Giles Lawrence's, at the old Crown Tavern in Bristol
(13 Jan.)

PYLE, Joseph, living at the mill that was John Bezer's
near Marchus-hook - has for sale a plantation of 334
acres in Bethlehem Twp., Chester Co. (13 Jan.)

MORGAN, John, at his store, late White & Taylor's, in
Water St., Phila. - sells cloth, hats, pipes, ironmongery (13 Jan.)

Water-lot in Water St., near Market St., Phila., is for
sale; enquire of Robert Hopkins, at Samuel Coats's in
Market St. (13 Jan.)

Tanyard in upper end of Germantown is for sale; enquire of
Anthony Benezet, living on the premises, or of Frederic
Ax (13 Jan.)

COFFIN, Capt., commander of a vessel belonging to Boston -

had both his thighs broken by the bursting of a cannon in the Bay of Honduras and died 3 weeks after - Boston item of 20 Dec. 1742 (18 Jan.)

ROBINSON, Thomas, a young merchant of New York - on Tuesday last shot himself through the head with a pistol - New York item of 10 Jan. (18 Jan.)

RYAN, John, sufferer in the late fire - offers reward for apprehension of an impostor woman who claims to be Mrs. Ryan and has been seeking gifts in the city (18 Jan.)

FRENCH, David, Esq., late of Newcastle, dec'd - accounts with estate to be settled with executors, John Finney and John Legate (18 Jan.)

House and lot in Elbow Lane, adjoining to John Eyres, are for sale; enquire of John Hall, living at David Evans, at the Sign of the Crown, Phila. (18 Jan.)

Plantation in Upper Darby, about 6 miles from Phila. and 2 from Darby Town, estate of Francis Pullan, dec'd, is for sale - by Amy Pullan and Richard Wall, executors (18 Jan.)

CURRIE, Ebenezer, at store of John Wallace and Comp., in Front St., Phila., opposite to Sam. Hazell's, Esq. - sells cloth, stationery, guns, maps, pictures, etc. (18 Jan.)

BRADLEY, George, opposite the house in which Mr. Merrewether formerly lived and near the Baptist Meeting-house in Second St., Phila. - sells cloth, hats, knives, buttons, etc. (18 Jan.)

STRETTLE, Robert and Amos, at their store in Front St., near Chesnut St., Phila. - sells cloth, hardware, whips, etc. (18 Jan.)

McCALL, Samuel, Jr., at his house in Front St., below the drawbridge, Phila. - sells cloth, tea, cutlery, pewter, gunpowder, pepper (18 Jan.)

RUTHERFURD, William, at James Mackey's store in Front St., Phila. - sells cloth, tea, cutlery, sugar (18 Jan.)

Writings collected and prefaced by Magnus Falconer may be supplied by Isaiah Warner, in Chesnut St. or by the author at Mr. Kirk's in Second St., Phila. (18 Jan.)

McKEE, Thomas, an Indian Trader, who came to Phila. a few days ago - tells of an unfortunate clash between Indians

of the Five Nations and English inhabitants of the upper parts of Virginia; mention is made of a Justice
Hog of Lancaster Co. who had given a pass to some Indians (27 Jan.)

Reward offered for recovery of 2 leather buckets, marked
B. Franklin & Co., that were lost at the late fire in
Water St. (27 Jan.)

Plantation of 150 acres in Lower Merion is for sale; enquire of Reece Lloyd in Phila. (27 Jan.)

Lots in Phila. in Walnut and Third Sts. for sale; enquire
of Andrew Hamilton (27 Jan.)

Chocolate is sold by Bard and Lawrence, Jr., at their
store in Water St., Phila., or at Dr. John Bard's in
Market St. (27 Jan.)

BARBER, Joseph, at the Temple Bar in Second St.,Phila. -
The Magic lanthorn may be seen at his establishment
(27 Jan.)

WENTWORTH, Capt., in a privateer belonging to St. Kitts,
drove off 2 Spanish privateers and retook an English
brigantine - New York item of 24 Jan. (2 Feb.)

WOOLFORD, Capt., in a privateer, found a Spanish wreck on
the east side of Porto Rico; his men got intoxicated,
were attacked by the Spaniards, who killed 9 of the
English - New York item of 24 Jan. (2 Feb.)

McKEE, Mr., the Indian trader - has left Phila. (2 Feb.)

REECE, Capt., from Antigua, reports at Phila. that 2
preachers who went from these parts to Tortola, John
Eastaugh and John Cadwalader, both died on that island
and were buried, one on each side of Thomas Chalkley,
who died there on the same mission about a year ago
(2 Feb.)

ARMIT, John, in Front St., Phila. - will pay reward for
recovery of 2 leather buckets lost at the late fire
marked W. Plumsted & Co., one marked E. Shippen & Co.,
one zenbrigs bag marked A R & Co., one ditto marked
W P & Co., 2 ditto marked S A & Co., and one ditto
marked R S & Co. (2 Feb.)

Plantation of William Klinkenburg, in Northampton Twp.,
Bucks Co., is for sale; apply to Bernhard Vanhorn,
living near said place, or to Solomon Fussel, chair-
maker, in Phila. (2 Feb.)

VAN METER, Isaac - offers for sale tract of 400 acres in
    Salem Co., on Delaware River, about 7 miles from Salem,
    and also 400 acres in Salem Co., near Alloway's Creek;
    Van Meter has given a note to James Ross for purchase
    of land on south branch of Potomack but Ross cannot give
    title (2 Feb.)

BLEAKLY, Henry, Irish servant (who has changed his name to
    John Sempell), who came from Mirock or Mackerlin in
    Ireland - runaway from John McMackin, of Buckingham
    Twp., Bucks Co. (2 Feb.)

Tract of 700 acres, within 1½ miles of Trenton, Hunterdon
    Co., is for sale; enquire of Thomas Cadwalader at Tren-
    ton (2 Feb.)

VERBRYCH, Bernardus, Esq., of Freehold Twp., near the
    Court-house, Monmouth Co. - offers reward if his stolen
    gelding is brought to him or to Joseph Steinard, of
    Phila. (2 Feb.)

SMITH, Charles, English servant, age c. 20, who pretends
    to be a blacksmith or bloomer - runaway from Peter
    Grubb's Ironworks, Lancaster Co. (2 Feb.)

MAY, Thomas, English servant, age c. 30 - same as above

SPENCER, John, late of Trenton, age c. 22, much addicted
    to gaming - has sold to David Witherspoon, of Newcas-
    tle Co., near Maryland, bills of exchange, signed
    Theophilus Severns, drawn on Lawrence Williams, of
    London; bills are not genuine; reward will be paid, if
    Spencer is brought to justice, by William Crosthwaite,
    of Phila., or the genuine John Spencer, living near
    Newtown, in Kent Co., Md. (2 Feb.)

PARSONS, Joseph, near Chester, will sell 100 acres and
    dwelling in Marple Twp., Chester Co., about 6 miles
    from Darby, on Conestogoe Road; apply to said Joseph
    Parsons or to Robert Pearson, near the said place (2
    Feb.)

BELL, Tom - arrived Thursday last in Phila. from Maryland
    pretending to be a son of Mr. Levingston in New York;
    the Mayor of Phila. committed him to prison; in Bar-
    bados he was the Thomas Burnet "that raised the Perse-
    cution against the Jews" (10 Feb.)

Notice concerning quit-rents, signed by Lyn Ford Lardner,
    Receiver-General (10 Feb.)

WARDWELL, William, coach-and chaise-maker - his shop is

in Market St., corner of Fourth St., Phila. (10 Feb.)

DICKSON, James, of Twp. of Little Britain, Lancaster Co.
- offers reward for intelligence about his 3-year-old
daughter Margaret, missing since last 26 Dec.; news of
her should be given to her father or to the Rev. Samuel Blair in Forks Manor, Chester Co., or to George
Gibson in Lancaster Town (10 Feb.)

MEREDITH, Reese - sells cloth, hardware, etc., at his
store on Carpenter's wharf, Phila. (10 Feb.)

SCHLEYDORN, Henry, sugarbaker - is removed to Norris's
Alley in Phila. (10 Feb.)

Plantation on west side of Schuylkil, in Blockley Twp.,
about 5 miles from Phila., is to be let; enquire of
Lewis Jones, living on the premises (10 Feb.)

REYNOLDS, Francis, sub-sheriff- reports that when David
Griffith, who has several times been convicted of
horse-stealing, was taken up and committed to the County Goal of Lancaster, he had in his possession a bay
stallion (10 Feb.)

Corner house below the drawbridge in Phila. is to be sold
or let; enquire of Edward Evans, dwelling in said house
(10 Feb.)

NOBLE, Anthony, painter and glazier - is removed to Society Hill, near Cherry Garden (10 Feb.)

Bay mare, belonging to James Read in Edgmont, has strayed
or been stolen from Phila.; reward will be paid if
mare is brought to Read or to Cadwalader Evans, tanner,
in Edgmont or to John Snowden, in Phila. (10 Feb.)

Brigantine **Batchelor**, Benj. Burke master, will sail for
Ireland; for passage agree with William Dames, at
Thomas Gordon's, on Powel's wharf, or with the master
(10 Feb.)

Tract of land in New Brunswick, Middlesex, N.J., will be
sold at Widow Baldwin's in New Brunswick; enquire of
John Deare, Esq., at Perth Amboy, or Paul Miller, Esq.,
in New Brunswick; sale is by virtue of writ issued at
suit of Conradus Desmith against property of Christopher Gildemeester, dec'd, which was in hands of Samuel
Nevil, administrator of said Gildemeester, dec'd, and
by virtue of writ issued at suit of John Nevil (administrator of property of Peter Sonman, dec'd, unadminis-
tered by Sarah Sonman, also dec'd, late executrix of

said Peter Sonmans, against property of Christopher
Gildemeester, dec'd) (17 Feb.)

Richardson & Eversley - are lately removed from the house
where they dwelt in Water St. into the house where
Nathan Levy lately lived in Front St. (17 Feb.)

CRANE, Charles, an Irishman, age c. 24, sailor - has absented himself from on board the snow Prince of Orange;
reward will be paid if he is apprehended and notice
thereof given to Messers Davey and Carson, merchants,
in Phila., or to Ann Baird, at the Sign of the Bowling
Green, in Water St., near Arch St. (17 Feb.)

HOW, William, of Perkiomum Twp., Phila. Co. - offers reward for recovery of strayed or stolen mare (17 Feb.)

Long account of the Moravians, who have been the subject
of much conversation since the arrival of Count Zinzendorff in Pennsylvania, extracted from the journal of
the Rev. John Wesley (24 Feb.)

ASHMEAD, John, late of Germantown, blacksmith, dec'd -
accounts with estate to be settled with Sarah and Samuel Ashmead, executors, who have for sale a house,
stable and lot in McCombs's Alley and adjoining a lot
of John Leech (24 Feb.)

LEWIS, Jenkin, servant, this country born, age c. 23, who
served his time with David Jenkin, of Uwchland, Chester
Co., but for sheep-stealing and other theft was made a
servant - runaway from William Hartley, of Charlestown,
Chester Co. (24 Feb.)

FOWLER, Peter, Irish servant, age c. 20 - same as above

House near Croswicks Meeting-house in West New Jersey and
also house and lot in Borden's Town are to be sold or
let; enquire of Joseph Borden in Bordentown (24 Feb.)

Soon will be published a letter from Lewis Thurnstein
(Deacon of the Moravian Church) to the people of Pennsylvania, translated from the Latin by Philip Reading,
of University College, Oxford (24 Feb.)

House and lot, now in occupation of Thomas Hunloke, Esq.,
in Water St., Burlington, are for sale; apply to Bennet
Bard or Hugh Hartshorne in Burlington (24 Feb.)

WILLIAMS, Capt. James - arrived Saturday last at Newport,
R.I., from St. Kitts, with news of prizes taken in the
West Indies by Capts. Woolford and Wentworth - Newport

item of 28 Jan. (3 Mar.)

FORBES, Alexander, master of the brigantine <u>Ann</u>, bound
from Jamaica to New York, in a letter dated St.
Christophers, Dec. 31, 1742, describes a terrible
storm which forced him to put in at St. Christophers -
New York item of 11 Feb. (3 Mar.)

OGLETHORPE, General, after a messenger from Chigley, King
of the Cowetaus, informed him of the capture of a
Spanish captain, sent Lt. Francis of the Rangers to
bring down the Spanish prisoner; Oglethorpe ordered
Capt. Croggs with a party of Rangers to watch the path
from Carolina to Augustine to intercept some 30 runaway Negroes from Carolina trying to join the Spaniards
at Augustine - New York item of 21 Feb. (3 Mar.)

CHANCELLOR, William, dec'd - accounts with the estate to
be settled with Elizabeth Chancellor, executrix and
administratrix (3 Mar.)

LOGAN, William - warns persons settled on Laetitia Penn's
(now Aubrey's) Manor in Chester Co. to procure surveys
and titles for their possessions; he also warns tenants
on Laetitia's other Manor (commonly called Stening) to
pay arrears of quit-rents (3 Mar.)

CLIFTON, John, at Richard Swan's, hatter in Market St.,
or at George Hedmer's, shopkeeper - sells Vidonia Wine
(3 Mar.)

BRADFORD, William, at the Sign of the Bible in Second St.,
Phila. - sells <u>The</u> <u>Interest</u> <u>of</u> <u>New-Jersey</u>, just published
(3 Mar.)

DAVIS, Capt. George, in Chesnut St., Phila. - has for
sale a Negro wench (3 Mar.)

Five acres on Hay Creek, lately belonging to John Ogden,
dec'd, and given by will to his son Joseph, are to be
let; apply to Diana Glover, grandmother and guardian of
said Joseph (3 Mar.)

The owner of a quantity of silver money that was taken up
on the big road leading from John Frew's towards Maryland is desired to apply to Thomas or Richard Woodward,
both of East Bradford, Chester Co. (3 Mar.)

WOOLLEN, Joseph, dec'd - accounts with estate to be settled with John and William Barge, appointed guardians
of Joseph Woollen, son of the dec'd (3 Mar.)

Plantation of about 50 acres in Whitemarsh Twp., Phila.
Co., about ½ mile from Spring Hill, is for sale; apply
to Francis Colly, living on the premises (3 Mar.)

MORGAN, Evan (who has lately suffered considerable loss by
fire) in Market St., Phila., gives notice to those indebted to him to make payment; he will dispose of real
estate, some adjoining property of Abraham Bickley in
Phila., and some in Chester, of which one tract on the
east side of Chester Creek is just by Thomas Morgan's
property (3 Mar.)

DURORE, Col. - his forces at Charlestown are ordered to
return to England (10 Mar.)

Address of inhabitants of Savannah to James Oglethorpe;
true copy of the original signed by Thomas Coleman (10
Mar.)

BURROWS, Capt., arrived at Phila. from Jamaica - has
brought news of operations against the Spaniards in
the West Indies (10 Mar.)

HUDSON, William, late of Phila., dec'd - accounts with estate to be settled with executors, William Hudson and
William Mode (10 Mar.)

Tract of about 200 acres, adjoining Mathew Signar's land,
in Mecunigy, Bucks Co., will be sold on 25 Mar. (10 Mar.)

Plantation of 100 acres in Newtown Twp., Chester Co., will
be sold 8 Apr. at house of Robert Tipping, dec'd, in
said town and county (10 Mar.)

Lot of ground in Phila. is to be sold 22 Apr. at house of
Joseph Cobourn, at the Three Tuns, in Chesnut St.,
Phila. (10 Mar.)

HART, Charles, of Shanandore - offers reward for capture
of John McGuire, who pretends to be an Indian trader;
the thief stole a horse from Hart and money, cost, hat,
and jacket from Widow Mary McGuire, of Shenandore; if
thief is capture, notice is to be given to Roger Hunt
in the Great Valley, Pa. (10 Mar.)

JONES, Malachi - offers for sale a plantation in Abington
Twp., 10 miles from Phila. and 4 from Germantown; there
is a convenience for erecting a mill on the same creek
that turns Leech's Mill (10 Mar.)

SMITH, John, dec'd - lots in burrough of Wilmington, belonging to his estate, are for sale; enquire of Nicholas

and Hester Bishop at the house (between Market and Front Sts.) in Wilmington (10 Mar.)

GREW, Theophilus - teaches school in Walnut St., Phila., in house where Joseph Claypole formerly lived (10 Mar.)

DARREL, Capt., from Providence - reports at Charlestown that a privateer schooner fitted out at Rhode Island has taken a Dutch sloop - Charlestown item of 24 Jan. (17 Mar.)

McKEAY, Capt., from Glascow - reports at Boston that Rev. Whitefield set out for London and plans to visit Boston - Boston item of 17 Feb. (17 Mar.)

Monday last 19 of the men lately belonging to the privateer schooner Capt. Griffiths returned; each man received 500 pieces of eight from a prize and the owners will get 10,000 pounds; their schooner was formerly a Spanish privateer taken by Capt. Allen - Newport, R.I., item of 14 Feb. (17 Mar.)

BOYD, Capt. - arrived last week at New York from Jamaica with news from the West Indies - New York item of 28 Feb. (17 Mar.)

BARNS, Capt. - arrived 27 Feb. at New York from Georgia (17 Mar.)

Letter dated New Providence, 26 Jan., from Capt. Sibbald, commander of the George privateer, of Phila., to one of the owners in Phila.; he mentions Capt. Dowel and Capt. Hogg (17 Mar.)

To be sold at Roberts's Coffee House in Phila. by public vendue: 2 houses in tenure of Stedman and Robinson; 2 houses in tenure of Philip Doz and John Mears; store bounded on north by tenement of John Dillwyn and on east by Rees Meredith's stores; house in tenure of John Cross, at the Sign of the Blue Anchor, bounded on north by store of William Fishbourn and on south by house of Mary Andrews; plantation in Phila. Co., near Horsham Meeting-house, in tenure of Rebecca Iredel (17 Mar.)

GRIFFITTS, Widow Elizabeth - will sell tenement and lot in Second St., Phila. (17 Mar.)

LEADAME, Richard - his wife Mary abuses him so much that he cannot live with her; he will not pay debts contracted by her in future (17 Mar.)

WILLIAMS, John, a West-Country-man, age c. 32, who says

he came into western part of Virginia with one Capt.
Taylor from Bristol - has been lately committed to Goal
of Sussex Co. upon Delaware as a suspected runaway
servant; notice given by Sheriff Peter Hall at Lewestown (17 Mar.)

ROGERS, Thomas, age c. 25, said to have come a freeman
with the above Williams from Bristol - same as above

Plantation of 230 acres in Deptford Twp., Gloucester Co.,
West New Jersey, 5 miles from Gloucester on the Salem
Rd., will be sold by Abraham Chattin, who lives on said
plantation; he also has for sale 400 acres near Turky
Point, Salem Co. (17 Mar.)

CARY, Samuel - will let a house in Newtown, Bucks Co. (24
Mar.)

FOX, James - teaches reading, writing, arithmetic, navigation, surveying in Lancaster Co. (24 Mar.)

ROBINSON, Valentine, of Brandywine Hundred, Newcastle Co.
- has for sale or to let house in Burrough of Wilmington in Hight St., fronting the upper Market-House (24
Mar.)

WHARTON, Joseph - will sell or let pastures in Myamensing
and Wicaco and lots on Society Hill and in Second St.,
Phila. (24 Mar.)

LIGHTFOOT, Jane, servant, age c. 24 - runaway from Francis Maybury, Jr., of North East (24 Mar.)

COLLINS, Michael, native Irish servant, age c. 25 - runaway from John Scott, of Hanover Town, Morris Co., East
New Jersey (24 Mar.)

KELLY, Patrick, native Irish servant, age c. 26 - runaway
from David Wheeler, of Hanover Town; they have stolen
2 silver spoons, one marked WB; notice of their capture
is to be given to their masters, to Benjamin Franklin,
to Manuel Crell at Wells's Ferry or to James Johnston,
at Trenton (24 Mar.)

SOUMAIEN, Samuel - offers reward for apprehension of Isaac
Marks (alias Dr. Marks), late of Annapolis, who is in-
debted to Soumaien and has forged bills of exchange (24
Mar.)

BRADFORD, Andrew, late of Phila., dec'd - accounts with
estate to be settled with Cornelia Bradford, executrix
(24 Mar.)

Account given by English prisoners brought to Charlestown
by a Spanish flag of truce; mentioned are General Oglethorpe, Capt. Hardy, Col. Cook and his newly invented
machine or carriages for guns, Capts. Parris, Morris
and Gale (who were taken prisoners in May last and carried to St. Augustine) (31 Mar.)

Account of engagement between inhabitants on frontiers and
a party of Shawan Indians as given by James McDowell
(brother of Capt. McDowell) who was in the action; mentioned are Col. Patten, Capts. Buchanan, Robinson and
McDowell - Williamsburg item of 11 Mar. (31 Mar.)

TRIMBLE, Capt., arrived at Phila. from Lisbon - gives account of engagement between H.M.S. Saphire, Charles
Holmes commander, and the fort and town of Vigo (31 Mar.)

BELL, Capt., from Madeira, at Phila. - tells of engagement
on 29 Jan. between an English sloop, the Diamond's
Prize, Capt. Garrish, and a Spanish privateer (31 Mar.)

DAVIES, Capt., from Providence - reports at Phila. that
our privateers convoyed the Register Ship to Havana
(31 Mar.)

GOODWIN, Joseph, bookbinder - is removed from his shop in
Second St. into Black Horse Alley, Phila. (31 Mar.)

Speech of H. E. Lewis Morris of New Jersey - is published
and sold by B. Franklin (31 Mar.)

Tract of 200 acres, between plantations of Edward Roberts
and William Nixon, in the Great Swamp, Bucks Co., is
for sale; enquire of Thomas Lightfoot, at his store on
Pemberton's wharf, Phila. (31 Mar.)

SEATON, Alexander, of Wilmington - persons who have de-
mands on him are to send accounts to Robert Strettell,
John Reynell or Samuel Sansom, of Phila., or Joseph
Peters, of Wilmington (31 Mar.)

BOOKMAN, Sarah, servant, age c. 20 - runaway from Thomas
Pierce, opposite to the Workhouse, in Third St., Phila.
(31 Mar.)

SMITH, Abel - runaway from on board the shallop Molly, belonging to Salem, taking with him sundry sums of money;
reward for his capture is offered by Thomas Rice (31
Mar.)

DAVENPORT, Rev., who lately came to New London, induced
his followers to burn certain religious books; Daven-

port said some of the people made idols of their gay
clothes, and these were turned over to him but he did
not have them burned - Boston items of 14 and 21 Mar.
(7 Apr.)

STORY, Capt., arrived at Boston from Lisbon - reports confirmation at home of condemnation of ship <u>Grand Taste</u>,
brought in by Capt. Thompson of H.M.S. <u>Success</u> (7 Apr.)

CUNNINGHAM, Capt. - was in the Downs the latter end of
Dec., bound for Boston (7 Apr.)

WARDELL, Nathaniel, of Boston, hay-weigher - Thursday
last baptized 2 women in the sea at the south end of
town - Boston item of 21 Mar. (7 Apr.)

PLUNKET, Capt. - arrived at New York Friday last from New
Providence - New York item of 28 Mar. (7 Apr.)

FORBES, Capt. - arrived at New York Monday last from St.
Kitts - New York item of 4 Apr. (7 Apr.)

COATAM, Capt., from Charlestown, S.C., reports at Phila.
that the people of Charlestown expect a Spanish invasion (7 Apr.)

VANDERPOOL, Malgert, a miner, at or near Neward, N.J. -
fell 114 ft. into a mine on Saturday last and died
within an hour - New York item of 4 Apr. (7 Apr.)

KINSEY, John, late attorney general, has been appointed
Chief Justice of Pennsylvania (7 Apr.)

Translation made by P. Reading, of letter from Lewis
Thurnstein, Deacon of the Moravian Church, to the
people of Pennsylvania (7 Apr.)

Brick tenement in Walnut St., next door to Capt. Philips's
and 4 doors from James's Coffee House, in Phila. will
be sold; it formerly belonged to Thomas Annis and is
now in possession of John Sober (7 Apr.)

BOEHLER, Peter - gives notice that the Moravian Brethren
at Bethlehem will cause such things as they consider
useful to be translated (7 Apr.)

HINDS, Thomas, of Phila., shopkeeper, dec'd - accounts
with estate to be settled with Anne Hinds, administratrix (7 Apr.)

ARMIT, Stephen - will sell or let grist-mills at Pennypack (7 Apr.)

BILES, Thomas, near the Post Office in Phila. - has for
sale a Negro woman and all sorts of pewter, brass and
copperware (7 Apr.)

McCOOLE, Walter, of Rockhill Twp., Chief Ranger of Bucks
Co. - lists horses taken up by him (7 Apr.)

WENTWORTH, Capt., on board the privateer Castor - describes
in a letter attack by Commodore Knowles on Laguira (14
Apr.)

DEVOU, Daniel, Jr. - on 3 Apr. his house near Morrisania
was burnt down (14 Apr.)

HALL, Capt. James - arrived 8 Apr. in South River from
London, with news of press for seaman in London (14
Apr.)

WEBB, Hugh, farmer, and a youth, his kinsman - drowned
Monday last when their boat, overloaded with fish,
filled and sank near League Island (14 Apr.)

Plantation in Goshen, Chester Co., is offered for sale by
Isaac Roberts, in Second St., Phila. (14 Apr.)

HOPKINS, Robert or Samuel Coates in Phila. - offer for
sale a Negro, baker by trade (14 Apr.)

PARR, Samuel, at his store in Water St., near Chesnut St.,
Phila. - sells sundry sorts of merchandize (14 Apr.)

KOCK, Peter - offers for sale 50 acres of Liberty land,
about 2 miles on the other side of Schuylkil, about ½
mile from Mr. Asheton's sawmill (14 Apr.)

STRAWBRIDGE, Ann, Irish servant, age c. 20 - runaway from
Benjamin Armitage, of Phila. (14 Apr.)

Reward will be paid for recovery of gelding, strayed or
stolen from pasture of John Salkeld in Chester; horse
is to be brought to Abraham Darlington in Birmingham
or John Salkeld in Chester (14 Apr.)

McONAGEL, Charles, Irish servant, age c. 20 - runaway from
Morgan Evans, of Carnarvon Twp., Lancaster Co. (14 Apr.)

Account of expedition to Laguira by the fleet under Commodore Knowles (21 Apr.)

Deposition of Obadiah Brown, of the snow Otter, taken before George Francis, Esq., 25 Mar. 1742 at Montserat
(21 Apr.)

Privateer <u>George</u>, Capt. Sibbald, of Phila. - arrived in Phila. Friday last from Providence; she brought in 55,000 pieces of eight and 30 of the English prisoners (21 Apr.)

TEMPEST, Robert, plush-weaver - is removed into Strawberry Alley, next door to the Widow Jordan's, in Phila. (21 Apr.)

KNIGHT, William - gives notice regarding taking up of the lots in Charles-Town, situated at Long Point, on North East River, in Cecil Co., Md. (21 Apr.)

CANADEY, Thomas, age <u>c</u>. 23 - runaway from his bail, John Jones, of Charles Town, Chester Co. (21 Apr.)

Prize sloop taken by Capt. Allen - arrived 15 Apr. at Newport (28 Apr.)

CLINTON, George, Gov. of New York - intended to embark from England sometime this summer according to Capts. Griffith and Bryant from London (28 Apr.)

Snow <u>Princess</u> <u>Anne</u>, Roger French master, belonging to New York - was wrecked in January last on the back of the Isle of Wight; the captain and most of the men perished (28 Apr.)

FORSTER, Moses, opposite to John Warder's, in Second St., Phila. - makes and repairs chaises (28 Apr.)

Ship <u>Ranger</u>, Peter Reeve master, now at Fishbourn's wharf - will sail for London; for freight or passage agree with Matthias Aspden or the master (28 Apr.)

Ship <u>Argyle</u>, Charles Stedman commander - will sail for South Carolina; for freight or passage agree with the commander or with Stedman, Robertson & Co. (28 Apr.)

BOEHLER, Peter, of the Moravians - claims that letter to Mr. Newman is falsified (28 Apr.)

House and lot in Third St. (now in occupation of the Dutch locksmith) and annuity arising on a gristmill in Christiana Hundred, Newcastle Co., are to be sold; enquire of Richard Hall or Amy Puling (28 Apr.)

MAES, John, at upper end of Front St., near Sassafrass St., Phila. - sells cocoa (28 Apr.)

OWEN, Owen and Ann Owen, both dec'd - accounts with their estates are to be settled with John Biddle and Robert

Owen, administrators (28 Apr.)

ROBERTS, Hugh, at the Tobacco Pipe in Market St., Phila. -
sells linseed oil and painting colours (28 Apr.)

KENNARD, John, of Manor of Moreland, Phila. Co. - his wife
Margaret has eloped from him (28 Apr.)

HASELL, Samuel - offers reward for recovery of gelding
strayed or stolen out of a pasture near Phila. (28 Apr.)

List of books sold by Stephen Potts, at the Bible and
Crown in Front St., Phila. (28 Apr.)

Plantation of 93 acres in Whipping Twp. is for sale; enquire of William Hawkesworth on the premises or of
Elizabeth Franks in said twp. (28 Apr.); plantation of
95 acres in Whitpain Twp., Phila. Co., between Skippack
Great road and Monatawny Great road; agree with William Hawkesworth on the premises or Elizabeth Franks,
living very near the premises (9 June)

One of General Oglethorpe's scout boats, commanded by
one Jones, arrived at Savannah from St. Joan's River
with letters to Col. Stephens, advising of the General's
landing in Florida; one of the General's vessels is a
ship of 20 guns commanded by Capt. Thomson - Charlestown
item of 4 Apr. (5 May)

WOOLFORD, Capt. - has taken and carried into St. Kitts a
rich Spanish prize (5 May); Capt. Meas, arrived at
Phila., from Antigua, states account about Capt. Woolford is false (12 May)

Report has reached Newport, R.I., that Commodore Knowles
had taken Laguira and placed there a garrison under
Capt. Somers; also it is said that Knowles is dead -
Newport item of 22 Apr. (5 May)

Account from Barbados of activities of 2 English privateers, one commanded by Capt. Charles Gwin and the other
by Capt. Le Gall - Boston item of 25 Apr. (5 May)

Snow _Seneca_, Mathew Wartberough master, will sail for
Bristol; for freight or passage agree with John Inglis
or master of the vessel, now at Messers. Allen and
Turner's wharf, below the drawbridge (5 May)

OSBORN, Jonas, lace-weaver from Dublin - may be spoke
with at Mr. Price's, cooper, in Front St., near Mc-
Combs's Alley, in Phila. (5 May)

CHANCELLOR, William, dec'd - 3 Negro sail-makers belonging
to his estate are to be sold; also all accounts with
estate are to be settled with Elizabeth Chancellor and
the trustees (5 May)

McKENNY, Peter, servant - runaway from William Gardiner
and Adam Farquhar, of Nutt's Ironworks, Chester Co. (5
May)

A bank house and lot, opposite to John McCombs's, bounded
on north by lot of Thomas Green and on south by a house
belonging to Caleb Ranstead, will be sold at Roberts's
Coffee House; enquire of Jane Fishbourn (5 May)

MARSHALL, Christopher, at the Sign of the Golden Ball, in
Chesnut St., opposite the end of Strawberry Alley -
sells all sorts of oils and colours (5 May)

TYSON, Richard, at the Sign of the Globe, on Germantown
Rd. - offers reward for recovery of strayed gelding (5
May)

Plantation of 300 acres in the Falls Twp., Bucks Co.,
fronting Delaware River, is for sale; enquire of Joseph Warder in Phila. (5 May)

BLAIR, Rev. James, Commissary of Virginia, President of
College of William and Mary, Rector of Bruton Parish,
sometime President of Virginia - died Monday last in
his 88th year - Williamsburg item of 22 Apr. (12 May)

DOWELL, Capt., in the privateer _Joseph_ _and_ _Mary_, consort
to the _George_ - arrived Saturday last at Phila. from
Providence (12 May)

NICHOLS, Mrs. Margaret - died Tuesday last at Phila.,
aged 74 (12 May)

Gold and silver buttons, lace, loops and thread are sold
at Dr. Farmer's in Second St., near Market St., Phila.
(12 May)

MORGAN, Evan, Jr., cooper, at his house near the drawbridge in Phila. - has a Negro lad for sale and also
wines, brandy, rum and cinnamon (12 May)

VAUSE, Ephraim, of Evesham Twp., Burlington Co., West New
Jersey - offers reward for recovery of mare strayed or
stolen from his plantation (12 May)

HANSON, Thomas, servant, this country born, age c. 24,
blacksmith - runaway from Peter Hall, of Lewestown,

Sussex Co. on Delaware (12 May)

MINES, John, Irish servant, age c. 20, blacksmith - same
   as above

GREEN, William - on Wednesday last was chosen Governor of
   Rhode Island, to succeed Gov. Ward; Joseph Whipple was
   chosen Deputy Governor - Newport item of 5 May (19 May)

On 31 Mar. Capt. Horton returned to Frederica, Ga., on
   board Capt. Thompson's ship; news is given of Oglethorpe's operations against St. Augustine; mention is
   made of Capts. Hardy and Coats (19 May)

SCUT, Capt. - last Friday at Boston the lightning shattered 3 masts of his new ship - Boston item of 9 May
   (19 May)

Among Spanish privateers lately fitted out at Havana the
   snow called the King's Snow, which lately took Capt.
   Phenix of New York, and a Bermuda built sloop, lately
   Capt. Whitney's (19 May)

List of killed and wounded in attack on Laguira is given
   for each ship; commanders and ships involved were Com.
   Knowles, Suffolk; Capt. Lushington, Burford; Capt.
   Callis, Assistance; Capt. Smith, Advice; Capt. Gregory,
   Norwich; Capt. Smith, Eltham; Capt. Walkins, Lively;
   Capt. Lisle, Scarborough - from letter from Curacoa
   dated 8 Apr. 1743 (19 May)

DOWERS, Capt. - lately arrived at Phila. from Lisbon (19
   May)

POWELL, Samuel, founder, next door to James Parrot's in
   Second St., Phila. - sells items of copper, iron, brass
   and pewter (19 May)

WALL, William, young Irish servant, who pretends to be a
   shoemaker - runaway from Samuel Thompson, of Newcastle
   Hundred (19 May)

Caesar, Negro, carpenter - runaway from Antil Deaver, of
   Baltimore Co., Md. (19 May)

WIMBLE, Capt. J., commander of privateer - arrived Saturday last at Newport; together with Capt. J. Allen, of
   Newport, he had taken a rich prize near Havana - Newport item of 13 May (26 May)

It is reported that Mr. Whitefield disapproves of Rev.
   Tennent's treatment of the Moravians - Boston item of
   16 May (26 May)

OXLEY, John - died Monday last at Phila., aged 61; he was born at Chester, Pa., but mostly resided in Island of Barbados; he was for upwards of 40 years an eminent preacher among the Quakers (26 May)

GREEN, John, Irish servant, age c. 25 - runaway from George Ward, Jr., of Deptford Twp., Gloucester Co. (26 May)

ALEXANDER, William, Col/lector/ - gives notice that the Custom House will be removed from Mr. Evans's to John Nelson's, in Chesnut St., Phila., next Monday (26 May)

HARRISON, John, over the drawbridge in Phila. - has for sale a parcel of Negroes, rum, sugar and dry goods (26 May)

The following real estate in Hunterdon Co., N.J., will be sold to the highest bidder: tract of 500 acres above the falls and bounded on the east by Mary Tomkins's land; tract of 166 acres bounded on west by Benjamin Olive's land, on east by Mary Tomkins's; these tracts were conveyed by Francis Cowper, of Northampton in Great Britain, to Nathaniel Palmer and by said Palmer mortgaged to Messers. Francis Willis and James Hubbard, of Virginia (26 May)

TILDEN, Charles, apprentice, age c. 16 - runaway from Andrew Jolley, of Wilmington (26 May)

BURROWS, Stephen or Evan, of Amwell, Hunterdon Co., N.J. - will pay reward for capture of 2 runaway servants, Edward Banbury, age c. 40, blacksmith, and William Cooper, Englishman, a collier (26 May)

CARMAN, Macaja, apprentice, age c. 19 or 20 (who has been seen at house of his brother, Joseph Carman, near the head of Sassafras River in Maryland) - runaway from John Read, of Phila. (26 May)

REDMON, Thomas, Irish servant, age c. 25 - runaway from John Edwards, of Salem, West New Jersey (26 May)

CRELLIUS, J. - has begun to publish a newspaper in German; advertisements are to be sent to him or to David Dashler, both living in Market St., Phila. (26 May)

JEFFERIES, Thomas, of East Caln Twp., Chester Co. - offers reward for recovery of strayed or stolen mare (26 May)

MIERS, Alexander, of Upper Dublin, near Morris's mill, Phila. Co. - has taken up a horse and a mare (26 May)

CONNOLY, William, of New Providence, near Perkiomen, Phila. Co. - has taken up a horse (26 May)

Plantation of 114 acres, at Kalconehook, Darby Twp., Chester Co., about 9 miles from Phila., on Darby Creek, is for sale; apply to Matthew Johns, now on the premises (26 May)

Most unfavorable report of the orphanage erected by Mr. Whitefield in Frederica, Ga., is given by Capt. James Hutchinson at Boston; General Oglethorpe was with him when he visited the building (2 June)

Poem in memory of Robert Jordan, late of Phila., dec'd, a preacher among the Quakers (2 June)

INGLIS, John, intending to leave Phila. for England - wishes to settle all accounts (2 June)

LEWIS, Henry, of Hilton Twp., Bucks Co. - has found on the Great Road, on Chesnut Hill, a feather bed, 2 pillos and a sheet (2 June)

Parcel of molasses for sale by Richard Smith, Jr., in Burlington, or John Smith, at Israel Pemberton's store in Phila. (2 June)

CREDE, John, of Buckingham Twp., Bucks Co. - will not pay debts contracted in future by his wife Elizabeth (2 June)

Address, in name of the Presbyterian Synod, signed by David Cowell, moderator, to Gov. George Thomas; this was on account of a paper brought into the synod by Thomas Cookson, Esq., containing illegal and seditious principles of some persons in Lancaster Co. who call themselves Presbyterians; answer of the Governor (9 June)

BURCHAL, Capt., who arrived Friday last at New York from Jamaica - informs that Commodore Knowles has taken Porto Cavally (9 June)

Answer to Capt. James Hutchinson's declaration about the orphanage in Georgia (9 June)

Ship Nancy, Joseph Arthur master, now at McCall's wharf, Phila. - will sail for London; for freight or passage agree with Samuel McCall, Jr., John Searle or the master (9 June)

SEARLE, John - offers reward for recovery of strayed gelding (9 June)

JONES, William, age c. 25, born in Wales, imported as indented servant into Maryland belonging to Dr. Charles
Carroll, of Annapolis - runaway from on board the
schooner Annapolis, lying in North East River in Maryland (9 June)

CAVENOR, Charles, committed for house-breaking - made his
escape from Edward Richardson, Constable of Apoquinomy
Hundred; after his escape he broke into the house of
Thomas Lewis and stole clothing (9 June)

Water lot on Chester Creek, bounded southward on street
that leads to Widow Loyd's plantation and on the north
joining to George Ashbridge's granary, is for sale; enquire of Isaac Williams, in Phila., or Jacob Howel, at
Chester (9 June)

Last night the privateers Wilmington and George, fitted
out by gentlemen in Phila., fell down our river to proceed on their cruize (16 June)

BROCKDEN, Charles, of Phila. - offers for sale his plantation of 100 acres at Moyamensing (16 June)

FLOWER, Benjamin, in Walnut St. - desires to let his house
and tanyard (16 June)

HARDING, John, at William Masters's houses on Market St.
wharf - sells flour (16 June)

McCLAINE, Hugh, mariner, of Phila. - his wife "Ann or
Nancy" (daughter of Jane Lepel, late of the Northern
Liberties of Phila.) has eloped from him (16 June)

TAYLOR, John, servant, who sometime ago was servant to
William Ellis, near Gloucester - runaway from Benjamin
Davis, of Chester, Pa. (16 June)

MILLER, Alexander, peruke-maker, in Second St., Phila. -
after 22 Aug. will leave off shaving business (16 June)

Second volume of State Trials, with "William Shaw" written
on the title-page - was lent to Capt. Lawrie and left
by him with some acquaintance in Phila.; person who has
it is to bring it to the printer (16 June)

PARSONS, John, West-Country man, convict servant, age c.
30 - runaway from V. Denton, of Annapolis (16 June)

WETHERIDGE, Isaac, West-Country man, convict servant, age
c. 30, shoemaker - runaway from John Senhouse, of
Annapolis (16 June)

OVERTON, Thomas, convict servant, age c. 30, weaver - runaway (taking with him a Negro belonging to Antill
Deaver, at the head of Bush River) from Michael Lawrless
(16 June)

NORTHOVER, Capt. Richard, commander of the ship Hanover
Pink, of Bristol, who was lately cast away - arrived 8
May at Providence in his long-boat from Crooked Island;
Friday last he married one of his passengers, Miss
Elizabeth Barnes, of Jamaica, who has a fortune of
10,000 pounds sterling - Providence item of 16 May (23
June)

FRANKLAND, Capt. Thomas, of H.M.S. Rose - Friday last married Miss Sarah Rhett, a young lady with a large fortune - Providence item of 30 May (23 June)

A white Negro girl of Negro parents is to be seen at house
of Joel Pointlet, in Charlestown, S.C., for one week,
at entrance price of 5s. - advertisement in South Carolina Gazette of 30 May (23 June)

Friday last arrived at New York the privateer sloops,
Castor and Pollux, commanded by Capts. Wentworth and
Woolford; they brought in as prizes 2 brigantines and
a sloop - New York item of 20 June (23 June)

McDONEL, Michael - at Court in Gloucester, West New Jersey,
last week was sentenced to death for the murder last
September of Richard Filpot (23 June); McDonel was
executed Monday last (30 June)

McDENNIS, Barnaby - was committed to Phila. Goal for house-
breaking; it is suspected he was accessary in the murder
of Mr. Bunting about 3 years ago; he was concerned in
some robberies with Callaghaun and Kaines (23 June)

VANURDER, Peter, baker, and Lawrence Hortwick, a German -
broke out of Goal of New Brunswick; John Deare, Sheriff,
offers reward for their capture (23 June)

YEOMANS, William, at his store upon Fishbourn's wharf in
Phila. - sells imported goods, knives, lancets, buttons,
gloves, etc. (23 June)

SUNLEY, Richard, dec'd - several plantations and tracts of
land in Bucks Co. belonging to his estate, are for sale;
apply to Thomas Brown, living in Third St., Phila., or
Robert Smith, in Buckingham Twp., Bucks Co. (23 June)

WALL, Joseph, servant - runaway from Henry Smith, of
Tulpehocken (23 June)

COLSON, Edward, servant - same as above

BELL, Tom, born in New England - broke out of prison on 11
June (23 June)

LAVERDY, Alexander, indented Irish servant, age c. 22,
something of a scholar, weaver by trade - runaway from
Thomas Cockran, of Earl-Town, Lancaster Co. (23 June)

ZEIGLER, Michael, of Perkiomium, Phila. Co. - has taken up
a mare (23 June)

LIGHTFOOT, Samuel - of Burrough of Chester - offers reward
for recovery of a horse and mare, stolen or strayed
from Thomas Millard's mill upon Schuylkil, in upper
part of Chester Co. (23 June)

Ship Angola, brought into Newport, R.I., by Capts. Allen
and Wimble, was condemned Friday last - Newport item
of 17 June (30 June)

Friday last Capt. Foster arrived at Boston from London and
on Tuesday last Capt. Collingwood from New Providence
(Collingwood reported that Capt. Rouse of the privateer
Young Eagle, of Boston, had retaken from the Spaniards
a small English ship); Wednesday last Capt. Scut returned in a miserable condition after a storm and Thursday Capt. Tyng arrived - Boston items of 20 June (30
June)

Capt. Waddel, who arrived Friday last at New York from the
Bay of Honduras, and Capt. Long, who arrived Saturday
in a brigantine from Curacoa, reported that they saw a
ship taken by a sloop off Barnagat - New York items of
27 June (30 June)

Remarks of Rev. Gilbert Tennent about the Moravians, with
mention of Count Zinzendorff, Mr. Boeler and Henerick
Visher (30 June and 7 July)

Letter, dated Charlestown, S.C., 5 June, 1743, from Rev.
Josiah Smith to Rev. William Cooper, of Boston (mentioned is Rev. Cooper's son William and letter he wrote
from Bethesda on 1 Jan. 1742) about the orphanage in
Georgia (30 June)

DOBBIN, Joseph, at Passunk, near Phila., offers for sale
a frame and log-house, adjoining on west George Mifflin's
ground and on north part of George Fitzwater's (30 June)

Sloop Mary Ann, Joseph Cox master, now at Warner's wharf
in Phila. - will sail for Jamaica; for freight or passage

agree with the master or with Samuel Hassell (30 June)

CANAAN, David, Irish servant, age c. 20 - runaway from
Henry Pennington, of Caecil Co., Md. (30 June)

BURK, Elenor, Irish servant, age c. 22 - same as above

BROTHERS, Daniel (alias Daniel Broderick), Irish servant,
age c. 19 - runaway from John Hughes, of Upper Merion,
Phila. Co. (30 June)

Plantation of 630 acres in Baltimore Co., on Draughts of
Deer Creek, about 6 miles from head of Bush River, is
for sale; agree with Abraham Boyd on the premises (7
July)

MOOR, Roger, native Irish servant, age c. 23 - runaway
from William Walker, at the Forks of Neshaminy, Bucks
Co. (7 July)

MAKFERON, Patrick, Irish servant, age c. 50, who talks
Scotch and has been a soldier - runaway from James
Whithill, of Lancaster Co. (7 July)

GILBERT, Robert, in Market St., Phila. - offers reward
for recovery of a mare and colt, strayed or stolen from
Commons of Phila. (7 July)

SMITH, John, an English servant, nailor by trade - runaway
from John Naylor, of Phila. (7 July)

CORBY, William, an English servant - runaway from John
Dabbin, of Phila., blacksmith (7 July)

Ship Henry, Capt. Little, is arrived in York River from
Africa with about 300 slaves; the brigantine Sea Horse,
Richard Tillidge master, is also arrived in York River,
with rum and sugar; the snow Betty, William Soper master, is arrived in James River from the Isle of May,
laden with salt - Williamsburg items of 10 June (14
July)

LYNCH, Head, Esq., Post-Master General of America - died
Monday last at his house in Caroline Co. - Williamsburg
item of 10 June (14 July)

PINSON, Capt. John, of the Princess Louisa, who had been
bound to India and was cast away, came in the snow
Betty - Williamsburg item of 17 June (14 July)

Ship London, Capt. Newham, the Restoration, Capt. Aylward,
and the Prince of Wales are arrived in James River,

from London; Capts. Belcher and Lane are arrived in
York River from London and Capts. Canders and Romny
from Bristol - Williamsburg item of 17 June (14 July)

NELSON, Thomas, Jr. - has been appointed Attorney General
and Judge of the Court of Vice Admiralty of Virginia in
place of Edward Barradell, dec'd - Williamsburg item of
17 June (14 July)

Thursday last arrived at Boston Capt. Rouse's prize ship
and Friday Capt. Frankland of H.M.S. Rose; the merchants
of Charlestown, S.C., lately gave him a 2-gallon silver
punch bowl - Boston item of 4 July (14 July)

BELL, Tom - on 11 July was at the ferry opposite New York
(14 July)

A brigantine, the Betty, Capt. Bibbe commander, belonging
to Liverpool, bound to Virginia - was taken up abandoned at sea and brought to Madeira and sold (14 July)

The Pretty Bettsy, Capt. Tilledge, belonging to Col.
Lewis of Virginia, was taken by the Spaniards but re-
taken 7 May by the brigantine St. George of Liverpoole,
Capt. Brathwait (14 July)

DANDRIDGE, Capt., of H.M.S. South Sea Castle - by end of
August will convoy from the Capes of Virginia to England (14 July)

MACKY, James, in Front St., Phila. - has lime juice for
sale (14 July)

OVERINGTON, Thomas, servant, age about 25 or 30, tanner -
runaway from Samuel Hilldrup, of Annapolis (14 July)

PARKER, William - offers reward for recovery of horse
strayed or stolen off the Commons of Phila. (14 July)

RICKALY, Thomas, convict servant, age c. 26 - runaway
from Charles Green, in Gunpowder Forest, near My Lady's
Manor, Md. (14 July)

WATERS, William, who says he served his time with William
Rodgers, of Baltimore Co., Md. - was taken up and committed to Goal of Newcastle; Samuel Bickley, sheriff,
says Waters will be discharged after 6 weeks unless
claimed (14 July)

RICHARDS, Owen, boatswain - runaway from on board ship
Philip and Peter, Benjamin North commander (14 July)

COLLINGS, Richard, sailor, age c. 24 - same as above

Minto, Negro, age upwards of 20 - runaway from John Pennington, innholder, in Frederickstown, Cecil Co., Md.
(14 July)

Adam, Negro, age c. 22 - runaway from Thomas Hynson, Jr.,
near Sassafrax (14 July)

COLE, Mary, residing at Henry Wood's, in Waterford, Gloucester Co., N.J. - will let for 10 years plantation in
Greenwich Twp., Gloucester Co., N.J. (14 July)

BAYNTON, Peter - has for sale a shallop and a schooner (14
July)

HYATT, John, Sheriff - will sell at Roberts's Coffee House
in Phila. land belonging to estate of William Chancellor, dec'd, as follows: lot adjoining Capt. Thomas
Bourn's rope-walk; lot in Northern Liberties near Hugh
Roberts's lot; lot in Northern Liberties adjoining lot
of John Warder's; lot in Third St., Phila., adjoining
lot of Henry Clifton's (14 July)

JACKSON, Joseph, Sheriff - announces sale at Giles Lawrence's, at the old Crown Tavern in Bristol, of land,
being the estate of John Bourke, dec'd, taken in execution at the suit of William Whitacre, Esq.; among the
tracts is one known as Mill Land, another called
Homer's Fields and another adjoining John Abraham
Denormandie's and Nathan Watsons' land (14 July)

HAYGEN, John, Irish servant - runaway from Isaac Baker,
of Cunnecocheg; reward for his capture will be paid
by Isaac Baker or Joshua Baker, near Lancaster (14 July)

Died 1 July at Williamsburg the son and only child of the
late William Gooch, Jr., and grandson of the governor
(21 July)

STACKEY, Mrs., of New York, widow - Monday last was
thrown down and rid over by a chair, so that she died
in a few minutes - New York item of 11 July (21 July)

SINCAU, Peter, of Elizabethtown - Monday last was kicked
to death by a horse - New York item of 11 July (21 July)

GARRITSON, Peter, of Hackensack - on Monday last was run
over by a wagon and killed - New York item of 11 July
(21 July)

JAUNCY, Capt. - arrived 16 July at New York from Jamaica

with news that the sloop <u>Young Batchelors</u>, Capt. David Griffith, was cast away but all the people saved - New York item of 17 July (21 July)

BELL, Tom - last week on Long Island was taken by a person whom he had defrauded by pretending to be a son of Col. Floyd - New York item of 17 July (21 July)

<u>The Nature and Necessity of Regeneration</u> (with some remarks on a discourse of Dr. Waterland's) by Jonathan Dickinson, Minister at Elizabeth-town, N.J. - sold by the printer hereof (21 July)

SNEED, Mary, dec'd - her house in High St., Phila., adjoining to David Evans's, is for sale; inquire of Edward Brooks (administrator of the estate) in Second St. or John Hood, living in said house (21 July)

TURNER, Peter - house where he now lives in Front St., Phila., is for sale (21 July)

FENEX, Robert, mulatto, age <u>c</u>. 27 or 28, sawyer - runaway from Philip Alexander, of Stafford Co., Virginia (21 July)

HOMES, Richard, Englishman, and Joshua Bevan, servant to Abraham Ingram, of Somerset Co., Md., have both been committed to Newcastle Goal, according to notice of Samuel Bickley, sheriff (21 July)

DUN, Owen, of Nantmel Twp., Chester Co. - his wife Elizabeth has eloped from him (21 July)

SADLER, Alexander, rope-maker, living in one of Charles West's houses, between his house and Second St. - has for sale a deck boat (which has been an oyster boat) at Capt. Goodman's wharf, Phila. (21 July)

Ship bound into Virginia from Aberdeen, Capt. Stuart master, ran ashore Friday last at Cape May (28 July)

<u>Divine Influence</u> by Rev. Alexander Webster of Edinburgh is sold by the printer hereof (28 July)

WRIGHT, Nathan, of Trenton - his wife Elizabeth has eloped from him (28 July)

CHANCELLOR, William, dec'd - 3 Negro sail-makers, belonging to his estate, are to be sold at the Indian King in Phila. (28 July)

BENEZET, John Stephen - intends to leave off trading (28 July)

Two supposed runaway servants, one from William Walker, at
the Forks of Neshaminy, and the other from James Whitehill, of Lancaster Co., have been taken up and committed to Burlington Goal (28 July)

Discourses on Various Important Subjects by Jonathan Edward, Pastor of the Church of Christ in Northampton, is
sold by the printer hereof (28 July)

BOGLE, Samuel, at Mrs. Harper's, in Second St., Phila. -
sells rum and sugar just imported in the ship Warren,
Capt. Cox master (28 July)

TUNSTALL, Richard, Clerk of Court of King and Queen Co.,
Va. - his 2 daughters, aged c. 12 and 11, last Sunday
se'nnight went into the River Mattapony to wash and
were drowned - Williamsburg item of 8 July (4 Aug.)

SMITH, Capt. Arthur, of Surry, only son of, aged c. 10 or
11 - Sunday last went into the creek to wash and was
drowned - Williamsburg item of 8 July (4 Aug.)

CLINTON, George, Gov. of New York - reported ready to
leave for New York end of May or early June (4 Aug.)

POWERS, Capt. - arrived Saturday last at New York from
Antigua - New York item of 1 Aug. (4 Aug.)

NEAVE, Joel (brother of Samuel Neave, merchant of Phila.)
- died Tuesday last (4 Aug.)

WELLS, Thomas - offers reward for recovery of mare strayed
or stolen off Society Hill; she was bought from Horsham
Twp. and grazed near Dr. Graeme's plantation (4 Aug.)

Squallo, Negro, age c. 26, country born, who was bought
from Dr. Rodman, who lives near Burlington - runaway
from Stephen Onion, of Baltimore Co., Md.; it is supposed that Squallo went away with a Mulatto belonging
to Charlestown Waters (4 Aug.)

BROWN, Michael, silk-dyer from London - is removed from
Chesnut St. to Sassafras St. or Race St., at Mr. William
Maugridge's, ship-joiner, in Phila. (4 Aug.)

GUICHARD, William, at Parr's wharf, Phila. - sells rum,
sugar, and molasses; he may be met with at Mrs. Meredith's, corner of Chesnut St. (4 Aug.)

About 2 months ago 3 Portuguese seamen in the night murdered Capt. Newark Jackson, of Boston, on board a
schooner of which Jackson was commander; they also

killed Capt. Charles Ledain, merchant (who was a passenger), and Capt. Jackson's boy and wounded William Blake (the boatswain); Mr. Blake brought the vessel to Currentine, where 2 of the murderers were seized and taken to Surinam; the other criminal escaped - Boston item of 1 Aug. (11 Aug.)

Monday last a young woman, age c. 18, was convicted at Boston of wearing men's apparel; she had been a sailor, made a number of voyages and used the name of Jemmy Hubbard; she had been a sailor on ship of Capt. Davis - Boston item of 1 Aug. (11 Aug.)

Sloop Virgin Queen, John Hornor master - will sail from Port Burlington to Boston; for freight or passage agree with Preseve Brown, Jr., or said master at Whitehill, N.J. (11 Aug.)

Sloop Dolphin, John Norton master, now at Fishbourn's wharf - will sail for Boston; William Norton, at his store on said wharf, sells rum, mackrel, chairs, pots, kettles, etc. (11 Aug.)

FARREL, Andrew, in Chesnut St., Phila. - offers reward for recovery of 2 horses strayed or stolen from Northern Liberties of Phila. (11 Aug.)

LAW, Robert, at Evan Morgan's, cooper, in Front St., near the drawbridge - has for sale a Negro wench (11 Aug.)

Malt-house and dwelling near the dock in Second St., Phila., is to be let for 7 years; apply to Elizabeth Griffits, of Phila. (11 Aug.)

WHARRY, John, at Mr. Goodwin's in Walnut St. - has for sale glass and looking-glasses, just imported from London in the ship Williams Galley, Henry Harrison master (11 Aug.)

BARD, Widow, in Burlington - has for sale a large house near the water in Front St. (11 Aug.)

OWEN, Owen, late of Phila., innholder, dec'd - accounts with estate to be settled with John Biddle, administrator (11 Aug.)

CREGIER, Capt., from Jamaica reports that Madam Beckford (daughter of our present governor) died in Jamaica the beginning of July last - New York item of 15 Aug. (18 Aug.)

DURELL, Capt., from Georgia, reports that James Oglethorpe embarked for England on 23 July - New York item of 15 Aug. (18 Aug.)

Two houses in Burrough of Bristol, Bucks Co., fronting Mill St., between John Abraham Denormandie's and Henry Tomlinson's, are to be let by the owner John Large, living on the premises, who intends to leave for New England (18 Aug.)

Lot of land in Burrough of Wilmington, New Castle Co., between Henry Hunter's and Stephen Foulkes's lots - apply to Joseph Tucker, of Lower Merion, Phila. Co. (18 Aug.)

HACKET, John, servant, this country born, age c. 28 - runaway from Benjamin Thompson, of Cohansie (18 Aug.)

LANE, Richard, servant, this country born, age c. 28 - same as above

RAGAN, William, servant - runaway from Joseph Harlen, of Kennet Twp., Chester Co. (18 Aug.)

BEDDALL, John, servant - runaway from Ruth Harlen, of Kennet Twp., Chester Co. (18 Aug.)

JONES, Daniel, dec'd - accounts with estate to be settled with Hannah and Ann Jones, execs. (18 Aug.)

McCALL, Samuel, next to Mr. Allen's in Water St., Phila. - sells sugar and European goods (18 Aug.)

COGDILL, John, Irish servant, age c. 17 or 18 - runaway from John Michener, of Manor of Moreland, Phila. Co. (18 Aug.)

DUCHE, Anthony, dyer - is removed from his house in Front St., to the upper end of Chesnut St., near the State House in Phila. (18 Aug.)

JEKYL, Margaret, at Charles Willing's, merchant in Phila. - has land for sale, including a water lot lying between the lots late belonging to the estate of Alexander Woodropp, dec'd, and those late belonging to Edward and Joseph Shippen (18 Aug.)

PERRY, Samuel - is lately removed from the corner of Carpenter's wharf to the corner of Hamilton's wharf, in Phila. (18 Aug.)

NOBLE, Anthony, at the Sign of the Painters and Glaziers Arms on Society Hill - has a Negro woman for sale (18 Aug.)

BICKLEY, Samuel, sheriff, gives notice that a Negro, who says he belongs to Benjamin Hill of North Carolina, has been committed to the Newcastle Goal (18 Aug.)

European and India goods are sold by Cuzzins and Smyter in one of the new stores on Hamilton's wharf in Phila. (18 Aug.)

TILL, William - offers reward for recovery of a box supposed to have been stolen out of the ship Williams Galley, Capt. Harrison, from London, lying at Hamilton's wharf (18 Aug.)

CUTLER, Capt. John, late commander of a snow belonging to Boston, who sailed for Leona - was murdered, with 2 or 3 of his men by some Portuguese, who took away his slaves; some slaves were recovered, the vessel was fitted out and Friday last was brought into Newport, R.I., by Capt. Wickham - Boston item of 15 Aug. (25 Aug.)

One of the 3 murderers of Capts. Ledain and Jackson was killed by Indians - Boston item of 15 Aug. (25 Aug.)

HOPKINS, Capt. William, in the privateer sloop Prince Frederick, of Newport, R.I., arrived Wednesday last at Newport, after taking 7 prizes - Newport item of 12 Aug. (25 Aug.)

ABEEL, John (son of David Abeel, merchant, of New York) - Saturday last accidently had his arm shattered when a gun went off; the arm was then amputated - New York item of 22 Aug. (25 Aug.)

Saturday last arrived at New York the Rhode Island privateer schooner Fame, Capt. Griffis commander, bringing in a Spanish sloop taken as a prize - New York item of 22 Aug. (25 Aug.)

NORTH, Capt. - has just arrived at Phila. from Cowes with European news (25 Aug.)

PEASLEY, Jonathan, of Phila. - his wife Dorcas has eloped from him (25 Aug.)

VANRIK, Stephen and Robert Reynolds warn people not to accept their notes fraudulently obtained from them by Samuel Patterson (25 Aug.)

CONWAY, Patrick, at Mr. Hamilton's wharf - sells rum, molasses, cotton and indigo (25 Aug.)

WEISER, Conrad, in Tulpehocken, offers reward for recovery of 2 bundles of Indian ware and goods, lost near Capt. Cressop's on Conechoche (25 Aug.)

Sloop at Capt. Bourn's wharf is for sale; inventory to be seen on board or at William Crosthwaite's in Front St. (25 Aug.)

VACHEN, Michael, Irish servant, age c. 26 - runaway from Robert Boyle, tanner, of Fallowfield, Chester Co. (25 Aug.)

WEISER, Conrad, in behalf of Virginia, on 31 July, at Onondaga - exchanged belts and strings of wampum with the Great Council of the Six Nations (1 Sept.)

NORTH, Capt., with 400 Germans, and Capt. Cowie, with 300, lately arrived at Phila. (1 Sept.)

JONES, Cadwalader, of Uwchland, Chester Co. - offers reward for recovery of horse strayed or stolen (1 Sept.)

Reward offered for recovery of mare strayed or stolen from plantation of Alexander McKinsterey, Buckingham Twp., Bucks Co.; reward will be paid by McKinsterey, Thomas Dufell or Joseph Mills (1 Sept.)

Ship Warren Galley, John Cox commander - will sail for London; for freight or passage agree with William Attwood, merchant, or the master on board at Hamilton's wharf (1 Sept.)

Snow Cape Fear Merchant, Israel Alleyne master - will sail for Cape Fear; for freight or passage agree with the master on board at Market St. wharf or with Robert Ellis (1 Sept.)

ROACH, John, Irish servant, age c. 20, sadler - runaway from owners of Iron Works near Burdenstown; reward will be paid for his capture if notice thereof is given to Joseph Peace or Andrew Read at Trenton or Francis Bowes at Christiana Bridge (1 Sept.)

HANSON, John, weaver, from England but late from Nicholas Austin's, of Abington, into Third St. in Phila. and now returned again to Nicholas Austin's, into Caleb Fisher's business, the said Caleb Fisher being dec'd (1 Sept.)

Brigantine Elizabeth, Edward Gill master - will sail for Antigua; for freight or passage agree with said master or with Samuel Hasell (1 Sept.)

OGLETHORPE, General - has fitted out a ship and taken with him to England Col. Heron and Mr. Brun - Williamsburg item of 12 Aug. (8 Sept.)

THOMPSON, Capt., at York Town, on 18 Aug. bought the Palarcha - Williamsburg item of 19 Aug. (8 Sept.)

HAWN, Lodowick, a Dutchman, when hunting squirrels at Piles Grove, Salem Co., shot a man and woman, killing the man and wounding the woman; Hawn has absconded (8 Sept.)

DAVIS, Benj., sheriff, gives notice that James Allen, an Englishman, servant to Stephen Hampton, planter, in St. Mary's Co., Md., has been committed to Chester Goal (8 Sept.)

JONES and Beddome, at their store in Market St., Phila., behind Sam. Grizley's - have for sale cloth and hardware (8 Sept.)

About 120 acres on Passyunk Road, about 2 miles from town, are for sale; apply to Richard Hill, Jr. (8 Sept.)

TOY, Elias, of Chester Twp., Burlington Co. - offers reward for apprehension of Robert Fryar, an Irishman, who stole from him cloth, a gun, a silver spoon and shirt buttons (8 Sept.)

CROCKLAND, John, servant, a Norforkshire man - runaway from William Towson, blacksmith, living in Baltimore Co., near the Red Horse, at Patapsco (8 Sept.)

REDIKEN, Edward, Irish servant, age c. 22, weaver - runaway from Thomas Mershon, of Maidenhead, Hunterdon Co., West New Jersey; a George Duckworth is supposed to be with Rediken (8 Sept.)

Cicero, a Negro, age c. 20 - runaway from the sloop Vernon, John Matchet master, now at Market St. wharf in Phila. (8 Sept.)

HILLS, William, a young man, transported for a crime from England - was executed on 26 Aug. at Upper Marlborough, Md., for the murder of his master's child (15 Sept.)

Extract of letter (about battle fought on the Rhine) from Judge Keene at Newfoundland, dated St. John's, 6 Aug. 1743, to Stephen Bouteneau, merchant, in Boston (15 Sept.)

Two barns at Charlestown, Mass., on Tuesday last were

burned with goods and merchandize, all the property of
Mr. Foster, sheriff of Middlesex Co. - Boston item of
5 Sept. (15 Sept.)

PRESTON, Samuel, long a member of the Council and Treasurer
of Pennsylvania - died Sunday last at Phila., aged
nearly 80 (15 Sept.)

LEWIS, Stephen, dec'd - house, shop, tanyard in Newcastle
on Delaware, part of his estate, are to be sold by the
administrators, Benjamin Swett and Josiah Lewis (15
Sept.)

House on Rariton River, about a mile above New Brunswick,
is for sale; apply to Gilbert Tennent; also a house in
New Brunswick in which the Widow Vanclief lives will be
sold by Gilbert Tennent or David Chambers (15 Sept.)

GIBSON, George, in Lancaster, is removed from the Sign of
the Crown and Three Horses to the Sign of the Three
Tons (15 Sept.)

Plantation of 140 acres in Cheltenham Twp., near Richard
Martin's mill, one mile from Oxford Church and 8 from
Phila. - will be sold by Thomas Nesmith (15 Sept.)

POORE, Richard, Irish servant - runaway from John Blackwood, fuller, of Gloucester Co., upon Timber Creek (15
Sept.)

SHARP, Thomas, Jr., of East Nottingham, Chester Co. - offers reward for recovery of horse stolen from him (15
Sept.)

DAVIS, David, at his store on Arch St. wharf, Phila. -
sells imported goods (15 Sept.)

CLARKE, Henry, at the Coach and Horses, opposite the State
House - sells turnspit dogs and wheels for roasting
meat (15 Sept.)

FALKNER, Capt. Lester, arrived at Phila. from Colerain in
Ireland, with European news (22 Sept.)

CLARKE, John - his sloop is stranded at Barnegat but the
men all saved - New York item of 19 Sept. (22 Sept.)

HARTLEY, William, near William Mores, Esq., in Charles
Town, Chester Co. - reward will be paid for recovery of
his horse strayed away from him; horse is to be returned
to him or to John Smith in Market St., Phila. (22 Sept.)

PULLEN, Francis, dec'd - accounts with estate to be settled with Ann Hall, executrix to the executor of said estate (22 Sept.)

Snow Friendship, David Began master, at Woodrop's wharf in Phila. - will sail for Beauford, N.C.; for freight or passage agree with master on board or at his house in Walnut St. (22 Sept.)

BRIEN, Daniel, Irish servant, age c. 18 - runaway from Francis Costigin, of New Brunswick (22 Sept.)

JONES, Isaac, intending for Europe, desires to settle all accounts (22 Sept.)

SCHLEYDORN, Henry, sugar baker, in Norris's Alley, Phila. - sugar, candy, molasses, indigo, tea, coffee, pepper (22 Sept.)

MARSHAL, John, English servant - runaway from Isaac Forman, of New Hanover, Burlington Co., West New Jersey (22 Sept.)

CLINTON, George, Gov. of New York - arrived Wednesday last at New York in H.M.S. Loo, Capt. Utting commander, who had under his convoy from Plymouth the Pegasus, Capt. Patterson, and the Neptune, Capt. Foot - New York item of 26 Sept. (29 Sept.)

COULTER, William, age c. 22, indicted for ravishing a Dutch woman of fourscore - acquitted 28 Sept. of rape but found guilty of assault (29 Sept.)

Snow Hercules, Capt. Anderson - returned 28 Sept. to Phila. to refit after damage from a hurricane; he reports that the Queen of Hungary, Capt. Blackburn, had only a main- mast left, while the Fame Gally, Capt. Sunderland, foundered (29 Sept.)

DOWEL, Capt., in the George privateer, of Phila. - has just arrived with a prize; Capt. John Evans's vessel, of Phila., was captured by the Spaniards but has been re- taken (29 Sept.)

Ship Loyal Judith, James Cowie master, now at Edward War- ner's wharf - will sail for Charlestown; for freight or passage agree with the master or with Robert and Amos Strettell (29 Sept.)

Sloop Diana, Hubbard Outerbridge master, now at Bourn's wharf - will sail for Barbados; for freight or passage agree with the master (29 Sept.)

Ship <u>Katherine</u>, Gurnay Wall master, now at Hamilton's wharf - will sail for Bristol; for freight or passage agree with Edward or Joseph Shippen or the master (29 Sept.)

WOLFF, Henry, Dutch servant, age <u>c</u>. 18 - runaway from Jacob Bouman, of Germantown (29 Sept.)

THOMAS, Moses, house-carpenter, of Phila. - is removed into Market St., next door but one to the Presbyterian Meeting-house in Phila. (29 Sept.)

NEAVE, Joel, lately dec'd - accounts with estate to be settled with Samuel Neave, administrator (29 Sept.)

FLING, Rebecca, Bristol servant girl (who sometimes calls herself Rebecca Hussey) - runaway from John Hamilton, tanner, near Lancaster (29 Sept.)

On 1 Oct. the following were elected for Phila. Co.-- representatives: John Kinsey, Thomas Leech, Isaac Norris, Edward Warner, James Morris, Joseph Trotter, Owen Evans, Robert Jones; sheriffs: John Hyatt, Morde- cai Lloyd; coroners: Henry Pratt, Jacob Duché; com- missioner: Philip Syng; assessors: Evan Jones, Robert Jones, Moses Hughs, Jeremiah Elfreith, John Lessher, James Paul; burgesses: Israel Pemberton, Oswald Peel; city assessors: John Stamper, Richard Parker, William Fisher, Thomas Howard, Stephen Armit, John Langdale (6 Oct.)

On 1 Oct. the following were elected for Bucks Co.: repre- sentatives: Mahlon Kirkbride, John Watson, Abraham Chapman, John Hall, Mark Watson, Benjamin Field, Garrat Vansant, Joseph Shaw; sheriffs: John Hart, Timothy Smith; coroners: Joseph Chapman, Joseph Hampton; com- missioner: John Hall; assessors: John Williamson, Barthol. Longstretch, Adam Harker, Thomas Paxon, Thomas Owen, Abraham Vastine (6 Oct.)

On 1 Oct. the following were elected for Chester Co.-- representatives: Jeremiah Star, James Gibbons, Thomas Chandler, Joseph Harvey, Samuel Levis, Joseph Pennock, George Ashbridge, Jr., Francis Yarnal; sheriffs: John Owen, Nathan Worley; coroners: Thomas Morgan, John Hanley; commissioner: Jacob Howel; assessors: Thomas Hughs, Awbry Roberts, Joseph Mendinghall, Joshua Pusey, Samuel Bunting, Thomas Pennel (6 Oct.)

On 1 Oct. the following were elected for Lancaster Co.-- representatives: Anthony Shaw, Arthur Patterson, Thomas Linley, John Wright; sheriffs: James Galbraith, James

Mitchel; coroners: Joshua Low, John Morris (6 Oct.)

On 1 Oct. the following were elected for Newcastle Co.--
representatives: John McCoole, William Armstrong, John
Vance, James McMahan, Samuel Clements, Daniel Corbet;
sheriffs: Samuel Bickley, Gideon Griffitths; coroner:
Benjamin Cook (6 Oct.)

On 1 Oct. the following were elected for Kent Co.--repre-
sentatives: Mark Manlove, John Tilton, John Robinson,
William Farson, Hugh Durbrow, James Gorrel; sheriffs:
Thomas Green, John Hunter; coroners: Edmund Badger,
Timothy Comings (6 Oct.)

SIBBALD, Capt. John, commander of the privateer Wilmington
- writes from Cape Nicholas about how Capt. Dowel of
the schooner George retook the vessel of Capt. Evans of
Phila. (6 Oct.)

Auction to be held at house of Widow Reeve in Burlington,
West Jersey (6 Oct.)

ANDERSON, Capt. Mark, of the privateer Eagle, of Charlestown, S.C. - on 17 Aug. returned there after taking a
Spanish privateer (13 Oct.)

On 1 Oct. the following were elected for Sussex Co.--
representatives: Jacob Kollock, John Clowe, Woolsey
Burton, Enoch Cummings, Daniel Nunez, Ryves Holt;
sheriffs: Peter Hall, William Shankland; coroners:
John Hall, Charles Perry (13 Oct.)

Ship Phaenix, William Willson master - will sail for
Charlestown, S.C.; for freight or passage agree with
the master or Benjamin Shoemaker (13 Oct.)

Jacob, Mulatto, age c. 19, who formerly lived with Mrs.
Jane Grant - runaway from Capt. John Spence, of Phila.
(13 Oct.)

OKILL, George, of Phila. - offers reward for capture of
the following 4 sailors, runaways from the ship Neptune:
Daniel Fox, John Guy, John Margison and Mundo McKixsey
(13 Oct.)

JONES, John, of Gloucester Co., Racoon Creek, N.J. — offers
reward for recovery of horse, strayed or stolen away
from Bethlehem on the Forks of Delaware; horse is to be
taken to Tho. Herbert, at the Sign of the Turk's Head
in Phila. (13 Oct.)

HAWKSFORD, John, Irish servant, age c. 25 - runaway from

John Dodd, of St. George's Hundred, Newcastle Co. (13 Oct.)

Servant lad, age c. 17, shoemaker - runaway from Zachariah Robbings, of Upper Freehold, East Jersey, near Allentown (13 Oct.)

JONES, Edward, storekeeper in Apoquinemy, Newcastle Co. - warns all persons from trusting anyone on his account (13 Oct.)

STANLEY, Valentine - has a Negro man for sale (13 Oct.)

ANDERSON, Capt. - arrived Friday last at Newport, R.I., from Charlestown, S.C.: with him came as passenger Capt. Clement Stanton, whose ship was taken on 27 Feb. - Newport item of 7 Oct. (20 Oct.)

TYNG, Capt., in the Province snow - has been ordered out after a Spanish privateer sloop - Boston item of 10 Oct. (20 Oct.)

MASTERS, William - will sell at auction at Roberts's Coffee House in Phila. 286 bushels of wheat (20 Oct.)

PERRY, Samuel, intending for England - desires to settle all accounts (20 Oct.)

Ship St. Andrew, Robert Brown master, now at Fishbourn's wharf - will sail for Charlestown; for freight or passage agree with the master or with Stedman, Robinson & Co., at their store in Water St., Phila. (20 Oct.)

Ship Lydia, James Abercrombie master, at Fishbourn's wharf - same as above

Two houses and lots in Phila., both in tenure of Stedman & Robinson, and a plantation in Phila. Co., near Horsham Meeting-house (now in tenure of Rebeccah Iredel) will be sold at Roberts's Coffee House (20 Oct.)

LOGAN, James - offers reward for recovery of one of his chaise horses, stolen from his plantation near Germantown (27 Oct.)

REEVE, John, late of Burlington, West New Jersey, dec'd - accounts with estate to be settled with Matthias Aspden, executor (27 Oct.)

JONES, George, lately living in Blackhorse Alley, Phila., now gone to England - accounts with him are to be settled with his attorney Lawrence Anderson, living in

Second St., Phila. (27 Oct.)

Tract of 171 acres, part of the place called South Hampton, joining to Derrick Oglin and on the other side to Lamberd Vandike, Thomas Duffil, Richard Clayton and Isaac Bolton, is for sale; enquire of John Jones, in Phila. (27 Oct.)

Tract of 200 acres in Monmouth Co., by Beaver Dam, near Crosswicks Creek, joining to land of Clement Plumstead, Esq., which George Willcocks, late of Perth Amboy, dec'd, by his will dated 3 Jan. 1728 left to be divided among the churches of Burlington, Shrewsbury and Hopewell, is for sale; apply to Rev. Campbell at Burlington or Rev. Miln at Shrewsbury; adv. is signed by Colin Campbell (27 Oct.)

Prince, Mulatto slave, who has lived on Tenicum Island in the Jerseys - runaway from Joshua George, in Bohemia, Cecil Co., Md. (27 Oct.)

HOMER, John, Irishman, shoemaker - has run away from his bail, John Leik, of Middletown, Chester Co. (27 Oct.)

THOMPSON, Edward, of East Caln, Chester Co. - has taken up a mare (27 Oct.)

FULHAM, Peter, Irish servant lad, tailor - runaway from William Craddock (3 Nov.)

WALKERS & GRIFFITH, at their store on Fishbourn's wharf, Phila. - have for sale Manchester goods and haberdashery ware (3 Nov.)

Ship Mary, Nicholas Stephenson master, now at Master's wharf, Phila. - will sail for London; for freight or passage agree with John Reynall or the master (3 Nov.)

Snow Sarah, Richard Berrill commander - will sail for Ireland; for freight or passage agree with William Dames, in Phila. (3 Nov.)

HOPWOOD, Samuel - mare belonging to him was stolen from plantation of Mary Reason, near Caecil Meeting-House in Maryland - reward is offered for return of the mare to Israel Pemberton in Phila. or in Virginia to John Pleasants at Currls or Samuel Jordan at Nancemond (3 Nov.)

Books just imported from London are for sale by Rev. Jones, Rev. Tennent, Samuel Hazzard, merchant, in Phila., by Rev. David Davis at the Welch Tract and by Dr. Reece

Jones at Christiana Bridge (3 Nov.)

CURRIE, Ebenezer, at his store next door to James Mackey's in Front St., Phila. - sells cloth, cards, tea, guns, cheese, etc. (3 Nov.)

RAFFARDY, Henry, Irish servant, age c. 22 - runaway from Joseph Bartholomew, in Whiteland, Chester Co. (3 Nov.)

ULRICH, Gaspar - offers reward for recovery of his horse strayed or stolen from his stable in Phila.; horse may be brought to him or to Christopher Bastian, on Chesnut Hill (3 Nov.)

PARSONS, John, West Country convict servant, age c. 30 - runaway from Vachel Denton, living near Annapolis, Md. (3 Nov.)

COOPER, Robin, Negro, age c. 50 - same as above

BAYNTON, Peter - has for sale a schooner and a brigantine (3 Nov.)

MORRIS, Lewis - speech to the New Jersey Assembly and address of the House by And. Johnston, Speaker (10 Nov.)

WILSON, William, master of the ship Phoenix - offers reward for apprehension of 3 runaway sailors, James Sutherland (a Yorkshire man, a ship-carpenter), Gray Patterson and William Finch (10 Nov.)

Sloop Sea Nymph, Samuel Brown master, now at Parr's wharf in Phila. - will sail for St. Christophers (10 Nov.)

INGLIS, John - has removed his store in Front St. to Plumb St., below the drawbridge, next door to the Ship (10 Nov.)

Creature called a mouse, about the size of a horse - to be seen at the house of John Saunders, huntsman, the upper end of Second St., Phila. (10 Nov.)

House fronting the roads leading from Phila. to Trenton and from Bristol to Newtown is to be sold by public-vendue at the 4 lane-ends, Middletown, Bucks Co.; enquire of William Huddleston (10 Nov.)

HUGHES, John, Irish servant, age c. 18 - runaway from John Mackey, of Fallowfield Twp., Chester Co. (10 Nov.)

FARMAR, R., at the Unicorn, in Second St., near Market St., Phila. - has a young Negro man and 4 years time of a servant woman for sale (10 Nov.)

HILLIS, George - will not pay debts contracted in future by his wife Jane (10 Nov.)

CRELLIUS, Joseph - designs to open his winter evening school for the German language and to continue to publish his weekly German newspaper; he lives in Arch St., next door to the Sign of the Blue Bell, in Phila. (10 Nov.)

Speech of Lewis Morris to the New Jersey Assembly (16 Nov.)

WEST, Thomas, late of Wilmington, dec'd - accounts with estate to be settled with the administrators, Thomas West, at Concord, or William West and Thomas Canby, at Wilmington (16 Nov.)

SCHUPPY, J., living in Strawberry Alley, at the Sign of the Book, in Phila. - designs to teach French and German in evening school (16 Nov.)

BARKLEY, George, Irish servant, age c. 26, tailor - runaway from William Thompson, living in Joppy, Baltimore Co., Md. (16 Nov.)

COVELL, Jacob, servant, age c. 17, tailor, whose indenture was signed by Richard Guess and Thomas Sheridine, Esqrs. - same as above

BAY, Thomas, master of the Indian Queen Oppess, lately taken by the Spaniards - states that the Spaniards computed that the chest of John Ryan on board was worth 600 pounds sterling; John Ryan states the chest contained about 200 pounds (16 Nov.)

RICHARDSON, John, late of Bristol Twp., Phila. Co., dec'd - accounts with estate to be settled with Aubrey and Edward Richardson, administrators (16 Nov.)

Sloop Susannah, Richard Newboald master, at Mr. Clymer's wharf in Phila. - will sail for Barbados (16 Nov.)

Ship George and Henry, George Bowler master, arrived Friday last at Charlestown, S.C., from Jamaica - Charlestown item of 7 Nov. (24 Nov.)

CLINTON, Gov. George - speech of New York Assembly (24 Nov.)

KIP, Capt. - arrived Friday last at New York from Curacoa and gave news of Spanish vessels taken by H.M.S. Litchfield, William Barnaby commander - New York item of 21 Nov. (24 Nov.)

Two New York privateers, the brigantine <u>Hester</u>, Capt. Rosewell, and the sloop <u>Polly</u>, Capt. Jefferies, sailed 20 Nov. against the Spaniards (24 Nov.)

ALISON, Mr. - a free school has been opened at his house in Chester Co. (24 Nov.)

A new map of Pennsylvania and maps of each county are intended by William Parsons, Surveyor General of Pennsylvania (24 Nov.)

FORTESCUE, Charles (late Free-School-Master of Chester) - has opened school at his house in the alley commonly called Mr. Taylor's (24 Nov.)

WALN, Richard, Jr., of Whitemarsh - offers reward for recovery of a strayed or stolen horse (24 Nov.)

DOLLARD, Patrick, Irish servant, age <u>c</u>. 30, hatter - runaway from Roger Connor, of Lancaster Town (24 Nov.; 3 Jan. 1744)

SMITH, Samuel, from Ireland, age <u>c</u>. 27 - has been missing for 6 weeks; news of him is desired by Michael Wallace, of Elk River, or it may be sent to the printer (24 Nov.)

READ, James, next door to the Post Office in Market St., Phila. - has for sale many books just imported in the <u>Mary</u>, Capt. Stevenson, from London (24 Nov.)

PARKER, William, living in the alley called Gilbert's or sometimes Preston's Alley, between Front St. and Second St., Phila. - offers reward for detection of person or persons who carried off several grafted apple-trees from his young orchard adjoining to the east Dr. Lloyd Zachary's plantation in the Northern Liberties of Phila. (24 Nov.)

BOWES, Francis, living near Christine Bridge - offers for sale a third part of a forge and grist mill upon Black Creek, near Burdens-Town, West Jersey; apply to said Bowes or to Joseph Peace or Andrew Read of Trenton (24 Nov.)

Address of General Assembly of New York, Adolph Philipse, Speaker, to Gov. George Clinton and the Governor's reply (1 Dec.)

BROWN, Michael, silk-dyer from London - is removed into Sassafras or Race St., at William Maugridge's (1 Dec.)

RAWLE, John, in Phila. - offers for sale real estate: a

tract of 120 acres, with plantation and sawmill joining to Charles Brockden's land in Morris Co., N.J. (apply to Capt. Joseph Thomson, who lives near it, or to Benjamin Canby at the ferry), and a tract of 800 acres in West New Jersey, near a branch of Prince Morris's River, called the Island Branch (1 Dec.)

Partnership of Hamilton and Coleman, who sell English goods, is about to expire (1 Dec.)

PRICHARD, Rees, Jr. - has for sale plantation of 250 acres in White Land Twp., Chester Co. (1 Dec.)

BOOGWALTER, Darst - offers reward for recovery of mare stolen from his stable, living in Lampister, Lancaster Co. (1 Dec.)

SMITH, George, Irish convict servant, age c. 45, blacksmith - runaway from Ellis Gill, living in Northumberland Co. on Wiccomico River, Va. (1 Dec.)

Ship Charming Polly, Capt. Solomon Goad commander, arrived Saturday last at Boston from Jamaica; a passenger with him was Colin Campbell, a member of the Council of Jamaica (6 Dec.)

Address of the Council (Cadwalader Colden, Speaker) of New York to Gov. Clinton and the governor's reply (6 Dec.)

House in Burrough of Wilmington in High St., fronting the Market House, is to be let by Joshua Littler, now living on the premises (6 Dec.)

HARRISON, John, of Phila. - offers reward for recovery of a boat taken from the sloop Joseph and Mary (6 Dec.)

JONES, Hugh, of Merion, Phila. Co. - offers reward for recovery of strayed horse (6 Dec.)

FITZGERALD, James, Irish servant - runaway from John Cross, of Baskenridge, Sommerset Co., East New Jersey (6 Dec.)

LEHMAN, Christian, at his house in Germantown, opposite to Mathias Adam Hogermaed - draws up documents in German or English and does surveying (6 Dec.)

Message from Gov. George Thomas to the Pennsylvania Assembly (15 Dec.)

Four tracts of land, each of 250 acres, in the Great Swamp in Bucks Co., adjoining to land of Benjamin Gilbert; enquire of Morris Morris, at the Great Swamp, or

William Logan in Phila. (15 Dec.)

TENNENT, Gilbert - calls attention to an error in the last
Gazette (15 Dec.)

KOCK, Peter - is removed from the corner house (formerly
called Charles Read's Corner) to his house in Water
St., Phila., next door to William Till, Esq. (15 Dec.)

The American Magazine and other items are sold by B.
Franklin (15 Dec.)

HALL, Robert, gardener, who came from Bayres in Parish of
Haddingtown, East Leuthain, Scotland - desires his
brother Patrick Hall, gardener, to write to him "gardener to Esquire Brinlie, in Roxbury near Boston" (15
Dec.)

RICHARDSON, Francis, designing for London - desires that
all accounts with Richardson and Eversley be settled
(15 Dec.)

John Wallace & Co., at their store in Front St., opposite
Samuel Hasell's, Esq. - sells cloth, books, snuff and
glass (15 Dec.)

ROCK, Henry, servant, weaver - runaway from John Henderson
of Freehold, East Jersey (15 Dec.)

ERWIN, Thomas, Irish servant, age c. 16 — runaway from
Robert Givanes, living on Elk River, Caecil Co., Md.
(15 Dec.)

DOYLE, David, Irish servant, age c. 30, cooper - runaway
from Thomas Sligh, living near the Red House in Baltimore Co., Md. (15 Dec.)

THOMAS, William, English apprentice, age c. 14, tailor -
runaway from Mathias Lamy, of Whiteland, Chester Co.
(15 Dec.)

Extract of Votes of the Pennsylvania House of Representatives mentions John Hall, Samuel Levis, James Gibbins,
Jeremiah Star, Mark Watson, Benjamin Field, Joseph
Pennock, Mahlon Kirkbride, Joseph Harvey, Isaac Norris
and Edward Warner (20 Dec.)

TIPPIN, Robert, late of Newtown, Chester Co., dec'd - accounts with estate to be settled with William Reiley,
executor, of Whiteland Twp., Chester Co. (20 Dec.)

SMITH, John, at one of Israel Pemberton's stores - sells

cloth, lead, sugar, molasses, etc. (20 Dec.)

Extract from the Votes of the General Assembly of New Jersey mentions Col. Farmar, Judge Allen, Mr. Nevill, Mr.
Cook, Mr. Mott and Mr. Vreeland and deals with the case
of Caleb Brown, Jr., charged with murder, who is in the
Monmouth Co. Goal (29 Dec.)

Anyone with plantation of 500 acres not above 30 miles
from Phila. to let is desired to enquire at Henry Dexter's, in Market St., Phila. (29 Dec.)

DAVEY & CARSAN offer reward for 2 sailors, Joseph Bowle
and Mathew Chambers (a Guernsey man), runaways from the
ship Catharine in the Bite of Newcastle (29 Dec.)

SIBBALD, Capt., defeated the Spaniards in ship (the schooner
Indian Queen Opess) they had taken from Capt. Bay, of
Phila. (29 Dec.)

DOWERS, Capt. - arrived Monday last at Phila. from Barbados (29 Dec.)

The Seneca, Capt. Wasborough, from Bristol, bound to Phila.
on 16 Dec. was driven ashore to northward of Cape May
(29 Dec.)

MORGAN, Evan, near the Court House in Phila. - sells cloth,
etc. (29 Dec.)

PARR, Samuel - intends shortly to leave Phila. (29 Dec.)

EDONOVAN, Patrick, servant, age c̲. 21, tailor - runaway
from James Baxter, of Apoquinimy in Newcastle Co.; reward for his capture will be paid by said Baxter or Mr.
Mollen, of Phila., tailor, or Anthony Duchee, tavernkeeper at Apoquinimy (29 Dec.)

1744

DARLING, Capt. - lately arrived at Piscataway from London
in a mast ship, with European news - Piscataway item of
3 Dec. 1743 (3 Jan.)

BELL, Tom - escaped last week from Charlestown, Mass.,
Goal - Boston item of 7 Dec. 1743 (3 Jan.)

TAYLOR, Alexander - executed Friday last at Annapolis for
the murder of his wife - Annapolis item of 28 Dec. 1743
(11 Jan.)

MALCOLM, John - executed Friday last at Annapolis for passing counterfeit money of Maryland - Annapolis item of 28 Dec. 1743 (11 Jan.)

Plantation of 143 acres in Passyunck Twp., about 3½ miles from Phila., is for sale; enquire of Hugh Davey or Joseph Sims, executors to Alexander Woodrop, dec'd (11 Jan.)

REED, William - intends to decline the business of tanning he now follows on Thomas Chalkley's plantation at Frankfort (11 Jan.)

HILLEGAS, Michael - has taken up a mare (11 Jan.)

SMITH, Benjamin - comments on a "Politico Letter" directed to the freeholders of the County of Hunterdon (11 Jan.)

Negro men and women are to be sold by Dr. Brown in Arch St. or Andrew Farrell, tanner, in Chesnut St., Phila. (11 Jan.)

Last week an ox weighing 1,749 pounds was killed at Mr. Malbone's farm in Newport - Newport item of 2 Dec. 1743 (19 Jan.)

The Leghorn Galley, Capt. Ellis master - arrived Saturday last at Boston from Spithead with artillery for Castle William - Boston item of 2 Jan. (19 Jan.)

Sugar, candy, molasses and tea are sold in Phila. by Buckridge Sims, at the house of Joseph Turner, and by William Wallace, sugar-baker, at the Sugar House, at the north end of Front St. (19 Jan.)

WHEELER, Maurice, Irish servant, age c. 22 - runaway from Paul Koul, of Amwell Twp., Hunterdon Co., N.J. (19 Jan.)

Proclamation of Lt.-Gov. William Bull, of South Carolina (26 Jan.)

MORGAN, Evan, cooper, near the drawbridge in Phila. - sells brandy, wines, indigo, etc. (26 Jan.)

Report of Committee of both Houses of Assembly of South Carolina is just published and is on sale by B. Franklin, at the New Printing Office in Market St., James Read, next door, Warner and Bradford, at the Bible in Front St. and W. Bradford, at the Bible in Second St. (26 Jan.)

PHIPPS, John, in Uwchland Twp., Chester Co. - has taken up 2 mares (26 Jan.)

BARGE, William, in North Wales Twp., Phila. Co. - has taken up a mare (26 Jan.)

CAVENOUGH, Eleanor (alias Plunkett), Irish servant, age c. 35 - runaway from Abraham Shelly, keeper of the Workhouse in Phila. (26 Jan.)

BELL, Capt. - has just arrived from Barbados with news that Commodore Knowles is on a secret expedition (2 Feb.)

Plantation of 116 acres in Passyunk Twp., about 3 miles from Phila. is for sale; apply to Andrew Haney in said township (2 Feb.)

RASH, John, of Bristol Twp., near Germantown, miller at Lukeens Mill, intending to move - desires to settle all accounts (2 Feb.)

CURRIE, Ebenezer - is removed from James Mackey's store in Front St. to his house on opposite side of same street between Norris's and Gray's Alleys (2 Feb.)

Plantation of 143 acres, in Passyunk Twp., about 3½ miles from Phila., is to be let; enquire of Hugh Davey or Joseph Sims, executors of Alexander Woodrop, dec'd (2 Feb.)

Ship Trafford, Capt. Goad, arrived 29 Jan. at New York from Liverpool; Goad reports that a snow belonging to Mr. Lucas of New York ran into a Spanish privateer and escaped, arriving at Baltimore Harbor in Ireland (8 Feb.)

TATNAL, Ann - makes her powders, which may be purchased at Thomas Shipley's in Ridley Twp. or Samuel Bunting's in Darby, Chester Co. (8 Feb.)

CALLENDER, William - sells hay at his plantation on Delaware, within 4 miles of Phila., or at his stable in Phila. (8 Feb.)

DAY, Bryan, English servant - runaway from Charles Ridgely, living near Patapsco Ferry in Baltimore Co. (8 Feb.)

Tract of 290 acres at Maiden Creek, Phila., is for sale; apply to James Starr, in Charlestown, Chester Co. (8 Feb.)

Plantation of 374 acres in Whiteland Twp., Chester Co., about 23 miles from Phila., is to be let; apply to Peter Osborne, living on the same (8 Feb.)

ELLIS, John, glazier, late from Dublin - may be reached at

Alexander Miller's, peruke-maker, in Second St., Phila.
(8 Feb.)

EVANS, Edward - has for sale books concerned with the Moravians (8 Feb.)

SMITH, Mr. - Tuesday last his body was found floating in
the river near Point No Point (16 Feb.)

Answer to paper subscribed John Allen which was lately
printed in the Pennsylvania Journal ('16 Feb.)

CARTER, Thomas, late of Phila., stay-maker, dec'd - accounts
with estate to be settled with Elizabeth Grant, administratrix; Michael Connor, who served his time with said
Carter, continues the business (16 Feb.)

VERNON, Catherine, Dutch servant, who has been in the
country about 3 years - runaway from William Baker, in
Chesnut St., Phila. (16 Feb.)

Report from Rhode Island, dated 3 Jan., that Capts. Allen
and White in consort have taken a prize worth almost
one million pounds (22 Feb.)

BARNS, Capt. - arrived Saturday last at New York from South
Carolina with news that Gov. James Glenn has arrived at
South Carolina - New York item of 13 Feb. (22 Feb.)

JAUNCY, Capt. - arrived last night at New York from Corracoa, with news of the activities in the West Indies -
New York item of 13 Feb. (22 Feb.)

Ship Patty, Capt. Jory, bound for Phila. from London, is
reported lost but all the people saved (22 Feb.)

SAUNDERS, John, huntsman - makes and sells jockey caps at
his house in the Northern Liberties of Phila. (22 Feb.)

ASHETON, Ralph - has a sawmill to let and sells stones for
building at his ferry; apply to him or Thomas Feglar at
said ferry (22 Feb.)

GREGORY, Richard, servant, age c. 30, joiner - runaway from
Nathan Rigbie (22 Feb.)

DALE, Joseph, Thomas Howard's convict servant, shoemaker,
runaway - is supposed to have stolen a mare from the
plantation of William Hammond (22 Feb.)

REILY, John (late clerk to Charles Brockden), at his office at Joseph Stretch's, hatter, in Second St., Phila.

- draws up deeds, leases, wills, etc. (22 Feb.)

REED, William, intending to decline his business of tanning at Thomas Chalkley's plantation at Frankford - will
let said plantation for 4 years (22 Feb.)

Thursday last a schooner from Phila. to Burlington overset and the following were drowned: Peter Baynton (merchant of Phila.), John Stapleford (his apprentice, who
had lately married Baytnon's niece), a Dutch man and
boy (1 Mar.)

Sloop Elizabeth, John McKay, master - will sail for South
Carolina; for freight or passage agree with John Wallace or with the master (1 Mar.)

Saturday last Capt. Warner, in a sloop from the West Indies, belonging to Messers. Lippets of Warwick, was
cast away on the rock off Point Judith; all the men were
saved - Newport, R.I., item of 10 Feb. (9 Mar.)

WALDO, Capt. - arrived last week at Boston from Jamaica;
with him came Capt. Breed, of Boston, whose brig was
taken by the Spaniards; Capt. Vincent of Rhode Island
was a prisoner at St. Jago de Cuba; Capt. Fennel in the
brigantine Hawk, privateer of Boston, had taken a prize
- Boston item of 13 Feb. (9 Mar.)

UTTING, Capt. Ashby, of H.M.S. Loo - arrived Friday at
Charlestown from Port Royal; he had taken a rich
prize but it struck on some rocks and was lost -
Charlestown item of 14 Dec. 1743 (9 Mar.)

Report brought to Frederica, Ga., on 15 Jan. that at Capt.
Carr's plantation some Yamasee Indians took 5 men;
Capt. Horton sent forces under Lt. Francis and Daniel
Demetrie (commander of a guard boat) to intercept the
Yamasees; Capt. Carr's 5 men were retaken; Tooanohowi
(nephew of Tomochachi) was shot and killed; 2 years ago
Lt. Francis's wife and young child were murdered by the
Yamasees - letter from Frederica, dated 1 Feb. 1744 (9
Mar.)

Recantation on Rev. George Gillespie, minister at the head
of Christiana Creek, Newcastle Co., before the Presbytery of Newcastle (9 Mar.)

Person unknown about a year ago put 2 hogheads of flax-
seed into Oswald Peele's store (9 Mar.)

Plantation of 110 acres on the Franckfort Road, about 2
miles from Phila., is for sale; enquire of George Peter

Hellegas, living on said place (9 Mar.)

Tract of 200 acres in Lower Merion Twp., Phila. Co., is to be sold; enquire of Issachar Price in Phila. (9 Mar.)

DAVIDSON, William, at his store on Fishbourn's wharf, sells cloth, gloves, stockings, etc. (9 Mar.)

BRITTON, William, Irishman, age c. 25, weaver - has escaped from custody of John Opdike, of Amwell, constable (9 Mar.)

Proclamation of Gov. George Clinton of New York requiring inspection by a physician of incoming vessels (15 Mar.)

Two brick houses in Fourth St. (part of estate of Benjamin Clark, dec'd), adjoining house of Peter Garrick, are for sale; enquire of Mary Clark and Benjamin Hooton, executors (15 Mar.)

BINGHAM, William, within 3 doors of the Baptist Meetinghouse in Phila. - has for sale sadlery ware, 2,000 acres in Orange Co., Va., 600 acres in Salem Co., 1,250 acres at Egg Harbour and 5,000 acres at the Forks of Delaware; house in Third St., Phila., is to be let; enquire of Ann Bingham (15 Mar.)

GALLACHAR, Thomas, Irish servant - runaway from William Foster, of Paxton, Lancaster Co. (15 Mar.)

Account of the capture of the brigantine Loyal William, Capt. Mark Anderson, which was later cast away on the rocks of Cape Florida - Charlestown item of 14 Dec. 1743 (15 Mar.)

Speech of Gov. William Shirley to the General Court of Massachusetts, with mention of Agent Kilby (21 Mar.)

SHEAFE, Mr., of Boston - on Thursday last his malt-house and brewery were destroyed by fire - Boston item of 27 Feb. (21 Mar.)

LAMPIER, Capt., of the privateer Fame - has taken and carried into Jamaica a large Spanish sloop - Newport, R.I., report in Boston item of 27 Feb. (21 Mar.)

Cicero's Cato Major, translated by James Logan, Esq. - is printed and sold by B. Franklin (21 Mar.)

AUSTIN, Samuel - warns that 2 coils of cordage put in his store will be sold unless the owner removes them (21 Mar.)

Furnace, sawmill and forge, within 13 miles of Lancaster,
will be let by Peter Grubb (21 Mar.)

House and lot (belonging to estate of Elizabeth Beere,
dec'd) on south side of Chesnut St., bounded on east
by house of George Sharswood and on west by house of
Caleb Cash, is to be sold by Thomas Bourne, George
Spafford and Jonathan Beere, executors (21 Mar.)

Tract of 202 acres in Bristol Twp., Bucks Co., on River
Delaware, about 2 miles from Bristol, known by name of
"Edward Wanton's Land" is for sale; apply to John Smith
at his store on Pemberton's wharf (21 Mar.)

Edward, Joseph and William Shippen have to sell or let lots
on Society Hill in Front St. and Second St., a water
lot joining to Mr. Woodrope's stores and wharf, a lot
fronting Mr. Powel's house in Third St., 300 acres on
the west side of Susquehannah, where Henry Hendricks
lived, 8 miles from John Wrights ferry, 395 acres on
the same side where Thomas Eastland lived, 375 acres
near Powtomeck where Redmond lived, 250 acres at Pex-
tan, fronting the river where Thomas Rennix lately kept
a ferry (21 Mar.)

DOWERS, Capt., arrived at Phila. from Antigua, brought
some officers from Antigua in recruit in Phila. (29
Mar.)

Brigantine <u>St</u>. <u>Andrew</u>, William Jones commander, will sail
for Cork; for passage apply to Jaspar McCall or said
master at Nixon's wharf (29 Mar.)

BREINTNALL, J. - gives notice of meeting of the Library
Co. of Phila. (29 Mar.)

BICKLEY, Samuel - will sell real estate in Wilmington (29
Mar.)

Fulling-mill, house and tanyard are offered for sale by
Job Harvey, the owner, living in Darby (29 Mar.)

ADDER, Scilis, servant - runaway from Benajmin Town, of
Bristol Twp., Bucks Co. (29 Mar.)

Reward will be paid by John Baldwin if the following 2
deeds are brought to William Atkinson, of Bristol,
Bucks Co., or to the printer hereof: deed from Charles
Lavalley to John Rowland and deed from Edmund Lovett to
John Rowland (29 Mar.)

Speech of Gov. James Glen to Assembly of South Carolina
(5 Apr.)

FRANKLAND, Capt. Thomas, of H.M.S. Rose - has taken 3 prizes (5 Apr.)

Privateer brigantine of Rhode Island, Capt. Allen - arrived Friday last at Charlestown, S.C. - Charlestown item of 12 Mar. (5 Apr.)

Saturday last arrived at Newport the Rhode Island privateer Prince Frederick, Capt. J. Dennis, and on Tuesday his consort, Capt. W. Allen (5 Apr.)

A Newport item of 23 Mar. gives information of the following privateers: Capts. Lamprier, James Allen, Griffitts, Wimble, Clark, Hunter, Maine and Frankland (5 Apr.)

KAY, John, late of Phila., butcher, dec'd - accounts with estate to be settled with Thomas Steward, of Phila., shipwright, one of the executors (5 Apr.)

MORGAN, John, at his store on Market St. wharf - sells cloth, gloves, hats, shoes, snuff, rum, etc. (5 Apr.)

McCALL, Samuel, Sr. - sells cables and rigging (5 Apr.)

Robin, Negro, age c. 20 - runaway from Joseph Taylor, of Freehold Twp., Monmouth Co., N.J. (5 Apr.)

Book of 23 sermons by Gilbert Tennent will be printed by subscription by W. Bradford in Second St., Phila. (5 Apr.)

Partnership of Bard and Lawrence, Jr., expires 1 May (5 Apr.)

Tract of 80 acres in Bristol Twp., within 5 miles of Phila., known as Pott's Mill, is for sale; enquire of Judeth Sharp, living near the place (5 Apr.)

COGING, Nicholas, Irish servant, age c. 18 - runaway from George Marpole, of Bristol (5 Apr.)

Address of South Carolina Assembly, by Benj. Whitaker, Speaker, to Gov. James Glen and reply of the governor (12 Apr.)

Ship Totness Galley, John Skillicorne master - will sail for Barbados; for freight or passage agree with Robert and Amos Strettell or the master (12 Apr.)

LLOYD, Richard, Welch servant, age c. 20, potter - runaway from John Cox, of Upper Freehold, Monmouth Co., N.J. (12 Apr.)

BRAME, John, on board the ship <u>Agnes</u> <u>and</u> <u>Betty</u>, at Fishbourn's wharf - has for sale cordage and sail cloth
(12 Apr.)

BEVAN, Aubrey, at Chester - has taken up a stray horse
(12 Apr.)

GOODIN, William, servant lad - runaway from William Gray,
bisket-baker, in Phila. (12 Apr.)

McKIM, William, Irishman, employed as skipper on a sloop
in Back River - abandoned the sloop; reward for his
capture offered by Alexander Lawson, at the Baltimore
Iron Works or Charles Ewell (12 Apr.)

McCOOLE, Walter, of Windor, in Rockhill Twp., Chief Ranger
of Bucks Co. - lists horses in his custody (12 Apr.)

HILTON, Capt., who arrived in New York from London, lost all
his masts on 25 Feb. in a gale but got into Dover; he
reports that Capts. Cox, Griffiths and Bryant were to
sail for New York (19 Apr.)

Persons dwelling in the Jerseys are to settle accounts
with estate of Peter Baynton, late of Phila., dec'd, with
Mary Baynton. executrix; others are to settle accounts
with Joshua Madddox and Thomas Bourne, executors (19
Apr.)

SMITH, Benjamin - offers for sale real estate in Trenton
(19 Apr.)

HUTCHESON, James, intending to move to New England - offers
for sale lot and house on Water St. in Wilmington, Newcastle Co. (19 Apr.)

The following are inlisted in Lt.-Gen. Dalzel's Regt.:
Patrick O'Neal, John Dennison, Thomas Phillips, John
Argell, Edward Comen, William O'Bryant and Bartholomew
McGee; if any of these are servants, their owners may
have them by applying to Capt. Charles Alexander, in
Phila. (19 Apr.)

HARTLEY, William, of Charles-Town, Chief Ranger for Chester
Co. - lists strays in his hands (19 Apr.)

Persons indebted to estate of Peter White, dec'd, and his
legatees are to meet at house of Joseph Ruckels in Burlington by order of Timothy Matlack and Richard Summers,
executors (19 Apr.)

RICHARDSON, Joseph, goldsmith, in Phila. - offers for sale

a case of gold scales (19 Apr.)

Ship <u>Barwick</u>, Capt. Harwood, from London, after escaping
from a Spanish privateer, arrived Sunday last in Pian-
ketank River - Williamsburg item of 3 Apr. (26 Apr.)

GRIFFITHS, Capt. - arrived at New York Wednesday last from
London - New York item of 23 Apr. (26 Apr.)

STEED, Capt., in passage from Corocoa to New York, was
taken by a Spanish privateer; 4 of the crew, however,
retook the vessel - New York item of 23 Apr. (26 Apr.)

BENGER, Hon. Elliott, of Virginia, is appointed Postmaster-
General of H. M.'s dominions in America (26 Apr.)

ARMSTRONG, John, and Indian trader, and 2 of his servants,
as they were going with goods to Allegany, were murdered by 3 Delaware Indians; the murderers are taken
and put into Lancaster Goal (26 Apr.)

HUGILL, George and William, Mulattos, brothers, this
country born - runaways from George and Valentine Robinson, of Brandywine Hundred, Newcastle Co. (26 Apr.)

BEASLY, Stephen - has for sale a house fronting Water St.,
Phila. (26 Apr.)

BAKER, George, at Kensington, near Phila. - has for sale
50 or 60 barrels of pickled herring (26 Apr.)

WILKINSON, Anthony, in Water St., Phila. - has for sale
pickled sturgeon (26 Apr.)

SPENCER, Dr. - will begin his first lecture of the second
course of experimental philosophy on 10 May (26 Apr.)

WALKER, Roger, intending to leave Pennsylvania - desires
all persons indebted to Roger Walker & Co. to pay their
balances (26 Apr.)

BIEDEREY, John Barnhard, Dutch servant, age c. 20 - runaway from Marcus Kühl, of Phila., baker (26 Apr.)

BOUTINEAU, Capt., arrived at Boston from the Bay of Honduras - reports that Capt. Fiske, in a sloop belonging
to Boston, was attacked and killed by a Spanish privateer; the owner, Capt. Richardson, and Capt. Bell, a
passenger, carried on a fight for some hours but were
finally taken - Boston item of 23 Apr. (3 May)

MILLER, John, carpenter, from Pequa - stole a horse from

Joseph McCoole, at George Parks's, tavernkeeper, of Fallowfield Twp., Chester Co.; reward will be paid to person who brings Miller or the horse to William Dickie's mill (3 May)

BLAIR & McILVANE, at their store in Water St., Phila. (where Stedman & Robertson formerly kept) - sell cloth, thread, oil, Bibles and cutlery (3 May)

HILL, Richard, Esq., dec'd - persons indebted to estate for rent are to make payment or be prosecuted by Lloyd Zachary and Mordecai Lloyd (3 May)

ALEXANDER, Timothy, English servant, age c. 35, shoemaker - runaway from James Bayard, living on Bohemia River in Maryland (3 May)

Indian murderer of John Armstrong was brought from Lancaster to Phila. Goal; he told of dispute in course of which Armstrong struck him, whereupon he killed Armstrong; he was in company with 2 other Indians, Little John and Billy; he killed one of Armstrong's men (who was coming to strike him with an ax) and Little John killed another servant of Armstrong (10 May)

TANNER, Philip, of Nottingham, Chester Co. - on 18 Apr. a fire consumed his mill (10 May)

Snow Brothers, John Evans master, will sail for London; for freight or passage agree with Stedman, Robertson & Co. at their store in Water St., Phila., or with the master on board (10 May)

A Spanish prize ship will be sold at Andrew Hamilton's wharf (10 May)

Third part of schooner Hope, now at Wilmington (property of John Boyd, dec'd) will be sold by David Bush, administrator (10 May)

FLEESON, Plunket, upholsterer, at the Easy-Chair, in Chesnut St., Phila. - will sell maple chairs as cheap as those imported from Boston (10 May)

H.M.S. Woolwich, Capt. Herbert, on 3 Apr. brought into Carlisle Bay a rich Spanish prize, the Asencion del Senor, Don Luis Port commander; the Spanish officers had their swords returned to them by Thomas Stevenson, Provost Marshal of Barbados; on 6 Apr. Capt. Herbert, Mr. Rawlin and others went to see the prisoners at the Town Hall, where Capt. Herbert gave a purse of money to Capt. Mackcleur, captain of the Guard, to distribute among the prisoners - Bridgetown item of 4 Apr. (17 May)

Tuesday Capt. James Allen in the privateer Revenge arrived
at Newport, R.I., with a prize sloop - Newport item of
4 May (17 May)

Ship Wilmington, John Sibbald commander, and the schooner
George, William Dowell commander, are fitting out for
a cruising voyage; those who wish to enter either
privateer may repair to the commanders or to the Sign
of the Boatswain-and-Call, near the drawbridge, Phila.
(17 May)

Ship Delila, James Navine master, will sail for Antigua;
for freight or passage agree with Ebenezer Currie or
the master of the ship now at Samuel McCall's wharf (17
May)

Caution to all persons not to accept assignment of a bond
given by David John, of Charlestown, Chester Co., to
Morgan Humphry of the same place (17 May)

BRADLEY, Edward, late of Phila., dec'd - accounts with estate to be settled with Esther Bradley, executrix, and
Ebenezer Kinnersly and Thomas Leech, executors (17 May)

DOWNY, James, servant, age c. 35 - runaway from Zebulon
Cook, of Upper Freehold, Monmouth Co., N.J. (17 May)

JONES, David, Welsh servant, age c. 21 - runaway from
Nathan Yarnall, of Edgmont Twp., Chester Co. (17 May)

KATTS, Ludowick, servant, age c. 19 - runaway from Christian Warner, blacksmith, in Germantown (17 May)

REEVE, John, late of Burlington, dec'd - accounts with estate to be settled with Matthias Aspden, executor (17
May)

HUTCHINS, Capt., from Phila., arrived at Charlestown yesterday se'nnight, having escaped 2 Spanish privateers
which chased him - Charlestown item of 7 May (24 May)

Ship Tartar, John Mackey commander, will sail as a privateer; persons who wish to go on the voyage are to repair to the Sign of the Crown and Thistle in Front St.,
Phila. (24 May)

DENING, William, at Joseph Stretch's - offers reward for
recovery of a lost gold seal, engraved with coat of
arms (24 May)

446

Curiosities are to be seen at John Baker's house, near
the upper end of Second St., 2 doors above the Sign of
the Ship, in Phila. (24 May)

BOYD, John, dec'd - accounts with estate to be settled with
William Davison (24 May)

Plantation of 140 acres in Newcastle Co., 8 miles from Newcastle and 5 from Christiana Bridge, is for sale; enquire of John Crawford, living on the premises (24 May)

CARDIFF, John, Irish servant, age c. 40 - runaway from
William Bonar (24 May)

FORDAM, John, of New York City, tailor - poisoned 20 May
by drinking the decoction of a root given him by a person to cure the stomach ache (31 May)

Newly appointed trustees of the Pennsylvania Loan Office
are John Kinsey, Thomas Leech, John Watson, Thomas
Chandler and John Wright (31 May)

Inn at Christiana Bridge, Newcastle Co., is to be let; enquire of Dr. Reese Jones at said bridge (31 May)

COLEMAN, William - offers for sale cloth, china, cutlery,
etc., just imported in the Warren, Capt. Cox, from London; the partnership of Hamilton & Coleman has expired
(31 May)

HASELL, Samuel - has for sale a Negro man, age c. 25 (31
May)

HAMILTON, John, Irish servant, age c. 15 - runaway from
Joseph Kaighin, of Gloucester Co., N.J. (31 May)

DOWDLE, Michael, Irish servant, age c. 20, who formerly
belonged to William Cook - runaway from John Scholey,
of New Hanover, Burlington Co. (31 May)

RANKIN, Capt. - arrived Wednesday last at Boston from Newcastle, with news that France has declared war on England - Boston item of 28 May (7 June)

TYNG, Capt. - arrived 27 May at Boston from Annapolis
Royal, with report that Canso is taken by the French
and Indians - Boston item of 28 May (7 June)

Capts. Woolford and Love, commanders of 2 privateer sloops
arrived 3 May at St. Kitts; they lost a prize, as the
French captain blew it up (7 June)

STEAD, Capt., in sloop <u>Griffin</u>, arrived Saturday last at New York; his vessel was taken by the Spaniards, who took out one Benjamin Herring and his wife; Capt. Stead later retook his ship and brought it into Port Royal - New York item of 4 June (7 June)

LANE, Hon. Henry, Esq., member of the Council for New York - died Monday last in New York - New York item of 4 June (7 June)

House, lot and stables ½ mile out of Trenton for sale; apply to Jane Atlee, administratrix of estate of her husband, Wm. Atlee, dec'd (7 June)

PRICE, Jonathan - offers reward for recovery of a strayed horse (7 June)

McCOLHEM, John, Irish servant, age <u>c</u>. 26 - runaway from Wm. Noblit, of Middletown, Chester Co.; it is supposed he went away with a New Englander named John Hoyet (7 June)

Tract of 100 acres, near the new road from Gloucester to Great Egg Harbour, lately belonging to Robert Jones, of Gloucester Co., yeoman, has been attached at the suit of John Blackwood and will be sold (7 June)

Proclamation of Gov. George Thomas of Pennsylvania (14 June)

BELL, Capt. Thomas, who went passenger from Boston in the sloop <u>Merrimack</u>, Wm. Richardson commander, bound to the Bay of Honduras, arrived a few days ago at Boston; Richardson's ship was taken off Chappel Key; later Capt. Bell was taken by Capt. Allen, of Rhode Island - Boston item of 4 June (14 June)

Saturday last arrived at New York 2 New York privateers, the brigantine <u>Hester</u>, Capt. Bayard, and the sloop <u>Polly</u>, Capt. Jefferies - New York item of 11 June (14 June)

Sloop <u>Le Trembleur</u>, John Sears commander, will sail on a cruising voyage; those inclined to enter on board may repair to the commander, at the Sign of the Jolly Trooper in Arch St. or to the Sign of the Pewter Platter in Front St., Phila. (14 June)

RADMONT, Henry, servant - runaway (with a native Irish freeman named Patrick Silver) from Walter Thetford, of Newcastle Co.; reward will be paid if he is taken and brought to Joseph Ramage (14 June)

A new schooner, at Peter Bard's wharf, will be sold by
Israel Pemberton and Robert Strettell (14 June)

PETERS, William - offers reward for recovery of a mare
strayed from his plantation in Blockley Twp., Phila. Co.
(14 June)

Reward will be paid by James Hunter or Peter Robinson if a
horse, strayed off the Commons of Phila., is brought to
Peter Robinson, at the Indian King (14 June)

WILSON, Edward, Irish servant, age c. 17 - runaway from
Edward Woodward, of Middletown, Chester Co. (14 June)

ATKINS, John - has taken the fulling-mill belonging to
John Marshall near Darby and intends to take in cloth
at the house of John Warner, at the Sign of the Horse
and Groom, in Strawberry Alley, near Market St., Phila.
(21 June)

GORHAM, Capt., from Jamaica, reports at Boston that Capt.
Lampier, in the privateer schooner Fame, of Rhode Island, and Capt. Hall, in a small Jamaica privateer,
have taken a valuable prize - Boston item of 11 June
(21 June)

Three privateers, Capt. Cranston, in the King George, Capt.
Dennis, in the Prince Frederick and Capt. W. Allen, in
the Prince William, have sailed from Newport and 5 more
commanded by Capts. J. Allen, Marshall, Bennetland,
Thurston, and Jennison, are preparing to sail - Newport
item of 4 June (21 June)

JAUNCY, Capt., arrived 18 June at New York from Madeira
(21 June)

HARGRAVE, Capt. - arrived in the Mercury Tuesday last at
Phila. from London (21 June)

CHEW, Samuel, Esq., Chief Justice of the Lower Counties -
died last week at Dover, Kent Co. (21 June)

GEORGE, George, in Blockley Twp., Phila. Co. - has taken
up 2 stray calves (21 June)

Tract of 2,000 acres on the branches of Pickering Creek,
Chester Co., is for sale; enquire of Michael Lightfoot
in Arch St., Phila. (21 June)

CUZZINS & SMYTER, at their store on Mr. Hamilton's wharf
in Phila. - sell cloth, cutlery, snuff, etc. (21 June)

House and lot in Kensington, on the River Delaware, extending from low water mark to Queen St., where William Hayes formerly kept tavern, are for sale; apply to William Hayes in Kensington (21 June)

WALN, Joseph, English servant, age c. 20, who speaks Dutch and Welsh and formerly lived with Peter Shaver - runaway from James Keimer, of East Nantmel (21 June)

DUNEVAN, Charles, Irish servant lad - runaway from Samuel Flower, at Reading (21 June)

Tract of 500 acres in New Hanover Twp., on main branch of Perquiominy Creek, Phila. Co., is for sale; enquire of Margaret Jekyll (21 June)

WEAD, Connerd, Dutch servant, age c. 30 - runaway from George Kastner, of Whitpin Twp. (21 June)

COULTAS, James, at the ferry - offers reward for recovery of a horse that strayed from the Middle Ferry on Schuylkill (21 June)

DAILEY, Dennis, Irish servant, age c. 22 - runaway from William Bird, of Amity Twp., Phila. Co. (21 June)

RANNELS, Edward, Irish servant, age c. 21 - same as above

Snow Limpston, William Wood master - arrived 15 June at Newport; she had been taken 20 May by a French privateer, which had also taken the Ranger, Peter Reeve from Phila., the ship Samuel, William Warden from South Carolina, and the sloop Queen Elizabeth, Robert Hewen, from Jamaica (28 June)

On 17 June Capt. Tyng, in the Massachusetts Province snow Prince of Orange, sailed from Boston on a cruize; Capt. Waterhouse is ready to sail; Capt. Fletcher is fitting out in a Province Sloop (28 June)

Proclamation of W. Shirley, Gov. of Massachusetts, countersigned by J. Willard, Secretary, for raising volunteers to reinforce the garrison at Annapolis Royal (28 June)

Saturday last, Commodore Warren, in H.M.S. Launceston, brought a rich French prize into New York, the 15th he has taken - New York item of 25 June (28 June)

JAUNCY, Capt. Ja., arrived 25 June at New York from Jamaica (29 June)

The following privateers have sailed or will soon sail
from Phila.: the Wilmington, the George, the Tartar
and Le Trembleur (28 June)

LYNN, Sarah, of Phila. (widow of Joseph Lynn, dec'd) –
offers for sale a water lot in Bristol Twp., Bucks Co.,
between the lots of John Hall and Samson Cary (28 June)

CASTOLO, John, servant, age c. 22 – runaway from Samuel
Webb, tanner, living in Baltimore Co. (28 June)

BURGE, Samuel, residing in Phila. – offers for sale land
in Morris Co., N.J. (28 June)

HARTLEY, William, Chief Ranger of Chester Co. – lists
strays in his possession (28 June)

JONES, Edward, of Phila. – he wishes his wife to be ex-
cepted from his advertisement that no one should be
credited on his account (28 June)

BROWN, Charity, widow, dec'd – messuage and bank lot, belonging to her estate, in Front St., bounded on south
by land of Thomas Hart and west by messuage and lot of
Edward Farmer – will be sold by William Cunningham and
Priscilla his wife, admins. (28 June)

RANSTED, Caleb, intending to remove to England, offers for
sale the following: tenement in Front St., where John
Jackson and Joseph Hordil live; adjoining tenement
where Randal Yeaton lives; tenement in Fourth St., near
John Linton's; tenement in High St., next door to John
Wister's, where Richard Warder lives; 2 tenements on
the bank in Front and Water St., over against John Ma-
combs, where John Henby and one Eaton now live; tenement next door to said Ransted's house; house where
said Ransted lives (28 June)

Speech of Sir Thomas Robinson, Gov. of Barbados (5 July)

HUNTER, Capt. – Wednesday last arrived at Boston from Holland, with European news – Boston item of 25 June (5
July)

ALLEN, Capt. J., sailed Tuesday last from Newport in the
Revenge and Capt. N. White in a Massachusetts priva-
teer lately took a French ship – Newport item of 22
June (5 July)

Account of taking of Canso by the French under Capt. De-
levere – Boston item of 25 June (5 July)

451

Boasts made by an Irishman named Murphy, now in command
of a French privateer (5 July)

TYNG, Capt. - has brought in a large French prize - Boston
item of 25 June and New York item of 2 July (5 July)

From New York 2 privateers, the brigantine Hester, Capt.
Bayard, and the sloop Polly, Capt. Jefferies, have
sailed and the sloop Clinton, Capt. Seamour, and the
Mary Anne, Capt. Tucker, will sail today - New York item
of 2 July (5 July)

REES, Capt. - Friday last arrived at Phila. from Antigua
(5 July)

The privateer Tartar, which sailed Sunday last from Phila.
- overset in the bay; the captain and about 6 officers
and men were saved in her longboat; Capt. Plasket took
up 14 in a pilot boat; Capt. Claes, coming from Barbados, took up 47 (5 July)

CUNNINGHAM, Capt. Thomas, age c. 30 - runaway from Capt.
Thomas Anderson; reward for his apprehension will be
paid by his master or by Samuel Welsh (5 July)

CARTY, Henry, Irish servant, age c. 19 - runaway from Benjamin Field, of Chesterfield, Burlington Co. (5 July)

House and lot, between Jacob Shoemaker's and John Durborow's, over against the prison in Phila. - will be
sold by Nicholas Ashmead, living on the premises (5
July)

CAMPBELL, Mr., in Burlington - will teach young men the
Classic authors (5 July)

MILLS, John, Irish servant, age c. 21 - runaway from Job
Sheppard, of Cohansie, Salem Co. (5 July)

SOUTH, William, Irish convict servant, age c. 24, who has
been about 18 months in this country and taught school
ever since - runaway (in company with James McGraugh,
Irish servant belonging to Robert Massey, of Stafford
Co.) from Richard Foote in Stafford Co. (5 July)

REYNOLDS, David, of Springfield Twp., Phila. Co. - offers
reward for recovery of horse strayed or stolen (5 July)

Negro woman and her child will be sold at Peter Robeson's
at the Sign of the Indian King in Market St. (5 July)

RATSEY, Robert, late commander of the ship David, of New

York, died on 26 Mar.; his death was reported by Job Pinkham, who now is in command of said ship arrived at Newport, R.I., on 19 July /probably an error for 19 June/ (12 July)

Monday last the Massachusetts Province snow Prince of Orange, Capt. Tyng, arrived at Boston with a French privateer prize, Capt. Delabroitz commander, a gentle-man well known in Boston and who has a son in school about 6 miles off - Boston item of 2 July (12 July)

Tuesday last Capt. Fletcher and Thursday last Capts. In-gerson and Gatman sailed from Boston on a cruize against H.M.'s enemies - Boston item of 2 July (12 July)

Thursday last arrived at Boston Capt. Roach from Cape Cod; his sloop was taken by a French privateer - Boston item of 2 July (12 July)

On 2 July the Massachusetts Province snow and a transport sailed from Boston for Annapolis Royal with a company commanded by Capt. Foye (12 July)

Thursday last privateer sloop Elizabeth, Capt. Thomas Barnes commander, sailed from New York on a cruize and on 8 July Capt. Eady arrived at New York from Rhode Island (12 July)

BELL, Tom, the famous sharper - was apprehended a few days ago in Phila. and committed to prison for an old mis-demeanour (12 July)

Solar microscope and musical clock are displayed at Mr. Vidal's in Second St., Phila. (12 July)

Brick house on east side of Passayunk Rd., near southern bounds of Phila., is for sale; enquire of Joseph Scull at said house or Nicholas Scull in Arch St. (12 July)

JONES, John, apprentice lad - runaway from James Davis, of Phila., carpenter (12 July)

JONES, Morgan, Welsh servant, age c. 20 - runaway from George Emlen, of Phila. (12 July)

GOODSON, Andrew, English servant - runaway from Timothy Matlack, of Haddonfield, Gloucester Co. (12 July)

COLLEMORE, William, servant - runaway from Abraham Car-lisle, of Phila. (12 July)

HAYNES, Richard - has for sale a Negro woman, sugar, and

rum; enquire at Richard Swan's, hatter, in Market St.,
Phila. (12 May)

Four persons, Moses Coates, John David, John Thomas and
Daniel Humphry, state they have seen 2 bonds, one from
Daniel John to David John, Jr., assigned to Morgan
Humphry, which was paid and cancelled, while the other,
from David John, of Pickering, Chester Co., to Morgan
Humphry is unpaid (12 July)

Isaac, Negro, age c. 26, who formerly lived in New England
- runaway from Bryan Murry, of Reading Furnace, collier
(12 July)

Among tracts of land in Burlington Co. to be sold or let
by John Burr are the following: a tract called Goshen
Neck, a tract in partnership with Philo Leeds, called
Bards Neck, a tract in partnership with Philo Leeds
joining to Bards Neck, 4 tracts in partnership with
Philo Leeds, at Cedar Swamps, by Bards Neck, tract
joining to plantation of Cauelear, on Mullicus River,
4 tracts of cedar swamps, near Cripp's sawmill, etc.
(12 July)

GRAHAM, Capt. John, late of sloop St. Andrew, of Jamaica,
who was taken on 27 Mar. last, carried to Porto Rico,
but escaped - arrived Monday last at Charlestown -
Charlestown item of 4 June (19 July)

DEAN, Capt. Grafton, commander of sloop Dolphin of Charlestown, was taken by the Spaniards, according to Capt.
Graham (19 July)

Two privateers belonging to Capt. Malbone of Newport, R.I.,
Capts. Thurston and Jennings, sailed Tuesday last and
2 more, Capts. Porter and Bennetland, are under sail -
Newport item of 6 July (19 July)

FLETCHER, Capt., who returned to Boston Wednesday last in
the Province sloop, sailed again yesterday on a cruize
- Boston item of 9 July (19 July)

Saturday last the Massachusetts commissioners and the delegates from the 6 nations of Indians above Albany embarked on board Capt. Sanders to treat with Indians to
the eastward - Boston item of 9 July (19 July)

The Phila. Galley, John Houghston commander, at Hamilton's
wharf in Phila., will sail for London; for freight or
passage agree with Cuzzins & Smyter or with the commander (19 July)

ALLEN, Nathaniel, of Phila., cooper - sells beef and pork in barrels (19 July)

NUTT, Anna - will sell or let ¼ part of French Creek Iron Forge (19 July)

WALSH, Martin, late of Chester Co., dec'd - accbunt with estate to be settled with Joseph Greaton, of Phila. (19 July)

ATTWOOD, William - will dispose of men and lads lately imported from England (19 July)

LEWIS, Walter, dec'd - his late dwelling in Arch St., near Schuylkill, is to be sold; apply to his widow, Ursula Lewis, executrix, living on the premises (19 July)

Privateer Caesar, Capt. Griffis, on 8 July brought into Newport a Spanish prize commanded by Don Juan Gonsal. de Valdez, and Thursday last Capt. John Dennis, in the privateer Prince of Newport, brought in another Spanish prize - Newport item of 13 July (26 July)

TYNG, Capt., in Province snow Prince of Orange, arrived Friday last at Boston from Annapolis Royal, after landing there reinforcements to serve under Gov. Mascarine; the fort there was repaired under the direction of Mr. Bastide, chief engineer of Nova Scotia - Boston item of 16 July (26 July)

LONG, Capt. - arrived Friday last at New York in a brigantine from Belfast - he had been taken by the Spaniards but released by Commodore Barnet; Capt. Morgan, in a sloop belonging to New York, was taken by the Spaniards but he and his men rose and killed all the Spaniards save one Negro; the English, however, all got drunk, whereupon the Negro killed them all (26 July)

ALBERTSON, Capt., in a small sloop belonging to Phila., was surprized and runaway with by some French prisoners at the Island of Providence; soon after, however, the sloop was retaken (26 July)

MATTHEWS & CHARLTON, peruke-makers, in Chesnut St., Phila., advertise (26 July)

RAYMER, John, convict, age c. 35, a West Country Englishman, blacksmith - runaway from William Walker, of Stafford Co., Va. (26 July)

BURN, Patrick, Irish convict servant, age c. 25 - same as above

McFEE, Robert, Irish servant, age c. 22, cooper - runaway
from John Hawthorn, living near Christine Bridge, Newcastle Co. (26 July)

Message of Gov. George Thomas to the Pennsylvania Assembly
(2 Aug.)

DALE, Capt., who arrived Wednesday last at Boston from
Liverpool, reports that Capts. Philips, Craige and Wood,
all bound for Boston, were waiting at Portsmouth for
convoy - Boston item of 23 July (2 Aug.)

SMITHERS, Capt. - sailed Monday last from Boston on a
cruize; Capt. Loring, in a privateer brigantine, is
ready to sail from Boston; Capt. Tyng sailed yesterday
from Boston for Annapolis Royal; Friday last Capt.
Batcheldor arrived at Boston from South Carolina with
news that Capt. Frankland in H.M.S. Rose had taken 3
prizes; Saturday last Capt. Murray arrived at Boston
from Gibraltar - Boston item of 23 July (2 Aug.)

KANE, Capt. - arrived Tuesday last at Newport, R.I., in a
sloop from the West Indies; on 19 July the Connecticut
guard sloop, Capt. Prentice, and the Rhode Island Colony
sloop Tartar, Capt. Fones, sailed from Newport on a
cruize; Capt. Griffiths, arrived at Newport, brought
letters with news of an Indian revolt against the
Spaniards in Peru - Newport item of 20 July (2 Aug.)

GREAR, George, of New York City, hatter, was murdered
Saturday morning in the street near the door of the
house where he lodged - New York item of 30 July (2
Aug.)

Sloop Fanney, Henry Dorrel master, now at Hamilton's wharf
in Phila., will sail for Barbados (2 Aug.)

CLAYPOOLE, James, in Walnut St., Phila. - has for sale a
tract of 200 acres in Wrights Town, Bucks Co., and a
lot on the south side of Walnut St. in Phila. (2 Aug.)

JONES, Rachel (wife of William Jones, of East Nantmel,
Chester Co.) - has absconded (in company with one John
Chapman, formerly founder at William Branson's Iron
Works, who has gone to Mr. Irish's in the Jerseys) from
her husband and children (2 Aug.)

FOULK, Edward, of Guynedd Twp., Phila. Co. - has taken up
a horse (2 Aug.)

O'CADEN, Patrick, native Irish servant, age c. 25 - runaway
from John Prosser and James Downey, near Wilmington,

Newcastle Co. (2 Aug.)

CATRINGER, Thomas, stay-maker from London - has removed
from Front St. to Chesnut St. and keeps the Sign of the
Green Stays (2 Aug.)

Grist mill about 7 miles from Chester is to be let; apply
to Joseph Pratt and Cadwallader Evans, living in Edgmont
Twp., Chester Co. (2 Aug.)

KENNEDY, Robert, of the adjacendy of Bedminster Twp., Bucks
Co. - has taken up a horse (2 Aug.)

BODDY, John, arrived from England - wishes to have an assembly of religious people on Sunday the 12th at the
Market Place in Phila. (2 Aug.); assembly is dropped,
as place deemed inconvenient by the Mayor (9 Aug.)

LINSEY, Michael, Irish servant, age c. 25 - runaway from
Joseph Baker and Stephen Beakes, both of Goshen,
Chester Co. (2 Aug.)

RILEY, Timothy, Irish servant, age c. 30 - same as above

HUTTON, John - offers reward for recovery of 2 fillies
strayed or stolen from his plantation on Pike Land in
Chester Co. (2 Aug.)

Tuesday last a French privateer near Sandy Hook took a
large ship, Robert Hamilton master; the privateer Marlborough, Capt. Morris, went in pursuit of the Frenchmen
- Newport item of 27 July (9 Aug.)

MARTINBOROUGH, Capt., in the Jolly Robin privateer - plundered the French port of St. Martins and carried off the
governor and his family as prisoners to St. Kitts -
Boston item of 30 July (9 Aug.)

WATERHOUSE, Capt., in a privateer belonging to Boston,
took a French brigantine; he met Capt. Barns, commander
of a New York privateer - Boston item of 30 July (9 Aug.)

FLETCHER, Capt., bound from Boston to Jamaica - was chased
by a large French ship - Boston item of 30 July (9 Aug.)

Prize lately taken by Capts. Hall and Lemprier should yield
about 200 pounds per man - New York item of 6 Aug. (9
Aug.)

Thursday last the privateer sloop Don Carlos, Capt. Abraham
Kip commander, sailed out of the Hook - New York item of
6 Aug. (9 Aug.)

SERGEANT, John - gives text of speech of our tribe of Indians to the Mohaws and their reply - New York item of
6 Aug. (9 Aug.)

Message to the New York House from Gov. George Clinton;
Mr. Catherwood brought a message from the governor -
New York item of 6 Aug. (9 Aug.)

French prize brigantine Seven Brothers, John Baptista
Testier late commander, taken by the Wilmington, arrived 9 Aug. at Phila. (9 Aug.)

BELL, Tom - disclosed operations of gang of counterfeiters
in remote part of the Jerseys (9 Aug.)

RONEY, John (alias John Fleming), Irish servant - runaway
from John Cuthbert, of Whiteland, Chester Co. (9 Aug.)

CHEW, Dr. Samuel, late of Kent Co., dec'd - accounts with
estate to be settled with Mary Chew, administratrix (9
Aug.)

Plantation of 313 acres in Chester Co., near Hamilton's
mill, is for sale; apply to Thomas Cearell at the
Crooked Billet in Phila., or William Hamilton at his
mill, or Thomas Hicklin, living on the premises (9 Aug.)

Message to the Governor of Pennsylvania from the Assembly,
J. Kinsey speaker (16 Aug.)

The guarda la coast sloop is fitted out under the command
of Mr. Hume - Williamsburg item of 19 July (16 Aug.)

SMITH, Samuel, merchant in Norfolk, in a letter to James
Mitchell in New York reported that on Tuesday arrived
at Norfolk Capt. Wakely from Liverpool, who spoke with
Capt. Gordon off the west of Ireland; he also stated
that the Carter Frigate, Capt. Malbone, and the Whitaker,
Capt. Dansie, were taken on their passage from London
to Virginia - Williamsburg item of 19 July (16 Aug.)

Wednesday last Capt. Styles arrived at Charlestown, S.C.,
from Jamaica, and with him came as passenger Capt.
Walter Graven (late of the sloop Honest Industry), who
was taken by the Spaniards - Charlestown item of 24
July (16 Aug.)

On 2 Aug. Capt. Morris in the Marlborough privateer, returned to Newport, having sighted only fishing vessels
(16 Aug.)

Prizes have been taken by Capts. Woolford, Martinborough

458

Rouse (in the Young Eagle privateer of Boston), Ingor-
sal and Gatman - Boston item of 6 Aug. (16 Aug.)

STEVENS, John, late of Ash Swamp, East New Jersey - was
lately sentenced to death for counterfeiting and passing false bills - New York item of 13 Aug. (16 Aug.)

Thursday last arrived at New York 4 privateers, the sloops
Clinton, Mary Ann, and Polly and the brigantine Hester,
commanded by Capts. Seymour, Tucker, Jefferies and
Bayard - New York item of 13 Aug. (16 Aug.)

Poem in memory of Archibald Home, late Secretary of the
Jerseys (16 Aug.)

House on Passyunk Rd., near Phila., is offered for sale by
Joseph Scull (16 Aug.)

Shallop, now lying at Austin's Key, near Mulberry or Arch
St. wharf, Phila., is for sale; enquire of Christopher
Taylor, of Tinnicum Island, or William Crosthwaite, in
Front St., Phila. (16 Aug.)

BOLTON, Robert, late of Phila., dec'd - accounts with estate to be settled with Edward Shippen, administrator
(16 Aug.)

GRACE, John Clark, servant, country born, age c. 30, who
has travelled through Pennsylvania, Maryland and Virginia - runaway from Edward Rumney, William Roberts and
Bridget Donaldson at Annapolis (16 Aug.)

PEARCE, Benjamin, convict servant, West-Country man, age
c. 30 - same as above

GRIFFIN, Edward, convict servant, age c. 45 - same as above

LLOYD, Mordecai - intends to run for office of sheriff of
Phila. Co., together with his brother, Thomas Lloyd (16
Aug.)

STRICKLAND, Myles, in Market St., Phila. - sells drops and
elixirs and London pewter and brass kettles (16 Aug.)

Plantation of 90 acres in Oxford Twp., Phila. Co., lying
by the mill called Potts's Mill and joining the land of
Thomas Potts, James Logan, John Marl, Matthew Phillips
and Joseph Jones, is for sale; apply to Caleb Ransted
in Phila. or Richard Hillin, who lives on the place
(16 Aug.)

Time of a Dutch servant to be disposed of by Andrew Robinson or Peter Robinson in Phila. (16 Aug.)

Governor of Massachusetts reproached the owners of the Hawk privateer because her commander, Capt. Waterhouse, allowed a French privateer to escape - Boston item of 9 Aug. (23 Aug.)

TYNG, Capt., arrived Wednesday last at Boston from Annapolis Royal, with news that the main body of Indians investing the fort have retired to Menis - Boston item of 13 Aug. (23 Aug.)

GORHAM, Capt., from North Carolina, reports at Boston that the master of a snow told him that Capts. Philips and Craige, both bound to Boston, were at Portsmouth, awaiting a convoy - Boston item of 13 Aug. (23 Aug.)

LEPPINGTON, Capt. - arrived in Boston with news from the West Indies (23 Aug.)

WATERHOUSE, Capt. - last week sent into Boston 3 French prizes he had taken - Boston item of 13 Aug. (23 Aug.)

Monday last sailed from Newport the country sloop Tartar and the Connecticut sloop Defence and on 10 Aug. Capt. Morris sailed from Newport in the privateer snow Marlborough - Newport item of 10 Aug. (23 Aug.)

It is reported that Capt. Waterhouse's commission is taken from him and that Capt. Barnes continues cruising off Cape Breton - New York item of 20 Aug. (23 Aug.)

KETELTAS, Capt. - arrived last week at New York in a brigantine from Coracoa - New York item of 20 Aug. (23 Aug.)

Saturday last arrived at Phila. the ship Medusa of Nants, John Gillet master, taken by Capt. Sibbald in the Wilmington privateer of Phila. (23 Aug.)

BATE, Humphrey, of Concord, Chester Co., weaver - will not pay debts contracted in future by his wife Margery (23 Aug.); he withdraws said notice (30 Aug.)

Prize ship Medusa at Mr. Hamilton's wharf and brigantine Seven Brothers will be sold (23 Aug.)

ROUSE, Capt., in the Young Eagle privateer of Boston, has taken 15 prizes; a Frenchman, on board a schooner belonging to Boston, one Kenney master, killed the captain, mate and boy; Capt. Donnel with 30 men went to bring the vessel to Boston; the sloop Dolphin, N. Young master, was taken by the Spaniards on 1 Aug.; Capt. Waterhouse sailed Friday last from Boston on a cruize; on 19 Aug. Capt. Robinson arrived at Boston from Liverpool - Boston items of 20 Aug. (30 Aug.)

Privateer ship David, William Axon commander, and the privateer brigantine Batchelors, Thomas Greenel commander, are about to sail from New York - New York item of 27 Aug. (30 Aug.)

STILLWELL, Capt., of Gravesend on Long Island - Thursday evening his barn was set on fire by lightning and entirely consumed - New York item of 27 Aug. (30 Aug.)

STEPHENS, John, of Ash Swamp, was executed Friday last at New York for counterfeiting - New York item of 27 Aug. (30 Aug.)

Message from Gov. G. Clinton was brought by Mr. Catherwood to the General Assembly of New York (30 Aug.)

It is reported from Bermuda that the Lancashire Witch, Capt. Fowler, bound from Barbados to Phila., is cast away (30 Aug.)

Schooner, now at Capt. Goodman's wharf, will be sold at Roberts's Coffee House; apply to Israel Pemberton or Robert Strettell for private contract (23 Aug.)

REYNOLDS, Francis, sub-sheriff - offers reward for capture of John Dennis, native Irishman, age c. 25, who lately escaped from the Goal of Lancaster (23 Aug.)

SCULL, Nicholas - will run for office of sheriff for Phila. Co. (23 Aug.)

Account of engagement on 23 July between the Banff sloop, Capt. James Hume, and a Spanish sloop - Williamsburg item of 2 Aug. (30 Aug.)

Fifteen French prisoners of war, brought to Norfolk by Capt. Wallace, escaped in a large boat belonging to Capt. Frip - Williamsburg item of 2 Aug. (30 Aug.)

Sloop Banff, Capt. Thompson, is arrived at Madeira - Williamsburg item of 2 Aug. (30 Aug.)

Prizes have been brought into Newport, R.I., by Capts. Potter, Bennetland, Cranston and W. Allen; Capt. Griffith is about to sail in a privateer belonging to Newport - Newport item of 17 Aug. (30 Aug.)

Ship belonging to Phila., Capt. Stamper master, is taken
and sent into St. Sebastians (30 Aug.)

Plantation of 700 acres, within a mile of the head of N.
East, formerly belonging to Major John Copson, dec'd,
is to be sold or let; enquire of John Read, Sr., at
Christeen Bridge (30 Aug.)

BELL, William, below the drawbridge, near Mr. Powel's
wharf, in Phila. - has Negroes for sale (30 Aug.)

HILL, Elizabeth, dec'd - accounts with her estate to be
settled with John Armit, of Phila., by order of Cadwallader Colden, executor (30 Aug.)

Notice to prospective volunteers for cruize in the brigantine Raleigh, Walter Coode commander, now fitting out
at Norfolk, Va.; notice is signed by Durham Hall for
the company (30 Aug.)

PRICE, Richard, English servant - runaway from Edmund
Briggs, of Bucks Co.; reward for his capture will be
paid by said Edmund Briggs or by William Briggs (30
Aug.)

CANON, Capt. - arrived at New York last week from Boston
and stated that on 1 July, when he was in Tarpaulin
Cove, Capt. Smith, in a sloop belonging to New London,
arrived there from the West Indies; on 8 July Capt.
Alexander Troup, late master of the brigantine William
and Sarah, of New York, arrived at New York; he had been
taken 8 Feb. by a Spanish privateer - New York items of
8 July /apparently out of place/ (30 Aug.)

POTTER, Capt., who arrived at Phila. Tuesday last from
St. Christophers, reports that the snow Otter, Capt.
Smith, had taken 2 enemy privateers; last night the
brigantine Hannah, Capt. England, arrived at Phila.
from Antigua, with news that a schooner belonging to
Phila., Capt. Cox master, had been taken by the French
- Phila. item of 11 July /apparently out of place/
(30 Aug.)

RICHARDS, Capt. - arrived Wednesday last at New York from
Bristol, with foreign news (6 Sept.)

LONG, Capt. - arrived 26 Aug. at Boston from Cagliari (6
Sept.)

Ship Legunea, Capt. Phaenix, of New York, and ship Little
Strength, Capt. Gladman, bound from New York to Amsterdam, are both taken by enemy privateers - New York item
of 3 Sept. (6 Sept.)

It is reported from St. Christophers that Capts. Woolford and Wilkinson have brought in 2 large French ships (6 Sept.)

Plantation in Newtown Twp., Gloucester Co., West New Jersey, fronting Delaware on one side and Newtown Creek on the other, is for sale; apply to Robert Stephens, living on the premises (6 Sept.)

GOODWIN, Thomas, Irish convict servant, age <u>c</u>. 45 - runaway from John Jackson, living in Cecil Co., Md. (6 Sept.)

Snow <u>Francis and Anne</u>, lying at George Allen's wharf in Phila., and sails and rigging, to be seen at Sims & Davie's storehouse, will be sold at Roberts's Coffee House (6 Sept.)

BEAZLEY, Stephen - has a brick house for sale; he offers reward for recovery of a boat, hired by one Joseph Twight, that was stolen or went adrift from Newcastle (6 Sept.)

WALLACE, Joseph, living in Bucks Co. - offers reward for recovery of a horse that strayed from Richard Walker (6 Sept.)

Tanyard in Germantown Rd., about a mile from Phila., is to be let; apply to Isaac Whitelock on said place or to Richard Brockden in Phila. (6 Sept.)

TYNG, Capt., arrived Friday last at Boston from a cruize; Saturday a privateer sloop commanded by Capt. Donahew sailed from Boston; Capt. Richardson will sail in a day or 2; Saturday Capt. Smithers arrived at Marblehead with an account of an attack made upon him by Indians at Port Roseway - Boston items of 3 Sept. (13 Sept.)

LEECH, John, near the church in Phila. - sells oil, chocolate, indigo (13 Sept.)

MORGAN, John, intending for England - desires all accounts to be settled; his store is on Market St. wharf in Phila. (13 Sept.)

MARIT, Jane, living on Society Hill, next house to Thomas Penrose's - has for sale a Negro woman and her 2 children (13 Sept.)

LEGATE, John, of Newcastle - requests that the person to whom he entrusted 100 pounds to be delivered in Phila. either deliver it or return it to Archibald McSparan, administrator (13 Sept.)

SCHUTZ, Anne Elizabeth, wife of Philip Schutz, of Lancaster Town - has eloped from her husband and gone away with one Jacob Frederick Kurtz (13 Sept.)

LAWRENCE, Giles, at Bristol - intends to take horses to pasture at the Friends Yearly Meeting (13 Sept.)

HALL, Peter, upholsterer, living at Mrs. Pugh's in Chesnut St., Phila. - makes beds and other furniture (13 Sept.)

ROBERTS, Robert, maltster, in Merion, has taken up a horse and a mare (13 Sept.)

MURPHY, Robert, Irish servant lad - runaway, together with John Smith, age c. 18 or 19, born near Stratten Island, from William Branson's Ironworks, at Reading Furnace; reward will be paid if the runaways are brought to William Branson in Phila. or to Samuel Flower at Reading Ironworks (13 Sept.)

BOONE, George, of Exeter, Chief Ranger of Phila. Co. - lists horses he has in his possession (13 Sept.)

Brigantine Expedition, John Millet master, at Fishbourn's wharf in Phila., will sail for Jamaica; for freight or passage agree with Stedman, Robertson & Co. or the commander on board (13 Sept.)

Privateer sloop Prince Charles, Capt. Simeon Potter, is now under sail - Newport item of 7 Sept. (20 Sept.)

BARNES, Capt., in privateer sloop Elizabeth, of New York - arrived Wednesday last at New York from his cruize to the eastward - New York item of 17 Sept. (20 Sept.)

YOUNG, Capt., commander of a 40-gun ship - now he's in harbor of St. Johns in Newfoundland (20 Sept.)

SHIPPEN, Edward and Joseph - have for sale men servants and sundry goods (20 Sept.)

Brick house where William Hays now lives is for sale; enquire of Samuel Hastings in Front St., Phila., or Susannah Hays at Kensington (20 Sept.)

A sugar-refiner and distiller wishes to engage with any gentlemen to carry on his business; he is at Thomas Bell's in Water St., Phila. (20 Sept.)

RUSSEL, Clement, plaisterer, near the drawbridge in Phila.

- offers reward for recovery of a strayed cow (20 Sept.)

DOYLE, Michael, Irish convict servant, who pretends to be a blacksmith - runaway from William Berry, in Kent Co., Delaware (20 Sept.)

SHIPPEY, J., who does bookbinding and lives in Strawberry Alley - intends to open a German evening school (20 Sept.)

GREW, Theophilus - will conduct his school in Norris's Alley (20 Sept.)

Schooner William & Mary, New England built, will be sold to the highest bidder at Roberts's Coffee House in Phila.; her tackle may be seen at Capt. George Spafford's, living in Water St. (20 Sept.)

CHASE, Capt., from Bristol, arrived at Boston, informs that a privateer fitted out at Bristol overset and 125 men were drowned; Capt. Martinborough from St. Kitts, informs that Capts. Woolford and Wilkinson have taken 6 prizes; a few days ago Capt. Smithers sailed from Boston to convoy a company of volunteer Indians to Annapolis Royal; Capt. Waterhouse, in a Boston privateer, came in Saturday; Capt. Richardson sailed from Boston 16 Sept. on a cruize - Boston items of 17 Sept. (27 Sept.)

A few days since a flag of truce came to St. John's in Antigua with English prisoners, including the master of a brigantine belonging to Mr. Odiorne, of Piscataqua - letter from St. John's dated 31 July (27 Sept.)

JOHNSON, Capt., from Rhode Island, and Capt. Gerritson, from New York, have both been taken - Boston item of 17 Sept. (27 Sept.)

WHITE, Capt., of Rhode Island - his privateer was destroyed by 2 French privateers (27 Sept.)

GALLOWAY, Peter, living near Dover - offers for sale numerous tracts of land in Kent Co. on Delaware (27 Sept.)

ELIOT, John - will teach French or Portuguese to those who wish to learn them, either at their own rooms or at his lodgings at John Cottinger's, near the George in Arch St., Phila. (27 Sept.)

BAXTER, James - offers reward for recovery of a gelding strayed or stolen from North East Forge, in Cecil Co., Md.; the gelding came from one Ogleby's, 15 miles above Phila. (27 Sept.)

ORD, John, at his shop at the corner of Grey's Alley in Front St., in the house where John Armit lived - sells cloth (27 Sept.)

HAYDOCK, Eden, late from England, at Paul Chanders, in the upper end of Second St., Phila. - does plumbing, glazing and painting (27 Sept.)

LOWENCE, James, dec'd - at his plantation his cattle, horses, cart, etc. will be sold at auction (27 Sept.)

RAMBO, Andrew, of Passyunk Twp. - offers reward for recovery of a colt (27 Sept.)

ROUSE, Capt., in a privateer schooner of Boston, with other vessels, took a French settlement on Newfoundland and brought 70 of the prisoners into St. John's; in August 2 vessels taken by Capts. Woolford and Wilkinson were brought to St. Kitts; Capt. Love, in the snow Dreadnaught, has taken a sloop loaded with sugar and coffee; Friday last Capts. Tyng and Fletcher sailed from Boston on a cruize; Capt. Gatman, in a privateer schooner of Boston, was taken at Porto Bass, by a French man-of-war; Capt. Loring, in a brigantine privateer belonging to Boston, has been taken; Capt. Samuel Richards, in a sloop bound from New York to Piscataqua, and Mr. Tufton Mason, a passenger, were taken off Cape Cod; Capt. Morepang has resigned as commander of a privateer and is made third lieutenant of a ship of war - Boston items of 24 Sept. (4 Oct.)

The following on Monday last were elected for Phila. Co.-- representatives: Isaac Norris, Thomas Leech, John Kinsey, Robert Jones, Edward Warner, James Morris, Owen Evans, Joseph Trotter; sheriffs: Nicholas Scull, Peter Robinson; coroners: Henry Pratt, Jacob Duche; commissioner: John Johnson; county assessors: James Paul, Moses Hughes, Robert Jones, Evan Jones, Jeremiah Elfreth, John Lasher; burgesses: Israel Pemberton, Oswald Peel; city assessors: John Stamper, Stephen Armitt, William Clymer, William Fisher, John Langdale, Thomas Howard (4 Oct.)

The following on Monday last were elected for Bucks Co.-- representatives: John Hall, Mark Watson, Mahlon Kirkbride, Abraham Chapman, Benjamin Field, John Watson, Garret Vansant, Joseph Shaw; sheriffs: John Hart, Timothy Smith; coroners: Joseph Chapman, Joseph Hampton; commissioner: John Hill; assessors: Adam Harker, Thomas Owen, John Williamson, Abraham Vastine, Bartholomew Longstretch, George Logan (4 Oct.)

The following on Monday last were elected for Chester Co.
--representatives: George Ashbridge, Francis Yarnal,
Joseph Pennock, Samuel Levis, James Gibbons, Joseph
Harvey, Thomas Cummings, Thomas Chandler; sheriffs:
John Owen, Richard Jones; coroners: Thomas Morgan,
Abraham Darlington; commissioner: Joseph Mendinghall;
assessors: Thomas Pennel, Samuel Bunting, Thomas
Hughs, Isaac Davis, Joshua Pusey, Joseph Gilpin (4 Oct.)

HOCKLEY, Richard, in Market St., Phila. - offers reward
for recovery of mare (which formerly belonged to John
Ross, of Susquehanna) that strayed from a pasture near
Phila. (4 Oct.)

BEVAN, Evan - has for sale a New England built brigantine
(4 Oct.)

Goods just imported in the ship Catharine, Gurney Wall
master, from Bristol - are sold by Robert and Amos
Strettell (4 Oct.)

Notice of fairs to be held in Charles-Town, on N. East
River, in Cecil Co., Md., is inserted by William Knight,
Regr. (4 Oct.)

CHESTERFIELD, Thomas, servant - runaway from Edward Barnes,
living in Oxford, Md. (4 Oct.)

Goods imported from Bristol in the ship Catharine - are to
be sold by Jevon & Perry, upon Hamilton's wharf in
Phila. (4 Oct.)

MUNDLE, James, servant, age c. 20 - runaway from Robert
Lewis, of Kennet, Chester Co. (4 Oct.)

ROACH, Edmond, servant, age c. 16, who served some time
with Joshua Littler at Wilmington and is a scholar -
same as above

Reward will be paid if horse stolen off the Commons is
brought to Joseph Coburn, at the Three Tuns in Chesnut
St., Phila., or to Joseph Hallowell, next door (4 Oct.)

HOPKINS, Robert - offers for sale the plantation on which
he now lives at Richmond, commonly called Point no Point
(4 Oct.)

Of the 4 gentlemen blown up with gunpowder at Newport,
R.I., last week 3 are since dead, Capt. Grant, Mr. Cod-
dington, Mr. Taylor, and one, Mr. Gidley, is in dangerous condition - Newport item of 28 Sept. (11 Oct.)

467

Letter from St. John's, dated 5 Sept., from a man who
sailed from Boston with Capt. Rouse - Boston item of
1 Oct. (11 Oct.)

STEWART, Capt. - brought report of arrival at London of
2 New York ships, the Queen of Hungary, Capt. Hilton,
and the Britannia, Capt. Griffith - New York item of 8
Oct. (11 Oct.)

ANDERSON, Capt. - arrived at New York Saturday last from
Jamaica - New York item of 8 Oct. (11 Oct.)

French privateer ship, the Experience, of Cape Breton, John
Joseph Le Gross commander, has taken the following: the
sloop Rover, Capt. Francis Frewen commander, a Bermudas
sloop, Capt. Dickinson master, a Rhode Island sloop,
Capt. Spencer master, a Boston sloop, David Ellinwood
master; the English prisoners were put ashore about 9
miles south of Cape Henlopen, on Capt. William Faucitt's
land (11 Oct.)

On the 1st Monday in October the following were elected for
Lancaster Co.--representatives: James Mitchell, Samuel
Blunston, Arthur Paterson, John Wright; commissioner:
Andrew Work; assessors: Martin Millin, Robert Allison,
Andrew Boggs, Patrick Hays, John Davies, Jacob Milin;
sheriffs: Samuel Scot, John Sterret; coroners: Robert
Thomson, Alexander Gibbony (11 Oct.)

On the 1st Monday in October the following were elected for
Newcastle Co.--representatives: John McCoole, William
Armstrong, John Vance, James McMahan, Samuel Clements,
Daniel Corbet; sheriffs: Samuel Bickley, Gideon Grif-
fith; coroners: Benjamin Cooke, James McMullen (11 Oct.)

On the 1st Monday in October the following were elected for
Kent Co.--representatives: Mark Manlove, James Gorrel,
John Tilton, John Robinson, Abraham Alle, Andrew Cald-
well; sheriffs: Thomas Green, John Hunter; coroners:
John Clayton, Jr., Thomas Parks (11 Oct.)

On the 1st Monday in October the following were elected for
Sussex Co.--representatives: Woolsey Burton, Jacob
Kollock, William Fassit, Abraham Wynkoop, Luke Watson,
Ryves Holt; sheriffs: William Shankland, Peter Clows;
coroners: Robert Gill, Alexander Lermouth (11 Oct.)

On 2 Oct. Edward Shippen was chosen Mayor of Phila. (11 Oct.)

Two books just published by B. Franklin: Pamela and A
Letter from the Rev. Dr. Coleman of Boston, to the Rev.
Mr. Williams of Lebanon, upon reading the Confession and

Retractions of the Rev. Mr. James Davenport (11 Oct.)

Remarks upon Mr. Geo. Whitefield by George Gillespy, minister of the Gospel in the County of New-Castle - published by John Stevens, at the Harp & Crown, in Third
St., opposite the Work-House (11 Oct.)

During Court in August a sum of money was left at the
house of Samuel Scot in Lancaster (11 Oct.)

WILLIAMS, Thomas, hatter - is removed from Strawberry Alley
to Second St., next door to Joshua Maddox, Esq., almost
opposite the Quaker Meeting-House (11 Oct.)

CROCKLAND, John, servant from Norfolkshire, age c. 25 -
runaway from William Towson, living in Baltimore Co.,
Md., near the red house (11 Oct.)

Time of an English servant lad, a plumber, to be disposed
of; enquire of Jonathan Durell (11 Oct.)

SMITHURST, Capt. - arrived Monday last at Boston, after
taking Capt. Gorham and his company of Indian Rangers
to the garrison at Annapolis Royal, under siege by the
French under Monsieur Duvivier; Duvivier withdrew when
Capt. Smithurst arrived; Capt. Allen of Boston was
killed by the French as he was at the helm of his sloop
- Boston items of 8 Oct. (18 Oct.)

Thursday last Capt. Smithurst sailed from Boston on a
cruize and Saturday 30 of the men taken with Capt. Gatman at Newfoundland arrived at Ipswich - Boston items
of 8 Oct. (18 Oct.)

Ship Jacob, Capt. John Keteltas commander, arrived last
night at New York from Amsterdam, with European news;
the privateer brigantine Hester and the sloop Polly are
ready to sail on a cruize - New York item of 13 Oct.
(18 Oct.)

JERRARD, Richard, at Spring Garden, near Phila. - does malt
barley and wheat (18 Oct.)

Tract of 1,400 acres, in Gloucester Co., at the head of
Timber Creek, is for sale; apply to the house of Henry
Roe, living near said land (18 Oct.)

BEDDOME, Joseph, about to remove into the country - desires
all balances to be settled (18 Oct.)

Messages of Gov. Geo. Thomas to the Pennsylvania Assembly;
in the second he mentions that Mr. Partridge, Agent for

Rhode Island, has engaged Mr. Paris in behalf of that colony; the House directed Samuel Levis and Abraham Chapman to wait on the governor (25 Oct.)

PAINTER, Capt. - arrived yesterday at New York from Turk Islands, with news that Capt. Harriot, in a privateer belonging to St. Kitts, took a French merchant ship (25 Oct.)

McCLELLAN, Hugh, of Pequay, Lancaster Co. - will not pay debts contracted in future by his wife Margaret (25 Oct.)

LEWIS, Mordecai, late of Newtown, Chester Co., dec'd - accounts with estate to be settled with William Lewis, of Haverford, or William Lewis, of Newtown, executors (25 Oct.)

MORRIS, James - will sell or let house, bake-house, stores and a landing in Newport, on Christiana Creek (25 Oct.)

Plantation in Ridley Twp., Chester Co., about 1¼ miles from the best landing in the county, is to be let; apply to Job Harvey at the said place (25 Oct.)

DONAHEW, Capt., commander of a Boston privateer sloop, was attacked by a brigantine lately commanded by Capt. Loring - Boston item of 22 Oct. (1 Nov.)

HOAR, Capt., from Newfoundland, informs at Boston that Capt. Rouse has taken several prizes and that Capt. Solomon Davis now commands the Young Eagle - Boston item of 22 Oct. (1 Nov.)

BEAL, Capt., in a privateer schooner, has returned to Portsmouth, N.H., with great booty - Boston item of 22 Oct. (1 Nov.)

WALTON, Capt. - arrived at New York last week from Madeira - New York item of 29 Oct. (1 Nov.)

REES, Capt. - arrived Monday last at Phila. from Antigua; his ship had been taken by a French privateer (1 Nov.)

HUSTON & CAMPBELL, at their store in Front St., opposite to Samuel Hasel, Esq., have for sale goods imported from London in the brigantine Argyle, John Seymour commander (1 Nov.)

PATERSON, Joseph, Negro, who formerly lived with Samuel Ogle, late governor of Maryland, and as such has procured a writing under the hand of Rev. Jacob Henderson

- runaway from Philip Key, of St. Mary's Co., Md. (1 Nov.)

WHITEFIELD, Rev. - preaches 26 Oct. at the Isle of Shoals and 27 Oct. at Portsmouth, N.H.; his only child died since he left England (8 Nov.)

Friday last arrived at Boston Capt. Craig and Capt. Jeffries, both from London; they report that Capt. Philips sailed for Antigua - Boston item of 29 Oct. (8 Nov.)

HERTELL, Capt., who arrived at New York Tuesday last from Georgia, describes an encounter with Spaniards near St. John's Beach - New York item of 5 Nov. (8 Nov.)

Monday last at Phila. the Indian Mushemelon, who murdered Armstrong the trader, and his 2 men received sentence of death (8 Nov.)

Monday last at Phila. Michael Milchdeberger, a Dutch wagoner, who drove his wagon over a chair, by which a boy was so wounded that he died, was found guilty of manslaughter and burnt in the hand (8 Nov.)

WHITEPAIN, Capt., bound from Dublin for Phila. with 140 servants and passengers, was taken by a Spanish privateer (8 Nov.)

Sloop, a French prize, taken by the _Wilmington_, Capt. Sibbald, arrived 8 Nov. at Phila. (8 Nov.)

CALAGHAN, Cornelius, Irish servant - runaway from Peter Matson, of Upper Merion (1 Nov.)

Tract of 218 acres in Charles-Town twp., Chester Co., is for sale; enquire of Emanuel Jones and David Emanuel, living on the same (1 Nov.)

MORGAN, Thomas, coroner - announces vendue, to be held at house of Aubrey Bevan, in Chester, of a flat that was George Watson's, in which Watson was drowned when the flat sank in Chester Creek; the money will be used to pay cost of the inquest and funeral charges (1 Nov.)

HAMILTON, WALLACE & CO., at the house where Widow Fishbourn formerly lived, the store fronting Fishbourn's wharf - have for sale goods imported from London in the _Argyle_, John Seymour master, and the _Williams_, Henry Harrison master (1 Nov.)

AHIERN, Morris, Irish servant - runaway from John Rolfe, of Salem, West New Jersey (1 Nov.)

Three mast ships, Capts. Noble, Darling and Forwood, arrived 26 Oct. at Portsmouth, N.H. (8 Nov.)

Snow Warren, Alexander Katter commander, and the old schooner George, John Dougall commander, are fitting out for a cruize; those desiring to enter on board may repair to the commanders at the Boatswain & Call, near the drawbridge in Phila. (8 Nov.)

NEAVE, Samuel, intending for England, wishes to settle all accounts; his store is in Water St., fronting Fishbourn's wharf (8 Nov.)

Items of real estate from the estate of Thomas Story, to be sold by Israel Pemberton and Anthony Morris, include property, now in the tenure of Charles Quinon, a lot fronting on Vine St., extending to James Mackey's lot and a lot in the Burrough of Chester, situated near the dwelling-house of John Wade; some items are to be sold at the Widow Roberts's Coffee House in Phila. and others at the house of Aubrey Bevan in the Burrough of Chester (8 Nov.)

House where William Read lately lived at Franckfort is to be let; enquire of Martha Chalkley, adjoining, or of Jacob Le Gay at his house in Arch St. (8 Nov.)

GRANT, Capt., in a mast-ship, has arrived at Piscataqua; Capts. Long and Adams will sail in mast-ships next week; Mr. Whitefield is very ill at York - Piscataqua items of 2 Nov. (15 Nov.)

GAYTON, Capt. Clark - arrived Friday last at Boston from Antigua - Boston item of 5 Nov. (15 Nov.)

Thursday last 3 New York privateers, the brig Hester and sloops Polly and Delight, commanded by Capts. Bayard, Morgan and Langdon, sailed in consort from New York - New York item of 12 Nov. (15 Nov.)

Privateer sloop commanded by Capt. Richards on 11 Nov. fell down to the Hook to proceed on a cruize - New York item of 12 Nov. (15 Nov.)

Privateer brig Greyhound, commanded by Capt. Jeffery (late commander of the Polly), will soon sail (15 Nov.)

French prize, now called the Prince Charles, Capt. Jacobus Kierstade commander, is fitting up for a privateer (15 Nov.)

New ship, the Clarendon, Capt. John Jauncey, and a brig

commanded by Capt. Rosewel are fitting out at New York
to sail in consort - New York item of 12 Nov. (15 Nov.)

French privateer snow, commanded by Le Gross, has been
taken by the <u>Comet Bomb</u> from Antigua (15 Nov.)

MEAS, Capt. - arrived Sunday last at Phila. from Barbados
(15 Nov.)

Mushemelon, the Indian, who murdered Armstrong the trader,
and one of his men, were executed 14 Nov. at Phila. (15
Nov.)

Just published by B. Franklin are <u>A Preservative from the
Sins and Follies of Youth, An Account of the New-Invented
Pennsylvania Fire-Places</u> and <u>Poor Richard's Almanack
for the Year 1745</u> (15 Nov.)

Articles may be signed at the Pewter Platter in Front St.,
Phila., for cruize of the ship <u>Marlborough</u>, Christopher
Clymer, commander, at the Sign of the Crown and Scepter
in Front St. for cruize of the snow <u>Cruizer</u>, William
Clymer commander, at the Boatswain & Call for the snow
<u>Warren</u>, Alexander Kattur commander, and for the old
schooner <u>George</u>, John Dougall commander (15 Nov.)

FIELD, Benjamin, tobacconist - is located next door to the
Sign of the Bell and nearly opposite to the Baptist
Meeting-house in Second St., Phila. (15 Nov.)

EVANS, Lewis, in Strawberry Alley, Phila. - sells fine
crown soap (15 Nov.)

CLARK, Andrew, an Edinburgh man, a silversmith by trade,
who counterfeits pisterines and served his time to Col.
John Taylor at the copper mines - deserter from his sergeant at Fredericksburg, Va., from H.M.'s Regt. of Foot
commanded by Edward Trelawny; reward will be paid by
Frederick Shenton if deserter is taken to Mr. Whitehead,
Goaler in Phila. (15 Nov.)

FITZGERALD, James, an Irishman, who served his time to Mr.
Richard Bristow - same as above

The <u>Ranger</u> privateer, of Boston, Capt. Richardson - on 29
Sept. had an engagement with a French privateer -
Boston item of 12 Nov. (22 Nov.)

The 2 Capt. Donnels, in a schooner and a sloop from Boston, were taken by a French ship - Boston item of 12
Nov. (22 Nov.)

Capt. Rouse has disposed of all save 3 of his prizes -
Boston item of 12 Nov. (22 Nov.)

GRIFFITHS, Capt., in the privateer <u>Caesar</u> - returned to
Newport, R.I., Tuesday last - Newport item of 9 Nov.
(22 Nov.)

BRYANT, Capt. - is just arrived at New York from London -
New York item of 19 Nov. (22 Nov.)

Ship <u>William</u>, Capt. Semple, of New York - has been taken
by the French but retaken by an English privateer -
New York item of 19 Nov. (22 Nov.)

WHITEFIELD, Rev. - is reported to be dangerously ill at
Boston (22 Nov.)

Plantation of between 300 and 400 acres, in Solebury Twp.,
Bucks Co., lying upon York Rd., about 1½ miles from the
River Delaware, is for sale; apply to James Hamilton at
said place (22 Nov.)

AMBORN, Christopher, of Nantmell Twp., Chester Co. - will
not pay debts contracted in future by his wife Susanna,
who has eloped from him (22 Nov.)

Plantation of 100 acres, on the York Road, about 18 miles
from Phila., is for sale; apply to William Tenant,
living on said plantation (22 Nov.)

BENNET, Capt., in a Newport privateer, sailed from Newport
Saturday last and on Tuesday Capt. Allen, Sr., and Capt.
Marshall - Newport item of 16 Nov. (29 Nov.)

On 16 Nov. Capts. Long and Adams were cleared and ready to
sail from Piscataqua (29 Nov.)

Two ships from the Governor of Cape Breton took the 2 Donnels just as they were going into Annapolis Royal, when
the French discovered a letter from the Governor of
Massachusetts to Col. Mascarene; this revealed that relief was on the way from Boston, so the vessels sent
from Cape Breton at the request of Mr. Duvivier sailed
away - Boston item of 19 Nov. (29 Nov.)

Letters from Jamaica give details on prize money to be
shared by the crews of Capts. Hall and Lemprier; Capt.
Smee had sent in a Dutch brigantine - New York item of
27 Nov. (29 Nov.)

COATAM, Capt., has arrived at Phila. with news from Lisbon;
all Phila. privateers are in except the <u>New George</u>,

Capt. Dowell (29 Nov.)

PETERS, Richard, Secretary - publishes order of the Governor of Pennsylvania, offering a reward for the seizure of Adam Hains, "a profligate young Man," in the neighborhood of Conrad Weiser, Esq., in Tulpyhockin, Lancaster Co.; on the night between the 15 and 16 Nov. it is believed that Hains set fire to Weiser's house; Hains was apprehended but escaped from the constable (29 Nov.)

MEREDITH, Rees, Clerk of the Union Fire Company of Phila., offers reward for apprehension of person or persons who stole the nozzels of most of the pumps in Market St. and several other streets (29 Nov.)

HODGKINSON, Peter Aris, of Burlington - offers reward to anyone who will care for his son John or send word to his father; John, age 13, was taken by a Spanish privateer in his passage from Dublin to Phila. in a brigantine commanded by Zacharia Whitepaine (29 Nov.)

NORTON, Thomas, of Charles-Town, Cecil Co., Md. - offers reward for recovery of 2 horses, strayed or stolen (29 Nov.)

WEISER, Conrad, of Heidelberg, Chief Ranger of the Northeast Corner of Lancaster Co. - lists horses on his hands (29 Nov.)

BOLTON, Robert, dec'd - his creditors are desired to bring their accounts to Edward Shippen (29 Nov.)

KOCK, Peter - offers reward for recovery of a lost gold seal ring, with letters P K drawn in one another (29 Nov.)

Tract of 21,000 acres in Albermarle Co., Va., is to be purchased for life or leased for 21 years; apply to Andrew Campbel, Esq., in Frederick's Co., Va., or to George Braxton, Esq., in King and Queen's Co., Va. (29 Nov.)

JONES, Daniel, late of Phila., dec'd - accounts with estate to be settled with Joseph Price and Anne Jones, executors (29 Nov.)

Sunday last the brigantine Defiance, Capt. John Dennis, and the sloop Queen of Hungary, Capt. Conkland, sailed from Newport, R.I., in consort - Newport item of 30 Nov. (14 Dec.)

WHITEFIELD, Rev. - preached in Boston on Wednesday at Dr.
Colman's Meeting-house and on Saturday at Mr. Webb's -
Boston item of 3 Dec. (14 Dec.)

Prize taken near Newfoundland by Capt. Donahew, in a privateer of Boston, arrived Tuesday last at Boston - Boston
item of 3 Dec. (14 Dec.)

On 30 Oct. a small sloop, going over from Nantucket to the
main land, sank near the Horseshoe Shoal; doubtless all
on board were drowned, namely David Folger (master and
owner), his son, Richard Swain and another white man,
2 Indian men, a squaw and a papoose - Boston item of 3
Dec. (14 Dec.)

BASS, Capt. in the Hawk privateer - sailed 2 Dec. from
Boston (14 Dec.)

Ship Warren, Capt. Strawbridge, inward bound from Ireland,
was driven ashore at Primehook Bay; 4 men and 5 women
were drowned - report from Lewestown (14 Dec.)

Ship Hannah, Capt. Peddie, that sailed from Phila. for
Ireland, was taken by a French privateer (14 Dec.)

STEVENSON, Capt. - arrived Sunday last at Phila. from
Holland with Palatines (14 Dec.)

BOURN, Capt., at his lower store on Market St. wharf -
sells cider, fish, oil, etc. (14 Dec.)

Partnership of Richardson & Eversley is dissolved (14 Dec.)

HAWKINGS, William, at the Sign of the Jolly Sailor, in
Front St., Phila. - has taken up a mare (14 Dec.)

Abbe, Negro wench - runaway from Samuel Walsh, in Phila.
(14 Dec.)

DRURY, Edward, in Vine or Race St., Phila. - sells Epsom
salts (14 Dec.)

DICKSON, Mrs., from Scotland, lodging at Mrs. Harper's, at
the corner in Second St. - will teach young ladies to
draw, paint or play the flute (14 Dec.)

Persons desiring to go on a cruize in the privateer ship
Prince Charles, Jacobus Kierstede commander, may re-
pair to Benjamin Kierstede's, at the Sign of the Pine
Apple, on the New Dock at Phila. (14 Dec.)

ANDREWS, Isaac, a New England man, age c. 26 or 27, carpenter - escaped from Henry Casse, Under Sheriff of Orange Co.; reward will be paid for his capture by applying to John Currey, at the upper end of Second St., Phila. (14 Dec.)

ANDREWS, John (brother of Isaac), New England man, age c. 26 or 27, carpenter - same as above

REEVE, John, late of Burlington, dec'd - accounts with estate are to be settled with Robert Hartshorne, attorney-at-law in Burlington, by order of Matthias Aspden, executor (14 Dec.)

Ship Salley, Capt. Lane - arrived 25 Oct. in York River from London (18 Dec.)

It was ordered by vote of the New Jersey Assembly that Richard Smith and William Cook urge Richard Patridge, Agent of New Jersey at the Court of Great Britain, to do his utmost to prevent passage of a bill to prevent issuing of paper bills of credit (18 Dec.)

It is reported that persons suspected of setting fire to Mr. Weiser's house are committed to prison (18 Dec.)

ACWORTH, John, formerly an eminent wine merchant in London, died Saturday last in Phila. (18 Dec.)

DEAN, Thomas, servant, age c. 21 - runaway from Michael Cario (a jeweller) in Phila. (18 Dec.)

KENNEY, Timothy (schoolmaster), late of Gloucester Co., dec'd - accounts with estate to be settled with John Snowden or John Wilkins, of Woodberry, Gloucester Co., executors (18 Dec.)

TYLE, Matthias, Dutch servant, age c. 30 - runaway from James Bayard, of Bohemia, in Maryland (18 Dec.)

Extracts from Votes of the House of Assembly of New Jersey, with mention of Mr. Eaton (chairman), Mr. Smith (from the Council), Charles Read (Cl. Con.), Mr. Young, Mr. Vreland; representation of the Council to Gov. Lewis Morris (25 Dec.)

DURRELL, Capt. - arrived Friday last at Phila. from Holland but last from Poole, with Palatines (25 Dec.)

ROBINSON, Peter, at the Sign of the Indian King in Phila. - offers reward for recovery of a strayed horse (25 Dec.)

Plantation of 110 acres in Tredyffryn, Chester Co., within

18 miles of Phila., on Conestogo Rd., is for sale; apply
to Humphrey Wayn or Richard Iddings, of Newtown (25
Dec.)

Gristmill and other real estate in Southampton, Bucks Co.,
for sale; apply to John Bond, living at said mill (25
Dec.)

1745

LE GALLES, Capt. - returned Tuesday last to Boston from
Cape Breton with 35 prisoners, among whom Capt. Loring,
Major Little, Capt. Hope and the 2 Donnels - Boston
item of 10 Dec. 1744 (1 Jan.)

Governor of Cape Breton died suddenly about 2 months ago
- Boston item of 10 Dec. 1744 (1 Jan.)

Account of engagement between Capt. Richardson and a
French privateer commanded by one St. Martin - Boston
item of 10 Dec. 1744 (1 Jan.)

Prisoners taken in arms on board the French privateer snow
lately commanded by Capt. Legrotz will be tried next
Wednesday in Boston - Boston item of 10 Dec. 1744 (1
Jan.)

WHITEFIELD, Rev. - preached in Boston at meeting-houses of
Rev. Colman, Rev. Webb and Rev. Gee and proposes to
preach at Dr. Sewall's - item from the Boston Gazette
of 4 Dec. 1744 (1 Jan.)

Capts. Griffith and Hilton, at New York, brought news of
Admiral Balchen's fleet; Capt. Stedman, bound to Phila.,
was chased by 2 ships; Capt. James, who arrived at New
York from Boston, learned at Martha's Vineyard from a
schooner from St. Kitts, one Baker commander, that
Capts. Kip, Seymour, Tucker, and Martinborough were at
St. Kitts; Capt. Baker took up at sea one Capt. Darling
and crew, who had been bound from Boston to North Carolina - New York items of 17 and 24 Dec. 1744 (1 Jan.)

Schooner Prosperity, John Lee master, bound from Phila.
to Boston - was driven ashore at Cape May (1 Jan.)

CURRIE, Ebenezer, whose store is between Gray's and Norris's Alley, in Front St., Phila. - intends for England;
he offers reward for capture of Cesar, a Negro, age c.
34, who lately belonged to William Vaughan, of Marcus
Hook, and who broke out of the workhouse Saturday
night (1 Jan.)

Screws are cut by Jonathan Humphreys, of Blockley, within
5 miles of Phila., near Conestogo Road; screws may
also be bought by applying to Joseph Gray, in High St.,
Phila., at the Sign of the Conestogo Wagon (1 Jan.)

WOOD, John, _alias_ Joseph Wood, servant, born in the Jerseys, a wheelwright and millwright - runaway from W.
Worthington, Jr., of Newfoundland, Baltimore Co., Md.;
notice of the runaway may be sent to the care of Thomas
Hughes, at Nottingham, Pa., or William Hopkins, on Susquehanna, in Maryland (1 Jan.)

BROWN, Dr. - has taken up a mare at his plantation in the
Northern Liberties of Phila. (1 Jan.)

McCOOLE, Walter, of Windsor, in Rockhill Twp., Chief
Ranger of Bucks Co. - lists horses in his hands (1 Jan.)

Continuation of representation of the Council of New Jersey (8 Jan.)

NORTH, Capt., in the _Cesar_ privateer, has brought into
Cowes a French prize; the ship _Hardman Galley_, Capt.
Warner,bound from Maryland to London, was cast away 31
Oct. on Hunger Shoals; at Lancaster an Indian named
Robin Hood is in goal, charged with ravishing a white
girl; the privateer _Le Trembleur_, Obadiah Bowne comman-
der, is fallen down to proceed on a cruize - Phila.
items (8 Jan.)

HARRISON, John, below the drawbridge in Phila. - sells gunpowder (8 Jan.)

HOUSE, Joseph, in Chesnut St., Phila. - sells New England
rum (8 Jan.)

GAMBLE, Richard, English servant, age _c._ 26, who has been
10 years in the country - runaway from Thomas Hanaway,
of Sadsbury, Lancaster Co., cooper (8 Jan.)

According to account of Capt. Bangs, who arrived Tuesday
last at Boston from South Carolina, Capt. Hamar, in
H.M.S. _Flamborough_, took a rich prize from Havana -
Boston item of 15 Dec. (15 Jan.)

Schooner privateer, commanded by Capt. Beezley of Montserrat, blew up - Boston item of 13 Dec. 1744 (15 Jan.)

PHILIPS, Capt., from London, but last from Antigua, ar-
rived Thursday last at Boston, and on Monday arrived the
Eltham man-of-war, Capt. Durrel - Boston item of 13
Dec. 1744 (15 Jan.)

MARTINBOROUGH, Capt. - is fitting out a privateer snow,
designed for the West Indies; the Queen of Hungary privateer, Capt. Groochy, is ready to sail - Boston item of
13 Dec. 1744 (15 Jan.)

On 20 Dec. the snow Britannia, William Allen commander,
and the sloop King George, Benjamin Cranston, sailed
in consort from Newport (15 Jan.)

HANDLIN, Capt., arrived at New York from St. Thomas, with
an account of vain pursuit of some French vessels by 2
English privateers - New York item of 31 Dec. 1744 (15
Jan.)

PENISTON, Capt., who arrived 6 Jan. from Bermuda - reports
that the governor, collector and parson of that island
lately died; Capt. Richardson brought in a French
prize - New York item of 7 Jan. (15 Jan.)

Privateer ship Prince Charles, Capt. Kierstede, has fallen
down from New York to proceed on her cruize - New York
item of 31 Dec. 1744 (15 Jan.)

The George, Capt. Dowel, had an engagement with a French
ship and is now refitting at Bermudas; his consorts,
Capts. Harvey and Keil, did not aid him in the fight
(15 Jan.)

If finder of a silver watch (maker is Handyside) will
take it to B. Franklin, he will receive a reward (15
Jan.)

WHITE, Townsend, intending for England, desires to settle
all accounts; he sells European and West India goods
(15 Jan.)

Four tracts, each of 250 acres, in the Great Swamp, Bucks
Co., adjoining to land of Benjamin Gilbert and Lawrence
Growden,for sale; enquire of William Logan (15 Jan.)

JACKSON, Joseph, of Borough of Bristol, Bucks Co. - his
assignees, Ennion Williams and William Buckley, give
notice to all persons indebted to Jackson to adjust
their accounts (15 Jan.)

BUTLER, Sarah, servant, who in May last ran away from one
Delaplane in Bucks Co. - runaway from John Cottinger,
tailor, at the corner of Arch St., over against the
Sign of the George (15 Jan.)

SMOUT, Edward, at Lancaster, in Lancaster Co., Ranger of
part of that county, lists strays in his hands and of-

fers for sale a tract of between 600 and 700 acres adjoining to the Manor in Lancaster (15 Jan.)

Wednesday last arrived at Phila. the prize taken by Capt.
Dowell (she was bound to Bourdeaux, master's name Can-
nonier) and on Friday a ship and snow, from the Warren
privateer, Alexander Kattur, and the Old George schooner,
William Dougall; the ship, the Lewis Joseph, was commanded by Capt. Piedsnoirs; the snow is the St. Anne,
Pierre Dalheu master (22 Jan.)

Ship Argyle, Capt. Stedman, bound to Phila. from Holland,
was taken by 2 Spanish men-of-war (22 Jan.)

ALEXANDER, William, Collector of Customs for Port of Phila.
- died Wednesday night last in Phila.; Abraham Taylor
succeeds him (22 Jan.)

HOPKINSON, Thomas - is appointed Judge of the Admiralty in
Pennsylvania (22 Jan.)

SMITH, John, at his store on I. Pemberton's wharf - sells
goods just imported from London (22 Jan.)

McCALL, Samuel, in Water St., and Michael Helligas, in
Second St., have for sale copper stills, imported in
the ship Mary, Capt. Bernard Martin from London (22
Jan.)

WILLING, Charles - has for sale a parcel of men and boys
just imported in the ship Dorothy, John Nicholls master,
from Bristol (22 Jan.)

Brick house on Water St., Phila., where Simon Beezley now
lives - will be sold at auction (22 Jan.)

Ship Musley Galley, George Durrel commander, now at Goodman's wharf - will sail for South Carolina (22 Jan.)

HUMPHREYS, John, country-born, age c. 23 - absconded from
his bail in Northampton Twp., Bucks Co.; reward for his
capture will be paid by John or Bernard Vanhorn, Jr.
(22 Jan.)

Brigantine Argyle, John Seymour commander, now at Fishbourn's wharf in Phila., will sail for Barbados; for
freight agree with the commander on board or at Mrs.
Mary Stapleford's in Second St. (22 Jan.)

On 20 Nov. last the privateers Fame, Capt. Clement Lampeer,
the Hector, Capt. Thurston, and the Betty, Capt. Jennings, engaged with a Spanish man-of-war and a Spanish

sloop - Charlestown, S.C., item of 3 Dec. 1744 (supplement to Gazette No. 841)

French ship, Le Sendra, taken by Capt. Hamar, was condemned 10 Dec. 1744 (supplement to Gazette No. 841)

FRANKLAND, Capt. Thomas - has taken a rich prize, the Conception, M. de Marean and Sig. Don Piedro De Leffagrate commanders; after the engagement the prize was committed to the care of Lt. Payne; in the action John Mitchel was wounded; Lt. Hector Vaughan, in command of the marines, behaved with great bravery (supplement to Gazette No. 841)

Thursday last arrived at Charlestown Capt. Scarling, in an Antigua privateer, and the St. Andrew, Robert Brown master - Charlestown item of 24 Dec. 1744 (Supplement to Gazette No. 841)

STEEL, James, late of Phila., dec'd - accounts with estate to be settled with Richard Renshaw and Rebecca Steel, executors (supplement to Gazette No. 841)

Real estate of James Steel, dec'd, which is to be sold includes the following: lot on Mulberry St., adjoining Peter Bizailon's; pasture opposite Clement Plumsted's and Israel Pemberton's; 16 acres adjoining Samuel Seller's plantation near Phila.; 310 acres on the branches of Apoquinimy, on the road leading to Andrew Peterson's; 150 acres called Black Jacobo's settlement; 310 acres on the west line of James Hamilton's land, on the southwest side of Duck Creek; enquire of Richard Renshaw and Rebecca Steel, of Phila., or Mary Hillyard, of Duck Creek, executors (22 Jan.)

YERKS, Anthony, late of Lower Dublin Twp., Phila. Co., dec'd - accounts with estate to be settled with John Harrison, of the Manor of Moreland, or James Eaton, of Lower Dublin Twp. (22 Jan.)

FRIVALL, Harmon, Dutch servant, age c. 24 - runaway from the plantation of his master, Robert Meade, in the Northern Liberties of Phila. (22 Jan.)

Nineteen lots in Germantown are to be sold at auction at the house of Thomas Carwell in Germantown (22 Jan.)

Mermaid man-of-war, Capt. Douglas, and privateer Raleigh, Capt. Cold, both sailed last week from Virginia (29 Jan.)

MANSFIELD, Capt. Thomas, master of the ship King's Meadow, bound from Jamaica for London - was murdered at sea by

482

3 Frenchmen and a Spaniard; ship was retaken by Capt.
Loney; Pierre Desmuer and Manuel Castanon have been
examined before John Grymes and Thomas Nelson, 2 of
the commissioners appointed for the trial of pirates;
the other 2 Frenchmen, Dom Serres and Jaques Bullister,
were put on board the ship Britannia, Capt. John Hutchinson, and carried to Maryland - Williamsburg item of 27
Dec. 1744 (29 Jan.)

VICKERY, Capt., in a brigantine belonging to Boston - has
been taken in the West Indies - Boston item of 31 Dec.
1744 (29 Jan.)

Last week a sloop (supposed to be Capt. Holmes from Phila.)
overset in our bay; it is reported from Newport that a
privateer commanded by Capt. S. Potter plundered some
French settlements; last week Capt. Baker arrived at
the Hyannas from St. Kitts; a brigantine belonging to
Mr. Grigs and commanded by Capt. Breeding sank in the
West Indies and the men were taken up by 2 privateers
(one was the Queen of Hungary, Capt. Powell); Capt.
Powell took a large French prize and in the engagement
Mr. Murry (Capt. Breeding's mate) was killed - Boston
items of 31 Dec. 1744 (29 Jan.)

Last week 4 sloops were brought into St. Kitts by New York
privateers, of which Capt. Kip of New York commanded
one; at St. Kitts the Hercules is fitted out and is commanded by Capt. Charles Palmer - letter from St. Kitts
dated 18 Nov. 1744 (29 Jan.)

All the Newport privateers are out except 2, a ship commanded by Capt. Thompson and a snow commanded by Capt.
Griffyth - Newport item of 4 Jan. (29 Jan.)

Wednesday last the ship Lincoln, Capt. John Jauncey, fell
down to the Watering Place and today her consort, the
brigantine Triton, Capt. Francis Rosewel, joins her;
Capt. Kierstede in the privateer ship Prince Charles,
sailed Saturday last - New York items of 21 Jan. (29
Jan.)

Brigantine Catharine and Mary, Capt. England, inward bound
from the West Indies, is ashore at the Capes (29 Jan.)

James and Daniel Benezet, at their store adjoining to
Samuel Grisley's in Market St., Phila. - have imported
goods for sale (29 Jan.)

GRIFFITHS, Isaac, at his store at Arch St. wharf - sells
rum, pickled fish, train oil (29 Jan.)

BARD, John, next door but one to Evan Morgan's corner - sells drugs, chemicals, oil, turpentine, rozin, chocolate (29 Jan.)

Servant woman's time to be disposed of; enquire of John Cottinger, tailor, near the George in Arch St., or Andrew Farrel, tanner, in Chesnut St., Phila. (29 Jan.)

HAMILTON, William, Irish servant, age c. 20 - runaway from John Brandon, of Hempfield Twp., Lancaster Co. (29 Jan.)

SMITH, Frederick, of Phila., hatter - proposes to build, upon subscription, a privateer (29 Jan.)

ACKWORTH, John, late of Phila., dec'd - accounts with estate to be settled with Richard Farmer, administrator (29 Jan.)

PARSONS, William, in Second St., Phila. - sells tea and clover-seed (29 Jan.)

House in Front St. and a cooper's shop adjoining in Water St., Phila., next door to Nicholas Crone's, are for sale; enquire of Widow Peters, at Reese Peters's, in Chesnut St. (29 Jan.)

LARDNER, Lynford, R. G. - gives times and places for collection of quit rents (5 Feb.)

BOURNE, Thomas and Samuel Hazard - offer reward for discovery of person or persons who broke into the New Building in Phila. (5 Feb.)

HYATT, John - sells sugar, spirits, copper stills, kettles, scales, weights and London pewter (5 Feb.)

LUCAND, John, dec'd - his house and lot and 200 acres on Cushapen Rd., joining Schippack Creek, near Guchal Guchal's mill, are to be sold; enquire of Abraham and Joseph Lucand, in Towmenson, executors (5 Feb.)

LIGHTFOOT, John, English convict servant, born in Cheshire, age not above 26 or 28, mason and bricklayer, an old runaway - runaway from Thomas Rutherford, High Sheriff of Frederick Co., Va. (5 Feb.)

LIGHTFOOT, Anne (wife of John), Irish convict servant, age c. 36 or 38 - same as above

WALKER, Capt., in a privateer from Island of Providence, brought in there a large prize schooner - Charlestown, S.C., item of 7 Jan. (12 Feb.)

The privateer sloop <u>Reprisal</u>, Capt. John Hopkins commander - arrived 17 Jan. with a prize snow at Providence, R.I. (12 Feb.)

Saturday last Capt. Snelling arrived at Nantasket from London - Boston item of 14 Jan. (12 Feb.)

INCHES, Capt., commander of a brigantine belonging to Boston, was taken on 20 Oct. by a French sloop - Boston item of 21 Jan. (12 Feb.)

Brigantine <u>Abigail</u>, Samuel Tingley commander, arrived Friday last at New York from Leghorn and on the same day the brigantine <u>Catharine</u> of New York, Robert Stevenson late master but now Robert Young; the <u>Catharine</u> had been taken by the Spaniards, but in the night Capt. Young and 2 men rose on the Spaniards, overcame them and retook the vessel; Capt. Young spoke with Capt. Fisher in a brig belonging to Phila. in a very shattered condition - New York items of 28 Jan. (12 Feb.)

A letter from Capt. Frankland's clerk to a friend in Boston mentions 9 tons of silver taken in a prize - New York item of 4 Feb. (12 Feb.)

LEVERING, Wichart - died last week not far from Phila., aged 109 (12 Feb.)

French prize ship <u>Lewis Joseph</u> will be auctioned off at James's Coffee House in Phila.; the inventory may be seen at said coffee house or at the house of William Allen (12 Feb.)

Plantation of 227 acres, in Newgarden Twp., Chester Co., is offered for sale by Samuel Hill, of Newgarden, owner of the property (12 Feb.)

LEECH, Isaac, dec'd - accounts with estate to be settled with Rebecca Leech, his widow and executrix (12 Feb.)

PATTON, Col. James - offers for sale land in Beverly Manor and Augustus Co., Va., including a tract where said Patton lives, a tract near Capt. Cresly's, a tract near Capt. Thomas Parson's pace and 4 tracts near Robert Looney's on James River (12 Feb.)

Ship <u>Carolina</u>, Stephen Mesnard commander, now at Mifflin's wharf in Phila. - will sail for London; for freight or passage apply to Matthias Aspden or the commander (12 Feb.)

RICHARDS, Richard, of Lancaster Co., lately dec'd - if

anyone has his will, he is desired to bring it to Nathan
Gibson, of Kingsess, Phila. Co., who after a month will
proceed to administration (12 Feb.)

McDONALD, William, Highland servant, age c̲. 30 - runaway
from Patrick Doral, of Annapolis, Md.; reward will be
paid if runaway is brought to his master or to Andrew
Farrell in Phila. (12 Feb.)

POTTER, Capt. Simeon, commander of the Prince Charles of
Lorrain - in a letter to his owners at Newport he gives
an account of how he took and plundered a French settlement on Y'opoch River - Newport item of 10 Jan. (19
Feb.)

COLVERT, Capt., from St. Kitts - reports that 9 privateers
belonging to that island have taken between 20 and 30
prizes off Martineco (19 Feb.)

Sunday last at Phila. the privateer ship Marlborough,
Christopher Clymer commander, fell down to proceed on
a cruize (19 Feb.)

COOK, Samuel, servant, country-born, age c̲. 18 - runaway
from Joseph Gilbert, of Biberry, Phila. Co. (19 Feb.)

CAVENAUGH, Thomas, servant - runaway from George Kelly of
Phila., blacksmith (19 Feb.)

SMITH, Samuel, in Market St., Phila., at Capt. Bourne's
lower store, near Market St. wharf - sells rum, molasses, sugar, oil, fish (19 Feb.)

Plantation of 250 acres in Oxford Twp., about 5 miles from
Phila. - is to be sold by the owner, Griffith Jones,
living on the premises, or Judah Foulk, near the Court
House in Phila. (19 Feb.)

Series of complaints published by Job Noble, living at
Warminster, Bucks Co. (19 Feb.)

McBROOM, Andrew, of Moreland, Phila. Co. - his wife Eleanor
has eloped from him (19 Feb.)

Copper stills, just imported in the ship Mary, Capt. Martin,
are for sale by Samuel McCall in Water St. or Michael
Helligas in Second St., Phila. (19 Feb.)

HART, Thomas, near William Parsons's, in Second St., Phila.
- grinds chocolate (19 Feb.)

DOUGLASS, Capt., in the Mermaid - writes that he took a

French ship - Kingston, Jamaica, item of 12 Jan. (26 Feb.)

The _Swallow_ sloop of war, Capt. Jelph, has been lost on Abaco Keys - Charlestown item of 21 Jan. (26 Feb.)

SPRING, Capt., commander of a snow belonging to Boston, was murdered by several of his prisoners in the Windward Passage - Boston item of 4 Feb. (26 Feb.)

BOURDET, Capt. Samuel, who arrived last week at New York, brought English prisoners from Hispaniola, including Capt. Brown (late master of the sloop _Garrit_ of New York) and Capt. Low (late master of a Bermuda sloop); Capt. Brown was told that a brigantine, Thomas Hill master, had been taken - New York item of 11 Feb. (26 Feb.)

JAUNCEY, Capt., in the brigantine _Mary Anne_, arrived last week at New York from Jamaica, bringing a Negro named Hanover, sent for trial by Gov. Trelawney; a House-Negro on Jamaica revealed a plot to kill all the white people, for which the Negro has been made free and Jamaica has settled on him 30 pounds a year for life; Capt. Jauncey brings news that Capt. Cunningham, in a privateer sloop, has taken a Spanish privateer - New York item of 18 Feb. (26 Feb.)

GRENALL, Capt., commander of the privateer brigantine _Batchelor_ of New York, arrived end of October last at Jamaica; it is reported that 3 privateers, commanded by Capts. Bayard, Langdon and Morgan, have carried 2 prizes into Barbados - New York item of 18 Feb. (26 Feb.)

REES, Capt., from Coracoa, informs that 3 New York privateers have taken a Spanish privateer; Capt. Evans, from Antigua reports that the ship _Molly_, Capt. Stamper, of Phila., sank at Antigua; Capt. Condy, from Madeira to Phila., put in at Antigua; Capt. Clay, from St. Christophers, informs that the privateer ship _Hercules_, Capt. Charles Palmer, was cruizing off Martineco; the brigantine _Jane_, Capt. Wright, belonging to Phila., is taken and carried into Guadeloup - all Phila. items (26 Feb.)

Recruiting officer for Gov. Trelawny's Regt. attends from 12 to 2 at Mrs. Roberts's Coffee House in Front St., Phila. (5 Mar.)

SCHLEYDORN, Henry, sugar-baker - is located in Norris's Alley, Phila. (5 Mar.)

Volunteers for cruizing voyage of the ship _Wilmington_, Adam

Lister commander, may repair to the Sign of the Boatswain and Call, near the drawbridge, in Phila. (5 Mar.)

Collection of books is to be auctioned off at the large
room over Mr. Vidal's school in Second St.; a catalogue
is available at Joseph Goodwin's, bookbinder, in Black
Horse Alley, Phila. (5 Mar.)

BICKLEY, Samuel, Sheriff of Newcastle Co. - has taken up a
Welshman named Thomas George, who says he served his
time with James Powel, of Baltimore Co., Md. (5 Mar.)

MARSHAL, John, at Richard Pitts's, silversmith, in Front
St., Phila. - sells books, linen, hats, rum, fish (5
Mar.)

POWEL, Evan - forbids anyone to trust his slave, Molatto
Bess, with money or goods (5 Mar.)

Turlington's balsam is sold at Mr. Josiah's, near Mr.
Powel's, over the bridge, in Phila. (5 Mar.)

GALLBRETH, James, Ranger for the Western Division of Lancaster Co. - lists strays in his hands (5 Mar.)

Letter from Capt. Bayard, commander of the privateer brigantine Hester, at sea, dated 29 Jan., tells of his activities; letter was brought to New York by Capt. Wolf
from Coracoa; it was reported at Coracoa that Capt.
Axon, in the ship David of New York, has taken 2 prizes
(12 Mar.)

Sunday last arrived at Phila. the brigantine Cleaveland,
Capt. Robinson, with European news (12 Mar.)

PEALE, Charles - advertises his Kent County School, near
Chester Town, Md. (12 Mar.)

WRAGG, James - has removed into Second St. to the house
where Dr. Thomas Bond lived; he sells ironmongery and
brass-work; he intends to go to England (12 Mar.)

HILLIARD, Philip, late of Phila., dec'd - accounts with
estate to be settled with Evan Morgan, Jr. (12 Mar.)

RUTHERFORD, John, commander of H.M.'s Independent Company
of Foot at Albany - gives notice that the following deserters will be prosecuted if they do not return to
Duty before 25 Apr.: Lawrence Waters, tailor, who
served his time in Phila.; Benjamin Jolly, son of a
farmer and miller, near Bristol; William Morrison, tanner and currier, and John Morris, son of a farmer at

Redclay Creek, Newcastle Co. (12 Mar.)

DOLLAHA, William, Welsh servant, age c. 30 - runaway from
Mary Lownes, of Myomenson (12 Mar.)

BELL, William, late of Phila., merchant, dec'd - accounts
with estate to be settled with James Bell and Samuel
Powel, Jr., executors (12 Mar.)

MAXWELL, Capt., from St. Christophers, reports that Capt.
Purcel, of that place, has taken a Spanish privateer
(19 Mar.)

Privateer ship Wilmington, Adam Lister captain, is fallen
down to go on a cruize (19 Mar.)

STEEL, George (malster and brewer to Mr. Preserve Brown in
Bordentown) in going thither from Phila. on 9 Mar. fell
overboard and was drowned (19 Mar.)

SHENTON, Frederick - offers reward for arrest of 2 deserters from the officer recruiting H.M.'s Regt. of
Foot under the command of Col. Trelawny, namely:
Richard Styles, born at Stamford in Lincolnshire, age
22, who has struck for some months under a blacksmith
in Phila., and Benjamin Jackson, age c. 25, a blacksmith (19 Mar.)

THOMAS, Thomas - warns against a strolling woman named
Elizabeth Castle (alias Morrey), who had done damage in
Newtown, Chester Co.; she pretends to be a school-mis-
tress, tayloress, staymaker, embroiderer and doctoress
(19 Mar.)

ALLEN, Ulrick, of Phila., designing soon to leave this
place - persons indebted to him are desired to make payment to John Ox in Germantown (19 Mar.)

HACKNEY, Samuel, intending for England - sells cordial
water (19 Mar.)

Wednesday last was launched at Boston the Massachusetts,
built by Capt. Berry and bought by the province, under
the command of Capt. Edward Tyng; Capt. Smethurst now
commands the Prince of Orange and Capt. Fletcher commands a brigantine in the service of the province -
Boston item of 25 Feb. (26 Mar.)

On 26 Dec. a brigantine from Barbados, bound to New London,
Charles Short master, was retaken from the French; on
28 Dec. Capt. Warren took a sloop commanded by Capt.
Nicholas Gouget; in Jan. Capt. Stanney, of Boston, and

Capt. Farrel both foundered in a storm; Capt. Miller,
of Boston, was taken and carried into Guadaloup - Boston
items of 25 Feb. (26 Mar.)

WHITEFIELD, Rev. - has preached for Rev. Jewet, of Rowley,
Rev. Chandler, Rev. Emmerson of Topsfield, Rev. Parsons
at Byfield; he is accompanied by several ministers, including Rev. White, of Cape Anne - Boston items from the
Boston Gazette of 26 Feb. (26 Mar.)

Extract of a letter from Thomas Tucker, commander of the
privateer sloop Mary-Anne, in consort with the sloop
Clinton, Thomas Seymour commander, both of New York,
dated at Providence, 18 Jan. - described their encounter with one Spanish and 2 French privateers - New York
item of 11 Mar. (26 Mar.)

GRENALL, Capt. in privateer brigantine Batchelors of New
York - has taken a small prize - New York item of 11
Mar. (26 Mar.)

JEFFERY, Capt. Richard, in the brigantine Greyhound and
Capt. N. Richards, in the sloop Williams, both of New
York - have taken 2 French sloops over St. Lucia - New
York item of 11 Mar. (26 Mar.)

Thursday last Capt. Beak, who arrived at Phila. from Bermuda, reported that the Comet Bomb, Capt. Spry, was
taken by a Spanish privateer (26 Mar.)

Letter from Barbados informs that the privateer snow Cruizer,
of Phila., William Clymer commander, has been there
(26 Mar.)

Ship Jane, Capt. Cribbs, belonging to Phila., bound to Barbados from Ireland, has been taken by a French privateer
(26 Mar.)

LEVY and FRANKS, in Phila., sell alom, copperas, gunpowder,
tea, spices, sugar, indigo, shot, nails, etc. (26 Mar.)

An Abstract from Doctor Berkley's Treatise on Tar-Water -
is sold by B. Franklin (26 Mar.)

Corner lot of 17 ft. front on Second St. and 70 on Sassafras
St. is for sale; enquire of Ulrick Allen, near Mr. Branson's, in Phila. (26 Mar.)

Lot on west side of High St. in Burlington, not far from
the Court House and Market, is for sale; apply to James
Inskeep (26 Mar.)

WEISER, Conrad, Ranger for Northeast Corner of Lancaster Co. - lists strays in his hands (26 Mar.)

BINGHAM, William, within 3 doors of the Baptist Meeting in Second St., Phila. - sells gunpowder, tea, cloth and land at the Forks of Delaware, Virginia and Cape May (4 Apr.)

POWEL, Samuel, Jr., below the drawbridge in Phila. - has for sale a young Negro man and woman (4 Apr.)

DRURY, Edward, in Vine or Race Sts., Phila. - sells Epsom salts (4 Apr.)

CARIO, Michael, jeweller, from London - is located in Front St., at the Crown and Pearl, next door to Mr. Wood's, clockmaker (4 Apr.)

Tony, Negro slave, Virginia born, age c. 30 - runaway from Benjamin Hill, in Bertie Co., N. C. (4 Apr.)

GREEVY (or REEVES), John, native Irish servant, age c. 35 - runaway from James Dougherty, of Nottingham, Chester Co. (4 Apr.)

BROWN, William, under sheriff - reports that John Parra, age c. 24, hatter, has been taken up as a runaway and is now in Trenton Goal (4 Apr.)

MARRIOT, Thomas, of Borough of Bristol - lists much real estate for sale (4 Apr.)

JONES, Griffith - mares, colts, horses, cows, etc., will be sold at his dwelling house near Franckfort (4 Apr.)

Twenty-eight lots in Germantown will be sold at the house of Henry Shryber, near Thomas Carwell's, in Germantown: some are opposite the lots lately sold by Mr. Hall (4 Apr.)

Plantation of 143 acres in Roxbury Twp., Phila. Co., will be sold by John Bawlde, living on the premises, 2 miles beyond Robinson's mill (4 Apr.)

HALL, Peter, upholsterer, in Chesnut St., Phila. - sells furniture and drums (4 Apr.)

Plantation of 116 acres in Phila. Co. on Franckfort Rd., formerly belonging to Peter Helligas, dec'd; enquire of George Biesie, next door to Michael Helligas, in Second St. (4 Apr.)

THOMPSON, Capt. Richard, commander of a small privateer
from Providence, has taken a Spanish prize - Charlestown, S.C., item of 18 Feb. (supplement to the Pa.
Gazette No. 851)

DENNIS, Capt. J., in the privateer Defiance, rescued Capt.
S. Carr (bound to Newport from Guinea), whose vessel
was a mere wreck - Newport item of 15 Mar. (supplement
to Pa. Gazette No. 851)

FREEMAN, Capt. - reports at Boston the safe arrival in
France of ships from Cape Breton - Boston item of 18
Mar. (supplement to Pa. Gazette No. 851)

BASS, Capt., in a privateer brig of Boston - with great
difficulty got to St. Kitts - Boston item of 18 Mar.
(supplement to Pa. Gazette No. 851)

KIP, Capt. Abraham - reports his taking a brig; Capt.
Greenall, in privateer brigantine Batchelors has brought
a small prize into Jamaica - New York items of 25 Mar.
and 1 Apr. (supplement to Pa. Gazette No. 851)

HOWELL, Joshua - Monday last, when traveling on horseback
from Trenton to Burlington, was attacked by 2 footpads;
he beat them off and escaped (supplement to Pa. Gazette
No. 851)

Schooner Kensington, Capt. Greenaway, from Barbados for
Phila., is ashore on the Capes; the Burlington, Capt.
Condy, of Phila., was taken the day he left Antigua by
a French privateer; the Marione, of Phila., Capt. Kollock, sank at Antigua; from St. Christophers it is reported that, in an engagement between the Hercules
privateer, Capt. Palmer, and a large ship, Capt. Palmer
lost his first lieutenant; Capt. Barns from South Carolina reports that 2 Rhode Island privateers have taken
a large French ship; Capts. Hargraves and Elves, both
from Maryland, have arrived in England - Phila. items
(supplement to the Pa. Gazette No. 851)

LECRAW, Capt. - returned to Marblehead from the West Indies
with letters and messages from Capt. Warren; Capt. Richardson, commander of the privateer Ranger of Boston,
died October last in Newfoundland; Capt. McNeal, now
commander of the Ranger, has taken 2 prizes; Capt.
Gruchy, in a Boston privateer, has taken a schooner and
sent her into St. Kitts - Boston items of 25 Mar. (12
Apr.)

WHITEFIELD, Rev. - preached 3 Mar. at General Pepperill's
in Portsmouth, N.H. - Boston item of 25 Mar. (12 Apr.)

BARDET, Capt. - arrived Saturday last at Boston from Antigua - Boston item of 1 Apr. (12 Apr.)

According to letter of 2 Feb. from Jamaica a Negro plot to
kill all whites on the island was revealed to the wife
of a planter; she sent a note to a neighbor, Sir Simon
Clark, who at once had the Council meet; horse and foot
were gathered and many Negroes were secured and punished
- Boston item of 1 Apr. (12 Apr.)

The Philadelphia Galley, Capt. Hughston, of Phila., has arrived in England (12 Apr.)

BREINTNALL, Joseph, Secretary - announces a meeting of the
Library Company of Phila. (12 Apr.)

MAYER, Jacob, of Shippack, Polford Twp. - his wife Agnes
has eloped from him (12 Apr.)

List of books to be sold by James Read, next door to the
Post Office in Phila. (12 Apr.)

HARTLEY, William, of Charles-Town, Chief Ranger of Chester
Co. - lists strays in his hands (12 Apr.)

PARSONS, Joseph, late of Marple, Chester Co., millwright,
dec'd - accounts with estate to be settled with Robert
Pearson, administrator, at the house of Joshua Thomson
in Ridley (12 Apr.)

BRAND, Jonathan, next door to the One Tun Tavern, in Water
St., Phila. - sells cheese, dry goods, rum, sugar and
coffee (12 Apr.)

WALL, Joseph, servant, age c. 20 - runaway from Thomas
Ricketts, at the head of Elk River, Md.; he took with
him Peter Dean, age c. 20 (12 Apr.)

ORD, John, late clerk to Charles Brockden, carries on business of scrivener and conveyancer at his office, facing
the Baptist Meeting-house in Second St., Phila., where
the late Collector lived (12 Apr.)

Plantation of 200 acres, in Cheltenham Twp., Phila. Co.,
3 miles from Germantown, will be sold by Thomas Carvell
in Germantown (12 Apr.)

DENNIS, Capt., and his consort have arrived at Providence,
R.I., to careen; prize sent home by Capts. Allen and
Marshal was lost a few days ago near Cape Cod - Newport
items of 5 Apr. (18 Apr.)

McNEAL, Capt., in the _Ranger_ privateer - arrived Thursday
last at Boston - Boston item of 8 Apr. (18 Apr.)

Thursday last arrived at New York the sloop _Sea Nymph_,
Capt. Vardil, from St. Christophers; Capt. Jeffery, in
the brigantine _Greyhound_, Capt. Richards, in the sloop
William, and Capt. Hyder, in their tender, all of New
York, have sent 9 prizes into Barbados and 4 into St.
Christophers - New York items of 15 Apr. (18 Apr.)

SCHLEYDORNE, Henry, of Phila. - offers reward for the ap-
prehension of Joseph Shaw, late post-rider between
Phila. and New York, age c. 30, whose family lives at
Prince Town in the Jerseys; Shaw has made off with about
150 pounds, of which about 70 belong to Schleydorne (18
Apr.)

Ship _Pandour_, William Dowell commander, and brigantine
George, Robert Wood commander, are now fitting out;
persons wishing to enter on board may repair to the
said commanders or to the Sign of the Boatswain and
Call, near the drawbridge in Phila. (18 Apr.)

DALEY, Dennis, Irish servant, age c. 22, and Thomas Jennings, English servant, who can speak Swedish - runaways from William Bird and Marcus Hulings, both of
Amity Twp., Phila. Co. (18 Apr.)

Plantation of 270 acres, in the Great Swamp in Bucks Co.,
will be sold by John Evans, of North Wales, and Griffith
Jones, of Oxford, executors of the estate of Arthur
Jones, of Oxford, late dec'd; enquire of Michael Lightfoot in Phila. (18 Apr.)

Lot at Kensington, fronting King St. and Queen St., is for
sale; apply to John Spencer, in Arch St., Phila. (18
Apr.)

WILCOCKS, John, below the drawbridge, Phila. - has Negroes
for sale (18 Apr.)

LYNN, Joseph, dec'd - his executors have for sale a lot at
the upper end of Market St., Phila. (18 Apr.)

WOOLLEY, Thomas, late of Marple, Chester Co. - has removed
to Phila. to the Sign of the White Horse, in Elbow Lane,
over against the Presbyterian Meeting-house, near the
Market, to keep a public house (18 Apr.)

Speech of Gov. William Shirley to the General Assembly of
Massachusetts (25 Apr.)

The privateer <u>Surprize</u>, Capt. William Edwards commander, fitted out at Charlestown, S.C., will sail in a few days - South Carolina item of 11 Feb. (25 Apr.)

MACLESTER, Capt. George, of the snow <u>Flying Fish</u>, belonging to Maryland, was taken by a French privateer, Sieur Jean Baptiste Roulleau, in the sloop <u>St. Andrew</u>, of Martineco; the snow was ransomed but Sunday last was driven ashore at New Point Comfort - Williamsburg item of 14 Mar. (25 Apr.)

Brigantine <u>Leah</u>, Capt. William Andrew, arrived 9 Mar. at Hampton from Glasgow; she had been chased by the privateer <u>Marlborough</u>, Capt. Clymer, from Phila.; the <u>Leah</u> rescued 2 Portuguese in a small boat - Williamsburg item of 21 Mar. (25 Apr.)

SHOARS, Capt. Peter - arrived at Piscataqua from Barbados; he had been chased by a French privateer (formerly commanded by Capt. Loring, of Boston); Shoars informed that the French ship that had taken Capt. Spry in the <u>Comet Bomb</u> was chased ashore at Corracoa and entirely lost - Piscataqua item of 11 Apr. (25 Apr.)

Prize taken by Capt. Dennis and consort was lately lost on coast of Georgia; Sunday last the Rhode Island Colony sloop <u>Tartar</u> sailed to New London; last night arrived at Newport Capts. Marshall and Allen; Capt. Marshall had lost his sloop on the Florida shore but returned safe in the other privateer and the prize; Capts. Morris and Ingersoll have taken a French snow and carried her into New Providence - Newport, R.I., items of 13 Apr. (25 Apr.)

WARREN, Commodore - took on board one Chapman, skipper of a fishing schooner of Marblehead, as a pilot - Boston item of 15 Apr. (25 Apr.)

KIP, Capt., of the privateer sloop <u>Don Carlos</u> of New York - lately put into Bermuda with a prize he had taken - New York item of 22 Apr. (25 Apr.)

KORTRECHT, Cornelius, baker, of New York - Monday last was crushed to death between the wharf and a sloop alongside of it - New York item of 22 Apr. (25 Apr.)

Schooner <u>George</u>, William Dowell commander, arrived last week at Phila., who says he spoke with Capts. Bayard, Langdon and Morgan, all of New York, who had taken a Dutch sloop (25 Apr.)

SHIRLEY, Gov. - received word that the French were fitting

out a force to take Annapolis Royal; it is reported
that Capt. Warren ordered the Eltham and Capt. Clark
Gayton to follow him; The Trembleur privateer of Phila.
has arrived at Lewestown and retaken an English ship
(25 Apr.)

BARGE, William, living in North Wales Twp., Phila. Co. -
will sell at his plantation the said plantation of 200
acres with Wisohicken Creek running through it (25 Apr.)

Four lots in Germantown to be let; apply to Samuel Ashmead
or Thomas York, at Germantown (25 Apr.)

DOUGLAS, George, of Trenton - his wife Athelanah has eloped
from him (25 Apr.)

Seventy lots in Wilmington are to be set up, by way of
lottery, by Nicholas Bishop and his wife Hesther (25
Apr.)

PRICE, William, dec'd - accounts with estate to be settled
with Anna Elizabeth Price and Edward Evans, executors
(25 Apr.)

MATLOCK, Timothy - will sell several houses and lots in
Hadonsfield, Gloucester Co., West New Jersey (25 Apr.)

HOPMAN, Andrew - will sell a plantation of 100 acres in
Greenwich Twp., Gloucester Co., near Old Man's Creek
Bridge (25 Apr.)

Message of Gov. George Thomas in Council to the Pennsylvania Assembly; Gov. mentions he engaged Conrad Weiser
to undertake a journey to Onontage and that Peter Chartier has gone over to the enemy (2 May)

Message to the Governor from the Assembly (2 May)

Speech of Gov. William Shirley to the General Assembly of
Massachusetts; he mentions Mr. Warren and Gov. Wentworth of New Hampshire - Boston item of 22 Apr. (2 May)

Upon orders from Commodore Warren, on Tuesday Capt. Durrell
in the Eltham, sailed from Piscataqua and Capt. Gayton in
H.M.S. Bien Aime has orders to sail - Boston item of 22
Apr. (2 May)

Saturday last arrived at Piscataqua a sloop taken by Capt.
Fletcher, in a brigantine in the government service -
Boston item of 22 Apr. (2 May)

Letters from General Pepperil, dated as Canso on 10 Apr.,

inform that troops raised in Massachusetts and New Hampshire have arrived at Canso; Capt. Donahew took 3 of the Cape Sable Indians, who informed that M. Duviviere had ordered Indians to be at Menis by last of May; Wednesday arrived at Boston Capt. Gould from New Providence, with whom came Capt. Inches, who was taken last fall in his passage from London; when Capt. Inches was in a flag of truce the vessel was retaken by one Capt. Walker; Capt. Dennis, of Rhode Island, took a Dutch sloop and put some of his men aboard but it sprung a leak, so they were forced to put in at Cape Francois, where they were imprisoned - Boston items of 22 Apr. (2 May)

BAYARD, Capt., of the privateer brigantine Hester, in consort with the sloops Polly and Dolphin, all of New York, took a sloop bound from Carthagena for Coracoa; it is reported that M. Crosoque is designing for our coasts with 7 privateers; Capt. Kierstede, in the privateership Prince Charles of New York, has lately taken 2 prizes - New York items of 29 Apr. (2 May)

Petition was presented to the Pennsylvania Assembly that all the upper part of Lancaster Co. above McCall's Manor be made a new county (2 May)

An Essay on the West-India Dry-Gripes, by Dr. Cadwalader, is printed and sold by B. Franklin (2 May)

WILKINSON, Anthony, in Water St., Phila. - sells pickled sturgeon (2 May)

Dwelling-house on Society Hill where Joseph Scull now lives is for sale; enquire of Robert Grace in Phila. (2 May)

LINCOLN, Abraham, late of Springfield, Chester Co., dec'd - his late dwelling-house is to be sold by Robert Taylor and Joshua Tomson, executors (2 May)

BROWN, Thomas - will sell a lot in Germantown, near the Market House and also 14 or 15 lots fronting on the road that leads to Andrew Robinson's mill (2 May)

BRYN, Arthur, Irish servant, born in Dublin, age c. 38 - runaway from the Clinton privateer, Capt. Seymour of New York; reward will be paid for his capture by John Muirhead and Hugh Mecan, both living near Prince-Town, N.J. (2 May)

KNOWLES, John, late of Phila., victualler, dec'd - accounts with estate to be settled with Joseph and Catherine Knowles, executors (2 May)

STRICKLAND, Myles - desires that his creditors bring in their accounts (2 May)

Sloop is offered for sale by Thomas James, cooper, in Walnut St., over against Joseph Marks (2 May)

A bundle of compasses was found between Coultas's ferry and Schuylkill mill; apply to Richard Meggs, at Andrew Hamilton's plantation, near the Lower Ferry (2 May)

Pennsylvania House of Representatives considers a petition from sundry inhabitants of Bucks Co. relating to obstructions on Neshamineh Creek (9 May)

The privateer Raleigh, Capt. Codd, fitted out in Virginia, has taken a French ship and a sloop - Williamsburg item of 18 Apr. (9 May)

Schooner, belonging to Capt. Perrin, on 26 Mar. sailed out of York River but was sunk near Fleet's Bay; all aboard were drowned, including George Sibbald (brother of Capt. Sibbald of Phila.) and Graves Packe, age c. 18 (son of Mrs. Sarah Packe), of Williamsburg (9 May)

Message of Gov. Shirley to the Massachusetts Assembly (9 May)

POTTER, Capt. Simon, in a privateer of Newport - arrived Wednesday at Bristol; he and his consort, Capt. Gruchy of Boston, took a French prize, which Capt. Potter left in the custody of Capt. Gruchy; account of engagement of the 2 privateers with the French is given in detail in a New York item of 29 Apr. and more briefly in a Newport item of 26 Apr. (9 May); the above privateers lay claim to part of a prize lately taken by Capts. Richards and Jeffery; Capt. Sommers, at the order of Commodore Knowles, carried them into Antigua (9 May)

WISHMAN, Capt. - arrived at Phila. this morning from St. Kitts and yesterday the snow Hope, Andrew Andrews master, sent in by the privateer ship Marlborough, Christopher Clymer commander (9 May)

MEREDITH, Hugh, of Phila. - after the ensuing fair he will be ready to take in and print or stamp linen, cotton, etc. (9 May)

ROBESON, Peter - offers reward for recovery of horse strayed or stolen out of a pasture near John Cox's; horse may be brought to the Sign of the Indian King in Phila. (9 May)

BOOD, John - will sell 40 lots in Frankfort (9 May)

ALLEN, Nathaniel, Jr., in Front St., near Market St., Phila.
- sells Carolina reed (9 May)

Brick house in Burrough of Chester, on High St., is for
sale; enquire of the owner Edmund Bourk, living on the
premises (9 May)

Thirty-four lots, on Germantown Rd., in the Northern Liberties, between the Rising Sun and Mr. Logan's plantation;
apply to Anthony Nice, at the Rising Sun, or William
Parsons in Phila. (9 May)

WILLIAMS, Lewelin, Welsh servant, age c. 20 - runaway from
Thomas Bate, of Montgomery, Phila. Co. (9 May)

ROUSE, Capt. - arrived Thursday last at Boston from Canso;
Commodore Warren was at Canso, as was Capt. Durrell;
among prizes brought into Canso was a brigantine for-
merly commanded by Capt. Loring of Boston; this brigan-
tine, just before it fell into our hands, had taken
Capt. Adams in a schooner bound to Newfoundalnd; a
French ship was engaged by a Rhode Island sloop, by
Capt. Fletcher of Boston and later by Capt. Rouse, but
outsailed them; Capt. Donahew has taken 5 more enemy
Indians; Friday last Capt. Gayton sailed from Boston for
Canso; Capt. Partridge arrived at Boston yesterday from
Tinkouth near Newcastle, with European news; yesterday
arrived at Boston H.M.S. Princess Mary, Richard Edwards
commander - Boston items of 6 May (16 May)

EDWARDS, Richard - has been appointed Commander-in-chief
over Newfoundland and the forts and garrisons of Placentia - Boston item of 6 May (16 May)

Monday last arrived at New York the brigantine Clinton,
Capt. Bowne, from Belfast, who reported that the brigantine Antigua Pacquet, Capt. Helme, of New York, was
taken by a French privateer; Tuesday arrived at New
York the privateer Don Carlos, Abraham Kip commander,
and the same day arrived Capt. Troup, of New York, who
was taken as he was going into Coracoa; on Wednesday
arrived at New York Capt. Powers from Jamaica, who met
Capt. Brown in a sloop belonging to New York; Capt.
Powers spoke with Capt. Kierstede of New York; 3 days
before Capt. Powers sailed from Jamaica the ship Ruby,
Capt. White, arrived there from Bristol, in company
with the Salisbury, Capt. Harman - New York items of 13
May (16 May)

Thursday last arrived at Phila. the privateer Warren,

Capt. Kattur, and on Sunday her consort, the Old
George, Capt. Dougal; Capt. Middleton from Bermuda re-
ports that he was chased by 2 sloops; Capt. Bay from Ja-
maica reports that the Rosanna, Capt. Reason, bound to
Phila., was lost on one of the Keys; Capt. Howel from
Winyaw reports 3 enemy privateers on the Carolina coast;
Capt. Stanley, who arrived at Phila. on Tuesday last
from Boston, met Capt. Dennis with a Spanish prize;
Dennis and Conkland in concert have taken 17 prizes
since November last (16 May)

Two Indian traders returned to Phila. empty from Allegheny
as they were plundered by Peter Chartier (16 May)

ROBINSON, Thomas, in Second St., Phila. - will dispose of
the times of men and women servants (16 May)

Sugar and rum taken in the prize sloop St. Nicholas will
be sold on Mr. Hamilton's wharf in Phila. (16 May)

PASCHAL, Benjamin, late of Phila., smith, dec'd - accounts
with estate to be settled with Margaret Paschal, administratrix (16 May); his trade is elsewhere mentioned
as "cutler" (23 May)

BIDDLE, John - will sell tract of 100 acres in Towamenson
Twp., Phila. Co., about 6 miles from North Wales Meeting-
house; auction will be held at house of William Tennis,
innkeeper, in Towamenson (16 May)

GRIFFITTS, Isaac, at his store in Water St., Phila. -
sells raisins (16 May)

TIREWICK, Nicholas, convict servant, age c. 40, a miner -
runaway from Robert Cooke, of St. Mary's Co., Md. (16
May)

GOODMAN, William, Irish servant, age c. 30 - runaway from
Richard Loyd, of Darby, Chester Co. (16 May)

BOWNE, Capt. - arrived Saturday at Phila. from Providence
with news that Capt. John Gardner had taken may small
Spanish craft; Capt. Bowne on 4 May parted with Capt.
Ingoldsby in the privateer Dispatch of Rhode Island and
Capt. Thomas Hammond in the sloop Jenny bound for New
York; Ingoldsby, Hammond and Mr. Winslow were all well
(23 May)

A letter from Charlestown, S.C., confirms that Capt. William Clymer, of Phila., in company with the above
privateers, has carried in 2 French prizes (23 May)

A ship belonging to Phila., Capt. Young, was taken last
winter and carried into St. Maloes (23 May)

People of the _Polly_ privateer of New York, Capt. Morgan,
report that on Saturday last they struck on a shoal
halfway up our bay, called the Brown, but got ashore
at Muskmelon Creek (23 May)

Prize ship _Victory_ will be sold at auction at James's Coffee House in Phila.; inventory is to be seen at the
coffee house or at the house of Samuel Hasell (23 May)

WORRELL, Isaiah - will sell or let his plantation of 75
acres in Oxford Twp., near Franckfort, about 5 miles
from Phila. (23 May)

Reports have come from Albany that a body of French and
Indians is fitting out in Canada under M. Bilatre as
commander and with a son of M. Lanoo's and a M. Artel
under him, presumably against Annapolis Royal - Boston
item of 6 May (23 May)

It is reported that a large force of French and Indians
arrived at Menis and it was expected that troops would
come with M. Duvivier from France and Louisburg; an account of the importance of Annapolis Royal is given -
Boston item of 13 May (23 May)

COOPER, Capt., arrived at New York from Antigua, reports
that Capts. Jeffery and Richards were at Antigua awaiting the outcome of a suit; on Friday Capt. Conyers from
South Carolina reported that the snow _Cruizer_, Capt.
Clymer, of Phila., in company with Capt. Lemprier of
Jamaica and Capt. Pon of Charlestown, had brought in 2
large French prizes; Saturday arrived the privateer _Dol-
phin_, Capt. Langdon, and on 20 May Capt. Bayard from
Providence, who reported that the Dutch sloop taken by
them and the _Polly_, Capt. Morgan, has been condemned;
as they were going out of Providence, Capt. Grenall was
coming in; Capts. Gardner and Edwards have taken a
large ship bound from Havana to Augustine - New York
items of 20 May (23 May)

House near Franckfort, by the Race Bridge, in Oxford Twp.,
between the house and lot belonging to Samuel Finney and
the house late in the possession of Standish Ford, is
for sale; enquire of the Widow Finney, at Martha Chalkley's in Franckfort (23 May)

Eighteen lots fronting on Second St. in Trenton are for
sale; enquire of Ephraim Bonham, next door to William
Fisher's, hatter, in Arch St., Phila. (23 May)

Plantation of 152 acres, on the upper York Road, 16 miles
from Phila., in the Manor of Moreland, Phila. Co., is
for sale; enquire of Patrick Hunlon, near the place, or
Andrew Farrell, tanner, in Phila. (23 May)

Ship Hanover, Capt. Churchman, and the James River, Capt.
Kennon, bound from Bistol to Virginia, are taken and
carried to France - Williamsburg item of 9 May (30 May)

Ship Cunliff, Capt. John Pritchard, on passage from Maryland to Liverpool, fought engagement with a French privateer; Capt. Pritchard died of his wounds 3 days after
- Annapolis item of 17 May (30 May)

The Virginia privateer, Capt. Codd, has taken and sent into St. Kitts a prize - Annapolis item of 17 May (30 May)

MESERVY, Capt., late skipper of a schooner belonging to
Marblehead - came to Boston Friday last; his schooner
has been taken near the Isle of Sables by a French pri-
vateer, whose captain praised the bravery of Capt.
Rouse; the same day arrived Capt. Bennet from Cape
Breton - Boston items of 20 May (30 May)

Account of landing of English forces off Louisburg as given
by an officer on board the Massachusetts, Capt. Sanders;
Capt. Thompson informs that the English flag was flying
at the Light-house - Boston item of 20 May (30 May)

On Saturday arrived at Boston Capt. Donahew from Cape
Breton; he reports that Capt. Durrell in the Eltham and
Capt. Tyng in the Massachusetts had taken 2 ships near
Louisberg and Capt. Smethurst in the Prince of Orange
was to sail soon for Boston with several prizes - Boston
item of 20 May (30 May)

A letter from on board the Prince of Orange, Capt. Adams,
dated in Nantasket Road, 21 May, informs that on 29 Mar.
Capt. Knox arrived at Gravesend, that Capt. Griffiths
was taken and carried into Bayonne and that Capt. Bryant
was to sail a month after Capt. Adams - New York item of
27 May (30 May)

Saturday last Capt. Thomas Grenall, in the privateer
Batchelors, arrived at New York - New York item of 27
May (30 May)

French squadron has arrived at Martinico under M. Caylus,
who is to succeed the Marquis de Champigny in the land
command of the French islands; it is learnt that 2
French ships under M. Latouch were to cruise on the English trade; Admiral Medley was expected in the West Indies
(30 May)

502

TOWNSEND, Capt. (late commander of the brigantine _Tyger_,
of Rhode Island) arrived Monday last at Phila.; he was
taken by a Spanish privateer, Julian Joseph de la Vega
commander, just off the bar of Charlestown; Capt. Townsend reports that the Spaniards dare not stir out of
Augustine for fear of General Oglethorpe's Indians (30
May)

Saturday last the ship _Bohemia_ arrived at Chestertown in
Maryland, with news that the _Juliana_, Capt. Spencer, the
Revolution, Capt. Mills, and the _Swan_, Capt. Whitehair,
were all taken (30 May)

Capt. Morgan, late commander of the sloop _Polly_, lost in
our bay, has hired a sloop and set out for North Carolina from Chestertown (30 May)

Letter from Capt. William Clymer tells of engagement with
3 French ships and a sloop (30 May)

Tuesday last arrived at Phila. Capt. Kollock from Antigu
(30 May)

PLUMSTED, Clement, many years merchant and magistrate of
Phila., died Saturday night last; each mourner at his
funeral was given a copy of one of Bishop Tillotson's
sermons (30 May)

The new privateer ship _Pandour_, Capt. Dowel, and the new
George brigantine, Capt. Wood, are sailing in consort
(30 May)

MORGAN, Joseph, of Hopewell, N.J., sets forth a method for
the longitude (30 May)

House and lots in Germantown, adjoining to John Johnston's
are for sale; apply to Abraham or Joseph Luckon in Towamenson (30 May)

Tract of 250 acres in Plumsted Twp., Bucks Co., is offered
for sale by Benjamin Kendall; for conditions of sale apply to Henry Hudelston in said twp. or Peter Stretch in
Phila. (30 May)

Tract of 102 acres, in Roxbury Twp., about 8 miles from
Phila., joining on the River Schuylkill and Whissebickon
Creek and on the land of Isaac Cook, is to be sold; apply to Rebecca Gorsuch, living in Providence, Chester Co.
(30 May)

ROCKHILL, Edward - offers reward for recovery of gelding
strayed or stolen from his plantation in Bethlehem,

Hunterdon Co. (30 May)

MATTHIAS, John, of Franconia Twp., Phila. Co. - his wife, Jane Matthias (<u>alias</u> Jane Jones), has eloped from him (30 May)

GRIFFITH, David, often convicted of horse-stealing - escaped from Goal of Lancaster; reward for his capture will be paid by Joseph Pugh, sub-sheriff of Lancaster Co. (30 May)

TRONE, Michael, native Irishman, convicted of felony - same as above

DAVIS, John, servant, age <u>c</u>. 18 or 19 - runaway from Daniel Cooper, of Phila. - servant may be brought to Peter Brown's, at the ferry-house in Phila. (30 May)

SCOTTON, Samuel, living at Nicholas Croan's in Front St., Phila. - offers reward for recovery of pocket book lost about Market St. wharf (30 May)

Account of the Cape Breton expedition; mentioned are Capts. Bennet and Donahew, Lt.-Gen. Pepperrell, Commodore Warren, Capts. Fletcher, Saunders and Bosch, Col. Bradstreet, Col. Waldo, Capt. Tyng, Col. Moulton, Capt. Rouse, Capt. Jacques and M. Duvivier - Boston item of 21 May (6 June)

On Saturday last Capt. Donahew sailed from Boston for the fleet before Louisburgh and today Capt. Bennet sails for the same - Boston item of 27 May (6 June)

POATE, Capt., in an ordinance schooner which lately sailed from Boston for Annapolis Royal, has been taken - Boston item of 27 May (6 June)

Friday last arrived at New York the privateer sloop <u>Clinton</u>, Capt. Seymour, and the sloop <u>Mary Anne</u>, late Capt. Tucker, now Capt. Leonard; Capt. Tucker had been shot - New York item of 3 June (6 June)

Gentlemen appointed at New York to receive subscriptions to buy supplies for the forces before Louisbourg are to meet at Mr. De Joncourt's Wednesday next - New York item of 3 June (6 June)

COULTAS, James, at the Middle Ferry on Schuylkill, has taken up a mare (6 June)

HILLEGAS, George Peter, late of Franckfort, dec'd - accounts with estate to be settled with John Philip Told and George Beshishee, administrators (6 June)

WHITE, Thomas - offers reward for recovery of mare, strayed or stolen from his plantation in Bristol Twp., Phila. Co. (6 June)

FOULK, Judah, gives notice that he has been appointed Collector of Excise for City and County of Phila., in place of Rees Meredith, resigned (6 June)

SHENTON, Frederick - offers reward if John Harris, born in Monmouth Co., age 28, who deserted from Col. Trelawny's Regt., is delivered to Mr. Whitehead, keeper of the Phila. Goal (6 June)

Plantation of 400 acres on Neshaminy Creek, adjoining to the ferry, is to be sold by the owner, Archibald Anderson, living on the premises, adjoining to Baldwin's ferry (6 June)

WILSON, John, Irish servant, age c. 20 - runaway from Thomas Allfree, of Thoroughfare Neck, Newcastle Co. (6 June)

CARREL, John, Irish servant, age c. 26 - runaway (taking his wife, who may go by name of Mary Umphrey, Cochran or Carrel) from William Williams, of Radnor Twp., Chester Co. (6 June)

VEPON, William, servant, age c. 50 - runaway from Anthony Lee; reward for his capture will be paid by said Lee or by Joseph Gray, at the Conestoge Wagon, Phila. (6 June)

A fine sloop, belonging to Col. Mackenzie, is being made ready by the Governor and Council to defend the Virginia coast - Williamsburg item of 23 May (6 June)

Thursday last arrived at Boston Capt. Smith with expresses from Lt.-Gen. Pepperel and Commodore Warren; on 18 May the Mermaid, Capt. Douglass, and the Shirley Galley, Capt. Rouse, engaged the Vigilant, the Marquis de Maisonfort commander; she struck, and command of her was given to Capt. Douglass, while command of the Mermaid was given to to Mr. Montague; list of ships in the fleet before Louisbourg is given, including Capts. Edwards and Cornwall - Boston items of 3 June (13 June)

BASTIDE, Capt., Chief Engineer in Nova Scotia, has joined the army before Louisburg - Boston item of 3 June (13 June)

Yesterday Capt. Ingersol, in a privateer belonging to Boston, arrived at Salem with a French ship he had taken in

company with Capt. Morris of Rhode Island - Boston item
of 3 June (13 June)

A small sloop commanded by one Loyd took and brought into
Nevis a French Guineaman with 370 Negroes and a great
quantity of gold dust and elephants' teeth - Letter from
Nevis dated 5 May (13 June)

Tuesday last arrived at New York the sloops Castor and
Pollux, Capt. Easom and Capt. Burgess, with a snow re-
taken from a Spanish privateer - New York item of 10
June (13 June)

REES, Capt., from Antigua - reports at Phila. that the
schooner Charming Peggy, Capt. Strawbridge of Phila., was
taken and carried to Guadeloup (13 June)

MEAS, Capt., from Jamaica, reports at Phila. that Capt. Renton and the Drake brought in prizes and that Capt. Rolans
in the privateer sloop Henry, of Barbados, brought in a
Swedish ship as a prize (13 June)

The Art of Preserving Health, by Dr. Armstrong - is printed
and sold by B. Franklin (13 June)

Tract of land in Franckfort Road, about 1¼ miles from Phila.
is for sale; agree with Timothy Scarth, tanner, in the
Northern Liberties (13 June)

TREGO, James, dec'd - accounts with estate to be settled
at late dwelling-house of said Trego with James Trego,
administrator (13 June)

MORGAN, William, English servant, age c. 37, who lately
followed flatting up Delaware - runaway from Henry Fagan
of Marple Twp., Chester Co. (13 June)

MARTIN, Richard, of Cheltenham Twp., Phila. Co. - has taken
up a horse (13 June)

The Tryal snow, William Jefferies master - has been seized
and sold at Havana; the Henry and Mary privateer, Capt.
Joseph Scarling, has sailed on a cruize - Charlestown
items of 18 and 25 May (20 June)

PERKINS, Capt. - arrived 2 June at Boston from St. Kitts,
in whom came Capt. Dourick, who had been taken and carried into Porto Rico; Dourick gives the following list
of masters whose vessels were taken and carried there:
Bromedge, Harman, Dowrick, Narin, Myrine, Boggs, Durham,
Gullifer, Hudson, Jennins, Herod, Frost, Troop, Hutchins,
Buffen, Jones - Boston item of 10 June (20 June)

One M. Gautie, a man of note among the French inhabitants
near the fort at Annapolis Royal, went away with the
countrymen (20 June)

McDANIEL, Capt. - was taken by the enemy - Boston item of
10 June (20 June)

SALTER, Capt., arrived at Boston from Newfoundland - reports that no men-of-war had arrived at Newfoundland -
Boston item of 10 June (20 June)

MORRIS, Gov., of New Jersey - had Assembly of New Jersey
prepare bill to send 2,000 pounds to Gov. Shirley of
Massachusetts for use of H.M.'s subjects at Cape Breton
- Boston item of 10 June (20 June)

List of Massachusetts naval vessels in N.M.'s service
against Cape Breton includes those commanded by Capts.
Tyng, Snelling, Rowse, Smethurst, Fletcher, Donahew,
Saunders, Bosch; also a ship, Capt. Griffin, and a snow,
Capt. Thompson, both hired of Rhode Island merchants -
Boston item of 10 June (20 June)

MESNARD, Capt., from Coracoa, reports at New York that
Capt. Stiles, in a sloop from New York, was taken by a
French privateer - New York item of 17 June (20 June)

SCHERMERHORNE, Capt., from South Carolina - reports on
movement of naval vessels - New York item of 17 June (20
June)

MARTYN, Richard, of Cheltenham, an eminent man in that
neighborhood, on 12 June stuck his heel against a scythe
that lay on the ground and died in a few hours (20 June)

BURROUGHS, Capt., arrived Saturday at Phila. from Ireland;
the snow George, Capt. Ambler, from Phila., was cast away
on the North Bull; Capt. Darrel, from Barbados, reports
2 more men-of-war have arrived there; Capt. Evans arrived Saturday at Phila. from Newcastle; the Caesar privateer, Capt. Noarth (belonging to Cowes, but bound to
Phila.), was taken in the Channel; Capt. Rivers of
Phila. was coming home, passenger in the Caesar; Capt.
Christopher Clymer, commander of the privateer Marlborough of Phila., has taken a small sloop; the Trembleur
privateer of Phila. lately careened at Bermudas; the
prizes carried into Charlestown, S.C., by the privateer
Cruizer, Capt. William Clymer, and 2 others, are divided
into shares; each man in the Cruizer gets about 70 pounds
- Phila. items of 20 June (20 June)

EVANS, Peter, Esq., eminent counsellor at law and many

years Collector of Customs for Phila., died Friday last
at Phila. (20 June)

SHENTON, Frederick - offers money to masters who will allow
their servants to enlist under Col. Trelawny (20 June)

COTTINGER, Thomas, from London - has removed from the Sign
of the Green Stays in Chesnut St. to the Sign of the
Green Stays in Arch St., next door to Septimus Robinson
(20 June)

Brigantine Argyle, John Elliot commander, now at Mr. Powel's
wharf - will sail for Barbados; for freight or passage
agree with Capt. John Seymour at Mrs. Stapleford's in
Phila. (20 June)

BRISTOL, Dan - will sell 8 lots in Oxford Twp., on Burlington Road, ¼ mile beyond Franckfort (20 June)

MILLER, George - offers reward for recovery of a horse
strayed or stolen off the Commons of Phila. (20 June)

WILSON, John, convict servant, age c. 27 - runaway from
Gunpowder Ironworks, Baltimore Co., Md.; reward for his
capture will be paid by Stephen Onion (20 June)

SOWARD, Lawrence, Irish servant, age c. 20 - runaway from
Thomas Shipley, of Ridley Twp., Chester Co. (20 June)

DANIELS, Richard, English servant - runaway from Joseph
Beaks, of Phila., drayman (20 June)

John, Negro, born in Dominica, who speaks French but little
English - runaway from the sloop Sparrow, lately arrived
from Barbados, Joseph Perry commander; whoever brings
him to John Yeats, merchant, at Phila., will receive a
reward (20 June)

LOVE, Joseph - offers reward for recovery of pair of silver
shoe-buckles, lost between the market-house and the Middle Ferry, marked I L and A S; reward will be paid if
they are brought to the Indian King in Phila. (20 June)

NIXON, Thomas, in Strawberry Alley, opposite the Butchers
Shambles in Phila. - sells spirit of Lavender (20 June)

H.M.S. Tartar, Henry Ward commander, arrived Thursday last
at Charlestown from a cruize - Charlestown item of 10
June (27 June)

On 15 June a schooner, Capt. Giddings master, arrived at
Boston from Cape Breton with expresses from Lt.-Gen.

Pepperell and Commodore Warren; Mr. Bastide had arrived at Canso; Commodore Warren sent Capts. Rouse, Tyng and Thomson to assist the garrison at Annapolis Royal - Boston items of 17 June (27 June)

MORGAN, Capt. (late commander of a New York privateer) has been apprehended in Norfolk on the road to North Carolina and committed to prison - extract of letter from Williamsburg dated 14 June (27 June)

Whaling vessel belonging to Cape Cod, Edmund Freeman master, arrived Friday last at Phila., bringing 83 English prisoners who had been taken by a Spanish privateer off the coast of Virginia from the vessels of the following masters: Capts. Brown, McMullen, Joseph Coleman; Capt. McMullen had rescued the crew of the bilander Warren, Capt. Gordon master (27 June)

A privateer snow belonging to Jamaica, Capt. Mackey, is lost on the coast of Florida (27 June)

Last night arrived at Phila. a vessel from Providence, with Capt. Spafford of Phila. (whose ship had been taken by Don Juan Fernando) and Capt. Spry (late of the Comet Bomb) (27 June)

TUCKER, Capt., from New York, was taken and carried into Havana; Capt. Rouse took 3 mortars and shells from Annapolis Royal for the use of the army at Cape Breton; Capt. Gayton was expected at Boston with transports and some 900 prisoners (27 June)

Plantation of 1,250 acres, between Capt. Nichols and Mr. Smith, in Orange Co., 4 miles from the waterside, is for sale; apply to Dr. Dupuy in New York or Daniel Dupuy, goldsmith, in Phila. (27 June)

WILLIAMS, John, Welsh convict servant, tinker, and convict woman servant who calls herself Margaret Williams, both bought together at Annapolis on 16 Jan. 1744 - runaways from Hugh Conn, near Bladensburg, Prince George's Co. (27 June)

JOHN, David, Sr., carpenter - cautions people not to take any mortgage on tract of land in Charles-Town, Cheste Co., belonging to him from John Jones and David John, Jr., who have not complied with the conditions of the rights they had to the land (27 June)

TURNBULL, Thomas, at the house of John Stoup, tailor, next door to Mr. Currie's in Front St., Phila. - has times of a parcel of Scotch servants to dispose of (27 June)

Twenty-one lots, 6 of which front on Burlington Road and house (where James McVough now keeps public house, on Franckfort Rd., 5 miles from Phila.) are for sale by auction at said house, where attendance will be given by Rebecca McVough, executrix of Isaac Worall, dec'd (27 June)

Eight acres, frame house, brick house and tanyard in Salem, N.J., are to be sold by Rebecca Edgell; apply to William Murdoch at Salem (27 June)

FOWLER, Peter, servant, born in Ireland, age c. 22, who has been in Pennsylvania nearly 4 years - runaway from William Hartley, living in Charles-Town, Chester Co.; reward for his capture will be paid by said Hartley or by Joseph Goodwin, bookbinder, in Black Horse Alley, Phila. (27 June)

NEAL, Valentine, Irish servant - runaway from Jacob Warrick, of Upper Freehold, Monmouth Co., N.J. (27 June)

GALLOWAY, John, servant, age c. 25, shoemaker - runaway from Hinson Wright, living in Queen Anne's Co., Mid. (27 June)

EVANS, John, servant - runaway from George Monrow, of Newcastle (27 June)

LEE, Thomas, of Upper Marlborough, Md. - offers reward for recovery of a bay gelding (brought from the northward by Anthony Whitehead Waters for John Darnall and by him disposed of to Charles Carroll, Esq., of whom Thomas Lee bought him), strayed or stolen; reward will be paid if horse is delivered to Thomas Lee at Upper Marlborough, John Frazer at Annapolis, Alexander Lawson in Baltimore Co., or Alexander Campbell in Phila. (27 June)

TUNIS, John, of Elizabeth Town, East Jersey - offers reward for recovery of his horse, which was stolen from James Banks, of Newark, East Jersey (27 June)

WHELLEN, John, Irish servant - runaway from Joseph James, of Willistown, Chester Co. (27 June)

Among ships arrived at Boston from the fleet before Louisbourg are those of Capts. Gayton, Snelling and Griffiths; Capt. Rouse, in an engagement with a French privateer, had not one man hurt; account from Annapolis Royal of activities of Capts. Rouse and Tyng and the engineer, Mr. Bastide; Capt. Snelling will sail from Boston with seamen to help man the Vigilant man-of-war - Boston items of 24 June (4 July)

BROWN, Capt., of New York (who was lately taken and car-
ried to Martineco) arrived this morning at New York from
Antigua; Capt. Threlkeld of New York, in the brigantine
William, and Capt. Arrowsmith, of New York, in the sloop
Emilia, have been taken by the same privateer who took
Capt. Stiles; Capt. Kierstede of New York has taken a
French privateer - New York items of 1 July (4 July)

GARDNER, John, in a letter from New Providence dated 10
May, describes his activity as privateer, tells how the
Spanish prisoners on his vessel rose against him and how
he saved the life of his lieutenant, Roger Bow (4 July)

Capt. Stiles from Bermuda reports the vessels of the following English captains recently taken in the West Indies: Harvey, Butterfield, Henry Jennings, Richard
Durham, Francis Cooper, Benjamin Wilkinson, William Cox,
William Tucker and Benjamin Jones (4 July)

LYFORD, Capt. William, whose ship was crippled in a storm,
put in at Havana, where he was generously allowed to refit
and pursue his voyage (4 July)

It is reported from Tenton that on 21 June 2 lads, Benjamin
and Severns Albertis, brothers, were fishing near the
falls; their canoe overset and Severns was drowned (4
July)

HOLMES, John, belonging to a Phila. privateer, was accidentally drowned a few days ago when he fell into the
river between the boat and the vessel (4 July)

CARTER, Charles, living near the falls of Rappahanock, will
dispose of tracts of land in Virginia at Fredericksburg
at the October Fair (4 July)

House and lot of the late William Chancellor, now in the
possession of James Murgatroyd, in Second St., Phila.,
will be sold at James's Coffee House (4 July)

Persons having books belonging to the estate of Peter Evans,
gent., dec'd, are desired to bring them to Peter Robertson or leave them at the house of David Franks, where the
dec'd lately dwelt (4 July)

Ferry over Delaware River, in Plumstead Twp., Bucks Co.,
near the mouth of Towhicon, is for sale; apply to Daniel
Dawson, hatter, in Phila. (4 July)

Capts. Allen and Cranston, in 2 Rhode Island privateers, a
few days ago off Martineco took a French ship - extract
of letter from Antigua, dated 3 June (11 July)

CANNON, Capt., who arrived at New York last week from Boston, informed that on 1 July Capt. Smith, in a sloop belonging to New London, arrived at Tarpaulin Cove; Smith had been taken by the French and ransomed; yesterday Capt. Alexander Troup, late master of the brigantine William & Sarah, of New York, arrived at New York; he had been taken by a Spanish privateer; on 7 June he sailed on board the brigantine Tryal, J. Evans master, bound to Phila., but this also was taken by the Spaniards, who then took a schooner belonging to Tortola, bound to New York, Peter Blunder master; Capts. Evans and Blunder were carried away prisoners - New York items of 8 July (11 July)

Capt. Potter arrived Tuesday at Phila. from St. Christophers and last night the brigantine Hannah, Capt. England from Antigua; a schooner belonging to Phila., Capt. Cox, has been taken; Capt. Martin has safely arrived in England - Phila. items of 11 July (11 July)

Partnership between Blair and Macilvaine in Phila. - has expired (11 July; 1 Aug.)

HARTLEY, William, of Charlestown, Ranger for Chester Co., lists the strays in his hands (11 July)

SIMS, Joseph, in Front St., Phila. - has for sale a young Negro woman and her 3 children (11 July)

HOGAN, Dominick, Irish convict servant - runaway from the Patapsco Ironworks in Baltimore Co., Md.; he belongs to Benjamin Tasker, Esq., and Co.; reward for capture of the runaway will be paid by Richard Croxall (11 July; 5 Sept.)

JOLLY, Matthew, Irish convict servant, age $\underline{c}$. 22 - same as above

KIRK, Henry, Irish convict servant, age $\underline{c}$. 22, butcher - same as above

CARPENTER, Abraham - offers reward for recovery of periagua, stolen or gone adrift from Nehemiah Allen's wharf in Phila. (11 July)

HASTINGS, Samuel - will sell 12 lots in Vine St., Phila. (11 July)

MALBONE, Godfrey - made a celebration at this house yesterday when news came of the surrender of Cape Breton - Newport item of 5 July (18 July)

Account in letter from Coracoa of action in which Capt.

Leary in a Barbados privateer took a Spanish sloop;
Capt. Brown who arrived 14 July at New York from Coracoa
gave a further notice of the affair; a French privateer
has taken a sloop commanded by Capt. Paul Painter and the
brigantine Habakkuk, commanded by Capt. Woodford - New
York items of 15 July (18 July)

Friday last arrived at New York 3 privateers, the ship Lincoln, Capt. Jauncy, the brigantine Triton, Capt. Rosewel,
and a sloop belonging to Antigua - New York item of 15
July (18 July)

ALBERTSON, Capt., who arrived at Phila. Saturday last from
Providence, reports that the Havanna Galley, commanded
by Capt. Thomson, is gone out on a cruize (18 July)

FRANKLIN, Benjamin, in Market St., Phila. - has just published a Collection of Sermons (by Ebenezer Erskine and
Ralph Erskine, with preface by Rev. Thomas Bradbury)
(18 July)

Plantation of 250 acres in Willistown, Chester Co., is for
sale; apply to Samuel Pennock, Third St., Phila., or
Joseph Pennock, West Marlborough, Chester Co. (18 July)

CARPENTER, Samuel - will sell mares, colts, horses, cows,
etc., at Dr. Zachary's plantation near the vineyard,
on the road to Andrew Robeson's mill (18 July)

CLARK, Henry, at the Sign of the Coach and Horses, opposite
to the State House in Phila. - sells dogs and wheels for
roasting meat; a variety of entertainment is to be
seen there (18 July)

McCALL, William, Scotch servant, age c. 40, carpenter -
runaway from John Nelson, of Phila. (18 July)

DEWEES, William, of Whitemarsh Twp. - has taken up a stray
mare and horse (18 July)

CLARK, Thomas, of West Caln, Chester Co. - has taken up a
stray mare (18 July)

Tuesday arrived at Nantasket from the harbour of Louisbourg H.M.S. Hector, Capt. Cornwall, with 100 French inhabitants of the place; 14 July arrived at Boston Capt.
Saunders from Cape Breton; Capt. Rouse was to sail for
England; Capt. Donahew has had engagements with several
vessels manned by French and Indians - Boston items of
15 July (25 July)

It is reported at New York that the ship Albany, Capt.

Bryant, bound from London to New York, was in the Downs on 23 May - New York item of 22 July (25 July)

A letter from Anguilla dated 29 May 1945 gives account of French attempt to take the island on 21 May; they were repulsed by Gov. Arthur Hodge, Capt. Richardson and some 95 men; among the killed were M. Le Touch, Capt. Rolough, Bonar (the French pilot), the son of the Gov. of St. Bartholomew's (25 July)

Capt. Hogg, from St. Christophers, brings news that Capt. Christopher Clymer of Phila. and 2 New York privateers have taken a register ship (25 July)

GOUVERNEUR, Nicholas and Isaac, merchants now residing at Corocoa, by Brandt Schuyler, offer reward for discovery of author or authors of report that they are concerned with a French privateer (25 July)

CROWLEY, Dennis, Irish servant, age c. 16 - runaway from Joel Bailey, of West Marlborough, Chester Co. (25 July)

Fourth part of grist-mill, commonly called Richard Thomas's Mill, in the Great Valley, Chester Co., is to be sold; enquire of Samuel Jones, in Uwchland, Chester Co., or Samuel Austin, in Mulberry St., Phila. (25 July)

KING, Thomas, Irish servant, age c. 36, who has been in this country about 20 years - runaway from Edward Mortimore, of Baltimore Co., Md. (25 July)

Account of the reduction of Louisbourg as reprinted from the Boston Evening-Post of 15 July (1 Aug.)

Paragraph of a letter from Capt. David Donahew, commander of the sloop Resolution, dated Canso Passage, 26 June he mentions Capts. Becket and Fones - Boston item of 22 July (1 Aug.)

DONAHEW, Capt. - on the 4 or 5 July, being in the Gut of Canso, went ashore where he, his brother (Lt.), master, chief mate, gunner, steward, quartermaster and boatswain were all killed by the Indians - Boston item of 22 July (1 Aug.)

At desire of Commodore Warren, all vessels carrying provisions to Louisbourg, by order of the Governor of Pennsylvania, will trade free of duty or impositions (1 Aug.)

STUTESBERRY, Robert, of Wrights Town, Bucks Co. - offers for sale a plantation of 171 acres (1 Aug.)

RADLEY, Daniel, late of Phila., dec'd - his late dwelling, containing 22 feet in breadth on Walnut St. and bounded north by Dr. Zachary's lot, is offered for sale by Samuel Powel, executor to the estate of said Radley (1 Aug.)

PARKER, William - offers for sale about 30 lots in Kensington, adjoining upon Franckfort Rd., opposite the Bell Inn (1 Aug.)

HART, John - offers for sale a large new brick house, in which he lives, on Front St., Phila., adjoining Jonathan Mifflin's (1 Aug.)

DAVIS, David, of Lower Merion, Phila. Co., fuller - designs to take in work in Phila. at Thomas Wooley's, at the Sign of the White Horse, opposite to the Prebyterian Meetinghouse (1 Aug.)

RIGHBY, John, who says he came from Cheshire, England - stole various items from Benjamin Harvey, of Maxfield Twp., Bucks Co., and a horse from Anthony Tate of Newtown (1 Aug.)

KANTON, Francis, servant, age c. 22 - runaway from John Harper, of the Manor of Moreland, Phila. Co. (1 Aug.)

HUGHS, John, servant, age c. 15 - runaway from Samuel Butcher, of Moreland, Phila. Co. - reward will be paid for his capture by Samuel Butcher and Joseph James (1 Aug.)

THOMPSON, John, who pretends to be a surgeon - runaway from on board the Brigantine Rebecca, John Childs commander; reward for his capture will be paid by Charles Edgar, Joseph Marks or Archibald Montgomery (1 Aug.)

JAMES, John - has for sale 2 houses on High St. in the Borough of Wilmington, Newcastle Co. (1 Aug.)

George, Mulatto Spanish slave, age c. 24, born at Havana, shoemaker, who says he was several years with Don Blass - runaway from Bennet Bard, of Burlington (1 Aug.)

MALONEY, Timothy, Irish servant, age c. 20 - runaway from Fretwell Wright, of Burlington (in company with Bennet Bard's man) (1 Aug.)

CARMICHAEL, William, Irish servant, age c. 30 - runaway from William Macarslon, in Laycock Twp., Lancaster Co. (1 Aug.)

DAVIS, James, Irish servant, age between 30 and 40, weaver - runaway from Samuel Richey, of Phila., weaver (1 Aug.)

HUMPHREYS, Jonathan, of Blockley, within 5 miles of Phila.,
near Conestogo Rd. - makes and sells screws; they also
may be bought from Joseph Gray, in High St., Phila., at
the Sign of the Conestogo Waggon (1 Aug.)

STRETTELL, R. & A. - sell wine, cloth, cutlery, ironmongery
(1 Aug.)

Tract of 250 acres in Plumsted Twp., Bucks Co., is for
sale; apply to Henry Hudelston, of Plumsted Twp., or
Peter Stretch in Phila., or Benjamin Kendall, the owner,
in Chester (1 Aug.)

ROBESON, Peter - will pay reward if horse strayed or stolen
out of a pasture near John Cox's is brought to the Sign
of the Indian King in Phila. (1 Aug.)

Call for volunteers for Edward Trelawny's Regt. of Foot in
Jamaica; the recruiting officer attends from 12 to 2 at
Mrs. Roberts's Coffee-house in Front St., Phila. (1 Aug.)

Account of the siege and surrender of Louisburg; dispatches
of the surrender were brought from General Pepperel and
Commodore Warren by Capt. Bennet; mention is made of 2
brave French officers, Mr. Boullarderie and Mr. Morpang;
a 64-gun French ship was engaged by Capt. Douglass in the
Mermaid and then taken by the Commodore and the rest of
the American fleet (supplement to the Pa. Gazette No.
868)

PICKET, Mr. (steward to the late Capt. Donahew) - arrived
Saturday last at Boston from Annapolis Royal and related
the story of the murder of Capt. Donahew - Boston item
of 29 July (8 Aug.)

THOMPSON, Capt., in the Rhode Island ship in the service of
the Massachusetts govt. - arrived at Boston Saturday last
in 17 days from Louisburg - Boston item of 29 July (8 Aug.)

SNELLING, Capt. - arrived last night at Boston from Louisburg; he reported that Capt. Fletcher had taken a large
schooner; Capt. Tyng in the Massachusetts is daily expected at Boston - Boston item of 29 July (8 Aug.)

RAPER, Caleb, Mayor of Burlington - died there Saturday
last (8 Aug.)

GRIFFITTS, Isaac - offers reward for discovery of thief who
stole new tackle rope from his granary in Phila. (8 Aug.)

SULLIVAN, Daniel, Irish servant, age c. 30, carpenter -
runaway from Samuel Smith, of Annapolis (8 Aug.)

BOURNE, Jesse, who lately removed to Samuel Neave's store, opposite Fishbourne's wharf in Phila. - all persons indebted to him are desired to make payment (8 Aug.)

SMITH, John, intending for England - wishes all accounts to be settled (8 Aug.)

SHENTON, Frederick - offers reward for delivery to him of any soldier attempting to sell his regimental clothing (8 Aug.)

HOLAND, Richard, English servant, age c. 20, shoemaker - runaway from Zachariah Robins, of Upper Freehold, Monmouth Co., East Jersey (8 Aug.)

GEORGE, Richard, of Merion, Phila. Co. - has taken up a horse (8 Aug.)

TYNG, Capt. - arrived last Monday at Boston and in a day or 2 will sail for Louisburg; Capt. Fletcher has taken a schooner - Boston item of 5 Aug. (15 Aug.)

WHITEFIELD, Rev. - in July preached for Rev. White at Hardwicke, at Quabin (where there is no minister), for Rev. Abercrombie of Pelham, for Rev. Edwards at Northampton, for Mr. Judd at Northampton, for Rev. Williams at Hadley, for Rev. Parsons at the Swamp, for Rev. Billings at Cold Spring, for Rev. Trowbridge, for Rev. Harvey at Kensington - Boston item of 5 Aug. (15 Aug.)

Thursday last arrived at New York Capt. John Smith and Saturday last Capt. Asa King, both from Jamaica - New York item of 12 Aug. (15 Aug.)

MOOR, Peter - was convicted Monday last in New York of uttering counterfeit pieces of eight (15 Aug.)

WRIGHT, Capt., from Bermudas reports that Capt. Skinner in a privateer had retaken a sloop commanded by Capt. Hinson (15 Aug.)

MORRIS, Capt., from Jamaica, reports that Capt. Wallace, bound from Phila. to Jamaica, was taken and carried to Leoganne (15 Aug.)

Ship Sarah Galley, Capt. Letchford, from Phila. - ran ashore on the Breakers at Port Morant (15 Aug.)

Schooner King Tammony, Capt. Bay, belonging to Phila., bound to Newfoundland - ran upon the rocks when warping into St. John's (15 Aug.)

N. Walton and W. Hetherington, in the sail loft late belonging to William Chancellor - teach writing, arithmetic and accounting (15 Aug.)

Plantation on the upper York Rd., 16 miles from Phila. in
the Manor of Moreland, Phila. Co. is for sale; enquire
of Patrick Hunlon, near the place, or Andrew Farrel,
tanner, in Phila. (15 Aug.)

Plantation of 50 acres, 2 miles from Oxford Church, is for
sale; enquire of Barnard Taylor at said plantation or
Solomon Fussell in Phila. (15 Aug.)

SCOT, Robert, of Whitemarsh, Phila. Co. - has taken up a
grey horse (15 Aug.)

MACCOY, Alexander, Highland Scotch servant, age c. 30 -
runaway from Patrick Doran, living in Annapolis (15 Aug.)

KING, Charles, English convict servant, age c. 30 - runaway
from George Brown, at Joppa, Baltimore Co., Md. (15 Aug.)

EWINGS, George, master of the Talbot County School, an
Irishman - runaway from said school; he took with him a
Negro named Nero; reward for their capture is offered by
William Goldsborough, Register of said school (15 Aug.)

RIDGWAY, John, born in Cheshire, age c. 40 - escaped from
Anthony Tate, near Newtown Goal, Bucks Co. (15 Aug.)

Iron-plaiting works and smith's shop, of the estate of Isaac
Harrow, dec'd - to be sold in Trenton; enquire of Anthony
Morris in Phila. or William Morris in Trenton (15 Aug.)

GRAFTON, Mary, on Society Hill - sells cloth, needles,
knives, books, sealing wax, etc. (15 Aug.)

MACMULLEN, John, Irish servant, age c. 17 - runaway from
Enos Lewis, of North Wales Twp., Phila Co. (15 Aug.)

HODGES, Capt. - arrived Tuesday last at Boston from Louisburg
with news of a very rich prize taken - Boston item of
12 Aug. (22 Aug.)

TYNG, Capt. - sailed Thursday last from Boston for Louisburg
in the Massachusetts frigate - Boston item of 12 Aug. (22
Aug.)

Paragraph of letter from Commodore Warren, dated Louisburg
17 July, to Thomas Lechmore, Esq., mentions General
Pepperell (22 Aug.)

GRACE, Capt. - arrived Friday last at Boston from Gibraltar - Boston item of 12 Aug. (22 Aug.)

The following vessels are fitting out at Boston to cruise in consort: privateer Brigantine Hawk, Capt. Philip Bass, and brigantine Ranger, Capt. Edward Fryer - Boston item of 12 Aug. (22 Aug.)

GREEN, Capt. from Providence - reports that the Havannah Galley (taken by Capt. Dennis and now commanded by Capt. Thompson) has taken 2 French prizes (22 Aug.)

Snow Dreadnaught, John Cunningham commander - is fitting out for a cruizing voyage; those wishing to join may repair to the commander or to the Sign of the Boatswain and Call near the drawbridge in Phila. (22 Aug.)

MORGAN, John, intending for England - wishes to settle all accounts (22 Aug.)

HARTLEY, William, ranger, of Chester Co. - has taken up some horses (22 Aug.)

JENKINS, John, of Trenton - has for sale tract of land in Bethlehem Twp., Hunterdon Co., West Jersey, joining to John Anderson's plantation, within half a mile of Irish's Works (22 Aug.)

House on east side of Second St., where Dr. Farmer now lives, is for sale - enquire of John Knight, at Joseph Stretch's, hatter, in Second St., Phila. (22 Aug.)

JARVIS, Thomas, at the Sign of the Free Mason, in Front St., Phila. - offers reward for recovery of a gelding, belonging to Robert White of Phila., that strayed or was stolen from a field near William Coats's pasture (22 Aug.)

BAZELEY, Stephen, late of Phila., dec'd - accounts with estate to be settled with Hannah Bazeley, widow of the dec'd and administratrix; she has blockmaker's tools to dispose of (22 Aug.; 3 Oct.)

Dick, a Negro, called "Preaching Dick" - runaway from Robert Grace, of Phila. (22 Aug.)

LOYD, Richard, Welsh servant, age c. 26 - runaway from Arthur Murphy, of Bucks Co., in the Falls Twp., Pensbury (22 Aug.)

SHELLEY, Abraham, Keeper of the Phila. Workhouse - has taken up a man who calls himself John White, age between 20 and 30 (22 Aug.)

STROUD, James - has taken up a mare at his plantation at Whitemarsh, Phila. Co. (22 Aug.)

KENARD, John, of Phila. - his wife Margaret has eloped from him (22 Aug.)

DUTHY, Capt. William, late of the sloop _Triumvir_, of and from Charlestown, for Rattan, which was taken by a French privateer, has returned to Charlestown and reports that Capt. Cars, from Scotland, bound for Charlestown, was also taken - Charlestown item of 12 July (29 Aug.)

Account of capture of a 22-gun French ship by Capts. Fletcher and Durell - extract of a letter from a sea officer at Louisburg - Boston item of 19 Aug. (29 Aug.)

Privateer sloop _Clinton_, Thomas Bevan commander - brought a French prize into New York Friday last - New York item of 26 Aug. (29 Aug.)

Privateers brigantine _Castor_, Capt. Easom, and sloop _Pollux_, Capt. Burges - have left New York to proceed on a cruize (29 Aug.)

Privateer brigantine _Hester_, Capt. Grenall - has taken a prize - New York item of 26 Aug. (29 Aug.)

TATEM, Capt. - Friday last arrived at Phila. from Jamaica; he reported that a vessel from New York, Capt. Stout, was taken but soon retaken by an English man-of-war (29 Aug.)

Privateer snow _Cruizer_, of Phila., Capt. William Clymer - arrived Saturday last at Phila. from South Carolina (29 Aug.)

REES, Capt. from Antigua - arrived at Phila. last night and reported that the _Fame_ sloop-of-war sprung a leak and had to run ashore at Anguilla (29 Aug.)

CORBET, Thomas, age 29, labourer - has deserted from Edward Trelawney's Regt.; reward for his capture will be paid by Frederick Shenton (29 Aug.)

COMPTON, Richard, of Phila. - his wife Lydia has eloped from him (29 Aug.)

RENSHAW, Richard - will sell or let lots, of which 8 are 14 ft. deep on the south side of Walnut St., Phila., opposite to Charles and James Townsends (29 Aug.)

A vendue will take place 2 Sept. at Andrew Hamilton's wharf in Phila. (29 Aug.)

RONEY, Thomas, Irish servant, age c. 23 - runaway from John Baldwin, in Cecil Co., Md. (29 Aug.)

RONEY, John (brother of Thomas), servant - runaway from Dr. John Jackson, of Cecil Co., Md. (29 Aug.)

NOWLAND, John, servant - same as above

KENNEDY, Bryan, of Phila. - his wife Judith has eloped from him and left her child of 21 months (29 Aug.)

CARIO, Michael, jeweller, in Front St., near Chesnut St., Phila. - will dispose of nearly 4 years time of an English servant maid (29 Aug.)

HOPKINSON, Thomas - has lots for sale in Phila.; one is in Second St., adjoining a lot of Charles Willing's (lately Stephen Armitt's) on the north and a lot of Nathan Levy's (being the corner of Norris's Alley) on the south (29 Aug.)

Tract of land, called Griffith Part, in Prince George's Co., Md., between the upper and lower falls of Potomack, on the mouth of Capt. John's Creek, is for sale - enquire of James Edmondson, near Belt Town, Prince George's Co., or of John Thompson, in Cecil Co. (29 Aug.)

The Wager man-of-war, Capt. Forest - is arrived in James River from Cape Breton - Williamsburg item of 8 Aug. (5 Sept.)

OLIVER, Capt. - arrived Tuesday last at Boston from St. Eustatia - Boston item of 26 Aug. (5 Sept.)

CLEVES, Capt., commander of a Bristol privateer and another privateer captured 2 South Sea ships and carried them to Newfoundland - Boston item of 26 Aug. (5 Sept.)

Privateer ship Lincoln, Capt. Jauncy, and the brigantine Triton, Capt. Rosewel, are ready to sail (5 Sept.)

WHITEFIELD, Rev. - arrived at New York Tuesday last from Long Island and preached - New York item of 2 Sept. (5 Sept.)

Ship Albany, Capt. Bryant, from London, arrived Thursday last at New York; there came with him as passengers Capts. Griffith and Woodford of New York Capt. Stevens of Amboy and Capts. Parker and Jackson, both of New Eng-

land, all having lately been taken by the enemy - New
York item of 2 Sept. (5 Sept.)

It is reported at Phila. that the ship Little Gipsy, Capt.
Coatam, and another Phila. vessel were lately taken when
coming through the Windward Passage (5 Sept.)

Capt. Lister of the privateer Wilmington, on 17 July put
his chief mate on board the schooner Phenix, of Marblehead, whose master, William Dixy, had died on their passage from Barbados (5 Sept.)

House in Market St., Phila., in which Robert Grace lives,
is to be let - enquire of Thomas Holland (5 Sept.)

The Necessity of Praising God, by Gilbert Tennent - just
published by William Bradford, in Second St., Phila. (5
Sept.)

EWING, George, at Elizabeth Town, N.J. - states that he had
not run away from the Talbot County School but on his return journey from New York was taken sick at Elizabeth
Town of the bloody flux and continues very ill and un-
able to travel (5 Sept.)

FOULK, Judah, Collector - gives notice that all retailers
of wine, rum, etc. in City and County of Phila. must pay
their excise quarterly (5 Sept.)

COX, William, late of Phila., merchant, dec'd - accounts
with estate to be settled with George Rock, administrator (5 Sept.)

A black horse is taken up at the Sign of the Bear in Franckfort (5 Sept.)

HARRIS, John, of Phila. - his wife Hester has eloped from
him (5 Sept.)

DUN, Owen, of East Nantmel Twp., Chester Co. - his wife
Elizabeth has eloped from him (5 Sept.)

LE GALLIS, Capt. - Wednesday last left Marblehead with 80
French prisoners for Brest, France, and Thursday last
Capt. Boutin left Boston with 168 French prisoners for
Brest; Capts. Bonner, Mulberry, Holloway, and Paramour
will soon leave for France with prisoners - Boston item
of 2 Sept. (12 Sept.)

TILESTONE, Capt. - Saturday last arrived at Boston from
Jamaica; he was chased by a privateer but escaped -
Boston item of 2 Sept. (12 Sept.)

WHITEFIELD, Rev. - arrived Thursday last at Phila. from New York (12 Sept.)

SCULL, Nicholas - plans to stand candidate for sheriff of City and Co. of Phila. (12 Sept.)

EVANS, Peter, Esq., dec'd - sale of his library will begin 24 Sept. at the house of Peter Robertson in Front St., Phila. (12 Sept.)

Tract of 200 acres in Warwick Twp., Bucks Co., next adjoining the plantation of John Wilkinson, Jr., and that of Jonathan Bavinkton is for sale - enquire of James Claypole, in Walnut St., Phila. (12 Sept.)

Thirty lots in Kensington, in the Franckfort Rd., almost opposite to the Blue Bell Tavern, are for sale - attendance at the place of the auction will be given by Timothy Scarth (12 Sept.)

The house where Jonathan Mifflin lives, with privilege of an alley into Letitia Court, in Phila., will be sold by George and Jonathan Mifflin (12 Sept.)

MYERS, Philip, country-born servant - runaway from Aylmer Grevill, on Society Hill (12 Sept.)

Ship Victory, now at Peter Kock's wharf in Phila. - will sail for London; for freight or passage agree with Samuel Hassell or Peter Kock (12 Sept.)

Accounts with the Loan Office of Pennsylvania are to be settled promptly, by order of John Kinsey (12 Sept.)

NICHOLAS, Anthony, of Phila. - offers reward for return of an old Negro woman who has run away (12 Sept.)

WITT, Caril, Dutch servant, age between 30 and 40, smith - runaway from Peter Conrad, of New Hanover Twp., Phila. Co. (12 Sept.)

BICKLEY, Samuel, sheriff - has taken up and confined in the Newcastle Goal an Irishman named John Coulton, age c. 28 (12 Sept.)

DALLEY, John, of Kingston, N.J., surveyor - desires subscriptions for a projected map of the road from Amboy to New York and Trenton to Phila. - subscriptions are taken by A. Reed in Trenton, James Leonard in Kingstown, Paul Miller in Brunswick, James Parker in New York and B. Franklin in Phila. (12 Sept.)

PATTERSON, William, near Christine Bridge in Newcastle Co. - will sell cows, oxen, sheep, etc. (12 Sept.)

MORGAN, Evan, near the Courthouse in Phila. - sells tea, rum, oil, dry goods (12 Sept.)

WYNGAARD, Luykas Johannes, of Albany, N.Y., merchant - offers reward for recovery of gelding stolen out of the great pasture of the City of Albany; the horse may be delivered to Benjamin Shoemaker, of Phila. (12 Sept.)

Squallo, Negro, age c. 30, born near Burlington in New Jersey, who formerly belonged to Dr. Redman - runaway from Stephen Onion at the Gunpowder Ironworks, Baltimore Co., Md. (12 Sept.)

BARD, John, in Market St., Phila., next door but one to Evan Morgan's corner - sells saffron and Jesuit's bark (12 Sept.)

HOLLAND, Thomas - has to let the house in Market St., Phila., where Robert Grace lives (12 Sept.)

Message from Gov. George Thomas to the Pennsylvania Assembly and the Assembly's answer (19 Sept.)

SCHERMERHORNE, Capt. - arrived at Charlestown Tuesday last; he reports he saw a brigantine (supposed to be the Defiance, Capt. Williams, from New York to Charlestown) taken by a Spanish privateer (19 Sept.)

Sloop Black Joak, Capt. Marsh, of and from Cape Fear for Charlestown, was chased ashore into Poole's Inlet; the privateer had a schooner belonging to Mr. Shute of Charlestown, with Percival Pawley and Col. Pawley's son passengers on board - Charlestown item of 19 Aug. (19 Sept.)

A sloop from Jamaica for Charlestown, Henry Dickenson master - was taken by a privateer Monday or Tuesday night - Charlestown item of 19 Aug. (19 Sept.)

DAVIS, Capt., in the guard schooner - took a brigantine at anchor off St. Simon's Bar - Charlestown item of 26 Aug. (19 Sept.)

STILES, Capt. R., from Jamaica - arrived Thursday last at Charlestown - Charlestown item of 26 Aug. (19 Sept.)

Ship Fame, Capt. Thompson commander - sailed Monday last from Newport, R.I. - Newport item of 6 Sept. (19 Sept.)

Saturday last the <u>Massachusetts Frigat</u>, Capt. Tyng command-
er, arrived at Boston from Louisburg and will sail for
Louisburg in a few days - Boston item of 9 Sept. (19
Sept.)

PROCTOR, Lt. - arrived 8 Sept. at Boston, bringing an Indian prisoner named Col. Job; on 1 Sept. the English
came upon 4 Indians, of whom they killed Col. Sam and
Lt.-Gov. Moxus, took prisoner Col. Job, while the other
Indian escaped; all 4 were leaders of the Penobscut
tribe - Boston item of 9 Sept. (19 Sept.)

Reported at New York that the Brigantine <u>Warren</u>, of New
York, Capt. Long, sailed 7 Aug. from Port Morant; it was
taken by a privateer but then retaken by the <u>Seahorse</u>
man-of-war - New York item of 16 Sept. (19 Sept.)

Privateer sloop <u>Hillary</u>, of Barbados, Capt. Rowland, from
Jamaica - arrived Sunday last at Phila., with Capt. Wallace a passenger, who informs that the ship <u>Little Gipsy</u>,
Capt. Cottam, was taken by a Spanish privateer, but the
brigantine <u>Conclusion</u>, Capt. Edes, of Phila., got clear
and returned to Kingston; Capt. Green, of the ship <u>Hawk</u>,
of Jamaica, was cast away on Morant Keys (19 Sept.)

Brigantine <u>Trial</u>, John Evans master, taken off our coast
when coming from Antigua - is thought to be the vessel
carried into Georgia (19 Sept.)

Privateer ship <u>Marlborough</u>, of Phila., Christopher Clymer
commander - arrived Tuesday last at Phila.; in lat. 33
he spoke with Capt. Brame for Phila. and Capt. Stedman
for Virginia (19 Sept.)

Sloop <u>Elizabeth</u>, William Wallace, Jr., master, at Edward
Warner's wharf, will sail for Charleston, S.C.; for
freight or passage agree with the master or with Robert
and Amos Strettell (19 Sept.)

KOCK, Peter, of Germantown Twp. - offers reward for recovery of a mare and colt (19 Sept.)

MOORE, Thomas, in Marple Twp., Chester Co. - has taken up a
stray horse (19 Sept.)

KERLAN, Patrick, Irishman, age <u>c</u>. 19 - runaway from Robert
Nivin, of Whiteclay Creek, near Christine Bridge (19
Sept.)

WEISER, Conrad, Ranger of the northeast corner of Lancaster Co. - gives a list of strays he has taken up (19
Sept.)

Sunday last arrived at Phila. the snow George, Capt.
Nathaniel Ambler, from Dublin; he was taken by a privateer but ransomed; he has servants whose time is to be
disposed of; enquire at Thomas Gordon's, near Powel's
wharf, or of the master on board (26 Sept.)

CATHRALL, Edward, who is leaving off shopkeeping - wishes
to settle all accounts (26 Sept.)

Address sent by the Synod of Phila. to William Gooch, Esq.,
Lt.-Gov. of Virginia, and address of the governor to Rev.
Robert Cathcart, moderator, and the Synod of Phila. (26
Sept.)

Twelve lots to be sold at the house of the late George
Traut, dec'd, at the upper end of Germantown, Phila. Co.,
by the executors, John Fridrick Ax and Richard Robb (26
Sept.)

Hamilton, Wallace (John) and Company have for sale goods
just imported in the ship Agnes and Betty, Capt. Brame,
and the ship Mercury, Capt. Hargrave (26 Sept.)

FARMER, R., at the Unicorn in Second St., Phila. - has
medicines and drugs for sale (26 Sept.)

BENEZET, James, in his store adjoining Nathaniel Allen's in
Front St., Phila. - sells many items imported in the
ship Agnes and Betty, Capt. Brame, and the Mercury, Capt.
Hargrave (26 Sept.)

BARNES, Henry, age c. 40, in 1736 or 1737 left England, intending for Virginia - he arrived and remained there
until 1740, when he wrote friends in England that anything sent him should be left with William Davis, near
Onoquan Ferry on Potomack; there is information that
Barnes went on the expedition against Cartagena; an estate has descended to him in England; he is to apply to
John Ross, in Phila., attorney-at-law, who seeks news of
Barnes from William Davis or anyone else (26 Sept.)

TURNER, Peter, in Front St., Phila. - has for sale goods imported in the Agnes and Betty and the Mercury (26 Sept.)

SHUPPY, John, living in Strawberry Alley, Phila. - designs
to open his winter evening school to teach German (26
Sept.)

Fourteen lots in Oxford Twp., fronting Burlington Road, ¼
mile beyond Franckfort - are to be sold by Dan Bristol
at the house of James McVough (26 Sept.)

House and lot fronting Mulbery St., extending 140 feet to Apple Tree Alley - will be sold by the executrix of John Knowles, dec'd (26 Sept.)

SWAM, John, servant - runaway from Joseph Forman, of Freehold, Monmouth Co., N.J. (26 Sept.)

WILLIAMS, Moses, half Indian and half Irish servant, this country-born - runaway from Samuel Shivers, of Greenwich, N.J. (26 Sept.)

CLARK, Capt. - Wednesday last arrived at Boston from Louisburg (3 Oct.)

Extract of a letter from Louisburg with account of a French squadron, Capt. Spry and Capt. Richardson in the sloop formerly Donahew's - Boston item of 23 Sept. (3 Oct.)

Several of the Jamaica fleet report having met 2 privateers of St. Kitts, commanded by Capts. Purcell and Rouse, going to Jamiaca - Newport item of 20 Sept. (3 Oct.)

Thursday last James Hamilton, Esq., was elected Mayor of Phila. (3 Oct.)

The following were elected on Tuesday last for Phila. Co.: representatives--John Kinsey, Isaac Norris, Edward Warner, Joseph Trotter, Thomas Leech, James Morris, Robert Jones, Owen Evan; sheriffs--Nicholas Schull, Peter Robeson; coroners--Henry Pratt, Richard Sewell; commissioner --Joseph Fox; assessors--Jeremiah Elfreth, Evan Jones, Moses Hughs, James Paul, John Jones Carpenter, Francis Parvin (3 Oct.)

On Tuesday last the following were elected for Chester Co.: representatives--Joseph Pennock, Thomas Cummings, George Ashbridge, Jr., Francis Yarnall, Robert Lewis, Joseph Harvey, Samuel Levis, Thomas Chandler; sheriffs--John Owen, Nathan Worley; coroners--Thomas Morgan, David Coupland; commissioner--John Davis; assessors--Samuel Bunton, Thomas Pennell, Isaac Davis, John Churchman, Thomas Park, Aaron Ashbridge (3 Oct.)

On Tuesday last the following were elected for Bucks Co.: representatives--Benjamin Field, Mahlon Kirkbride, John Hall/?/, Mark Watson, Abraham Chapman, John Watson, Richard Mitchell, Cephas Child; sheriffs--John Hart, Timothy Smith; coroners--Jo. Chapman, Jo. Hampton; commissioner-- Benjamin Taylor; assessors--John Williamson, Abra. Vastine, George Logan, Thomas Owen, Bartholomew Longstretch, Adam Harker (3 Oct.)

Wednesday last the following were chosen for Phila. City:
burgesses--Israel Pemberton, Oswald Peele; city asses-
sors--William Clymer, William Fisher, Thomas Howard,
Francis Richardson, William Callender, Stephen Armit (3
Oct.)

BLUNSTON, Samuel, Esq., of Hempfield, Lancaster Co., one
of the representatives of that county - died there Monday last (3 Oct.)

Ship Ann-Galley, George Houston commander - will sail for
London; for freight or passage agree with John Inglis
or the master on board at McCall's wharf, Phila. (3 Oct.)

Persons indebted to Stedman, Robertson & Co. are desired to
settle accounts (3 Oct.)

SCOTT, James, at one of Mr. Hamilton's stores, next door to
Messrs. Jevon and Perry's store in Phila. - sells cloth,
paper, shoes, tea, etc. (3 Oct.)

BILES, Thomas, 3 doors below the Post Office in Market St.,
Phila. - sells pewter, copper, tin, brass (3 Oct.)

HARDING, John, on William Master's wharf, at lower end of
Market St., Phila. - sells wire screens (3 Oct.)

ELLIOT, Maurice, of East-Town, Chester Co., on Conestogo
Rd., 18 miles from Phila. - will let his house there, as
he intends to leave Pennsylvania (3 Oct.)

HASSERT, Arent, in Laetitia Court, Phila. - sells boulting
cloths and other goods imported from London by Capts.
Brame and Hargrave (3 Oct.)

MILLORD, William, servant, age c. 20 - runaway from Peter
Browne, at the Old Ferry, in Phila. (3 Oct.)

CURTIS, John, servant, age c. 17 or 18 - same as above

HOLLINGTON, Hannah, age c. 16, who says she was born in
Spain but came from Dublin in the Draper, Capt. Basnet -
runaway from John Douglas (3 Oct.)

Owners are desired to call for a hogshead of rum and 12 barrels of lime on board the sloop Royal Ranger, Samuel
Brownlow master, from Barbados (3 Oct.)

Tract of between 600 and 700 acres, joining on one side the
Conestogo Manor and on the other side the River Susquehannah, is for sale - enquire of Edward Smout in Lancaster (3 Oct.)

At Barbados a collection was taken up for the widows and
children of the men lost with Capt. Smithurst (10 Oct.)

KINGSTON, Capt. E., who sailed from Boston for the West
Indies, was taken by a French privateer but retaken by
the ship _Pandour_, belonging to Phila. (10 Oct.)

TYNG, Capt. - sailed from Boston for Louisburg in the _Mass-
achusetts Frigate_ (10 Oct.)

GIBBS, Capt., from Antigua - informs that Commodore Lee had
sent in a French privateer (10 Oct.)

BROWN, Capt., from Bermudas - reports that Capt. Kiel in a
privateer of Bermudas had brought in a French sugar
ship (10 Oct.)

WHITEFIELD, Rev. - arrived at Annapolis, Md., 27 Sept. (10
Oct.)

Last week the following were elected for Lancaster Co.:
representatives--John Wright, Arthur Patterson, James
Mitchel, James Wright; sheriff--James Starret; coroner--
William Hamilton (10 Oct.)

Last week the following were elected for Newcastle Co.:
representatives--John McCoole, William Armstrong, John
Vaunce, James McMahan, Daniel Corbit, John Edwards;
sheriffs--Henry Newton, Gideon Griffith; coroners--James
McMullen, Benjamin Cooke (10 Oct.)

Last week the following were elected for Kent Co.: repre-
sentatives--James Gorrel, Mark Manlove, Andrew Caldwell,
John Tilton, Joseph Dowding, Abraham Allee; sheriff--
Thomas Green; coroner--Thomas Parks (10 Oct.)

Last week the following were elected for Sussex Co.: repre-
sentatives--Woolsey Burton, Jacob Kollock, John Klows,
Benjamin Stockley, Joseph Draper, James McElwane; sheriff
--William Shankland; coroner--Robert Gill (10 Oct.)

Almanacks for sale by B. Franklin (10 Oct.)

Ship _Friendship_, Henry Lisle master, at Fishbourne's wharf
in Phila. - will sail for London; for freight or passage
agree with the master or Joseph Noble, John Armit or
William Callender (10 Oct.)

HARTLEY, William, Chief Ranger for Chester Co. - lists the
strays in his hands (10 Oct.)

COLEMAN, William - has for sale copper stills (10 Oct.)

House, malt-house and brew-house, in King's St., Trenton,
Hunterdon Co., West New Jersey are for sale - apply to
Thomas Hooton, living at Trenton Ferry; also for sale is
a lot 1½ miles above Trenton, belonging to estate of
William Atlee, dec'd; enquire of Jane Atlee, living in
Trenton, or Thomas Hooton (10 Oct.)

Plantation of 290 acres in Evesham, Burlington Co., West
New Jersey, about 12 miles from Phila., late of John Kay,
dec'd, now in the possession of Nathaniel Hopewell, will
be sold at auction at the Widow Roberts's Coffee House
in Phila.; for terms and title enquire of Thomas Say, of
Phila., sadler, one of the executors of said John Kay,
dec'd (10 Oct.)

Alexander Jamieson, Scotch servant, weaver by trade, and
John Skerum, English servant, who pretends to be a baker,
both belonging to David Galloway, of Northumberland,
stole a schooner when returning from Norfolk and murdered the skipper, Tobias Horton; William Gooch, Gov.
of Virginia, offers reward of 10 pounds for apprehension
of the murderers; David Galloway will pay 10 pistoles
for return of the schooner to him at Wicomico River,
Northumberland Co. or to Archibald Taylor at Norfolk (10
Oct.)

Saturday last arrived at Charlestown from South Edisto
Philip Thomas, mate, and several seamen belonging to the
ship _Dundee_, William Vaughan commander, from New Providence to Charlestown; the ship was chased till aground
by a Spanish privateer - Charlestown item of 9 Sept. (17
Oct.)

ROUSE, Capt. John -- brought news of rejoicing in England
over fall of Louisburg; General Pepperell is knighted;
Mr. Warren is made a Rear Admiral and is ordered to buy
Rouse's snow - Boston item of 7 Oct. (17 Oct.)

Ship _Eaton_, Capt. Syers - arrived Monday last at New York
from Jamaica, with news that the _Merlin_ man-of-war has
taken the Spanish privateer sloop lately commanded by
Capt. Hall (17 Oct.)

KOLLOCK, Capt. - his sloop was driven ashore at the east
end of Antigua by a French privateer (17 Oct.)

OSWALD, Capt., in the ship _Hampshire_, of Phila., bound to
Dublin, has been taken by a French privateer and carried
into Brest (17 Oct.)

CURRIE, Ebenezer, at his store between Norris's and Gray's
Alley, in Front St., Phila. - has for sale cloth, weapons,

tea, spices, glasses, etc., for sale (17 Oct.)

Testimonials as to the virtue of Mr. Torres's Chinese Stones
are as follows: Thomas Saquin, William Hatton, Samuel
Hobert, all of Rhode Island; Col. George Pawley, of
Charlestown, S.C., certifies that a neighbor, William
Poole used said stones to save life of his dog that had
been bitten by a snake; William Allen, of Goose Creek,
S.C.; Francis Bremar, of Orange Quarter, S.C.; Peter Du-
may and John Girar of French Santee, S.C.; James Benoist
of English Santee, S.C.; Peter Rambert, of English San-
tee, S.C.: John Barksdale, of George Town, Winyaw, S.C.;
Benjamin Hillyard, of Wilmington, N.C.; daughter of Col.
Moore of Cape Fare, N.D., was cured of toothache; wife
of minister of Pamphlicoe, N.C.; William Hardy, of Isle
of Wight Co., Va.; Madam Grimel, of Prince George Co.,
Va.; Benjamin Aikins, of Brunswick Co., Va.; wife of
Thomas John, Manakin Town, Va.; Mr. Milks, Charles City,
Va.; William Corington, King William Co., Va.; wife of
J. Jakey, Prince George's Co., Md.; William Usher; Samuel
Smith, Jr., of Anne Arundel Co., Md.; Mr. Torres's pow-
ders - may be bought from him at Jacob Duche's in Market
St., Phila., or at Anthony Duche's, the dyer (17 Oct.)

RAY, James, Irish servant, age c. 18 - runaway from Joseph
Rogers, of Vincent Twp., Chester Co. (17 Oct.)

Eighty acres on Chesnut Hill, Germantown Twp., between the
land of Anthony Dennis, near Peter Kook's land, and the
land of John Barge - will be sold at auction by Derrick
Rebenstock (17 Oct.)

Friday last arrived at New York the brigantine Jamaica
Packet, Capt. Albuoy, from Newcastle with European news
- New York item of 21 Oct. (24 Oct.)

Friday last arrived at New York from a cruize the privateer
Dolphin, Capt. Richard Landon commander, of New York, who
has taken a French snow - New York item of 21 Oct. (24
Oct.)

BOWNE, Capt., who arrived at New York from Coracoa - reports
he spoke with the privateers Warren and George of Phila.
- New York item of 21 Oct. (24 Oct.)

DOWERS, Edward, at his house in Water St., next door to the
Widow Beazley's, in Phila. - has for sale a parcel of
servants, Cheshire and Gloucester cheese and Irish linens
(24 Oct.)

Snow George, Nathaniel Ambler master, now at Plumsted's
wharf in Phila. - will sail for Dublin: for freight or

passage apply to Robert Wakely, at Thomas Gordon's or to the master on board (24 Oct.)

Brigantine **Elizabeth**, John Strawbridge master - will sail for Antigua; for freight or passage agree with Samuel Hasell or the master (24 Oct.)

NEAVE, Samuel, intending for London with Capt. Houston - wishes to have all accounts settled (24 Oct.)

GALBREATH, James, Ranger for the West Division of Lancaster Co. - lists strays in his custody (24 Oct.)

MARTIN, Richard, late of Cheltenham, Phila. Co., dec'd - accounts with estate to be settled with Mary Martin, executrix (24 Oct.)

JEWERS, John, of Phila., mariner - married Margaret Cooke (wife of William Cooke), supposing her husband was dead; it has been discovered, however, that said William Cooke is alive and on board one of H.M.'s ships; John Jewers will not pay debts contracted by Margaret in the future (24 Oct.)

TENNANT, Robert, of Phila. - his wife Mary has eloped from him (24 Oct.)

L'Amilie, French prize sloop, taken by Capt. Langdon of New York - was brought into Newport, R.I., Monday last by Capt. Thomas Randal - Newport item of 18 Oct. (31 Oct.)

Ship **Prince of Wales**, Capt. Thomas Brewer commander, and ship **Duke of Cumberland**, Capt. Benjamin Cranston commander - will sail from Newport as privateers in November (31 Oct.)

French and Indians on 11 Oct. attacked Ft. Dummer but failed to take it; they killed Neh. How and David Rugg but Robert Baker escaped; these 3 were outside the fort - Boston item of 21 Oct. (31 Oct.)

COX, Thomas, of New York, butcher - Monday last was killed when a pistol accidentally went off - New York item of 28 Oct. (31 Oct.)

Tuesday last the **Clinton** privateer, Capt. Began, sailed from New York and the privateer sloop **Polly**, Capt. Helme, will sail in a few days - New York item of 28 Oct. (31 Oct.)

Letter to Mr. Franklin claims that the Chinese Stones and powders of Mr. Torres are made from remnants of buckshorn (31 Oct.)

B. Franklin will publish Monday next his <u>Poor</u> <u>Richard's</u> <u>Almanack</u> <u>for</u> <u>1746</u> and he has for sale <u>Gospel</u> <u>Sonnets</u> by Rev. Ralph Erskine and Mrs. Rowe's <u>Devout</u> <u>Exercises</u> <u>of</u> <u>the</u> <u>Heart</u> (31 Oct.)

Quantity of pig iron has been left on Andrew Hamilton's wharf (31 Oct.)

IRWINE, Mathew - has a Negro wench for sale (31 Oct.)

Persons wishing to join the privateer ship <u>Marlborough</u> are to repair to the commander, Christopher Clymer, at the Sign of the Pewter Platter in Front St., Phila. (31 Oct.)

Lots on west side of the Great Road from Phila. to German-town, late the estate of John Rigley, dec'd, and since of James Holt, will be sold at auction at the house of Anthony Nise, being the Sign of the Rising Sun, on said Great Road; plan of the whole may be seen at Nise's house, or in Phila. at William Parsons's or Walter Good-man's; attorneys of John Holt are Rebecca Holt and Wal-ter Goodman (31 Oct.)

COOPER, William - offers reward for recovery of horse stolen from his stable (31 Oct.)

KEY, Philip - gives notice that a brigantine, brought into Britton's Bay in Potomack River, Md., by John Bebby, master of the ship <u>William</u> <u>and</u> <u>Betty</u> from Liverpoole, will be sold, with its cargo, at Leonard's Town in St. Mary's Co., Md. (31 Oct.)

Sam, a Negro, age <u>c</u>. 26, enticed by one Isaac Randall (an apprentice of Thomas Marriot, Jr.) - runaway from Thomas Cadwalader, of Trenton (31 Oct.)

RYAN, John, Irish servant - runaway from Tho. Ebtharp, liv-ing on Bohemia Manor in Caecil Co., Md.; reward will be paid if runaway is brought to Elk River Ferry, to John Kankey or John Altum (31 Oct.)

KEY, Philip, of St. Mary's Co., Md., offers reward for Negro Jo (who was cook of Samuel Ogle, Esq., Gov. of Maryland), who ran away from Key and served on a privateer out of Phila. (31 Oct.)

JONES, John, of Worcester - has taken up a horse (31 Oct.)

WOOLEY, Thomas, at the White Horse, in Market St., near the Presbyterian Meeting-house in Phila. - has taken up a horse (31 Oct.)

A black cow has been since June at the plantation of Jacob
Levering, in Roxburgh Twp., Phila. Co. (31 Oct.)

FULLEN, James, of Phila. - will not pay debts contracted
in future by his wife Barbara (31 Oct.)

DONNEL, Capt. - arrived Wednesday last at Boston from Louisburg - Boston item of 28 Oct. (7 Nov.)

ADAMS, Capt., in a mast ship from Piscataqua bound to England - has been taken by a French man-of-war (7 Nov.)

The Dutch snow, Capt. Andries, taken by the privateer ship
Marlborough but discharged has arrived in Amsterdam (7
Nov.)

Schooner Unity, Capt. Balitho, of Phila. - has been taken
by a Spanish privateer (7 Nov.)

Capt. Green from Providence informs that Capt. Canton, in
a privateer of that place - has brought in a French
sloop (7 Nov.)

Peter Turner, William & David McIlvaine (at their store in
Water St., opposite to Charles Willing's) and George
Emlen, Jr. (near the Post Office in Market St.) all ad-
vertise for sale goods brought to Phila. in the ship
Carolina, Stephen Mesnard master, from London (7 Nov.)

SMITH, John, at his store on Israel Pemberton's wharf, in
Phila. - offers imported goods for sale (7 Nov.)

Reward for recovery of a gelding, strayed or stolen from
the pasture of William Donaldson in Derby, will be paid
if the gelding is brought to Peter Middlecalf or William
Donaldson, at the Sign of the Ship in Derby, Chester Co.
(7 Nov.)

BROWN, William, Under Sheriff - offers reward for capture
of James Johnson, an Irishman (whose right name is White)
who broke out of Trenton Goal; he had lately run from
his bail and entered on board the Dreadnaught, Capt. Cunningham, who put him ashore (7 Nov.)

Tract of 119 acres in Eastown Twp., Chester Co., will be
sold at the late house of Evan Ellis, dec'd, in said township; enquire of Samuel Roads or John Nickinson, of
Blackley Twp., Phila. Co. (7 Nov.)

NORTON, Richard, of Charles-Town, Caecil Co., Md. - offers
reward for recovery of 2 horses, strayed or stolen (7
Nov.)

TUFTS, Capt. - arrived Friday last at Boston from England - Boston item of 4 Nov. (14 Nov.)

Ship Carolina, Stephen Mesnard commander - will sail for London; for freight or passage agree with Matthias Aspden or the master on Fishbourn's wharf (14 Nov.)

Cows, horses, hogs, etc., will be sold at plantation formerly belonging to Aaron Goforth (14 Nov.)

MORGAN, John, at his store on Market St. wharf - sells cloth, cutlery, rum, wine, cocoa, coffee (14 Nov.)

Building and lot extending into Black Horse Alley, now in the occupation of Dr. Farmar - will be sold at Roberts·'s Coffee House in Phila. (14 Nov.)

ROCK, G. - directs that accounts with estate of William Cox, merchant, dec'd, be settled with John Langdale, tanner, near Mr. Cox's late dwelling; the sadlery goods are to be disposed of by William Paschal, sadler, in Market St. (14 Nov.)

Pennsylvania Fireplaces, made by Robert Grace - are sold by Lewis Evans in Strawberry Allen (14 Nov.)

GARDNER, James, servant, age c. 30, skinner or leatherdresser by trade - runaway from John Howell, of Phila., tanner (14 Nov.)

BURK, James, Irish servant, carpenter, who came to these parts about 12 or 14 years ago - runaway from Charles Ridgeley, of Baltimore Co., Md., near Patapsco Ferry (14 Nov.)

RYAN, Daniel, Irish servant, age c. 26 - runaway from John Hackett, of Newgarden, Chester Co. (14 Nov.)

SEARLE, John, below the drawbridge, in Phila. - sells leather soles (14 Nov.)

Tanyard in Marlborough Twp., Chester Co., belonging to the Widow Jackson, is to be let (14 Nov.)

LE FAVRE, Capt. - Saturday last arrived at Boston from Ratan, near the Bay of Honduras - Boston item of 11 Nov. (21 Nov.)

WHITEFIELD, Rev. - arrived 19 Oct. at Bath Town, N.C., on his way to Georgia (21 Nov.)

A sloop, Thomas Glentworth, Jr., master - is ashore and

lost within a few miles of the Cape - report from Lewistown (21 Nov.)

WILLIAMS, Francis, Welsh servant - runaway from the brigantine Kouh Kan; reward will be paid for his return to
James Templeton at Alexander Lane's store (21 Nov.)

DURHAM, Bartholomew, Irish servant, age c. 20 - runaway
from Ann Burn - reward will be paid by Ann Burn or Peter
Robeson if the runaway is brought to the Indian King in
Phila. (21 Nov.)

THOMAS, William, English servant, age c. 17 - runaway from
Matthias Lamey, of Whiteland, Chester Co. (21 Nov.)

RAMSEY, Thomas, of Phila. - his wife Elizabeth has absented herself from him (21 Nov.)

FLETCHER, John, of Plymouth Twp., Phila. Co., Deputy Ranger
- gives list of strays in his hands (21 Nov.)

Four lots in Phila. will be sold at Peter Robeson's, at the
Indian King (21 Nov.)

ARCHER, Tho., of Charlestown, Caecil Co., Md., lists among
items stolen from his pocket the following: a demand
due from Alexander McConnell to Robert Stephenson; a
penal bill due from James Harrison to Moses Ruth; a note
from James Read to Tennet Stevenson; a note from Philip
Cazier to Tho. Archer; a note from Samuel Blith to James
Thompson; a note from Samuel Blith to John Shields (21
Nov.)

Yesterday arrived at New York the prize sloop lately taken
by Capt. Langdon in the privateer brigantine Dolphin, of
New York - New York item of 25 Nov. (28 Nov.)

Privateer ship Prince Charles is fitting out for a cruize
under Capt. Samuel Tingly from New York (28 Nov.)

BALCHEN, Capt., of the Pembroke man-of-war - captured 2
Martinico sugar ships (28 Nov.)

RAMSAY, Capt., master of a Scotch ship at Charlestown, S.C.
- with a schooner went out and took a Spanish privateer
(28 Nov.)

The New George privateer, Capt. Wood, of Phila., came up on
Friday last (28 Nov.)

The Friendly Instructor, with preface by Rev. Dr. Doddridge
- is reprinted and sold by B. Franklin in Phila., who

also has lately published <u>Poor Richard's Almanack</u> <u>for</u>
<u>1746</u> (28 Nov.)

KENSEY, John, Scotch servant, age <u>c</u>. 19 - runaway from
Richard Naylor, of Montgomery, Phila. Co. (28 Nov.);
Kensey is in custody at Annapolis (17 Dec.)

Jack, Mulatto slave, age <u>c</u>. 35 - runaway from Alexander
Lockhart, Esq., of Trenton, West New Jersey (28 Nov.)

James Starling, over Tohecan, Bucks Co., or Colin McSweney,
in Abington, Phila. Co. - will pay reward for recovery
of horse that strayed or was stolen from Phila. (28 Nov.)

HONETTER, Andrew, near Robinson's mill - offers reward for
a mare and colt that strayed or were stolen from his
plantation (28 Nov.)

FARMER, Edward, of Whitemarsh, dec'd - accounts with estate
to be settled with John and Peter Robeson and Joseph Farmer, executors (28 Nov.)

Plantation of 300 acres, where Patrick McConwey lately
lived, near Duck Creek - is for sale; enquire of Richard
Harrison, near Phila. (28 Nov.)

Malt-house, brew-house, dwelling-house and tanyard are to
be let in Noxontown, Newcastle Co. - apply to John Ross
in Phila. or Abraham Gooding and John Vance, in Newcastle
Co., executors of Thomas Noxon, dec'd (28 Nov.)

New brick house in Second St., Phila., opposite the New
Market Place, now in the occupation of John Kerlin, will
be sold at auction (28 Nov.)

Naman's Creek Mills and about 85 acres adjoining (part of
the real estate of Thomas Moore, dec'd) - will be sold
1 Jan., with Joseph Cloud, administrator of the dec'd,
in attendance, by order of the Orphan's Court (Richard
McWilliam, Deputy Clerk) (28 Nov.)

About a week ago a French sloop flag of truce arrived at
Tarpaulin Cove from Cape Francois with 30 English prisoners, among whom is Capt. Clark - Boston item of 25 Nov.
(6 Dec.)

HALL, Capt. - Friday last, when coming into New York in a
sloop from Cape Breton and when he was as far as Gravesend, was forced ashore - New York item of 2 Dec. (6 Dec.)

CHILD, Capt., from Jamaica, reports that the <u>Blast</u> snow-of-
war was taken by 2 row galleys from Havana (6 Dec.)

BROWN, Capt., from St. Chrstiophers, reports that the privateers <u>Betsey</u> and <u>Bonetta</u>, Capts. Rouse and Purcel, of that island, have been taken (6 Dec.)

SHARP, Thomas, merchant, dec'd - persons indebted to the estate are to pay Walter Goodman, of Phila., merchant (attorney of John Thomas, executor of said Sharp); the administrators of John Hopkins and John Inglis have delivered the books and papers of said Thomas Sharp to the executor (6 Dec.)

DAVIS, David (son of Ellis Davis) dec'd, carpenter, late of Horsham, Phila. Co., who left Pennsylvania about 10 or 12 years since and went to New England - by applying to Thomas Fletcher, of Abington, Phila. Co., he will hear something to his advantage (6 Dec.)

MULLIN, John, Irish apprentice, age 17 - runaway from the ship <u>Catharine</u>, Joseph Smith, master; reward for return of the apprentice will be paid by Cunningham and Gardner, merchants in Phila. (6 Dec.)

Grist mill, bakehouse and oven are for sale in Southampton, Bucks Co. - apply to John Bond at said mill (6 Dec.)

BLEAKLEY, John, at Kensington - has hay for sale (6 Dec.)

MURRAY, Richard, of Lower Dublin, Phila. Co. - persons indebted to him are desired to pay him in order that he may satisfy his creditors (6 Dec.)

FARRALL, Roger, Irish servant, age 45 - runaway from Isaac Whitelock, of the Borough of Lancaster (6 Dec.)

ADDIS, John, dec'd - accounts with estate to be settled with Mary and Joseph Addis, executors (6 Dec.)

Tract of 300 acres is offered for sale by Jacob Coladay, of Cresem, in Germantown Twp. (6 Dec.)

SHELLY, Abraham, Workhouse-keeper in Phila. - has for sale the time of a servant girl (6 Dec.)

SHEPPARD, John - has taken up a mare at the Sign of the Swan, on Chesnut Hill, Germantown Twp., Phila. Co. (6 Dec.)

Account of attempt made by Nathaniel Hasey, Deputy Sheriff, to impress in Boston 15 men for service on H.M.S. <u>Wager</u>, Capt. Forest commander; the press gang entered the house of Capt. Cowley and took 5 sailors belonging to his ship; the gang then entered at the north end of town the house

of one Mr. Poor, where were 3 men formerly belonging to
the sloop commanded by Capt. Downahew, later by Capt.
Richardson; the gang so wounded 2 of these men that they
died; Hasey and the boatswain of the Wager are committed
to prison - Boston item of 25 Nov. (10 Dec.)

WEISER, Conrad, Ranger of the northeast corner of Lancaster
Co. lists the strays he has on hand and George Boone,
Chief Ranger of Phila. Co. lists strays on hand (10 Dec.)

ROCK, George, administrator - has for sale a Negro called
Sam that belonged lately to Mr. Cox (10 Dec.)

Ship William and Anne, of Annapolis, Capt. Strachan - was
taken near the Banks of Newfoundland and ransomed for
1,500 guineas - Annapolis item of 15 Nov. (17 Dec.)

Ship Pandour, William Dowell commander, and brigantine
George, Robert Wood, commander, seek volunteers; those
inclined to join are to repair to the commanders or to
the Sign of the Boatswain and Call, near the drawbridge,
Phila. (17 Dec.)

CONELY, Briant, Irish servant, age c. 17 - runaway from
John Reed, Sr., of Christine Bridge, Newcastle Co.; reward will be paid if the servant is brought to his master or to John Harding, at the lower end of Market St.,
Phila. (17 Dec.)

Tract of 200 acres, in Newtown, Chester Co., is for sale;
apply to Thomas or Caleb Reece, living on the premises
(17 Dec.)

A lease and release from James Steel to George Ward for 112
acres and a lease from Nathaniel Poole for 100 acres are
both lost; reward for their recovery will be paid by
John Parrot, of Phila., or George Ward, at the head of
Timber Creek (17 Dec.)

CARR, Capt. B., in the privateer Marlborough of Newport,
R.I. - took a Spanish sloop - Newport item of 29 Nov.
(24 Dec.)

Letter dated Deerfield 25 Nov. - reports that body of Indians have burnt Lydius's blockhouse and taken his son
- Boston item of 2 Dec. (24 Dec.)

Monday last the privateers, the brigantine Greyhound, Capt.
Jeffery, and the snow Dragon, Capt. Seymour, sailed from
New York - New York item of 9 Dec. (24 Dec.)

VARDIL, Capt. - arrived at New York 15 Dec. from Jamaica;

on the passage he spoke the <u>Clinton</u> privateer of New
York, who informed them that with the privateers <u>Hester</u>
and <u>Batchelors</u> of New York, she had taken a Spanish
brigantine (24 Dec.)

From 2 Indians Major Swartwort has leared that the French
and Indians have ready great numbers of snowshoes for an
attack on Albany and back parts of Pennsylvania and New
Jersey; Peter Chartier has deserted to the French (24
Dec.)

On 11 Dec. was taken from the Post Office at Phila. a silver
spoon, marked T.C., Philip Syng maker; person who took
it is desired to return it or be exposed (24 Dec.)

BARD, Dr. John, of Phila. - wishes all accounts with him to
be settled (24 Dec.)

WATERMAN, John - has for sale at his store on Carpenter's
wharf in Phila. choice claret and sundry West India
goods; he has for sale also a Barbadian Negro girl; enquire of him at Capt. John Elliot's in Second St. (24
Dec.)

HELLICAS, Michael, in Second St., Phila., has taken up a
horse (24 Dec.)

HESTON, Thomas, of the Falls Twp., Bucks Co., near Trenton
Ferry - offers reward for recovery of a strayed or stolen
mare; reward will be paid if she is taken to Josiah Woods
near said ferry, or to John Lacy's in Wrights Town (24
Dec.)

Saturday last arrived at Hampton the brigantine <u>Globe</u>, Daniel Rees master, belonging to Phila.; he had been taken
on 30 Nov. by Mons. Letouch, who also took a snow privateer, Joshua Wilkinson commander, who ransomed the <u>Globe</u>;
Rees took on board at Antigua Capt. Joseph Arthur, Jr.,
master of a vessel belonging to Phila., which had been
taken prize and carried into Martineco; Capt. Arthur's
journal is printed - Williamsburg item of 12 Dec. (31
Dec.)

GREEN, Capt., who arrived at Charlestown, S.C., last week
from Providence, reported that Capts. Fennel and Pumell
had taken 2 Spanish schooners - Charlestown item of 25
Nov. (31 Dec.)

BARNES, Capt. - arrived Thursday last at New York; he had on
board Capt. Collet, late of the brigantine <u>Catherine</u>
(taken 30 Oct. by the Spaniards) and Capt. Twaits of the
<u>Tartar</u> (also taken by the Spaniards) - New York item of
23 Dec. (31 Dec.)

Brigantine <u>Grafton</u>, Capt. Taylor of Phila., was taken in
passage to Jamaica but soon after retaken by the <u>Drake</u>
snow-of-war (31 Dec.)

DAMES, William, intending for Europe and wishing to settle
all accounts - will be at the following places for that
purpose: at John Tillotson's, on Corsica Creek, Queen
Ann's Co., Md., on 11 Jan.; at Samuel Massey's, Chester
Town, Kent Co., Md., on 15 Jan.; at his own plantation,
on Back Creek, Cecil Co., Md., on 18 Jan.; at Capt.
Slayter Clay's, at Newcastle, Pa., on 22 Jan.; at Mr.
Coburn's, at the Three Tuns, in Chesnut St., Phila., on
25 Jan. (31 Dec.)

REBENSTACH, Derrick, late of Germantownship, dec'd - accounts
with the estate to be settled with the executors,
Christian Lehman and Wigard Miller (31 Dec.)

WHEALON, Daniel, Irish convict servant, age <u>c</u>. 30, smith
by trade - runaway from William Parks from Hanover Courthouse, Va., taking a horse stolen from Abraham Bedel,
living near the place where the Upper Southanna Bridge
stood, in Hanover Co.; he had run away before from a
former master, John Fitzgerald, of King William Co. (31
Dec.)

1746

SHIRLEY, Gov. and wife - arrived 8 Dec. 1745 at Boston from
Louisburg in the <u>Massachusetts</u> <u>Frigate</u>, Capt. Tyng commander; Gov. Shirley was attended by troops under Col.
Jacob Wendell, Col. Estes Hatch and Col. Benjamin Pollard - Boston item of 12 Dec. 1745 (7 Jan.)

Large sum was collected for relief of widows and children
of the men lost in the province snow <u>Prince</u> <u>of</u> <u>Orange</u>,
Capt. Smethurst, in the expedition against Cape Breton
- Boston item of 16 Dec. 1745 (7 Jan.)

DAVIS, Laurence, born in England, age <u>c</u>. 24 - has stolen
clothes and money from Hezekiah Bye, of Solebury, Bucks
Co. (7 Jan.)

CODGDILL, John, servant - runaway from Samuel Morris, of
Whitemarsh, Phila. Co. (7 Jan.)

HUMPHREYS, James - last Saturday lost in the Market in
Phila. a pocketbook, in which is a note payable to Ralph
Asheton from William Finley (7 Jan.)

BASKER, John, Irishman, supposed to be a servant, age <u>c</u>.

35 - was committed to Phila. Goal, Joseph Scull keeper
(7 Jan. supplement)

BUTLER, Thomas, Irishman, supposed to be a servant, age c.
21 - same as above

SHELLEY, Abraham, Keeper of the Workhouse in Phila. -
wishes to buy yarn, thread, linen (7 Jan.)

Proposal of John Bood, of Phila., for sale of buildings and
land; plans may be seen at his house or houses of Richard Sewell and Robert Greenway; tickets may be bought at
Phila. from John Bood, Richard Sewell and Robert Greenway; at Trenton from John Jenkins; at New York from Daniel Bellergrau, post rider (14 Jan.)

MARTIN, Capt. - has arrived from London at New York (14 Jan.)

WHITEFIELD, Rev. - has arrived in Georgia (14 Jan.)

HARTLEY, William, Ranger of Chester Co. - lists strays in
his hands (14 Jan.)

ORIN, Joseph, servant, age c. 16 - runaway from Daniel Mercer, of East Marlborough (14 Jan.)

Ship Expedition, Capt. Robert Robinson, from York River,
and the ship Restoration, Capt. John Wilcox, from James
River, have been taken and carried into France - Williamsburg item of 19 Dec. 1745 (21 Jan.)

Ship Success, Capt. Maclentoch, from Scotland, struck a-
ground, with loss of the ship and 5 of the men - Williamsburg item of 2 Jan. (21 Jan.)

Brigantine Boston Packet, Capt. Hunter, sailed Tuesday last
from Boston for Louisburg but met with a storm, cut away
from his masts and was towed into Marblehead - Boston
item of 30 Dec. 1745 (21 Jan.)

Sloop Mary, Capt. Man, arrived at New York Tuesday last from
Jamaica; he gave an account of a battle between the
British fleet and the French off Cape Nicholas on 15
Dec. - New York item of 13 Jan. (21 Jan.)

MACKENNY, Westlock, age c. 32, sailor, carpenter by trade -
runaway from privateer ship Marlborough, Christopher
Clymer commander; owners of the ship, Peter Bard and
John Howell will pay reward for his capture (21 Jan.)

GANTHONY, James, age c. 35, sailor - same as above

BRYAN, Joseph, age c. 40, sailor - same as above

HICKKEY, Francis, age c. 24, sailor - same as above

HUSBANDS, Thomas, age c. 23, sailor - same as above

HAZELY, John, age c. 30, sailor - same as above

HARRIS, Robert, age c. 40, sailor - same as above

MORGAN, William, English servant, age 29, who can talk
   Welsh - runaway from Henry Fagan, of Marpole Twp., Chester Co. (21 Jan.)

BROWN, Margaret, servant woman, who has had 4 or 5 children
   - runaway from John Leadlie, of Bristol Twp., Phila. Co.
   (21 Jan.)

McCOLLUM, John, late St. George's Hundred, Newcastle Co.
   upon Delaware - has run away from his special bail,
   John McFarland (21 Jan.)

Since 3 Dec. last a bay horse has been at Thomas Murry's,
   at Point-No-Point, the Widow Lynn's plantation (21 Jan.)

Tract of 66 acres in Twp. of Haverford, Chester Co. (part
   of estate of Lewis Davis, dec'd) - to be sold at auction
   by John Davis, administrator (21 Jan.)

PLUMSTED, Clement, Esq., dec'd - accounts with estate to
   be settled with Mary Plumsted and William Plumsted,
   exec. (21 Jan.)

GOODWIN, Joseph, bookbinder, in Black Horse Alley, Phila.
   - will dispose of 3 years of a servant girl's time (21
   Jan.)

JOHNSTON, Widow, at Wicaco - will dispose of 3 years of a
   Dutch servant girl's time (21 Jan.)

Messuage and lot in Market St., where he now lives, bounded
   northward with Market St. and eastward with Richard
   Brockden's, will be sold by Anthony Siddon, of Phila.,
   joiner (21 Jan.)

Message of Gov. George Thomas to the Pennsylvania Assembly
   and Assembly's answer to the governor (28 Jan.)

Privateer brigantine Hester, Capt. Grenall - arrived Friday last at New York - New York item of 20 Jan. (28 Jan.)

Brigantine Industry, Capt. Pearse, has arrived in the

Sound - New York item of 20 Jan. (28 Jan.)

Wednesday last Nehemiah Baldwin and 2 others were committed
to jail in Newark for being concerned in a riot; the
next day one of the men, being taken to a judge to be
admitted to bail, was liberated by a mob which broke
into the jail and freed all prisoners - New York item
of 20 Jan. (28 Jan.)

The privateer Raleigh, Capt. Millar, of Virginia, has taken
a French sloop (28 Jan.)

STEVENS, Capt., his mate and another man were murdered by
a French Mulatto on sloop bound for Jamaica (28 Jan.)

Little credit is due, according to a letter from Louisburg
of 30 Nov., to Mr. Bastide, the Engineer of Nova Scotia
(28 Jan.)

PEACOCK, Marmaduke - persons indebted to him are desired to
make immediate payment to Thomas Robinson, merchant, in
Phila. (28 Jan.)

RYLEY, Bryan, Irish servant, age c. 18 - runaway from
George Walker, of Pyke's Land, Chester Co. (28 Jan.)

BURGE, William, dec'd - accounts with estate to be settled
with Samuel Burge, executor, in Arch St., Phila. (28 Jan.)

MORGAN, Evan, cooper, near the drawbridge, in Front St.,
Phila. - sells wine, spirits and women's silk stockings
(28 Jan.)

WRAIT, Capt. - arrived 1 Jan. at Cape Anne, with Lt.-Col.
Ryan a passenger; other officers came with Capt. Lawson,
who arrived at Boston Thursday last; Capt. Lawson saw
Capt. Nevin off Cape Sables - Boston item of 13 Jan. (4
Feb.)

EMERSON, Mary, at the Sign of the Chest of Drawers in Front
St., Phila. - sells household goods (4 Feb.)

Ship Mary, Bernard Martin commander - will sail for London;
for freight or passage agree with John Reynell or with
the master on board at Fishbourne's wharf, Phila. (4 Feb.)

CLAY, Slater - has opened a public house in Newcastle, the
house where Mr. Curtis formerly lived (4 Feb.)

Dwelling and bakery, fronting Ratcliff St., in the Borough
of Bristol, Bucks Co., now in the possession of John
Hall, Esq. - will be sold at auction by Anthony Wilson,

FRAPPEL, Richard, dec'd - accounts with estate to be settled with Richard Sewall, impowered to act by Joseph
Turner, administrator (4 Feb.)

CARNALT, John, servant, age c. 23, from Darbyshire, Eng.,
who talks North-country English - runaway from George
Curry, of New London Twp., Chester Co. (4 Feb.)

Servant of Mr. Hannam, of Nantmel Twp., Chester Co., when
attempting to fell a tree, was accidentally killed on
Saturday se'nnight (11 Feb.)

BLACKWELL, Capt., bound from Phila. to Antigua - is reported to have lost all his masts 3 days after he left
the capes (11 Feb.)

Ship Aurora, Capt. Pickeman, from Holland via Plymouth -
arrived 28 Jan. at Annapolis with nearly 200 Palatines
(11 Feb.)

LARDNER, Lyn-ford - gives notice of payments of quit rent
due the Hon. Proprietaries (11 Feb.)

SEYMOUR, John, in Norris's Alley, Phila. - sells tea, pepper, coffee, rice and chocolate (11 Feb.)

HARGRAVE, Charles, in Front St., Phila., next door to the
Bank Meeting-house - sells muskets, pistols, tea, oil,
figs, glassware, china, pewter, pictures and wall-paper
(11 Feb.)

DURBOROW, Joseph, in Wackacoe - will sell lots at auction
at house of John Clifton in Wickacoe (11 Feb.)

DAVID, John, living near James Trego's - offers 10 pounds
reward for the apprehension of Samuel Prichard, taken
for forgery, who escaped from the constable in Donnegall,
Lancaster Co.; Prichard once lived in this twp., but now
lives about 8 miles from John Harris's ferry, on Susquehannah (11 Feb.)

BROGDEN, Edward, Irishman, age c. 25, carpenter - runaway
from his bail, John Hanly, in Chester (11 Feb.)

BEAKS, Stacy, late of Trenton, dec'd - accounts with estate
are to be paid to the executors, Mary Beaks and Gideon
Bickerdike (11 Feb.)

SMYTER, Capt., in a ship from London for Charlestown, S.C.,
and a brigantine for Cape Fear were taken 3 Dec. in sight
of Capt. Liddel, who arrived in Charlestown last Tuesday
- Charlestown item of 20 Jan. (18 Feb.)

TUCKER, Thomas, in his passage from Edisto to Charlestown last week, met a Dutch sloop taken by Capt. John Brown in a Rhode Island privateer - Charlestown item of 20 Jan. (18 Feb.)

NEVIN, Capt. - arrived 19 Jan. at Boston, having taken on board the crew of a sinking sloop, I. Wade master - Boston item of 20 Jan. (18 Feb.)

Friday last arrived at Boston Capt. Dummet from Bristol and on 19 Jan. Capt. Sherburn in a snow - Boston item of 20 Jan. (18 Feb.)

Friday last arrived at New York the ship Ruby, Capt. William Starkey from Gibraltar; in her company came out the following transports: Unity, Capt. Perry; Spencer, Capt. Sadler; Ridley, Capt. Jackson; Seanymph, Capt. Morecroft; the Friend's Glory, Capt. Milner; the Fell, Capt. Ormsby; the snow Katharine, Capt. Brown, all bound to Cape Breton - New York item of 3 Feb. (18 Feb.)

SHOURT, Capt., who arrived at New York Wednesday last from New Providence - reports that the privateer schooner George of Phila. lost her doctor and his mate and many men by sickness; the Castor and Pollux privateers of New York have put into one of the Bahama Islands to refit - New York item of 10 Feb. (18 Feb.)

Four lots in Phila. will be sold at the Widow Roberts's Coffee House; Patrick Baird is the vendue master (18 Feb.)

LUNAN, Alexander, on Sassafras River - has salt for sale (18 Feb.)

VAN AKEN, Henry, in Chesnut St., Phila., opposite to Charles Brogden's - sells coffee and coffee-mills, teakettles, looking glasses, etc. (18 Feb.)

Accounts with William McCormick are to be settled with him, assisted by William Attwood, at the Sign of the Indian King, in Market St., Phila. (18 Feb.)

Plantation of 100 acres in Oxford Twp., on road from Franckfort to Oxford Church, about 10 miles from Franckfort, on which Charles Harper now lives, is for sale; apply to Charles Harper or to John Boutcher, in the Manor of Moreland (18 Feb.)

Volunteers to serve in Lt.-Gen. Dalzell's Regt. of Foot at St. Christophers or Antigua may repair to Capt. Lewis Stevens, at the Indian King, Market St., Phila. (18 Feb.)

SAUNDERS, Richard, dec'd - accounts with his estate to be settled with William Russel, administrator (18 Feb.)

HOW, James, English convict servant - runaway from Major Andrew Campbell, Esq., of Frederick Co., Va. (18 Feb.)

Peter Robeson, Joseph Farmar and Jonathan Robeson, executors of Edward Farmar, Esq., last of Whitemarsh, dec'd - have for sale a tract of 250 acres in Bucks Co., above the Forks of Delaware, on a branch of a creek called McMuckle's Creek; other tracts, situated in the township of Whitemarsh, Phila. Co., one in the tenor of Samuel Erwin, one in the tenor of Robert Scott, one in the tenor of George Harkness, one in the tenor of Daniel Rynor (18 Feb.)

Privateer snow Warren, Capt. Kattur, of Phila., arrived Thursday last at Phila.; he told of Capt. Cunningham's engagement with some French ships (25 Feb.)

PLUMSTED, William - offers reward for jailing of the following mariners who ran away from the ship Westmoreland, John Dod Bonell commander: Richard Edwards, George Todder, John Pipe, Samuel Field, John Jackson, William Gessop and James Carroll (25 Feb.)

Notice to volunteers for service in the Regt. of Foot of William Shirley, Gov. of Massachusetts, are to repair to the Sign of the George, in Second St., Phila.; signed by Charles Proctor and Philip Gottfried Kast (25 Feb.)

House, lot and tanyard in Darby, Chester Co., to be sold or let; apply to John Justice, at Boon's Island, Kingsess Twp., Phila. Co. (25 Feb.)

COULTAS, James, at the Middle Ferry on Schuylkill - has a Negro girl for sale (25 Feb.)

PETERS, William, who served his clerkship in the Town-Clerk's Office at Liverpool, has moved from his office in Walnut St. to one in Chesnut St., the house where the late Mr. Cox lived; he serves as Register of the Court of Admiralty, notary public or conveyancer (25 Feb.)

Real estate is to be sold in Germantown - enquire of George Bringhurst in Germantown (25 Feb.)

HAMMET, Capt. - arrived Tuesday last at Nantasket from Lisbon - Boston item of 10 Feb. (4 Mar.)

Brigantine Mary, Thomas Desborough master, of New York -

reported taken by a French privateer - New York item of 14 Feb. (4 Mar.)

HERON, Col., late of General Oglethorp's regt. - has been appointed Gov. of Bermuda, in the room of Mr. Popple, Esq. (4 Mar.)

RENSHAW, Richard - will sell at an auction at the house of Peter Robeson, at the Sign of the Indian King, in Market St., Phila., 14 lots, some of which are bounded by property of Joseph Gardner (4 Mar.)

Collection of some 600 books will be sold at auction at the large room over Mr. Vidal's school in Second St., Phila. (4 Mar.)

Five lots in Wickacoe, between Second and First Sts., from the River Delaware, bounded southward on the north side of Almond St., westward on Joseph Richards, northward on Edward Shippen, Esq., and eastward by William Preston; sale will be at house of John Clifton in Wickacoe (4 Mar.)

CARVER, Jacob, at the Sign of the Stays, in Market St., Phila., over against the Prebysterian Meeting-house - makes all sorts of stays (4 Mar.)

CATREL, Mrs., from Dublin, at Mr. Burk's periwig-maker, in Front St., Phila., between Chesnut St. and Walnut St., and almost facing Gray's Alley - makes caps, bonnets, cloaks, and turbans for Negroes (4 Mar.)

CONDY, Capt., who was taken by a French privateer, came home in Capt. Greenway (11 Mar.)

Brigantine Hannah, Capt. Stamper, of Phila. - is said to be stranded in the Bay of Bantry in Ireland (11 Mar.)

MARSHAL, Capt. Peter, in the Prince Frederick privateer of Rhode Island - on 6 Jan. drove off 2 French privateers near Barbados (11 Mar.)

Two persons of note deceased in February were Ralph Asheton, Esq., of Phila., a member of the Governor's Council, and Jacob Taylor, formerly Surveyor General of Pennsylvania and "a very ingenious Astronomer and Mathematician" (11 Mar.)

SHIRLEY, W. - assures that persons enlisted for a definite period in his regiment or that of Sir William Pepperrell will be released at the time specified (11 Mar.)

ROCK, G., administrator of William Cox's estate, advises
that he will attend at Peter Warraws in Lancaster the
2 first days of the May Court (11 Mar.)

MELLOR, Jacob - will sell lots 9 miles from Phila., near
the Three Tons, on the Great Conestogoe Road (11 Mar.)

STEUART, William, Irish servant, age c. 37, shoemaker -
runaway from William Moode (11 Mar.)

BROOKS, Capt. - arrived at Portsmouth, N.H., about a week
ago from Plymouth, England, with European news - Boston
item of 24 Feb. (15 Mar.)

LISLE, Capt. - arrived at Plymouth, England, from Phila.,
on 20 Dec. (15 Mar.)

Philip Gottfried Kast or Charles Proctor will pay a reward
if the following 3 persons, who deserted from the officers recruiting for Gov. Shirley's Regt., are brought
to the Sign of the George, in Second St., Phila.; Moses
Larken, Daniel Shie and Barney Maclauchlan (15 Mar.)

Plantation of Herman Groethousen, late dec'd, in the Manor
of Springfield, adjoining Germantown Twp. - will be sold
by the executors, John Groethousen and Wigard Miller (15
Mar.)

Several houses and lots at Hadonfield will be sold by Timothy
Matlock and David Elwell (15 Mar.)

COOK, Samuel, servant, country born, age c. 19 - runaway
from Joseph Gilbert, of Biberry, Phila. Co. (15 Mar.)

HOPKINS, Capt. John, of Rhode Island, commander of the Re-
prizal - was killed in engagement 1 and 2 Feb. with a
Biscayan ship - Charlestown, S.C., item of 10 Feb. (27
Mar.)

Thursday last arrived at Charlestown the privateers Marlborough, Capt. Carr, and Reprizal, Capt. Dunbar, lately
Capt. John Hopkins of Rhode Island - Charlestown item
of 10 Feb. (27 Mar.)

HARVEY, Capt., from Jamaica - informs that the Spaniards
have several gallies on the cruize - Charlestown item of
10 Feb. (27 Mar.)

TURNER, Capt. Lewis - sailed 19 July from St. Kitts and was
taken by a French ship, the Lamoma, which also took the
mast ship Prince of Orange, Capt. Adams, with Gov. Clark
of New York and his family on board - Boston item of
25 Feb. (27 Mar.)

Ship <u>Balance</u>, Capt. Gill, sailed from New York to Phila.,
is ashore a little to the south of Barnagat - New York
item of 24 Mar. (27 Mar.)

MEAS, Capt. - has arrived at Phila. from Jamaica (27 Mar.)

The man-of-war <u>Sheerness</u> is commanded by William Bulley,
son of the Mr. Bulley who is Comptroller of the Customs
at Phila. (27 Mar.)

BARTRAM, John, botanist - has 2 specimens of the English
ash-colored ground liverwort, sent him by Dr. Dillenius,
chief Professor of Botany at Oxford (27 Mar.)

Privateer ship <u>Lincoln</u> of New York, Capt. John Jauncy commander - accidentally overset to the leeward of Cayan
and went to the bottom; 7 men were drowned but the rest
got aboard the <u>Triton</u>, Capt. Rosewel (27 Mar.)

NEALL, Daniel, Irish servant, age <u>c</u>. 28 - runaway from Daniel Onell, of Timber Creek, Gloucester Co. (27 Mar.)

MACKINNEY, William, servant, this country born - same as
above

BROGDEN, Edward, Irishman, age <u>c</u>. 27, house-carpenter -
runaway from his bail, John Hanley, in Chester Co. (27
Mar.)

LEECH, John, dec'd - accounts with estate to be settled
with Mary Leech, in Second St., Phila., near the church;
lots belonging to the estate are to be sold, including
one in Kensington on Marlborough St. and crossing Crown
St. 386 ft. in length to Benjamin Shoemaker's; another
lot of 4 acres is at Pegg's brick-kilns (27 Mar.)

CROASDALE, Thomas - will sell brick house on west side of
Front St., Phila., now in his possession (27 Mar.)

Snow <u>Warren</u>, Alexander Katter commander - will sail on a
cruising voyage; volunteers may repair to the commander
or to the Sign of the Boatswain and Call, near the drawbridge in Phila. (27 Mar.)

PRESTON, Samuel, late of Phila., dec'd - sundry ground-rents
in Phila. are offered for sale by his executors, Samuel
Preston Moore and Preston Carpenter (27 Mar.)

DRURY, Edward, in Vine or Race St., Phila. - sells Epsom
salts (27 Mar.)

LEWELLIN, John, acting for the public school of St. Mary's

Co., Md. - seeks a master for said school (27 Mar.)

SMITH, Joseph, Irish-born servant, age c. 22, weaver - runaway from Jacob Hindman, of Talbot Co., Md. (27 Mar.)

MILLAR, John, servant, a Scotchman or from the North of England, age c. 30, cooper - runaway from Robert Newcom, of Talbot Co., Md. (27 Mar.)

LYLIS, James, young Irish servant, weaver - runaway from Margaret Lowe, of Talbot Co., Md. (27 Mar.)

ALLEN, Nathaniel, Jr., in Front St., near Market St., Phila. - has for sale a quantity of Carolina reed, fit for stay-makers (27 Mar.)

Brigantine _Defiance_, of Newport, Capt. John Dennis, took a French ship on 30 Jan.; Capt. Dennis lost 15 men, one of whom was Mr. Calder, the quartermaster - Newport, R.I., item of 21 Mar. (3 Apr.)

ERSKINE, Capt. - last week arrived from Antigua at Rhode Island in a sloop belonging to Boston, with Capt. Mills (who had been taken by the French) on board as a passenger - Boston item of 24 Mar. (3 Apr.)

BASS, Capt., in a privateer of Boston, has taken a French sugar-ship in the West Indies - Boston item of 24 Mar. (3 Apr.)

Friday last at a Court of Assize for Suffolk Co., Mass., John Fowle (boatswain of H.M.S. _Wager_) and John Warren (lad of c. 17) were found guilty of the barbarous murder of William Conner and John Bryant - Boston item of 24 Mar. (3 Apr.)

WHITEFIELD, Rev., in a letter from Charlestown, S.C., to a friend in Boston, relates that he has settled his family at Bethesda - Boston item of 24 Mar. (3 Apr.)

JAUNCY, Capt. John, late commander of the privateer ship _Lincoln_, of New York - arrived Wednesday last at New York with a French prize, the _Annunciation_, Mons. Rapouillet commander; Capt. Higgins, of the Rhode Island privateer _Hector_, claims a share of the prize - New York item of 31 Mar. (3 Apr.)

Sloop _Mary Anne_ of New York, Capt. Burchal, when attacked by 2 privateers, fought her way through them and got in safe - New York item of 31 Mar. (3 Apr.)

TANNER, Capt., arrived at New York from Coracoa - informs

that the privateer sloop <u>Polly</u>, Capt. Helms, of New York, has taken 3 prizes - New York item of 31 Mar. (3 Apr.)

WITTER, Capt. - arrived at New York Saturday last from Jamaica - New York item of 31 Mar. (3 Apr.)

Ship <u>Balance</u>, Capt. Gill, which was ashore at Barnagate, is got off - New York item of 31 Mar. (3 Apr.)

The <u>Dragon</u> privateer of New York, Capt. Seymour - has retaken a Boston sloop - New York item of 31 Mar. (3 Apr.)

2 Apr. arrived at Phila. the prize ship <u>Judith</u>, which was bound from Marseilles to Cape Francois, John Baptist Troupez Martin commander, and was taken by the Phila. privateer ship <u>Marlborough</u>, Capt. Christopher Clymer (3 Apr.)

Capt. Eve from Barbados informs that the French privateers are very brisk thereabouts (3 Apr.)

PITTS, Capt., from Barbados, reports that he spoke with 2 privateer brigantines, Capt. Richards of New York and Capt. Bass of Boston, and the next day with Capt. Tingley of New York (3 Apr.)

<u>A</u> <u>Protest</u> <u>against</u> <u>Popery</u>, by Hugh Jones - has been lately published at Annapolis by Jonas Green and is also sold by B. Franklin (3 Apr.)

KING, John, convict servant, age <u>c</u>. 25 - runaway from Robert North and Alexander Lawson, of Baltimore Co., Md. (3 Apr.)

SALTER, Samuel, convict servant, "a dapper little fellow" - same as above

FARRINGTON, Capt., of schooner <u>Dolphin</u> - on 15 Mar. was cast away on Block Island - Newport item of 28 Mar. (10 Apr.)

French prize ship <u>St. Joseph</u>, Mons. Jacob Mariene commander, was taken by the <u>Pollux</u> privateer, of New York, Capt. Burget, the <u>Castor</u>, Capt. Easom, and the <u>Diana</u>, Capt. Skinner, of Bermuda - New York item of 7 Apr. (10 Apr.)

RICHARDS, Capt., in brigantine <u>William</u>, of New York, and Capt. Bass, of Boston, have taken a large Dutch ship - New York item of 7 Apr. (10 Apr.)

HOWELL, Capt., from Statia - was chased on his passage to New York - New York item of 7 Apr. (10 Apr.)

SEMPLE, Capt. - arrived yesterday at New York and brought letters from Capt. Tingley - New York item of 7 Apr. (10 Apr.)

TANNER, Capt. - Friday se'nnight arrived at New York from Corocoa and brought an extract from Capt. James Burchall bound from New York to Coracoa - New York item of 7 Apr. (10 Apr.)

Sloop from Barbados, Capt. McKitrick - was taken by a French privateer, Capt. Cadiz - New York item of 7 Apr.; Capt. Cadiz also took a ship from Barbados, Capt. Bullock commander, with the owner, Mr. Gibbs, on board - New York item of 7 Apr. (10 Apr.)

Privateer brigantine Caesar, Capt. Griffith, of Rhode Island - was cast away on the west end of Bermuda (10 Apr.)

The following ships from Phila. have arrived as follows: the Highlander, Capt. Watson, at Plymouth; the Anne Galley, Capt. Houston, at Falmouth; the Carolina, Capt. Mesnard, at Portsmouth; the ship Boulton, Capt. Downes, at Belfast (10 Apr.)

Capt. Bryant, of New York, was taken by a French privateer between Portsmouth and the Downs (10 Apr.)

French ship, sent by the Marlborough privateer, Capt. Christopher Clymer, was condemned Monday last at Phila. as a lawful prize (10 Apr.)

Goods taken out of the prize ship La belle Judith will be sold at auction at Oswald Peele's wharf in Phila., as will the ship; an inventory is to be seen at Peter Bard's, merchant, in Water St. (10 Apr.)

WILKINSON, Anthony, in Water St., Phila. - sells pickled sturgeon (10 Apr.)

DAWSON, Daniel, hatter, late of Phila., dec'd - accounts with estate to be settled with executors, Solomon Fussell and Jeremiah Warder (10 Apr.)

Eight lots in Phila. are to be sold at auction at Roberts's Coffee-house; one house is late dwelling of Paul Preston, dec'd; another lot, on Gilbert's Alley, has a smith's shop, now in the possession of William Parker; apply to Joseph Oldman, William Fisher or William Parker (10 Apr.)

At David Sekell's, at Spring Garden, is to be seen an ox weighing 1,892 pounds (10 Apr.)

HOLDER, John, millwright, late of Trenton, N.J., but now
of Derby in Chester Co. - will not pay debts contracted
in future by his wife Johanna, who has gone to Trenton
and taken their child (10 Apr.)

Philip Gottfried Kast or Charles Procter, at the Sign of
the _George_, in Second St., Phila., will pay reward for
the capture of the following deserters from Gov. Shirley's
Regt.: Moses Larken, Daniel Shie, John Price, Richard
Brazier, Thomas Leech, Joseph Bragden, Barney Maclauchlan, Daniel Lion, John Macgloughlin, Albert Leopolt and
Charles Burnes (10 Apr.)

WOOD, David, servant, age _c_. 23, millwright - runaway from
Thomas James and Robert Murray, of Lancaster, Pa. (10
Apr.)

At Templebar, Salisbury, Bucks Co., are to be seen the confession of R.R. and a tame dolphin (10 Apr.)

Testimonials to efficacy of the China-stones and powders of
Mr. Torres are given by the following: Ann McDonald, of
Phila.; Daniel Fossit, of Phila.; William Hodge; Robert
Johnston, of Merrion Town, Phila. Co.; Mr. Mares's wife
(10 Apr.)

TINGLEY, Capt. - has arrived at New York with a very rich
prize (17 Apr.)

A Spanish man-of-war snow took the following prizes: the
ship _Postilion_, Capt. Doughty and Capt. Curling of the
storeship (17 Apr.)

Privateer _Galgoa_, Capt. Arracouchea, was lately careening
(17 Apr.)

DENNIS, Capt., of Rhode Island - is being detained by the
Gov. of Havana (17 Apr.)

The _Trembleur_, Capt. Bowne, of Phila. - has taken a Spanish
sloop and is now in consort with the _Bumper_, a privateer
of Montserrat, Capt. Beesley commander (17 Apr.)

Reflections on Courtship and Marriage - has just been published by B. Franklin (17 Apr.)

TURNER, Peter, over against the Post Office, in Market St.,
Phila. - has for sale goods imported in the ship _William_,
Capt. Henry Harrison, from London; Samuel Emlen, at the
Sign of the Golden Heart, opposite the Market, in High
St., Phila., sells items imported in the same ship (17
Apr.)

MATLACK, Timothy - is removed and settled in Phila., against the Jersey Market, a little above the Post Office in Market St., at the Sign of the Two Sugar-Loves, marked T M in gold letters (17 Apr.)

LEYCET, John, servant brass button- and buckle-maker - runaway from Thomas Morgan, of Borough of Chester, Chester Co. (17 Apr.)

HOLLAND, William, apprentice, age c. 16 - runaway from Thomas Manle, joiner, in Front St., Phila. (17 Apr.)

MACGEACH, William, late of Abington, dec'd - accounts with the estate to be settled with Abigail Macgeach, executrix (17 Apr.)

LE GALLEE, Capt. - has arrived at Boston - Boston item of 14 Apr. (24 Apr.)

Capt. Tingley's prize ship was condemned at New York Tuesday last - New York item of 21 Apr. (24 Apr.)

JOHNSTON, Capt., of the privateer brigantine Dolphin - has taken a French sloop (24 Apr.)

Woodstock Galley, of Phila., Capt. Exeter, bound from Phila. to Londonderry - ran on the Three Tuns and was lost (24 Apr.)

Tuesday last the prize schooner Magdalene, taken by the Trembleur, arrived at Phila. (24 Apr.)

Parcel of servants has arrived in the snow Dublin's Prize, William Rankin master, now off Chesnut St. wharf and will be sold by Israel Pemberton, Jr., or by the master (24 Apr.)

The prize sloop Mary, the prize schooner Magdalene, sugar, coffee, bulls hides, tortois shells, earthenware and mahogany planks will be sold at Mr. Hamilton's wharf in Phila.; an inventory may be seen at Townsend White's in Front St. (24 Apr.)

SEYMOUR, John, in Mr. Norris's Alley - sells silk (24 Apr.)

OSWALD, Andrew, at Joseph Turner's store, in Front St., Phila. - sells maps (24 Apr.)

LITTLE, William, dec'd, late of Duck Creek, Newcastle Co., master of a shallop - accounts with estate are to be settled with William McCrea, administrator, in Front St., Phila. (24 Apr.)

WYER, Simon, at the Sign of the Globe in Market St., Phila.
- mends pewter articles (24 Apr.)

WORTHINGTON, James, sailor, who pretends to be a carpenter
- absconded from ship <u>Ballance</u> (now at Phila.), Richard
Gill master (24 Apr.)

CLEMMONS, Hugh, Irish sailor - same as above

HALL, Archibald, Irish sailor - same as above

BOWLER, John, of Phila., mariner - will not pay debts contracted in future by his wife Rose (24 Apr.)

Real estate in New Jersey is to be sold or let by William
Morris and William Morris, Jr., in Trenton (24 Apr.)

House on Society Hill is for sale; enquire of Robert Grace,
merchant, in Phila. (24 Apr.)

LENDRUM, Andrew, late of Trinity College, Dublin - has
opened school in New Brunswick to teach Latin, Greek,
logic (24 Apr.)

PORTER, Mary, a prisoner woman - runaway from house of
Arthur Foster, of Paxton Twp., Lancaster Co. (24 Apr.)

VAN VEGHTY, Mr., a farmer - scalped by French and Indians
close by his house at Shaatacook, about 18 miles from
Albany (1 May)

Privateer sloop <u>Polly</u>, Capt. Helme, last from Rhode Island
- arrived 27 Apr. at New York (1 May)

Snow <u>Wexford</u>, Capt. Lyon, of Phila. - has arrived at Lisbon (1 May)

Ship <u>William</u> <u>and</u> <u>Mary</u>, of Phila., Capt. William Blair, bound
for Ireland - has put into Fial (1 May)

SIMS, Joseph, at his house in Front St., Phila. - sells
goods imported in the ship <u>William's</u> <u>Galley</u>, Capt. Harrison, from London (1 May)

Tract of land in Bucks Co. belonging to Richard Murray -
is to be sold by Abraham Chapman and Henry Vanaken, in
Phila. (1 May)

FLETCHER, John, of Plymouth, Deputy Ranger for George
Boone, Esq., Chief Ranger for Phila. Co. - lists strays
in his hands (1 May)

WOLDRIDGE, Michael, servant, age between 17 and 18 - runaway from James Payne, cooper, living on Society Hill (1 May)

OKILL, George - has a small bale imported in the ship William Galley, Capt. Harrison; owner proving his claim and paying costs may have it (1 May)

MARRIOTT, Thomas, living in Borough of Bristol, Bucks Co. - has lots of land there for sale (1 May)

BRIANT, Mr., of Gorham Town, about 10 miles from Falmouth - on 19 Apr., together with 4 of his children, was killed by a party of Indians - Boston item of 28 Apr. (8 May)

Gov. William Shirley, of Massachusetts - directs the militia officers on the eastern and western frontiers to order the inhabitants to carry arms on Sundays and other days (8 May)

GRIFFIS, Capt. - last week arrived at Boston from New York - Boston item of 28 Apr. (8 May)

JAUNCY, Capt., who arrived at New York last week from Jamaica - had been in company with 2 New York privateers, the Clinton sloop and brigantine Triton; he tells of an engagement between H.M. snow Drake, Capt. Clarke, and a Spanish privateer - New York item of 5 May (8 May)

SMITH, Capt. - arrived 4 May at New York from Jamaica (8 May)

Indians in New York have burnt the barn of Matthys Vandenbergh, opposite to Col. William Schuyler's, within 4 miles of the City of Albany, and a barn in Schenegtade belonging to William Teller - New York item of 5 May (8 May)

A Negro of Mr. Sanders Glen, within ½ mile of Schenegtade, seized a gun from an Indian - New York item of 5 May (8 May)

Lottery tickets may be obtained from Peter Valete, Peter Van Brugh Livingston and Gabriel Ludlow in New York and from B. Franklin in Phila. (8 May)

House and lot in Market St., next door to Jacob Shoemaker's, at the Sign of the Spinningwheel, are to be let; enquire of James Meredith at said house (8 May)

Two lots in Phila. are to be sold at auction by order of Mary Leech, executrix of John Leech, dec'd, at John Saunders's, at the Sign of the Huntsman and Hounds (8 May)

GREEN, Thomas, Sheriff, of Dover - has in the goal there an
Englishman who goes by the name of James Young, age c.
40, thought to be the person who escaped August last
from Anthony Tate, near Newtown Goal, Bucks Co. (8 May)

DAVIS, David, fuller, at Lower Merion, Phila. Co., within a
mile of the Three Tuns and 10 miles of Phila. - offers
for sale his 100-acre tract, dwelling and mill, as he has
removed to Darby to the fulling mill late Job Harvey's;
he will continue to take in work at John Chappel's, at
the Sign of the Black Bull, in Market St., Phila. (8 May)

WELLS, Moses, living in Lower Dublin, Phila. Co. - offers
reward for recovery of mare strayed or stolen (8 May)

BOYER, Theobald - will sell 10 lots at auction at the Sign
of the Rising Sun, on Germantown Rd. (8 May)

JACOBS, James, apprentice, carpenter, age c. 18 or 19, born
at New York - runaway from Isaac Taylor, of Phila. (8
May)

WARKINS, Richard, of Phila., tobacconist - will not pay
debts contracted in future by his wife Catharine (8 May)

Detailed account of the murder on 5 Apr. of Richard Waters,
tailor, in Kent Co., Md., by 2 Papist servants, Hector
Grant, a Highlander, and James Herney, an Irishman; a
West-country convict woman servant and an orphan apprentice girl knew of the projected murder, were sworn to
secrecy but finally confessed (15 May)

It is reported that Capts. Ellis, Binney, Mackenzie, Perchard,
with tobacco from Maryland, were taken on their way home
and Capt. Kemp, from Barbados for Maryland, is taken (15
May)

OGILVIE, Capt. - his ship is lost, with its cargo and all
the men except the captain and one man - Annapolis item
of 22 Apr. (15 May)

BROWN, Capt. - was taken up, along with his crew, as his
ship, belonging to Maryland and bound for London, was
sinking just within the Capes - Annapolis item of 29
Apr. (15 May)

Letter, dated St. Malo, France, 26 Jan., of Capt. Isaac
Prince, of Boston, tells how he was taken, as was Capt.
Curtis from Boston - Boston item of 5 May (15 May)

COLE, Capt., in a brigantine, foundered and was taken up by
a French ship - Boston item of 5 May (15 May)

TERREL, Capt. - has taken a rich ship and carried her into Antigua - Boston item of 5 May (15 May)

BENNET, Capt. - arrived 4 May at Boston from Louisburg in the brigantine _Boston Pacquet_ (15 May)

Letter from a gentleman at Albany, dated 5 May, recounts deeds committed by Indians: at Stonearabia 2 Negroes (one belonging to Levinus Winne and the other to the heirs of Mrs. Wendell) were taken prisoner; at Kinderhook the houses and barns of Tunis Van Slyck and Peter Vosburgh were burnt; at Schengtade Simon Grant and 2 of his brothers were killed and the house and barn burnt; one Indian is supposed to be a son of Tom Wileman; Major Collins and Major Glen are gone in pursuit of the Indians - New York item of 12 May (15 May)

GRANT, Capt. - arrived Tuesday last at Phila. from South Carolina, with Rev. Whitefield on board; Capt. Grant reports that Capt. Clymer, of Phila., in company with Capt. Lampree of Charlestown, has taken a Spanish sloop (15 May)

LYON, Capt. - has arrived at Phila. from Barbados (15 May)

REILY, James, a servant of Quintane Moore, of Ridley Twp. - hanged himself on 8 May (15 May)

Partnership of Stedman and Robertson, in Phila., has expired (15 May)

STUART, William, Irish servant, age c. 37, shoemaker - runaway from William Moode, of Phila. (15 May)

Plantation of 250 acres in Lower Merion, Phila. Co., between Conestogoe Rd. and Schuylkill, is for sale by Joseph Tucker, on said place (15 May)

JACKSON, Samuel, whip-maker, of the southern liberties of Phila. - offers reward for strayed cow (15 May)

PASCHALL, Elizabeth, shopkeeper, in Market St. - intends to take down and rebuild the house where she lives and remove for 3 months to the house where Robert Jordan formerly lived, in Strawberry Allen, Phila.; accounts with estate of her dec'd husband, Joseph Paschall, are to be settled with her (15 May)

By order of the Orphans Court of Phila., Thomas Hopkinson clerk, the following items will be sold at the house of Margaret Ingram, at the Sign of the Rose and Crown, in Front St., Phila.: tenement now in the possession of Samuel Shoemaker, merchant, fronting Water or King St., late the estate of Stephen Bazeley, dec'd (15 May)

Audit of Orphan House accounts in Georgia (original vouchers
are at Savannah in hands of Mr. Habersham), sent by Rev.
Whitefield to Mr. Franklin; William Woodroofee, William
Ewen and William Russel, who had examined accounts, swore
to accounts before Henry Parker and William Spencer,
bailiffs of Savannah (22 May)

At Contocook on 4 May a Mr. Cook and a Negro man were killed
by Indians and a Mr. Jones is missing - Boston item of
11 May (22 May)

Report from Albany of the following attacks of Indians:
fired (but missed) upon Lt. Burrows, as he was riding between Mr. Johnston's house and his mill; burnt the house
and barn of Nicholas Fisher at Canistagajon; at Mr.
Livingston's farm took prisoner Jacob Egmont and killed
his brother-in-law, Mr. Hogg - New York item of 19 May
(22 May)

H.M.S. _Torrington_, Capt. Hardy commander - arrived Thursday
last at Sandy Hook from Cape Breton - New York item of
19 May (22 May)

WHITEFIELD, Rev. - arrived at Phila. Saturday (22 May)

Four Negroes and 2/33 of the privateer ship _Marlborough_ -
will be sold at auction at Widow Jones's Coffee House in
Water St., Phila. (22 May)

COOK, Zebulon, at corner house over the drawbridge in Front
St., Phila. - offers reward for recovery of bag, con-
taining 295 pistoles and one moidore - dropped between
Phila. and Frankford (22 May)

CONNOLY, Simon, native Irishman, age c. 24, who served his
time in the upper part of Chester Co., near James Way's
- escaped from John Owen, Sheriff of Chester Co., who offers reward for Connoly's capture (22 May)

Toney, Negro slave, Virginia born, age c. 30, a good sawyer
- runaway from Benjamin Hill, of Bertie Co., N.C.; reward will be paid if slave is brought to his master or
to John Blakeley, in Phila. (22 May)

The following 3 names are added to list of deserters from
the officers raising men for Gov. Shirley's Regt.: Henry
Mactheron, Richard Mackalley and Daniel Lewen (22 May)

SHERBURN, Capt. - arrived Thursday last at Boston from
Louisburg - Boston item of 19 May (29 May)

MINVEIELLE, Mr., merchant, of Barbados - repaid sum taken out of a French flag of truce by Capt. Helme, which made possible the release of English prisoners held at Martinico - New York item of 26 May (29 May)

MORRIS, Lewis, Gov. of New Jersey - died Wednesday last at Trenton at an advanced age - New York item of 26 May (29 May)

NORWOOD, William, a son of, belonging to the garrison at Saraghtoga - on Tuesday last was killed by the Indians, while a German who used to live with Col. John Schuyler was taken prisoner - New York item of 26 May (29 May)

DICKISON, Capt., arrived at Phila. from Antigua - reports capture of 2 brigantines (29 May)

GLENTWORTH, Capt., of Phila. gives the following list of captains who were prisoners with him at Martinique: Stanly, Robinson, Adams, Mansfield, Howard, Gross and Loveit from Boston; Walden and Slayton from Piscataway; Heverlan and Smith from New York; James from Rhode Island; Mitchell from Virginia; Kemp and Blake from Barbados; Jones from Lisbon; Gladman from London; Gibbins and Dyer (29 May)

Deposition of 23 May 1746 of John Cunningham (commander of privateer snow Dreadnaught), John Gardner (lieutenant) and David Logan (carpenter of said snow) before James Hamilton, Mayor of Phila., concerning action at sea against French ships; English ships present were brigantine Castor, of New York, Capt. Easom, and Capts. Burgess and Skinner (29 May)

NEGLEE, John, at auction at his plantation (opposite to Mr. Logan's) will sell 36 lots, extending along the road leading from Phila. to Germantown; a plan may be seen at said Neglee's, or at his son John Neglee's in Phila. (29 May)

CROXALL, Richard - offers reward for capture of the 3 following convict Irish servants belonging to Benjamin Tasker and Co., who have run away from the Baltimore Ironworks: Matthew Jolly, age c. 25; Henry Kirk, a young fellow, butcher by trade; Terence Flanagan, age c. 24; they took with them a Dutch servant woman belonging to William Williams at the said works; she stole from her master, among other things, a bond from Fielding Turner to William Williams and another bond from Alexander McCollum to Williams (29 May)

SHEERLOCK, John, Irish servant, age c. 25, who served part

of his time with John Tree of Caecil Co. - runaway from
Alexander Lawson and Company, from a plantation commonly
known as White Marsh, in Baltimore Co., formerly belonging to Daniel Dulany, Esq. (29 May)

VOMABLE, James, Irish servant, who served his time near
where Sheerlock did, weaver by trade - same as above

Toney, Negro, age c. 24 - runaway from John Pawling at
Perkiomen (29 May)

GRAY, Joseph - employed B. Franklin to print 2d., 3d. and
6d. notes of hand to meet the need for small change (29
May)

GREEN, John, of Lancaster Co. - by applying to Thomas Wil-
liams, hatter, in Second St., Phila., opposite the Quakers
Meeting-house, will hear something to his advantage (29
May)

McCAMANT, Alexander, of Salisbury Twp., Lancaster Co. - has
taken up a stray horse (29 May)

BLUNSTON, Samuel, Esq., late of Lancaster Co., dec'd - accounts with estate to be settled with James Wright,
executor (29 May)

CRAIGE, Capt. - arrived 25 May at Boston from Bristol (5
June)

The _William_ _and_ _Mary_, William Blair master, of Phila., has
arrived at Belfast and the _Euryale_, Lawrence Anderson
master, of Phila., has arrived at Madeira (5 June)

NORRIS, Charles - requests that the person who borrowed
Conyers Middleton's _Life_ _of_ _Cicero_ from Samuel Morris
return the book (5 June)

LEECH, Mary, executrix of John Leech, dec'd - will sell at
auction at the Sign of the Swan in Kensington several
lots (5 June)

SWEECKHOUSE, Conrad, living next door to Thomas Myer in
Third St., Phila. - makes and gilds picture frames (5
June)

KIRK PATRICK, John, of Charlestown, in North East - offers
reward for recovery of a stray mare (5 June)

SIMS, Buckridge, at house of Joseph Turner, and William Wallace, at the Sugar House, the upper end of Front St.,
Phila. - sell sugar, candy and molasses (5 June)

Ship **King Ahasuerus**, Abraham Le Messurier master, will sail for Barbados (5 June)

BROOKS, John, Irish servant, shoemaker - runaway from Alexander Cruikshank, of Phila., shoemaker (5 June)

Proclamation of Lt.-Gov. George Thomas of Pennsylvania (12 June)

RAMSEY, WILLIAM, sailor, who came from Londonderry - runaway from the snow **Entwistle**, Capt. William Davison; reward will be paid if Ramsey is brought to George Okill, merchant, in Phila. (12 June)

YOUNG, David, servant, from Londonderry - same as above

LAWRENCE, Thomas, Jr. - is removed to his house in Second St., Phila., where Samuel Sansom lately dwelt, near to Peter Stretch's (12 June)

HARTLEY, William, Chief Ranger of Chester Co. - lists strays in his hands (12 June)

SADOWSKI, Andrew, of Amity Twp. - offers reward for recovery of 30 pounds in gold coin, lost on 4 June, if it is sent to Marcus Hulings (12 June)

BAYNTON, Peter, dec'd - accounts with his estate to be settled with the executors, Mary and John Baynton, Joshua Maddox and Thomas Bourne (12 June)

LINUS, Thomas, of New Providence Twp., Phila. Co. - will not pay debts contracted in future by his wife Jane (12 June)

WHITELOCK, Isaac, of Borough of Lancaster, tanner - offers reward for recovery of strayed gelding (12 June)

MAN, John, of Warwick Twp., Bucks Co. - has taken up a brown horse (12 June)

HARKNESS, George, in Whitemarsh - has taken up a bay horse (12 June)

Sloop of Capt. Dickenson, bound for Corocoa, struck upon Bonira and was lost but the men were saved, according to a report of Capt. Tanner - New York report of 10 June (19 June)

Snow **Two Sisters**, a French prize, taken by the letter of marque ship **Wilmington**, of Phila., commanded by Capt. Sibbald, arrived Friday last at Phila. (19 June)

READ, James, at upper end of Chesnut St., Phila., has been
commissioned notary and tabellion public within Pennsylvania (19 June)

ROBESON, Malchum, Scotch servant, who can talk Welsh - runaway from James Davis, of Tredyffryn (19 June)

Tickets for the New York lottery may be purchased from Peter
Valete, Peter Van Brugh Livingston and Gabriel Ludlow in
New York and from B. Franklin in Phila. (19 June)

OBARE, Michael, Irish servant, age c. 20 - runaway from Rees
Price and Henry Glasford, of London Britain Twp., Chester
Co. (19 June)

MARTIN, William, Irish servant, age c. 20 - same as above

ASHETON, Susannah, administratrix of the estate of Ralph
Asheton, dec'd - offers for sale a malthouse, brew-
house, sawmill and lots on the Haverford and Merion Rds.
and a hop garden formerly belonging to Walter Lewis (19
June)

Plantation, formerly belonging to Peter Shilbert, dec'd, at
Sommerhousen, joining to Matthew Muris's papermill, in
Wisahickon, and to the plantation of Mr. Kock, merchant,
of Phila. - to be sold by Shilbert's widow (19 June)

Persons indebted to George Jones, formerly of Black Horse
Alley - are to settle accounts with his attorney, Lawrence Anderson in Second St., Phila. (19 June)

COTTER, Thomas, who served his time to John Allison, of
Donegall, Lancaster Co. - is desired to apply to his
brother, John Cotter, who is now in Phila. (19 June)

KELLY, Patrick, of Biberry - will not pay debts contracted
in future by his wife Elizabeth (19 June)

Meeting between the Gov. of South Carolina and the leaders
of the Catawba Indians, Yanahe Yaiengway, Capt. Taylor,
Nasserhee and others; some Chicesaws, under French Jemmy,
had killed a Catawba Indian (26 June)

Thursday last arrived at New York the privateer brigantine
Dolphin, of New York, commanded lately by Capt. Johnson
but now by Capt. Randall, as Johnson was killed in an
engagement with a French ship, the St. Jaques, Mons. Dela-
motte commander; the Dolphin's consort was the privateer
brigantine Prince Frederick, Capt. Marshal, of Rhode Island, who lost his master and 2 other men - New York
item of 23 June (26 June)

Saturday last privateer schooner <u>The Seeker</u>, Capt. Harriot, sailed from New York - New York item of 23 June (26 June)

HARVEY, Capt., arrived at New York from Turks Island, reported that a Boston sloop, Capt. Hancock, was taken - New York item of 23 June (26 June)

Tuesday last arrived in Phila. a schooner taken by the privateer snow <u>Warren</u>, Capt. Katter, of Phila. (26 June)

ASHTON, Capt. - Tuesday last arrived at Phila. from Barbados but last from St. Kitts; he had been taken by a French privateer but retaken by the <u>Lyme</u> man-of-war (26 June)

It is reported from Virginia that the following 3 ships have been taken: ship <u>Jenny</u>, Capt. Bogle, from Glasgow; the <u>John</u>, Capt. Bland, and Capt. Higgins from Rappahanock (26 June)

Privateer ship <u>Marlborough</u>, of which an inventory is to be seen at Peter Bard's, will be sold at vendue at Oswald Peel's wharf (26 June)

REISER, Bernard - offers for sale his place of 70 acres in Germantown; for terms inquire of Balthas Reiser, living on the premises (26 June)

WEISER, Conrad, Ranger of the Northeast Corner of Lancaster Co. - lists strays in his hands (26 June)

MOORE, Thomas, in Fourth St., Phila. - offers reward for recovery of a horse strayed or stolen from the Commons, Phila. (26 June)

HOLMS, Thomas - offers reward for recovery of a mare, strayed or stolen from the Rising Sun, between Phila. and Germantown; the mare or information thereof may be brought to the owner at Mr. Armitage's, the Rising Sun, or the Crooked Billet (26 June)

Messages from Lt.-Gov. George Thomas to the Pennsylvania Assembly (3 July)

LONG, Capt. - arrived 22 June at Boston, with European news (3 July)

CUMMINGS, Timothy - about a fortnight ago was killed by Indians near St. George's Fort - Boston item of 23 June (3 July)

HAWKS, Gershon - wounded in the arm by Indians in Hampshire Co., Mass.; one Mr. Perry escaped to Fort Pelham (3 June)

Tuesday last arrived at New York the privateer brigantine
<u>William</u>, Capt. Nathaniel Richards; Capt. Richards, with
Capt. Bass of Boston, took a sloop on 17 Apr. (3 July)

BILL, Capt. - arrived Wednesday last at New York; he had
been taken but ransomed (3 July)

GOOCH, Brig.-Gen. of Virginia - plans to set out for New
York about 12 July (3 July)

At Kinderhook the Indians have taken captive a son of John
Vosburgh and a daughter of Isaac Tewise Van Deusin -
New York item of 30 June (3 July)

LIGHTFOOT, Capt. - has sent into Providence a large Spanish
ship (3 July)

MORGAN, Evan - will let the Three Crown Tavern, next door
to Peter Bard's, in Water St., Phila. (3 July)

FRANKLIN, B. - will publish Saturday next Gen. Blakeney's
<u>The New Manual Exercise</u>, with <u>The Evolutions of the Foot</u>
by Gen. Bland (3 July)

Tom, Negro, age <u>c</u>. 22 or 23, who formerly belonged to Dr.
Shaw of Burlington - runaway from Samuel McCall, Jr.,
of Phila. (3 July)

WARDE, Thomas, English servant, age <u>c</u>. 19 - runaway from
George Emlen, of Phila. (3 July)

WARD, Barnet, Dutch servant, age <u>c</u>. 24 - same as above

Jack, Negro, age <u>c</u>. 22 - runaway from Hugh Martin, of
Lebanon, Hunterdon Co. (3 July)

HUTCHISON, John - runaway from John Buckingham, of Newcastle Co. (3 July)

SWAM, John, servant, age <u>c</u>. 26, this country born - runaway
from Joseph Forman, of Freehold, Monmouth Co., N.J.
(3 July)

WARREN, John, a felon, Westcountryman, age between 50 and
60 - escaped from Newtown Goal, Bucks Co.; reward for his
capture is offered by John Penquite (3 July)

PUGH, Joseph, Sub-Sheriff of Lancaster Co. - offers reward
for capture of the 3 following women who broke out of the
goal of that county: Jane McCoun (age <u>c</u>. 20), committed
for murder; Ann Guttery (age <u>c</u>. 13), committed for murder;
Mary Porter, convicted of felony (3 July)

DRURIE, Edward, in Vine or Race St. - sells Epsom salts
and English rub stones (3 July)

ZUILLE, Matthew, at the store where Alexander Lane formerly lived, in Front St. - sells handkerchiefs, stockings,
thread, paper, hardware (3 July)

RUSHBROOK, Thomas, of Phila. - will not pay debts contracted
in future by his wife Ann (3 July)

Tuesday last arrived at Boston from Louisburg H.M.S. Chester,
Capt. Spry commander, with Admiral Warren and Sir William
Pepperell on board - Boston item of 30 June (10 July)

At Louisburg Gov. Knowles is arrived; one regt. there is to
be commanded by Col. Frampton; Capt. Starkey arrived
with 200 soldiers from New York; Col. Choat returned from
St. John's - Extract of a letter from Louisburg, dated
3 June - Boston item of 30 June (10 July)

On 28 June near the fort at Schenegtade the Indians killed
John Quackenboss and Thomas Meebee and carried off a
Negro - New York item of 7 July (10 July)

Saturday last arrived at New York the privateer sloop
Clinton, Capt. Bevan, and yesterday a French prize snow
taken by Capt. Byard in the Hester, of New York - New
York item of 7 July (10 July)

Sloop Katie, of Phila., Cornelius Bowne master, bound to
Providence, was cast away on the north end of Abico (10
July)

Messuage and lot of George Wensell, on one side of the road
between Germantown and Whitemarsh, was attached at suit
of William Branson; Richard Sewell, Robert Greenaway and
Samuel Smith, who were appointed auditors, will sell the
real estate (10 July)

FLOWER, Samuel, of Reading - offers reward for recovery of
horse strayed from Reading Furnace, Chester Co. (10 July)

RAY, James, a felon, age c. 19, who was a servant to Abraham
Underhaven in New Providence and later to Joseph Rogers,
of Chester Co. - has escaped from Phila. Goal; Joseph
Scull offers reward for his capture (10 July)

COLSON, William, Negro, Bermudian born - runaway from William
Hugg, of Gloucester Town (10 July)

McCORMICK, John, Irish servant, age between 30 and 40 - runaway from Benjamin Davis, of Upper Merion, Phila. Co.
(10 July)

Proclamation of Lt.-Gov. George Thomas of Pennsylvania (17 July)

It is reported at Boston that Capt. Rouse had returned to Louisburg from St. John's, where the inhabitants who were supposed to come away refused, some having gone to Canada and others concealed in the woods - Boston item of 7 July (17 July)

Saturday last a prize snow, taken by Capt. Bayard and sent to New York, was condemned; French prisoners on board reported that Capt. Vardil, who sailed from New York for Jamaica, was taken by a French privateer - New York item of 14 July (17 July)

WHITEFIELD, Rev. - will preach Tuesday next at the Crooked Billet in the Manor of Moreland (17 July)

HAMILTON, William, administrator of William Hamilton, dec'd, will sell at auction the mills and plantation of 200 acres, late of the dec'd, at West Marlborough, Chester Co. (17 July)

Plantation of 500 acres on Timber Creek, Gloucester Co., West New Jersey, which formerly belonged to Abraham Porter, dec'd - is offered for sale by the owner, Daniel Hingston, on the plantation; in Phila. enquire of Joseph Sims, in Front St. (17 July)

BROCKDEN, Richard, opposite the Butcher's Shambles, in Phila. - offers reward for recovery of a mare and a colt (17 July)

Mark, Negro, age c. 25 - runaway from John Hinson, of Pine Forge, refiner (17 July)

McENTIRE, Nicholas, Irish servant, age c. 17 - runaway from Samuel Ralston, of Whiteclay Creek Hundred, Newcastle Co. (17 July)

Masters of vessels taken by French (20 May to 1 July) and carried into Martinique: Charles Donavan, John Simmonds, Jacob Parsons, Owen Fergus, Francis Frewen, Nathaniel Pierce, Elisha Wells, Thomas Oliver, Thomas Clauge, John Bush, Fobes Briggs, John Vavassor, Hugh Hedges; masters of vessels taken into Guadaloupe: John Brown, Samuel Coverly, Capt. Parmeyter, James Townshend, Capt. Coker, Capt. Evans, Capt. Webber (24 July)

CLYMER, Capt. William, commander of the privateer snow Cruizer, of Phila. - was taken prisoner and sent to Spain (24 July)

House in Second St., Phila., near the Baptist Meeting, in which William Bingham now lives, is to be let; enquire of James Bingham (24 July)

Ned, Negro - runaway from Reynold Howell, on Whiteclay Creek, in Newcastle on Delaware (24 July)

Plantation in Radnor Twp., Chester Co., within a mile of Radnor Meeting-house is for sale; enquire of Peter Jones of Lower Merion (24 July)

SEATON, Alexander - has opened a writing office in a front room at the house of Widow Drinker's, almost opposite to William Branson's in Second St., Phila. (24 July)

CLYMER, Christopher - requires all men inlisted in his company to appear at the Sign of the George in Phila. or the Bear in Frankford on Monday at 10 or be considered deserters; he names 2 men as deserters, Richard Williams, a butcher, whose mother lives in New York, and Samuel Swanson, a tailor, who lived in Second St., Phila., and was lately seen in Darby (24 July); the deserters are given as belonging to the company of Capt. William Trent (31 July)

PRICE, David, servant, age c. 24, born in Somerset Co., Md. - runaway from Thomas Nixon, of Dover, Kent Co. on Delaware (24 July)

FAIRBROTHER, Thomas, English servant, age c. 27, carpenter - runaway from John Philips, of Phila., house-carpenter (24 July)

SCULL, Nicholas, Sheriff - gives notice that there will be sold at the house of Jacob Hall, at Tacony, Oxford Twp., Phila. Co., a tract of land, late the estate of Arthur Jones, dec'd; a plan thereof may be seen at Michael Lightfoot's or Griffith Jones's in Phila.; also a 100-acre tract in Upper Merion will be sold on 16 Aug. at Richard Hughs's, on Conestogoe Rd. (24 July)

FREMAN, Capt. - last Tuesday arrived at Marblehead from the Orkneys - Boston item of 21 July (31 July)

Vessel from Piscataqua, John Clark master - was lost 2 days ago to westward of Chapeaurouge Bay - extract from a letter from Louisburg of 25 June (31 July)

GRIFFITS, Capt., in a Rhode Island privateer, has lately taken 2 prizes - Boston item of 21 July (31 July)

BARNES, Capt. - arrived at New York 27 July from Louisburg (31 July)

WOODFORD, Capt. - arrived at New York last Wednesday from Antigua, with news that 2 privateers, Capt. Place and Capt. Higgins, both of Antigua, have taken a pirate sloop, the <u>Pearl</u>, commanded by Capt. Ward, who had stolen the sloop (then commanded by Capt. Maybury) from St. Christophers in the night - New York item of 28 July (31 July)

Brigantine <u>Townsend</u>, Capt. Anthony, of Phila. - was towed into Bermuda on 7 July, bottom uppermost (31 July)

Thursday last arrived at Phila. Capt. Dorrell, from Barbados (31 July)

WHITEFIELD, Rev. (not yet 32 years old), after preaching in Phila., has left for New York (31 July)

HARTLEY, William, Chief Ranger of Chester Co., at Charlestown, Chester Co. - lists strays in his hands (31 July)

MILLER, Alexander, peruke-maker - has removed from his house in Second St. to Front St., Phila., next door to Mr. Thomas Ellis, glazier, almost opposite Roberts's Coffee House (31 July)

BRUCE, John, at store lately used by Samuel Neave, opposite to Capt. Coombes's, in Water St., Phila. - sells cloth, stocking, patterns, Bibles, snuff, etc. (31 July)

BRAND, Jonathan, in Water St., next door to the One Tun Tavern, near Carpenter's wharf, Phila. - sells Indian corn (31 July)

BAYLIE, Thomas - directs delinquent members of the Cornwall Company (whose Ironworks are in Lancaster Co.) to pay what is due (31 July)

KENTING, Thomas, of Oxford Twp., Phila. Co. - offers reward for recovery of a horse, stolen or strayed (31 July)

ISERLO, Engel, in Rockhill Twp., Bucks Co. - has taken up a horse (31 July)

GREEN, James, in Fourth St., Phila - offers reward for recovery of a strayed horse (31 July)

HOLLYDAY, James, Jr., sheriff - offers reward for apprehension of the following prisoners who escaped from the Queen Anne's Co. Goal in Maryland; John Murphy, Irishman, age between 30 and 40, committed on suspicion of felony, and Isaac Jones, born in said county, age <u>c</u>. 30, prisoner for debt (31 July)

COLE, William, servant, age c. 20 - runaway from Elizabeth Jefferis, of East Bradford Twp., Chester Co.; reward will be paid if the runaway's horse is taken and
sent to Joseph Gray's in Phila. (31 July)

FENBEY, John, of Phila., potter - his wife Mary has eloped
from him (31 July)

WENYAM, James, Mulatto, age c. 37 - runaway from Richard
Colegate, of Kent Co. on Delaware; reward will be paid
if runaway is taken to his master or to Abraham Gooding,
Esq., or to the High Sheriff of Newcastle Co. (31 July)

Tony, Negro, age c. 24, who speaks good English and High
Dutch - runaway from John Pawling, of Parqueoman (31
July)

O'DURISH, Patrick, servant - runaway from David Sheerer, of
Nantmill Twp., Chester Co. (31 July)

CONNER, Bryan, servant, age 35, who speaks English, Irish
and French - runaway from William Oakford, of Alloway's
Creek (31 July)

BROWN, Capt., on passage from Boston to Louisburg, was attacked but escaped - Boston item of 28 July (7 Aug.)

It is reported that the Shirley Galley, Capt. Rous, and
another ship were taken by Indians when part of their
crews were on shore - Boston item of 28 July (7 Aug.)

The following 3 men, Roman Catholics, taken on board a
French privateer, were executed Thursday last at Boston:
Peter Ferry, Thomas Rigby and James Cattee - Boston item
of 28 July (7 Aug.)

At Kinderhook the Indians killed one Brown but Woodcock and
Wheeler who were with him escaped - New York item of 4
Aug. (7 Aug.)

FENBY, Mary, of Phila., whose husband John had advertised
that she eloped, states that they parted by consent; she
desires that no one trust him on her account (7 Aug.)

BURN, Simon, Irish servant - runaway (supposedly in company
with Sarah Rothness, who lately eloped from her husband
in Queen Ann's Co.) from the schooner Bennett, now in
Chester River; reward for his capture will be paid by
Hamilton & Wallace in Phila. (7 Aug.)

WILLARD, Joseph, servant, born in Bucks Co. - runaway from
Thomas Clemson, who lives at John Heath's (7 Aug.)

JONES, Barbara, late of Phila., shopkeeper, dec'd - accounts
with estate to be settled with John Jones, Jr., executor
(7 Aug.)

READ, John, Jr., late of Newcastle Co., dec'd - accounts
with estate are to be settled with William Patterson,
near Christine Bridge; Read's house is to be let by
said Patterson or Samuel Hazard, administrator (7 Aug.)

Jack, Bermudian Negro, age c. 19 - runaway from Stafford
Somersall, commander of the sloop Elizabeth and Mary,
lying at Hamilton's wharf in Phila. (7 Aug.)

Schooner Elizabeth Marianne, Capt. George Wardlin, from New
York, bound to Frederica - Friday last was chased into
Charlestown, S.C., by a French privateer - Charlestown
item of 14 July (14 Aug.)

Sloop Diamond, Edward Evans, master, from Charlestown,
bound to Antigua, has been taken by the French - Charlestown item of 21 July (14 Aug.)

Brigantine Abigail, Capt. Carlisle, of New York, bound for
Jamaica, has been cast away on the Grand Key; news was
brought by Capt. Stiles - New York item of 11 Aug. (14
Aug.)

Indians killed 8 men of Capt. Mackintosh's Company about 6
miles east of Albany, at the plantation of a Mr. Collins - New York item of 11 Aug. (14 Aug.)

SMITH, Capt., from Antigua, reports that the ship Ballance,
Capt. Gill, of New York, has arrived at Antigua - New
York item of 11 Aug. (14 Aug.)

BAYARD, Capt., of the privateer brigantine Hester, of New
York - has taken a French privateer and retaken an English vessel - New York item of 11 Aug. (14 Aug.)

The brigantine Argyle, of Phila., and the brigantine Addi-
son, Capt. Peele, of Phila., were taken by the French
(14 Aug.)

DINGEE, Charles - states that the infamous Tom Bell, call-
ing himself Lloyd, came on board his ship about 3 miles
above Newcastle and stole clothing (14 Aug.)

THOMPSON, Caesar, dec'd - accounts with his estate to be
settled with William Spafford and Thomas Ellis, executors (14 Aug.)

SCOTT, James, is removed from store upon Hamilton's wharf

to the house where Edward Shippen formerly lived, at the corner of Walnut St. next Front St. - sells dry goods (14 Aug.)

GOODFELLOW, William, servant, age c. 15 - runaway from James Claxton, at the Sign of the Bear, in Frankford (14 Aug.)

Snow George, Nathaniel Ambler master, just arrived from Ireland with servants; enquire of George Meares at Thomas Gordon's on Powell's wharf (14 Aug.)

Negro woman and Negro boy for sale; enquire of Lawrence Growdon, at Trevase, Bucks Co. (14 Aug.)

BENNETT, John, apprentice, age 19, country born - runaway (taking with him an English convict servant, brass-founder by trade) from Charles Miller, of Ogletown, near Newcastle (14 Aug.)

PRATT, Henry - is removed from the Sign of the Ship a Ground in Front St. to the Royal Standard in Market St., opposite the Butcher's Shambles, where he keeps tavern (14 Aug.)

LONG, Moses, convict servant, who talks broad Yorkshire - runaway (with Anne Fetcham, convict servant) from Samuel Hart, of Potapsco (14 Aug.)

HART, William, Irish convict servant, age c. 26 - runaway from William Dames, of Chestertown, Md. (14 Aug.)

VAN AKEN, Henry, in Chesnut St., opposite Charles Brockden's office, at Phila. - will sell lots in Germantown; enquire of Paul Kripper opposite the Quaker's Meeting, Phila.; he also has for sale land along Mill St. in Germantown, joining in length with Daniel Mackennet's land, opposite Benjamin Shoemaker's land (14 Aug.)

Corks are sold at William Davis's, chair-maker, near the upper end of Second St., Phila. (14 Aug.)

WILLIAMS, Capt., who arrived at Boston Thursday last from Louisburg, reported that Capts. Rouse and Starkey were returned there from St. John's; an Indian fellow belonging to Capt. Rouse escaped and saved the life of a son of Gov. Clinton of New York - Boston item of 11 Aug. (21 Aug.)

Saturday last, when wives of Capt. John Rouse and Capt. Clark Gayton were riding in a chair through Pleasant St., a lad shooting at a mark on a tree accidentally wounded slightly Mrs. Gayton on the nose but killed Mrs. Rouse - Boston item of 11 Aug. (21 Aug.)

MIDDLETON, Capt., in a Bermudas sloop, decoyed a French privateer onto a reef, so that the privateer stove to pieces (21 Aug.)

HAZLETON, Capt. - arrived Tuesday last at Phila. in a flag of truce from Havana (21 Aug.)

WHITEFIELD, Rev. - arrived Saturday last at Phila. from New York (21 Aug.)

SHUMLEY, Rachel, late of Phila., dec'd - accounts with estate to be settled with Richard Sewell, administrator (21 Aug.)

WENZELL, George, late of Cresham, in the German Twp. - his creditors are to present their accounts to the auditors, Richard Sewell, Samuel Smith and Robert Greenway, on 29 Aug. at the house of William Dewees in Germantown and on 1 Sept. at the house of Henry Pratt, near the Court House in Phila. (21 Aug.)

RAKESTRAW, William, at the upper end of Fourth St., Phila. - offers for sale a brick house in Front St., at the corner of Jones's Alley, commonly called Pewter Platter Alley (21 Aug.)

MEDCALF, Jacob, dec'd - his plantation in Town of Gloucester is to be sold by the executors, Joseph Cooper, William Hudson and William Cooper (21 Aug.)

Potts's Mills are for sale; apply to Thomas Shoemaker in Phila. (21 Aug.)

ELVES, Henry, in Water St., corner of Market St., Phila. - sells glue, sweet oil and ship chandlery goods (21 Aug.)

EATON, Richard, ivory-, hard wood- and horn-turner - lives in Front St., opposite to Coombes's Alley (21 Aug.)

NORRIS, Thomas - will sell at auction stone house and lot in Germantown, on the north side and on the entrace of the town of Phila. (21 Aug.)

FRY, William, late of Middletown, dec'd - accounts with estate to be settled with the administrators, Joseph Richardson, Jonas Preston and Thomas Tomlinson (21 Aug.)

Two brick houses in Burlington are for sale; apply to Peter Bard, merchant, in Phila., or Dinah Bard, at Burlington (21 Aug.)

PARSONS, William - offers for sale 2 brick houses on the west side of Second St., Phila., between his dwelling house and the corner house on Mulberry St., where Ebenezer Kinnersly lives (21 Aug.)

ALEXANDER, James - offers reward for recovery of a mare and colt, strayed or stolen from plantation of John Atkins, of Lower Dublin (21 Aug.)

WILKINSON, Anthony, in Water St., Phila. - has pickled sturgeon for sale (21 Aug.)

SHARP, Thomas, dec'd - George Emlen, Jr., and John Nicholas are empowered to collect debts due the estate (21 Aug.)

DELATUSH, Henry - offers for sale real estate at Reckles Town, near Crosswicks Meeting House, Burlington Co. (21 Aug.)

BINGHAM, William - has removed from house (2 doors below the Baptist Meeting) in which he formerly lived to a house near Black Horse Alley, 2 doors below William Bradford's, printer, in Second St., Phila. (21 Aug.)

Ship Mary, Capt. Martin, from Phila. - has arrived in England (28 Aug.)

WHITEFIELD, Rev. - preached Sunday last in Phila. (28 Aug.)

PEACOCKE, Marmaduke - sells wine vinegar at his store in the alley where Stephen Vidal keeps school in Second St., Phila. (28 Aug.)

DAWSON, Robert, dec'd - accounts with estate to be settled with George Emlen, Jr., and James Benezet, administrators (28 Aug.)

RUE, Joseph, apprentice, age c. 19, shoemaker - runaway from William Baker, of Bensalem, Bucks Co. (28 Aug.)

FITZ SIMMONS, Richard, Irish servant, age c. 22, who pretends to be a baker by trade - runaway from Samuel Bettle, of Birmingham, Chester Co. (28 Aug.)

HANRATY, Thomas, Irish servant, age c. 19 - runaway from James Maxwell, of Londongrove Twp., Chester Co. (28 Aug.)

Brigantine Le Trembleur, Obadiah Bowne commander - will sail as a privateer; persons wishing to enter on board may repair to said commander or to the Sign of the Le Tremoleur in Water St., Phila. (28 Aug.)

Reward will be paid for horse strayed from plantation of
Edward Grizzel, of Middletown Twp., Chester Co.; horse
may be brought to the owner or to William Guy, of Edgmont Twp. (28 Aug.)

ATTERBURY, Francis, servant, age c. 27, who calls himself
an Englishman - runaway from Thomas Shepherd, of Cohansey
(28 Aug.)

Privateer brigantine Hester, Capt. Samuel Bayard commander,
of New York - arrived at New York yesterday with 3 fine
prizes - New York item of 1 Sept. (4 Sept.)

LINCH, Patrick, Irish servant, age c. 20 - runaway from
George Taylor, at Warwick Furnace, in Chester Co. (4
Sept.)

BUDDELL, William, late of Mount Holley, dec'd - his house,
for upwards of 15 years a good and accustomed inn, is to
be let; accounts with the estate are to be settled with
Nathaniel Thomas and John Monroe, executors (4 Sept.)

Brick house, below the drawbridge, Phila., near William
Plumsted's, now in the tenure of John Harrison, is for
sale; apply to James Stuart, in Front St. (4 Sept.)

Several lots in Germantown are for sale; apply to Isaac
Shoemaker in Phila. or John Shoemaker in Germantown (4
Sept.)

Auction will be held at house of Robert Dawson, next the
Quaker's Meeting House, in Second St., Phila. (4 Sept.)

House where Thomas Bourne now lives, in Market St., Phila.,
is to be let; enquire of Thomas Holland (4 Sept.)

Britain's Mercies, and Britain's Duty, by George Whitefield
- has just been published by William Bradford, at the
Sign of the Bible in Second St. (4 Sept.)

Distilling done at John White's, in Fifth St., between Market St. and Chesnut St., Phila. (4 Sept.)

THOMAS, Samuel - will sell at auction the fulling mill in
Lower Dublin, Phila. Co., which formerly belonged to
Richard Thomas (4 Sept.)

MEDDIN, Roger, Irish servant lad - runaway from John Pass,
of Mount Holley, Burlington Co. (4 Sept.)

Lot and House, adjoining the house Mr. Levy now lives in,
will be sold at auction (4 Sept.)

Mona, Spanish Negro, age c. 18 or 30 - runaway from Thomas Mayburry, at Hereford Furnace, Phila. Co. (4 Sept.)

PATTERSON, Alexander, servant, age c. 17 or 18, who knows something of the tailor's trade - runaway from Timothy Grunon, of Bohemia, Md. (4 Sept.)

Dick (commonly called "Preaching Dick"), Negro, age c. 29 - runaway from Thomas Rutter, of Phila. (4 Sept.)

Wife of Governor of Massachusetts - died 29 Aug. at Dorchester, Mass. (11 Sept.)

CONNOLY, Capt. - arrived yesterday at Boston from Annapolis Royal - Boston item of 1 Sept. (11 Sept.)

Five companies of volunteers raised in New Jersey for expedition against Canada are commanded by Capts. Parker, Dagworthy, Stephens, Ware and Leonard (11 Sept.)

Ship Hope, Capt. Ritchie, from Phila. - was taken by a French privateer but retaken by English men-of-war; Capt. Shaw, in a Rhode Island privateer, took the Frenchman that took Capt. Ritchie (11 Sept.)

WHITEFIELD, Rev. - last night returned to Phila. after an excursion of 9 days into East Jersey (11 Sept.)

MILLS, Daniel, English servant, tanner - runaway from George Aston, of Whiteland, Chester Co. (11 Sept.)

SCULL, Nicholas - intends to run for office of sheriff in Phila. Co. (11 Sept.)

STUART, Edward, late of Newcastle, chapman, dec'd - accounts with estate to be settled with Redmond Conyngham, administrator (11 Sept.)

COX, William, West County servant, age c. 25 or 30, butcher - runaway from Thomas Holmes, of Annapolis; reward will be paid if Cox is brought to John Nelson in Phila. or Peter Robeson, at the Sign of the Indian King (11 Sept.)

WILSON, Abraham, carter, dec'd - accounts with estate to be settled with John McCulla's, in Water St., Phila. (11 Sept.)

House in Fourth St., Phila., between Race and Arch Sts., is for sale; apply to John Norwood, in Front St. (11 Sept.)

SENSEBACH, Adam, German, age c. 22, farmer, from Telpahoken - deserted from Foot Company of Capt. John Diemer (11 Sept.)

Just published, and to be fold by B. Franklin,

MOOR's *American Country Almanack* for the Year 1746.

Lately publish'd, and to be fold by B. FRANKLIN,
THE Votes of the laft Seffions of the Affembly of the Province of Pennfylvania. Price 2s.

Just Imported in the Ship Carolina, Stephen Mefnard from London, and to be fold by William & David M'Ilvaines at their Store in Water Street, oppofite to Charles Willing's, very reafonably, for ready Money or the ufual Credit,

BRoadcloths, broad and narrow fhalloons, buttons and mohair, plain callimancoes, worfted damafks, tammies, florettas, ftripp'd lincy woolcy, embofled flannels, white and coloured Kendall cottons, plains, half-thicks, ruggs, blankets, red, green and blue baze, yarn hofe, mens and womens worfted ftockings, mens and womens thread ditto, double and finle worfted caps, fingle cottton caps, gartering, 7-8 garlix, yard wide tandems, 6-4, yard wide and 3-4 Manchefter checks, yard wide, 7-8 and 3-4 Scotch ditto, 7-8 and yard wide ftripp'd Hollands, yard cotton Hollands, 7-8 and 3-4 bed ticks, linnen handkerchiefs, filk handkerchiefs, tufted fuftines, ftript and diced ditto, cambricks, callicoes, quilts, needles, pins, fhoe and knee buckles, painted fnuff boxes, fcizers, mens and womens thimbles, buck fcale tables, bone ditto, black tipp'd ditto, buck fpring knives, piftol capt ditto, buck penknives, buck handled cuttoes, and fundry other Merchandize too tedious to mention.

N. B. As the Term of Partnerfhip between William Blair and William M'Ilvaine is now expired, all Perfons indebted to them are defired to pay their refpective Debts, they both intending for Britain in Fourteen Days.

Just Imported from Europe, and to be fold by John Smith at his Store on Ifrael Pemberton's Wharff, the following Goods, viz.

FIne ozenbrigs, yard wide and 7-8 garlix, tandems, nuns holland, long lawns, cambricks, filefiar, yard wide and 7-8 Irifh linnen, diapper, dowlas, 6-4 bed ticks, white heffens, yard wide, 6-4, 7-8 and 3-4 cotton and linnen check, fine, fuperfine and coarfe bro d cloths, forreft cloths, fine and coarfe plains, ditto kerfeys, napt coatings, frize, half-thicks, London and Yorkfhire fhalloons, tammies, durants, buttons and hair, black taffaties, changeable ditto, white, pink, changeable and ftriped Perfians, black and blue alopeens, bandanos, velvet caps, bellad filk, filk and worfted hofe, worfted damafks, red and white flannel, cotton romals, fundry forts fleeve buttons, flat white mettal coat and veft buttons, pins & needles, Kirby's fifh hooks, buck rivitted, bone, horn & cocoa-cafe knives & forks, piftol capt buck fpring knives, ditto penknives with feals, taylors fheers, fheep fheers, fciffars, brafs inkpots, horn and ivory combs, fnuff-boxes, nuns thread, flates and flate pencils, quarto bibles, writing paper, maps, fealing-wax, wafers, ink-powder, mens and womens horfe whips, falt petre, brown and white buckram, nonfopretties, cloth coloured thread, felt hats, womens fhammy gloves and lamb mittins, coffee mills, pepper boxes, hungary, tapes, bobbins, camblets, filk and linnen handkerchiefs, cord, galloon, ferrits, worfted qualities, gartering, cotton caps, fhirt buttons, crates of yellow porringers, and white flint ware, &c.

Just imorted from London, and to be fold very cheap, by Wholefale or Retail, three Doors below the Poft-Office, in Market-Street,

ALL Sorts of Pewter, hard Metal and common Brafs, Copper and Tin-ware, of all Sorts; where is alfo given the higheft Price in Cafh, for any Quantity of old Pewter, Copper or Brafs, by
THOMAS BILES.

Now fitting out for a Cruizing VOYAGE *againft his Majefty's Enemies, and will fail in three Weeks at fartheft,*

The Privateer SHIP MARLBOROUGH, *CHRISTOPHER CLYMER*, Commander, Burthen 300 Tons, to carry 20 Carriage Guns, 2 Nine, and 18 Six Pounders, 20 Swivels, with all Kinds of warlike Store, and 150 Men.

ALL Gentlemen Sailors and able body'd Landfmen, inclined to enter on board the faid Privateer, may repair to the Commander aforefaid, or to the Sign of the *Pewter-Platter*, in *Front-Street*, where the Articles are to be feen and fign'd by thofe who have a Mind to go the Cruize.

For NEWRY:

The SNOW GEORGE, *FRANCIS BOGGS* MASTER, Will be clear to fail in Fifteen Days.

For Freight or Paffage, agree with John Erwine in Second Street, next Door to Samuel Sampfon's, or the Mafter on Board.

N. B. *Said Erwine has feveral Sorts of Irifh Linnens, Sheetings and Diapers, to be fold cheap, for ready Money or fhort Credit.*

October 6. 1745.

BRoke out of Trenton Goal, on Saturday Night laft, one James Johnfton, a lufty, ftrong built Man, about fix Foot high, of a frefh Complexion, and fair infinuating Speech: He is an Irifhman, and his right Name is White; he lately ran from his Bail, and entered on board the Dreadnought, Capt. Cunningham, who upon Application caufed him to be fet on Shore at Newcaftle, and committed to Goal there, from whence he was brought laft Thurfday. Whoever fhall apprehend the faid Johnfton, and fecure him, fhall have Five Pounds Proclamation Money as a Reward.
William Brown, Under Sheriff.

Philadelphia, November 7. 1745.

JESSE BOURNE, intending for England with Capt. Mefnard, defires all Perfons indebted to him to pay immediately. There is a neat Affortment of European Goods, very cheap for ready Money, to be difpofed of by faid Jeffe Bourne.

Part of a page from *The Pennsylvania Gazette* of November 14, 1745.

SEYDMAN, John, German, age <u>c</u>. 21, who came from Boston - same as above

SHAFFER, Adam, German, age <u>c</u>. 23, who came from over Schuylkill - same as above

GERLACH, Wendell, German, tailor, who came from Schippack - same as above

DOUGHTY, Neil, Irishman, from Lancaster - same as above

SEYMOND, Bernard, young man, smith, who came from Goshehopen - same as above

MAYER, John, joiner, who came from Goshehopen - same as above

HARRIS, John, of Peckstan, and his wife Esther have parted; he will not pay debts contracted by her in future (11 Sept.)

COATS, William, Jr., of Phila. - will not pay debts contracted in future by his wife (11 Sept.)

HART, John, Sheriff - will sell plantation of 300 acres in the Forks of Delaware, late belonging to Moses Tatamy, taken in execution (11 Sept.)

Variety of European goods - are for sale by Jones and Beddome, at their store in Second St., Phila., between the Baptist Meeting House and the George (11 Sept.)

Two or 3 vacancies for schools exist in Bethlehem Twp., Hunterdon Co., West Jersey; apply to John Emley in Bethlehem (11 Sept.)

WEISER, Conrad, Ranger for northeast corner of Lancaster Co. - lists strays in his hands (11 Sept.)

Harry, Mulatto slave - runaway from Jane Brent, in Charles Co., near Port Tobacco (11 Sept.)

MURRAY, Bryan, native Irish servant, age <u>c</u>. 24 - runaway from Stephen Jenkins, of Abington Twp., Phila. Co.; reward will be paid by Robert Beard if runaway is brought to said Jenkins or to John Beard, at Neshaminy (11 Sept.)

Reward will be paid by John Stapler in Wilmington or Stephen Stapler in Phila. for recovery of a boat that was stolen or went adrift from Wilmington in Newcastle Co. (11 Sept.)

Admiral Warren on Friday last hoisted his flag on board the

Massachusetts Frigat, Capt. Tyng commander - Boston item of 8 Sept. (18 Sept.)

Ship Oswego, Capt. John Waddel, who arrived Friday last at New York, states that about 5 weeks ago he parted with the Four Brothers, Capt. Brasher, for New York, the Carolina, Capt. Mesnard, the Friendship, Capt. Lisle, and the Anne Galley, Capt. Houghston, for Phila. (18 Sept.)

BELL, Tom - has enlisted in a New Jersey company under Capt. Stevens (18 Sept.)

SCHUYLER, Capt. - commands the militia at Saraghtoga (18 Sept.)

Arrived at Newcastle on Delaware are the ship William and Mary, Capt. William Blair, from Belfast and Larne, the brigantine Rebecca, Capt. Burk, from Dublin and Capt. Marshal from Londonderry (18 Sept.)

FARMER, Edward, late of Whitemarsh, dec'd - accounts with estate to be settled with Peter Robeson (18 Sept.)

Plan of Louisburgh, done by Mr. Pelham from original drawing of Richard Gridley, Esq., Commander of the Train of Artillery at the Siege of Louisburgh - has been published by J. Smibert, In Queen St., Boston (18 Sept.)

Five lots of land in Germantown, some touching upon Jacob White's land, will be sold at house of Bernard Reser in Germantown; enquire of Charles Brockden, in Phila. (18 Sept.)

BROWN, Mary, Irish servant, age c. 19 or 20 - runaway from John Stinson, in Walnut St., Phila. (18 Sept.)

REY, James, Irish servant, age c. 18, who can talk Dutch - runaway from Conrad Waltecker, of Phila., butcher (18 Sept.)

HUDDELL, Joseph, cooper, over against the Tun, in Water St., Phila. - sells the Universal Balsamick Tincture (18 Sept.)

TAYLOR, John, at Sarum, Chester Co. - sells rod-iron and hoops (18 Sept.)

Plantation of 152 acres in Manor of Moreland, Phila. Co. is for sale; enquire of Andrew Farrel in Phila., who has a Negro, a tanner by trade, to sell (18 Sept.)

CRAVEN, Capt., of H.M.S. Rye - on his approach, in a bay north of Gaspia, the crew of a snow at anchor blew up their ship (25 Sept.)

NORTON, Rev. John, at Fort Massachusetts, in a letter dated
20 Aug., states that they have surrendered to the French
and Indians and that a Mr. Knolton was killed - Boston
item of 15 Sept. (25 Sept.)

Thursday last arrived at New York the French prize ship St.
Joseph, taken 29 Aug. by the privateer brigantine William,
Capt. Arnold, of New York - New York item of 22 Sept.
(25 Sept.)

Last week a sergt. of Capt. Livingston's company, quartered
at Mr. Van Veghten's fort near Albany, was shot and killed
by Indians - New York item of 22 Sept. (25 Sept.)

BLAIR, Capt. informs at Phila. that about a fortnight ago
he spoke with a French prize snow going to New York,
taken by the Triton privateer of New York (25 Sept.)

Ship Arundel, late Capt. Henderson, from Londonderry to
Phila., has arrived at Newcastle; she was taken by a
Spanish privateer and in the passage the captain, both
mates and some passengers died (25 Sept.)

Yesterday arrived at Phila. the sloop Jane and Sarah, Capt.
Phinehas Hubble, from Barbados; they had an engagement
with a French privateer schooner; Capt. Grant, from
Georgia for Phila., spared Hubble some hands and a sail
(25 Sept.)

WHITEFIELD, Rev. - left Phila. Thursday last (25 Sept.)

WALDO, Brig.-Gen. is to command the army assembled at Albany
(25 Sept.)

The Carolina, Capt. Mesnard - arrived at Phila. this morning from London (25 Sept.)

Deeds are drawn by Alex. Stuart and Lewis Gordon at their
office in Front St., Phila., opposite the house of Joseph Turner, merchant (25 Sept.)

FOULKE, Col. J. - warns that quarter's excise on rum, wine,
brandy is due (25 Sept.)

RANSTED, Caleb, at his house next door to the King's Arms
in Front St., near the Bank Meeting, Phila. - sells tea,
sugar, spices, paint, hardware, glassware, snuff (25 Sept.)

HYND, Robert, at upper end of Walnut St., Phila. - has for
sale horses and carts (25 Sept.)

McCOOMBES, John, tailor, late of Phila., dec'd - accounts
with estate to be settled with Thomas Hartley, administrator, at John Hamilton's, at the Sign of the Scales,
in Front St. (25 Sept.)

MACGUNNIGAN, Edward, native Irish servant, age c. 22 - runaway from William Armour, of Newcastle (25 Sept.)

DAVIS, David, fuller, at fulling mill in Darby, late of Job
Harvey - offers reward for recovery of strayed or stolen
horse, if horse is brought to him or to John Davis, fuller,
in Lancaster Co., 6 miles from the town (25 Sept.)

HASKELL, Joshua, master of a fishing schooner belonging to
Gloucester, deposed that he saw a great number of ships
on Cape Sable Shore - Boston item of 22 Sept. (2 Oct.)

Thursday last arrived at New York a French prize taken on
14 Aug. by the privateer Triton, Capt. Man commander -
New York item of 29 Sept. (2 Oct.)

HOLMES, Mrs. Elizabeth - died Tuesday last at her house in
the Out Ward of New York City, wanting but about 2
months of being 108 years of age - New York item of 29
Sept. (2 Oct.)

Oct. 1 the following were elected for Phila. Co.: repre-
sentatives: John Kinsey, Isaac Norris, Joseph Trotter,
Thomas Leech, James Morris, Owen Evans, Edward Warner,
Hugh Evans; sheriffs: Nicholas Scull, Richard Sewell;
coroners: Henry Pratt, Jacob Duchee; commissioner: Wil-
liam Clymer; assessors: John Jones Carpenter, James
Paul, Hugh Roberts, Abraham Daws, John Morris, Abraham
Levant (2 Oct.)

HARDING, John, on William Master's wharf, lower end of
Market St., Phila. - sells rice (2 Oct.)

HAMILTON, Alexander, of Phila. - intends soon for England
and wishes all accounts to be settled (2 Oct.)

BENEZET, Daniel, at his store in Front St., Phila., at
corner of Morris's Alley, in the house where Francis
Richardson formerly lived - sells goods imported from
London in the Carolina, Stephen Mesnard commander (2 Oct.)

GILCHRIST, Lawrence, age c. 23, sailor - runaway from ship
Griffin, John Chubbard master; George Okill in Phila.
will pay reward for his capture (2 Oct.)

FERGUSON, John, sailor, age c. 22 - same as above

JORDAN, James, sailor, age c. 20 - same as above

DAVIS, Richard, sailor, age c. 18 - same as above

CUNNINGHAM, Thomas, servant, age c. 18 - same as above

DUNBAR, John, servant, age c. 18 - same as above

McCALL, George, at his store on the other side of the drawbridge in Phila. - sells imported goods from London (2
Oct.)

BECKER, Peter, in Germanton, will sell 24 acres there (2
Oct.)

ASHMEAD, Sarah, widow, in Germantown - offers reward for
recovery of a horse strayed or stolen from her pasture
(2 Oct.)

Land on west side of Schuylkill, the greatest part between
Schooten's and Morton's land - to be sold at Roberts's
Coffee House in Front St., Phila. (2 Oct.)

HARTLEY, William, Chief Ranger for Chester Co. - lists
strays in his hands (2 Oct.)

HANMER, John, in Kent So. - offers reward for recovery of a
mare stolen or strayed from a lot in Chester Town, Md.
(2 Oct.)

GALE, Nicholas, near the Widow Began's in Arch St., Phila.
- will make or mend cane bottoms for chairs (2 Oct.)

HARLEY, William, Irish servant, age c. 19 - runaway from
George Dowllenger, of Strasburgh Twp., Lancaster Co. (2
Oct.)

HILLEGAS, Michael, in Second St., Phila. - offers reward
if mare stolen or strayed from his stable is returned
to him or to Henry Pawling, upon Schuylkill (2 Oct.)

Cloth and nails are sold by Norris and Griffitts at their
store in Front St., Phila. (2 Oct.)

COLLINS, David, apprentice, born at Stanford or Stratford,
on road leading to Boston - runaway from Matthias Meuris's
paper mill, on Wissahickon Creek, about 3 miles from
Germantown (2 Oct.)

Abraham Lincoln, of Springfield, Chester Co., or Michael
Hilton, in Lower Dublin, Phila. Co., will pay reward for
recovery of horse strayed from Lincoln's plantation (2
Oct.)

SMOUT, Edward, Esq., Ranger in Lancaster Co. - lists strays in his hands (2 Oct.)

The 6 following convict servants, lately arrived from Ireland in the <u>Rebecca</u>, Capt. Burk, have run away from William Ellis's plantation on Bohemia River, Cecil Co., Md.: Timothy Whaland, Thomas Lynagh, Thomas Walker, Peter Duffey, Donald Macdonald and James Dilland; reward for their capture will be paid by William Ellis or James Maclauchlan (2 Oct.)

HOOPER, Capt. - Saturday last returned to Boston from Annapolis Royal with information that the <u>Shirley Galley</u>, Capt. Rouse, had sunk - Boston item of 29 Sept. (9 Oct.)

H.M.S. <u>Fowey</u>, Capt. Taylor commander - arrived Tuesday last at Sandy Hook from Virginia - New York item of 6 Oct. (9 Oct.)

Thursday last Israel Pemberton, Sr., and Oswald Peele were chosen burgesses for Phila., and on Tuesday William Attwood, Esq. was chosen mayor (9 Oct.)

The following are chosen for Lancaster Co.--representatives: James Mitchell, John Wright, James Wright, Arthur Patterson; sheriffs: James Starret, John Starret; coroners: Isaac Saunders, Robert Wallace; commissioner: Patrick Hays; assessors: Evan Price, Daniel Ferre, Thomas Cox, Andrew Mays, Robert Murray, David Taylor (9 Oct.)

The following were chosen for Bucks Co.--representatives: Richard Mitchell, Derrick Hoogland, Abraham Chapman, Mahlon Kirkbride, John Watson, John Hall, Cephas Child, Joseph Hampton; sheriffs: Amos Strickland, Timothy Smith; coroners: John Chapman, John Hart; commissioner: Samuel Cary; assessors: John Williamson, George Logan, Abraham Vastine, Bartholomew Longstretch, William Edwards, Thomas Paxon (9 Oct.)

The following were chosen for Chester Co.: representatives: Francis Yarnall, George Ashbridge, Samuel Levis, Thomas Worth, Robert Lewis, Thomas Chandler, John Owen, Peter Dicks; sheriffs: Benjamin Davis, Thomas Morgan; coroners: Isaac Lea, Aubrey Bevan; commissioner: Joshua Thompson; assessors: Thomas Pennel, Aaron Ashbridge, Thomas Park, James Few, Elisha Gatchell, Jr., Isaac Davis (9 Oct.)

The following were chosen for Newcastle Co.--representatives: John Macool, William Armstrong, James Macmechen, John Vance, John Edwards, Daniel Corbit; sheriffs: Gideon Griffith, Henry Newton; coroners: James Macmullin, Samuel Silsby (9 Oct.)

The following were chosen for Kent Co.--representatives:
James Gorrel, Andrew Caldwell, Thomas Green, Robert
Wilcocks, Hugh Durborrow, John Brinckle; sheriff: John
Hunter; coroner: George Goforth (9 Oct.)

The following were chosen for Sussex Co.--representatives:
Jacob Kollock, Woolsey Burton, Joseph Draper, Ryves Holt,
James Macilvaine, John Clowes; sheriff: William Shank-
land; coroner: John Molleston (9 Oct.)

Just imported and to be sold at Charles Hargraves, in Front
St., next door to the Bank Meeting, mezzetinto prints,
including South Prospect of the City of New York and also
a new map of Scotland by Emanuel Brown, his Majesty's
Geographer (9 Oct.)

WHITE, Joseph, in Bristol Twp., near Germantown - offers reward for recovery of mare stolen or strayed out of Robert
Hopkins's pasture at Point-No-Point, Phila. Co., if mare
is brought to the owner or to Mr. Dewees, tavernkeeper
in Germantown (9 Oct.)

The snow George and equipment will be sold by auction at
John Parrock's wharf in Phila. (9 Oct.)

MACLEHEANY, John, agent for the hostages, Robert Macleheany
and William Calhoun - gives notice of meeting to deter-
mine the proportions of ransom money of persons or
freighters concerned, who arrived at Newcastle on Delaware from Ireland, in the ship Arundel Galley, which was
taken by a Spanish privateer and ransomed by the commander, Matthew Rowen (9 Oct.)

A brick tenement on west side of Second St., now in the
possession of Moses Thomas, will be sold (9 Oct.)

Plantation of 300 acres, on the Forks of Delaware, late belonging to Moses Tatamy, taken in execution at the suit
of Gerrard Williamson, will be sold by John Hart, late
sheriff (9 Oct.)

LESHIRE, Johan Henry, of Germantown - his wife, Maria Mar-
garetta, has eloped from him (9 Oct.)

White Horse Tavern (lately possessed by James Trego, dec'd)
in Whiteland Twp., Chester Co., for 30 years a tavern,
on the great Conestogoe Rd., 25 miles from Phila. - is to
be sold; to learn of the title and conditions of sale,
apply to James Trego, now living thereon, or to Richard
Richison, living near said place; also part of the estate
and for sale is a brick house, a tavern, where Israel
Hendrickson now lives, opposite the courthouse in the

Borough of Chester; apply to Thomas Cummings or Jacob Howell in said borough (9 Oct.)

MACRAW, Daniel, Scotch Highland servant - runaway from Charles Dick, merchant, in Fredericksburgh (9 Oct.)

ROSS, John, Scotch Highland servant, age c. 16 - runaway from John Mitchell, merchant in Fredericksburgh (9 Oct.)

HAILY, Thomas, Irish servant, age c. 20 or 21 - runaway from Dr. William Lynn in Fredericksburgh (9 Oct.)

PIPINEAU, John James, age between 40 and 50, native of France, who speaks French and Low Dutch but little English -runaway from James Richard, of Patapsco, Md. (9 Oct.)

RODINQUEZ, Anthony, master of La Judith, from Rochelle, bound to Quebec, has news of French fleet - Boston item of 6 Oct. (16 Oct.)

BUNKER, Capt. - arrived at Boston Saturday last from Louisburg - Boston item of 6 Oct. (16 Oct.)

BARNES, Capt. - arrived Friday last at New York from Louisburg - New York item of 13 Oct. (16 Oct.)

Ship Friendship, Capt. Lisle, arrived Monday at Phila., from London, and on Tuesday the ship Anne Galley, Capt. Houston from London (16 Oct.)

Creditors of George Wensell, alias Wahnsidel, are notified that a dividend will be made on the estate at the house of Henry Pratt, near the courthouse, Phila.; the auditors are Richard Sewell, Samuel Smith and Robert Greenway (16 Oct.)

Neate and Smith, at their store, opposite to the Sign of the Bible, in Front St., Phila. - sell goods imported from London in the Anne Galley, Capt. Houston (16 Oct.)

BARTOW, Theodosius, of Westchester, N.Y. - offers reward for recovery of a horse stolen from him (16 Oct.)

RAMPOON, John, late of Salem Co., N.J. - escaped from William Barker, under sheriff - reward will be paid if the fugitive is taken and brought to Barker or to Nicholas Gibbon, High Sheriff of Salem Co. (16 Oct.)

COBB, Capt., who sailed a week ago for the coast of Acadia - returned Friday last to Boston with report about the French forces - Boston item of 10 Oct. (23 Oct.)

DAVIS, Capt. - arrived Saturday last in a sloop from Annapolis Royal, with news: one soldier in Capt. Prebble's company has been wounded; Capt. Gorham of the Rangers took a party of Frenchmen - Boston item of 10 Oct. (23 Oct.)

DENNIS, Capt., of Rhode Island - has taken a French sloop bound for Martineco (23 Oct.)

JAUNCEY, Capt. - arrived Thursday last at New York from Jamaica, with news of death of Admiral Davers there - New York item of 20 Oct. (23 Oct.)

Indians lately killed and took 16 men at Saratoga, belonging to the companies of Capts. Langdon and Hart; Lt. Johnstone of Hart's company and Barent Bradt, of Langdon's company, behaved well - New York item of 20 Oct. (23 Oct.)

Ship Neptune, Capt. Wilkinson, from Holland, with Palatines, is on the river at Phila. (23 Oct.)

LIGHTFOOT, Thomas, at house where Israel Pemberton, Jr., lately removed, fronting Chesnut St., Phila. - sells cloth, cutlery, sugar, rum, pork, shot, etc. (23 Oct.)

MORGAN, John, at his store on Market St. wharf - sells cloth, cutlery, brandy, sugar, indigo, etc. (23 Oct.)

MARSHAL, Christopher, at the Sign of the Golden Ball, opposite the end of Strawberry Alley, near the Three Tun Tavern, Chesnut St., Phila. - sells painting materials and other goods (23 Oct.)

MORGAN, Evan, in Market St., Phila. - has to let a house in Water St., Phila., next door to Peter Bard's, merchant; also a corn merchant mill in Chester Co., about 15 miles from Whiteclay Creek landing (23 Oct.)

Ship La Pomone, of Londonderry, William Gregg commander, will sail for Wilmington in Cape Fear; for freight or passage apply to Alexander Boyd, at Messers. Cunningham and Gardner's or to William Faris, at Col. Spafford's (23 Oct.)

NORMAN, Anna Maria, Low Dutch convict servant - runaway from William Williams of the Baltimore Ironworks (23 Oct.)

TAYLOR, Thomas, born in Maryland - broke out of goal; reward for his capture is offered by John Risteau, Sheriff of Baltimore Mo. (23 Oct.)

WHITE, Nathaniel, of West Caln, Chester Co. - offers reward for recovery of 2 strayed horses (23 Oct.)

GILLEYLIN, John - offers reward for apprehension of the following 5 sailors who ran away from the snow Anne, Robert Macky, then lying at Reedy Island: Bartholomew Barrell (who lodged in Pewter Platter Alley), Bartholomew Thomas, John Dean, Robert Anderson and Archibald Mackeloy (23 Oct.)

On 14 Sept. arrived at Charlestown, S.C., the Fame privateer, of Rhode Island, Capt. Thomas Thompson commander; on 1 Sept. the Fame and the privateer Industry, Capt. Ellis, belonging to Providence, engaged a Spanish privateer sloop; a shot in her powder room blew up the Industry and only 44 men survived; on the 3 Sept. a hurricane drove the Fame on a reef and the vessel was saved only with the utmost difficulty - Charlestown item of 22 Sept. (30 Oct.)

BESWICKE, Capt. - arrived last week at Charlestown from St. Augustine with English prisoners, among whom were Capts. William Service, Charles Stewart and James Doughty; they report that a French privateer sloop, Capt. Borneau, took a Phila. sloop, John Adams master, and the ship Susannah, Capt. Service; other English prizes taken are the ship Elizabeth, of Liverpoole, Capt. Stewart, the sloop Brunswick, James Strike master, the St. George, Capt. Richard French, and the schooner Increase, C. Badley master - Charlestown item of 22 Sept. (30 Oct.)

Brigantine Argyle, John Seymour commander, will sail from Phila. for London; for freight or passage agree with the master or Joseph Shippen (30 Oct.)

FLEESON, Plunket, at the Easy Chair in Chesnut St., a little above Third St., Phila. - wishes to buy hog's bristles (30 Oct.)

Brigantine Elizabeth, Edward Gill commander - will sail from Phila. for Newry or Belfast - for freight or passage agree with the master on board or Samuel Hasell or John Meas (30 Oct.)

WILLARD, Joseph, servant, age c. 19, blacksmith - runaway from William Parker, of Phila. (30 Oct.)

The following have deserted from Capt. John Diemer's company at Albany, N.Y.: Casper John, a German, age 26; Peter Grodhouse, age 19, who lived in Telpahoken; Conrad Cornman, age 21, who lived at Coshehopen; Bernard Sharnbach, age 21, who lived at Coshehopen; George Redelff, age 19, who lived at Kennet-hill; Philip Smith, age 23, a German; Andrew Bushon, a Swiss, age 28, cooper by trade; William Lower, age 19, who lived at Schupack; Henry Plat, age 21, a German (30 Oct.)

BOOD, John - gives notice that lots of ground in Smithfield, Manor of Moreland, and in Kensington will be sold at the house of Michael Hillegas in Second St., Phila. (30 Oct.)

PAXTON, James, of Salsbury, Lancaster Co. - has taken up a mare (30 Oct.)

MELCHOR, William - offers for sale a plantation in Upper Dublin, Phila. Co., upon the great road from Phila. to North Wales (30 Oct.)

STEELE, James - offers reward for recovery of a horse stolen from him between Phila. and Frankford (30 Oct.)

ASHFORD, Thomas (commonly called "The Farmer"), convict servant - runaway from D. Dulany's plantation on Wye River, in Maryland (30 Oct.)

DE PREFONTAINE, Peter - teaches reading, writing and arithmetic in the house where Jonathan Biles lately lived, in Race St., Phila., almost opposite the Moravian Meeting-house (30 Oct.)

Account of the death of the Duke d'Anville on 15 Sept. and the suicide of the commandant at Jelrute -Boston item of 22 Oct. (6 Nov.)

DELAMONT, Mr., a wagoner, was scalped by the Indians about 18 miles from Albany - New York item of 3 Nov. (6 Nov.)

Last week arrived at New York an English prize sloop, Joseph Dickinson master, retaken from the Spaniard Don Pedro de Aracochia by the Castor and Pollux, privateers of New York - New York item of 3 Nov. (6 Nov.)

SCOTT, James, who intends to go to England this winter - sells cloth at his store in Walnut St., Phila. (6 Nov.)

William Atwood, Samuel Mickle and Cadwallader Evans request that the creditors of Henry Camm, of Upper Providence Twp., Chester Co., meet at the house of Peter Robeson, at the Sign of the Indian King, in Market St., Phila. (6 Nov.)

MORRIS, William, Jr., at his store in Trenton, opposite to John Jenkins's - sells rum and salt (6 Nov.)

MEARIS, Matthias, at his paper mill in Germantown Twp., 3
miles from Germantown - has taken up a cow (6 Nov.)

MORGAN, Thomas, of Chester - offers reward for recovery of
a strayed or stolen mare (6 Nov.)

WHITE, Josiah, of Mount Holy, near Burlington, N.J. - seeks
a journeyman shearman (6 Nov.)

A lot of land in the Northern Liberties of Phila. is for
sale; enquire of William Adams living on the premises
(6 Nov.)

THOMAS, Richard, of Hilton Twp., Bucks Co. - has taken up
a roan filley (6 Nov.)

INGHAM, Jonathan, fuller, of Solebury, Bucks Co. - offers
reward for recovery of cloth stolen from his shop (6 Nov.)

DENTON, John, of Phila. - offers reward for recovery of a
raft that was stolen or went adrift from Pool's Bridge
(6 Nov.)

Ship Friendship, Henry Lisle master - will sail for Bristol;
for freight or passage agree with William Callender or
with the master at Israel Pemberton's wharf in Phila. (6
Nov.)

TERRET, George, Irish servant, stocking-weaver - runaway
from John Needham, of Phila. (6 Nov.)

POPE, Charles, of Duck Creek Hundred, Kent Co. on Delaware
- his wife Anne has eloped from him (6 Nov.); on 20 Nov.
Charles cancels the above (20 Nov.)

LOGAN, William - desires return of Locke's Essay on Human
Understanding and the 2 volumes of The Guardians;
Locke's essay has the name J. Logan (father of William)
in the title page (6 Nov.)

PURNELL, Capt. - was killed in engagement with a French
privateer; Capt. Stamper was retaken by 2 English men-
of-war (13 Nov.)

Letter of H. Jones, at Bohemia, Md., to the Jesuits in Maryland and Pennsylvania (13 Nov.)

Cuzzins and Smyter - have removed their store from Front
St. to the house where John Stamper lately dwelt in
Water St., near Chesnut St., Phila. (13 Nov.)

DAVID, Amos, Welch servant, age c. 19 or 20 - runaway from

John Rowland, of Whiteland, Chester Co. (13 Nov.)

Tract of 200 acres in the Northern Liberties, about 4 miles from Phila. and 2 from Germantown, is offered for sale; apply to Robert Meade, near the premises, or the owner, John Michael Browne (13 Nov.)

WARREN, John, age between 50 and 60 - escaped from Newtown Goal, Bucks Co.; Sheriff Amos Strickland offers reward for his capture (20 Nov.)

HANNIS, John, at his plantation at Passyunk - sells cows, sheep and horses; enquire of him or of Andrew Hannis, living near the road leading to John's plantation (20 Nov.)

WHITE, William, age between 40 and 50, who pretends to be a tinker - has absconded from his bail, David Wilson, in Southampton, Bucks Co. (20 Nov.)

LEECH, John, late of Phila., dec'd - debts owing his estate or his widow are to be paid at once (20 Nov.)

MARSHALL, David - offers reward for boat lost from his shallop, Happy Return, at Newcastle; reward offered if news of the boat is given to Thomas Jones, at the coffee house in Phila., or to George Monroe, at Newcastle (20 Nov.)

CLARKE, Michael, servant, age c. 40 - runaway from Samuel Atkinson, of Chester Twp., Burlington Co. (20 Nov.)

HOPKINSON, Thomas, in Front St., Phila., who draws deeds and conveyances - seeks to sell or let Pool Forge, on Manatawny Creek (20 Nov.)

LACEY, Mary (widow and administratrix of Thomas Lacey, dec'd) - will sell at auction at the house of Widow Breintnall, the Sign of the Hen and Chickens, in Chesnut St., Phila., 2 lots of ground in Pewter-Platter Alley, one in the occupation of the Widow Moore, the other in the occupation of Daniel Philatoung (20 Nov.)

The following ships sailed for Phila.: ship Mary, Capt. Martin, and Capts. Hargrave, Crosthwaite and Redman (27 Nov.)

Ship Judith, Capt. Holland - has run upon a rock in Catwater Harbor and bilged (27 Nov.)

Brigantine Louisburg, Capt. Budden, of Phila. - has arrived at Dover on his way to Holland (27 Nov.)

Brigantine **Delaware**, Capt. Taylor, of Phila., and Capt.
Forbes were taken by a French privateer; the brigantine
Dolphin, Capt. Dewers, of Phila., was cast away off the
west end of Cuba; privateer **Defiance**, of Rhode Island,
Capt. Sweet, struck upon the Hen and Chickens, to south-
ward of Cape Henlopen, and ran ashore on the Cape (27
Nov.)

Norris and Griffitts - have for sale cloth imported from
London per the **Mercury**, Charles Hargrave commander; Peter
Turner, opposite the Post Office, in Market St., sells
goods imported on the **Mercury**, as does James Scott, in
Walnut St. (27 Nov.)

WHARTON, Joseph - has taken up a cow, which is now in his
meadow (27 Nov.)

PETERS, William, Register, Office of Vice-Admiralty, Pennsylvania - gives notice that Messers. Willing, Sober
and Coleman are appointed auditors and that all freighters
and persons concerned, who arrived at Newcastle on Delaware from Ireland in the ship **Arundel Galley** (taken by a
Spanish privateer and ransomed by Matthew Rowan) are to
meet at the house of John Cleary, the Sign of the Fleece,
in Second St., Phila. on 9 Dec. (27 Nov.)

DE CASTRO, Daniel Mandus, merchant in Lancaster - intends
for Corocoa by way of Phila. and New York (27 Nov.)

HUTCHINSON, John, dec'd - accounts with estate to be settled
with the executors, John Burge and Mah. Kirkbride (27
Nov.)

FRETZEL, Joannes Harmonius and his wife, Dutch servants -
runaways from Robert Meade of Phila.; it is said they are
settled in a place called the camp, back of New York (27
Nov.)

HUNT, Roger, of East Caln Twp., Chester Co. - will not pay
a bond given by him to William Hamilton, of West Marlborough, near Doe Run, Chester Co., as the bond was il-
legally obtained (27 Nov.)

HARRIS, Alexander, late of Deptford, Gloucester Co., waterman, dec'd - accounts with estate to be settled with
Solomon Fussell, executor; said Fussell has for sale a
house on west side of Front St., over the drawbridge, in
Phila., joining to John Inglis, merchant, on the north,
and Capt. Hartley, on the south (27 Nov.)

A gristmill, called Kinsey's Mill, near Germantown - offered
for sale by Christian Kinsey, living on the premises (27
Nov.)

MAYER, Mons., the priest who came over with the French
fleet - tells of disinclination of French for the expedition - Boston item of 10 Nov. (2 Dec.)

BENNET, Capt., in the Boston Packet - arrived Friday last
at Boston from Louisburg - tells of his engagement with
a French privateer and its prizes in Prospect Harbor -
Boston item of 10 Nov. (2 Dec.)

Saturday last a party of 12 Indians arrived at New York in
a sloop from Albany and marched with troops, headed by
Col. Johnston, to the Governor's - New York item of 24
Nov. (2 Dec.)

Ship Wilmington, Capt. Sibbald, of Phila. - has arrived at
the Downes (2 Dec.)

People of Barbados paid Capt. Fielding, of the Leostaff
privateer, of Bristol, to cruise off the island for 12
days to protect their trade (2 Dec.)

The following sell goods imported by Capt. Hargrave in the
ship Mercury: Hamilton, Wallace and Co. in Water St.;
Ebenezer Currie, in Front St.; Buckridge Simms, at Joseph Turner's, in Front St.; James Trotter, at store of
Samuel Welsh in Front St. (2 Dec.)

Ship Neptune, Thomas Wilkinson commander, will sail from
Phila. for Charlestown, S.C.; for freight or passage
agree with Robert and Amos Strettell (2 Dec.)

PORTER, Robert, of Whitepain Twp., Phila. Co. - has taken
up a cow (2 Dec.)

Mark, Negro, age c. 24 - runaway from John Hanson, of Manhatawny Forge (2 Dec.)

The following have deserted from Capt. Beverly Robinson's
Company of Foot, now at Fort George, N.Y.: James Shaw,
Irishman, age 23; Philip Radman, Irishman, labourer, age
c. 20; William Harris, born in Maryland, age c. 20, carpenter; Hugh Tully, Irishman, sawyer by trade, age c.
30, who has been a drummer in the dragoons in Ireland (2
Dec.)

REYNOLDS, David, of Springfield Twp. - will sell lots of
ground on great road leading from Phila. to Sammuel Morris's mill, 10 miles from Phila. (2 Dec.)

Sloop Swallow, James Whittwood master, of and from Jamaica
for Phila. - struck on 11 Oct. when trying to reach
Charlestown (9 Dec.)

BINNEY, Capt., who arrived at Phila. last week from Boston, reports that Capt. Langstaff, in a sloop from Boston to Phila., is cast away on Nantucket Shoals (9 Dec.)

Sloop Mary from London, Capt. Martin - arrived 8 Dec. at Phila. (9 Dec.)

GROVES, Capt., from Boston - arrived 8 Dec. at Phila.; in his passage he took up people of a French prize (which had been taken by Capt. Carr in a Rhode Island privateer) that was cast away on Nantucket Shoals (9 Dec.)

It is reported from Antigua, via Virginia, that Capt. Rodd and 2 other captains named Dickinson, all Bermudas sloops, have been taken by a French privateer (9 Dec.)

At plantation of John Hannis in Passyunk Twp., are to be sold livestock and utensils (9 Dec.)

Plantation of 100 acres in Haverford Twp., Chester Co., about 9 miles from Phila. - will be sold by Joseph Lewis, living on said place (9 Dec.)

CONOLY, Peter, native Irish servant, age c. 20 - runaway from Samuel Evans, of Marple Twp., Chester Co. (9 Dec.)

BOURNE, Jesse, at store in Water St., opposite Dickenson's wharf in Phila. - sells goods imported in ship Mercury, Capt. Hargrave (9 Dec.)

John Mifflin in Phila. or Robert Beeby in Wilmington will pay reward for recovery of small boat, stolen or broke loose from sloop Speedwell, Robert Beeby master, lying at Powell's wharf in Phila. (9 Dec.)

House and lot in King St., Borough of Lancaster are for sale; enquire of George Sanders in King St., or Abraham Johnston near the Gap (9 Dec.)

BREINTNALL, John, whalebone-cutter, in Chesnut St., Phila. - sells telescopes, spy-, reading-, burning- and magnifying glasses (9 Dec.)

McGENNIS, Andrew, of Chester - his wife Elizabeth has eloped from him (9 Dec.)

House and lot in Kensington, near the batchelor's hall - are to be sold at auction on 11 Dec. by John Lodowick Siepel, of the Northern Liberties, locksmith (9 Dec.)

House, formerly in the possession of Jane Watson, on Society Hill, now belonging to Patrick Wiley, surgeon, is to be

sold at auction on 1 Jan.; it is on Water St., extending
back to a lot of Edward Shippen, Esq., bounded on the
south east by a lot in possession of John McEntire and on
north-east by lot in possession of Alexander Alexander
(9 Dec.)

Speech of Gov. William Shirley to General Assembly of
Massachusetts (16 Dec.)

On 16 June the brigantine Expedition, Capt. Millet, a flag
of truce, with 57 prisoners, sailed from Kingston, Jamaica, for Havana; the prisoners rose, took the ship and
would have killed the English had not Mr. Wolf, who un-
derstood Spanish, dissuaded them; the prisoners were put
ashore at Cape Cruz; the ship sank in a tornado - Kingston item of 6 Sept. (16 Dec.)

Account of piracy carried out by 5 Negroes; they seized a
sloop of Capt. Taylor; eventually 4 were arrested and
committed to Acomack Goal in Virginia (16 Dec.)

A transport, having on board Capt. Sayer's company, drove
ashore at Martha's Vineyard; the men were saved (16 Dec.)

On 14 Nov. the privateer snow Duke of Marlborough, Benjamin
Carr commander, arrived at Newport, R.I.; in an engage-
ment with 2 French ships 3 of his men were killed, James
Smith of Phila., John Hall of South Carolina and Jehoe
Jones of Cape Fear - Newport, R.I., item of 7 Nov. (16
Dec.)

Saturday last H.M.S. Mermaid, Capt. Gayton commander, and a
merchantman, Capt. Powers, arrived at Nantasket - Boston
item of 17 Nov. (16 Dec.)

Wednesday last a sloop from the West Indies, Capt. Gatty,
was cast away on Lynn Beach; the captain and 8 of his
men died - Boston item of 24 Nov. (16 Dec.)

Tuesday last arrived at Boston Capt. Cobb, who reported
that Capt. Bourne had arrived safe with a company of
soldiers at Annapolis Royal; Capt. Cobb further informed
that 350 troops under Capt. Gorham embarked on board
Capt. Conolly for Minas but after 10 days returned because of tempestuous weather; Capt. Davis is under orders
to sail towards Minas to discover what he can - Boston
item of 24 Nov. (16 Dec.)

Account of a Mohawk Indian named Hendrick, who got letters
from the Gov. of Canada for Crown Point, but brought the
same to Albany - New York item of 4 Dec. (16 Dec.)

Capt. Leybourn, in a privateer brigantine of Bermudas, brought in there a large French ship he had taken - New York item of 8 Dec. (16 Dec.)

GRIFFITTS, Thomas - died Tuesday last at Phila.; he was Keeper of the Great Seal of Pennsylvania, had been a judge of the Supreme Court and twice Mayor of Phila. (16 Dec.)

LARDNER, Lyn-ford, succeeds Griffitts as Keeper of the Great Seal (16 Dec.)

WHITE, Thomas, at his house in Market St., between Fourth and Fifth Sts., where Robert Grace formerly lived and Capt. Bourne lately dwelt - sells cloth and other goods (16 Dec.)

SWAN, Richard, hatter, in Market St., Phila. - sells coffee, sugar, wine, brandy, dry goods (16 Dec.)

WEISER, Conrad, Ranger of North East Corner of Lancaster Co. - lists strays in his hands (16 Dec.)

CARR, Joseph, servant, age c. 20, who has been a soldier - runaway from James Evins at the Gunpowder Ironworks in West Nottingham, Chester Co. (16 Dec.)

REARDON, William, Irish servant, age between 20 and 30, born near Cork, who has been privateering, served some time with Hugh Evans of Merion and was a longtime prisoner in Chester Goal - runaway (in company, it is supposed, with one Mary Sullivan) from William Reynolds, living in Charlestown, Chester Co. (16 Dec.)

Brick house in Water St., Phila., next door to Peter Bard's, merchant, near Market St. wharf, is to be let by Evan Morgan, in Market St., as is also a corn merchant mill in Chester Co., about 15 miles from Whiteclay Creek Landing (16 Dec.)

THOMAS, Evan, late of Byberry, dec'd - accounts with estate to be settled with the executors, Rachel and Evan Thomas (16 Dec.)

BISPHAM, Benjamin - offers for sale a plantation of 200 acres on Oldman's Creek, in Penn's Neck, Salem Co., West Jersey (16 Dec.)

McCOOLE, Walter, of Rockhill Twp., Bucks Co. - lists strays in his hands (16 Dec.)

TOWERS, Robert - offers reward for recovery of 12 buckskins,

a side of mutton, 2 bushels of oats and a sheet, all in
a bag, lost on Germantown Rd., between William Masters's
mill and Isaac Norris's plantation; the items may be
brought to Isaac Coren's, in Market St., Phila. (23 Dec.)

PRITCHARD, Griffith, of Charlestown, Chester Co. - offers
reward for recovery of a mare strayed between Phila. and
the middle ferry; it may be brought to Pritchard, or to
John Jones at the Plow and Harrow in Phila., or John
Samuels, near Radnor Meeting-house (23 Dec.)

MURRAY, Richard, of Cheltenham - will prosecute if anyone
cuts timber off his land (23 Dec.)

Plantation of 200 acres in Manor of Moreland, 13 miles from
Phila., is for sale; apply to Joseph Dubree, in the
Northern Liberties of Phila., or James Dubree, living on
the premises (23 Dec.)

Pool Forge, on Manhatawny Creek, is to be let or sold; apply
to Thomas Hopkinson (23 Dec.)

Case of Macleheany and Calhoun vs. Owners and freighters of
ship _Arundel_ in Court of Vice-Admiralty of Pennsylvania;
Willing, Coleman and Sober are the auditors; J. Moland
is advocate for the complamants (23 Dec.)

PICKERIN, Rachel, English servant, age _c_. 30, who has enquired for one Timothy Conner (supposed to be her bastard's father; he served his time with William Peters,
fuller, living near Concord) - runaway from Matthias
Kerlin, tavernkeeper, in Concord, Chester Co. (23 Dec.)

Capts. Dowrick and Farrington, both of Boston, were taken
in their passage to Jamaica (30 Dec.)

Capt. Howland, in a brigantine belonging to Plimouth, was
cast away upon Atlin's Keys (30 Dec.)

DENNIS, Capt. - has taken a French privateer (30 Dec.)

EMMET, Capt., who sailed from Boston for Holland, was cast
away on the northern coast of Scotland; the captain and
his mate, Mr. Eggleston, were both drowned (30 Dec.)

About 40 soldiers under Capt. Kinslaugh are apparently
drowned in wreck of a schooner sent out from Louisburg -
Boston item of 8 Dec. (30 Dec.)

KNOWLES, Gov. - reported to be very ill at Louisburg -
Boston item of 8 Dec. (30 Dec.)

COWLEY, Capt. - has arrived at Boston from Londonderry -
Boston item of 8 Dec. (30 Dec.)

Thursday last the sloop <u>Trial</u>, William Smith master, of Bermuda, and a sloop from Maryland, Duncan Murray master,
were cast away near Sandy Hook - New York item of 15 Dec.
(30 Dec.)

The following have arrived at the Capes: Capts. Crosthwaite
from London, Scott from Dublin, Reese from Antigua and
Ware from Madeira (30 Dec.)

GRIFFITTS, Thomas, dec'd - accounts with estate to be settled with executors, Mary and Isaac Griffitts (30 Dec.)

Lot of land in the Northern Liberties of Phila. is for sale;
enquire of William Adams, living on the premises (30
Dec.)

WILLIAMS, Thomas - desires to let the house where he lately
lived, at Frederickstown, on Sassafras River in Maryland;
apply to Capt. Peter Bayard, merchant, on Bohemia River,
or to Thomas Williams, at Mrs. Mary Andrews's, on Fishbourn's wharf, Phila. (30 Dec.)

SUGAR, Thomas - will sell at auction at the Sign of the
George in Second St., Phila., a new brick messuage on
south side of Sassafrass St., Phila.; for title, enquire
of Charles Brockden (30 Dec.)

1747

Account (from on board H.M.S. <u>Lenox</u>, at Jamaica, 13 Sept.
1746) of the behaviour of Commodore Mitchell in letting
a French fleet get into Cape Francois; besides Mitchell
are mentioned Capts. Lawrence and Dent (6 Jan.)

Last night arrived at New York the privateer brigantine
<u>Triton</u>, Capt. Abraham Man commander; the <u>Triton</u> had taken
2 large French ships and had run another ashore - New
York item of 29 Dec. (6 Jan.)

VEALE, Joseph - wounded in Westchester Co. by a Negro, who
is now committed to goal - New York item of 29 Dec. 1746
(6 Jan.)

Sloop <u>Catherine</u>, Capt. Smith, from Londonderry, has arrived
at Newcastle; she was taken by a French privateer but
ransomed for 5,000 pounds (6 Jan.)

BOND, Thomas and Phineas - give account of the healing

virtue of wells newly discovered in Virginia (6 Jan.)

BROWNE, John Michael - has for sale tract of 200 acres in the Northern Liberties, about 4 miles from Phila., 2 from Germantown and 2 from Franckfort; offers will be received by the owner or by Robert Meade, near the premises (6 Jan.)

Snow John, Thomas Crosthwaite commander - will sail for South Carolina; for freight or passage agree with the master on board or at William Crosthwaite's in Front St., Phila. (6 Jan.)

HUGHES, John, servant, age c. 17 - runaway from Joseph Jeanes, of Manor of Moreland, Phila. Co. (6 Jan.)

WARNER, Mary, living in Wrightstown, Bucks Co. - has found parcel of silk handkerchiefs between Phila. and Franckfort (6 Jan.)

COCKRAN, Thomas, of Haverford Twp., Chester Co. - offers reward for recovery of mare strayed or stolen; it may be brought to the owner or to William Bell's, at the Sign of the Buck, on Conestogo Rd., about 9 miles from Phila. (6 Jan.)

COATS, William, Sr., at the Northern Liberties of Phila. - has appointed Thomas Say, of Phila., his attorney (6 Jan.)

Address of Lt.-Gov. of Pennsylvania and Council to the King, transmitted to Thomas Penn, Esq. (13 Jan.)

DENNIS, Capt., in a Rhode Island privateer, has taken 5 or 6 French privateers - Boston item of 16 Dec. (13 Jan.)

MACFARLAND, Capt. - arrived Friday last at Boston from Hull; he disabled a dogger and scuttled her - Boston item of 22 Dec. (13 Jan.)

Tuesday last arrived at New York a French prize taken off west end of Porto Rico by the privateer snow Dragon, of New York, Capt. Thomas Seymour commander - New York item of 5 Jan. (13 Jan.)

MANN, Capt., in company with the privateers Castor and Pollux, of New York, on 4 Nov. last took a large French ship - New York item of 5 Jan. (13 Jan.)

Capts. Samson, Snow and Langstaff, all from Boston, are arrived at Cape May (13 Jan.)

WHELDON, William, butcher, in Front St., Phila. - has for

sale a Negro girl and 3½ years of a servant girl's time (13 Jan.)

JEVON, William, lately removed from Hamilton's wharf (late the store of Jevon and Perry), next door to John Mifflin's in Market St., has just imported ironmongery and cloth from London in the _Mary_, Capt. Martin (13 Jan.)

A fulling-mill, near Mr. Branson's iron-works, in Carnarvan Twp., Lancaster Co., is to be let; apply to John Morgan (13 Jan.)

JACOB, Job, of Wilmington, Newcastle Co. - asks that owner claim a hogshead of molasses which was supposed to be for Hannah Harlon, in Kennet, Chester Co.; he also has to be sold or let a large lot in the Borough of Wilmington, Newcastle Co., on the west side of Thorn St. (13 Jan.)

Stone house, called the Sign of King Tamony and in possession of William Dewees, is for sale; apply to Jacob Vonderwite, carpenter, living in Germantown (13 Jan.)

COATS, William, Sr., of the Northern Liberties of Phila., is incapable of transacting his affairs; his heirs, therefore, William Coats, Jr. (his son), Elizabeth Edge (his daughter), John Coats, Sr., in right of Ann Kilcrese (another daughter), Peter Brown in behalf of his children by Prisciller (another of his daughters, dec'd), have impowered Thomas Say, of Phila., sadler, to receive income from the estate and pay debts of the estate (13 Jan.)

Sloop _Molly_, of Annapolis, Charles Giles commander, bound to Barbados, is taken by a French privateer - Annapolis item of 30 Dec. (20 Jan.)

DOWELL, Capt., of the privateer ship _Pandour_, of Phila., together with Capt. Wood in the brigantine _George_ and the _Dragon_ of New York, has taken a French ship and ransomed her for 17,000 dollars (20 Jan.)

KINNETT, Thomas (given later as Thomas "Skillien"), who is to be spoken with at the house of Richard Swan, in Market St., Phila. - teaches art and science of defense, pursuit of the small sword and dancing (20 Jan.)

WILKINSON, Anthony - has to let a house and wharf between the sugar-house and Poole's bridge (20 Jan.)

MOLAND, John, in the Northern Liberties of Phila. - has a Negro girl for sale (20 Jan.)

WARNER, Thomas, of Phila. Co. - his wife Mary has eloped from him (20 Jan.)

BRADY, Daniel, Irish servant, age c. 20 - runaway from William Hudson, of Phila., tanner (20 Jan.)

House, within 2 doors of the White Horse, in Elbow Lane, opposite the Presbyterian burying-ground, is to be let; enquire of Henry Dexter, corner of Strawberry Alley, opposite the Shambles, Phila. (20 Jan.)

Plantation of 200 acres, formerly Gayan Miller's, in Kennet Twp., Chester Co., is to be let for 5 years; for terms agree with George Miller (living on the premises), William Cooper and Robert Lewis, adjoining the same (20 Jan.)

SAY, Thomas - is impowered to manage estate of William Coats, Sr., by his children William Coats, Jr., Elizabeth Edge, John Coats, Sr., and Peter Brown (20 Jan.)

House and lot in Second St., Phila., opposite to Samuel Rhodes's, is for sale; enquire of Adam Rhodes, in Walnut St. (20 Jan.)

Tuesday last arrived at Charlestown, S.C., the sloop Victory, of Charlestown, Peter Bostock master, who brought 16 English prisoners from Havana, one of whom is Richard Whyte, late master of the ship Loyal Catherine, from London, who was taken July last by Francisco Lorenzo - Charlestown item of 15 Dec. 1746 (27 Jan.)

Lately taken and carried into Havana are the following: a ship from Jamaica, one Dellison master, and a sloop from New York for Georgia, one Shourt master - Charlestown item of 15 Dec. 1746 (27 Jan.)

English vessels lately seized at Cuba are as follows: the schooner Charming Nelly, Capt. Cox and the sloop Industry, Capt. Williams, both of Charlestown; a ship from New York, Capt. Walton; a sloop from Rhode Island, Capt. Clark; a sloop from Jamaica, Capt. Bedlow - Charlestown item of 15 Dec. 1746 (27 Jan.)

The Success frigate, Capt. Thompson, with about 50 recruits for General Oglethorp's Regt., has arrived at Frederica - Charlestown item of 15 Dec. 1746 (27 Jan.)

Sloop Diamond, Capt. Hooper, was taken 16 Oct. last by the French but retaken by Capt. Jefferies in a New York privateer and carried into St. Kitts - Boston item of 5 Jan. (27 Jan.)

TARR, Capt. Othniel, arrived at Boston from the West Indies, related that he had been taken and carried to Martinico - Boston item of 5 Jan. (27 Jan.)

Capt. Benjamin Hallowell's account of his engagement in the ship Duke of Cumberland with 2 privateers - Boston item of 5 Jan. (27 Jan.)

SEAGERS, Capt., of Maryland - his ship was taken near St. Eustatia but he escaped - Boston item of 5 Jan. (27 Jan.)

It is reported from Louisburg that Gov. Knowles is recovering - Boston item of 5 Jan. (27 Jan.)

It is reported from Newport, R.I., that William Clagget, of that town, in his electric experiments has set fire to spirits of wine - Boston item of 5 Jan. (27 Jan.)

Last week a sloop from Shrewbury, Capt. Price master - was driven ashore on Coney Island - New York item of 12 Jan. (27 Jan.)

KETELTAS, Capt., arrived at New York Saturday last in a snow from Jamaica, with report of French vessels taken - New York item of 12 Jan. (27 Jan.)

Monday last arrived at New York a French prize sloop taken by Capt. Jefferies in the Greyhound privateer of New York - New York item of 19 Jan. (27 Jan.)

Brigantine Seahorse, Capt. Handlin, from St. Thomas, was cast away near the east end of Long Island - New York item of 19 Jan. (27 Jan.)

Sunday last arrived at Phila. Capt. Collis, from North Carolina, who was taken and carried into Havana, as was Capt. Donaldson in the ship Elizabeth (27 Jan.)

TYLEY, Capt., of New London - was taken by a Spanish privateer; Capt. Twaitts, of New York, was overset 150 leagues northeast of the Caycos; he got to Havana and is gone to Jamaica in a flag of truce (27 Jan.)

GREENWAY, Capt., in a schooner of Phila., has put into North Carolina (27 Jan.)

WHITEFIELD, Rev. George - arrived at Charlestown the middle of last month (27 Jan.)

GREENWOOD, Joseph (son of Daniel Greenwood, of Enfield, England), who went to Maryland from England in the ship Expedition, Capt. English, about 3 years ago; news of

him is sought, and it is requested that it be sent to
the Post Office in Phila. (27 Jan.)

Silver watch was found on the great road between Gabriel
Shoulder's and John Trump's; owner is to apply to John
Davis, cordwainer, in North Wales (27 Jan.)

REED, Margaret, midwife, formerly of Phila. - has returned
from Carolina to practise in Phila.; she is at Mrs.
Penelope Hayley's, in Second St., near the Church (27
Jan.)

CRESSON, Solomon, dec'd - accounts with estate to be settled with John Cresson, executor (27 Jan.)

CRISPIN, Joseph, apprentice, cooper by trade, age c. 19 -
runaway from Nehemiah Allen, of Phila. (27 Jan.)

Speech of Gov. William Shirley to General Assembly of
Massachusetts (3 Feb.)

Sloop Abigail, George Mitchel commander - arrived Monday
last at Portsmouth, N.H.; they had chased away a French
snow from the mouth of St. John's Harbour - Boston item
of 5 Jan. (3 Feb.)

Last week a vessel belonging to Mr. Dames, of Newtown, Md.,
was entirely cut to pieces by the ice (3 Feb.)

A currier, a single person, by applying to William Reed, at
his lodgings at the Widow Bridges in Front St., Phila.,
may secure 100 pounds Jamaica money per year for 4 years
if he will go to Jamaica (3 Feb.)

BLAND, John (alias of Uttie Perkins), age c. 24 - was committed to Phila. Goal on suspicion of having stolen 2
horses and a Negro boy named Peter, age c. 10, from one
Gistin, living at Poff Pon, S.C.; Nicholas Scull, Sheriff
of Phila. Co., states that Bland is said to have been a
noted horse-stealer in Virginia and South Carolina (3
Feb.)

A bakehouse to be let for 3 years; enquire of Benjamin
Franklin (3 Feb.)

Two French prizes have been sent into Newport, one taken
by Capt. Dennis in the Prince Frederick, the other by
Capt. William Dunbar, of Providence - Newport, R.I., item
of 10 Jan. (10 Feb.)

NORTON, Lydia, celebrated Quaker preacher - died last second
day at Hampton Falls at an advanced age - Hampton Falls

item of 1 Jan. (10 Feb.)

BURT, Capt., in a mast ship - arrived Saturday last at
Boston from Plymouth, England - Boston item of 12 Jan.
(10 Feb.)

NORRIS, Capt., in ship bound from Boston to New York - on
4 Jan. was cast away near Scituate; the men were saved,
except for the mate - Boston item of 19 Jan. (10 Feb.

KNOX, Capt., of Boston - has safely arrived at St. Kitts -
Boston item of 19 Jan. (10 Feb.)

DENNIS, Capt., commander of Rhode Island privateer - has
taken several French prizes; the gentlemen of St. Kitts
have presented him with a golden oar and a purse of 500
pistoles - Boston item of 19 Jan. (10 Feb.)

Tuesday last at Musketto Cove, Long Island, Dennis Lawrence
(apprentice to Capt. Walton of New York) and Thomas
Brooks, a labourer, having got the itch, agreed to take
flour of brimstone to cure themselves; by mistake they
took ratsbane and both died - New York item of 2 Feb. (10
Feb.)

GOODWIN, Joseph, late of Phila., bookbinder, dec'd - accounts with estate to be settled with the administrators, William Hartley and Lewis Evans (10 Feb.)

POPE, Charles, of Duck Creek - his wife Anne has again
eloped from him (10 Feb.)

HARTLEY, William, Chief Ranger for Chester Co. - lists
strays in his hands (10 Feb.)

BOWES, Francis, near the Tun, in Water St., Phila., where
Robert Ellis lately lived - sells rum, wine, sugar, tea,
coffee, chocolate, pepper, ginger (10 Feb.)

VANDERSPIEGEL, William, at lower end of Arch St., Phila. -
has for sale New York lottery tickets (10 Feb.)

Corn and saw mills, late of John Baldwin, of Newcastle Co.,
dec'd, are to be let for 14 years; apply to Elizabeth
Baldwin, executrix, living on the premises, Jacob Hollingsworth, executor, or Robert Lewis, of Chester Co.
(10 Feb.)

Letter from Gov. William Shirley of Massachusetts to the
Duke of Newcastle (17 Feb.)

The Warren privateer, Capt. Katter, of Phila., on 25 Dec.

was refitting at Heneago after an engagement with a 36-gun ship (17 Feb.)

Imported goods are advertised for sale in Phila. by Daniel Benezet at his store in Front St., by Francis Richardson at the corner of Front and Pine Sts. and Isaac Griffitts at his store in Water St. (17 Feb.)

Brick house at the head of Market St., formerly the Sign of the Dove, is to be let by William Russell (17 Feb.)

NEVILL, William, late of Greenwich Twp., Gloucester Co., dec'd – accounts with estate to be settled with David and Hannah Jones and Mary Nevill, administrat., at the Widow Doze's, the corner of King St., on Walnut St. wharf (17 Feb.)

CLARK, Michael, Irish servant, age c. 40 – runaway from Samuel Atkinson, of Chester Twp., Burlington Co. (17 Feb.)

A shallop, formerly property of John Baizley, is to be sold; apply to William Rush or Joseph Lynn, in Phila. (17 Feb.)

COFFY, Hugh, house-carpenter – escaped from Gloucester Goal; West New Jersey; reward for his capture will be paid by Francis Haddock, Under-Sheriff (17 Feb.)

Plantation of 81 acres in Lower Merion, about 5 miles from Phila., is to be sold; apply to Griffith Griffiths, living on the premises (17 Feb.)

CLARKE, Capt. – arrived at Newport, R.I., 5 Feb., in a flag of truce from Havana (24 Feb.)

DONALD, Capt., in schooner from Boston, was cast away at or near Mt. Desert and 34 men were drowned – Boston item of 3 Feb. (24 Feb.)

NOBLE, Col. – has arrived at Annapolis Royal to take command of the forces that belonged to Brig.-Gen. Waldo's Regt. – Boston item of 3 Feb. (24 Feb.)

JAUNCEY, Capt., who arrived at New York last week from Jamaica, reported the total loss by fire of the ship London, Capt. Porter, of New York, at anchor in Port Royal Harbor on 22 Dec. – New York item of 16 Feb. (24 Feb.)

WITTER, Capt. – arrived Thursday last at New York from Coracoa – New York item of 16 Feb. (24 Feb.)

BRYANT, Capt. John, in the Prince Charles, of New York, has arrived at Gibraltar – New York item of 16 Feb. (24 Feb.)

Two privateers, a snow commanded by Capt. Woolford and a
   brigantine commanded by Capt. Dennis of Rhode Island,
   were sighted off St. Christophers in pursuit of French
   vessels (24 Feb.)

Capt. Hazelton, of Phila., and Capt. Edgar, of Phila., have
   both been taken by a French privateer (24 Feb.)

HALL, Capt., from Anguilla, reports that Capt. Goddard, in
   a New York sloop, has been taken off Antigua (24 Feb.)

Ship Friendship, of Phila., Capt. Lisle, proved so leaky that
   part of the cargo was thrown overboard and the ship with
   difficulty reached Antigua (24 Feb.)

Ship Neptune, Thomas Wilkinson commander, now riding off
   Market St. wharf in Phila. - will sail for Charlestown,
   S.C.; for freight or passage apply to the commander or to
   Robert and Amos Strettell (24 Feb.)

LOGAN, William, at his house in Second St., Phila., and
   William and David McIlvaine in their store in Water St.,
   opposite Charles Willing's - sell goods imported in the
   snow John Galley, Thomas Crosthwaite master, from London
   (24 Feb.)

NICOLS, Henry, Rector of St. Michael's Parish, Talbot Co.,
   Md. - seeks an unsettled clergyman, of a fair character,
   and in full orders (24 Feb.)

CAVENAUGH, Hugh, native Irish servant, age c. 20 - runaway
   from John Stevenson, of Norrington Twp., Phila. Co. (24
   Feb.)

WOODWARD, Japheth, hatter, late of Hattonfield, dec'd - accounts with estate to be settled with Elizabeth Woodward,
   administratrix (24 Feb.)

House at Charles Town, Md., to be sold; apply to Alexander
   Cochran, in Charles Town (24 Feb.)

An overshot sawmill, 3½ miles from Coultas's Ferry and 2 from
   Darby, in Darby Twp., Chester Co. - apply to John Marshall,
   of Darby Twp. (24 Feb.)

The Acts of the Rebels (abstract of the journal of James Ray,
   of Whitehaven) - just published by B. Franklin (24 Feb.)

To ship freight on the brigantine Greyhound for London apply
   to Jasper McCall (24 Feb.)

Lot, called "Hudson's Square," from High St. to Mulberry St., opposite to John Kinsey's, is to be let; apply to Isaac Williams or William Moode (24 Feb.)

American Balsam is sold by Samuel Robeson, in Vine St., Phila., between Second and Front Sts. (24 Feb.)

KNOWLES, Gov., in Louisburg, is reported to be seriously ill - Boston item of 9 Feb. (3 Mar.)

RAMSEY, Mons. - is reported to have fled, with a number of French and Indians, from Menis; Col. Noble had decided to pursue him - Boston item of 9 Feb. (3 Mar.)

Capts. Winslow, Rouse and Cobb lately marched to the head of Annapolis River - Boston item of 9 Feb. (3 Mar.)

Capt. Bruce reports that the French man-of-war Mercury has been taken - Boston item of 9 Feb. (3 Mar.)

The following captains were among those taken by enemy privateers: Carey, Buckley, Nevin, Dumaresque, Mulberry and Moody; Capts. Fones and Clarke arrived safely at London (3 Mar.)

Capt. Bruce came out with Capt. Craige and Capt. Dunn, both for Boston, with the Birginia fleet (3 Mar.)

On 21 Nov. the schooner Speedwell, of Phila., Capt. Greenaway, arrived at Edenton from Barbados (3 Mar.)

Schooner Nancy, Capt. William Jackson, from England, and Capt. Seager, of Annapolis, both arrived at Annapolis - Annapolis items of 10 and 17 Feb. (3 Mar.)

DICKINSON, Capt. Benjamin, in a Bermudian sloop, bound for Jamaica from Phila., has been taken (3 Mar.)

Plantation in East-town, joining the Conistogoe Road and about 17 miles from Phila., will be sold at auction by Maurice Elliot, living on the premises (3 Mar.)

SEIPEL, John Ludwick, at the Locksmith's Sign, in Second St., Phila. - has for sale a house in Northern Liberties of Phila., between William Branson's and John Kampher's, 2 lots in Kensington and a lot in Oxford Twp. (3 Mar.)

REED, William, at his store on Rees Meredith's wharf - has for sale claret, cider, cloth, etc. (3 Mar.)

CROSTHWAITE, Thomas - warns of legal action against James Camton and John McCluire, who have not paid him their passage money (3 Mar.); both men are Irishmen; Camton is a joiner and McCluir a spinning-wheel-maker (24 Mar.)

Tanyard and house in Northern Liberties of Phila. are to be let; enquire of Andrew Edge, living on the place (3 Mar.)

Thursday last Capt. Benjamin Goldthwait arrived at Boston from Annapolis Royal; he gives an account of French attack on the Grand Pré in Menis, where the following were slain: Lt.-Col. Noble, his brother Ensign Noble, Lt. Jones, Lts. Lechmere and Pickering; Capt. How was wounded and captured; other English officers taken were Capt. Doare, Lt. Gerrish and Ensign Newton; English troops surrendered were allowed to go to Annapolis Royal - Boston item of 4 Mar. (16 Mar.)

Letter of P. Mascarene, Lt.-Gov., from Annapolis Royal to the party returning from Menis; Col. Gorham was sent to receive the party - Boston item of 2 Mar. (16 Mar.)

Letter of Lt.-Col. Noble, dated Grand Pré at Menis, 28 Jan. 1747; it mentions Capt. Perkins and Major Phillips, quartermaster (16 Mar.)

A letter from Annapolis Royal of 23 Jan. tells of attempt made by Mons. De Ramsay to incite the people at Menis against the English (16 Mar.)

Two men of Martha's Vineyard, who were captives in Canada, saw there Capt. Bagley of Newbury, Capt. Jonathan Salter of Boston, Mr. Richardson of Boston, who was taken with other of Capt. Rouse's men, and some of Capt. Donahew's men - Boston item of 2 Mar. (16 Mar.)

Land on the south branch of Mantua Creek, in Gloucester Co., West Jersey, and sawmill and plantation in possession of Jonathan Fisher are to be sold; for satisfaction in the title, apply to George Emlen, in Phila. (3 Mar.)

JONES, John, late of Salem, attorney-at-law, dec'd - accounts with his estate to be settled with Mary Jones, administratrix (3 Mar.)

FOWLER, Peter, Irish servant, age c. 25 - runaway from William Hartley, of Charlestown, Chester Co. (3 Mar.)

Plantation of 232 acres, in St. George's Hundred, Newcastle Co., on Appoquimmony and Drayer's Creek, known by the name of High Hook - is to be sold; apply to Garret Dushane (3 Mar.)

Plantation called "the Trap," in Newcastle Co. - is for sale: enquire of John Vaunce and Charles Robinson (3 Mar.)

Plantation of 114 acres in Haverford Twp., Chester Co., 10
miles from Phila., late the property of Humphrey Ellis,
dec'd - is to be sold; apply to Edward Williams, of
Blockley Twp., or Henry Lawrence and Jeremiah Ellis,
living near the above premises (3 Mar.)

CARRIL, Patrick, Irish servant - runaway from Walter Thetford, of Mill Creek Hundred, Newcastle Co. (3 Mar.)

LANG, Alexander, at his store in Front St., Phila., at the
house where Samuel Neave lately dwelt - sells European
goods just imported in the ship Mary, Capt. Martin, from
London (3 Mar.)

Plantation of 100 acres, joining to John Brown's plantation
in Maxfield, Bucks Co., 5 miles from Trenton, is for
sale; apply to Richard Houghs, near Thomas Yardley's (3
Mar.)

Plantation late belonging to Joseph Naylor, of Montgomery
Twp., Phila. Co., dec'd, is for sale; apply to the execu-
tors, Richard Naylor, John Foreman and John Williams (3
Mar.)

WHITEFIELD, Rev. - reached Charlestown, S.C., the Saturday
before 16 Dec. - Boston item of 12 Feb. (10 Mar.)

HALL, Capt., from Anguilla, reports that Capt. Elbertson,
in a sloop of New York, has been taken (10 Mar.)

Privateer brigantine Hester, Capt. Troup, of New York -
took a French sugar-ship (10 Mar.)

DENNIS, Capt., of Rhode Island, according to Capt. Hazelton,
challenged the Gov. of Martinico to send out 2 vessels
against him; this was done but they chased the Leostaff
privateer of Bristol, Capt. Fielding, which obliged one
to sheer off and captured the other (10 Mar.)

H.M.S. Lyme, Capt. Tyrrel, has retaken a London ship (10 Mar.)

WARREN, Mrs. Sarah - died last Saturday night in Phila.,
aged 107 (10 Mar.)

HYSLOP, William, at his store in Water St., which formerly
belonged to Stedman and Robertson - sells Scotch checks,
handkerchiefs, snuff (10 Mar.)

A new house, within 2 doors of the White Horse, in Elbow
Lane, Phila., opposite the Presbyterian burying-ground
is to be let; enquire of Henry Dexter, at the corner of
Strawberry Alley, opposite the Shambles (10 Mar.)

Five hundred acres, known by the name of Christeen Mills, 3/4 mile from Christeen Bridge, Newcastle Co., and also 230 acres, now in the tenure of Hugh Owens, are to be sold by William Patterson (10 Mar.)

LOLLER, Edward, Irish servant, age c. 17 - runaway from John Climson, of Salisbury Twp., Lancaster Co. (10 Mar.)

Plantation of 175 acres in North Wales Twp., Phila. Co. - to be sold or let; apply to Daniel Williams, in Phila. (10 Mar.)

TRUMAN, Thomas, living near the Quakers Meeting-house, in Second St., Phila. - offers reward for recovery of 2 strayed or stolen horses (10 Mar.)

THORNTON, Joseph, in Newtown, Bucks Co. - wishes to sell the Half Moon Inn, which he has kept for 14 years; it is nearest to the courthouse and the court is pleased to dine at it (10 Mar.)

SCARTH, Timothy - announces the coming sale by auction of some 30 lots in Kensington, lying on Franckfort Rd., 1½ miles from Phila., almost opposite the Sign of the Wheatsheaf (10 Mar.)

BARLY, James, Irish servant, age c. 17, who speaks pretty good English and good Dutch - runaway from John Keppler, of Perkyoman, by Pawling's Mill, Phila. Co. (10 Mar.)

Brick house on south side of Market St., between Third and Fourth Sts., Phila., lately possessed by Benjamin Eastburn, dec'd, is to be let; enquire of Thomas Woolley, or David Clarke, now in possession of said house (10 Mar.)

The ship Charming Rebecca, Thomas Stamper master, will sail for Antigua; for freight or passage agree with Thomas Phillips, at Plumstead's wharf, or at his lodgings on Society Hill, or with the master on board (10 Mar.)

Tuesday last Capt. Fryer arrived at Boston from Anguilla - Boston item of 2 Mar. (16 Mar.)

It is reported that H. E. Samuel Ogle, Esq., with wife and family, is bound for Maryland to resume the government of the province - Annapolis item of 3 Mar. (16 Mar.)

WHITEFIELD, Rev. George - is reported to have arrived in Georgia (16 Mar.)

AMBLER, Capt. - arrived Thursday last at Phila. with report that Commodore Knowles has recovered and intends for

England (16 Mar.)

ROBERTSON, Peter, in Front St., Phila. - has books for sale (16 Mar.)

WESTLEY, Mandlin, Welsh servant, who came from Bristol, age c. 25 - runaway from Robert Gelton, of Boston in New England; reward for her commitment to any goal in New Jersey or Pennsylvania will be paid by Thomas Lightfoot in Phila. (16 Mar.)

STOCKEY, Anne Carrola, English servant, age c. 25 - same as above

FOULKE, Samuel - assails advertisement of Thomas Skillvin, who proposed to open a fencing and dancing school in Phila. (16 Mar.)

Peter Robeson, Joseph Farmer and Jonathan Robeson design to sell on 6 Apr., at the house of Christopher Robins, in Whitemarsh Twp., 14 lots in said township; a plan of them may be seen at Peter Robeson's, at the Indian King, Phila. (16 Mar.)

The following soldiers, all Irishmen, have deserted from the Virginia Company, quartered at the fort in New York: Michael Holland, joiner, age c. 22; Thomas Ormand, planter, age c. 20; James Gabbott, carpenter, age c. 24; George Malcolm, age c. 36; Archibald Hanna, sawyer, age c. 22; James Row, weaver, age c. 25 (16 Mar.)

CARROLL, John, Irish servant, age c. 40 - runaway from Jonathan Woodland, of St. George's Hundred, Newcastle Co. (16 Mar.)

A country seat, adjoining to Rariton Rd., which leads from Wells's Ferry down to Rariton Landing, 7 miles from said landing and 9 from New Brunswick, is for sale; apply to Dr. William Farquhar in New York, Benjamin Franklin in Philadelphia, or Jacob Janeway, living on the premises; Joseph Read, merchant in New York, has woodland adjoining the premises (16 Mar.)

Plantation of 315 acres in Darby Twp. is for sale; enquire of Joseph Levis, living in Oxford Twp., near Franckfort (16 Mar.)

JOHNSTON, Patrick - offers reward for recovery of bay horse that strayed from James Snodgrass's plantation in Martick Twp., Lancaster Co.; horse may be brought to James Macconnell, tavernkeeper at Ochterara (16 Mar.)

LANGDALE, John, late of Phila., tanner, has gone to settle
in Virginia; accounts with him are to be settled with
his attorney, Philip Syng (16 Mar.)

BEVAN, Aubrey, innkeeper in Chester - is removed and now
lives opposite to the courthouse in that borough, at the
Proprietor's Arms (16 Mar.)

In the engagement at Menis the French commander, Capt.
Coulon, was dangerously wounded; Ensign Newton of Boston,
one of the prisoners, has been released - Boston item of
9 Mar. (24 Mar.)

Excerpt from a letter of James Gardner, of Nantucket, who
lately arrived there from Canada, dated Nantucket, Feb.
19: 2 French warships in March took the following: a
brigantine, J. Holdam commander; a snow, R. Roberts mas-
ter; Capt. Salter of Boston; Capt. Bagley of Newbury;
Capt. Jordan of Newport; Capt. Philips of Marblehead;
Zephaniah Pinkman of Nantucket; Capt. Johnston of Amboy;
a schooner of Salem, Francis Cox master; a schooner of
Cape Ann, Joseph Dennie master; sloop of Norwich, Conn.,
Capt. Story; Capt. Colebay; among prisoners at Quebec were
Capt. Chapman of London, Capt. Southerlin of Cape Cod;
Capt. Poet of Casco - Boston item of 9 Mar. (24 Mar.)

JEFFERIES, Capt., in the privateer Greyhound of New York -
has lately retaken an English ship - New York item of 16
Mar. (24 Mar.)

BEEZLEY, Capt., in the privateer Dolphin, of New York - has
lately been at Barbados - New York item of 16 Mar. (24
Mar.)

TULL, Simon, of Schenegtade - his stable, with grain and
horses, was entirely destroyed by fire the night of 22
Feb.; a Negro confessed the crime and was burnt for the
same 5 days after - New York item of 16 Mar. (24 Mar.)

Thursday last H.M.S. Foulkstone, Capt. Gregory, arrived within the Capes, with Samuel Ogle and wife on board; the
Ogles went on board the Neptune, Capt. Grindall, and proceeded to Annapolis; on 16 Mar. Mr. Ogle, attended by
Thomas Bladen, then Governor, went to the Council Chamber,
where the Commission appointing Samuel Ogle governor was
opened and published - Annapolis item of 17 Mar. (24 Mar.)

The brigantine Friendship, Capt. Rossiter, lately foundered
southwest of Bermuda, as did a Bermudian sloop, Capt.
Todd master (24 Mar.)

Capt. Wood on Thursday last brought to Phila. the people of

the ship <u>William</u> and <u>Mary</u>, Capt. Cowen, of Phila., which
sank; Capt. Wood reached them just in time to save them
(24 Mar.)

It is reported from Maryland that 4 French men-of-war on 10
Sept. took the snow <u>Glasgow</u>, Capt. Montgomery, and the
ship <u>Prince George</u>, Capt. Coulter (24 Mar.)

Capt. White, from Providence, reports that Capt. Bevan, of
New York, had carried there 2 French sloops and that
Capt. Lawrence, of New York, brought in there a brigan-
tine belonging to Boston (24 Mar.)

RIVERS, Capt., from Anguilla - advises that the privateer
<u>Trembleur</u> took a French prize but that Capt. Dennis of
of Rhode Island was in sight before she struck; that
Capt. Troup, of New York, took a French sloop; that Capt.
Woolford, in a St. Kitts privateer took a French sloop;
Capt. Ashton, of Phila., came passenger with Capt. Rivers
as his ship was taken by a French privateer (24 Mar.)

CROSTHWAITE, William, in Phila. - has dry goods for sale;
he has 2 chests of medicines brought from London in the
<u>John Galley</u>, Thomas Crosthwaite master (24 Mar.)

ALLEN, Nathaniel, Jr., in Front St., near Market St., Phila.
- has for sale a parcel of Carolina reed (24 Mar.)

JOHNSON, John, tailor - is removed from Water St. to Market
St.; his tavern Sign of the Phoenix is for sale (24 Mar.)

FEW, James, of Kennet - has rented from 1 May next the house,
wharf and stores of Job Jacobs in Wilmington (24 Mar.)

HYSLOP, William, at his store in Water St., Phila., which
formerly belonged to Steadman and Robertson - has for
sale goods just imported from Scotland, via Boston, in
the sloop <u>Endeavour</u>, James Nicholls master (24 Mar.)

GRIFFITH, Gideon, sheriff - on 13 Mar. took up and committed to the Newcastle Goal one Thomas Gilpin, who says
he is a shoemaker (24 Mar.)

O'DENNYSEY, Laughlin, native Irish servant, age 30 - runaway from William Moore, of St. George's Newcastle Co.
(24 Mar.)

Capt. Troup boarded and took a French privateer, Capt. Lat-
touch commander; Capt. Long saw the <u>Hester</u> pass by St.
Eustatia - New York item of 23 Mar. (2 Apr.)

SWEETING, Capt., in a Rhode Island privateer, has sent in

a French prize (2 Apr.)

A large French ship from Havana was taken on Christmas Day
by 2 English men-of-war, the Gloucester, Capt. Saunders,
and the Lark, Capt. Cheape; the prize had 1,000,000 pounds
sterling aboard (2 Apr.)

REED, Capt. William, at his store in Water St., Phila -
sells cloth and other items just imported from Glasgow
(2 Apr.)

Plantation, late of Edward Nicholas, dec'd, in Limrick Twp.,
Phila. Co., fronting the River Schuylkill, is to be sold
at auction by William Currie and Thomas Bull, executors
(2 Apr.)

FARMAR, Richard, at the Unicorn, in Second St., Phila. -
has for sale an assortment of drugs and medicines imported from London in the Fortune, Capt. Russel (2 Apr.)

MAURICE, Matthias, paper-maker, late of German Twp., Phila.
Co. - accounts with estate to be settled with Jacob and
William Levering, executors (2 Apr.)

WILSTIN, John, convict Irish servant, age c. 30 - runaway
from Stephen Onion, living at Gunpowder Ironworks (2
Apr.)

NEALE, John, convict Irish servant, age c. 28 - same as above

STAR, Jeremiah, Collector of Excise for Chester Co. - will
receive entries from retailers both at his own house and
also at the house of John Salkeld in Chester (2 Apr.)

Cloth, glassware, tools, paper and cutlery, just imported
by John Graham, are for sale at Matthew Zuill's store,
opposite to the Sign of the Pewter Platter in Front St.,
Phila. (2 Apr.)

MARRIOTT, Thomas - will sell at auction real estate in the
borough of Bristol, Bucks Co. (2 Apr.)

A brick house on the west side of the road leading from
Phila. to Germantown and Frankfort, next adjoining to
the house where William Coates now lives, will be sold
at auction (2 Apr.)

RUSSELL, William, at the head of Market St., formerly the
Sign of the Dove, will let brick house and wooden tenement (2 Apr.)

George Okill and Robert Greenway, attornies of Leonard Mor-

rey, will sell at the house of Robert McCunty, in
Springfield, Phila. Co., said plantation and also 2
plantations, each of 200 acres, on the River Delaware,
Gloucester Co., West New Jersey, about 3 miles from
Phila., opposite Fairman's Island, now in the tenure of
James Wilson and Samuel Tue (2 Apr.)

LUNAN, Alexander - gives details of a fair to be held on
30 Apr. at Frederick Town, Caecil Co.; horses are to be
entered with James Hughes 3 days before the fair (2 Apr.)

REA, James, Irish servant, age c. 19, who can talk Dutch -
runaway from Jost Dubs, at Reading Iron-works (2 Apr.)

VONDERWEID, Jacob, of Germantown, carpenter - has 2 houses
to be sold; both in Germantown; one is a tavern, with the
Sign of the Indian King, on the main street; the other is
in the lane near the market place, commonly called As-
mead's Lane, belonging to Andrew Robeson's mill (2 Apr.)

TROUP, Capt., in the privateer brigantine Hester - lately
took 8,000 pieces of eight from a Spanish merchant on a
Danish vessel - New York item of 6 Apr. (9 Apr.)

It is reported that Capts. Griffith and Bryant, both of New
York, have arrived in England, while Capts. Riven and
Davies, bound from New York to Holland, have been taken
(9 Apr.)

Thursday last arrived at New York the privateer sloop Revenge, Capt. Helme; the Polly, Capt. Elmes, was cast
away Thursday night on the south side of Long Island -
New York item of 6 Apr. (9 Apr.)

SCHERMERHORN, Capt., from South Carolina - reports that before he sailed 5 vessels from London were taken by a
Spanish privateer - New York item of 6 Apr. (9 Apr.)

CUNDY, Capt. - arrived yesterday at Phila. from Jamaica and
reports that H.M.S. Experience, Capt. Holmes, has taken
a large French ship (9 Apr.)

From Antigua is advice that the ship Anne Polley, Capt.
Houston, of Phila., has been taken by a French privateer
(9 Apr.)

SWEETIN, Capt., of Rhode Island, has taken 7 prizes (9 Apr.)

McKAGHAN, Archibald, Irish servant - runaway from John
Foulks, tanner, of Borough of Lancaster (9 Apr.)

Sam, Negro, age c. 26, who was sold by Dr. Cadwallader to

Thomas Tindall, of Trenton - runaway from said Tindall
(9 Apr.)

FOWLER, Peter, Irish servant, age c. 25 - runaway from William Hartley, of Charlestown, Chester Co.; reward will
be paid if news of the runaway is given to Benjamin
Franklin, in Phila., so that his master may have him
again (9 Apr.)

HUTCHISON, George, at Mrs. Griffitts's store in Water St.,
Phila. - sells goods imported from Scotland (9 Apr.)

At Roberts's Coffee House in Phila. will be sold part of
Pool Forge in Phila. Co.; enquire of George Mifflin in
Market St., Phila. (9 Apr.)

MOORE, John, of Brandywine Hundred, Newcastle Co. - his
wife Elizabeth has eloped from him (9 Apr.)

WILLIAMS, Rees - has for sale 2/3 of a grist-mill, on Chester
Creek, Chester Co., 2 miles from tide water (9 Apr.)

ROBESON, John, Irishman, age c. 21 - deserted from Lt.
Dwight, recruiting for Sir William Pepperell's Regt. at
Louisburg (9 Apr.)

McCARTNEY, Charles, Irishman, age c. 35 - same as above; if
either deserter is brought to the George, in Second St.,
Phila., a reward will be paid by John Scutt for Lt. Dwight
(9 Apr.)

Lot of ground on Society Hill, adjoining to a lot of Daniel
Harrison's, will be sold at auction (9 Apr.)

Indian attack made last Sabbath evening on Shattuck's fort,
above Northfield; the Indians were repulsed - Boston item
of 6 Apr. (16 Apr.)

Capt. Trent this morning went down with Lt. Proctor's party
but the height of the water in the Swamp obliged them to
go as far up as where Capt. Schuyler's house stood to get
to the other side. At Mr. Tenbrook's farm they were attacked by French and Indians in ambush, and, after fight-
ing an hour, retreated to the Swamp. Capt. Livingston
had sent Ensign Bratt towards the Swamp and Lts. Johnson
and Hall round the Swamp. One Frenchman, Julian Fortain,
age 29, was taken prisoner - Extract of letter from
Saraghtoga dated 7 Apr. - New York item of 13 Apr. (16
Apr.)

The following were killed in sight of Saraghtoga Fort:
Daniel Ireland, John Reade, Richard Brown, Peter Stiles

616

and John Smith (all of Capt. Wraxell's company); John
Loyd and Isaac Brown (both of Capt. Richards's company);
George Pentaw (of Capt. Honeyman's company); one Kelly
(of Capt. Hart's company) - New York item of 13 Apr.
(16 Apr.)

It is reported from Kinderhook that a party of French and
Indians on 10 Apr. killed Peter Vosburgh and Matthew Van
Duesen and took captive a son and daughter of Vosburgh,
a child of Van Duesen, a daughter (and her child) of Jan
Gardenier, a Negro belonging to Jan Van Alstyn and another
Negro belonging to Bata Van Duesen - New York item of 13
Apr. (16 Apr.)

A passenger who came with Capt. Andrews, who lately left
Havre de Grace, reports that 5 ships with stores for
Canada were to sail about 20 Mar. (16 Apr.)

Snow Peggy, Capt. Hamilton, of Phila. - was taken on 17 Feb.
by the privateer Tavignon, of St. Maloes (16 Apr.)

Two men from the Jerseys, Maynert Johnson and William Cas-
way, have been passing counterfeit 12s. bills (16 Apr.)

Goods just imported from Glasgow in the brigantine Endeavour,
John Andrews master, are being sold by Hamilton, Wallace
& Co., at their house in Water St., by William Andrews,
at his store on Pemberton's wharf in Phila., and goods
imported from Scotland in the same vessel are for sale
by Robert Hamilton at Mr. Fishbourn's store in Water St.
(16 Apr.)

A company of servants, just imported from Ireland in the
ship Euryale, Lawrence Anderson, Jr., commander, are to
be sold by William Masters at his house or by Lawrence
Anderson on board said ship, opposite to the Market St.
wharf (16 Apr.)

Lt. Mackinney or John Baron, at the George, in Phila. will
pay a reward for capture of the following deserters from
Sir William Pepperrell's Regt. of Foot: John Dundas,
born in Edinburgh, age 25, labourer; George Carbright,
born in Dublin, age 24, weaver; Goerge Tarrett, born in
Dublin, age 25, stocking-weaver; John Cox, born at Mantua
Creek, age 26, cooper; Nicholas Connor, born in Dublin,
age 25, labourer; John Cullicut, born at Devonshire, age
32, labourer; Benjamin Ford; Dennis Hays, born in Cork,
age 22, tobacconist; Elijah Bruster, born at Connecticut,
age 21, labourer; Isaac Provender, age 21; Joel Clark;
Thomas Barnard, born in old England, age 30, tailor
(16 Apr.)

MURPHY, John, having declined riding post to Maryland - will serve gentlemen as messenger to any part of Pennsylvania or the neighboring provinces (16 Apr.)

CRESSON, Solomon, dec'd - accounts with estate to be settled with John Cresson, executor (16 Apr.)

SMITH, Isaac, late of Hattonfield, dec'd - accounts with estate to be settled with Elizabeth Smith, administratrix (16 Apr.)

Lot of land on the crossroad leading from Isaac Norris's, on the Germantown Rd., to Jacob Dubree's, on the Wysahickon Rd., will be sold by William Adams, gardiner, in the Northern Liberties of Phila. (16 Apr.)

JOCHAM, William, English servant, age c. 19 - runaway from Augustine Muse, living in Caroline Co., Va. (16 Apr.)

WILSON, John, servant, age c. 21 - runaway from Benjamin Fred, of New Garden Twp., Chester Co. (16 Apr.)

ANDERSON, William, Irish servant - runaway from Alexander Crage, of New London Twp., Chester Co. (16 Apr.)

HANSON, John, late of Abington, dec'd - accounts with estate to be settled with Nicholas Austin and William North (16 Apr.)

Twenty-five acres of land in Passyunk Twp. and Moyamenson, 2 miles from Phila. (part of estate of James Lownes, dec'd) will be sold by Mary Lownes, widow (by order of the Orphan's Court) at Widow Roberts's Coffee House in Phila. (16 Apr.)

The following arrived at Boston: Gov. Knowles on Friday last; Capt. Haugh on Tuesday last from South Carolina; Capt. Samuel Allyn Tuesday last from Virginia - Boston items of 13 Apr. (23 Apr.)

On Western frontier Capt. Melvil, with 27 men, was hemmed in for a day about 15 miles above Ft. Dummer, by a body of Indians (23 Apr.)

Monday last arrived at New York a French snow, taken on 18 Mar. by the privateer Hester, Capt. Troup, and the Dragon, Capt. Seymour, both of New York; on Friday last arrived the Spanish privateer sloop, now under command of Capt. Kip, taken 21 Mar. off Porto Rico by the Greyhound privateer of New York - New York item of 20 Apr. (23 Apr.)

Saturday last the Virginia company under Capt. Beverly

Robinson embarked from New York for Albany - New York
item of 20 Apr. (23 Apr.)

The following were taken and carried in Leoganne: Capt.
Godfrey, Capt. Harvey (belonging to Piscataqua) and
Capt. Durell (belonging to Boston) - New York item of
20 Apr. (23 Apr.)

MANN, Capt. James, who arrived 19 Apr. at New York, reports
that Capt. Beazley, in the Dolphin privateer of New York,
has taken 3 Dutch sloops - New York item of 20 Apr. (23
Apr.)

Letter of the Rev. Josiah Smith, of Charlestown, S.C.,
about the Rev. Mr. Whitefield (23 Apr.)

Tract of 2,700 acres, called Green's Manor, in St. George's
Hundred, Newcastle Co., is to be sold; enquire of John
Inglis, merchant, in Phila., or John Moland, of the
Northern Liberties Twp. (23 Apr.)

MORGAN, Bryant, Irish servant, age c. 40 - runaway from
Arthur Lee, of Kent Co., Md. (23 Apr.)

MORGAN, Evan, cooper, at his house near the drawbridge in
Phila. - sells wines, spirits, spices, chocolate, cheese,
nails (23 Apr.)

Plantation of 200 acres in Haverford Twp., Chester Co., is
for sale; enquire of Rees Price, of Merion (23 Apr.)

Meadow land near Myomensing is for sale; enquire of Ebenezer
Currie, in Front St., Phila. (23 Apr.)

Plantation of 146 acres in Biberry Twp., Phila. Co., is to
be sold; apply to Isaac Delavau, living at said plantation (23 Apr.)

LEITH, Alexander, at Mr. Glentworth's house in Market St.,
Phila. - sells cloth imported from Scotland (23 Apr.)

GALLOWAY, John, administrator, will sell at auction in
Chester Town, Kent Co., (for the advantage of John Owen,
of London, and the proper representatives of William
Belch, dec'd) 18 years lease of one moiety of a lot in
Chester Town, belonging to the estate of Capt. Richard
Lux, dec'd (23 Apr.)

DUNLAP, James, at his store in Water St., next door to
Messieurs Hamilton, Wallace and Co., in Phila. - sells
goods just imported from Scotland (23 Apr.)

ROGERS, James, linen-bleacher, on Society Hill - whitens, cleans, washes, removes stains (23 Apr.)

ATHETON, Susannah, widow, by order of the Orphan's Court, at Roberts's Coffee House in Phila., will sell real estate: one lot, taken off the west end of 840 acres (formerly called Roch's land and lately the land of Ralph Asheton, dec'd, on the west side of Schuylkill, in Twp. of Blockley); persons mentioned in bounding the lots are Barnabas Wilcox, John Marshall, John Ball, Richard Marsh; other persons whose land is mentioned are John Simcock and William Warner; also to be sold is a ground-rent arising out of a lot in Chesnut St. occupied by Jonathan Beers, George Sharswood, James Bainbridge and George House; a plan of the lots may be seen at James Humphreys's living at Carpenter's Brewhouse, behind the Governor's (23 Apr.)

Gilbert Mawhorter offers reward for recovery of a horse strayed or stolen from Robert Mawhorter's door in Lower Dublin Twp., Phila. Co.; the horse may be brought to Thomas Kenten's, in Oxford Twp. (23 Apr.)

A brew- and malt-house in Borough of Bristol, 20 miles from Phila., is to be let; apply to Peter Bard, merchant, in Phila., or John Denormandie, on the premises (23 Apr.)

CLARK, William, in Phila. - will let lots on northwest side of Frankfort Rd., about 4 miles from Phila., part of plantation on which John Strickland now lives (23 Apr.)

COWELL, Capt. - arrived a few days ago at Marblehead from Sardinia, with European news - Boston item of 20 Apr. (30 Apr.)

TANNER, Capt. - arrived at New York Monday last from Jamaica - New York item of 27 Apr. (30 Apr.)

Sloop of New York, Capt. Hutchenson, has been taken by a Spanish privateer; one Loyd (the mate) and 2 men escaped in the boat and arrived at South Carolina (30 Apr.)

Privateer Pandour of Phila. arrived at Phila. 29 Apr. (30 Apr.)

Ship Mary, Capt. Anderson, of and from London, has been taken near Barbados (30 Apr.)

CARTER, Capt., a Jamaica storeship, has been cut out of Torbay (30 Apr.)

Agreement has been made that Capt. Grantham, in a Bermuda

privateer, is to cruise on the coast of Barbados (30 Apr.)

A prize schooner from the privateer brigantine <u>Trembleur</u>, Capt. Bowne, of Phila., is in the river at Phila. (30 Apr.)

WHITEFIELD, Rev. - has arrived at Bohemia in Maryland (30 Apr.)

William Adams's vendue is postponed to 7 May (30 Apr.)

Parcel of French claret will be sold on John Stamper's wharf, near the drawbridge (30 Apr.)

Snow <u>Jane</u>, Giles Heysham commander, will sail for Liverpool; for freight or passage agree with Israel Pemberton, Jr., or said commander (30 Apr.)

ZWIFFLER, John Andrews, Dr. of Physic, is removed from John Barcley's in Market St. to the Widow Nailor's in Arch St., opposite to Septimus Robinson, Esq. (30 Apr.)

Warning not to buy the prize money belonging to Benjamin Barker (who has lately gone from New York to Phila.), as he gave a bill of sale for said money to William Millinner, of New York, witnessed by Anthony Ham and Armor Viele (30 Apr.)

SCULL, Nicholas, Sheriff - announces annuity arising from lot on north side of Morris's Alley, taken in execution at the suit of William and Elizabeth Chancellor, will be sold (30 Apr.)

POLE, John, of Phila. - sells cables, anchors, iron pots, etc. (30 Apr.)

ALLEN, Nathaniel, Jr., in Front St., near Market St., Phila. - has Carolina reed for sale (30 Apr.)

COCHRAN, Robert, at John Frazer's on Society Hill, has for sale claret wine and oil (30 Apr.)

Lot in Water St., Phila., opposite to house where Thomas Griffitts, dec'd, lately lived, will be sold; enquire of Mary and Isaac Griffitts, executors, in Water St. (30 Apr.)

WOOLEY, Thomas, of Phila., innholder, is removed from the Sign of the White Horse in Elbow Lane to the Sign of the Horse and Groom in Strawberry Alley, near the market (30 Apr.)

CADWALLADER, Martha, dec'd - furniture will be sold by public vendue at her late dwelling house, next door to Hugh Roberts's, in Market St., Phila.; enquire at Samuel Morris's at lower end of Second St. (30 Apr.)

MAURICE, Matthias, dec'd - at his late house in German Twp., Phila. Co., will be sold a tract of land with a papermill; the executors of his estate are Jacob and William Levering (30 Apr.)

WISE, Jacob - will sell at auction 33 lots, of which 5 front Germantown main street; others front a street leading to York Rd., opposite to the lots lately sold by John Wister (30 Apr.)

Three Irish convict servants, Arthur Burns, Terence Burns and Bryan Morgan (age c. 40) - runaways from William Ellis, Arthur Lee and T. Bryan, all of Caecil Co., Md. (30 Apr.)

Reward offered for recovery of horse strayed away from Simon Butler's mill, in New Britain Twp., Bucks Co.; reward will be paid if horse is brought to said Butler, or to John Jones, tavernkeeper in Phila., or to James James in St. George's Hundred, Newcastle Co. (30 Apr.)

MOORE, Samuel Preston - offers reward for recovery of 2 horses that strayed from his plantation near Franckfort (30 Apr.)

Brigantine Greyhound will sail for London; for freight or passage agree with Jasper McAll (30 Apr.)

Speech of Lt.-Gov. George Thomas to the General Assembly of Pennsylvania on the death of John Penn (7 May)

DENNIS, Capt. John - arrived last Monday at Newport, R.I., in the privateer Prince Frederick of that place - Newport item of 24 Apr. (7 May)

Letter from Capt. Phineas Stevens, commander of the fort at No. 4, almost 40 miles above Northfield, dated 7 Apr.; he tells of his resistance against a force of French and Indians commanded by General Dobelina; only 2 men in the fort were wounded, John Brown, Jr., and Joseph Ealy; Commodore Knowles is having a silver sword presented to Capt. Stevens - Boston item of 27 Apr. (7 May)

Mons. Ramsay plans to attack Annapolis Royal, as is reported by vessels from that place (7 May)

NORTON, John - has liberty to preach to the English captives at Montreal (7 May)

Account of party of Indians sent out by Col. Johnston,
under the command of Lt. Walter Butler, Jr., against the
French - New York item of 4 May (7 May)

On 3 May Capt. John Wright arrived at New York from Savannah, Ga., with news of activities of French and Spanish
privateers (7 May)

Saturday last at Annapolis, Md., lightning struck the mast
of the Mercury, Capt. Hargrave - Annapolis item of 21
Apr. (7 May)

VAUNCE, Capt., from Barbados - arrived Sunday last at Phila.
with news that Capt. Maccullough, of Phila., had been
taken by a French privateer and then retaken by Capt.
Frankland in the Dragon man-of-war; also that the sloop
Katie, Capt. Bowne, of Phila., was cut out of Surinam
harbor but retaken by Capt. Grantham (7 May)

CLARKE, Capt., in a ship from Montserrat for London, has
been taken and carried into Guadeloupe (7 May)

A snow from Poole for Charlestown, S.C., Thomas Courtin commander, and a schooner from Charlestown for New York,
Isaac Colcock commander, have been taken by a Spanish
privateer; Capt. Colcock spoke with Capt. Crosthwaite,
formerly of the snow John, who had been taken by a privateer (7 May)

YERKAS, Herman - has taken up a horse at his plantation
(7 May)

JACOB, Thomas, at the head of Elk, Caecil Co., Md. - his
wife Martha has eloped from him (7 May)

The following have deserted from Capt. John Diemer's company of foot at Albany: William Echard, born in Germany,
age 33, who lived in Lancaster; Nicholas Fye, a German,
who lived in Lancaster; Jacob Wirt and George Fantx,
Germans, who both lived on Society Hill in Phila.; Jo-
seph Burriston, an Irishman, who lived in Phila.; John
Shaw, Dennis Carrol, Roger Mountain, John Burns (alias
Philip Campbell), Irishmen, who lived in Lancaster Co.;
James Lackey, Irishman, age c. 24; William Hart, an
Englishman, a sawyer by trade, who lived near German-
town; Anthony Bushong, a cooper, who lived in Lancaster
Co.; George Groff, Johannes Rittenbaun and George Rerer,
Germans, who lived at Tulpehocken; Arthur Macdonald, an
Irishman, tinker by trade; Isaac Daniel, an Irishman, who
lived near Germantown; W. Franklin offers a reward for

apprehension of any of these deserters (7 May)

GREGORY, Thomas, commander of H.M.S. <u>Folkstone</u>, will convoy
merchant ships from Hampton, Va., to England (7 May)

BENTLEY, Thomas, Englishman, age <u>c</u>. 25 - runaway from
bail, Vanhorne, in Northampton Twp., Bucks Co. (7 May)

COFFEE, John, Irish servant, age <u>c</u>. 17 - runaway from Thomas
Griffiths, of Vincent Twp. (7 May)

James, Negro, age <u>c</u>. 22 - runaway from James Pettigrew, of
Accomack Co., Va.; reward will be paid if slave is brought
to John Neal, attorney-at-law, at Lewistown, Sussex Co.
(7 May)

JONES, John, English servant, age <u>c</u>. 25 - runaway from Edward Wells, of Phila. (7 May)

HAIR, Margaret, living in house of Mrs. Carr, in Walnut St.,
Phila. - will instruct young ladies in French and fine
needlework (7 May)

Brigantine <u>Jane & Sarah</u>, Patrick Vaunce commander, at Hopkins's wharf in Phila. - will sail for Barbados; for
freight or passage agree with John Hopkins, merchant, in
Water St., or said master on board (7 May)

CARTWRIGHT, Abraham, age <u>c</u>. 21, who keeps about the forest
near Mr. Weatherspoon's, on the borders of Maryland -
deserter from Sir William Pepperrell's Regt.; reward will
be paid if deserter is brought to Lt. Mackinnen, at the
George Tavern, Phila. (7 May)

REYNOLDS, John, age <u>c</u>. 21 - same as above

BEASTON, John, age <u>c</u>. 19 - same as above

BYER, Blas - offers reward for recovery of mare strayed or
stolen from his plantation in Rockhill Twp., Bucks Co.
(7 May)

BROOKS, Edward, in Front St., near the Bank Meeting-house -
will sell house and lot on north side of High St., Phila.,
where Henry Pratt now dwells, at the Sign of the Royal
Standard, opposite to the butchers shambles (7 May)

Address of General Assembly of Pennsylvania (John Kinsey,
Speaker), to Lt.-Gov. George Thomas and the reply (14
May)

The Chactaw Indians renew treaty made with the English in

Charlestown, S.C., in 1738 by the Red King, brother to
Red Shoes, chief of the nation - Charlestown item of 20
Apr. (14 May)

Tuesday last arrived at Charlestown the privateer ship Mercury, Capt. William Duthy, of Charlestown, and Saturday
arrived the Elizabeth, Capt. Boyd, with 21 English prisoners from St. Augustine, including Capt. Thomas Crosthwaite
who had been taken by Capt. Stephen Berrard; Berrard has
also taken Capts. Paul, Hutchinson, Seymour, Green and
James Williams - Charlestown item of 20 Apr. (14 May)

Schooner Dorchester (owned by Mr. Prichard), Walter Humphreys
master, has just arrived at Charlestown from Providence,
but last from St. Augustine; she had been taken by a
Spanish privateer, commanded by St. Jago Gaultier, and
then ransomed - Charlestown item of 20 Apr. (14 May)

Friday last arrived at Charlestown the James, Samuel Ball
master; she was taken by a schooner commanded by Monsieur
Bruneau but retaken by H.M.S. Aldborough - Charlestown
item of 27 Apr. (14 May)

Sloop Stephen, of New York, Capt Chambers, was taken and
carried to St. Domingo; the sloop Unity, of New York,
Capt. Hunter, was cast away on the Anegada Rocks; the
sloop Swallow, of New York, Capt. Hewart, has been carried into St. Jago de Cuba - New York items of 11 May
(14 May)

Speech of Sir William Gooch of Virginia to the General Assembly and reply of the Council (14 May)

BEAZLEY, Capt. Michael, of the privateer Dolphin, of New
York, has brought into Cape Fear a rich prize (14 May)

MAGEE, Capt. Nathaniel, of Phila., who was taken in the
snow John, has arrived at Phila.; he was taken to St.
Augustine; the ship Catherine and Mary, Capt. Childs,
of Phila., has been taken (14 May)

The Warren privateer, Capt. Katter, is to sail from Phila.
tomorrow or the next day (14 May)

EVANS, Jonathan - has been constituted the officer for
executing the act "more effectually to prevent unfair
practices in the Packing of Beef and Pork for Exporta-
tion" (14 May)

ANTES, Henry, at his plantation near Nazareth, in the Forks
of Delaware, has taken up a horse (14 May)

BRANSON, William - offers reward for recovery of his horse,
strayed or stolen; it may be brought to the owner or to
Samuel Flower, Esq., at Reading Furnace (14 May)

Dwelling (lately in possession of George Okill), stores and
wharf, next door to the ferry house in Water St., Phila.,
are to be let; apply to Rebecca and Elizabeth Rawle,
living next door to the premises (14 May)

Between 2 and 4 years of time of a blacksmith are to be
sold; apply to William Rush, of Phila. (14 May)

Ten lots, on southeast side of a cross lane leading from the
main street of Germantown to Abington, will be sold by
John Frederick Ax, in behalf of Jeremiah and Balthazar
Traut; also there will be sold sundry lots, on opposite
side of said lane, by Matthys Adam Hogermoedt; sale is to
be near house of Balthazar Traut, living near the premises (14 May)

GILBERT, Robert, in Market St., Phila. - offers reward for
recovery of a horse and mare, hired from him by Francis
Kelly and George Nevill (14 May)

LEAMING, Aaron, late of Cape May, dec'd - accounts with estate to be settled with the executors, Aaron, Jeremiah
and Elizabeth Leaming (14 May)

MILLER, William, of New Garden Twp., Chester Co. - offers
reward for recovery of mare strayed or stolen (14 May)

MAAG, Jacob, in Second St., Phila., offers for sale a house
and lot in Kensington, one mile from Phila., joining upon
Queen St. and Hanover St. (14 May)

House within 2 doors of the White Horse, in Elbow Lane, opposite the Presbyterian burying-ground, is to be let; enquire of Henry Dexter, at the corner of Strawberry Alley,
opposite the shambles (14 May)

STEEL, James, late of Phila., dec'd - accounts with estate
to be settled with Richard Renshaw and Rebecca Steel,
executors (14 May)

BUNHILL, Ruth (formerly Ruth Thompson), late of Phila., dec'd
- accounts with estate to be settled with Richard Renshaw,
administrator (14 May)

House and lot in Front St., opposite to Capt. Goodman's
house, belonging to Samuel Redman, is to be sold at
auction at Mrs. Roberts's Coffee House in Phila. (14
May)

WOOD, John, watchmaker, in Front St., Phila. - offers reward for recovery of silver watch (made by William Bell
in London), which has been lost (14 May)

HAWKINS, John (alias Hawksford or OXFORD), Irish servant,
age c. 28, who has been some time in the country - runaway from Amos Garrett, of Baltimore Co., Md. (14 May)

RYAN, John, Irish servant, age c. 23, who pretends to be a
tinker - same as above

DUNN, Catherine, Irish servant, age c. 20 - same as above

TROSS, Jack, Negro, age c. 38, who speaks good English and
some Dutch - runaway from Matthias Gmelin, glazier, in
Worcester Twp., at Matachen, Phila. Co. (14 May)

Stephen, Negro, late property of Dr. Thomas Bond, of Phila.
- runaway from John Read, at Christine Bridge; reward will
be paid if runaway is delivered to James Mathews in Chester or Mr. Shelley, at the workhouse in Phila.; advertisement is signed by George Rock (14 May)

SACKETT, Simon, late of Bristol, Bucks Co., dec'd - accounts
with estate to be settled with William Buckley and Thomas
Dowdney, executors (14 May)

BUNKER, Capt. - Friday last arrived at Boston in a sloop
from Nantucket; he had been taken by a Spanish privateer
but ransomed his sloop; the same privateer took a schooner,
one Mayo master, and plundered it - Boston item of 11 May
(21 May)

BEAR, Capt., of Rhode Island - when off the Gold Coast the
slaves rose and killed all aboard except 2 mates, who
jumped overboard - letter from Coast of Guinea dated 14
Jan. (21 May)

A sloop from Virginia, Capt. Newbold, arrived 17 May at
New York (21 May)

The new governor and Commodore Legge have both arrived at
Barbados; Capt. Buckmaster, of Rhode Island, has been
taken in the harbour of Surinam; the brigantine Globe, of
Phila., Daniel Rees master, has been taken; Capt. Green-
away from Antigua reports that the sloop Tortola, of
Phila., George Morrison master, has been taken (21 May)

Brigantine Endeavour, John Andrew commander, now at Thomas
Wells's wharf in Phila., will sail for Virginia; for
freight or passage agree with the master on board or at
the house of Thomas Wells, ship-carpenter, in Front St.
(21 May)

House, formerly in the occupation of Joseph Scull, on Passyunk Rd., in the Southern Liberties of Phila., is to be
let; enquire of Maurice and Edmund Nihill, brewers, in
Phil. (21 May)

CROSS, William, Irish sailor, age c. 35 - runaway from the
snow Bonetta-packet, Charles Lyon master; reward for his
capture will be paid by Samuel Powell, Jr. (21 May)

McDONNELL, Patrick, Irish servant, age c. 28, who served
his time to John Clemson, of Pequa, on edge of Chester
Co., and is brought in again a servant for his fine and
prison-fee, being indicted for felony; he has been privateering in the New George from Phila. and with Capt.
Tingley from New York - runaway from John Hanly, of
Chester (21 May)

DOWERS, Edward (commander of the ship Bolton), at his store,
next door to Capt. Spafford's in Market St., corner of
Water St., Phila. - sells cloth, thread, tea (21 May)

SMITH and JAMES, at their store on Israel Pemberton's wharf
- sell cloth, hardware, glass, paper, maps, etc. (21 May)

CADWALLADER, Martha, dec'd - accounts with estate to be settled with Samuel Morris, tanner, at lower end of Second
St., Phila., or Thomas Cadwallader (21 May)

HARRISON, Henry, at his store on south side of Reese Meredith's wharf, sells cloth, shoes, hats, china, tea,
gloves, spices (21 May)

CURRIE, Ebenezer, in Front St., Phila. - has for sale a
meadow in Myomensing (21 May)

Tract of land called "Green's Mannor" in St. George's Hundred, Newcastle Co., is for sale; enquire of John Inglis,
merchant, in Phila., or John Moland, of the Northern
Liberties Twp. (21 May)

THOMAS, William, English servant, age c. 20 - runaway from
John Holland, of Whiteland Twp., Chester Co. (21 May)

Sundry lots adjoining the north side of Phila. (between the
sugar-house and Pool's bridge and between Front St. and
Third St.) are for sale; enquire of Anthony Wilkinson,
carver (21 May)

WEISER, Conrad, Ranger of the northeast corner of Lancaster
Co. - lists strays in his hands (21 May)

GRANT, Capt., at Mr. Hazard's wharf - sells rice and leather
(21 May)

SHELLEY, Abraham, Keeper of the Phila. Workhouse - buys
yarn and makes and sells hat-linings, oakum, etc. (21
May)

NICHOLSON, William, dec'd - tract called "Nicholson's Mannor," of 4,200 acres, belonging to his heirs, is for
sale; it lies in the forest of Baltimore Co., about 24
miles from Baltimore, on Patapsco River; enquire of John
Galloway (21 May)

MORRIS, Morris, of Phila. - offers reward for horse strayed
or stolen from his stable (21 May)

SCARTH, Timothy, of the Northern Liberties of Phila. - offers reward for recovery of gold and silver objects
stolen from his house (21 May)

RICHISON, Richard, Chief Ranger of Chester Co. - lists
strays in his hands (21 May)

BARKER, Charles, Irish servant - runaway from Samuel Meredith, at Coventry Forge, Chester Co. (21 May)

Cuffy, Negro, a Creole, born at Mortserrat, who speaks
both French and English - runaway from Richard Swan, of
Phila. (21 May)

GULDEN, Emanuel, carpenter - accounts with his estate to be
adjusted by Marcus Kuhl (21 May)

Wednesday last arrived at New York the privateer snow _Dragon_,
Capt. Seymour; in company with the _Greyhound_, Capt. Jefferies, he took 2 prizes, the _Beiname_, Capt. Dupey, and
the _Prudence_, Capt. _La Faveur_; Capt. Jefferies was later
taken by a French man-of-war - New York item of 25 May
(28 May)

Address of the Mayor (W. Atwood) and Commonalty of Phila.
to Gov. George Thomas (28 May)

WRIGHT, Henry, whip-maker, from H.M.'s Whipmaker, London,
but last from Annapolis, Md. - makes and repairs whips
in Chesnut St., 3 doors above Fourth St., Phila. (28 May)

DIGNAN, Bryan, Irish servant, age $\underline{c}$. 20, who formerly ran
away from Edward Goff and was taken up near the Forks of
Delaware - runaway from Randal Marshall, living near
Warwick Furnace, Chester Co. (28 May)

WENTWORTH, Sion, servant, born in New England, age $\underline{c}$. 25,
blacksmith - runaway from John Veneman, of Chester (28
May)

EVANS, Edward, shoemaker, of Phila. - offers reward for recovery of horse strayed or stolen off the Commons of Phila. (28 May)

MAGRA, John, of Phila. - his wife Jane has eloped from him (28 May)

House and lot (belonging to Samuel Redman) in Front St., Phila., opposite to Capt. Goodman's house, will be sold at auction at Mrs. Roberts's Coffee House (28 May)

FOULKS, John, late of Borough of Lancaster, dec'd - his house and tanyard in said borough are for sale; apply to Margaret Foulks (living on the premises), Thomas Doyle and Isaac Whitelock, executors, all of said borough (28 May)

New brick house and a slaughter-house, lately erected by Richard Frapwell, on the north side of Vine St. (there is a yearly rent payable to William Parsons), will be sold at auction at the Widow Roberts's Coffee House; enquire of J. Turner, administrator (28 May)

WHARTON, John, offers for sale various tracts of land in Chester, on Society Hill in Phila., and also 3 quarters of a forge and sawmill, where said John Wharton lives, in Ashston Twp., Chester Co., about 5 miles from Chester or Marcus Hook (28 May)

DOWNS, Capt. Richard, late of Cape May, dec'd - accounts with estate to be settled with Elisha Hand and Nathaniel Foster, executors (28 May)

HENDERSON, Francis, Irish servant, age c. 24 - runaway from John Potts, Esq., of Colebrookdale Twp., Phila. Co. (28 May)

WHITE, John, in Fifth St., between Market St. and Chesnut St., in Phila. - sells imported drugs (28 May)

Addresses of the Houses of New Jersey (Robert Lawrence, Speaker) and Pennsylvania (John Kinsey, Speaker) to King George II (4 June)

Address to Lt.-Gov. George Thomas from Christ Church in Phila. (signed for the vestry by Thomas Leech, Jacob Duchee, Wardens) and from the Presbyterian Synod of Phila. (signed by A. McDowell, Moderator) (4 June)

Capts. Fones and Snelling have arrived at Boston from London - Boston item of 25 May (4 June)

JOHNSTON, Col. - received a letter from Lt. Thomas Butler,

who had gone out as head of a party of Indians against the French of Canada - New York item of 1 June (4 June)

Thursday last arrived at New York from New London Capt. Thomas Hill (late master of the brigantine Ann and Elizabeth) and Capt. John Long (late master of the brigantine Lark), both of New York; both had been taken, Capt. Hill on 4 May and Capt. Long on 8 May; the Spanish privateer also took a bilander from Pool, Capt. White, and a sloop from Connecticut, Ezra Hubbel master (4 June)

H.S.M. Fowey, Capt. Policarpus Taylor, sailed last week from Hampton Road for Cape Breton and H.M.S. Folkstone, Capt. Taylor, is returned from a cruize - Williamsburgh item of 14 May (4 June)

Last week came to Phila. James Dawkins, Esq., who on his way to London in the ship Harrington was taken and carried to Havana (4 June)

WHITEHILL, Rev. - came to Phila. Friday last (4 June)

Monday last Gov. Thomas, his wife and daughter embarked for London on board the Greyhound, Capt. Budden (4 June)

Tuesday last arrived at Phila. the privateer brigantine New George, Capt. Wood, of Phila.; with him came as passengers Capts. Lusher and Conyers, both of Bermuda, who were taken by the Spaniards; the brigantine Catherine, Capt. Stewart, of Phila., is supposed to have been taken (4 June)

SAVAGE, Richard, Irish servant, age c. 25, cooper and butcher - runaway from Joseph Kelley, of Bristol Twp., Bucks Co.; reward will be paid for his capture by said Kelley or Charles Edgar, in Phila. (4 June)

REARDON, William, native Irish servant, age between 20 and 30, who formerly served Hugh Evans, of Merion, Phila. Co.; he has been confined in Chester Goal - runaway from William Moore, living in Chester Co. (4 June)

CLARK, Derby, native Irish servant, abe c. 28, weaver - runaway from James Star, living in Chester Co. (4 June)

Isaac, Negro, age c. 30 - runaway from Andrew Reed, of Trenton (4 June)

Reward will be paid for recovery of horse strayed from Henry Millar's pasture at Kensington, if horse is brought to Henry Apple in Kensington or to Jacob Maag, at upper end of Second St., Phila. (4 June)

Horse (which formerly belonged to Philip Hilliard, dec'd)
has strayed or been stolen from Evan Morgan, cooper; reward will be paid for its recovery by Evan Morgan, Jr.
(4 June)

Servant girl (4 years to serve) is to be let by John Huntsman, tailor, in Church Alley, Phila. (4 June)

SPENCE, Capt. John, late merchant in Phila., dec'd - reward
will be paid for discovery to the printer hereof of any
effects of debts due the estate of the dec'd (4 June)

WOODLAY, Jonathan, late of Limerick Twp., Phila. Co.,
dec'd - persons indebted to said estate are to make payment to Henry Peters, executor (4 June)

Four lots fronting Chesnut St. in the square where the
governor lately dwelt, called Carpenter's Square, are to
be sold or let by Dr. John Wright (4 June)

The following recruits, raised by Capt. John Huston for
William Shirley's Regt., have deserted: Richard Simmons,
labourer, born in the Jerseys, age c. 23; William Gil-
liams, wheelwright, born in the Jerseys, age c. 24;
George Gardner, labourer, born in the Jerseys, age c. 40,
who lately worked with John Pass, at the ironworks in
Mount Holly; William Scanlan, scrivener, born in Ireland,
age c. 40, who lately kept school in Gloucester Co., in
the Jerseys; Patrick Burnet, a miller, born in Ireland,
age c. 33, who dwells near Darby, Pa.; Manchester Holloway, blacksmith, born in Pennsylvania, age c. 20, last
seen a few days ago with his relations near Lancaster;
reward will be paid if a deserter is brought to Capt.
John Huston, at the Sign of the George, in Second St.,
Phila., or, if a deserter is lodged in goal, reward will
be paid by said John Huston or John Baron (4 June)

The following 16 soldiers, belonging to Sir William Pepperrell's Regt., have deserted from H.M.'s service from
on board the sloop Merrimack, Philemon Saunders master,
lying at anchor at the east end of Long Island: John
Whiston, Englishman, who has a wife and child with him;
William Dawhauty, Irishman; James Mackedue, Irishman;
Cornelius Grimes, Englishman; John Stewart, an old fellow; Luke Collems, born in Ireland, age 26, weaver; Thomas
Donahew, born in Ireland, age 24; James Macdaniel, born
in Ireland, age 26; David O'Dowley, born in Ireland, age
22; John Davis, born in Maryland, age 25; Hezekiah Shaw,
born in Pennsylvania, age 22; Robert Eiles, born in England, age 35; William Thompson, born in Pennsylvania, age
21; James Alexander, born in England, age 22; Charles
Wiggen, born in Maryland; James Macbribe, an old deserter;

if any deserter is apprehended, notice is to be given
to Sir William Pepperrell in Kittery, Lt. Dwight at
Boston, Capt. Wooster in New Haven, Capt. Huston, John
Baron or John Scutt in Phila. (4 June)

MACGUIER, James, Irish servant - runaway from Benjamin
Bradford, living at Bohemia Ferry, Cecil Co., Md. (4
June)

MEALEY, John, Irish servant, age c. 40 - same as above

LANE, Edward, in Providence Twp., Phila. Co. - has taken
up a mare (4 June)

BATES, Daniel, of Waterford Twp., Gloucester Co. - his wife
Elizabeth has eloped from him (4 June)

BULLOCK, Robert, of Phila. - will pay no debts contracted
in future by his wife Catherine, who has run him into
debt' (4 June)

Proclamation by Anthony Palmer, president, and the Council
(Richard Peters, Secretary) because of departure of
George Thomas for Great Britain (11 June)

On 7 June the privateer brigantine Hester, Robert Troup
commander, of New York, arrived there (11 June)

Thursday last arrived at Phila. Capt. Stevenson, late of the
brigantine William and Mary, which on 18 Apr. was taken
by Don Pedro Arracochea; the Spanish privateer, while he
was on board, took the following: the snow Catherine,
Capt. Brownette of London; Capt. Shaldon, in a Rhode Island brigantine; Capt. Wormstead, in sloop Expedition,
of Boston, and 2 other sloops (11 June)

STEWART, Capt., who arrived Saturday last at Phila., advises
that the following vessels had lately been sent there:
2 New York sloops (Capt. Burch is master of one); 2
brigantines and a sloop of Boston (Ruggles and Brown are
masters of 2 of them) and a Rhode Island brigantine (Capt.
Godrey is master) (11 June)

LEGGE, Commodore, at Antigua, remains inactive, waiting for
trial of Commodore Lee to take place - extract from letter from Antigua dated 19 May (11 June)

Brigantine Elizabeth, Capt. Gill, of Phila., bound to Antigua, is taken (11 June)

BEVAN, Capt., in the sloop Clinton, of New York, is taken
but Capt. Bowne in the privateer brigantine Trembleur,

of Phila., escaped, according to Capt. White from Providence (11 June)

William and David McElvaine have removed their store from
Water St. to the house, where Emerson and Graydon formerly lived, in Front St., near the drawbridge (11 June)

CARR, James - offers reward for recovery of a horse, strayed
or stolen (11 June)

FERGUSON, William, of Uuchland, Chester Co. - offers reward
for recovery of strayed or stolen horse (11 June)

House and lot on west side of King St., Phila., next door
to John Fisher's, merchant, is for sale; apply to Nixon
Chattin, living in said house (11 June)

Plantation of 100 acres in Lower Dublin Twp., about 10 miles
from Phila. on great road from Phila. to Newtown, is offered for sale by John Atkins, Jr., who lives in Bristol
Twp., about 4 miles from Phila. (11 June)

PALMER, William, Irish servant, age c. 18 - runaway from
Oley Forge in Phila. Co.; reward for his capture will be
paid by John Lesher and Company (11 June)

CONNOLY, Peter, native Irish servant, age c. 29 - runaway
from Samuel Evans, of Marple Twp., Chester Co. (11 June)

BUCKINGHAM, John, of Mill Creek Hundred, Newcastle Co. -
offers reward for recovery of 2 mares, strayed away from
William Emett, near Charles-Town, Md. (11 June)

DOCKERY, Matthew, of Chester Mill, Queen Anne's Co., Md. -
will furnish 2 wheel chair and horse and driver for persons desiring to travel between Newtown and Mrs. Elizabeth Wilsons' house at Kent Island or to Talbot Co.
Court-house (11 June)

PENEBECKER, Peter - offers reward for recovery of a horse,
strayed or stolen from plantation formerly belonging to
Henry Poland, of Bebber Twp., Phila. Co. (11 June)

HAWKSFORD, John (alias Hawkins or Oxford), Irish servant,
age c. 28 - runaway from Amos Garrett, of Baltimore Co.,
Md. (11 June)

DUNN, Catherine, Irish servant, age c. 20 - same as above

SLYERN B/?/N, Solomon, of Lancaster - his goods will be
sold Monday next under the Court-house (11 June)

Printer hereof will pay reward for recovery of horse
strayed or stolen out of pasture of Widow Ball, a little beyond Kensington (11 June)

Address of Consistory of Presbyterian Society of Phila.
(signed by Gilbert Tennent) to Lt.-Gov. Thomas and address of the Baptist Congregation in Phila. (signed by
Jenkin Jones and William Branson) to said George Thomas
(18 June)

Ship Antilope, Capt. Griffiths, and ship Oswego, Capt.
Bryant, have arrived at New York with news from Europe
(18 June)

A vessel that arrived Tuesday last at Boston from Pemaquid
reported on the mischief done by the Indians; bodies of
10 of our people have been found and buried, Capts. John
and Joseph Cox, Lt. Haws, Nathaniel Bull, George Clark,
Jacob Pett, George Caldwell, one Smith and 2 more (names
unknown.); 3 more are missing and supposed to be in the
hands of the Indians, Reuben Dyer, Benjamin Cox (son of
Joseph Cox aforesaid) and Benjamin Mayhew; Abner Lowel,
one of the company, escaped - Boston item of 8 June (18
June)

On 14 June arrived at New York the ship Jacob, Capt. Anderson, from Turk Islands; Capt. King, from Madeira, informs that the London and Garland, London privateers,
took a rich French prize, which, however, sank in rough
weather - New York items of 15 June (18 June)

MESNARD, Capt., in ship Carolina, for Phila., sailed with
Capts. Bryant and Griffitts but was parted from them in
the West Indies (18 June)

BOWNE, Capt. - has arrived at Phila. in the brigantine
Trembleur (18 June)

Lots of land on north side of Phila., between the Sugar House
and Pools's Bridge, are for sale; enquire of Anthony
Wilkinson the Bildschnitzer ("wood-carver") (18 June)

CROASDALE, Thomas, dec'd - effects belonging to his estate
will be sold at auction at the Sign of the George Inn, in
Phila; the items may be seen beforehand; Richard Renshaw
is administrator of the estate of said Thomas Croasdale,
innholder (18 June)

HIND, Robert, dec'd - accounts with estate to be settled
with Mary Hind, executrix (18 June)

Plantation lately in occupation of John Baptist Clark in

Derry Twp., at Swatarow Creek, on road that goes from
John Harris's to Lancaster, and also another plantation
in Pensborough Twp., on Yellow Breeches Creek, adjoining
to Andrew Millar's plantation, will be sold; they were
taken in execution by Sheriff James Sterett to satisfy
debt recovered against said Clark by Thomas Lightfoot and
John Smith, merchants, in Phila. (18 June)

JONES, Owen, of Phila., offers reward for recovery of
strayed or stolen horse (18 June)

PURTELL, Thomas, carpenter - runaway from his bail, Jacob
Giles, of Baltimore Co., Md. (18 June)

MACGUIRE, Patrick, Irish servant - runaway from Thomas
Fletcher, of Abington Twp., Phila. Co. (18 June)

MATTHEWS, Patrick, Irish servant - same as above

WHITE, John, English servant, age c. 40 - runaway from
Philip Ward, Strawborough Twp., Lancaster Co. (18 June)

HYNSON, Nathaniel, Jr. - keeps ferry from Easter Neck Island, in Kent Co., over to Annapolis and back (18 June)

WARNER, Robert, baker, of Phila. - offers reward for recovery
of horse strayed or stolen from off the Commons (18 June)

PERRY, Christopher, late of Phila., cutler, dec'd - accounts
with estate to be settled with Eleanor Perry, executrix
(18 June)

Reward is offered for recovery of silver watch (maker's
name Tomlinson, London), with 2 seals (one silver, with
a coat of arms, the other bathmetal, with glass faces, a
crown on one side, and King William's and Queen Mary's
heads on the other), lost between Germantown and Phila.
(18 June)

On 14 June the Boston Packet, Capt. Bennet commander, arrived at Cape Ann from Nova Scotia - Boston item of 15
June (25 June)

COATAM, Capt., arrived at Phila. from Barbados, reports
that a sloop was captured by the French in sight of the
fort at Barbados (25 June)

CUZZINS & SMYTER, at their store in Water St., near Chesnut St., Phila. - sell goods imported from London (25
June)

William and David Macilvaine, at their store in Front St.,

636

near the drawbridge (where Emerson and Graydon formerly
lived) - have for sale goods imported from London (25
June)

SIMS, Buckridge, at Joseph Turner's, in Front St., Phila. -
sells European and East India goods (25 June)

BENEZET, Daniel, at his store in Front St., at corner of
Martin's Alley, Phila. - same as above

BENEZET, Philip, at his store at corner of Arch St., opposite
the George Inn, in Second St., Phila. - same as above

EMLEN, Samuel, opposite the market in Phila. - sells Dr.
Benjamin Godfrey's cordial and Dr. Bateman's pectoral
drops (25 June)

JAMES, Thomas, Jr., will sell at auction, at James's Coffee-
house, a new house, near the corner of Walnut St. and
Second St., opposite the Golden Fleece and the house
where the Widow Falkner lives (25 June)

MARSHALL, Christopher, at the Sign of the Golden Ball, near
the Three Tun Tavern, in Chesnut St., Phila. - has for
sale a large assortment of goods (25 June)

EMLEN, George, Jr., near the Post Office, in Market St.,
Phila., has for sale goods imported in the Carolina,
Capt. Mesnard, from London (25 June)

CUMMING, Timothy, late of Dover, Kent Co., dec'd - house
where he dwelt is to be let by John David, administrator
(25 June)

DAVIS, David, of Goshen, Chester Co. - offers reward for
recovery of mare, strayed or stolen (25 June)

PATTERSON, William, Irish servant, age c. 22, whose father
is a miller at Christine Mills - runaway from Nicholas
Bayard, of New York; Patterson, who has changed his name
to John O'Connor, ran away with one James Williams and
his wife, also runaways (25 June)

Caesar, Negro, age between 20 and 30 - runaway from Jonathan
Ingham, of Salisbury, Bucks Co. (25 June)

O'HARRA, Catherine, Irish servant girl, who has been 10
months in the country - runaway from Moses Macilvaine,
of Lancaster Co. (25 June)

MILES, Bartholomew, Irish servant, age c. 26 - runaway from
Henry Cooper, of New Hanover Twp., Burlington Co., West
New Jersey (25 June)

GRIMES, Mary, Irish servant - same as above

Notice from John Kinsey of the General Loan Office of Pennsylvania for persons indebted to said office to make payment (25 June)

WILLING, Charles - has for sale Negro men and boys just imported in the brigantine George from Guinea (25 June)

BOSTOCK, Capt., from Providence, reports at Charlestown that
Capt. Purnell had taken a French bark - Charlestown item
of 4 May (25 July)

WHITEFIELD, Rev. - arrived last week at New York - New York
item of 29 June (2 July)

Thursday last arrived at New York a French flag of truce,
Monsieur Besse commander, with 85 English prisoners from
Cape Francois, among them Capt. Thomas Bevan of New York,
Capt. Tillage from South Carolina and Capt. Stanny from
Boston - New York item of 29 June (2 July)

DEXTER, John - on 28 June was taken up at New Haven, Conn.,
and committed to goal on suspicion of counterfeiting
pieces of eight and pistoles (2 July)

An Indian from Saraghtoga reports that Lt. Chew and some of
his men have been captured; Col. Peter Schuyler is now to
go there with his regiment - extract of letter from Albany dated 21 June (2 July)

Thursday last the snow Success, Capt. Ouchterlong, arrived
at Phila. from London and Monday last Capt. Green, late
of the brigantine Carpenter, of Phila., arrived; he had
been taken 12 May by a privateer, which also took a
schooner, Capt. Northcutt, from Virginia (2 July)

ROSS, Capt., in a brigantine from Piscataqua, bound to
Phila., is cast away on the Hog's Back in the Sound (2
July)

FRANKLIN, B. - lists books just imported by him (2 July)

HOLLAND, Nathaniel, bookbinder, almost opposite the Conestogoe Waggon, in Market St., Phila. - binds old and new
books (2 July)

Ship Carolina, Stephen Mesnard commander, will sail for
London; for freight or passage apply to James Pemberton
or said commander (2 July)

Brigantine Exchange, William Simpson commander, will sail

638

for Bristol; for freight or passage agree with Robert
and Amos Strettell or said commander (2 July)

PATTERSON, Walter, at his store at the Widow Welch's, opposite to John Bringhurst's, in Front St., Phila. -
sells cloth, pepper, etc. (2 July)

ZUILLE, Matthew, at his store in Front St., opposite to
the Sign of the Pewter Platter - sells cloth, powder,
shot, steel, lead (2 July)

DOWERS, Edward, at his store in Market St., Phila., at the
corner of Water St. - sells cloth, hats, cheese (2 July)

LANG, Alexander, at his store in Front St., in the house in
which Samuel Neave formerly lived - sells cloth (2 July)

Soldiers who have deserted from the 4 Pennsylvania companies
at Albany will be pardoned if they return to duty before
10 Aug.; notice is signed by Samuel Perry, William Trent,
John Diemer and John Shannon (2 July)

Tract of 27 acres, with house and barn, on outlands of Germantown, back of John Corgus's, on the road to be laid
out from Chestnut Hill to Lucan's mill is to be sold or
let; enquire of Reinard Vogdes, at said place, or of John
Johnson, sadler, in Germantown (2 July)

Tract of 200 acres (late the land of William Noble) in Warminster Twp., Bucks Co., is to be sold at the Crooked
Billet, on the York Rd.; enquire of John Macvaugh, living
on the premises, or apply to William Tidmash in Phila.
(2 July)

Brigantine George, John McCleland late master, now at Hamilton's wharf, will be sold at auction at Mrs. Roberts's
Coffee House (2 July)

MATHER, James, at Chester - has clover hay for sale (2 July)

MEARNS, Samuel, in Front St., near the drawbridge, in Phila.
- offers reward for recovery of horse strayed or stolen
from pasture of James Rogers on Society Hill (2 July)

JEWELL, Robert, of Phila. - offers reward for recovery of a
mare, strayed or stolen (2 July)

WALL, Margaret, who lately came to Phila. in quest of her
husband, Henry Wall, seeks news of him; Henry, born in
Warwickshire, England, went from Londonderry to Antigua
with Capt. Blacklock about 4 years ago and lately sailed
out of Rhode Island (2 July)

Proclamation of the President (Anthony Palmer) and Council
(Richard Peters Secretary) (9 July)

Col. Peter Schuyler, with his regiment, has arrived at
Saraghtoga; Lt. Chew is a prisoner; a party of Indians
and whites, under Hendrick, a noted Mohawk chief, were
discovered near Montreal and had to flee - New York items
of 6 July (9 July)

GERB, Andrew, in a French privateer sloop from Cape Francois, has taken the following prizes: Capt. Greenaway;
the brigantine Dispatch, William Bartha master, from
Boston; a sloop from Nantucket, Charles Gardner master;
a North Carolina sloop, Peter Winding commander; a Bristol ship, Capt. Walker, from St. Kitts; a Virginia brigantine, Capt. Nisbet (9 July)

Sunday last arrived at Phila. Capts. Houston, Catline, Darrel and Wells from Antigua (9 July)

Rob. Sutcliffe, of Antigua, gives his version of a financial
difficulty involving Thomas Clark, Os. Sprigg and Joseph
Belt, Jr., all of Maryland; his attornies are Philip
Thomas, Esq., and Sons; John Hepburn, Esq., is acting for
the Maryland gentlemen; Sutcliffe wishes to have matters
submitted to impartial Phila. merchants to arbitrate (9
July)

FARRELL, Andrew, of Phila., tanner - plans to leave Pennsylvania as soon as possible because bullets have been
fired through his windows and twice in a week windows
have been broken by brickbats (9 July)

GREGGE, Thomas, of Phila., brazier, intending for England,
wishes to settle all accounts (9 July)

Plantation of 230 acres in village of Woodbury, Gloucester
Co., 5 miles on the road from Gloucester to Salem and
about 9 from Phila., is for sale; enquire of Abraham
Chattin, living on the premises (9 July)

Brigantine George, Robert Wood late captain, now at Mr.
Inglis's wharf, will be sold at auction at Mrs. Roberts's
Coffee House (9 July)

HODGE, William - offers reward for recovery of horse,
strayed or stolen (9 July)

Brigantine Esther, Robert Savage commander, now at Thomas
Hay's wharf, will sail for Barbados (9 July)

Snow Esther, William Hall commander, now at Mr. Till's

wharf, will sail for Antigua (9 July)

BLACKWOOD, John - will sell or let a plantation of 300
acres, on the head of Timber Creek, about 8 miles from
Gloucester; there is a dwelling house and a fulling mill
on the property (9 July)

ERWIN, John, at his house in Strawberry Alley, where Robert
Jordan formerly lived, has for sale a parcel of servants
just arrived in the ship Sally, Capt. Boggs, from London
(9 July)

DONAHEW, Daniel, Irish servant, a miller, age c. 40 - runaway from John Yoder, of Oley Twp., Phila. Co. (9 July)

LYNCH, Thomas, Irish servant, age c. 20 - same as above

CAIN, Edward, Irish servant, hatter, age c. 35 - runaway
from Samuel Howell, of Phila., hatter (9 July)

CASTILLOW, David, Irish servant, hatter, age c. 22 - same
as above

Cesar, Negro, age c. 30 - runaway from the Widow Price, in
Kent Co.; reward for his capture will be paid by John
Booth, in Kent Co. (9 July)

Primis, Negro, age c. 25, bought of John Blackadore - runaway from John Fox, of Kensington, shipwright (9 July)

WEBSTER, John, Englishman, age c. 28, servant - has been
taken up on suspicion of being a runaway from Daniel
Cheston, Sheriff of Kent Co. (9 July); he left with an
Irish woman, age c. 28 (who, Webster says, is his wife);
her description fits that of a woman who has run away
from Henry Cooper (9 July)

Extract of letter from Major God. Clark, of Barbados, dated
10 June; mentioned are Mr. Warren and Capt. Kembell -
New York item of 13 July (16 July)

Extract of a letter from Barbados, dated 13 June, with mention of Admiral Anson - New York item of 13 July (16 July)

A sloop that arrived last week from Cape Breton sailed from
thence with the Fowey man-of-war, Capt. Taylor, and Capts.
Shirley and Rouse - New York item of 13 July (16 July)

Saturday last arrived at New York Capt. Hutchinson, who had
been taken by a Spanish privateer; the same privateer took
also vessels commanded by Capt. Stevens and Capt. Holmes
- New York item of 13 July (16 July)

Some of crew of Spanish privateer came up the bay as far as
Bombay Hook, landed at plantation of Mr. Liston (from
which they took 4 Negroes) and then went to the house of
James Hart (whose wife they shot and wounded); after this
they took 2 Phila. pilot boats, one of John Ayres and the
other of John Jones (16 July)

Tuesday last Capt. Richey arrived at Phila. from Coracoa;
he had been chased for 12 hours by a ship and a brigantine (16 July)

Real estate will be sold at public auction by the heirs of
John Cadwallader at Widow Roberts's Coffee House: included among other items are a messuage on the north side
of High St., Phila., lately in possession of Martha Cadwallader, dec'd, a lot in Phila. between Sixth and Seventh
Sts. from Schuylkill, bounded on east by ground now of
Evan Morgan, and a lot at Wicacoa, bounded by ground late
of Edward Roberts, dec'd, on the north and by Claypole's
ground on the south; apply to Samuel Morris, of Phila.,
tanner (16 July)

CLIFFTON, John - keeps the Sign of the George in Phila. (16
July)

STRICKLAND, Amos, sheriff - offers reward for capture of the
following who escaped from Newtown Jail in Bucks Co.:
Malachi Walton (who formerly kept an inn in Bristol);
Paul Messenger, a Dutchman, wheelwright by trade; Henry
Thornton, servant, belonging to said Amos Strickland (16
July)

MORGAN, John, at his store on Market St. wharf, Phila. -
sells sugar, rum, wine, cocoa, indigo and salt (16 July)

FORTESCUE, Charles Walker, who teaches Latin at his house in
Taylor's Alley - warns of a "vile imposter," Foster Pierce,
who deceived him by a false story of the death of Charles's
father and produced a forged letter purporting to be from
Charles's uncle, John Fortescue (16 July)

Two adjoining plantations, containing 14,000 acres, upon the
river Delaware, about 12 miles from Trenton, and a sawmill built by John Holder are to be let; apply to Daniel
Cox, living on the premises, or John Cox, at Trenton (16
July)

LARDNER, Lyn-Ford - will sell at auction at Walter Maccoll's,
in Rockhill Twp., 13 tracts, of from 100 to 260 acres
each, in Manor of Perkasy, Bucks Co., about 30 miles from
Phila.; plans may be seen at the Surveyor General's Office in Phila., at Joseph Thornton's in Newtown, Bucks

Co., at Christian Snyder's near Thomas Maybury's, at Peter Snyder's, about 2 miles from the premises, and at Walter Maccoll's in Rockhill Twp. (16 July)

PORTER, Robert, late of Cecil Co., Md., dec'd - accounts with estate to be settled with Eleanor Porter, executrix (16 July)

SCULL, Nicholas, sheriff - will sell goods taken in execution (16 July)

DENISON, John, Irish servant - runaway from James Pryor, of Kennet, Chester Co. (16 July)

ROBERTSON, Peter, merchant, in Front St., Phila. - will sell by public vendue, at the Widow Roberts's Coffee House, a messuage in Phila. and also 4 lots (all the property late of the estate of Peter Evans, Esq., dec'd) (16 July)

A stray mare has been taken up at the plantation of Thomas Kanten in Lower Dublin Twp.; owner may apply to Robert McWhorter, who lives on the place aforesaid (16 July)

GAY, Capt., reports at Boston that French privateers have taken the following, all of Boston: Capt. Prince in a brigantine, Capt. Bruce in a ship and Capt. Watts in a snow (23 July)

Thursday last arrived at New York the privateer brigantine Dolphin, Capt. Beezley, in whom came Francis Fresneau, merchant, of New York; Fresneau had been taken by a Spanish privateer but soon retaken by Capt. Obrien, from South Carolina (23 July)

PEMBERTON, Capt., in ship Johnson, from Liverpool, is arrived in Maryland (23 July)

MARTIN, Capt., late of ship Mary, from Antigua for Phila. - arrived Friday at Phila.; he was taken at the Capes by the Spaniards who were returning from Mr. Liston's plantation (23 July)

Tuesday last arrived at Phila. a Nantucket sloop, formerly commanded by Charles Gardner (which had been taken by Capt. Gerber); the sloop was later taken by the Spaniards but retaken by Capt. Waters in the ship Francis (26 July)

Armament of the privateer brigantine George will be sold at auction at Mr. Inglis's wharf in Phila. (26 July)

Stone house on Germantown Rd., in the Northern Liberties, 3 miles from Phila., will be sold at auction; for title enquire of John Naglee or the owner, Peter Wolbrough (23 July)

ROBINSON, Thomas - will sell house and lot in Front St., the fourth door from the Boatswain and Call, near the drawbridge, and next door to Thomas Hatton; there is also a cooper's shop for sale there on said lot (23 July)

Brigantine _Trembleur_, Obadiah Bowne commander, will leave on cruize; those who wish to sign may do so at The Sign of the Trembleur in Water St., Phila. (23 July)

HARDING, John - offers reward for recovery of a flat that is lost (23 July)

DURHAM, Bartell, Irish servant, age c. 23 or 24 - runaway from Thomas Anderson, of Upper Merion, Phila. Co. (23 July)

ERWIN, Thomas, Irish servant, brickmaker and miller, age c. 20 - runaway from Lawrence Potter, of Northern Liberties of Phila. (23 July)

ROUSE, John, in Market St., Phila., owner of horse that was stolen or broke out of the stable of William Reed, of Newgarden, Chester Co. - offers reward for recovery of horse if brought to him or to William Reed (23 July)

House, lot and tanyard in Lancaster (formerly in possession of John Foulk, late of Lancaster, dec'd) - to be sold by Margaret Foulk, Thomas Doyle and Isaac Whitelock, executors (23 July)

SHELLEY, Abraham, of Phila., intending for Europe - will sell at the workhouse furniture, a thread mill, a Negro lad, a set of joiner's tools, etc. (23 July)

A young woman is for sale; enquire of Dennis Flood, at the Sign of the Shoulder of Mutton, in Pewter Platter Alley, Phila. (30 July)

Plantation of 200 acres adjoining on Conestogoe Rd. about 20 miles from Phila. is to be sold or let; apply to Samuel Evans, living thereon (30 July)

WEIS, Frederick, of Phila. Co. - his wife Catherine has eloped from him (30 July)

Sunday last 2 sons (one aged 7 and the other 6) of William Reynolds, hatter, of Annapolis, were drowned - Annapolis item of 14 July (30 July)

Sunday last Madam Anne Ogle, wife of Gov. Ogle, gave birth to a son - Annapolis item of 21 July (30 July)

Thursday last the ship <u>Johnson</u>, Capt. Pemberton, arrived at Oxford in <u>Choptank</u> from Liverpool, with 2 English and 106 Scotch rebels - Annapolis item of 21 July (30 July)

SEAGER, Capt., in the sloop <u>Chester Town</u>, arrived 21 July at Annapolis from Barbados (30 July)

SWEETING, Capt., in a Rhode Island privateer, arrived at Newport 16 July with a prize (30 July)

BALL, Capt., who sailed from Boston some time since for Barbados, obliged 2 French privateers that attacked him to sheer off (30 July)

JAMES, Capt. - arrived 20 July at Marblehead from Lisbon (30 July)

RAW, Thomas, English convict servant - runaway from Kingsbury Furnace, Baltimore Co.; reward will be paid for his capture by Jonathan Chapman, on behalf of the Kingsbury Company (30 July)

REDSON, Thomas, at upper end of Second St., Phila., has a horse for sale (30 July)

Cuffy, <u>alias</u> Billy Farrell, Creole, born at Montserrat - runaway from Richard Swan, of Phila. (30 July)

COFFEL, John, Irish servant, age <u>c</u>. 17 - runaway from Thomas Griffith, of Vincent Twp., Chester Co. (30 July)

HANNAH, James, born in north of Ireland - runaway from the ship <u>Domville</u>, Robert Young commander, now at Mr. Goodman's wharf in Phila. (30 July)

REARDON, William, Irish servant, born near Cork, age between 20 and 30, who formerly served Hugh Evans, of Merion, Phila. Co. - runaway from William Moore, of Moorehall, Chester Co. (30 July)

Lot and 2 brick houses in Wilmington, in High St., near the Upper Market-House and adjoining to David Faris's, are for sale; enquire of William Warner, living in Wilmington, or John James, living in Willistown Twp., Chester Co. (30 July)

FORSTER, Reuben, in High St., Phila. - offers reward for recovery of horse, strayed or stolen out of a pasture in Phila. (30 July)

James, a Negro, Carolina born - runaway from John Winckles, painter, in Phila. (30 July)

Extract of letter from on board the schooner Spry, dated at Louisburg, 30 June - Boston item of 27 July (6 Aug.)

WITTER, Capt. - arrived 2 Aug. at New York from Coracoa (6 Aug.)

ALBERTSON, Capt., from Providence, arrived Thursday last at Phila. and informs that Capt. Gardner, in a privateer sloop of that place had taken a Spanish schooner and sloop (6 Aug.)

By the brigantine Louisburgh, Capt. Wright, from Jamaica, there is advice of arrival at Jamaica of Capt. Renton in a 70-gun ship (6 Aug.)

MARTIN, Capt., in a Boston brigantine, has been taken off the east end of Jamaica (6 Aug.)

Letter from Georgia, dated 22 July, mentions arrival there of Col. Heron (6 Aug.)

FRANKLIN, B. - offers reward for recovery of horse strayed or stolen out of his pasture near Phila. (6 Aug.)

COLEMAN, William, of Phila., has 12 copper stills, of English make, for sale (6 Aug.)

Hamilton, Wallace and Company, whose store is in Water St., Phila. - intends to give up store-keeping and to go to Britain (6 Aug.)

Meadow near Moyamensing, bounded on south by Hay's Creek, on north by the proprietaries meadow and east by Joseph Wharton's, is to be sold; enquire of Ebenezer Currie, in Front St. (6 Aug.)

MACGARVEY, John, a weaver - runaway from Thomas Jacob at the head of Elk River (6 Aug.)

PARKS, George, servant, age c. 17 - runaway from Samuel Hurford, of Phila. (6 Aug.)

YEATS, James, English apprentice, who came from Eling in Hampshire, age c. 18 (who was apprentice to Giles Lawrence, joiner, who lately lived at Bristol, Bucks Co.) - runaway from Thomas Priestly, joiner, of Phila. (6 Aug.)

SHERRETT, William, apprentice lad - runaway from Peter Lawrence, of Phila. (6 Aug.)

TUCKNESS, Henry, apprentice lad - runaway from Isaac Dawson, hatter, of Phila. (6 Aug.)

Negro man, age c. 21, is for sale; enquire of John Winckles, painter, in Third St., Phila. (6 Aug.)

DUGAN, James, Irish servant - runaway from Daniel Stuard, in Oxford Twp., Phila. Co. (6 Aug.)

O'HARA, Patrick, who was born in north of Ireland, apprentice - runaway from the Domville, Robert Young commander, now at Mr. Goodman's wharf in Phila.; reward will be paid for his capture by Allen and Turner or said commander (6 Aug.)

Capt. Twentyman, from Liverpool, and Capt. Crawford, from Glasgow, both have arrived in Virginia with European news (Supplement to Pennsylvania Gazette of 6 Aug.)

The Argyle, Seymour captain, from Phila., was taken by the Marshal de Saxe privateer, but since retaken - extract of letter from London of 19 May (Supplement to Pa. Gazette of 6 Aug.)

H.M.S. Enterprize, Capt. Holmes, at latter end of April took a prize and brought her into Jamaica - Williamsburg item of 22 July (13 Aug.)

FRANKLIN, B. - has just published Letters between Theophilus and Eugenio (13 Aug.)

MARTIN, Capt. John, at his store in Water St., opposite to Fishbourn's wharf - has white Irish linens for sale (13 Aug.)

Brick messuage on west side of Gallowhill Market, in the Northern Liberties of Phila., is offered for sale by John and Jacob Naglee, executors of Jacob Naglee, shopkeeper, dec'd (13 Aug.)

Parcel of leather will be sold by Nicholas Scull, sheriff, at the late dwelling house of John Howell, in Chesnut St., Phila. (13 Aug.)

MOORE, Samuel Preston - offers reward for recovery of horse and mare strayed from his plantation near Franckfort (13 Aug.)

GRACHAMS, Francis, Irish servant, age c. 21 or 22 - runaway from Isabella Nevins, of Mill Creek Hundred, Newcastle Co. (13 Aug.)

CLARE, John, next door to Capt. William Attwood, our present mayor, in Front St., Phila. - teaches mathematics (13 Aug.)

The trustees of the college in New Jersey, William Smith, Peter Vanbrugh Livingston, William Peartree Smith, gent., and ministers of the Gospel Jonathan Dickinson, John Pierson, Ebenezer Pemberton and Aaron Burr, have chosen as further trustees Rev. Gilbert Tennent, William Tennent, Samuel Blair, Richard Treat and Samuel Finley; Jonathan Dickinson has been chosen president and Caleb Smith tutor (13 Aug.)

McNEMARE, John, Irish servant, age 25 - runaway from Peter Downey; servant, if taken, is to be brought to Prince's Iron Works (13 Aug.)

MARTIN, William, Irish servant, age 22, a miller and cooper - runaway from Job Ruston, living in Londonderry Twp., Chester Co. (13 Aug.)

CONNER, Michael, staymaker, is removed from Cox's corner, in Chesnut St., to the house opposite the secretary's office in Walnut St. (13 Aug.)

Wednesday last arrived at New York the privateer brigantine Revenge, Alexander Troup commander, with a French prize, the Triumph, Mons. Francis Greshon late master - New York item of 17 Aug. (20 Aug.)

SMITH, Capt., who arrived at New York Thursday last from Jamaica, informs that he fell in with a French privateer sloop (lately that of Capt. Burch's of New York) - New York item of 17 Aug. (20 Aug.)

KELLY, Francis - on Monday last was committed to Phila. Goal on suspicion of counterfeiting French pistoles (20 Aug.)

Books published or sold by B. Franklin, including writings by Samuel Finley and by Abel Morgan, at Middletown, East Jersey (20 Aug.)

House and lot on the main street in Germantown are to be sold; enquire of Thomas Watts in Germantown (20 Aug.)

Two tracts of land in Gloucester Co., West New Jersey, fronting the River Delaware, about 3 miles from Phila., are for sale; on them are 2 small plantations, in possession of James Wilson and Samuel Fue (20 Aug.)

MORREY, Leonard, late of Cheltenham, Phila. Co. - persons indebted to him are to make payment to his attornies, George Okill and Robert Greenway (20 Aug.)

Stone house in Germantown, at the lower end, is for sale;
enquire of John Bartolot, sadler, living on the premises
(20 Aug.)

DOWERS, Edward - his store, formerly kept in Water St., the
corner of Market St., is removed to his dwelling house in
Water St., next door to Samuel Shoemaker's store; Dowers
sells cloth, thread, pins, buttons, tea (20 Aug.)

HOWSAR, Loranz, Dutch servant, age c. 20 - runaway from John
Jerret, of Horsham Twp., Phila. Co. (20 Aug.)

KERREGAN, Manus, native Irishman, age c. 30 - runaway from
Reading Furnace; reward for his capture will be paid by
his master, Richard Hughs, of West Caln, Chester Co., or
Samuel Flower, at Reading Furnace (20 Aug.)

Schooner Deborah, Edward Stecher late master, now at Israel
Pemberton's wharf - will be sold at James's Coffee House
in Phila. (20 Aug.)

POWELL, John, Irish servant, age c. 20, a good scholar, who
will pass for a miller or schoolmaster - runaway from
Robert Lewis, of Wilmington (20 Aug.)

PENDEGRASS, John, Irish servant, who will pass for ship-
carpenter or sailor - runaway from Edward Hopkins, ship-
carpenter, of Wilmington (20 Aug.)

COOKE, Richard, English servant, age c. 30, who has a discharge from Patrick Lynch, with whom he served his first
time (the discharge is attested by Dr. George Buchanan
as magistrate) - runaway from Charles Ridgely, near Patapsco Ferry, Baltimore Co., Md. (20 Aug.)

SPENCER, James, English convict servant, gardiner by trade,
age 27 - runaway from Thomas Lee, Esq., of Stratford, Va.
(20 Aug.)

BYRNE, Patrick, Irish convict servant, age c. 30 - runaway
from Major William Walker, of Stratford, Va.; Byrne and
Spencer have committed a felony, for which warrants are
out against them (20 Aug.)

MITCHELL, Patrick, Irish servant, age c. 22 - runaway from
James Lestrange, of Piles Grove Twp., West New Jersey
(20 Aug.)

Address of Council of Proprietors (Andrew Johnson, president)
to Gov. Jonathan Belcher of New Jersey; address from Corporation of Perth Amboy to Gov. Belcher; address of Corporation of Elizabeth Town (John Ross mayor; Rob. Ogden,

Cor. Hetfield and Jon. Hampton, members of Common Council; Mat. Hetfield, Sam. Woodruff, John Radley and Tho. Clark, aldermen) to Gov. Belcher; address of City of Burlington (Robert Smith, recorder) to Gov. Belcher (27 Aug.)

On 12 Aug. arrived at Newport, R.I., Capt. Durfey from Leoganne in a flag of truce (27 Aug.)

Account of engagement between Spanish privateer and ship Patience, Capt. Robert Brown, bound from South Carolina to London; the Patience was taken; Capt. Brown and his brother, John Brown, were wounded so that their lives were despaired of - Newport item of 14 Aug.(27 Aug.)

Last Thursday se'nnight the French Indians took at Schotack the following 4 prisoners and carried them to Canada: Abraham Valkenburgh (age c. 70), Jacob his son, his son-in-law Andries Huck, and his grandson, a lad of about 4 - New York item of 10 Aug. (27 Aug.)

TYRER, Capt., arrived at Phila. from Jamaica, informs that the trial of Commodore Lee has begun (27 Aug.)

Snow Sincere Friend, Thomas Tyrer commander, now at Oswald Peele's wharf in Phila. - will sail for Antigua; for freight or passage apply to George Okill or to said master (27 Aug.)

Schooner Squirrel, Edward Strecher master, now at Chesnut St. wharf - will sail for Providence; for freight or passage agree with said master or Anthony Whitley, at the Old Ship Aground (27 Aug.)

MACMAHAN, Alexander, Irish servant, age c. 25 - runaway from on board the snow City of Cork, Daniel Jappie commander; reward for his capture will be paid by Conyngham and Gardner (27 Aug.)

CRAIGE, William, apprentice, age c. 19 - runaway from Colin Ferguson, tailor, of George's Town, Kent Co., Md. (27 Aug.)

Servant boy, age c. 18 - runaway from Capt. Thomas Tyrer; reward will be paid if he is brought to his master at George Okill's, merchant, in Front St., Phila. (27 Aug.)

RANKIN, Thomas, convict servant, age c. 30, born in Cheshire, England, who served part of his time with Richard Barns, of Richmond Co., and is an old runaway - runaway from Thomas Rutherford, of Frederick Co., Va., near the mouth of Shanando River (27 Aug.)

STOMAN, Tobias, of Conestogo Twp. - offers reward for recovery of 2 mares, strayed away; they may be brought to
Robert Thornbrugh's, tavernkeeper, in Lancaster (27 Aug.)

Plantation of 200 acres in New Britain Twp., Bucks Co., will
be sold by Mary Craige, executrix of Thomas Craige, by
order of the Orphan's Court (27 Aug.)

JONES, Aquila - will sell by public vendue 2 lots of ground;
one is on the west side of Bread St., adjoining to house
and ground of Thomas Green; the other is on east of said
street, adjoining to still-house and ground of Peter
Chevalier (27 Aug.)

Tract of 62 acres in Oxford Twp., about 6 miles from Phila.
and ½ mile from the river (part of the estate of Arthur
Jones, dec'd) is for sale; for title and terms enquire
of Elizabeth Jones, living near the place, by the river
side, or of Michael Lightfoot, in Third St., Phila. (27
Aug.)

Detailed advertisements, one signed by Osborn Sprigg, Thomas
Clark and Joseph Belt., Jr., the other by John Hepburn;
mentioned is the attachment against the effects of Robert
Sutcliffe and Wells Bowen (27 Aug.)

Plantation in village of Woodbury, Gloucester Co., 5 miles
on the road from Gloucester to Salem, is for sale; enquire of Abraham Chattin, living on the premises (27 Aug.)

Plantation (formerly Aaron Goforth's, on the Delaware side,
about 6 miles from Phila.) is for sale; enquire of Joseph
Sims, merchant, in Phila. (27 Aug.)

BOYLE, Daniel (where John Hannis lately lived) in Passyunk -
has a good pasture for horses and cows; apply to John
Clare, at the Golden Fleece, Phila. (27 Aug.)

A country seat, adjoining to Rariton Rd., which leads from
Wells's Ferry down to Rariton Landing, 7 miles from said
landing and 9 miles from New Brunswick, is to be sold by
Joseph Read, merchant in New York; apply to Dr. William
Farquhar in New York, Benjamin Franklin in Phila., or
Sarah Janeway, living on the premises (27 Aug.)

Friday last Capt. Everton arrived at Boston, bringing with
him the company of a ship bound to Boston from Biddeford
in Wales, John Hunt master, that lately foundered at sea
14 leagues from Cape Pine in Newfoundland - Boston item
of 24 Aug. (3 Sept.)

Extract of letter, dated Albany, 19 Aug. 1747 from Col.

Johnston to Gov. George Clinton; Johnston had just come to Albany to desire assistance of Cols. Roberts and Marshal - New York item of 30 Aug. (3 Sept.)

On 24 Aug. Capt. Stevenson arrived at Boston from Plymouth with European news (3 Sept.)

Extract of a letter from Annapolis, dated 30 Aug., states that Capt. Burrey is arrived at Potowmack from London (3 Sept.)

DICKINSON, Capt. Benjamin, bound to Jamaica from Phila., has been taken and carried to St. Iago (3 Sept.)

SKERMERHORNE, Capt., who was taken off of Carolina Bar by a Spanish privateer but rescued by the Fowey, man-of-war, Capt. Taylor, arrived Tuesday last at Phila. (3 Sept.)

Flag of truce from Quebec brought the following people from the Jerseys, Pennsylvania and Maryland: Joseph Bryant, John Windridge and John Steward, of Pennsylvania, taken 13 Apr. 1746; Edward Loyd of Maryland; Susana Philips of Phila.; Wm. Scot and Richard Smith of the Jerseys; Wm. Davis of Phila., taken 20 Aug.; Philip Martin of Phila., taken 15 Apr.; Lt. Joseph Chew, Henry Smith, Thomas Harlow, James English, Martin Winyard, Robert Active and Tho. Archer of Maryland -- Turned to the French: Tho. McClothland and Katharine his wife of Phila. -- Dead during their captivity: John Bingham, Philip Scarfield, Arch. Gartrage and James Doyle of Phila.; Richard Bennet of New Jersey (3 Sept.)

Privateer brigantine Trembleur, Capt. Bowne, is falled down on a cruize (3 Sept.)

WHITEFIELD, Rev. - has preached in Boston in Dr. Coleman's and other churches (3 Sept.)

SEWELL, Richard - announces he will stand for office of sheriff of Phila. (3 Sept.)

Bilander Vernon, Thomas Reeks commander, at Fishbourn's wharf - will sail for Charlestown, S.C.; for freight or passage agree with Cuzzins and Smyter at their store in Water St., near Chesnut St., or with the master (3 Sept.)

MORRIS, Thomas, convict servant, age c. 35, lately transported from Ireland, belonging to the Rapahannock Company in Virginia - runaway from North-east Furnace in Baltimore Co.; reward for his capture will be paid by William Ballondin on behalf of the company (3 Sept.)

WRIGHT, Henry (Kindrick), whipmaker, is removed from Chesnut
    St. to Market St., near the Conestogo Wagon (3 Sept.)

Two Negro men are for sale; enquire of Peter Brotherson or
    Joseph Sims in Phila. (3 Sept.)

WILLING, Charles, being removed to his house in Third St.,
    Phila., sells rum, sugar, cloth, ironmongery, etc. (3
    Sept.)

MURPHY, John, of Phila. - has declined riding post to Mary-
    land (3 Sept.)

FITZ PATRICK, Patrick, Irish servant, age c. 22 - runaway
    from George Fudge, bricklayer, in Dock St., Phila. (3
    Se.t.)

MAHON, Paul, Irish servant, age c. 24, sawyer - runaway from
    Simon Shirlock, shipwright, on Society Hill (3 Sept.)

TRACY, Laughlin, servant, age 22, lately come from Ireland -
    runaway from Robert Boyle, tanner, of Fallowfield Twp.,
    Chester Co. (3 Sept.)

VAUGHAN, Michael, servant, age 30 - same as above

PURTILL, Thomas, age c. 35, joiner - runaway from Baltimore
    Co. from his bail; reward for his capture will be paid by
    Jacob Gales or Nathan Rigbie, Jr. (3 Sept.)

Lot in Kensington, extending in length from Queen St. to
    the river, with brick house (in which Mr. Priest lives);
    the plan may be seen at John Bleakly's, at Carpenter's
    Island, or at Oswald Peele's or Lewis Evans's in Phila.
    (3 Sept.)

JACOBS, Job, in Providence, Phila. Co. - has taken up a
    horse (3 Sept.)

SMITH, Benjamin, living at Prime-hope mills, in Hunterdon
    Co., West New Jersey, has real estate for sale, including
    a plantation in Hanover Twp., Burlington Co., whereon
    Thomas Seant now dwells (3 Sept.)

BINGHAM, James, late of Phila., dec'd - accounts with estate
    to be settled with Anne and William Bingham, executors
    (3 Sept.)

BINGHAM, William - has for sale tracts of land, including
    the following: a plantation in Lancaster Co., on Tulpe-
    hoken Creek, on which Reece Thomas now lives; 11 acres
    in Tracony, adjoining Jacob Hall's plantation; a bank

and water lot, between Jonathan Mifflin's and Preserve Brown's (3 Sept.)

DILLWORTH, James - will sell a lot of 40 acres and a log house on it in Bristol Twp., about 6 miles from Phila., 2 from Germantown and 3 from Frankford (3 Sept.)

MEREDITH, Rees - has a Negro man for sale (3 Sept.)

STERRET, James, sheriff, in Lancaster - will sell real estate taken in execution to satisfy a debt against Baptist Clark, on a judgment obtained by Thomas Lightfoot and John Smith, merchants in Phila.; included are the following: plantation and grist-mill in Hanover Twp., on Monody Creek; another plantation distant about a mile from said mill; a plantation in Pennsborough Twp., lying between Andrew Miller's and the mill formerly John Campbell's (3 Sept.)

CLIFTON, John, at his house in Second St., Phila. - sells cloth, gum, coffee, brandy, antimony, etc. (3 Sept.)

Speech of Gov. Jonathan Belcher of New Jersey to Council and General Assembly and address to Gov. Belcher from John Reading, Speaker of the Council, and address to the governor from Robert Lawrence, Speaker of the House (10 Sept.)

Report that Admiral Warren is appointed governor and Lt.-Col. Hopson lieutenant governor of Louisbourg - Boston item of 31 Aug. (10 Sept.)

Letter of Col. W. Johnson to the governor of New York (10 Sept.)

STAMPER, Capt., who arrived Tuesday at Phila. from Lisbon, reports that there was at Lisbon a privateer formerly commanded by Capt. Jefferies of New York (10 Sept.)

List of books published or sold by B. Franklin (10 Sept.)

WHITE, Thomas, at his house in Market St., almost opposite to the Sign of the Dutch Wagon, between Fourth and Fifth Streets, Phila. - sells cloth, shot, frying pans, thread, pins, books (10 Sept.)

BAKER, John - will sell water lots at Kensington (near John Blakely's lot) (10 Sept.)

House on Second St., about ¼ mile below the New Market, for sale - enquire of Peter Keen, living on Society Hill (10 Sept.)

BUDDINOT, Elias, silversmith, is removed from the house
next door to the Post Office, in Market St., to the
house where Joseph Noble lately dwelt, in Second St.,
4 doors above Black Horse Alley; clocks and watches are
repaired there by Emanuel Rouse (10 Sept.)

HUGHES, William, late of Chichester, Chester Co., dec'd -
accounts with estate to be settled with William Hughes,
administrator (10 Sept.)

CUISICK, Edward, Irish servant, age c. 20, a pretty good
scholar - runaway from Thomas Paxton, of Conestogoe
Manor, and Benjamin Ashleman, of Conestogoe Twp. (10 Sept.)

DOYLE, Thomas, Irish servant, age c. 24 - same as above

DUGAN, James, Irish servant, age c. 28 - runaway from Daniel
Steward, of Oxford Twp., Phila. Co. (10 Sept.)

Brigantine S. Stephen, Thomas Williams commander, now at
John Stamper's wharf, below the drawbridge - will sail
for Antigua; for freight or passage agree with John
Stamper or the master (10 Sept.)

Wednesday last arrived in Rhode Island a prize taken by
Capt. Sweet, commander of a Rhode Island privateer -
Rhode Island item of 4 Sept. (17 Sept.)

Two Spanish privateers at the Capes have taken the ship
Delaware, Capt. Lake, of Phila. (17 Sept.)

McCALL, Jasper, late of Phila., merchant, dec'd - accounts
with estate to be settled with Magdalene, Samuel and
George McCall, executors (17 Sept.)

YEATES, George, late of Newcastle Co. on Delaware, gent.,
dec'd - accounts with estate to be settled with Mary
and John Yeates, administrators (17 Sept.)

Books published by B. Franklin (17 Sept.)

Negro woman for sale; enquire of Joseph Sims, in Front St.
(17 Sept.)

TAYLOR, Thomas, of Middletown - his wife Chessen has eloped
from him (17 Sept.)

LEITH, Alexander, at the house of Mr. Boudinot, in Second
St., next door to Mr. Forbes's - has for sale a large
assortment of goods (17 Sept.)

SCULL, Nicholas, Sheriff - gives notice of forthcoming sale

at house of Standish Ford, on the great road leading from
Germantown to Phila., of stone messuage in Northern
Liberties of Phila., by said great road, near Fairhill
Meeting-house, belonging late to Peter Woolbrugh, taken
in execution at suit of John Naglee (17 Sept.)

Plantation, now in tenor of Samuel Irvine, and another late
in the tenor of George Harkness, in Whitemarsh Twp.,
Phila. Co., part of the estate of Edward Garmer, dec'd,
are to be sold by Peter Robeson, Joseph Farmer and Jonathan Robeson, executors; a plan of the lands may be seen
with Peter Robeson, at the Indian King, Phila. (17 Sept.)

DAVIS, Sarah, Welsh servant, age c. 27 - runaway from William Plaskett, of Trenton (17 Sept.)

HARRISON, John, over the drawbridge in Phila. - sells powder, sugar, cocoa, tea, olives, cloth, leather, cordage
(17 Sept.)

List of vessels taken by a French privateer sloop of Cape
Francois, the Marshal Vaudroy, M. Lahaye, commander:
Capt. Green from Providence; sloop Ranger, Capt. Smith
from Rhode Island; Capt. Ramsay from London; ship London,
Capt. Cary, and brigantine George and Mary, Capt. Hayton,
both from Virginia; ship London, Capt. Skinner, from Virginia; sloop Charity, C. Newbold from Phila.; ship Delaware, Capt.Lake of Phila.; ship Bolton, Capt. Eves of
Phila.; said French privateer chased the ship Cumberland,
Capt. Moor, from Londonderry for Phila., but could not
come up with her; he saw Capt. Tiffen but did not venture to engage his ship (24 Sept.)

PURNELL, Capt., of Providence - has sent in there 2 prize
sloops (24 Sept.)

Saturday last arrived at Phila. Gov. Jonathan Belcher, of
New Jersey (24 Sept.)

Brigantine Prosperity, of Phila., Robert Ritchie commander,
ran upon Brandywine Shoal (24 Sept.)

BENEZET, James, at his store at the house where Samuel Parr
lately lived, opposite Mr. John Hopkins - sells assortment of European goods, as do Philip Benezet, at his
store, the corner of Arch St., opposite the George Inn,
in Second St., and William and David McIlvaine, at their
store in Front St., near the drawbridge (24 Sept.)

RONEY, James, of Caecil Co., Md. - his wife Margaret has
eloped from him (24 Sept.)

WASTLE, Timothy, of Barnard Castle, Durham Co., England — at the Post Office in Phila. will hear something to his advantage (24 Sept.)

BENEZET, Daniel, at his store in Front St., at the corner of Morris's Alley, Phila. - sells European goods (24 Sept.)

Messers. Neat and Smith, next door to Townsend White, in Front St., Phila. - have European goods for sale; they intend for England in a few months (24 Sept.)

CURRIE, Ebenezer, dec'd - accounts with estate to be settled with Samuel McCall, Sr., and John Groves, administrators (24 Sept.)

MARKS, Joseph - will sell the stone house where Bernard Reser lately lived, at the lower end of Germantown (24 Sept.)

House on Passyunk Rd., in Southern Liberties of Phila., formerly in the occupation of Joseph Scull, is to be let; enquire of Maurice and Edmund Nihill, brewers, in Phila. (24 Sept.)

Negro man, age c. 25 - runaway from Thomas Harrison, of Prince William Co., Va. (24 Sept.)

Plantation of 600 acres in Passyunk Twp., about 4 miles from Phila., fronting the Schuylkill, is to be let; enquire of Dr. John Kearsley, Andrew Hannis or Bartholomew Penrose (24 Sept.)

Warning to pilots and military is issued by Jacob Kollock and Rives Holt (24 Sept.)

CRESSON, Solomon, dec'd - accounts with estate to be settled with John Cresson (24 Sept.)

PUGH, Mishael - will sell house and lot in Borough of Wilmington, on north side of Market St., near the Upper Market (24 Sept.)

GRAY, George, at the Falls Ferry, on Schuylkill - offers reward for recovery of a colt (24 Sept.)

In an engagement at St. George's Fort in September, 4 English, John Kilpatrick, Nathan Bradley, John Vole and Benjamin Harvey, were killed, while 3 Penobscot Indians --well-known to Capts. Bradbury and Bean--were killed by the English - Boston item of 21 Sept. (1 Oct.)

AUSTEL, Capt. - arrived a few days ago at Boston from Lisbon, with European news - Boston item of 21 Sept. (1 Oct.)

DEAN, Capt. - arrived Saturday last at New York from Jamaica (1 Oct.)

JOHNSTON, Col. - arrived last week at New York from Albany with 9 Indian chiefs - New York item of 28 Sept. (1 Oct.)

BELL, Tom - on 27 Sept. was committed to the Jail of New York City (1 Oct.)

BURCHILL, Capt., of H.M.S. Lyme - has had an engagement with Don Pedro to the windward of Antigua (1 Oct.)

DAVIS, Capt., in the Walker privateer schooner of Georgia, and Capt. Twist, in a galley from Charlestown, have taken a Spanish sloop called the Conquestador (whose boat took Capt. Martin in our bay and came up to Mr. Liston's plantation) (1 Oct.)

Snow Happy Return, Capt. Scott, from Londonderry, ran upon the Hen and Chickens Shoal, and about 50 people were drowned (1 Oct.)

A large Moses was Sunday last taken away or turned adrift from the ship's postilion, John Combes master, lying at Mr. Inglis's wharf (1 Oct.)

Ship Widow, now at John Inglis's wharf, will sail for London; for freight or passage agree with Samuel McCall, Sr., or John Groves (1 Oct.)

Cloth just imported in the ship Lydia, Capt. William Tiffin, from London, is sold by Charles and Alexander Stedman at their store in Water St., Phila. (1 Oct.)

DOWERS, Edward, at his store, next to the store of Benjamin and Samuel Shoemaker, in Water St., above Arch St., sells cloth and clothing (1 Oct.)

CANADA, John, Irish servant, age c. 23 - runaway from Joseph Burr, of Burlington Co. (1 Oct.)

Sampson, a Negro, age c. 50, and his son Sam by an Indian woman - runaways from Silas Parvin, of Cohansie Bridge (1 Oct.)

Negro girl of about 17 is for sale; enquire of Miles Strickland or the Widow Hilburn in Fourth St., Phila. (1 Oct.)

Two-wheel chair for sale; apply to Mr. Foster, chair-maker,

658

in Second St., Phila. (1 Oct.)

Person understanding paper-making is desired to apply to
Daniel Womelstorf (1 Oct.)

Publications printed and sold by B. Franklin (1 Oct.)

Household furniture will be sold at house where Jasper
McCall, late of Phila., dwelt, below the drawbridge in
Front St. (1 Oct.)

BURD, James, at his store opposite to John Bringhurst's in
Front St., Phila., sells cloth, spices, hats, cutlery,
ironmongery (1 Oct.)

SWIFT, John, at his store upon Mr. Hamilton's wharf - sells
cloth, books, gloves, paper, combs, etc. (1 Oct.)

McDONALD, Reynold, servant, age c. 26 - runaway from Robert
Miller, of Pensborough Twp., Lancaster Co. (1 Oct.)

McNAMEE, Catharine, servant, age c. 34 - same as above

FARRELL, Andrew, of Phila. - has for sale plantation of 152
acres in the Manor of Moreland and also the 4-wheeled
chaise that belonged to Gov. George Thomas (1 Oct.)

PATERSON, James, servant, age c. 25 - runaway from Francis
Graham, of Mill Creek Hundred, Newcastle Co. (1 Oct.)

WHITE, James - offers reward for recovery of strayed or
stolen gelding; news of gelding to be given to Geo. Goforth of Dover, to David Marshal of Duck Creek or Samuel
Sloss near the head of Bohemia (1 Oct.)

On 7 Sept. Capt. Brown arrived at Boston from Phila.; his
snow was taken by a Spanish privateer but he overcame
Spanish prize crew placed on his vessel - Boston item of
28 Sept. (8 Oct.)

FISHERMAN, Capt., of Penicook - was killed by Indians -
Boston item of 28 Sept. (8 Oct.)

Tuesday last Capt. Hayward arrived at Phila. from Bristol
(8 Oct.)

Thursday last the following were elected for Phila. Co.--
representatives: John Kinsey, Isaac Norris, Thomas
Leech, Edward Warner, Joseph Trotter, James Morris,
Owen Evans, Hugh Evans; sheriff: Richard Sewell; coroner: Henry Pratt; commissioner: John Jones Carpenter;
assessors: William Foulk, Joseph Stretch, Joseph Morris,

Abraham Levant, James Jones (8 Oct.)

Thursday last the following were elected for Bucks Co.--
representatives: Mahlon Kirkbride, Cephas Child, Joseph
Hampton, Derrick Hogland, Richard Walker, John Watson,
Abraham Chapman, John Hall; sheriff: Amos Strickland;
coroner: John Chapman; commissioner: John Watson, Jr.;
assessors: William Edwards, George Logan, Giles Knight,
William Murry, Abraham Vastine, Thomas Paxon (8 Oct.)

Thursday last the following were elected for Chester Co.--
representatives: Samuel Lewis, Francis Yarnall, George
Ashbridge, Thomas Worth, Peter Dicks, John Owen, John
Davis, Thomas Chandler; sheriff: Benjamin Davis; coroner:
Isaac Lee; commissioner: Thomas Pennell; assessors:
Elisha Gotebell, Jr., Thomas Parks, Isaac Davis, Aaron
Ashbridge, Isaac Pearson, John Jackson, Nathaniel Pen-
nock (8 Oct.)

Thursday last the following were elected for Lancaster Co.
-- representatives: John Wright, Arthur Patterson, James
Webb, Peter Worrell; sheriff: James Sterett; coroner:
Edward Dogherty (8 Oct.)

Thursday last the following were elected for Newcastle Co.
--representatives: William Armstrong, James McMahon,
John McCoole, John Vance, John Edwards, Jehu Curtis;
sheriff: Gideon Griffith; coroner: James McMullen (8
Oct.)

Thursday last the following were elected for Kent Co.--
representatives: John Brinckle, Hugh Durborough, Thomas
Green, John Robeson, James Gorrel, Abraham Allee;
sheriff: John Hunter; coroner: George Goforth (8 Oct.)

Thursday last the following were elected for Sussex Co.--
representatives: Jacob Kollock, Woolsey Burton, John
Clowes, Ryves Holt, James McIlvaine, John Neill; sheriff:
Peter Clowes; coroner: Isaac Wil/?/bank (8 Oct.)

Friday last Israel Pemberton, Sr., and Oswald Peele were
chosen burgesses for Phila. and for assessors Stephen
Armit, Thomas Howard, William Callendar, Philip Syng,
John Dilwyn, John Mifflin (8 Oct.)

List of books just imported by B. Franklin (8 Oct.)

Snow Charming Molly, Joseph Hayward commander, now at Powell's
wharf - will sail for South Carolina; for freight or
passage agree with the commander on board or William
Atwood (8 Oct.)

Privateer ship <u>Pandour</u>, William Dowell commander - all
   inclined to go on a cruize may repair to the Sign of
   the Pewter Platter in Front St. (8 Oct.)

SMITH & JAMES, at their store in Water St., above Arch St.
   - have imported goods for sale (8 Oct.)

ASHMEAD, John - has lots in Germantown for sale; 2 of these
   are about 80 perches from Germantown Market on a street
   leading to Andrew Robeson's mill; another lot is on a
   street leading by Reynier Costard's to Phila. (8 Oct.)

LOGAN, William in Second St. - sells imported goods (8 Oct.)

WILLING, Charles, at his store in Third St. - sells cloth,
   powder, ironmongery, canvas, cables, Bristol tobacco
   pipes, sugar (8 Oct.)

Plantation of 250 acres in Blockley Twp., 5 miles from
   Phila., is for sale; apply to Richard Pearne, living on
   the premises (8 Oct.)

SWINNY, Edward, Irishman, who lodged at Patrick Roberts's in
   Arch St., Phila. - runaway from the ship <u>Frere</u>, John
   Peters commander; reward will be paid if he is taken and
   brought to said commander or to Thomas Lloyd (8 Oct.)

If any deserter from Albany will enlist for Cape Breton with
   Capt. John Houston at the Kings Arms in Second St.,
   Phila., he will receive bounty (8 Oct.)

FINLEY, Samuel - designs to reply to Mr. Morgan's Antipoedo
   -Rantisen (8 Oct.)

MORGAN, Evan - offers reward for recovery of a lost gold
   stock-buckle, marked EM; he has removed from his house
   at the corner of Market St., against the Courthouse door,
   to his house in Water St., at the Sign of the Two Sugar
   Loaves, next door to Peter Bard's (8 Oct.)

WAINRITE, Ann, servant, who was brought up in Virginia -
   runaway from Francis Mines, in Appoquinimy, Newcastle
   Co. (8 Oct.)

Beck, Negro - runaway (in company with Ann Wainrite) from
   Jannet Balvaird (of Appoquinimy, Newcastle Co.) (8 Oct.)

HALL, Capt. - arrived 15 Oct. at Phila. from Antigua; he
   reports that in a hurricane on 19 Sept. a new ship from
   Phila. was lost and all the people were drowned except
   Capt. Faulkner, who was on shore (15 Oct.)

McCOLOUGH, Capt., in a brigantine of Phila., was taken within 5 leagues of Antigua and Capt. Douglas, in a sloop of Phila., is also taken, as are Capts. Harper, Hall and Worsdale, all from Phila. (15 Oct.)

ATWOOD, William, is re-elected Mayor of Phila., and Tench Francis, John Mifflin, John Stamper, Samuel McCall, John Sober, Joseph Sims, Phineas Bond and John Wilcocks are chosen members of the Common Council (15 Oct.)

CROOKSHANKS, Capt., of the Lark, is to be sent home from Cape Breton (15 Oct.)

Sunday last arrived at Phila. the ship Two Brothers, Capt. Arnot, from Holland, with Palatines (15 Oct.)

Reward will be paid for pocketbook, lost betwen Naaman's Creek and Phila., by B. Franklin at the Post Office or Thomas Robinson at Naaman's Creek (15 Oct.)

A parcel of paper money was left on the counter of the shop of Jacob Shoemaker, at the Sign of the Spinning-wheel, in Market St., Phila. (15 Oct.)

Ship Two Brothers, Thomas Arnot master, will sail for South Carolina; for freight or passage apply to Benjamin and Samuel Shoemaker or to said master (15 Oct.)

Ship Euryale, John Cox commander, at Masters's wharf in Phila. - will sail for Ireland; for freight or passage apply to said master, at William Spafford's, in Front St. (15 Oct.)

Three plantations in Fallowfield Twp., Chester Co., are to be sold or rented; apply to Evan Morgan, in Water St. (15 Oct.)

POWELL, Samuel, Jr., late of Phila., merchant, dec'd - accounts with estate to be settled with William Coleman and James Pemberton, executors (15 Oct.)

TROTTER, James, at his store in Front St., next door Nathaniel Allen - sells cloth, oil, anchovies, capers, mustard, wax, gunpowder, etc. (15 Oct.)

GREEN, Thomas - will sell 2 houses in Bread St., or Moravian Alley (15 Oct.)

HODGES, Hugh, tobacconist - is removed from his house in Water St., next door to Capt. Hopkins's, to the house where the Widow Harper lived, next door to Thomas Campbell's, opposite to the Court House in Phila. (15 Oct.)

HOUSE, Joseph, in Water St., a few doors above Market St., Phila. - sells cocoa (15 Oct.)

GRIFFITTS, Isaac, at his store at the upper end of Water St. - sells rum, salt, Jesuits Bark, Connecticut lottery tickets (15 Oct.)

Plantation (formerly Aaron Goforth's) on Delaware side, about 6 miles from Phila., is for sale; enquire of the owner, Nathaniel Johnson, at Mrs. Howell's in Market St., Phila., or of Joseph Sims (15 Oct.)

PYEWELL, William, tanner, is removed from Second St. to the house and tanyard near Chesnut St. where John Howell, tanner, lately lived; Pyewell will let or sell a house over against Samuel Rhodes's, at the lower end of Second St.; the tanyard lately occupied by John Langdon is to be let (15 Oct.)

HUGHES, John, Irish servant, age c. 20 - runaway from William Moses, Jr., of Phila., blacksmith (15 Oct.)

PETERS, Joseph, at his store in Wilmington - has for sale hardware and cloth (15 Oct.)

HENTON, Israel, a Newenglandman - has stolen goods from house of John Miller, of Plymouth Twp., Phila. Co. (15 Oct.)

FOSTER, Moses, chairmaker, in Second St., Phila. - has for sale a 2-wheel chair (15 Oct.)

ANDREW, William, at his store in Water St., where William Macilvaine formerly kept store - sells cloth (15 Oct.)

WAMSLEY, John, servant, age c. 23 - runaway from Daniel Williams, of Towamenson, Phila. Co. (15 Oct.)

WOODSIDE, Capt. - arrived 18 Oct. at New York from Providence (22 Oct.)

Verses written by a gentleman on reading Barclay's Apology (22 Oct.)

HARDING, John, Sr., dec'd - accounts to be settled with John Harding, Jr., and George Adams, administrators (22 Oct.)

ROBESON, Peter, at the Indian King in Market St., offers reward for recovery of a horse strayed from a pasture in the Northern Liberties of Phila. (22 Oct.)

Tracts of land in Gloucester and Salem Counties, belonging

to Col. John Alford, of Charles-Town in New England, are
to be sold by Edward Shippen, of Phila., and John Ladd,
of Gloucester Co. (22 Oct.)

Harry, Negro, age c̲. 20 - runaway from Thomas Meade; reward
for his capture will be paid by William Plumsted (22 Oct.)

Lot on south side of Chesnut St., between lots late of Samuel Norris, dec'd, will be sold at house of the Widow
Breintnall, at the Sign of the Hen and Chickens, in Chesnut St., Phila., by Mary Lacey, widow and administratrix
of Thomas Lacey, dec'd (22 Oct.)

CARPENTER, Abraham, cooper, who lives in Dock St., Phila.,
near the Golden Fleece, offers chairs, hoops, etc., for
sale (22 Oct.)

CLIFTON, John, at his house in Second St. - has for sale
cloth, brandy, tea, sugar, etc. (22 Oct.)

WAUGH, William, carpenter, will sell at John Faris's, at
the Sign of the Duke of Cumberland, opposite the premises,
a lot and kitchen on Society Hill (22 Oct.)

WALTER, Henry, blue-dyer, in Lancaster - has removed from
his former dwelling-house and dwells higher up in the
same street (22 Oct.)

PEARSON, Samuel,Irish apprentice, age c̲. 19 - runaway from
Hugh Lindsay, of Phila., house-carpenter (22 Oct.)

Reward is offered for recovery of mare and colt that strayed
away from Upper Milford Twp., Bucks Co., by Jacob Gar-
denheir, in Upper Milford, or Jacob Naglee in Germantown
(22 Oct.)

FRYE, John - has taken up a cow at his plantation in Coventry Twp., Chester Co., near Millard's mill (22 Oct.)

Ship Mary, formerly commanded by Capt. Martin, has been
taken by a privateer's boat (29 Oct.)

Ship Patience, Capt. Robert Brown late master, and a sloop,
late Capt. Schermerhorn's, of New York, are re-taken (29
Oct.)

The carpenter of the privateer that took Martin (being an
Englishman) has been sentenced to be hanged (he was one
of those at Mr. Liston's plantation) and the captain of
the privateer is to be tried for his life (29 Oct.)

The Dantzick Merchant, Capt. Brown, has been taken but retaken by H.M.S. *Adventure*, Capt. Hayman; Capt. Calcock, in a schooner belonging to Charlestown, has been taken and carried to Augustine (29 Oct.)

The snow *Jane and Jannet*, William Muir master, now at Fishbourn's wharf, will sail for Charlestown; for freight or passage agree with the master or Charles and Alexander Steadman, merchants (29 Oct.)

Ship *Beulah*, James Child master - will sail for London; for freight or passage agree with Benjamin and Samuel Shoemaker or said master (29 Oct.)

SCULL, Nicholas, late Sheriff - announces sale of lot in Wicacoa, Phila. Co., bounded by Thomas Williams's lot to south, by John Pelham's lot to north, on east by Swanson's St., late belonging to Daniel Dawson, dec'd, and taken in execution at suit of George Emlen, Jr.; auction will take place at Capt. Dollinson's at Wicacoa (29 Oct.)

Lot and house in Water St. near Market St., Phila., now inhabited by Capt. Oswald Peele, bounded to south by house late Capt. William Clymer's but now of Joseph House, Jr., and to northward by a house of Thomas Says; apply to Francis Bowes, of Phila. (29 Oct.)

GIFFORD, Samuel (formerly clerk to Charles Brockden and late clerk to James Hamilton, Esq.), at the Sign of the Key in Second St., next door to Richard Sewell, Esq., sheriff (between Chesnut and Walnut Sts.) draws deeds and other instruments (29 Oct.)

BACHLEY, Christian, coach-maker, in Market St., Phila. - offers reward for recovery of a horse that strayed away (29 Oct.)

STRICKLAND, Amos, Sheriff - offers reward for capture of the following, who escaped from Newtown Jail in Bucks Co.: Malachi Walton, who formerly kept an inn in Bristol; Paul Messenger, a Dutchman, a wheelwright (29 Oct.)

STRICKLAND, Amos, Sheriff - has taken up and had committed to Goal of Newtown, Bucks Co., a Negro named John Cuffee, age c. 26, who says he belongs to John Harding, master of a ship from Madeira to Patapsco, Md.; the Negro says his master was shot in the voyage by a Spanish privateer (29 Oct.)

MARSHALL, Christopher, at the Sign of the Golden Ball, facing Strawberry Alley, near the Three Tuns, in Chesnut St., Phila. - sells oils, colors, glass, vitriol, etc. (29 Oct.)

Plantation of 600 acres in Passyunk Twp., fronting River
Schuylkill, about 4 miles from Phila., is for sale; en-
quire of Dr. John Kearsley, Andrew Hannis or Bartholomew
Penrose (29 Oct.)

Account of treatment of Capt. Brown of the ship _Patience_, at
the hands of Capt. Bernard in a Spanish privateer, as
given by Capt. Brown's brother, who was mate (5 Nov.)

Snow _Rebecca_, Capt. Henderwell, who sailed from Charlestown,
S.C., has been taken - Charlestown item of 8 Aug. (5 Nov.)

RAMSAY, Capt., in a ship for London from Cape Fear has been
taken, as has the brigantine _John_ & _Mary_, Thomas Corbett
master, made prize by the _Francis_ _Gabriel_ the _Conqueror_,
Stephen Beard commander - Charlestown items of 31 Aug.
and 7 Sept. (5 Nov.)

The _European_, Benjamin Wright master, from Charlestown bound
to London, was taken 20 July; Capt. Wright was killed -
Charlestown item of 28 Sept. (5 Nov.)

The dispatch ship, Philip Marette master, from London for
Charlestown, is taken - Charlestown item of 14 Sept. (5
Nov.)

Account of attacks made by French and Indians upon a sergeant
and 18 men of Capt. Robinson's company, who were returning
from Dirk Van Slyk's, about 3 miles from their quarters at
Kinderhook - extract of a letter from Col. Roberts, dated
Albany, 24 Oct., to the Gov. of New York (5 Nov.)

A vessel arrived last week at Phila. from Barbados reports
the death of Commodore Legge (5 Nov.)

SCULL, Nicholas, Sheriff - announces forthcoming sale of
leather at late dwelling-house of John Howell, tanner,
in Chesnut St. (5 Nov.)

Reward offered for recovery of horse, strayed or stolen out
of Owen Roberts's yard in Black Horse Alley; horse is to
be brought to John Jones, of North Wales, or to Owen
Roberts (5 Nov.)

Plantation of 315 acres, in Derby Twp., is for sale; enquire of Joseph Levis, near Franckfort (5 Nov.)

SHUTE, Thomas, Jr. - has for sale oranges, potatoes and sole
leather, just imported in the sloop _Susannah_ and _Francis_,
Thomas Beazely commander, at Bickley's wharf (5 Nov.)

Mill on French Creek, near River Schuylkill, in Charles-

Town Twp., Chester Co., is for sale; apply to James
Starr, Jr., or Moses Starr (5 Nov.)

RICHARDSON, Edward, of New Providence Twp., Phila Co., has
taken up 2 mares (5 Nov.)

BOYDEN, James, late of Phila., merchant, dec'd - accounts
with estate to be settled with Robert Greenway, executor,
who will sell lot of about 43 acres in Oxford Twp.,
Phila. Co., fronting the Delaware about 6 miles from
Phila. (5 Nov.)

GODFREY, Thomas, of Phila., Gravesend - desires that volumes he lent may be returned (5 Nov.)

BALDWIN, Francis, living near John Frost's, on Back Creek,
Va. - offers reward for recovery of mare that strayed
away (5 Nov.)

GILBERT, Anthony, of Germantown - offers reward for recovery
of horse that strayed from his pasture; horse may be
brought to him, or to Henrick Capely, next door to John
Wister in Market St., Phila. (5 Nov.)

House (known by name of the Spread Eagle), in Borough and
Co. of Chester, on south side of Chester Bridge, bounded
by Bridge St. and Essex St., is for sale; apply to Isaac
Lee, living in said house, who keeps the Sign of the
Boar's Head, or Ebenezer Wollaston, in Newport, New-
castle Co., weaver (5 Nov.)

PRENTICE, Rev., Minister of Grafton - on 23 Oct. his letter
was accidentally shattered by gunpowder explosion, so
that he died the following Saturday - Boston item of 2
Nov. (12 Nov.)

Publications of B. Franklin (12 Nov.)

BURGESS, Thomas', late of Norriton, living at Fishbourne's
wharf in Phila. - sells grain and salt (12 Nov.)

CROSSDALE, Thomas, dec'd - accounts with estate to be settled at the Sign of the George in Phila. with Richard
Renshaw, administrator (12 Nov.)

Privateer snow Warren is to be sold; inventory may be seen
at Widow Roberts's Coffee House (12 Nov.)

WILSON, John, of Solebury Twp., Bucks Co., living near Thomas
Pryor's mill - offers reward for recovery of strayed mare
(12 Nov.)

ANDERSON, William, Irish servant, age c. 22 - runaway from
Alexander Craig, of New London Twp., Chester Co. (12 Nov.)

FURIO, John, Irish servant, age c. 30 - runaway from Frances
Scholey, of Springfield (12 Nov.)

WILLIAMS, James, of Rapho Twp., Lancaster Co. - offers reward for strayed or stolen mare; she may be brought to
the owner or to Robert Rigg, of Uchland Twp., Chester
Co. (12 Nov.)

STYLES, Capt. Richard - arrived a few days ago at Charles-
town, S.C., from New Providence; he reports that Capt.
Richard Thompson, of that island, has taken a large
Spanish ship - Charlestown item of 19 Oct. (19 Nov.)

A privateer of Frederica has retaken Capt. Campbell's
schooner of Port Royal; a Spanish privateer had in company a large ship supposed to be the European, lately
commanded by Capt. Wright - Charlestown item of 26 Oct.
(19 Nov.)

WHITEFIELD, Rev. - arrived in Charlestown Saturday last -
Charlestown item of 26 Oct. (19 Nov.)

Saturday last arrived at New York Capt. White, who had been
taken by the French, who eventually placed him in a snow
belonging to Liverpool, Capt. Threlsall master, which
they took on 26 July - New York item of 16 Nov. (19 Nov.)

EDWARDS, Capt., from Barbados, reports that the privateer
ship Antelope, of New York, Capt. Amory, put in there to
refit; Capt. Tyrrell, in one of H.M.'s ships, carried in
there 2 French privateers (19 Nov.)

Privateer ship Pandour, Capt. Dowell, is fallen down on a
cruize (19 Nov.)

At a Court of Oyer and Terminer in Phila. yesterday Patrick
and Michael Burne and William Ward were found guilty of
burglary and robbery, having broken open the house of
Mrs. Anne Cox of Moyamensing, and were sentenced to death
(19 Nov.)

DUFFIELD, Jacob - offers reward for recovery of horse stolen
from Robert Dixon's at the Center; horse may be brought
to Peter Robeson's or Joseph Gray's, at Phila. (19 Nov.)

Sloop John, John Barwick master, at Plumstead's wharf in
Phila. - will sail for New Providence (19 Nov.)

Deserters from Sir William Pepperell's Regt., if they will

report to N. Whiting at the George in Second St., Phila., will obtain indemnity and bounty money (19 Nov.)

McNEAL, William, of Horsham Twp.,.Phila. Co. - his wife Mary has eloped from him (19 Nov.)

COX, John - has house to be let on Passyunk Rd., about a mile from Phila. (19 Nov.)

BARTHOLOMEW, Joseph, of Whiteland Twp., Chester Co. - offers reward for 5 cattle that have strayed away (19 Nov.)

McALISTER, Archibald, of Pennsborough Twp., Lancaster Co. - has taken up a Negro named Joe, age $\underline{c}$. 30, who says he came from South Carolina (19 Nov.)

HUNTER, James, of Newtown, Chester Co. - offers reward for recovery of a gelding that strayed or was stolen from the plantation of John Hunter, of Whiteland, Chester Co. (19 Nov.)

HEAD, John, hatter, in Phila., opposite to the church - offers reward for recovery of a horse strayed or stolen out of the street in Phila. (19 Nov.)

BURK, John, late tavernkeeper at Whitemarsh, dec'd - accounts with estate to be settled with Huse Burk, of Whitemarsh Twp., or Edward Burk, of Upper Dublin Twp., executors (19 Nov.)

MARTIN, William, late of Whipton Twp., Phila. Co. - accounts with estate to be settled with Abraham Dawes, Richard Wall and Benjamin Davis, administrators (19 Nov.)

PATTERSON, John, Irish servant, age $\underline{c}$. 22, blacksmith - runaway from the shallop Speedwell, William Phillips master; servant may be brought to Capt. John Phillips in Water St., Phila. (19 Nov.

Harry, Negro, who speaks English and Dutch - runaway from Thomas Mayburry, of Phila. Co. (19 Nov.)

Wreck of a fishing vessel, supposed to be one belonging to Marblehead, Thomas Allen master, has been seen on a rock near Cape Sable Shore - Boston item of 16 Nov. (26 Nov.)

The French Indian who surrendered to the people at Capt. Van Renslaer's house escaped over the walls of the fort; Van Schaick and Abeel had been taken last spring - extract of letter from Albany dated 14 Nov. - New York item of 23 Nov. (26 Nov.)

GRANT, Capt., arrived Tuesday last at Phila. from Jamaica, reports that a privateer sloop of Bermuda, commanded by Capt. Griffitts, took into Jamaica a prize ship and sloop and that the brigantine William, of New York, was taken by a Spanish privateer (26 Nov.)

Saturday last numerous inhabitants of Phila. met at Mr. Walton's Schoolhouse in Arch St. and an association was formed for common security and defence; on Monday following another meeting was held at Roberts's Coffee House (26 Nov.)

The executors of the estate of Samuel Powell, Jr., dec'd, William Coleman and James Pemberton, will sell at J. Pemberton's store, fronting Chesnut St. wharf, adjoining to that from whence Smith and Jones lately removed, sundry sorts of English goods (26 Nov.)

STERRETT, James, sheriff - will sell 2 plantations lately belonging to Edward Edwards, one of 300 acres in Carnervan Twp., Lancaster Co., the other on which Edwards lived in Earl Twp., Lancaster Co. (26 Nov.)

SUMER, Richard, born in London, age c. 22, barber - deserted from Sir. William Pepperrell's Regt.; reward will be paid by Nathan Whiting if he is captured and brought to any goal or to said Whiting at the Sign of the George in Second St. (26 Nov.)

ANDERSON, Joseph, born in Devonshire, age 40, tailor - same as above

WILLING, Charles, at his house in Third St., Phila., has 2 Negroes for sale (26 Nov.)

BOONE, Andrew, of Derby Twp., Chester Co., dec'd - accounts with estate to be settled with Mounce Rambo and William Donaldson, administrators (26 Nov.)

CLINTON, Robert, Irish servant, age c. 20, weaver - runaway from James Greenfield, of Newlin Twp., Chester Co.; he was enticed away by one Sylvester Eagon, an Irishman, weaver (26 Nov.)

DAVIS, Sarah, Welsh servant - runaway from William Plasket of Trenton (26 Nov.)

Ship Pepperrell, William Grant master - will sail for Londonderry; for freight or passage agree with Samuel Hazard or said master (26 Nov.)

New messuage and kitchen on west side of Fifth St., Phila.,

is for sale; enquire of Elizabeth Wrag, living on the premises (26 Nov.)

DOYLE, Lawrence, Irish sailor, age c. 26 - runaway from snow Dragon, William Andrew master - reward will be paid if he is brought to William and David Macilvaine, in Front St., Phila. (26 Nov.)

CANGLING, James, Irish sailor, age c. 26 - same as above

WEISER, Conrad, Esq. - in a letter reports on activities of the Indians; he is Interpreter to the Province of Pennsylvania (3 Dec.)

Places assigned for persons in Chester Co. to meet to sign association are the following: for inhabitants of townships of East Nottingham, West Nottingham, New London, Londonderry, London Britain and London Grove--the house of John Frew, in New London Twp. on 14 Dec.; for inhabitants of West Marlborough, East Marlborough, New Garden, Kennet, East Fallowfield, West Fallowfield, Sadsbury and New Linton--the house of Nathaniel Ring in Kennet on 15 Dec.; for inhabitants of Upper Chichester, Lower Chichester, Chester, Concord, Middletown, East Bradford, West Bradford, Birmingham, Bethel and Edgmont--house of James Mathers in Chester on 17 Dec.; for inhabitants of Haverford, Marple, Springfield, Upper Derby, Lower Derby, Ridley, East-Town, Radnor, Newtown, Upper Providence and Lower Providence--house of Mr. Donaldson in Derby on 18 Dec.; for inhabitants of Charles-Town, Tredyffryn, Whiteland, Goshen, Willis-Town, West-Town and Pikeland--at the house of John Hambricht (where James Trago formerly dwelt) on 21 Dec.; for inhabitants of East Caln, West Caln, East Nantmell, West Nantmell, Coventry, Vincent and Uchland-- at the house of Thomas Park in the Great Valley on 22 Dec. (3 Dec.)

Tract of 200 acres in Limrick Twp., Phila. Co. (part of plantation of Edward Nicholas, dec'd) is for sale; apply to William Currie or Thomas Bull, executors (3 Dec.)

Articles of agreement between John Farrill, commander of the James Frigat, on behalf of himself and the owners and the ships company; those desiring to enter on board may repair to the commander at New York or to Joseph Redman at Phila. (3 Dec.)

WILSON, James, an Englishman (who was arrested for abusing a servant and found guilty of homicide by a coroner's inquisition) - escaped from John Holme, Constable of Waterford, Gloucester Co.; Holme offers reward for his capture (3 Dec.)

Cuffee, Negro, age <u>c</u>. 26 - runaway from David Smith, living
in Worcester Co., Md. (3 Dec.)

PAUL, Jonathan, late of Germantown Twp., miller, dec'd -
accounts with estate to be settled with Deborah Paul,
administratrix (3 Dec.)

GOODING, Jacob, living in St. Georges, Newcastle Co. - offers
reward for recovery of strayed or stolen stallion (3 Dec.)

DAWSON, Widow, in Second St., Phila. - has Negro man for
sale (3 Dec.)

BADMIN, Charles, apprentice, age <u>c</u>. 17, who speaks English,
French, Spanish and Dutch - runaway from William Hasleton
of Phila. (3 Dec.)

Cicero, Negro, age <u>c</u>. 23, blockmaker by trade - same as
above

Philadelphia Lottery will be under the management of William
Allen, Joshua Maddox, William Masters, Samuel McCall,
Sr., Edward Shippen, Thomas Leech, Charles Willing, John
Kearsley, William Clymer, Sr., Thomas Lawrence, Jr.,
William Coleman and Thomas Hopkinson; the 15% deducted
from the whole sum produced will be used for such purpose
as the above managers decide, together with William Wal-
lace, John Stamper, Samuel Hazard, Philip Syng, John
Mifflin, James Coultas, William Branson, Rees Meredith,
Thomas Lloyd and Benjamin Franklin (12 Dec.)

Saturday last Patrick and Michael Burns were executed but
William Ward was reprieved and remanded to prison (12 Dec.)

Yesterday the Rev. Mr. Jenny in the Church of England
preached on the lawfulness of self-defence (12 Dec.)

SCULL, Joseph, Keeper of Pound of Phila. - lists creatures
in his keeping (12 Dec.)

STAMPER, Thomas, in Arch St. - sells tea (12 Dec.)

KUHL, Marcus, in Market St., Phila. - has a Negro woman
for sale (12 Dec.)

CATTHRINGER, Thomas, of Phila., staymaker - his wife Elizabeth has eloped from him (12 Dec.)

UNDERHILL, James, a Dublin boy - runaway from the sloop
<u>William</u> and <u>Agnes</u>, Alexander Martin master, belonging to
Barbados; reward will be paid for his capture by said master or by John Harrison, merchant, in Phila. (12 Dec.)

COWREN, Elizabeth, Dutch servant, age c. 25 - runaway from John Spencer, of Phila., shipwright (12 Dec.)

BRITTON, Benjamin, baker, in Chesnut St., corner of Fourth St., Phila. - has for sale a Negro wench, age c. 20 or 21 (12 Dec.)

Messages from the President (Anthony Palmer) and Council to the Assembly and answers of the Assembly (John Kinsey, Speaker) (15 Dec.)

Early last week Capt. Coverly in a brigantine from New Providence bound to Boston was wrecked on rocks east of Marblehead and 11 people were drowned - Boston item of 30 Nov. (15 Dec.)

In same storm Capt. Hewet, in ship from Newcastle bound to Boston, was cast away near Scituate - Boston item of 30 Nov. (15 Dec.)

ELLIS, Joseph, of Dedham, Mass., on 12 Nov., in his 82nd year, married Mrs. Susannah Smith in her 68th year, his 3rd wife; together they have now living 230 children, grandchildren and great-grandchildren - Boston item of 30 Nov. (15 Dec.)

Monday last 2 men, Joseph Bradford, born in New London (who pretends to be a doctor) and John Lummis, born in Narraganset, a blacksmith, were arrested at Hackinsack and committed to Bergen Co. Goal for passing counterfeit New Jersey bills of credit - New York item of 7 Dec. (15 Dec.)

FITZPATRICK, Peter, an Irishman - runaway from his bail, Patrick Conner, from Newcastle Co. (15 Dec.)

ASTON, George, has to be let house where he lives (where a tavern has been kept several years past), adjoining to Conestogoe Rd. (15 Dec.)

Brigantine Pembroke, Arthur Burroughs commander - will sail for Dublin; for freight or passage agree with Norris and Griffitts or said master (22 Dec.)

HUGHES, John, of Green Hill, Lower Merion - proposes that associators of Upper Merion, Lower Merion and Blockley signify their intention of training to him or to Charles Jenkins (22 Dec.)

Cato, Negro, who has been 2 years in the country and says he raun away from John Bale or Bailey in Virginia - has been taken up by Sheriff Benjamin Davis and committed to Goal of Chester Co. (22 Dec.)

On Friday a fire broke out in a sail-makers loft upon Wentworth's wharf and consumed the whole building and Mr.
Fletcher's warehouse - Boston item of 7 Dec. (29 Dec.)

STEVENSON, Capt., in a large ship for the West Indies rode
out a storm last Thursday in Nantasket Rd., but the
Panther was driven upon the rocks near Rainford's Island
- Boston item of 7 Dec. (29 Dec.)

Spanish galley that was taken by Capt. Forrest and fitted
out as a privateer at Kingston, Jamaica, has taken a
Dutch ship - extract of a letter from Kingston, dated
14 Oct. (29 Dec.)

BRITAIN, Capt. - arrived at New York last Friday from Cape
Breton - New York item of 14 Dec. (29 Dec.)

COSINE, John, of New York City, wife of - Saturday last,
seized with a fit, fell into the fire and was burnt to
death - New York item of 21 Dec. (29 Dec.)

Schooner Two Sisters, Capt. Roney, of New York, is ashore
about 6 miles to east of Cape May (29 Dec.)

List of masters of English vessels carried into Havana from
1 Apr. to Nov.: Capts. Snow, Meredith, John Banes, Saltus,
Everton, White, Hill, Long, Bronker, Wright, Harvey,
Bronett, Stevenson, Sheldon, Wormshead, Broadback, Shaw,
Dickson, Elingwood, Lloyd, Gibb, Wilson, Cole, Houston,
Watts, Harris, Clase, Shick (29 Dec.)

TENNENT, Rev. Gilbert - Thursday last in Phila. in the New
Building preached a sermon on the lawfulness of war (29
Dec.)

Six sets of bills of exchange, all signed W. Shirley and
Cha. Knowles, have been stolen (29 Dec.)

GRUBB, Nicholas, of Wilmington - his wife Mary has eloped
from him (29 Dec.)

FARMAR, Richard, at the Unicorn, in Second St., Phila. -
sells cloth, drugs, medicines, varnish (29 Dec.)

HALL, Jacob, mason, dec'd - plantation late belonging to
him, in Oxford Twp., about 7 miles from Phila., is to be
sold by his executors, Edward Collins and Abraham Leech
(29 Dec.)

HENDERSON, William - offers reward for recovery of his stallion, strayed away; stallion is to be brought to owner or
to Peter Robeson, at the Sign of the Indian King in Phila.
(29 Dec.)

674

1748

Resolution voted by town meeting at Boston against riotous
assembly; Ezekiel Goldthwait, Town Clerk, was to prepare
a copy and Edward Hutchinson (moderator of the meeting)
and the Selectmen were to wait on Gov. Shirley, the Council and the House - Boston item of 27 Dec. 1747 (5 Jan.)

Ships that have gotten up the river to Phila. are as follows: ship Catherine, Capt. Moore, Capts. Pitts and
Airy, Joseph Greenway; Capt. Ganthony is arrived at Wilmington and Capts. Green and Rees are both below (5 Jan.)

GRINDLE, Capt., in a flag of truce, arrived at New York Friday last from Leoganne (5 Jan.)

BOWNE, Capt., of the privateer Trembleur, has taken a Spanish
privateer sloop (5 Jan.)

Friday last 9 companies of Associators of Phila. and one of
Myamensing, met at the State House; officers elected
were Abraham Taylor colonel; Thomas Lawrence lt.-col.;
Samuel McCall major; officers of the Companies are (No.
1) Charles Willing captain, Atwood Shute lieut., James
Claypole ensign; (No. 2) Thomas Bond captain, Richard
Farmer lieut., Plunkett Fleeson ensign; (No. 3) John
Inglis captain, Lyn-Ford Lardner lieut., Thomas Lawrence,
Jr., ensign; (No. 4) James Pelegrean capt., William
Bradford lieut., William Bingham ensign; (No. 5) Peacock
Bigger capt., Joseph Redman lieut., Joseph Wood ensign;
(No. 6) Thomas Bourne capt., Robert Owen lieut., Peter
/illegible/, ensign; (No. 7) William Cozzins capt.,
George Spafford lieut., Abraham Mason ensign; (No. 8)
Septimus Robinson capt., William Clemm lieut., William
Rush ensign; (No. 9) James Coultas capt., George Gray,
Jr., lieut., Abraham Jones ensign; (No. 10) John Rose
capt., Richard Swan lieut., Philip Benezet ensign; (No.
11) Richard Nixon capt., Richard Renshaw lieut., Francis
Garrique ensign (5 Jan.)

BARNES, Margaret, alias Hopping Peg, servant, born in Exeter,
England, a breeches-maker by trade - runaway from John
Langdale, of Norfolk, Va.; reward will be paid if she is
returned to him or to William Hudson in Phila. (5 Jan.)

HALL, Hugh, and Joseph Candour, in Conewago, Lancaster Co.,
and Derry Twp. - offer reward for return of 3 mares that
strayed away (5 Jan.)

RICHARDS, Joseph, late of Phila., merchant, dec'd - accounts
with estate to be settled with Mary Richards, executrix
(5 Jan.)

BOWES, Francis, in Water St., near the Tun Tavern - sells tea, cocoa, chocolate, pepper, etc., out of his store on Robert Ellis's wharf in Phila. (5 Jan.)

HARPER, Joseph, late of Oxford, dec'd - accounts with estate to be settled with Joseph Harper, of Phila., or Matthias Keen, of Lower Dublin, executors (5 Jan.)

678

Bass (cont'd), Capt. 551, 565; Philip 518
Basset, - Col. 198; Henry 32
Bastian, Christopher 429
Bastide, Capt./Mr. 454, 504,508,509,543
Batcheldor, Capt. 455
Bate, - Humphrey 459; Margery 459; Thomas 498
Bateman, - Dr. 118,149, 220,244,265,274,359, 636; Arthur 291₵lement 229; Daniel 195,216
Bates, - Daniel 632; Elizabeth 632
Bath, John 377;
Bathurst, Sir Francis 130
Battel, - Widow 96; W. 96
Battin, Simon 363
Bavaird, Jannet 660
Bavinkton, Jonathan 522
Bawlde, John 490
Baxter, - Capt. 1; Rev. 15; James 146,235,246, 434,464
Bay, - Capt. 499,516; Thomas 430
Bayard, & Co. 160; Capt. 252,259,260,447,451, 458,471,486,487,494, 496,500,567,571; James 444,476; Nicholas 636; Peter 362,597; Samuel 575
Bayeux, - John 256; Thomas 377
Baylis, George 208
Bayly, see Bailey
Baynton, - John 562; Mary 442,562; Peter 4,41, 111,114,180,218,260, 334,342,346,376,381, 415,429,438,442,562
Baynum, Thomas 291
Beach, John 291,310
Beak, - Capt. 489; Mr. 296
Beaks/Beakes - Joseph 507; Mary 544; Stacy 544; Stephen 456; William 362
Beal/Beale, - Capt. 469; Col. 379; Alexander 259; William 195
Bealey, Hugh 292
Bean, Capt. 146,656
Bear, - Capt. 626; Jacob, Sr. 273
Beard, - Mrs. 96; Archibald 138; Hannah 292; John 42,215,578; Robert 578; Stephen 665
Beaston, John 623
Beatley, Samuel 216
Beaton, Daniel 208
Beauchamp, Isaac 54
Beauclerk, Lord Vere 39
Beaumont, John 198,227, 381
Beazely/Beazley/Bazely/ Bazeley/Beasely/Beasley/ Beasly/Beezley/Beesley/ Baizley, - Capt. 326, 478,553,611,618,642; Widow 530; Hannah 518; John 604; Mary 292; Michael 624; Simon 480;

Stephen 121,235,245, 295,443,462,518,559; Thomas 137,665
Bebby, John 532
Bechtel, Johannes 292
Beck, Jeremiah 301
Becker, - Conrad 319; Peter 582
Becket, - Capt. 513; William 230
Beckford, - Col. 48; Madam 418
Beddall, John 419
Beddes, Richard 236
Beddome, Joseph 379,468
Bedel, Abraham 540
Bedford, - Capt. 259; Eleanor 292; John 292
Bedgood, Capt. 80
Bedlow, Capt. 213, 600
Bedon, Stephen, Jr. 378
Bee, Mr. 271
Beeby, Robert 593
Beech, Henry 223
Beeke, Thomas 292
Beekman, - Col. 239; Gerrard 139
Beeks, William 135
Been, Thomas 119
Beere, - Elizabeth 440; Jonathan 159,440
Beers, - Capt. 325; Jonathan 619
Began, - Capt. 531; Widow 582; David 424
Begs, David 292
Belch, William 618
Belcher, - Capt. 81, 150, 414; Mr. 81; John 69; Jonathan/J./Gov. 16,17, 19,24,26,28,29,32,35, 36,38,43,51,52,59,61, 68,78,81,82,86,87,90, 103,105,107,113,121, 124,173,191,219,221, 227,241,243,276,278, 290,322,327,328,648, 649,653,655
Belden, Samuel 109
Belknap, Samuel 261
Bell, - Capt. 71,188,293, 401,436,443; Arthur 292; Hamilton 208; James 488; John 19; Joseph 208,216; Thomas/ Tom 208,256,335,348, 394,412,414,416,434, 447,452,457,463,571 (alias Lloyd), 579,657; William 334,376,461, 488,598,626
Bellergrau, Daniel 541
Bellisle, Mrs. 268
Bellomont, Earl of 145
Belt, Joseph, Jr. 639,650
Benezet, - Mr. 286,363; Anthony 391; Daniel 482,581,604,636,656; James 482,525,574,655; J. Stephen/John Stephen 204,217,314,416; Philip 636,655,674;Stephen 257,285
Benford, Peter 214
Benger, Elliott 443
Benjamin, Capt. 38
Benn, - Henry 292; John 206

Bennet/Bennett, - Capt. 136,194,213,274,283, 473,501,503,515,558, 592,635; Mr. 6; Francis 338; James 154,292,297, 361; John 30,154,572; Richard 651
Bennetland, Capt. 448,453, 460
Benny, Elizabeth 2
Benoist, James 530
Benson, - Capt. 81; John 292
Bentley/Bently, - John 5; Tho./Thomas 87,623
Bere, George 306
Berkeley/Berkley/Bercley, - Rev. Dean 78,81,489; Geo. 67; John 246
Bernard, Capt. 665
Berram, Rev. 292
Berrard, Stephen 624
Berrill, Richard 428
Berry, - Capt. 306,488; Benjamin 22,36; Garrat 388; Michael 250; Samuel 120; William 273, 464; Withers 69
Bertram, see Bartram
Berwick/Barwick, - Capt. 77,213;Elizabeth 261; John 261,667; Margaret 183; Richard 297
Beshishee, George 504
Besse, Capt. 637
Best, John 208
Beswicke, Capt. 587
Bethel/Bethell, - Capt. 309; Samuel 102; William 292
Betson, Thomas 235
Betterfield, John 28
Betterton, Benjamin 369
Bettle, Samuel 333,574
Bevan/Beven, - Capt. 566, 612,632,637; Aubrey 204, 240,278,333,381,442,470, 471,583,611; Catherine 42; David 184; Evan 16, 78,195,466; Henry 42; Joshua 416; Thomas 159, 519; William 26
Bewly, John 81
Bezer, John 391
Biags/?/, Sarah 292
Bibbe, Capt. 414
Bickerdike, Gideon 544
Bickerstaff, Samuel 272
Bickford/Bickfords, Mr./ Messr. 126,364
Bickley, - Mr. 28,131,163, 168,173,184,187,189,206, 221,344,359,665; Widow 389; Abraham 57,204,385, 398; Samuel 57,94,280, 333,381,388,414,416,420, 426,440,467,487,522; William 152,171
Bicknel, Elizabeth 229
Biddle, - James 49; John 232,363,377,404,418,499; William 39,51,249,377
Biederey, John Barnhard 443
Biesie, George 490
Bigar, Robert 180
Biggelow, Capt. 10
Bigger, Peacock 155,198,

710

711